RUSSIAN FOLKLORE

RUSSIAN FOLKLORE

By ACADEMICIAN Y. M. SOKOLOV

TRANSLATED BY CATHERINE RUTH SMITH

INTRODUCTION AND BIBLIOGRAPHY BY
FELIX J. OINAS

DETROIT
Folklore Associates
1971

Library of Congress Catalog Card Number 79-134444

ISBN 0-8103-5020-3

INTRODUCTION

I

Yuriy Matveyevich Sokolov's *Russian Folklore* (Russkii fol'klor) was published in the Soviet Union in 1938, and again in 1941, primarily as a textbook for students of higher educational institutions. Although it was replaced by another text, edited by P. G. Bogatyrev,[1] some time later, it is still the best general work of its kind and best suited to give Western readers a picture of Russian folklore.

Russian Folklore, written in its final form by Yuriy Matveyevich Sokolov, is actually the result of a collaboration between him and his twin brother, Boris Matveyevich. Since the brothers Sokolov, during their whole lives, pursued the same interest and did a considerable part of their scholarly (especially collecting) work jointly, it is only proper to treat·them together here in giving some basic facts of their life and work.[2]

Boris and Yuriy Sokolov were born on April 19, 1889 in Nezhin. Their father, professor of Russian literature at the Historic-Philological Institute, was shortly thereafter appointed professor at Moscow University and the family settled down in Moscow. In 1906, Boris and Yuriy enrolled in the historic-philological faculty of Moscow University, where they began

[1] See item 3 in the Bibliography.

[2] More information on the lives of the brothers Sokolov can be found in E. Gofman and S. Mints, "Brat'ia B. M. i Iu. M. Sokolovy" (The Brothers B. M. and Yu. M. Sokolov), Iu. M. Sokolov, *Onezhskie byliny* (Onega Byliny), pp. 9-31. (See item 66 in the Bibliography.)

studying language, literature, and folklore. They both were especially influenced by V. F. Miller, the famous leader of the historical school in Russian folklore. Thanks to Miller's encouragement, they undertook two study and collecting trips to Novgorod province that resulted in the publication of *Songs and Tales of the Belozero Region* (Pesni i skazki Belozerskogo kraia, 1915). After graduating from Moscow University in 1911, they remained at the University for the purpose of preparing themselves for an academic career. At the same time they taught in high schools and in the Teachers Institute in Moscow. Boris's scholarly work centered around byliny, and Yuriy's around Russian literature of the 1830's and 1840's.

In 1919, the brothers became separated temporarily when Boris was appointed professor at Saratov University. Boris was actively engaged in the study of the ethnography of the Volga region and organized the ethnographic museum of the Saratov district. In 1925 he returned to Moscow, where the brothers jointly began to do intensive research work. In the next year, they published *Poetry of the Village* (Poeziia derevni), a guide for collectors of folklore. In the summer months from 1926 to 1928 they organized and directed an expedition, called "in the footsteps of Rybnikov and Hilferding," to the Olonets region, under the auspices of the State Academy of Fine Arts in Moscow. The purpose of this expedition was to investigate the fate of the heroic epic and historical songs in this area since the collecting of Rybnikov and Hilferding in the 1860's and '70's. The byliny collected on this expedition were not published until 1948.

Beginning from 1929, the brothers Sokolov published a series of booklets on Russian folklore (Russkii fol'klor) for the correspondence course in teacher training. The sections devoted to the historiography of folklore, byliny, and folktales were written by Boris, and those on the remaining genres and on Soviet folklore by Yuriy.

Boris devoted much energy to organizing the Central Museum of Ethnology, which became one of the greatest museums in

Europe. He was director of this museum almost until his death in July, 1930. Yuriy held the position, in the thirties, of professor of folklore in the Institute of History, Philosophy, and Literature and in the Moscow State Pedagogical Institute. His research was concerned primarily with the interrelationship between folklore and written literature. Among other things, he became actively involved in the discussions that arose in connection with the attacks launched by the government against the prevailing trends in folklore scholarship, especially in the question of the aristocratic origin of the heroic epic. Although he proved the untenability of some of the views of their over-anxious accusers, he had, nevertheless, to acknowledge that the basic positions held by himself and by his late brother concerning the aristocratic origin of the byliny were erroneous.[3]

In 1939, Yuriy Sokolov was elected a member of the Ukrainian Academy of Sciences and became director of the Folklore Institute of the Academy in Kiev. He began making plans for new publications, expeditions, and collection work, but could not carry them out. He died on January 15, 1941 from a heart attack, right after having given a speech at a festive meeting in honor of Academician A. E. Krymsky.

The idea for the compilation of *Russian Folklore* (1938) grew out of the survey of Russian folklore prepared for a correspondence course in teacher training (see above). It was this survey that became the nucleus of *Russian Folklore*. Certain chapters ("Religious Verses" and "Tales"), that were written by Boris Sokolov for the correspondence course, were only revised by Yuriy for inclusion in *Russian Folklore*. Many chapters, as Yuriy himself points out, were completely re-written and others were substantially revised. Thus, *Russian Folklore* is essentially the product of the revision and enlargement of the textbook for the correspondence course, and no doubt owes its existence to this text.

---

[3] See Iu. Sokolov, "Russkii bylinnyi epos" (Russian Bylina Epic), *Literaturnyi kritik* (Literary Critic), Moscow, 1937, No. 9, pp. 171-196.

Russian Folklore is very broad in scope, both diachronically and synchronically. The work includes information on Russian folklore beginning with the most ancient times (as found in the *Primary Chronicle* and the subsequent annalistic works) up to the 1930's. The work is, however, based essentially on the folklore material collected in the 19th and 20th centuries. Russian folklore of the czarist time is contrasted with that of the Soviet period, and the changes manifesting themselves in folklore and in the study of it have been brought out clearly.

One of the most interesting chapters in Sokolov's work is the "Historiography of Folkloristics." Sokolov gives, in more than a hundred pages, an excellent survey of all the major phases in the development of Russian folklore scholarship. He views this development as closely dependent upon the movements and schools in Western Europe, such as the mythological school, the diffusionist school, the Finnish school, the anthropological theory, and the historical school. He shows how the Western European ideas came to Russia and, after sometimes arousing controversy (for instance between the Slavophiles and Westerners), were eventually accepted. The merits of Sokolov's survey of the historiography of Russian folklore stand out especially clearly, if we compare it with the corresponding chapter in the Bogatyrev textbook (see below).

Sokolov's textbook covers all the genres of Russian folklore with the exception of the ballads. The study of ballads had been neglected in Russia up to the most recent times. This might have been partly due to the fact that Russian ballads do not represent a clear-cut genre, but are strongly influenced by other genres (by the byliny in the north, and by the lyrical songs in the south). There were no special collections of ballads published in Russia during the czarist time. The ballads were included in large collections of folksongs, such as in *The Songs Collected by P. V. Kireyevsky* (Pesni, sobrannye P. V. Kireevskim) as "the epic, princely songs," and in A. I. Sobolevsky's *Great Russian Folk Songs* (Velikorusskie narodnye pesni) as "lower epic songs." The latter term is symptomatic of the modest prestige that this genre enjoyed.

There were no signs of an increase in interest in ballads during the Stalin era. Only one collection of ballads was published in this period, with a lengthy introduction by N. P. Andreyev. Andreyev, however, failed in his attempt to define and to classify the Russian ballads. There were no studies devoted to ballads. The tragical events depicted in ballads could evidently not be reconciled with the striving for optimism in literature, encouraged by responsible Soviet circles.

While Sokolov omitted the ballads in his *Russian Folklore,* he, on the other hand, included discussions of such unpopular subjects as religious verses and mythology. Sokolov's survey of religious verses is impartial and without any intention as antireligious propaganda. This propaganda was perhaps not even necessary, since, as Sokolov himself observes, the religious verses were disappearing "owing to the general cultural development and the progress of the Soviet organization." Russian mythology is discussed in the chapter entitled "On the Origin of Poetry and the Early Stages of its Development," perhaps for the purpose of disguising it.

Sokolov's survey of the individual genres displays a well-rounded scholar, equally at home in all aspects of Russian folklore. He has avoided the schematism which is characteristic of the Bogatyrev textbook and has presented the essential problems concerning each genre. Even a casual acquaintance with the book shows that the author has been especially interested in the following problems: the origins, the narrators, and the structure and style.

Concerning the problem of origins, Sokolov endeavors to point out the ultimate inner forces that led to the rise of individual genres. It is only natural that he is inclined to prefer the theories that can be reconciled with Marxism. Thus he traces the origin of poetry back to the rhythm of work, as Karl Bücher did, and seeks the motivation for the rise of chastushki (folk rhymes) in the basic change of the social-economic conditions of life in Russia in the 1860's.

Hardly anywhere else has the personality of the individual singer and narrator been so much emphasized as in Russia.

Russian folklorists, beginning with Rybnikov and Hilferding, have stressed the close interrelationship between the personality of the teller and his creation. It is only natural that this aspect should figure prominently in Sokolov's textbook. His classification of the tellers of tales and singers of byliny into different categories while illustrating these categories with numerous examples is both interesting and illuminating. Here Yuriy Sokolov has been able to utilize his brother's work on the narrators (*The Tellers* [Skaziteli]).

One of the outstanding features of *Russian Folklore* is its discussion of structure and style. This is the more commendable, since concentration on esthetic aspects (the so-called "Formalism") in literature and folklore had been condemned in the Soviet Union since the second half of the 1920's. Sokolov discusses the structure of almost all folklore genres, but dwells especially on the structure of charms, byliny, tales, and lyric songs. He also devotes much attention to the poetics and style of the major genres. In his treatment of the structure and poetics, the author has drawn extensively on his brother's work, especially on his famous article, "An Excursus into the Field of the Poetics of Russian Folklore" (Ekskursy v oblast' poetiki russkogo fol'klora).

The survey of Soviet folklore contains many topics that are new and unusual for Western students of folklore. Such are, for instance, the use of folklore in the Soviet Union for propaganda purposes (which Sokolov readily admits), the concentration on the workers' songs, revolutionary songs (especially those connected with the October Revolution and the Civil War), and folklore about Soviet political and military leaders. We hear further of the arguments between Soviet folklorists on whether or not the "memorates," i.e. biographical narratives and memoirs (skazy), should be included in folklore. Despite some dissonant voices, they were actually included "as a kind of new phenomenon which belongs to the facts of oral creation." Especially interesting are certain incidents of the Party's and government's interference with the scholars' work, such as the condemnation of formalism and the great controversy about the origins of byliny. Both of them ended with the scholars renouncing their former trends. In the latter controversy, which was carried on in newspapers and journals, the scholars had to make public apologies for their "errors."

Although *Russian Folklore* is a solid work and can well be used even a few decades after its publication, there are certain details that would require revision. Such is for instance the elaboration of N.Ya. Marr's ideas about language and folklore, which has no justification for appearing in a folklore textbook, except to demonstrate the oddities of the Stalin era. Marr was, in the 1930's and '40's, one of the officially recognized leaders of Soviet philologists; his so-called "paleontological analysis" of semantics was interwoven with data drawn from archaeology, ethnology, and folklore. Attacked by Stalin himself at the beginning of the 1950's, Marr's theories were scrapped and Marrists degraded.

Sokolov's discussion of spring and harvest customs follows closely Wilhelm Mannhardt's views, as they appear in his *Wald- und Feldkulte* (which were taken up partly by James Frazer). For instance, the ceremonial reverence paid to the last sheaf in Russia is ascribed, in Mannhardt's manner, to the vegetation demon who was caught in it. Actually, these Mannhardtian ideas had been justly criticized as early as 1934 and in the following years by C. W. von Sydow, who traced the customs connected with the last sheaf back to the so-called "ominal magic."[4]

II

Soon after the publication of Sokolov's *Russian Folklore*, there occurred a change in the Soviet policy towards literature which also affected the study of folklore. At that time there

---

[4] See C. W. von Sydow's articles on the Mannhardtian theories in *Folk-Lore*, 45, London, 1934, pp. 291-309, and *Folk-Liv*, III, Stockholm, 1939, pp. 242-254.

began a most intensive campaign, led by A. A. Zhdanov, against all Western elements in Soviet literature and literary study. Among the folklore scholars, V. Ya. Propp and M. K. Azadovsky were accused of stressing the international character of folklore and of following the comparativist line. Propp's book, *Historical Roots of the Fairy Tale* [112][5] which contained abundant quotations from such internationally oriented scholars as Frazer, Boas, Kroeber, and others, were compared to a London or Berlin telephone directory. The change of direction that followed is clearly manifest in folklore studies after 1948 until the death of Stalin (1953). The folklorists now refrained from giving any references to Western scholarship in their works.

The new trend appears clearly in the folklore textbook edited by Bogatyrev. The chapter on the development of Russian folklore scholarship in its relationship to European schools (written by M. K. Azadovsky and Yu. N. Sidorova) comprises only fifteen pages and is entitled characteristically "The Bourgeois Schools in Russian Folklore Scholarship and the Fight Against Them." Much more attention has been paid to the description of the attitude of Russian writers and critics toward folklore. The obvious purpose of this description has been to show the development of Russian folkloristics from indigenous national roots and to diminish the role of foreign influence. The same reason probably accounts for not mentioning the first recorders of Russian folklore, the Englishmen Richard James and Samuel Collins, in the Bogatyrev textbook.

After Stalin's death and especially after the de-Stalinization in 1956, a certain liberalization has been noticeable in Russian scholarship. While Stalin still figured as an authority on folklore in the first edition of the Bogatyrev textbook, his name was completely erased from the second edition (1956). In the years that followed, it became possible to devote more attention to the problems of form than before. Especially characteristic is the republication of the major portion of a

---

[5] The numbers in the brackets refer to items in the Bibliography.

formalistic study on byliny by A. P. Skaftymov [82], condemned previously.

Despite the changes in trends, the interest manifested in folklore has continued with unabating vigor in the Soviet Union. As before, folklore materials are published in local papers and magazines, sent in by teachers, agronomists, and members of collective farms. Folklore clubs are continuing their work in numerous collective farms and factories. Folklore is taught as a special subject in pedagogical institutions and universities. There is hardly any doubt that this broad interest in folklore has been encouraged by official circles because of its propaganda value.

A number of large-scale conferences on folklore have been held during recent years. The Institute of Russian Literature (Pushkin House) and the Institute of World Literature co-operated in sponsoring conferences in Leningrad in 1953 and 1958. The former conference was devoted to the discussion of two problems—Soviet folklore (its nature, characteristic features, tasks, and methods of its study), and the history of Russian folklore and its periodization. In this conference there were 250 participants, all invited. The conference of 1958, with 240 participants, centered around the problems of contemporary folklore. In addition to the all-Union conferences, meetings of regional folklorists are arranged frequently for the discussion of special problems. Thus, a regional conference was held in Petrozavodsk (Karelian SSR) in 1957 on the collection and study of folklore in the North, and another in Ulan Ude (Buryat-Mongol ASSR) in 1959 on the study of folklore in Siberia and the Far East.

Scores of highly qualified folklorists have been actively engaged in collection, publication, and research. A number of collections of folklore materials have been published, especially in the series "Monuments of Russian Folklore" (Pamiatniki russkogo fol'klora), since 1960. The materials in this series are distinguished by competent introductions and detailed commentaries. A few significant studies on almost all genres have appeared. The results have been especially noteworthy in the study of byliny and historical songs, and also in ballads, ritual songs, etc. Following are some noteworthy examples of such studies.

A. M. Astakhova's study, *Russian Byliny Epic in the North* [68], is one of the most solid works of Russian folklore. Unlike V. F. Miller and other leading pre-revolutionary folklorists, Astakhova studies the byliny not as archaic stagnant phenomena, but as living processes. Analyzing the bylina tradition of the last one hundred and fifty years, she establishes basic laws pertaining to the creative process of the folk epic, and studies the significance of the environment and the influence of written literature on the byliny. V. Ya. Propp, in his *Russian Heroic Epic* [79], endeavors—following V. G. Belinsky—to formulate the basic idea of each bylina, contending that the idea of a bylina expresses the ideals of the corresponding epoch. P. D. Ukhov has studied some formal elements (epithets and commonplaces) in the byliny [87, 88].

The historical interpretation of the byliny which had subsided after the activities of V. F. Miller for a few decades, has recently been revived by M. M. Plisetsky and B. A. Rybakov. Plisetsky [78] traced the geographical names and the reflection of early feudal society in byliny. Rybakov [80] went even further than Plisetsky; he was inclined to see in byliny extensive traces of early historical events (up to the thirteenth century).

The historical songs have been studied successfully by B. N. Putilov and V. K. Sokolova. In addition to numerous articles, especially on the songs pertaining to the popular uprisings, they both wrote a general survey of the historical songs [91, 93].

The ballad genre became the object of study in the Soviet Union only in the late 1950's; this study has been carried on primarily by one man—D. M. Balashov. Balashov published a number of articles on ballads [123-125] and an anthology of them [117]. His work has, after the studies of V. V. Sipovsky,

N. F. Sumtsov, I. N. Zhdanov, etc., which had become anti-quated long ago, advanced ballad research considerably. Attempts at ballad studies by some others (e.g. I. I. Zemtsovsky)[6] have been less successful.

In the study of rites and ritual poetry, V. I. Chicherov's work on the winter period of the Russian agricultural calendar [36] is most significant. Chicherov concentrates especially on the celebration of Christmas and New Year festivals and gives a penetrating analysis of the rites and customs observed and the songs presented. V. I. Propp's book on the agrarian holidays [37] includes all the most important holidays during the entire year. It endeavors to prove that the celebration of holidays in Russia was prompted, almost exclusively, by economic considerations.

V. P. Anikin has pursued the study of the origin of riddles [46, 54]. Developing further the ideas expressed by some former scholars (e.g. M. A. Rybnikova), Anikin elaborated a fascinating theory of the genetic connection of riddles with allegorical, secret speech. The details of this theory still require further substantiation and study.

Research on Russian folklore has been carried on also outside the Soviet Union, often with very gratifying results. Carl Stief's *Studies in the Russian Historical Song* [94] was the first to define precisely the relationship between the historical songs and the byliny and to give thorough studies on a dozen historical songs. Roman Jakobson and Marc Szeftel made an interesting attempt to clarify the historical background of the bylina about Volkh Vseslavyevich [72]. Elsa Mahler's extensive work on wedding ceremonies and songs [44] contains much factual material, but is carelessly executed. On proverbs, two studies have appeared in the West, one by Andrew Guershoon [50] and the other by I. Klimenko [51]; the latter is, however, of little value.

---

6 See I. I. Zemtsovskii's article on the ballad of the daughter as a bird in *Russkii fol'klor* (Russian Folklore), VIII, M.-L., 1963, pp. 144-159.

We have touched here on only a few works in Russian folklore that have appeared after the publication of Sokolov's *Russian Folklore*. There are many other studies that would deserve mention, but considerations of space cause us to refer the reader to the attached bibliography.

Finally it should be mentioned that the English translation of Sokolov's textbook is not satisfactory. It contains a great number of blunders caused by misunderstanding of Russian and is inconsistent in its transliteration of titles and names. It is to be hoped that in the future this translation can be subjected to a thorough revision or a new translation be prepared.

FELIX J. OINAS

Indiana University
November, 1965

BIBLIOGRAPHY

The following bibliography contains works on Russian folklore that do not appear in Sokolov's textbook. Of the works in Russian, only the more important ones (including republications of the earlier collections and studies) published after 1938 have been given. The works in Western languages have been included irrespective of the time of their publication, since they are inadequately represented in Sokolov's book. A certain imbalance in favor of the works in English has been prompted by the desire to refer the users of this textbook to the material most easily accessible to them.

I. GENERAL WORKS

1. Astakhova, A. M., et al., ed., *Ocherki russkogo narodno-poeticheskogo tvorchestva Sovetskoi epokhi* (Studies of Russian Folklore of the Soviet Period). M.-L.,[1] 1952.

2. Baranov, S. F., *Russkoe narodnoe poeticheskoe tvorchestvo* (Russian Folklore). M., 1962.

---

[1] M. = Moscow; L. = Leningrad.

3. Bogatyrev, P. G., ed., *Russkoe narodnoe poeticheskoe tvorchestvo* (Russian Folklore). 2nd ed. M., 1956 (1st ed., 1954.)

4. Chadwick, H. Munro, and N. Kershaw Chadwick, "Russian Oral Literature," *The Growth of Literature,* II, New York, 1936, pp. 1-296.

5. Chicherov, V. I., *Russkoe narodnoe tvorchestvo* (Russian Folklore). M., 1959.

6. Chicherov, V. I., *Voprosy teorii i istorii narodnogo tvorchestva* (Questions on the Theory and History of Folklore). M., 1959.

7. Harkins, William E., *Bibliography of Slavic Folk Literature.* New York, 1953.

8. Harkins, William E., *Dictionary of Russian Literature.* Paterson, N. J., 1959.

9. Mel'ts, M. Ia., comp., *Russkii fol'klor; Bibliograficheskii ukazatel', 1945-1959* (Russian Folklore: Bibliographical Index, 1945-1959). L., 1961.

10. Pírková Jakobson, Svatava, "Slavic Folklore," *Funk and Wagnalls Standard Dictionary of Folklore, Mythology, and Legend,* II, New York, 1950, pp. 1019-1025.

11. Poltoratskaia, M. A. (Marianna A. Poltoratzky), *Russkii fol'klor; Khrestomatiia, stat'i i kommentarii* (Russian Folklore: Chrestomathy, Articles, and Commentaries). New York, 1964.

12. Pomerantseva, E. V., and S. I. Mints, comp., *Russkoe narodnoe poeticheskoe tvorchestvo; Khrestomatiia* (Russian Folklore: Chrestomathy). M., 1963.

13. Ralston, W. R. S., *The Songs of the Russian People.* London, 1872.

14. *Ruskii fol'klor* (Russian Folklore), I-IX. Ed. A. M. Astakhova et al. M.-L., 1956-1964 [continuing].

15. *Russkoe narodnoe poeticheskoe tvorchestvo* (Russian Folklore), I-II. Editor-in-chief V. P. Adrianova-Peretts (Vol. I); D. S. Likhachev (Vol. II). M.-L., 1953-1956.

16. Stender-Petersen, Ad., *Russian Studies.* Copenhagen, 1956. (Acta Jutlandica, Aarsskrift for Aarhus Universitet, XXVIII, 2, Humanistisk Serie, 43.)

II. HISTORIOGRAPHY OF FOLKLORE SCHOLARSHIP

17. Azadovskii, M. K., *Istoriia russkoi fol'kloristiki* (History of Russian Folklore Scholarship), I-II. Ed. by E. V. Pomerantseva. M., 1958-1963.

18. Azadovskii, M. K., "Sovetskaia fol'kloristika za 20 let" (Soviet Folklore Scholarship During Twenty Years), *Sovetskii fol'klor* (Soviet Folklore), VI, M.-L., 1939, pp. 3-53.

19. Chistov, K. V., "Folklore Studies and the Present Day," *Soviet Anthropology and Archaeology*, I, New York, 1963, No. 4, pp. 37-48.

20. Gippius, E. V., and V. I. Chicherov, "Sovetskaia fol'kloristika za 30 let" (Soviet Folklore Scholarship During Thirty Years), *Sovetskaia etnografiia* (Soviet Ethnography), M., 1947, No. 4, pp. 29-51.

21. Gusev, V. E., "Folklore Research in the USSR," *The Soviet Review*, II, New York, 1961, No. 1, pp. 51-58.

22. Oinas, Felix J., "Folklore Activities in Russia," *Journal of American Folklore*, 74, Philadelphia, 1961, pp. 76-84.

23. Razumova, A. P., *Iz istorii russkoi fol'kloristiki (P. N. Rybnikov, P. S. Efimenko)* (On the History of Russian Folklore Scholarship: P. N. Rybnikov, P. S. Efimenko). M.-L., 1954.

24. Schlauch, Margaret, "Folklore in the Soviet Union," *Science and Society*, VIII, New York, 1944, pp. 205-222.

25. Sokolova, V. K., "Sovetskaia fol'kloristika k 40-letiiu Oktiabria" (Soviet Folklore Scholarship on the Fortieth Anniversary of the October Revolution), *Sovetskaia etnografiia* (Soviet Ethnography), M., 1957, No. 5, pp. 72-85.

26. Zelenin, Dm. K., "The More Important Folklore and Ethnographical Archives and Institutes in the European Part of the U.S.S.R.," *Folk-Liv*, II, Stockholm, 1938, pp. 218-222.

See also items 2, 3, 5, 15, and 16.

III. MYTHOLOGY

27. Haase, Felix, *Volksglaube und Brauchtum der Ostslaven.* Breslau, 1939. (Wort und Brauch, Heft 26.)

28. Jakobson, Roman, "Slavic Mythology," *Funk and Wagnalls*

Standard Dictionary of Folklore, Mythology, and Legend, II, New York, 1950, pp. 1025-1028.

29. Krappe, Alexander H., "La chute du paganisme à Kiev," *Revue des Études Slaves,* XVII, Paris, 1937, pp. 206-218.

30. Máchal, Jan, "Slavic Mythology," Louis H. Gray, ed., *The Mythology of All Races,* III, Boston, 1918, pp. 215-314.

31. Machek, Václav, "Essai comparatif sur la mythologie slave," *Revue des Études Slaves,* XXIII, Paris, 1947, pp. 48-65.

32. Meyer, Karl H., "Slavic Religion," Carl Clemen, ed., *Religions of the World,* New York, 1931, pp. 243-253.

33. Schmaus, A., "Zur altslawischen Religionsgeschichte," *Saeculum,* IV, München, 1953, pp. 206-230.

34. Tokarev, S. A., *Religioznye verovaniia vostochnoslavianskikh narodov XIX nachala XX veka* (Religious Beliefs of the Eastern Slavic Peoples from the Nineteenth to the Beginning of the Twentieth Century). M.-L., 1957.

35. Unbegaun, B.-O., "La religion des anciens Slaves," *Les religions de l'Europe ancienne,* II, Pt. 3, Paris, 1948, pp. 387-445.

See also items 13 and 95.

IV. RITUAL POETRY CONNECTED WITH THE CALENDAR

36. Chicherov, V. I., *Zimnii period russkogo zemledel'cheskogo kalendaria XVI-XIX vekov* (The Winter Period of the Russian Agricultural Calendar from the Sixteenth to the Nineteenth Centuries). M., 1957. (Trudy Inst. Etnografii im. N. N. Miklukho-Maklaia, n.s., XL.)

37. Propp, V. Ia., *Russkie agrarnye prazdniki* (Russian Agrarian Holidays). L., 1963.

See also items 2, 3, 5, 11, 12, 13, 15, 118, and 126.

V. RITUAL POETRY CONNECTED WITH THE FAMILY

38. Bazanov, V. G., Intr. and comm., *Russkaia narodno-bytovaia lirika; Prichitaniia Severa v zapisiakh V. G. Bazanova i A. P. Razumovoi* (Russian Lyric Folk Poetry of Everyday Life: Laments of the North, Recorded by V. G. Bazanov and A. P. Razumova). M.-L., 1962.

39. Chistov, K. V., *Narodnaia poetessa I. A. Fedosova; Ocherk zhizni i tvorchestva* (Folk Poetess I. A. Fedosova: Sketch of Her Life and Creative Work). Petrozavodsk, 1955.

40. Chistova, B. E., and K. V. Chistov, ed., *Prichitaniia* (Laments). L., 1960.

41. Kozachenko, A. I., "K istorii velikorusskogo svadebnogo obriada" (On the History of Great Russian Wedding Rites), *Sovetskaia etnografiia* (Soviet Ethnography), M., 1957, No. 1, pp. 57-71.

42. Lineff, Eugenie, *Russian Folk-Songs as Sung by the People and Peasant Wedding Ceremonies Customary in Northern and Central Russia.* Chicago, 1893.

43. Mahler, Elsa, *Die russische Totenklage.* Leipzig, 1935. (Veröffentlichungen des Slavischen Instituts der Berliner Friedrich-Wilhelms-Universität, XV.)

44. Mahler, Elsa, *Die russischen dörflichen Hochzeitsbräuche.* Berlin, 1960. (Veröffentlichungen der Abteilung für slavische Sprachen und Literaturen des Osteuropa-Instituts (Slavisches Seminar) an der Freien Universität Berlin, XX.)

See also items 2, 3, 4, 5, 11, 12, 13, 15, 118, 126, and 136.

VI. CHARMS AND DIVINATIONS

45. Klagstad, Harold L., "Great Russian Charm Structure," *Indiana Slavic Studies,* II, Bloomington, 1958, pp. 135-144.

See also items 2, 3, 5, 11, 12, and 15.

VII. PROVERBS AND RIDDLES

46. Anikin, V. P., *Russkie narodnye poslovitsy, pogovorki, zagadki i detskii fol'klor* (Russian Proverbs, Sayings, Riddles, and Children's Folklore). M., 1957.

47. Dal', V., *Poslovitsy russkogo naroda* (Proverbs of the Russian People). Intr. by V. I. Chicherov. 4th ed. M., 1957.

48. Eyke, Wera von, *Russkie poslovitsy. Russische Sprichwörter* (Russian Proverbs). Zürich, 1947.

49. Graf, A. E., *1200 neue russische Sprichwörter.* Halle (Saale), 1963.

50. Guershoon, Andrew, *Certain Aspects of Russian Proverbs.* London, 1941.

51. Klimenko, I., *Das russische Sprichwort.* Bern, 1946.

52. Langnas, Isaac A., coll. and transl., *1200 Russian Proverbs.* New York, 1960.

53. Mel'ts, M. Ia., et al., ed., *Poslovitsy, pogovorki, zagadki v rukopisnykh sbornikakh XVIII-XX vekov* (Proverbs, Sayings, and Riddles in Manuscript Collections from the Eighteenth to the Twentieth Centuries). M.-L., 1961.

54. Sadovnikov, D. N., *Zagadki russkogo naroda* (Riddles of the Russian People). Ed. and Intr. by V. P. Anikin. M., 1959.

See also items 2, 3, 4, 5, 11, 12, and 15.

VIII. BYLINY

(A) COLLECTIONS

55. Astakhova, A. M., ed., *Byliny Severa* (Byliny of the North), I-II. M.-L., 1938-1951.

56. Astakhova, A. M., ed., *Il'ia Muromets* (Ilya Muromets). M.-L., 1958.

57. Astakhova, A. M., et al., ed., *Byliny Pechory i Zimnego berega (Novye zapisi)* (Pechora and Winter Coast Byliny: New Recordings). M.-L., 1961.

58. Astakhova, A. M., et al., ed., *Byliny v zapisiakh i pereskazakh XVII-XVIII vekov* (Byliny in Recordings and Retellings from the Seventeenth to the Eighteenth Centuries). M.-L., 1960.

59. Borodina, E., and R. Lipets, ed., *Byliny M. S. Kriukovoi* (Byliny of M. S. Kryukova), I-II. M., 1939-1941. (Letopisi Gosudarstvennogo literaturnogo muzeia, VI, VIII.)

60. Chadwick, N. Kershaw, *Russian Heroic Poetry.* New York, 1964.

61. [Danilov, Kirsha], *Drevnie rossiiskie stikhotvoreniia, sobrannye Kirsheiu Danilovym* (Ancient Russian Poems, Collected by Kirsha Danilov). Ed. by A. P. Evgen'eva and B. N. Putilov. M.-L., 1958.

62. [Gil'ferding, A. F.], *Onezhskie byliny, zapisannye A. F. Gil'ferdingom letom 1871 goda* (Onega Byliny, Recorded by A. F.

Hilferding in the Summer of 1871), I-III. 4th ed. Ed. by A. I.
Nikiforov and G. S. Vinogradov. M.-L., 1949-1951.

63. Hapgood, Isabel Florence, *The Epic Songs of Russia*. Intr.
Note by J. W. Mackail. London, 1915.

64. Magnus, L. A., *The Heroic Ballads of Russia*. London, 1921.

65. Propp, V. Ia., and B. N. Putilov, ed., *Byliny* (Byliny), I-II.
M., 1958.

66. Sokolov, Iu. M., *Onezhskie byliny* (Onega Byliny). Ed. by V.
Chicherov. M., 1948. (Letopisi Gosudarstvennogo literaturnogo
muzeia, XIII.)

(B) STUDIES

67. Anderson, Walter, "Die neuesten Schicksale der Byline
"Dobrynja und Marinka" im Onegagebiet," *Festschrift für Max
Vasmer zum 70. Geburtstag*, Berlin, 1956, pp. 39-44. (Veröffentlichungen der Abteilung für slavische Sprachen und Literaturen
des Osteuropa-Instituts (Slavisches Seminar) and der Freien Universität Berlin, IX.)

68. Astakhova, A. M., *Russkii bylinnyi epos na Severe* (Russian
Bylina Epic in the North). Petrozavodsk, 1948.

69. Chettéoui, Wilfrid, *Un rapsode russe, Rjabinin le père*.
Paris, 1942.

70. Kharkins, Vil'iam (William Harkins), "O metricheskoi roli
slovesnykh formul v serbokhorvatskom i russkom narodnom epose"
(On the Metrical Role of Oral Formulas in the Serbo-Croatian and
Russian Folk Epic), *American Contributions to the Fifth International Congress of Slavists, Sofia, September 1963*, II, The Hague,
1963, pp. 147-165.

71. Hartmann, Karl, "Die Rhapsodin M. S. Krjukova, ihre
sowjetischen Volkspoeme und deren Verhältnis zur Tradition des
grossrussischen Heldenliedes," *Die Welt der Slaven*, II, Wiesbaden,
1957, pp. 394-418.

72. Jakobson, Roman, and Marc Szeftel, "The Vseslav Epos,"
Memoirs of the American Folklore Society, 42, Philadelphia, 1949,
pp. 13-86.

73. Krżyzanowski, Juljan, *Byliny; Studjum z dziejów rosyjskiej
epiki ludowej* (Byliny: Study on the History of the Russian Folk
Epic). Vilna, 1934. (Instytut naukowo-badawczy Europy wschod-
niej, Sekcja filologiczna, No. 3.)

74. Lixačev (Likhachev), D. S., "Time in Russian Folklore," *International Journal of Slavic Linguistics and Poetics*, V, 'S-Gravenhage, 1962, pp. 74-96.

75. Linevskii, A. M., *Skazitel' F. A. Konashkov* (The Narrator F. A. Konashkov). Petrozavodsk, 1948.

76. Mazon, A., "Mikula, le prodigieux laboreur," *Revue des Études Slaves*, XI, Paris, 1931, pp. 149-170.

77. Mazon, A., "Svjatogor ou Saint-Mont le Géant," *Revue des Études Slaves*, XII, Paris, 1932, pp. 160-201.

78. Plisetskii, M. M., *Istorizm russkikh bylin* (The Historicity of Russian Byliny). M., 1962.

79. Propp, V. Ia., *Russkii geroicheskii epos* (Russian Heroic Epic). 2nd ed. M., 1958. (1st ed., 1955.)

80. Rybakov, B. A., *Drevniaia Rus'; Skazaniia, byliny, letopisi* (Ancient Rus': Legends, Byliny, Chronicles). M., 1963.

81. Schmaus, Alois, "La byline russe et son état actuel," *La Table Ronde*, No. 132, Paris, Décembre 1958, pp. 114-127.

82. Skaftymov, A., "Poetika i genezis bylin" (Poetics and the Genesis of the Byliny), *Stat'i o russkoi literature* (Articles on Russian Literature), Saratov, 1958, pp. 3-76. (1st ed., 1924.)

83. Stender-Petersen, A. N., "Problematika sbornika Kirshi Danilova" (Problematics of Kirsha Danilov's Collection), *Scando-Slavica*, IV, Copenhagen, 1958, pp. 70-93.

84. Stief, Carl, "Das Verhältnis zwischen der altrussischen Chronik und dem Volksepos," *Scando-Slavica*, III, Copenhagen, 1957, pp. 140-147.—The same article reworked and enlarged: "Vzaimootnosheniia mezhdu russkim letopisaniem i russkim narodnym eposom" (The Mutual Relationship Between the Russian Chronicle Writing and the Russian Folk Epic), *Scando-Slavica*, IV, 1958, pp. 59-69.

85. Stief, Carl, "Die Ausnützung der Motive in den Bylinen," *Festschrift für Dmytro Čyževs'kyj*, Berlin, 1954, pp. 290-296. (Veröffentlichungen der Abteilung für slavische Sprachen und Literaturen des Osteuropa-Instituts (Slavisches Seminar) an der Freien Universität Berlin, VI.)

86. Trautmann, Reinhold, *Die Volksdichtung der Grossrussen*, I: *Das Heldenlied (Die Byline)*. Heidelberg, 1935.

87. Ukhov, P. D., "Postoiannye epitety v bylinakh kak sredstvo tipizatsii i sozdaniia obraza" (Constant Epithets in the Byliny as a Means for Typification and Creation of the Image), *Osnovnye problemy eposa vostochnykh slavian,* pp. 158-171. (See item 89.)

88. Ukhov, P. D., "Tipicheskie mesta (*loci communes*) kak sredstvo pasportizatsii bylin" (Commonplaces as a Means of Localizing Byliny), *Russkii fol'klor* (Russian Folklore), II, M.-L., 1957, pp. 128-154.

89. Vinogradov, V. V., et al., ed., *Osnovnye problemy eposa vostochnykh slavian* (Basic Problems of the Epic of the Eastern Slavs). M., 1958.

See also items 2, 3, 4, 5, 6, 8, 11, 12, 15, 16, 99, and 127.

IX. HISTORICAL SONGS

90. Putilov, B. N., ed., *Narodnye istoricheskie pesni* (Historical Folk Songs). M., 1962.

91. Putilov, B. N., *Russkii istoriko-pesennyi fol'klor XIII-XVI vekov* (Russian Historical Folk Poetry from the Thirteenth to the Sixteenth Centuries). M.-L., 1960.

92. Putilov, B. N., and B. M. Dobrovol'skii, ed., *Istoricheskie pesni XIII-XVI vekov* (Historical Songs from the Thirteenth to the Sixteenth Centuries). M.-L., 1960.

93. Sokolova, V. K., *Russkie istoricheskie pesni XVI-XVIII vv.* (Russian Historical Songs from the Sixteenth to the Eighteenth Centuries). M., 1960. (Trudy Inst. Etnografii im. N. N. Miklukho-Maklaia, n.s., LXI.)

94. Stief, Carl, *Studies in the Russian Historical Song.* Copenhagen, 1953.

See also items 2, 3, 4, 5, 6, 11, 12, 15, 60, 61, 118, and 121.

X. RELIGIOUS VERSES

95. Fedotov, G., *Stikhi dukhovnye (Russkaia narodnaia vera po dukhovnym stikham)* (Religious Verses: Russian Folk Religion on the Basis of the Religious Verses). Paris, 1935.

96. Stammler, Heinrich, *Die geistliche Volksdichtung als Äusserung der geistigen Kultur des russischen Volkes.* Heidelberg, 1939.

See also items 4, 11, and 15.

XI. FOLK TALES AND LEGENDS

(A) Collections

97. Afanas'ev, A. N., *Narodnye russkie skazki* (Russian Folk Tales), I-III. Ed. by V. Ia. Propp. M., 1957.

98. [Afanas'ev, A. N.], *Russian Fairy Tales.* Transl. by Norbert Guterman; folkloristic commentary by Roman Jakobson. New York, 1945.

99. Astakhova, A. M., *Narodnye skazki o bogatyriakh russkogo eposa* (Folk Tales About Russian Epic Heroes). M.-L., 1962.

100. Bazanov, V. G., and O. B. Alekseeva, ed., *Velikorusskie skazki v zapisiakh I. A. Khudiakova* (Great Russian Tales Recorded by I. A. Khudyakov). M.-L., 1964.

101. Chernyshev, V. I., *Skazki i legendy pushkinskikh mest; Zapisi 1927-1929 gg.* (Tales and Legends from Places Where Pushkin Lived: Recordings from 1927 to 1929). Ed. by N. P. Grinkova and N. T. Panchenko. M.-L., 1950.

102. Magnus, Leonard A., *Russian Folk-Tales.* New York, 1916.

103. Moldavskii, Dm., ed., *Russkaia satiricheskaia skazka* (Russian Satirical Tale). M., 1958.

104. Nechaev, A., and N. Rybakova, ed., *Russkie narodnye skazki* (Russian Folk Tales). M., 1952.

105. Novikov, N. V., ed., *Russkie skazki v zapisiakh i publikatsiiakh pervoi poloviny XIX veka* (Russian Tales in the Recordings and Publications of the First Half of the Nineteenth Century). M.-L., 1961.

106. Pomeranzewa (Pomerantseva), Erna, *Russische Volksmärchen.* Berlin, 1964.

107. Pomerantseva, E. V., *Russkie narodnye skazki* (Russian Folk Tales). M., 1957.

108. Propp, V. Ia., ed., *Severnorusskie skazki v zapisiakh A. I. Nikiforova* (North Russian Tales, Recorded by A. I. Nikiforov). M.-L., 1961.

109. Ralston, W. R. S., *Russian Folk-Tales.* London, 1873.

(B) Studies

110. Anikin, V. P., *Russkaia narodnaia skazka; Posobie dlia uchitelei* (Russian Folk Tale: Handbook for Teachers). M., 1959.

111. Gerber, Adolph, *Great Russian Animal Tales*. Baltimore, 1891. (Publications of the Modern Language Association of America, VI, No. 2.)

112. Propp, V. Ia., *Istoricheskie korni volshebnoi skazki* (Historical Roots of the Fairy Tale). L., 1946.—The same in Italian: *Le radici storiche dei racconti di fate*. Transl. by Clara Coïsson. Torino, 1949.

113. Propp, V. Ia., *Morphology of the Folktale*. Ed. with an Intr. by Svatava Pirkova-Jakobson. Transl. by Laurence Scott. Bloomington, 1958. (Publications of the Indiana University Research Center in Anthropology, Folklore, and Linguistics, X.)

See also items 2, 3, 4, 5, 8, 11, 12, 15, 74, 136, and 140.

XII. FOLK DRAMA

114. Berkov, P. N., ed., *Russkaia narodnaia drama XVII-XX vekov* (Russian Folk Drama from the Seventeenth to the Twentieth Centuries). M., 1953.

115. Veletskaia, N. N., "On the Late Stage in the History of the Russian Folk Drama," *Soviet Anthropology and Archaeology*, II, New York, 1964, No. 4, pp. 41-51.

116. Vsevolodskii-Gerngross, V. N., *Russkaia ustnaia narodnaia drama* (Russian Oral Folk Drama). M., 1959.

See also items 2, 3, 5, 11, 12, 15, and 120.

XIII. LYRIC SONGS AND BALLADS

(A) COLLECTIONS

117. Balashov, D. M., comp., *Narodnye ballady* (Folk Ballads). M.-L., 1963.

118. Kolpakova, N. P., et al., ed., *Pesni Pechory* (Pechora Songs). M.-L., 1963.

119. Lopyreva, E., ed., *Liricheskie narodnye pesni* (Lyric Folk Songs). L., 1955.

120. Moldavskii, D. M., *Narodno-poeticheskaia satira* (Satirical Folklore). L., 1960.

121. Novikova, A. M., ed., *Russkie narodnye pesni* (Russian Folk Songs). M., 1957.

122. Propp, V. Ia., ed., *Narodnye liricheskie pesni* (Lyric Folk Songs). L., 1961.

(B) STUDIES

123. Balashov, D. M., "Ballada o gibeli oklevetannoi zheny" (The Ballad of the Destruction of the Slandered Wife), *Russkii fol'klor* (Russian Folklore), VIII, M.-L., 1963, pp. 132-143.

124. Balashov, D. M., "Iz istorii russkoi ballady" (On the History of the Russian Ballad), *Russkii fol'klor* (Russian Folklore), VI, M.-L., 1961, pp. 270-286.

125. Balashov, D. M., "Kniaz' Dmitrii i ego nevesta Domna" (Prince Dmitriy and His Bride Domna), *Russkii fol'klor* (Russian *Folklore*), IV, M.-L., 1959, pp. 80-99.

126. Kolpakova, N. P., *Russkaia narodnaia bytovaia pesnia* (The Russian Folk Song of Everyday Life). M.-L., 1962.

127. Shtokmar, M. P., *Issledovaniia v oblasti russkogo narodnogo stikhoslozheniia* (Studies on the Versification of Russian Folk Songs). M., 1952.

128. Sidel'nikov, V. M., *Poetika russkoi narodnoi liriki* (The Poetics of Russian Folk Lyric). M., 1959.

129. Sidel'nikov, V. M., comp., *Russkaia narodnaia pesnia; Bibliograficheskii ukazatel', 1735-1945 gg.* (Russian Folk Song: Bibliographic Index, 1735-1945). M., 1962.

See also items 2, 3, 5, 8, 12, 15, 55, 57, 58, 60, and 74.

XIV. CHASTUSHKI

130. Bokov, V., ed., *Russkaia chastushka* (Russian Chastushka). Intr. by L. Sheptaev. L., 1950.

131. Jarcho, B. J., "Organische Struktur des russischen Schnaderhüpfels (Častuška)," *Germanoslavica*, III, Brno, etc., 1934, pp. 31-64.

132. Lazutin, S. G., *Russkaia chastushka; Voprosy proiskhozhdeniia i formirovaniia zhanra* (Russian Chastushka: Questions on the Origin and Formation of the Genre). Voronezh, 1960.

133. Lopatin, Ivan A., "What the People Are Now Singing in a Russian Village," *Journal of American Folklore*, 64, Philadelphia, 1951, pp. 179-190.

134. Rozhdestvenskaia, N. I., and S. S. Zhislina, ed., *Russkie chastushki* (Russian Chastushki). M., 1956.

See also items 2, 3, 5, 11, 12, 15, 118, and 120.

XV. LITERATURE AND FOLKLORE

135. Astakhova, A. M., et al., ed., *Voprosy sovetskoi literatury, IV; Fol'klor v russkoi sovetskoi literature* (Questions on Soviet Literature, IV: Folklore in Russian Soviet Literature). M.-L., 1956.

136. Azadovskii, M. K., *Stat'i o literature i fol'klore* (Articles About Literature and Folklore). M.-L., 1960.

137. Eleonskii, S. F., *Literatura i narodnoe tvorchestvo; Posobie dlia uchitelei srednei shkoly* (Literature and Folklore: Handbook for High School Teachers). M., 1956.

138. Gibian, George, "Dostoevskij's Use of Russian Folklore," *Journal of American Folklore*, 69, Philadelphia, 1956, pp. 239-253.

139. Gorlin, Michel, "Le conte populaire dans la littérature russe vers 1830," Michel Gorlin and Raïssa Bloch-Gorlina, *Études littéraires et historiques*, Paris, 1957, pp. 7-28. (Bibliothèque Russe de l'Institut d'Études Slaves, XXX.)

140. Lupanova, I. P., *Russkaia narodnaia skazka v tvorchestve pisatelei pervoi poloviny XIX veka* (Russian Folk Tale in the Works of the Writers of the First Half of the Nineteenth Century). Petrozavodsk, 1959.

141. Matviichuk, N. F., *Tvorchestvo M. Gor'kogo i fol'klor* (The Works of M. Gorky and Folklore). Kiev, 1959.

142. Piksanov, N. K., "Dostoevskii i fol'klor" (Dostoyevsky and Folklore), *Sovetskaia etnografiia* (Soviet Ethnography), M., 1934, No. 1-2, pp. 152-165.

143. Rowland, Mary and Paul, "Pasternak's Use of Folklore, Myth, and Epic Song in *Doctor Zhivago*," *Southern Folklore Quarterly, XXV*, [Gainesville, Florida], 1961, pp. 207-222.

144. *Russkaia sovetskaia poeziia i narodnoe tvorchestvo; Sbornik statei* (Russian Soviet Poetry and Folklore: Collection of Articles). L., 1955.

145. Stenbock-Fermor, Elisabeth, "Elements of Folklore in an Early Work of Tolstoy," Morris Halle et al., comp., *For Roman Jakobson*, The Hague, 1956, pp. 540-546.

146. .Vykhodtsev, P. S., *Russkaia sovetskaia poeziia i narodnoe tvorchestvo* (Russian Soviet Poetry and Folklore). M.-L., 1963.

See also item 6.

RUSSIAN
FOLKLORE

FOREWORD

❦

The Russian Translation Project of the American Council of Learned Societies was organized in 1944 with the aid of a subsidy from the Humanities Division of the Rockefeller Foundation. The aim of the Project is the translation into English of significant Russian works in the fields of the humanities and the social sciences which provide an insight into Russian life and thought.

In the difficult problem of the selection of books for translation, the Administrative Committee has had the counsel and cooperation of Slavic scholars throughout the United States and Great Britain. It is thought that the books chosen will be useful to general readers interested in world affairs, and will also serve as collateral reading material for the large number of courses on Russia in our colleges and universities.

Since Russian history is a continuum, the volumes translated are of various dates and have been drawn from both the prerevolutionary and postrevolutionary periods, from writings published inside and outside of Russia, the choice depending solely on their value to the fundamental aim of the Project. Translations are presented in authentic and unabridged English versions of the original text. Only in this way, it is believed, can American readers be made aware of the traditions, concepts, and ideologies by which the thinking and attitudes of the people of Russia are molded.

It should, of course, be clearly understood that the views expressed in the works translated are not to be identified in any way with those of the Administrative Committee or of the Council.

THE ADMINISTRATIVE COMMITTEE
JOHN A. MORRISON, *Chairman*
HAROLD SPIVACKE
SERGIUS YAKOBSON
MORTIMER GRAVES
W. CHAPIN HUNTINGTON

CONTENTS

Contents

IN LIEU OF A PREFACE

The course in Russian folklore which is presented herewith is designed for students of the literary faculties in institutions of higher education. But, in view of the almost complete lack at the present time of general works on folklore, I have so arranged the book that it may be useful also for teachers, graduate students, and those who are beginning scientific work. This will explain the presence of somewhat voluminous bibliographical materials on the points which are dealt with in the book. It will explain also the comprehensiveness of the historiographic survey. It has been my wish that my book might serve as a primary source of assistance for the independent scientific work of young specialists.

My course deals with all the fundamental aspects of the oral poetic works of the old and new period. In it I have considerably enlarged the scope of the phenomena which are generally included in a survey of folklore. In considerably larger measure than in previous courses on Russian popular literature, I have assigned a place to the ancient literary evidences of oral works. I have considered it necessary to include in the historiographic survey rather extensive quotations from the works of the most outstanding investigators of folklore, since young students are insufficiently acquainted with the scientific monographs. Besides, very many of these books are difficult to find in the libraries.

In planning my course, I have followed the programs which have

[1]

been approved by the Committee on Higher Education for the faculty of letters of universities and teachers' colleges.

At the beginning of the list of chapters in my book, I have placed some material written by me for a correspondence course in teacher training (in 1930–1932). This course was drawn up in conjunction with my brother, Professor B. M. Sokolov, now deceased. The chapters on "Religious Verses" and "Tales" were prepared by B. M. Sokolov, and here have only been revised in part by me. Many of the chapters (for example, the introductory chapter on theory, the historiographic survey, the *byliny*, the historical songs, the section on Soviet folklore, and others) have been completely rewritten, and others have been substantially revised. Being restricted by space in the quotation of passages from texts on folklore, I have not felt it necessary to reproduce these texts in full, since many of them have been published in the *Anthology of Russian Folklore* by Professor N. P. Andreyev, where they are arranged in almost the same order as in my course. The use of my course presupposes the required collateral reading of the works of folklore themselves (from the *Anthology* or from the scientific collections of folklore indicated in the course).

In the main, the course is devoted to Russian folklore; but in view of the fact that in our time the folklore of the other peoples of the USSR has had such a great influence on the social life of the whole country of the Soviets, and since it is found to be most closely interrelated with Russian folklore, I have thought it necessary, at the end of the book, to give a general survey of the Soviet folklore of the fraternal peoples of the USSR, and to characterize the works of two celebrated popular poets who have been decorated by the government: Suleyman Stalsky and Dzhambul Dzhabayev.

PROFESSOR YURY SOKOLOV

PROBLEMS AND HISTORIOGRAPHY
OF FOLKLORE

THE NATURE OF FOLKLORE
AND THE PROBLEMS OF FOLKLORISTICS

"Folklore" is a scientific term, of English derivation. It was first introduced into scientific terminology in 1846, by the English scholar, William Thoms (W. G. Thoms). Literally translated, "folklore" signifies the wisdom of the people, the people's knowledge. This term was quite rapidly adopted by scholars in other countries, and soon became an international one.[1]

This term was at first used to denote only the materials included in the scope of this study; later on, it was frequently used to designate also the branch of science which devotes itself to the study of this material.[2]

At the present time, in accordance with the practice of the majority of European and Soviet scholars, the term "folklore" is used to designate the material of study; to indicate the science which deals with this material, the term "folkloristics" is employed.

Besides these international terms, other terms are also encountered in the scientific terminology of various countries. For instance, to

[1] The word is used with well known changes in pronunciation: in English. *folklore* (the English pronounce it "fo'klor"); German, *die Folklore* (pronounced. under the influence of the German word *Volk* [people], "folklor"); French, *le folklore*, "folklore"; Italian, *il folklore*, "folklore"; Spanish, *el folklore*, "folklore" —the latter two with the final *e* pronounced, and so forth.

[2] Cf., on this point, Dr. Kaindl, *Die Volkskunde, ihre Bedeutung, ihre Ziele und ihre Methode* (Leipzig und Wien, Franz Deutick, 1903), pp. 22-23; also Arnold van Gennep, *Le Folklore* (Paris, 1924).

See also the article by Prof. E. G. Kagarov, "What Is Folklore?" *Artistic Folklore*, Nos. IV-V, Moscow, 1929.

designate "folkloristics" the Germans use the word *Volkskunde* (meaning folklore as a science), or, in a narrower sense, the word *Volksdichtung* (the poetry of the people, folk creation); the French, besides using the word *le folklore*, refer to the material of study as *traditions populaires* (the traditions of the people, the legends of the people); the Italians, in conformity with this practice, speak of *le tradizioni popolari*, and so forth.

But if the term "folklore" has gradually become the prevailing one in the majority of countries, it does not follow from this that a single meaning has been definitively fixed for this term. On the question of the content and scope of the concept of folklore, and also concerning the nature of folkloristics and the boundaries which divide it from related disciplines, the greatest difference of opinion prevails in the scholarly world.

A number of western European scholars (for example, the French scholar van Gennep) identify folklore with ethnography, but some, especially the Germans, identify it with national and regional studies.

By "folklore" one should understand the oral poetic creations of broad masses of people.

If the term "literature" is employed, not in its literal sense (written materials), but more widely; that is, if we understand by it not only written artistic creations, but oral artistic productions in general, then folklore is a special branch of literature, and folkloristics thus is seen to be a part of literary scholarship.

The idea of the close connection of folkloristics with literary studies has also been expressed more than once by western European scholarship. It has been formulated more definitively during the past few years by Soviet scholars.[3]

But once the oral poetic creations of the masses of the people are included under the term "folklore," then the question may arise:

[3] Cf. my article, "Current Problems in the Study of Russian Folklore," *Artistic Folklore*, No. I, 1926, p. 5; also the public lecture of the deceased Academician S. F. Oldenburg at the Sorbonne in 1929, "Le Conte dit populaire, problèmes et méthodes," by S. F. Oldenburg, *Revue des études slaves* (Paris, 1929); my article "Folkloristics and Literary Scholarship," in the collection of *Studies in Memory of P. N. Sakulin* (Moscow, 1931), p. 280; the book by M. K. Azadovsky, *Literature and Folklore* (Leningrad, State Literary Publishing House, 1938), p. 4, Preface, and pp 196-201, "Russian Storytellers."

Why not make use of the old terminology which was formerly in current use—"literature of the people" or "poetry of the people"? Under these titles, in the nineteenth century, and even in more recent times, in the period before the revolution, lectures were read in the universities, and textbooks were issued for the middle schools.[4] At first glance, the use of this old term would seem to be expedient at least in this respect, that it is clearer and more readily understandable than the foreign word "folklore."

But it is only at first glance that this seems to be so. In actuality, however, the terms "literature of the people," "poetry of the people," in their application to the historical past, may call forth a whole series of inappropriate concepts and obsolete, fallacious interpretations which cannot pass the test of scientific criticism. The fact is that these terms, which had their origin in the first half of the nineteenth century, in the period of the romantic and Slavophile enthusiasms of the nobility, and which were widely used in the popular literature of the second half of the last century, contained in themselves the echoes of the class ideas of that time. The romantic and Slavophile nobility used the term "people" in accordance with the vaguely defined nationalistic teaching of that time, regarding the "popular spirit," the "popular soul," as a kind of unique, extraclass, socially nondifferentiated whole, opposed to other nationalities. The lower classes of the popular intelligentsia used the words "people" and "popular" mainly for the peasant masses, but again as a socially nondifferentiated whole. Hence these vague, indefinite, and fallacious categories in the romantic understanding of the word "popular" as pertaining to

[4] For example: *Introduction to the History of Russian Folklore* by P. V. Vladimirov (Kiev, 1896); the lithographed course in *Russian Popular Poetry* of Prof. Vsevolod F. Miller (Moscow, 1909–1910); *Introduction to Popular Literature*, lectures on popular literature by Prof. A. M. Loboda (Kiev, 1911); "Russian Popular Literature," a lecture by Prof. I. I. Zamotin (Warsaw, 1913–1914); No. 1 of the third volume of the great work of Acad. E. F. Karsky, *The White Russians*, under the heading, "Popular Poetry" (Moscow, 1916); *Introduction to the Study of Popular Literature*, by P. M. Sobolev (Orekhovo-Zuevo, 1922); N. I. Korobka, "Popular Literature," *An Essay Toward a Survey of the History of Russian Literature for Schools and Self-Instruction* (St. Petersburg, 1909) Pt. I, No. 1; V. V. Sipovsky, "Popular Literature," *History of Russian Literature* (St. Petersburg, 1906), Pt. I; also the sections in the textbooks for the middle schools by Nezelenov, Smirnovsky, Savodnik, and others.

the whole nation, or in the popular understanding of this term as pertaining to the whole peasantry, were usually introduced into the university courses and into the school textbooks on "popular literature," obscuring its real social basis. With these same fallacious categories were also linked, as we shall see later, incorrect juxtapositions of the "popular literature" and the artistic written literature.

The unsuitability of such a term, which involuntarily drew after it a train of false theoretical assumptions, was already acknowledged by many, even in the prerevolutionary period.

With the first decade of the twentieth century, in the years before the revolution, and in the first years after the Great October Socialist Revolution, another term began to gain favor: "oral literature." [5]

The term "oral literature" correctly characterizes folklore only in its technical aspect, but it is the more acceptable because, if it does not include in itself any of the sociological characteristics of the subject, still, on the other hand, it has the advantage of not containing any false sociological implications.

During the past few years, with the rapid growth of socialist culture, in the process of establishing a classless society in the USSR, the terms "popular works," "popular literature," "popular art," have again (and this time with full justification) come into general use for the contemporary mass creations of the working people. But with reference to the oral poetry of earlier periods created among the various classes, there remain in force the considerations set forth above, as regards difficulties of a theoretical and methodological character, which are involved in the use of these terms.

But in this course we prefer to make use of the word "folklore," both for the sake of consistency in terminology and because of the international character of this scholarly term, which facilitates international scientific work.

One of the peculiarities of folklore is seen to be the presence within

[5] Thus V. A. Keltuyala in his *Course in the History of Russian Literature*, Pt. I (St. Petersburg, 1906), Bk. 1, uses mainly the term "oral works"; Prof. M. N. Speransky calls his course, *Russian Oral Literature* (Moscow, 1917); N. L. Brodsky, N. A. Gusev, and N. P. Sidorov call their well known bibliographical reference work, *Russian Oral Literature* (Topics, Bibliography, Programs for the Collection of Oral Poetic Works) (Leningrad, 1924).

it of aspects of syncretism, that is, the inevitable connection between the oral works and elements of the other arts. Folklore falls within the realm of the scenic arts (mimetics, pantomime, dramatic art), not only in the presentation of the so-called "popular drama" and dramatized ceremonies—the wedding, funeral, agricultural, choral, and other performances—but also in the narration of *byliny*, the telling of tales, and the rendition of songs; it also falls within the realm of the choreographic art (popular dances, folk dances, choral dances) and of musical art (the tunes of the songs). Consequently, folkloristics also falls partly within the purview of such disciplines as the art of the theater, choreography, and musicology.

Oral productions (songs, tales, sayings, proverbs, riddles, and so on) have their roots in the very existence of the broad laboring masses. The folklorist, therefore, cannot help being at the same time, to a certain degree, an ethnographer. Otherwise, he runs the risk of making an altogether incorrect interpretation of the folklore which he is studying.

Finally, the folklorist must be, to a considerable extent, a linguist; he must be proficient in the language, dialect, and speech of the oral poetic productions which he is collecting and studying. Dialectology is one of the scholarly fields which are compulsory for everyone who wishes to be a genuine folklorist.

Thus, folkloristics cannot help invading the fields of the theater, choreography, musicology, ethnography, and linguistics. In their turn these disciplines cannot, of course, get along without the aid of folkloristics.

However, does the overlapping of folkloristics with related disciplines, on the one hand, deprive it of its right to an independent existence; and, on the other hand, does it do away with the proposition formulated above, that folklore is a branch of literary art (that is, of literature in the broad sense of the word), and that folkloristics is a branch of literary study?

No complex phenomenon of life can avoid being the object of study from various points of view, but every complex phenomenon has its own basic, specific characteristic. And this distinguishing characteristic of folklore proves to be something which defines it above all as a part of literary art, and folkloristics as a branch of literary study.

For a correct exposition of the relation between folklore and literature, between folkloristics and literary study, it is necessary at the very outset to break away from those views on this question which have persistently, during the course of many decades, been engrafted first upon the Slavophile, then upon the popular movements in the field of our science.

"Literature of the people," as folklore was then called, was contrasted to artistic literature in two particulars: first, "literature of the people" was, as it were, impersonal, whereas written literature always had a specific author; and, second, "popular literature" was, as it were, artless in contrast to the "artistic" written literature.

However, both of these contrasts, so long maintained in scholarship, fail to pass the test of criticism.

First of all, what is "impersonal" poetry, or, as they still used to say in the nineteenth century, "poetry of the whole people"? If one is speaking of the wide popularity, the extensive diffusion of this or that work, whether it be a tale, a *bylina*, or a song, if the name of the author, furthermore, is unknown, then does it follow from this, that there never was an author? Of course there was. On the contrary, there have never been works which could have been composed by no one, or by the "whole people."

The researches of folklorists since the end of the nineteenth century and during the first decades of the twentieth, especially those of the Russians, both in the prerevolutionary period and in our own time, have demonstrated in the most convincing manner how wrong those persons were who spoke of a supposedly impersonal popular creative work.

Systematic researches into the life and works of the narrators of *byliny*, the storytellers, the women who composed lamentations, the wedding attendants, and the other so-called "bearers" of folklore have shown what a vast role personal artistic skill, training, talent, memory, and the other aspects of the individual mind play in oral poetry. Besides, it has now been thoroughly established, and confirmed by hundreds, if not by thousands of examples, that every "bearer" of folklore, that is, performer of oral poetic works, is at the same time, to a considerable degree, their creator and author.[6]

Among them are people who are talented and people who have no gifts; those with a rich, original imagination and imitators lacking in independence; experienced hands and novices in the art; gay humorists and stern moralists; preachers who are devoted to religion and bold atheists; fantastic romanticists and realists. In other words, in their psychological and ideological attitudes, in their degree of mastery and endowment, we may encounter among the "bearers" of folklore (that is, its creators and performers) no less diversity in individual

[6] The first to introduce the custom of classifying the written texts of *byliny*, not by subjects, but by narrators, and of adding brief biographical notes concerning them, and characterizing the peculiarities of the individual repertory and the individual manner of performance, was A. F. Hilferding, *Onega Byliny* (St. Petersburg, 1873; 2nd ed., 3 vols., 1896; 3rd ed., Vol. II, 1938). From that time on it became compulsory for every collector of *byliny* and tales to adhere to this principle; see *White Sea Byliny*, by A. V. Markov (Moscow, 1901); *Pechora Byliny*, by N. E. Onchukov (St. Petersburg, 1904); *Archangel Byliny*, by A. D. Grigoryev (Vol. I, Moscow, 1904; Vol. III, St. Petersburg, 1910). The same principle has been adopted also by the collectors of tales. Such collections as the following: *Northern Tales*, by N. E. Onchukov (St. Petersburg, 1909); *Tales and Songs of the Belo-Ozero Region*, B. and Y. Sokolov (Moscow, 1915); *Great-Russian Tales from the Province of Vyatka*, by D. K. Zelenin (Petrograd, 1915); *Great-Russian Tales from the Province of Perm*, by the same author (St. Petersburg, 1914); *Tales from the Upper Lena Region*, by M. K. Azadovsky, No. I (Irkutsk, 1925); *Upper Lena Tales* (2nd ed., Irkutsk, 1938); *Tales and Legends of the Northern Region*, by I. V. Karnaykhova (Moscow, 1934), and others; and during the past few years collections of the works of individual storytellers or narrators have begun to appear. Thus, the following books have appeared: *Tales of Kuprianikha: A Transcript of the Tales, an Article on the Works of Kuprianikha, and Commentaries*, by A. M. Novikova and M. A. Ossovetsky, introductory article and general editing by Prof. I. P. Plotnikov (Voronezh, 1937); *White Sea Tales, Related by M. M. Korguev*, ed. A. N. Nechayev (The Soviet Writer, 1938).

The State Museum of Literature has in preparation editions of *Tales of I. F. Kovalev*, and *Byliny of M. S. Krukova*.

The results of the work of Russian folklorists, who have examined the life and work of individual narrators and storytellers, have been summed up in the German work of M. K. Azadovsky, *Eine sibirische Märchenerzählerin* (Helsinki, 1926), FFC No. 68; see also B. M. Sokolov, *Narrators* (Moscow, 1924); M. K. Azadovsky, *Russian Tales* (Academia, 1932); introductory article, "Russian Storytellers," reprinted in a condensed form in the above-mentioned book by M. K. Azadovsky; *Literature and Folklore* (Leningrad, 1938), pp. 196-272.

The works of Russian scholars enumerated above have had a deep influence on the work of Western folklorists (Heseman, Mason, Muiko).

types than we find in written artistic literature. Thus, it is not fitting to speak of folklore as though of an impersonal creation.

From what has just been said, there will readily become apparent also the fallaciousness of another characteristic which was thought to distinguish folklore from artistic literature: the notorious "artlessness" of folklore. Of what kind of "artlessness" of folklore is it possible to speak, when at every step in even the least thoughtful analysis of any text of folklore we shall necessarily discover elements of artistic crafts-manship or literary art?

The direct observations of folklorists make us realize how the nar-rators, storytellers, and singers strive for mastery in the knowledge and performance of their works, how, it frequently happens, some of them spend years in the study of their art. At times, if one looks closely, one can discover, as it were, "schools" of art, distinguishing certain masters from others both in repertory and in style, in their artistic manner of performance.

Under these conditions it is not fitting to speak of a certain "artless-ness" of folklore. On the other hand, one must consider as altogether fallacious the definition which has been given by earlier investigators to artistic written literature, as if it were "artificial," and consequently studied, unnatural, not organically living. Entirely unacceptable also, of course, from the contemporary point of view, is the definition of oral poetry as "artless" and of written literature as "artificial." Both the one and the other, being manifestations of one great literary art, are poetry.

Frequently, defending the theory of the "impersonality" of oral poetry, people argue with reference to the *anonymity* of works of folklore; but, as we have already pointed out above, this characteristic is purely external, and even, in the last analysis, accidental. Works of folklore are anonymous, nameless, for the reason that the names of the authors, in the vast majority of cases, have not been revealed, have not been discovered, because for the greater part they were not written down, but were preserved only in the memory of the people. But, in the first place, this was not the case always and everywhere. For in-stance, in the East (including the Soviet part of Central Asia and the Caucasus) many songs, composed both in the ancient and also in the later period, tenaciously preserve the names of their authors. These names are included in a fixed scheme of sounds (with rhymes, assonance, and alliteration), usually at the end of the song. This trick which the poets had of preserving their names in the texts is now widely known from the songs of the popular poets who have been decorated: the Lezgian *ashug* Suleyman Stalsky, and the Kazakh *akyn* Dzhambul. In the second place, during the past few decades the folklorists have begun to indicate exactly from whom, where, and when this or that poetic work was recorded, and as a result of this, they have sometimes discovered the authorship of local creators of folklore. In the third place, during recent times it has continually been discovered, with increasing frequency, that this or that popular song, which everyone had considered as truly a "folk song," proved to be a literary production of this or that well known or little known poet.[7]

One must suppose that through careful historico-literary work there will also be uncovered a still greater number of unknown authors of well known songs which many people had felt it necessary to consider "impersonal."

However, the names of the authors of many songs will never be revealed, because when they composed the songs they did not write them down, but disseminated them by word of mouth only. But, by analogy with the facts which we have just pointed out from the literature of the nineteenth and twentieth centuries, we may affirm that anonymity does not signify the "impersonality," the "lack of an author," of any oral production.

And, lastly, anonymity is not a kind of distinguishing mark of folklore in comparison with written literature. To secure for themselves, for their own name, the works of their personal creative genius has become the practice of the majority of peoples only since the beginning of the epoch of capitalism.

In the epoch of feudalism the authors of written literary works, and also the authors of works in the field of the graphic arts (architecture, sculpture, painting), often did not aspire to perpetuate their own names.

The theory of folklore as a special form of creative work, to be dis-

[7] See below, the section on singers and popular adaptations of songs.

tinguished in principle from literary creation, is tentatively based by several investigators also on the fact that works of folklore do not have a fixed text, but are always presented in a whole series of *variants*, while a literary production always has a text absolutely fixed by the author.

The role of variants in the history of folklore is, of course, very great; even so, they do not constitute the principal distinction between it and written literature.

Let us, in the first place, think of the written literature of the epoch of feudalism, before the invention of printing. The copying of books by hand brought with it involuntary mechanical changes, alterations, which, as they accumulated, gradually made the text other than it had been. A still greater role was played by deliberate revisions of the work, now of a quantitative character (abridgements and expansions), now of an ideological (those for which the accepted term in philology is "redactions"). One need only call to mind, for example, the complex history of the Russian chronicles, which represent an exceedingly intricate network of countless reworkings and redactions. It required the work of several generations of scholars, especially the work of that most talented scholar, Academician A. A. Shakhmatov, to disentangle the complicated puzzle, created through the centuries, of the chronicles and their transcriptions.

But even with the invention of printing, the variations in literary texts did not cease. Historians of literature, at every step, have had to deal with the facts either of a new version of an old work by another author, or, still more frequently, with different "variants" and "redactions" of one and the same work by its own author.

Naturally, in folklore, as predominantly oral poetry, the variation has a greater significance than in written literature. Not being written down, the once-created text is preserved only in the memory of the narrator, storyteller, or singer. And, as numerous investigations by folklorists have shown, the text never remains in an unchanged form, even on the lips of one and the same person. One must not lose sight of the fact that, in the narration of a *bylina* or a tale, or in the rendition of a song, there is always an element of *improvisation*. No matter how exceptional a memory the narrator or storyteller may possess, in the repeated performance of a *bylina* or a tale he unfailingly introduces this or that change, abbreviates or expands the text, adds or subtracts, centers his attention upon something other than he emphasized the first time. In such changes much depends on the mood of the narrator, and also on the audience which is listening to him (on its composition, moods, and tastes).

Nevertheless, this fact does not signify anything differing in principle from written literature. The role of the variants merely appears to be more distinct in oral works; but it is necessary to treat every variant as an artistic fact which has an independent significance. It is only necessary to make recordings, for example, of tales on one and the same subject by two different storytellers, to be convinced of the fact that we have to do with two different works, though similar in theme and subject matter.

From a theoretical point of view, there will in this respect be no radical difference from what is so often encountered in the history of any literature. The figure of Don Juan and the arrangement of the subject matter which was developed out of his amatory adventures, as is well known, have been worked over by very many authors (Molière, Byron, Pushkin, Alexis Tolstoy, and others); none the less, no one will deny the complete independence and intrinsic value of the works of each of these authors. It is precisely in this way that we must approach the material we encounter in folklore; it is necessary, behind any kind of general related scheme of subject matter, behind any kind of general similarity in the outlines of the hero of the tale—behind everything which is prompted by poetic tradition—to perceive the creative aspect of the storyteller, who must be considered not only as a transmitter, but above all as an author.

Here a question arises concerning *tradition*, which also is considered by certain investigators as an essential characteristic that distinguishes folklore from literature. But again we insist that the distinction between folklore and artistic literature, in this relationship too, is more of a quantitative than of a qualitative kind. Surely, apart from poetic tradition, one cannot even conceive of the development of literature In folklore this power of tradition appears to be stronger, because the oral creation, not being fixed in any outward form, has had to work out, in the course of many centuries of practice, such traditional mnemonic devices as would preserve in the memory sometimes very complicated subjects.

An analysis of the poetics of folklore will have to show how the stylistic and compositional devices worked out by tradition, on the one hand, contribute to the memorizing of artistic texts, and, on the other hand, facilitate their reworking or the creation of new texts by means of improvisation.

No matter how great may be the power of poetic tradition, in actuality, in the creative oral poetic process, there is no distinction in principle from the creative process in literature. The power of tradition and the force of personal initiative, of individual "improvisation" (in the broad sense of this word)—these two opposing factors, in the last analysis, also go to make up that unity which is known as a poetic creation. It differs from folklore only in degree. Folklore cannot be reduced to one tradition alone; otherwise it would be necessary to acknowledge in it only the source of stagnation, sluggishness, and conservatism.

Not so long ago, one still encountered the efforts of certain scholars to discern in folklore only this, or chiefly this aspect. A number of researchers tried to reduce the essence of folklore to the understanding of cultural "survivals," "relicts," as if even forming the specific character of folklore in contrast to literature. (On the reactionary theory of "relicts," see below.)

In the content and form of folklore, it is impossible to deny the presence of survivals of the old cultures of earlier social-economic structures (feudalism, tribal society). There is no aspect of the life and activity of human society which does not reflect, in one degree or other, the experience of past stages in human culture; but to isolate folklore, solely on the basis of this characteristic, into a special field of knowledge, is inexpedient and groundless. Those same surviving elements are to be observed also in material culture, as well as in customs, manners, opinions, language and, finally, in art; in a word, in the whole of social life. The historian of any phenomenon will discern individual elements of the past in the new, in the contemporary; elements, of course, which in an appropriate manner have been changed, worked over, and transformed.

None the less, to make all these "survivals" the basic object of a knowledge of folkloristics would be an unjustifiable extension, and at the same time a contraction, of its tasks.

Folklore is an echo of the past, but at the same time it is also the vigorous voice of the present. If we were to reduce folklore to the "living past" (as it has at times been called, under the influence of romantic idealization), this would mean that we must pass over the role played by folklore in contemporary times, and not picture to ourselves with sufficient clearness its social function.

Here we approach the cardinal questions of the social nature and the social significance of oral poetry. The folkloristics of the nobles in the first half of the nineteenth century, and the popular folkloristics of the second half of that century, obscured the social nature of folklore.

Folklore has been, and continues to be, a reflection and a weapon of class conflict; consequently, again, it is not distinguished in nature, in any way, from artistic literature, with reference also to its social function as a reflection and a weapon of class conflict.

The first efforts of Soviet folklorists to undertake a more detailed examination of the class nature of the works of folklore have already yielded very tangible results.

If prerevolutionary folkloristics (both of the nobles and of the bourgeoisie) concentrated on the collection and study almost exclusively of peasant folklore, Soviet folkloristics, on the other hand, has also included within the sphere of its knowledge the oral creations of the working class, both in its present and in its past. Besides, Soviet folklorists in their course have had to destroy many prejudices of the old scientific schools, which had discerned in the folklore of the factory and the mill nothing but "coarseness," "factory workers' efforts." (See on this point a more detailed discussion in the section "Folklore of the Factory and the Mill.")

The contemporary Soviet folklorists have not only continued the study of peasant folklore, but have also made the subject of their study the works of other intermediate social groups, which for the greater part had been ignored in the scholarly works of the prerevolutionary period; namely, the urban folklore of the petty bourgeois (middle class) surroundings. In this way folkloristics has illuminated the life of oral creations among all social classes, including also children's folklore, which had hardly been studied at all before.

But with reference to folklore there arises one exceedingly significant difficulty concerning method, which complicates the class analysis of oral poetry. The difficulty consists in this, that a work of folklore (a *bylina*, tale, song, proverb, riddle, and so on) frequently is seen to be not only a fact of contemporary life, but also includes in itself many elements of the past, survivals, relicts, of which we have spoken above. Traits of this kind, as we have made clear, are present also in the productions of written literature, but quantitatively there are more of them in folklore, for precisely the reason that folklore is chiefly oral poetry, preserved in the memory, and handed down—in continual reworkings, it is true—from mouth to mouth, from generation to generation.

There arises the problem of the social determination not only of that which characterizes a given production as a reflection of the epoch when its recorded form was produced, but also of those elements which are indisputably preserved in a given text as an echo of other epochs, remote or recent.

In a class analysis of folklore it is natural to begin first of all with an effort to understand its social function in contemporary times. We have been saying a great deal about the role of the creative personality of each of the "bearers" of folklore. We have emphasized the significance of this "bearer," not only as an artistic performer of a strange text, but above all as an artistic author, who to a certain degree freely arranges the poetic material which is being handed down by him. It is understandable why the contemporary folklorist strives not only to make an exact copy of the *byliny*, tales, and songs which have been communicated to him, but also to collect more or less detailed biographical information about the narrator or the singer, and to give the history and characteristics of his work.

But as in the study of literature, so also in folkloristics, biography must occupy a subordinate place in the series of fundamental tasks which await the investigator. It must serve for him only as secondary material for the settling of questions of a class nature, dealing with the social function of works of folklore.

Like the professional writer in literature, the "bearer" of a popular work is frequently also a *professional artist.* In disproof of the old Slavophile theories of the supposed "impersonality" and the supposed "artlessness" of popular creations, we have already said that not everyone is capable of being the creator and performer of this or that production of folklore. For this, both talent and training are demanded.

The researches of folklorists during the second half of the nineteenth century, and in the twentieth, have shown how many genres of folklore have indubitably been worked out and perfected by persons who had made a special study of their craft as poets and performers, and had developed this craft into a profession, that is, who had earned their bread by their skill in artistic creation and artistic performance.

Such, for instance, are the many wailers, weepers, mourners, creators and performers of funeral, wedding, and recruiting laments; such are the wedding attendants, frequently invited to manage the wedding ceremony, and to entertain the public, many times a year, at weddings in their district; such are the itinerant professional beggars, the blind men, the performers of religious verses; such are the many storytellers, and especially the narrators of *byliny,* and so forth. In its proper place (in the appropriate chapters) there will be a more detailed discussion of all these categories of professional performers of folklore in the recent past, and to some extent also in contemporary times, and information will be given also about the broader role of professional masters of the popular art in ancient times—buffoons, itinerant professional beggars, singers of the druzhina,* and so on.

These categories of performers and creators of Russian folklore, naturally, must be compared with the corresponding categories of professional masters of the popular art among other peoples of the

---

* *Druzhina:* a company or retinue serving as aids to the prince both as an armed force and as advisers and servitors. In general a *druzhina* did not exceed several hundred men.—Ed.

USSR: with the Ukrainian bandore players and lyre players, with the Karelian *cantelists*, with the Caucasian *ashugi*, the Uzbek *bakshi*, the Kirghiz and Kazakh *akyni* and *zhirshi*, the Yakutsk *olongokhuti*, the Mongolian *tulchi*, and also with the ancient Greek *aëdists* and rhapsodists, the medieval French jongleurs, the German *Spielmänner* and Meistersinger, and so forth.

Professionalism in a popular creation is a natural expression of its great complexity; it demands special teaching and training.

The researches of the collectors of folklore lead us to the conclusion that in the telling of *byliny*, the narration of tales, in the performance of laments, and so forth, one can determine the existence of various artistic "styles," or "schools," which are distinguished one from another, each having its own tradition, frequently going back into the distant past. This still further complicates the question of the history of oral poetry. Unfortunately, scientific investigations of the processes of popular creation began too late; very much that happened in the life of folklore in the past ages has irrevocably disappeared, and is being restored, with very great difficulty, by means of a retrospective transfer of conclusions from the contemporary period to the past.

From all that has been said, one may perceive how difficult it still is, in the present status of the science, to establish *periods* in the history of folklore, like the periods in the history of written literature. If, even in the field of literary studies, there are so many arguments being waged about the problem of establishing periods in the history of literature, then with reference to folklore it is still more difficult to do this, since the question depends not only upon the choice of a principle for determining the periods, but also upon the absence of any kind of fixed dates. It is true that there may come to our aid indirect references, drawn from ancient written monuments, which give us certain facts from the life of oral poetry (for example, accounts in the chronicles of the singing of songs, or of the existence of this or that ceremony), or which include within themselves direct echoes of oral productions (for example, proverbs, renderings of legends, and so forth, inserted into the chronicles), and finally, the testimonies of foreign travelers. But on the whole, these chance references cannot give us a picture of the development of folklore in all its fullness. It is necessary to base the work mainly upon a paleontological and historical analysis of the texts of folklore which have been preserved in later copies. As to the degree in which even such an analysis may not be considered reliable, this point will be discussed below.

In this connection, it must be remembered that we have been speaking about elements, concealed in one and the same text of folklore, which have reference in their origin to various epochs and to various social surroundings. And therefore, according to my deep conviction, it is still impossible to affirm that it may perhaps already be possible to build up a precise history of folklore. Such an effort must inevitably be reduced to a bare, abstract outline, the first parts of which it is almost totally impossible to substantiate by the filling in of concrete material. To assign periods to the history of Russian folklore (and that merely in the most general outline) is possible only from the time when there began to appear more or less systematic records of it; that is, for certain genres, since the end of the seventeenth century, but for the majority, only since the second half of the eighteenth. For the earlier epochs boundaries can be fixed only by conjectures and hypotheses.

Nevertheless, if at the present time it is impossible to give a full history of oral poetry, still, the specific results attained by scholarship must necessarily be made use of by historians of literature. In so far as the manifestations of folklore, by virtue of a specific oral creation, must be distinguished as a special branch of the general science of literature, folkloristics has the right to an independent existence within the history of literature. But at the present time it is constantly entering more and more into the consciousness of students that to write a history of literature without including information about the manifestations of contemporary oral poetry would mean that one had not covered the literary art in its entirety. For a number of periods this would mean restricting one's self to an account of the poetic creations of the ruling classes (and that in an incomplete form, because the ruling classes, in the epoch of feudalism, for example, created poetic works not only in written, but also in oral form), and ignoring completely what was going on in the artistic creative work of the exploited laboring masses.

Attempts at such an inclusion of oral poetic works in the historico-literary survey were already being made a long time ago. So, V. A. Keltuyala included facts dealing with folklore in his *Course in Russian Literature*,[8] in the survey of the literature of the feudal period, which, along with the written monuments, also included the *byliny*. It is true that this attempt, in respect to its methodology, was in many respects completely erroneous. For example, the *bylina*, in that form in which we know it from the lips of northern peasants, cannot in any case, either in its content or in its form, be traced back in toto to the feudal period. V. A. Keltuyala, however, took no account of this. On the other hand, even his attempt to arrange the phenomena of oral poetry according to the same periods as the literary monuments, proved to be only half successful. A very large number of the specific genres of folklore (charms and incantations, festival songs, songs describing the life of the people, tales, riddles, proverbs, and sayings) he found it necessary to collect into a special chapter, which preceded the whole historico-literary course, since it seemed impossible to assign them to fixed historic periods. (As to the gross perversion of the social nature of popular oral poetry, which V. A. Keltuyala permitted himself, this will be discussed later, in the historiographic survey.)

The problem of assigning periods to folklore has been treated in all its breadth, in comparatively recent years, by the late Academician P. N. Sakulin, first in his *History of the New Russian Literature* (1919), then in the brochure, *The Synthetic Structure of the History of Literature*, and, finally, in the book *Russian Literature* (1928). Even in 1919 he wrote: "We must consider the people's creative work as uninterrupted, but changing with time." It is possible to speak of well defined periods in the history of the people's creative work. "Unfortunately," adds Sakulin, "in this field learning is found to be power-

---

[8] V. A. Keltuyala, "History of Ancient Russian Literature," *Course in the History of Russian Literature; Materials for Self-Education*, Pt. I (St. Petersburg, 1906), Bk. 1. Still earlier, A. N. Pypin had made a slight attempt to place folklore before the account of the literature of the eighteenth century, in his *History of Russian Literature* (St. Petersburg, 1902).

less; but, none the less, certain periods are fixed." [9] Sakulin recognizes the fact that for the history of literature, of course, not only the newly created works are of interest, but also those modifications to which a traditional work is subjected. "The old poetic heritage is subject to modifications: every more or less talented narrator, singer, storyteller, and so forth, leaves the imprint of his creative spirit on these works, changing their form, their composition, and in part their subject. . . . Scholarship now places a very high value on these individual factors in the process of transmission." [10]

In the book which he published ten years later, *Russian Literature*, P. N. Sakulin was obliged to give up the idea of constructing a complete history of oral poetry according to periods. At the beginning of the book he gives a broad survey of the works of folklore according to their fundamental genres; but nevertheless, in his further exposition of the history of written literature, he does not forget "to remind the reader, even though by a few words, that oral poetry existed in every epoch." [11] And in reality, if scholarship is not yet able to give the history of oral poetry by periods, then, at any rate, one must strive toward this end. I am convinced that now there is not a single historian of literature who, in giving a general survey of the literature of this or that epoch, would not consider it necessary also to include in his historical survey information about the status of oral poetry at that time. However, the uncertainty as yet of the chronological, geographic, and social dating of the vast majority of concrete texts of folklore, and the specific traits of folklore as an oral poetic creation, having special conditions for its "existence," distinguish folkloristics as a separate branch of literary study. The history of literature cannot alone take the place of works on folklore.

But there are certain questions which can successfully be settled only by the closest cooperation between the folklorist and the histori-

[9] P. N. Sakulin, *History of the New Russian Literature: The Epoch of Classicism* (Moscow, 1919), p. 28.

[10] *Ibid.*, p. 28.

[11] P. N. Sakulin, *Russian Literature*, Pt. 1 (1928), p. 12. He follows the same procedure also in the second part of the course, where he gives an account of the history of Russian literature in the eighteenth and the beginning of the nineteenth century. See P. N. Sakulin, *Russian Literature*, Pt. 2 (Moscow, 1929), pp. 148-163.

an of literature. These are questions having to do with the mutual influences of oral poetry upon literature, and of artistic literature upon oral poetry. It is difficult to mention any number of outstanding authors from the eighteenth century to the twentieth century, who in some degree or other, with various motives, with different principles, did not approach oral poetry as the source of artistic forms, of vivid language, of the richest rhythms. Historians of literature and folklorists have already done a good deal to illuminate these facts. The vast role, already ascertained, of folklore in the literature of the eighteenth century; [12] the uncovering of special interests in folklore on the part of Pushkin,[13] Gogol,[14], Lermontov,[15] Melnikov-Pechersky,[16] Korolenko, Koltsov,[17] Nekrasov,[18] Turgenev,[19]

[12] See, for example, the work of N. N. Trubitsyn: *The Poetry of the People in Its Social and Literary Uses in the First Third of the Nineteenth Century* (St. Petersburg, 1912).

[13] V. F. Miller, "Pushkin as Poet and Ethnographer," *Ethnographic Review*, No. 1, 1899; M. K. Azadovsky, "Pushkin and Folklore," *Annals of the Pushkin Commission*, Vol. III (1937), pp. 152-182, reprinted in M. K. Azadovsky's book, *Literature and Folklore* (Leningrad, 1938), pp. 5-64. This book includes also the following essays: "Tales of Aripa Rodionovna," pp. 273-292, and "Sources of Pushkin's Tales," pp. 65-105, reprinted from the *Annals of the Pushkin Commission of the Academy of Sciences of the USSR*, Vol. I (Leningrad, 1935), pp. 134-163; Plotnikov, *Pushkin and Popular Creative Works* (Voronezh, 1937); Y. M. Sokolov, "Pushkin and Popular Creative Works," *The Literary Critic*, No. 1, 1937; N. P. Andreyev, "Pushkin in Folklore," *ibid.*; A. Babushkina, "Tales of A. S. Pushkin," *Children's Literature*, No. 1, 1937; M. A. Rybnikova, "Tales of Pushkin in the Elementary School," *The Elementary School*, No. 9, 1936, pp. 32-44.

[14] B. M. Sokolov, "Gogol the Ethnographer," *Ethnographic Review*, Nos. 2-3, Moscow, 1910; S. Mashinsky, "Gogol and the Popular Historico-Poetic Tradition," *Literary Studies*, No. 3, 1938.

[15] N. M. Mendelson, "Popular Motifs in the Poetry of Lermontov," in the collection *A Wreath for Lermontov* (Moscow, 1914).

[16] G. Vinogradov, "An Attempt to Examine the Folklore Sources of Melnikov-Pechersky's Novel *In the Forest*," *Soviet Folklore*, Nos. 2-3, Leningrad, 1935.

[17] A. I. Nekrasov, "Koltsov and Popular Lyric Poetry," *Annals of the Division of Russian Language and Literature of the Academy of Sciences* (1911), Bk. 2; P. M. Sobolev, *Koltsov and Oral Lyric Poetry* (Smolensk, 1934).

[18] V. Yelanskaya, "On Popular Song Motifs in the Works of Nekrasov," *October*, No. 12, 1927; I. N. Kubikov, *Commentaries on Nekrasov's Poem, "Who Can Live Happily in Russia"* (Moscow, 1933); N. P. Andreyev, "Folklore in the Poetry of Nekrasov, *Literary Studies*, No. 7, 1936; Y. M. Sokolov, "Nekrasov and Popular Creative Works," *The Literary Critic*, No. 2, 1938.

[19] B. M. Sokolov, "Peasants As Represented by Turgenev," in the collection *The Creative Work of Turgenev*, ed. I. N. Rozanov and Y. M. Sokolov (Moscow, 1918).

L. Tolstoy,[20] Shchedrin,[21] Dostoevsky,[22] Leskov, Gorky,[23] and others. In the twentieth century we see that almost every new literary school—the symbolists, the futurists, the imaginists—Balmont, Bryusov, Blok, Bely, Gorodetsky, Mayakovsky, Yesenin—reverts to folklore. Often folklore serves as a constant source of enrichment, with forms for the expression of revolutionary ideas and moods (for example, in the work of Editor Bagritsky, A. Prokofiyev,[24] A. Surkov, N. Aseyev, and others).

Many writers have not only, so to speak, passively experienced in their work the influence of oral poetry, but have also attentively and persistently studied the peculiarities of its artistic forms, language and content. Here are Pushkin's famous tributes to the language of Russian tales and proverbs:

A tale is a tale, but our language is a world in itself, and nowhere can it be given that Russian spaciousness, so well as in a tale. But how is one to achieve this? One should be able to learn how to speak Russian, even outside of a tale. But no, it is difficult, it is not yet possible! But what splendor, what meaning, what significance there is in every one of our proverbs! What gold is here! But it does not give itself into your hands, no! [25]

"What a delight these tales are! Every one is a poem!" [26] No less sig-

---

[20] Y. M. Sokolov, *L. Tolstoy and the Narrator Schegolenok* (in preparation); V. I. Sreznevsky, "Language and Legend in the Works of L. N. Tolstoy," in the collection *To the Academician S. F. Oldenburg, in Recognition of His Fifty Years of Scientific and Public Activity* (Leningrad, 1935).

[21] Y. M. Sokolov, "From the Folklore-Materials of Saltykov-Shchedrin," in the collection *The Literary Heritage*, Vols. 11-12, No. II, Moscow, 1934.

[22] N. K. Piksanov, "Dostoevsky and Folklore," *Soviet Ethnography*, Nos. 1-2, 1934.

[23] N. K. Piksanov, "Gorky and Folklore," *Soviet Ethnography*, Nos. 5-6, 1932, published in an expanded form as a separate book, *Gorky and Folklore* (Leningrad, 1935, 2nd ed. (Leningrad, 1938); idem, "Gorky on Folklore," *Soviet Folklore*, Nos. 2-3, 1935; the collection, *Pushkin and Gorky on Folklore* (State Textbook Publications, 1938); S. A. Bugoslavsky, "Gorky and the Russian Folk Song," *The Literary Critic*, No. 6, 1938.

[24] Y. M. Sokolov, "A. Prokofiyev and Popular Creative Works," *The Literary Critic*, No. 1, 1936.

[25] L. Maykov, *Pushkin* (St. Petersburg, 1899), p. 418.

[26] Pushkin, *Letters*, ed. with notes by B. L. Modzalevsky (1815–1825), Vol. I. *Proceedings of the Pushkin House of the Academy of Sciences of the USSR*, Leningrad, 1926, p. 97.

nificant are the numerous testimonies of Gogol to the beauty of oral poetry. Gogol, as it were spontaneously, blended his own creative work with his native poetry and tales: "My joy, my life—O songs, how I love you!"—the words burst from his lips. And in his well known article "Little-Russian Songs" he has chanted a hymn of rapture to them. Lev Tolstoy used to give preference to the popular creations over many of the recognized masterpieces of high art. In his treatise "What Is Art?" he distinguished the popular poetry for its sincerity, simplicity, and infectious quality.

Unswerving in his appreciation of folklore was A. M. Gorky. His stirring autobiographical works, *Childhood* and *My Universities*, are filled with recollections of the place held in his life by folk songs, tales, and legends. Gorky, in these and other works, appears as an eminent connoisseur and judge of folklore. One need only recall the last chapter of the first volume of *Klim Samgin*, in which there is such a skillful description of the appearance of the storyteller Orina Fedosova. But, in addition to the fact that, in his creative writing, Gorky often deals with folklore, he also, in his theoretical and critical discussions, repeatedly touches on the subject. Many times he advised writers to look more often and more deeply into the productions of oral poetry, thereby refreshing their literary language and enriching their creative powers.

As everyone knows, in his report at the First All-Union Congress of Soviet Writers, in 1934, A. M. Gorky devoted a great deal of attention to folklore. In particular, he maintained two propositions: (1) Oral poetic creations are closely connected with the laboring activity of mankind; (2) folklore has been able to create deep and clear images, of great generalizing power, precisely owing to this connection. Gorky said:

Again I call your attention, comrades, to this fact, that by far the deepest and most vivid, the most artistically fashioned types of heroes are created by folklore, by the oral creations of the working people. The perfection of such figures as Hercules, Prometheus, Mikula Selyaninovich, Svyatogor; further, Dr. Faustus, Vasilisa the All-Wise, the ironically successful Ivan the Fool, and finally Petrushka, who vanquishes the doctor, the priest, the police, the devil, and death itself—

these are all figures in the creation of which reason and intuition, thought and feeling have been harmoniously combined. Such a combination is possible only through the direct participation of the creator in the creative work of actuality, in the struggle for the renewal of life.[27]

In his concluding remarks A. M. Gorky again returned to folklore. The occasion was the noteworthy appearance at the Writers' Congress of the Daghestan (Lezgian) *ashug*, Suleyman Stalsky. Gorky said:

I turn again, with a word of friendly advice, which may also be understood as a request, to the representatives of the nationalities of the Caucasus and Central Asia. Upon me—and, I know, not upon me alone—the *ashug* Suleyman Stalsky has made a most profound impression. I saw this old man, illiterate but wise, sitting in the presiding council, whispering, creating his verses; then he, the Homer of the twentieth century, recited them most wonderfully.

Cherish the people who are able to create such pearls of poetry as Suleyman produces. I repeat: the beginning of the art of words is in folklore. Collect your folklore, make a study of it, work it over. It will yield a great deal of material both to you and to us, the poets and prose writers of the Soviet Union. The better we come to know the past, the more easily, the more deeply and joyfully we shall understand the great significance of the present which we are creating.[28]

At the Writers' Congress A. M. Gorky was not the only one who spoke about folklore. Many of the delegates touched upon it in their speeches, especially the delegates of the national provinces and republics—of Central Asia, the Caucasus, the Volga provinces, and Siberia. This is fully understandable. If oral creative work, as we have seen, serves as such a rich source for Russian literature, which stretches back a thousand years, then how much greater is its significance for those literatures which have begun to come into existence only recently, many only after the Great October Socialist Revolution, which gave them a literature. If Russian contemporary literature is being built up on the basis of our vast oral and written cultural-artistic heritage, then there is a whole group of other peoples of our Union whose

[27] A. M. Gorky, *On Literature: Articles and Speeches, 1928–1936,* 3rd ed., enlarged, ed. N. F. Belchikov (Moscow, 1937), p. 450.
[28] *Ibid.,* p. 481.

only cultural-artistic heritage in the field of literary art has been oral poetry.

The appearance at the Writers' Congress of the popular singer-*ashug*, Suleyman Stalsky, was significant in this respect, that thereby, as it were, public sanction was given to the idea of folklore, oral poetry, as one of the inalienable parts of the contemporary literary movement. This served as confirmation of the idea that folklore is just as much a part of contemporary social life, of the structure of the new socialist society, as is artistic written literature. And not without reason was there found at the Writers' Congress, among other tributes from the collective farmers' and workers' delegations, a brochure published by the Political Division of the Starozhilov machine-tractor service station,[29] and an issue of its newspaper *The Tractor*. Both contained new collective farm songs, recorded on the spot and in part composed by the farmers. The collectors and composers of the songs appealed to the Writers' Congress with the request that it help them in their further oral poetic work. They said in this appeal:

With all our collective farm people we have prepared this offering. There are thirteen village Soviets in the zone of our machine-tractor service station. In each of these, we have our collective-farm composers of folk songs, our poets, our dramatists. There are thirty-eight collective farms served by our machine-tractor service station, and only in two of them are there no authors and collectors of new folk songs. We give a report on the best of them in these pages. Of course, they are not all equally successful and interesting. But we want to present to the masters of literature a new collective-farm reader. We want to show the yearning toward literary creativeness, toward the literary word, on the part of the most widely diffused classes of population in the collective-farm countryside. . . . We do not regard our work as finished. We shall continue the work of collecting folk songs, and the creative guidance of young collective-farm poets and creators of popular songs. We are awaiting help from the writing public, from the Union of Soviet Writers, from the Writers' Congress.[30]

From the text of the appeal, it is obvious that the thesis, often repeated by the folklorists, of the necessity of "active intervention in

---

[29] *Collective Farm Songs*, ed. B. Holtzman (Voronovo, 1934).

[30] *The Tractor*, newspaper of the Political Division of the Starozhilov Machine-Tractor Service Station, No. 147 (1934).

the process of folklore," has begun to be realized in life. In my paper "The Significance of Folklore and Folkloristics in the Reconstruction Period," presented in 1931, this idea was set forth as follows:

In so far as oral poetic creation is one of the domains of literary art, *the actual tasks of the contemporary workers' and collective farmers' folklore are exactly the same as the actual tasks of proletarian literature.* In putting into practice the systematic class direction of literature, it would be inconsistent to leave the oral creations to the mercy of the elements—it is necessary that, in the oral creations also, the proletarian consciousness should subordinate to itself the elemental process.[31]

In the class struggle which took place in connection with the development of the collective-farm organization, the *kulaks*, who were being liquidated as a class, very often made use of oral literature as a means for their counterrevolutionary agitation and propaganda. In folklore there also found expression other influences which were alien or hostile to the socialist order: the petty bourgeois element, the declassed, the so-called "jailbirds," the criminal element. A most energetic war was waged with all these factors in folklore, and one of the most effective measures in this war was the effort to raise oral poetry to a higher ideological and artistic level.

During the past few years, during the periods of the two Stalin Five-Year Plans, the concern of the Party and of the Government for the poetic creations of the people has yielded vast results. With the victory over the last of the exploiting classes, with the consolidation of the socialist order in town and country, the creativeness of the people flowered.

The All-Union, republic, district, regional, and even collective-farm Olympiads for original art have revealed a multitude of talented masters of folk poetry, song, and dance. The radio, the sound-equipped

---

[31] Discussion on "The Significance of Folklore and Folkloristics in the Reconstruction Period," *Literature and Marxism*, No. 5, 1931, p. 92. This same idea was developed in detail by me, also, in a paper read at the First Folklore Conference, before the Organizational Committee of the Union of Soviet Writers, Dec. 15, 1933. See the reports of this conference in *Pravda*, Dec. 16, 1933, and in the *Literary Gazette* of Dec. 17, 1933; see also my articles in the *Literary Gazette* of Dec. 11, 1933, and in the *Soviet Regional Studies*, No. 10, 1933, the article entitled "Folklore and Regional Studies."

cinema, phonograph records, club and theatrical platforms, periodicals, central and district publishing firms, have cooperated in the broadest popularization of folk creations. This interest of the Soviet public, the corresponding selection of the best material and performance, the criticism of all that is least valuable, and the struggle with all that is false, antisocial, or hostile, have lifted folk creations to a very high and artistic level.

All these phenomena have been linked with the process that has been going on in Soviet scholarship dealing with folk creations, and in Soviet folkloristics, which has gradually mastered the theory and the method of Marxism-Leninism. I am speaking chiefly of the mastery of the general bases of dialectical materialism and their application to the study of the material of folklore.

But it is necessary to ask one's self what was the direct relation of the founders of Marxism and Leninism to folklore and to the science which deals with it.

We are still not in a position to give a strictly systematic history of Marxist ideas in the field of folkloristics, because the question has not been sufficiently worked over; but we consider it necessary to reproduce merely a few specific statements, dealing either directly with folklore, or with questions which are bound up with it in the most intimate way—statements made by Marx, Engels, Lenin, Stalin, and, in passing, also by Lafargue, who has left in Marxist literature the fullest judgment as to folklore.

The exceedingly broad education of Marx and Engels, their deep knowledge of the most diverse sciences, are well known. In particular this fact is known, that Marx and Engels were acquainted with Russian, along with other languages, that they read Russian authors in the original. Marx had attentively studied the famous *Tale of Igor's Raid*, that outstanding artistic monument of medieval Russian literature.[32]

But we are interested in the question of the relation of Marx and Engels to the productions of oral poetry, of folklore. There is a great deal of information on this point in the works and letters of Marx

[32] K. Marx and F. Engels, *Works*, Vol. XXII, p. 122.

and Engels, and also in the memoirs and biographical literature concerning them.[33]

There is preserved, among other things, a curious reminiscence of Lafargue to the effect that Marx himself was able, and loved, to tell folk tales.[34]

Marx and Engels not only knew the tales of folklore, but they read folk poems, the Norwegian and Danish sagas, and so forth.

Marx displayed an especial interest in the Greek epic; the comments on it, made in Marx's work, *Critique of Political Economy*, have a most exceptional significance for folklorists. There Marx raises a question of the greatest importance, as to the *uneven development of the forms of culture.* He points out that, where productive capacity is very backward, and production relationships are insufficiently developed, there sometimes grow up cultural superstructures of such richness and such power, that they exert their influence even upon succeeding epochs in the development of society.

With reference to art, it is known that the fixed periods of its greatest development do not correspond with the general development of society, nor, consequently, with the development of the material basis of the latter, which constitutes, so to speak, the skeleton of its organization. For instance, compare the Greeks and also Shakespeare with their contemporaries.

With reference to the various forms of art [continues Marx], for example, the epic, it is even acknowledged that they, in their classical form, constituting a period in world history, never could have been created, as soon as artistic production as such had begun; that, in this way, in the field of literature itself, these particular and highly significant forms, are possible only at a comparatively low stage of artistic development.[35]

[33] For a list of the basic statements of Marx and Engels on folklore, and also for examples of their use of the forms and works of folklore, see the article by V. I. Chicherov, "Karl Marx and Friedrich Engels on Folklore," *Soviet Folklore*, Nos. 4-5, 1936.

[34] See P. Lafargue, "Personal Recollections of Karl Marx," in the collection, *Marx—The Thinker, the Man, the Revolutionary* (State Publishing House, 1926); and extracts in the book, *Marx and Engels on Art*, ed. A. V. Lunacharsky, (*Soviet Literature*, Moscow, 1933), p. 207. See also, in the same work, V. Liebknecht, "In Field and Meadow."

[35] Karl Marx, Preface to the *Critique of Political Economy* (*Collected Works* [Marx, Engels and Lenin Institute, Party Press, 1933], Vol. XII, Pt. 1, p. 200).

Emphasizing the contradiction between high art in a specific period and the comparatively low level of that period's social development, Marx explains these contradictions. He says:

If this takes place in the field of art, in the relations among its various forms, then it is still less striking that this circumstance takes place in the relation of the whole field of art to the general social development. The difficulty consists only in the general formulation of these contradictions. It is only necessary to isolate each of them, to explain them. Let us take, for example, the relation of Greek art, and thereafter of Shakespeare, to their contemporaries. It is well known that Greek mythology constituted not only the arsenal of Greek art, but the very soil from which it grew. Is it possible that the attitude toward nature and social relationships, which lies at the basis of Greek fantasy, and therefore also of Greek art, could have existed in the presence of "self-acting mules" [Steam textile machines—Au.], railways, locomotives, and the electric telegraph? What could Vulcan do against Roberts & Co., Jupiter against the lightning rod, and Hermes against the *Crédit mobilier*! Every mythology overcomes, subjugates, and forms the forces of nature in imagination and with the help of imagination; it disappears, consequently, with the actual mastery of these forces of nature.[36]

"As the premise of Greek art we find Greek mythology, that is, nature and social forms which have already been worked over in an unconsciously artistic manner in folk fantasy. This is its material. . . . No such development of society as that which excludes every mythological relation to nature, every mythologizing of nature, which demands from the artist a fantasy that does not depend on mythology,"[37] could possibly, according to the opinion of Marx, furnish the soil for the development of Greek art.

Having made clear this indissoluble bond of Greek art with mythology, Marx again asked himself whether it was possible for the forms and aspects of old Greek art to arise in our contemporary civilization.

"On the other hand," he said, "is an Achilles possible in the era of gunpowder and lead? Or, in general, an Iliad alongside of the printing press and the typographical machine? And will there not disappear,

36 *Ibid.*, p. 203.   37 *Ibid.*, p. 203.

unavoidably, the tales, the songs, and Muses, and along with these, also, the necessary premises of epic poetry, with the appearance of the printing press?" [38]

This argument of Marx's has a great significance in principle, not only for the understanding of the Greek epic, but also for the understanding of the general laws of development of epic poetry; in particular, as we shall see in the proper place, for an answer to the question of the fate of the ancient Russian epic poetry in the modern period.

Marx expresses also another important thought, and raises still another new problem. "However, the difficulty," he continues, "does not consist in understanding that Greek art and the epic are bound up with the well known forms of social development. The difficulty consists in understanding that they still continue to give us artistic pleasure, and in a certain sense preserve the value of a standard and an unattainable example." [39]

And in fact, the Marxist science of history has now learned to erect upon definite social-economic relations a superstructure of ideological phenomena; but the Marxist students of the history of art are still constantly struggling with the problem of explaining why the poetic productions created under certain conditions should continue to give artistic pleasure in the course of many centuries, in an altogether different social and cultural setting.

Marx gives this explanation for the undiminished interest in the ancient Greek epic:

A man cannot be transformed again into a child, or he becomes childish. But does he not take delight in a child's naïveté, and is not he himself obliged to strive toward this end, that he may reproduce his own true nature at a higher stage? In the nature of a child, in every era, does there not come to life again the character of this era, in its artless truth? And why should not the childhood of human society, there, where it had the most beautiful development of all, possess for us an eternal charm, as a stage which never repeats itself? There are uneducated children, and there are children who have the wisdom of old age. Many of the ancient peoples belong to this [latter] category. The Greeks were normal children. The fascination which their art pos-

[38] *Ibid.*, p. 203.   [39] *Ibid.*, p. 203.

sesses for us does not lie in its contradiction to that undeveloped stage of society, upon which it grew up. On the contrary, that art appears to be the result of that stage of society, and to be indissolubly linked with the fact that the immature social relations under which it arose, and under which alone it could arise, can never be repeated again.[40]

A deep interest in that which was created in the early stages of human development, that is, in particular, an interest in the various forms of traditional folklore, is encountered in Marx and Engels from their early years.

Here is Engels' discussion, in one of his early articles (1839), on the "German popular books" which had enjoyed great favor. These books (half-literature and half-folklore) attracted Engels by their simplicity and naïveté. But it is noteworthy that Engels does not limit himself to a statement of their poetic and ethnographic significance; he emphasizes their possible political influence, their significance as propaganda in the struggle for freedom, against the nobility, against pietism. The young Engels writes:

A popular book has as its task to entertain the peasant, when, tired out, he returns in the evening from his heavy day's work; to divert him, enliven him, make him forget his burdensome toil, transform his stony field into a sweet-smelling garden; it has as its task to turn the workshop of the artisan and the pitiful garret of the exhausted apprentice into a world of poetry, into a golden palace, and to depict his buxom sweetheart in the guise of a wondrously beautiful princess; but it also has as its task . . . to clarify his ethical sense, to make him realize his strength, his right, his freedom, to awaken his manhood, his love for his fatherland.

Consequently, if the requirements which we may justifiably demand, in general, of a popular book, are to be summed up as a rich poetic content, a keenness of wit, and moral purity . . . then, besides this, *we have the right to demand that a popular book should be responsive to its own time* [Italics mine.—Au.], otherwise it ceases to be a popular book. In particular, if we turn our attention to our own time, to the struggle for freedom which characterizes it, to the developing constitutionalism, to the resistance to the oppression of the aristocracy, to the struggle of thought against pietism, of clearness of mind against the remains of a morose asceticism, then I do not see why we should not have the right to demand of a popular book that

[40] *Ibid.*, pp. 203-204.

in this respect it should lend assistance to the less educated circles, and should show them, though, of course, not by direct deduction, the truthfulness and reasonableness of these strivings—but never in any case should it have any connivance with hypocrisy, servile cringing before the nobility, and pietism. It goes without saying, however, that a popular book must keep alien from itself those customs of earlier times, which in our own era appear to be absurd or unjust.[41]

Engels, taking into account the social-political function of a popular book in contemporary times, decisively rebels against the exclusively esthetic approach to popular books on the part of the romanticists—Tieck, Herres, Marbach, Ziemrock—who, it is true, awakened an interest in them on the part of the bourgeois public. Engels boldly declares the necessity of a critical examination of popular books, a complete exclusion of some of them from use by the masses, and a revision of a number of others. Besides, he insists on a careful, sensitive attitude toward the popular style, in making such a revision.

But perhaps, O German people, perhaps the best of these books still deserve intelligent revision? Of course, not everyone is capable of this; I know only two authors possessing sufficient critical acumen and taste in selection, and the skill to handle the ancient speech—these are the Brothers Grimm; but would they have the inclination and the time for this work? [42]

As if anticipating those replies which Marx gave to the question of the cause of the unfading charm of the Greek epic, the young Engels writes: "These old folk books, with their ancient speech, with their misprints and poor engravings, possess for me an exceptional poetic charm. They carry me away from our over-tense time, with its contemporary 'conditions, confusion, and delicate interrelationships,' into another world, which is much closer to nature." "But," adds Engels, "as to that [the purely subjective esthetic approach.—Au.], this is not the place to speak of it. True, the main argument of Tieck consisted in this poetic charm, but what is the meaning of the authority of Tieck, of Herres, and all the other romanticists, when reason speaks against it, and when we are dealing with the German people?" [43]

[41] Marx and Engels, *Works*, Vol. II (1929), pp. 26-27..
[42] *Ibid.*, p. 33.   [43] *Ibid.*, pp. 33-34.

And so, the social-political function of a popular book, its contemporary significance in the life of the laboring masses, compel Engels to rise above a subjective esthetic valuation of it. Has Engels not left a legacy, in this respect, for us also? Do we not pay too little attention to such truly popular books (which play a vast role in the mode of life of the masses) as, for example, songbooks? But, broadening our conception of the "popular book" to include all oral poetry, we can see in Engels' words also a program for work on folklore, not only in the interests of artistic admiration (and, we add, in the interests of scientific investigation), but also in the social and political interests of the masses themselves. But of this we have already spoken.

The attitude of Engels—no longer the young Engels, but Engels in his declining years—toward the folklore of the old revolutions is also of interest in connection with all this. Engels has a very critical approach even to the revolutionary heritage in the poetry of the past. In these critical comments of his there is, as it were, a direct advice to us also, when we turn to the revolutionary motifs of the earlier peasant movements. "The 'Marseillaise' of the Peasant War," writes Engels, "was the hymn, 'Ein' feste Burg ist unser Gott' (A mighty fortress is our God). And although the text and the melody of this song are pervaded with the confidence of victory, nevertheless, at the present time, it is impossible, and incorrect, to interpret it in this sense [that is, in the sense of the 'Marseillaise.'—Au.]. Other songs of this era have been assembled in collections of popular songs, *Des Knaben Wunderhorn*, and so forth. There, possibly, something else will be found. But already, at that time, the *Landsknecht* occupied a significant place in our popular poetry. . . . There were many Chartist songs, but one cannot get hold of them now. . . . All this has long ago been forgotten; however, this poetry was not of much value. . . . Generally speaking," Engels concludes his argument, "the poetry of the past revolutions, with the exception of the 'Marseillaise,' seldom produces a revolutionary impression in later times, since, in order to influence the masses, it must reflect also the prejudices of the masses at that time. Hence the religious twaddle even among the Chartists." [44]

It is very interesting to observe at this juncture that those songs

44 *Ibid.*, Vol. XXVII, pp. 467-468.

which were created at the time of the Peasant War were taken up and revised by the enemy groups. ("*Already, at that time, the* Landsknecht *occupied a significant place in our popular poetry.*" Italics mine.— Au.)

In Russian folklore it is well known to us that the songs created at the time of the peasant movement of Stepan Razin, which were enormously popular among the masses of the people, were then taken up by those who were hostile to the peasant movement. Many songs of the era of Razin were transformed into soldiers' songs, and revised in the spirit of the Royalist politics of the eighteenth and nineteenth centuries.

As we have seen, Engels, both in his youthful years and in the last years of his political-philosophical activity, differentiated between the two sides to folklore—its artistic value and its politico-educational influence (its social-political function). More than once he emphasized, also, the historico-perceptive value of the productions of folklore.

So, for example, in his famous work, *The Origin of the Family, of Private Property, and of the State*, Engels, discussing the family mode of life in the peasant village communities, says: "With reference to family life within these large families, it must be observed that at least in Russia it is known that the fathers of the families violently abuse their position in relation to the young women of the community, especially their daughters-in-law, of whom they often form a harem for themselves; the Russian popular songs are very eloquent on this point." [45]

The historical significance of popular songs has been frequently and most persistently emphasized by one of the early Marxists, Lafargue. He has devoted a whole treatise to folklore. This is the unusually interesting article, "Les Chansons et les cérémonies populaires du mariage" (Popular Wedding Songs and Customs, 1886). It may be found also in a Russian translation in the collection of Lafargue's articles, *Sketches of the History of Primitive Culture*.[46] Lafargue

[45] F. Engels, *The Origin of the Family, of Private Property, and of the State* (*Collected Works*, Vol. XVI, p. 43).

[46] Paul Lafargue, *Sketches of the History of Primitive Culture* (Moscow, 1926; 2nd ed., Moscow, 1928).

makes clear the value of the wedding songs and ceremonies of various lands and peoples as an excellent source of information on the history of modes of life and social relations. He draws voluminous material from the works of Tylor and other ethnographers and folklorists, and reveals, by means of an analysis of this material, its significance for the history of the position of women in the family and in society. He rejects the theory of borrowing, and inclines rather toward Tylor's theory, toward the idea that at the basis of folklore there lie the general laws of development of mankind; but, in contrast to Tylor, he decisively raises the problem of the social-economic conditions of folklore.[47]

The works of Lafargue have a great methodological significance. Not only in this article, but also in the whole series of his works on political economy,[48] he frequently reverts to the material of folklore, and points out its exceptional significance, particularly for those peoples who had no written history:

A popular song bears, in general, a local character. The subject occasionally may be brought in from the outside, but it is accepted only in those cases when it corresponds to the spirit and customs of those who adopt it. A song cannot be put on like a new fashion in dress. Among the most diverse and distant peoples there have been found similar songs, legends, and customs. Scholars conjecture that they have either been handed down from one people to another, or have constituted a part of their spiritual heritage, which they possessed in common before their separation. The savages of the Stone Age in Europe gave their knives, hatchets, and other flint implements exactly the same shape as did the aborigines of Australia. It is impossible to assume that this coincidence was based on tradition or borrowing. The similarity of the raw material led man, in both places, to work it up in the same way. Precisely so, people who have received impressions from the same phenomena transmit them in similar songs, sayings, and customs. . . .

Folk poetry, the production of the masses, arises from the very

---

[47] On the views of P. Lafargue concerning general questions of folklore, see V. Hoffenshefer, *Paul Lafargue, a Practical Exponent of the Marxist Critique* (State Press for the Publication of Literature, Moscow, 1933), pp. 87 ff. On the theories of borrowing, and on the "anthropological theory" of Tylor, see the next chapter of this volume.

[48] See the above-mentioned work of Hoffenshefer.

mode of life of the popular masses; the people sings its songs under the immediate and direct impression of the passion which it is experiencing. . . . Owing to this exactness and truthfulness, oral literature possesses a greater historical value than any production of an isolated individual; therefore one may make use of it with confidence, without the danger of being led astray by it.[49]

These indications are very important for us, because the early history of very many peoples (particularly among us in the Soviet Union) can frequently be known only on the basis of the materials of folklore. That is why it is so important, not only for the study of literature, but also for historical science, to collect and study folklore.

The artistic, historic, and essentially political significances of oral poetry were highly valued by V. I. Lenin. In his article, "Lenin on Poetry," [50] V. D. Bonch-Bruevich recollects:

V. I. was continually studying Dal's dictionary of the Russian language, which stood on his book stand, and he took an interest in the sayings and proverbs which were included in it. . . . I do not remember now how it was, but the conversation turned to the folk epic, and when I said that I had in my library quite a good selection of books of *byliny*, folk songs, and tales, he immediately asked me whether I could give him an opportunity of looking them over. Of course, I was glad to comply with this request. And that very evening I observed how Vladimir Ilyich read attentively the *Smolensk Ethnographic Collection*, compiled by V. N. Dobrovolsky.

"What interesting material," he said to me, when I came to see him in the morning. "I have glanced rapidly over all these books, but I see that there is an obvious lack of the hands, or the desire, to generalize all this, to survey all this from the social-political point of view; for, you know, on the basis of this material, it would be possible to write a splendid study of the hopes and expectations of the people. See, in the tales of N. E. Onchukov, which I have leafed over, there certainly are remarkable passages. Here is a point to which we should call the attention of our historians of literature. This is an authentic folk creation, such as is necessary and important for the study of the popular psychology in our days."

Here, of course, it must be borne in mind that these are not the direct utterances of Lenin himself, but the recollections of another

---

[49] P. Lafargue, *Outlines of the History of Culture* (Moscow, 1926), pp. 51-54.

[50] Excerpts from this article have been printed in the anthology of Prof. N. P. Andreyev, *Russian Folklore* (Leningrad, 1936), p. 21; 2nd ed. (1938), p. 29.

person. Whether Lenin really made use of these expressions, it is difficult to determine. But as to the correct transmission of Lenin's basic ideas, there can be no doubt. Following the advice of Lenin, folklorists must generalize the phenomena of folklore, must survey them "from the social-political point of view," must uncover in the productions of folklore the history of the "hopes and expectations" of the working masses in the past, and must comprehend folklore as important material for the study of the psychology and ideology of the popular masses in our own time.

Like Marx and Engels, Lenin loved oral poetry, and was not only interested in it as a very rich source of artistic enjoyment, but also valued folklore as a historical record, and as something necessary in the political and social work of our days.

The study of the "hopes and expectations of the people," expressed in folklore, is one of the fundamental tasks of Soviet folkloristics.

At the present time, in accordance with this plan, work is being carried on throughout the USSR, with reference to Russian folklore, and also to that of the other Soviet peoples.

After the Great October Socialist Revolution, there was an extensive development of work in the collection, publication, and study of the folklore of the most diverse nationalities of the USSR. A vast, definitive role was played in this work by the wise national policy of Lenin and Stalin, and as a result of this policy there grew up a firm friendship among the fraternal peoples.

The study of the folklore of all nationalities in the Soviet Union is being guided by those theoretical principles of proletarian culture which have been given with admirable clarity in *Questions of Leninism*, by J. V. Stalin.

Proletarian culture, socialistic in its content, receives different forms and different modes of expression among various peoples who have been drawn into the socialist organization, depending on their differences in language, mode of life, and so forth. Proletarian in its content, nationalist in its form—such is that universal human culture toward which socialism is advancing. Proletarian culture does not replace nationalist culture, but gives it content. And on the other hand, nationalist culture does not replace proletarian culture, but gives it form.

And if it is a matter of the uniting of various nationalities with proletarian culture, it is hardly possible to doubt that this uniting will take place in forms corresponding to the language and mode of life of these nationalities.[51]

This uniting is in progress, as evidenced by the collectors and investigators of contemporary Soviet folklore among all nationalities in the USSR, and also in the ranks of nationalities beyond the border, side by side with other forms, through national songs and tales, through proverbs and sayings, through various other aspects of the national folklore, which grows up in conformity with the language and mode of life of these nationalities.

The volume published by the editorial office of *Pravda* to celebrate the twentieth anniversary of Soviet power, and entitled *Creative Works of the Peoples of the USSR*, serves as a striking demonstration of the role played by national folklore in the uniting of various peoples with the universal proletarian, socialist culture.

Numerous songs, popular rhymes, stories, tales, and proverbs, which have been translated into the Russian language from the multifarious languages of the Soviet peoples, show the great ideational and artistic heights attained by folk creation in our time, what a vastly important artistic force this is in the propagandizing of the resplendent ideas of Communism, what a great place folklore occupies in Soviet socialist culture.

[51] J. Stalin, "On the Political Tasks of the University of the Peoples of the East" (speech at a meeting of the students of the Communist University for the Toilers of the East, May 18, 1925), *Questions of Leninism* (1931), pp. 137-138.

HISTORIOGRAPHY OF FOLKLORISTICS

After we have become acquainted with the definition of the theme and the tasks of folkloristics, and before we approach the characterization of the concrete phenomena of folklore, it is necessary to become acquainted, even though briefly, with the history of our science, with the basic stages of its development.

It is not my purpose here to give exhaustive information on the history of the creation and study of folklore in Russia and abroad. This information may be drawn from other books, which are specially devoted to the historiography of our science.[1] I am trying to characterize, as I have said, only the basic stages in the historical development of folkloristics. Without such historiographic orientation it is impossible to think of undertaking independent scientific and pedagogical work. In the independent work of the student or the teacher, naturally, one has to turn back to the labors of earlier scholars—to Buslayev, Afanasyev, Veselovsky, Vsevolod Miller, and many others. Without a general idea of their theoretical views and methodological principles, a critical evaluation of their pronouncements on the concrete questions of folklore will be difficult.

Such a historiographic survey is necessary also for understanding how and why there arose this, that, and the other cardinal problem of folkloristics, and what efforts have been made to solve them; what have constituted the achievements and, on the other hand, the set-

---

[1] Efforts at historiographic surveys have already been made repeatedly in general university courses on popular or oral literature. See the courses by M. N. Speransky, P. V. Vladimirov, A. M. Loboda, I. I. Zamotin, S. K. Shambinago; also the more detailed one in the *History of Russian Ethnography*, by Acad. A. N. Pypin, Vols. I-IV (St. Petersburg, 1890–1892). Historiographic surveys have also been made in connection with the treatment of individual genres of folklore. Thus, the historiography of the old Russian epos is given in the following two works: A. M. Loboda, *The Russian Knightly Epos* (Kiev, 1896), and A. P. Skaftymov, Chap. IV, "Materials and Researches on the Study of the *Byliny* from 1896 to 1923," *Poetics and the Genesis of the Byliny: Essays* (Saratov, 1924). The historiography of the Russian tale (but with extensive digressions into the field of the study of the tale in western European science) is given in the book by S. V. Savchenko, *Russian Folk Tales: History of Their Collection and Study* (Kiev, 1914).

backs or errors in the progress of scientific thought. Finally, it is important to realize that the history of, so to speak, such a very special science as folkloristics, is found to be dependent upon the general social conditions of Europe and of Russia in the nineteenth and twentieth centuries, and that the specific stages of folkloristics have reflected the fundamental changes in social life.

We have no direct information as to the oral poetry of our ancestors in the most ancient times.

The literature of feudal Russia bore a predominantly religious character. The Christian Church viewed the oral poetry of the popular masses with stern hostility, seeing in this oral poetry an expression of "unclean," [2] that is, heathen, ideology, with which the church waged a violent struggle. And beyond a doubt, a great many songs, tales, games, and ceremonies must have contained in manifest form, or as survivals, some elements of the pre-Christian heathen cults, myths, and magic. However, the ecclesiastical writers, in their polemical zeal, were inclined to label as heathen, in general, every kind of diversion, amusements, esthetic pleasures, anything which even slightly went beyond the limits of the Church's teaching and regulations. This is also the reason why Russian literature of the feudal Middle Ages failed almost entirely to fix in written form the productions of oral poetry, of folklore.

Scattered accidental references to it must be sought, literally bit by bit, in the vast number of monuments of ancient Russian literature, which have come down to our time, and which are preserved in the manuscript divisions of the central and provincial libraries.

In the ecclesiastical precepts, the so-called "dicta" of the Fathers of the Church, in the collections of Church rules—*Gubernator, Mensurae,* in the guidebooks for confessors, in the canonical *Quaestiones,* in the collections of aphorisms, the so-called *Melissae,* in the individual lives of the saints, and in collections of them—patristics, prologues, "Monthly Readings in the Lives of the Saints," and in other forms of medieval Church literature, one may meet with a reference to this, that, or the other ceremony, combined with the singing of songs and with folk dances: now to the playing of musician-buffoons,

---

[2] Russian *pogany,* from the Latin *paganus,* heathen.

who shattered the solemn dignity of the ecclesiastical holiday; now to incantations and fortunetelling, now to some belief or other which had been made into a legend, and so on. But usually these references are exceedingly fragmentary and general, combined with the exaggerated interpretations of a fanatical Christian preacher, who considered it his moral duty to add to the description of the fact a militant "unmasking" of paganism and "demonic songs and games." [3]

The chronicle tales concerning the first princes, concerning the events of the tenth and the beginning of the eleventh century, are based, apart from the transferred historical material (Byzantine and Bulgarian), to a significant degree upon oral traditions, legends, perhaps on songs. The tales about the first princes, for example, about the calling of the princes, about the vengeance of Olga upon the Drevlyane for the death of Igor, the tale of the death of Oleg, caused by his horse, in accordance with the prediction of the sorcerer, and many others, have close parallels in the tales of other peoples, in particular, the Scandinavian. Such chronical tales as the tale (*circa* A.D. 992) of the wrestling match of the Russian athlete Yan Usmoshchvets (the tanner) with the Pechenegian wrestler, the tales of the feasts of Prince Vladimir, the tale of the siege of Belgorod, of the fight of Prince Mstislav with Rededya, and many others, are also based, apparently, on epic songs and tales of that time. As to the fact that, among the *druzhina*, there were singers and composers of songs, there is the testimony not only of the *Tale of Igor's Raid* (with its mention of the seer Boyan), but also of the chronicles. For example, about A.D. 1241, in the Volynian (a continuation of the Hypatian) Chronicle, there is mention of a certain "eloquent singer Mitus," who, beaten and bound, was brought by force to Daniel of Galicia, after the singer's refusal to serve the prince.

The princes valued the praises of the singers. In this same Volynian

[3] See the "Words of a Certain Lover of Christ and Contender for the True Faith," "The Teaching of Luke Thidyata" (eleventh century), "Life of Theodosius Pechersky" (eleventh century), "The Story of the Rich Man and Poor Lazarus" (twelfth century), "Canonical Answers of John II, Metropolitan of Russia" (eleventh century), "The Teaching of the Zarubsky Monk Georgius" (thirteenth century), and others. See the summary in the book by Nicholas Findeisen, *Survey of the History of Music in Russia* (State Publishing House, Music Section, Vol. I, Moscow-Leningrad, 1928), pp. 26-170.

Chronicle it is said, around A.D. 1251, that when the Galician princes, Daniel and Basilko, returned from a successful campaign, "a song of praise was sung to them."

There is also mention of the singing of songs of praise to the princes, in the *Tale of Igor's Raid*. Boyan composed songs "to the aged Yaroslav, to the brave Mstislav, who killed Rededya before the hosts of the Kosogi, to the handsome Román Svyatoslavovich." In the *Tale* mention is made of the fact that in Kiev songs were sung also by foreigners, who visited the ancient Russian capital: "There [in Kiev] Germans and Venetians, there Greeks and Moravians, sing the praise of Svyatoslav." The *Tale* ends with the ascription of praise:

Having sung a song to the old princes, let us sing a song to the young ones also. Glory to Igor, son of Svyatoslav—to the Fierce Wild Ox, Vsevolod—to Vladimir, son of Igor! All hail to the princes and their knightly band, who fought on the battlefield against the troops of the infidels for all Christian men! To the princes, glory! And to their knightly band—ay, verily, glory!

An analysis of the forms and artistic style of the *Tale of Igor's Raid*, of certain fragments of chronicles, narratives, and other productions of ancient literature, reveals the influence of oral popular poetry.[4]

All these and numerous other direct and indirect testimonies of medieval literature bear witness beyond a doubt that in the first centuries of the Russian state there existed diverse forms of oral poetry, and in addition, that these existed among various social classes. But, unfortunately, hardly any original records of the folklore of that time have been preserved. And the reconstruction of a picture of the ancient life of folklore is possible only by an indirect method—the method of comparing these broken and fragmentary testimonies of ancient literature with the very rich folklore material presented in the records of the last three centuries.

[4] On the connections of the *Tale of Igor's Raid* with popular oral poetry, see: E. V. Barsov, *The Tale of Igor's Raid as an Artistic Monument of the Kiev Period of Ancient Russia* (Vols. I-III, Moscow, 1887–1889); A. A. Potebnya, *Tale of Igor's Raid: Text and Comments* (1878, reprinted in 1914); A. Smirnov, *Tale of Igor's Raid* (Voronezh, 1879); V. N. Perets, *On the Study of the "Tale of Igor's Raid"* (Leningrad, 1926), and the same book in its Ukrainian edition, *Tale of Igor's Raid* (Kiev, 1926); Y. M. Sokolov, "The 'Tale of Igor's Raid' and Popular Creative Works," *The Literary Critic*, No. 5, 1938.

Special records of the productions of folklore are known to us from the seventeenth century on. For the first records of Russian folklore, scholarship is indebted to two foreigners. Thus, the most ancient collection of historical songs was compiled on the initiative of the English traveler Richard James, for whom, during his sojourn in the Archangel region in the years 1619-1620, there were written down historical songs dealing with the events of the era of "unrest." [5] The other traveler, also an Englishman, Collins, who had lived in Moscow for forty years, wrote down in the years 1660 and 1669 two curious tales connected with the name of Ivan the Terrible.[6]

Unfortunately, Collins kept only an English rendering of them. From purely amateur motives, as material for entertaining reading, people began in the seventeenth century to write down the texts of the *byliny*. (It is true that they destroyed the poetic rhythm, and that they interpolated elements of literary language.) From the seventeenth century, mostly from the end of it, five texts have come down to us, and from the eighteenth century, ten more.[7] At the end of the seventeenth century people also began to compile collections of popular proverbs.[8] So far as one can judge from the character of the writing, and from the notes which have been made in the manuscripts, notebooks filled with *byliny* and collections of proverbs were in circulation, in the seventeenth and eighteenth centuries among the minor nobility, the merchant class, the official class, the lower clergy, and the literate peasants. In the seventeenth century people began to

[5] P. K. Simoni, "Great-Russian Songs, Written Down in the Years 1619–1620 for Richard James in the Far North of the Kingdom of Moscow," *Annals of the Divisions of Russian Language and Literature of the Academy of Sciences*, Vol. LXXXII, No. 7, St. Petersburg, 1907. An original point of view on the songs written down for R. James, as the product of individual creativeness, has been expressed by V. V. Danilov in *Proceedings of the Division of Ancient Russian Literature*, Academy of Sciences of the USSR, Vol. II, 1935.

[6] A. N. Veselovsky, "Tales of Ivan the Terrible," *Old and New Russia*, No. 4, 1876, pp. 313-323; article reprinted in the *Collected Works* of A. N. Veselovsky, Vol. XVI (Leningrad, 1938), pp. 149-166.

[7] B. M. Sokolov, "Records of the Ancient *Bylina*" *Ethnography*, Nos. 1-2, 1926, pp. 97-123; No. 1, 1927, pp. 107-122, and No. 2, pp. 301-314.

[8] P. K. Simoni, "Ancient Collections of Russian Proverbs, Sayings, Riddles, etc., of the Seventeenth to the Nineteenth Centuries," Nos. I-II, *Annals of the Division of Russian Language and Literature of the Academy of Sciences*, Vol. LXVI, No. 7, St. Petersburg, 1899.

compile, under the influence of the formal schooling of the South-west, manuscript collections of religious songs, which were called "psalms" and "canticles." Gradually, secular songs found their way into these collections.[9] From the seventeenth century there are preserved also notebooks with the religious verses of the Old Believers.[10]

Similar records of the texts of folklore, designed to preserve what had, in a particular social setting, been diffused mainly by word of mouth, continued to be produced also in the later period—in the eighteenth and nineteenth centuries. With the exception of the records mentioned above, made for the cultured Englishmen James and Collins, folklore was at first written down in exactly the same milieu to which its "bearers" belong. But in the eighteenth century there also originate in Russia records which pursue quite different ends, the ends of satisfying the interests of curiosity among the ruling classes. The famous collection, *Ancient Russian Poems* (that is, *byliny*), compiled in the middle of the eighteenth century by a certain Cossack, Kirsha Danilov, for a rich man of the Urals, the millowner Demidov,[11] may serve as the clearest example.

The eighteenth century, especially the second half of it, is contradictory in its attitudes toward oral poetry. In the classical literature of the nobility, during the course of several decades, oral poetry was shunned, and looked down upon, as being the creation of the "base rabble." But on the noblemen's estates, and in the social life of the capital, it flourished.[12] Not only the middle class, but also the higher nobility, the court aristocracy, loved to watch the peasants' choral

[9] See "The Beginning of Artistic Poetry in Russia: An Investigation of the Influence of the Little-Russian Versification and Popular Poetry of the Sixteenth to the Eighteenth Centuries upon the Great Russian," from the "History of the Russian Song," Pt. I, of V. N. Perets' *Historico-Literary Researches and Materials* (Recueil Bogoglasnik, St. Petersburg, 1900), Vol. I.

[10] See, in the collection of P. Bessonov, *Vagrant Beggars*, Nos. I-VI, Moscow, 1861–1874.

[11] *Ancient Russian Poems*, collected by Kirsha Danilov (1st ed., Moscow, 1804; 2nd ed., Moscow, 1818; 3rd ed., Commission for the Publication of Records and Treaties, 1878; 4th ed., by A. Suvorin, Petrograd, 1893; scientific edition of the Public Library, ed. P. Sheffer, Petrograd, 1901; latest edition, ed. S. K. Shambinago, Moscow, 1938).

[12] The living role of folklore has been described in detail in the book of essays by N. N. Trubitsyn, *On Popular Poetry in the Social and Literary Usage of the First Third of the Nineteenth Century* (St. Petersburg, 1912).

dances, to listen to the peasants' songs. Besides that, it was precisely in the eighteenth century that the great lords, and the rest of the nobility who were striving to imitate them, had at their homes, along with the estate theaters at which French plays were chiefly presented, choruses of singers, orchestras of musicians, *corde-chasse* players, *gusly* players. At the court, in the palaces in the suburbs of Moscow, on the provincial estates, there were contests among troupes of the land-owners' singers and musicians.

The repertory of their concerts was generally made up of transla-tions and of original compositions, of ballads of gallantry and of songs written in the conventional style of classicism. On this plan, for ex-ample, there was compiled by G. N. Teplov, in the year 1759, a song-book with musical notes, *Intervals of Repose from Labor*. But toward the end of the century the repertory was considerably increased, be-cause of the Russian and Ukrainian popular songs, which, it is true, were slightly worked over to suit the ears of the court. Examples were the *Collections of Simple Russian Songs* with notes (four numbers) which appeared in the period 1776–1796, compiled by the court psaltery player V. F. Trutovsky; the *Collection of Russian Popular Part Songs, set to music by Ivan Prach* (Part 2, first edition, 1790), which was compiled by a friend of Derzhavin's, a fancier and connois-seur of Russian songs, N. A. Lvov. Then there also begin to appear "songbooks" without notes, with only the written texts, but usually with an indication of the tune to which the given text was to be sung.

But along with these noblemen's collections in the last third of the eighteenth century, there also come to light songbooks which are clearly intended for a more democratic public—for the city bour-geoisie, the minor officials, the merchant class, and also for the literate peasantry. Such is the famous songbook of the bourgeois— as he calls himself, the "insignificant"--writer M. D. Chulkov, *Col-lection of Various Songs*, Parts 1-4 (1770–1774). This collection was republished in 1776 by the author himself, and in 1780–1781 it ap-peared in an edition by N. I. Novikov, under the title *A New and Complete Collection of Russian Songs* (six parts). From the end of the eighteenth century and during the whole course of the nine-

teenth, and even going on into the twentieth, there appear a countless number of songbooks, including a great many songs and literary
ballads which had penetrated into the mass of the people, had been
worked over among them, and had in this way been transformed into
folklore. The song-books also contain a very great number of songs
which had been taken down from the lips of country and city singers,
traditional songs of the peasantry, the bourgeoisie, the soldiers, and
so forth.

In such a spirit, not with any scientific aims, but to satisfy the demands of the people, V. A. Levshin (or, as it was formerly thought,
M. D. Chulkov) published in 1780–1783 the ten parts of his *Russian
Tales, Containing the Most Ancient Narratives of the Renowned
Knights, Popular Tales, and Others Surviving Through the Retelling
of Adventures;* they represent an original stylization of traditional
popular tales in imitation of the knightly romance of adventure and
magic, so dear to the bourgeois reader. Even earlier, in 1766–1768,
Chulkov had published in four parts a collection of anecdotes and
narratives, *The Scoffer, or, Slovenian Tales.* There were a great many
people who continued Chulkov's work. His activity in the diffusion of
folk songs, tales, and anecdotes borders closely upon the manuscript
and so-called "bast" * literature, which preceded his work and which
continued to be developed even after his time. In the manuscript
collections and in the cheap "bast" editions, traditional folklore was
fantastically combined with the tendency to "literary pretentious-
ness," the latter material frequently being of very poor quality. But,
in spite of the liberties taken in the adaptations and revisions of the
authentic folklore, the general mass of the bourgeois cheap popular
and manuscript literature gave no small supply of material for the
history of oral poetry in the eighteenth century and in the later period, which, unfortunately, has not even yet been studied with sufficient thoroughness.

Folkloristics, as a science, has been in existence for a little more
than a hundred years. Its rise as a theoretical discipline dates from the

---

* Bast (*lubóchnaya*) literature, originally books printed from wood (bast) engravings. Now used of popular "educational" books published in former times,
crude in form and content, and without artistic quality.—Ed.

first decades of the nineteenth century. Up to that time there had been only sporadic amateur collections of oral poetic material, and literary reworkings of it. The origin of folkloristics is closely connected with that broad trend in the fields of philosophy, science, and history, at the beginning of the nineteenth century, which received the name of romanticism.

Among the ideas of romanticism, the most widespread at that time was the idea of the "popular mind," which confirmed the presence of national unity, and at the same time effaced the class differentiation of the nation. The youthful bourgeoisie was inclined to speak in the name of the whole nation, and to ascribe its class ideas to the nation as a whole. To the study of the "national spirit" or the "national soul" of the people, scholars of the most diverse fields of knowledge (philosophers, historians, historians of law, philologists, students of literature, and so forth) devoted their knowledge. The science of folkloristics, which also began at this time, is very basic to these ideas. The science of "folk literature" was born in an atmosphere of romanticism, and, as we have already seen in the preceding chapter, its very name itself bears witness of this. The memorials of popular literature, which people began to collect and study at that time with particular enthusiasm, were bound to reveal all the richness and all the depth of the so-called "popular (or national) soul."

In the idealistic romantic philosophy of that time, especially in the philosophical works of Schelling, and later of the youthful Hegel, the doctrine is developed that the meaning of world history consists of the successive changes of the various national cultures. The "national spirit" of every nation, in the long process of self-development, reaches its apogee, enriches with its national values the "treasury" of the whole human race, and then yields its place to the manifestations of another "national spirit," which becomes the dominant power over the ideas of the world of culture. According to the teaching of the German philosopher-romanticists, Germany's "national spirit" was becoming such a dominant power over the ideas of the world. It is not difficult to perceive, in such a philosophy of history, the nationalistic tendencies which have guided her.

Other sciences, with their resources, have sought to confirm these nationalistic tendencies. Historians have found in the data of the historical past of Germany indications of the fact that, just as German literature, going back with its roots into the depths of the centuries, possesses exceptional vigor and fullness of life, so in its "national spirit" there is the guarantee of a great future. The thoughts of the historians of law, the historians of literature, and the historians of language have tended in this direction.

At that time there originates the comparative, so-called Indo-European philology. Its romantic (idealistic and nationalistic) roots are now completely obvious. German scholars (Bopp, later Schleicher and others), by means of a comparative analysis of the linguistic phenomena of the European and some of the Asiatic peoples, established the relationship of these peoples. They explained the resemblance of linguistic phenomena in the field of phonetics, morphology, and lexicology as the result of the derivation of peoples who were related to one another by a common ancestor. Already, in itself, this nationalistic tendency, which had isolated a well known group of European and certain non-European languages from the countless other languages of the world, was being still more intensified in works on the history of the specific national languages of the Indo-European family.

In particular, the German scholar-romanticists, who had examined the history of the Germanic tongues, were proving in their works that it is precisely the Germanic languages which most fully and clearly preserve the common Indo-European heritage. According to the opinion of these scholars, it is precisely from the data of the Germanic tongues that one can reconstruct most distinctly the basic peculiarities of the so-called "parent language," that is, the ancestor of all the Indo-European languages. Consequently, in the German philology of that period and of the one following it, there was frequently to be noted a tendency even to supplant the very name "Indo-European languages" by the name "Indo-Germanic languages."

On the one hand, the general ideas and temper of romanticism, and on the other, precisely and exactly the influence of comparative linguistics, which received such a great development at that time, left their characteristic imprint also on the first stages in the history of folkloristics.

The people of the western European countries began to be fascinated by, and to study, the "popular literature," first of all in England, then in Germany, beginning with the second half of the eighteenth century. In England, great significance was attached to the poems of Macpherson, *Fingal* and *Songs* (1760), patterned by him after the works of the ancient bard Ossian. In 1765 T. Percy published a collection of genuine ancient popular songs. The beautiful songs of the Scotch peasant-poet, Robert Burns, were created on the basis of genuine folklore.

Under the influence of English literature, in Germany in the years 1778–1779, there was published by Gottfried Herder a famous collection of the songs of various peoples, *Stimmen der Völker in Liedern* (Voices of the People in Songs).

Herder's book had a great influence on the later work of the romanticists in the collection and publication of folklore. The main stimulus to the rise and development of folkloristics among the romanticists is seen to be the national urge. In the publication of the first of the romanticists' editions of folklore, the political aims are clearly and concretely manifested. For their elucidation it is necessary only to bear in mind that these first publications coincide with the period of the Napoleonic wars. Such are the famous collection of German popular songs, compiled by the poets Arnim and Brentano, *Des Knaben Wunderhorn* (The Boy's Wonderful Horn), 1805; *Die Altdeutschen Volksbücher* (The Old German Popular Books), Herres, 1807; and *Deutsche Kinder- und Hausmärchen* (Tales for the Children and the Family), by the Brothers Grimm, 1812–1815. Here must be added also the magazine published by Arnim, *Zeitung für Einsiedler* (A Magazine for the Recluse), 1808, devoted to national antiquities and popular poetry.

A leading role in the strictly scholarly treatment of folklore in the period of romanticism in Germany was played by the brothers Wilhelm (1787–1859) and Jakob (1785–1863) Grimm, particularly by

Jakob, an unusual connoisseur both of oral German poetry, of literature, of law, and of language.[13]

In his general theoretical judgments and in his works on the particular questions of the history of law, language, literature, and folklore, Jakob Grimm was guided, as he himself affirmed many times, "by patriotic motives." Collecting the riches of the language of the people for the German dictionary, attentively studying the local color of the living popular speech and the monuments of ancient literature for the *German Grammar* and the *History of the German Language,* searching out, in scholarly archives and in the current colloquial speech, in proverbs, sayings, tales, ceremonies, and customs, information on the "antiquities of German law," editing old medieval literary productions like *Songs of the Niebelungen* and *Reynard the Fox,* collecting, systematizing, and making a literary adaptation of "German folk tales"—through the course of their whole half-century of activity Jakob Grimm and his brother Wilhelm were motivated by one general idea: to reveal and to demonstrate the antiquity, beauty, and richness of the German national culture. In their works there is gradually sketched out a grand picture of German "folk creativeness" in all the fields of social, family, intellectual, religious, and everyday life. The idealization of everything that is national, that is traditional, that goes back to distant centuries, covering that past with a kind of rosecolored haze, was characteristic of the work of the Brothers Grimm, as also of other folklorist romanticists.

Oral poetry, or, as it was then called, "popular poetry," provided by far the most vivid and most diverse colors for the creation of this idealized picture of the national past. The Brothers Grimm possessed a deep knowledge of oral poetry, and, along with this, they beautifully

[13] The chief works of J. Grimm are: *Tales for the Children and the Family* (Deutsche Kinder- und Hausmärchen) (1812–1815); *German Grammar* (Deutsche Grammatik) (1819, 1826–1827); *Antiquities of German Law* (Deutsche Rechtsal tertümer) (1828); an edition, with a translation into the new German language, of the medieval poem, *Reynard the Fox* (Reinecke Fuchs) (1834); *German Mythology* (Deutsche Mythologie) (1835; 2nd ed., 1844); *History of the German Language* (Geschichte der deutschen Sprache) (1848); his minor articles have been collected in the *Kleinere Schriften* (Minor Articles), Nos. I-IV, 1864. The minor works of W. Grimm have been collected in his *Kleinere Schriften* (1st ed., Berlin, 1881).

adopted, as literary men, the stylistic peculiarities of the popular (peasant and bourgeois) speech, which is so powerfully revealed in that reworking to which they, with great artistic feeling, subjected the popular tales,[14] stylizing them anew to conform to the idealized conceptions of the traditional "popular spirit" which had been worked out at that time. The personal poetic sense of the Brothers Grimm preserved them from that lack of taste which many of their followers failed to escape (and not only in Germany, but in other countries as well). It must be said that this literary reworking by the Brothers Grimm of the tales which they had collected, this stylization, is not at variance with those theoretical demands of principle which they had set forth for the editing of popular productions. Having an excellent mastery of the popular speech, and having adopted the peculiarities of the popular poetics, the Brothers Grimm considered themselves to have the right to "restore" this folk quality to the texts which had lost it.

As we shall see later on, the example of the Brothers Grimm had its imitators, even in Russia, including the person of the first editor of *Russian Folk Tales*, A. N. Afanasyev. From the viewpoint of contemporary folkloristics, even a cautious reworking and stylization of the texts, written down from their performers, is considered absolutely inadmissible in scientific editions. But in the era of the Brothers Grimm, in the world of romantic ideas and principles, this was altogether permissible. To the credit of the Brothers Grimm, it must be added that they were almost the first to establish the principle of publication of the authentic, popular oral poetic productions (but, as we see, this principle was practiced by themselves and by their followers with noteworthy concessions and restrictions).

The ideological trend of the folklorist works of the Brothers Grimm,

14 On the stylistic reworking by the Brothers Grimm of the German popular tales, see the latest works: F. Schultz, *Die Märchen der Brüder Grimm in der Urform* (Tales of the Brothers Grimm in Their Original Form) (Zweite Jahresausgabe der Frankfurter Bibliofilengesellschaft Offenbach a. M., 1924); *Märchen, Urfassung nach der Originalhandschrift der Abteilung Oelenberg in Elsass* (An Original Version of the Tales, After the MS in the Oelenberg Department in Alsace) (J. Lefftz, Heidelberg, 1927).

The discovery of the original rough drafts and sketches of the Grimm tales casts light on the history of the creation of this famous book.

their general emotionalism, proceed entirely from romantic ideas and moods. But it is interesting also to understand the special methodological principles, and methods of scholarly treatment of the phenomena of folklore, which were applied by the Brothers Grimm, and thereafter by their followers.

If many of the humanistic sciences of that time followed from the general premises of romanticism, then with reference to methodology in that era the "leading" discipline was that of philology. During that period it made exceptional progress. Its methods led to definite, clear results, and in their fundamental lines of thought they continued to be dominant, for almost an entire century. The limitations and fallibility of these linguistic methods and results began to be revealed only in our own time, and particularly in the light of the "new science of language" of the Academician N. Y. Marr and his school. In the course of the nineteenth century, however, especially in the first half of it, the methods of Indo-European philology were considered most reliable. They also exerted a very powerful influence on the branches of scholarship related to linguistics, among which was the new science of folkloristics.

In his linguistic works J. Grimm employed the "comparative method" in settling questions on the history of the German language and its dialects, and on the place of the German language in the family of related languages. He began to make use of this comparative method, also, in settling questions on the productions of popular poetry. If in the field of linguistics the coincidence of words, sounds, and forms in various dialects of the German language leads us back to a general Germanic parent language, and the coincidence of these same elements in a series of several related languages leads us to an Indo-European parent language, then according to this same system of the "comparative method," similar elements also in the field of folklore, in fantastic forms and subjects, must also be treated as a heritage, which has come down to new peoples or their tribal branches from a common ancient ancestor. Such a train of scientific thought made it possible to project, over many centuries, the various phenomena of contemporary life, and to reconstruct the national culture of the most ancient time.

It is also certain that, because of insufficient caution and strictness in the use of this method, because of the presence of an obvious enthusiasm for those prospects which at first sight it promised, scholarly thought which was tempered with a bias, and followed a nationalistic slant, must have led, and did actually lead, the science of folkloristics into the jungle of fantasy.

One of the characteristic features of the majority of the branches of romanticism, along with idealism and nationalism, was mysticism, an overemphasized interest in religion. By virtue of this, in the national culture too, elements of religious consciousness were sought with particular zeal, an effort was made to establish its forms in the past, and the folkloristics of that time turned its steady attention upon the reflection of ancient religious concepts in oral poetry, upon religious myths.

In J. Grimm's investigations into folkloristics, myths occupied the central place. The views of Grimm on the nature of oral poetry, and on the progress of its development from the most ancient times, have been set forth by him in the greatest detail in the book *German Mythology*. On the basis of direct and indirect references in ancient literature, various historical data, but chiefly on the basis of that which, according to his opinion, was preserved in oral poetry—in proverbs, sayings, riddles, songs, legends, tales—Grimm reveals a picture of the most ancient beliefs of the Germans. This book produced an unusual impression upon contemporary scholars, and through the course of long years it was the scientific model which was followed by the folklorists of various countries. At the present time, all the methodological defects of this book are obvious: the overestimation of the degree of antiquity of this or that production, in spite of the fact that it had been handed down through later eras in legends, tales, and other productions; the too great confidence in outward (purely accidental) similarity or consonance; the hasty identification of that which bears only an approximate resemblance, and so forth. But in the course of many years these defects were, for the majority of investigators, imperceptible. They were impressed by the truly exceptional erudition of the author, the richness of his facts, the bold creative power of his scholarship.

This work of J. Grimm, devoted to the systematization and explanation of Germanic myths, was also, to a considerable degree, the reason why the whole scientific conception of Jakob Grimm in the field of folkloristics began to be known as the mythological theory, or the mythological school. This name persistently passed into the history of the science of folklore.

As I have said, Grimm had a great many followers: from among the chief of these, mention must be made of the German scholars Kuhn, Schwartz, Mannhardt, the English scholar Max Müller, the French scholar Pictet, and finally of the Russians—F. I. Buslayev, A. N. Afanasyev, and O. F. Miller.

Each of these also had his own scientific thematics and his own original theoretical propositions.

Adalbert Kuhn (1812–1881) was, like J. Grimm, before all else, a linguist.[15] Following the principles of Indo-European comparative philology, he also studied the myths of the Indo-European peoples, applying the comparative method still more widely than J. Grimm had done. In his book, *The Descent of Fire and of the Drink of the Gods*,[16] he explains the Greek myth of Prometheus, who brought down fire to earth, by means of a connection of the name Prometheus with the Sanskrit word "prâmathyas," which means "a borer," and with the primitive method of procuring fire by means of boring a tree. At a much later time, when he was in his seventies, he wrote a work of a general character, on *The Stages in the Development of Myths*.[17]

In the methodology of his mythological investigations, Kuhn followed with the greatest consistency along the paths which had been laid out by linguistics, making too great abuse, however, of the connection of names and titles. In his case, besides, there may already be noted a tendency to see at the foundation of the majority of myths a deification of the elemental forces of nature—the storm, the thunder, the lightning, the wind, the clouds; that is, here we already have the

---

[15] Beginning in 1852, he published a linguistic magazine, *Zeitschrift für vergleichenden Sprachforschung*, and later, together with Schleicher, the *Beiträge zur vergleichenden Sprachforschung, auf dem Gebiete der ärischen, celtischen und slavischen Sprachen* (beginning in 1858).

[16] A. Kuhn, *Die Herabkunft des Feuers und des Göttertranke* (Berlin, 1859).

[17] A. Kuhn, *Entwicklungsstufen der Mythenbildung* (Berlin, 1873).

beginning of the so-called "meteorological" or "storm" theory, which was developed with the greatest fullness and persistence by the follower of Kuhn, Schwartz.[18]

"All groups of myths," said Schwartz in his book *The Origin of Mythology*, "prove that thunderstorms have always been the main object of the content of myths. These phenomena, so terrible, so filled with life, are almost always associated with the embodiment of supernatural forces." There were very many myths which Schwartz related to the theme of the conflict of darkness and light, since primitive man, according to his opinion, now and again had a glimmering of this idea, observing how the clouds cover the sun, in order that, in the end, they may finally be overcome by it. But for all the narrowness and onesidedness of his interpretation of the myths, Schwartz, in his general theoretical judgment, made a notable step forward, as compared with Grimm. He established the point that many superstitious ideas, which have survived up to the present time among the masses of the people (the belief in wood spirits, goblins, and so on), which Schwartz called "inferior mythology," must be considered as original manifestations of primitive thought, and not as feeble echoes of complex ancient myths. Thereby the soil was prepared for the most distinct and realistic judgments of Mannhardt.

Kuhn and Schwartz had been interested chiefly in the question of the content of mythological concepts among the ancient Indo-Europeans. The question of the origin and rise of myths, the problem of the actual process of the creation of myths, served as the object of the scientific researches of one of the greatest scholars of the middle of the nineteenth century—Max Müller.

Max Müller, a German by origin, having passed through the German scientific school, spent the greater part of his life in England,

---

[18] Schwartz, *Der heutige Volksglaube und das alte Heidenthum mit Bezug auf Norddeutschland* (Popular Beliefs of the Present Time and the Ancient Paganism, Particularly in the North German Territories) (Berlin, 1849; 2nd ed., 1862). *Der Ursprung der Mythologie dargelegt an griechischer und deutscher Sage* (The Origin of Mythology According to the Materials of the Greek and German Tales) (Berlin, 1860); *Sonne, Mond und Sterne; Ein Beitrag zur Mythologie und Culturgeschichte der Urzeit* (The Sun, the Moon and the Stars) (1864). *Wolken und Wind, Donner und Blitz* (Clouds and Wind, Thunder and Lightning) (1878).

taught at Oxford University, and wrote the majority of his works in English.

He was an authority on Sanskrit, a student of literature and a philologist. In his famous works, *Essays on Comparative Mythology* [19] and *Lectures on the Science of Language*,[20] Max Müller expounded his theory of the origin of myths, which has left a very great imprint on the folkloristics of the world.

Max Müller explains the rise of myths by a phenomenon which he very characteristically called "the malady of language." He means by this term the process of the gradual obscuring of the original sense of words, what we would now call—employing the terminology accepted in contemporary linguistics—the process of semantic changes in language. Max Müller begins with the assumption that primitive man, particularly the ancestor of the Indo-Europeans, expressed his thoughts in words which possessed a wholly concrete meaning. He was not able to think abstractly, for the very reason that in his language there existed only concrete words. Every object, every natural phenomenon received its name from some concrete and outstanding characteristic. But the same object could also be named from some other characteristic. On the other hand, various objects and phenomena could naturally receive the same name, because of a resemblance as to specific characteristics. Consequently the primitive concrete language, so to speak, consisted entirely of epithets (usually metaphorical), and must have included a great many synonyms and homonyms. For example, to denote the sun, the words "the shining one," "the radiant one," "the burning one," "the bright one" might serve; to denote the woods, "the rustling one," "the green one." On the other hand, the words "the shining one" might be used to designate not only the sun, but also the moon, the stars, water, and so forth.

---

[19] Max Müller, *Essays* (1856, 2nd ed., 1881); transl. into French, *Essais sur la mythologie comparée, les traditions et les coutumes* (Paris, 1873). A preliminary survey under the title *Comparative Mythology*, in Russian, was published by N. S. Tikhonravov in *Chronicles of Russian Literature in Antiquity*, Vol. V (1863).

[20] Max Müller, *Lectures on the Science of Language* (1862–1864); Russian transl., *Lectures on the Science of Language* (St. Petersburg, 1865; Voronezh, 1870); French transl., *Nouvelles leçons sur la science de langage*, 2 vols. (Paris, 1867).

It is this diversity and lack of stability in terms which must in the course of time, according to Müller, have produced a continually greater confusion of ideas, a forgetting of the original sense of words, which must have resulted in the so-called "malady of language," forming fantastic concepts as to natural phenomena, that is, myths.

In order to understand how concretely Max Müller sketched for himself the process of the formation of myths, let us have recourse to a certain example, which he himself used more than once, borrowing a passage from A. Lang's book, *Mythology:* [21]

Let us suppose that in the period of the creation of myths someone said: "The shining one follows after the burning one," wishing to express the thought: "The sun follows after the dawn." Let us further suppose that the word which meant "the shining one" appears to be the Aryan prototype of the Greek word *helios*, "sun," and that the word which has the meaning "the burning one" is also the Aryan prototype of the Sanskrit word *ahanâ*, or *dahanâ*, "dawn." Let us suppose that the word corresponding to Helios becomes confused with Apollo, a god who has features in common with the sun; let us suppose that the word which means "the burning one" is transformed from some kind of word like *ahanâ* or *dahanâ* into Daphne, and let us assume that a well known tree also bore the name of Daphne, because it ignites easily.

Once all these transformations had come about, and had then been forgotten, the Greeks found in their language the following expression: "Apollo pursues Daphne." They would have seen that Apollo is a word of masculine gender, and Daphne of feminine gender. And in such a way, they would have come to the conclusion that Apollo is a young god in love, pursuing the beautiful, chaste nymph Daphne, and that Daphne, fleeing from his pursuit, transformed herself, or was transformed, into a tree, which bears the same name.

"To me, all this seems clear as day," says Max Müller, and in this way he educes a myth from linguistic phenomena.

From this example it is evident that Max Müller attached a meaning to grammatical categories, particularly to the category of gender, to the morphological gender endings, as well as to semasiological changes in language, as factors contributing to the formation of myths.

[21] A. Lang, *Mythology*, transl. and ed. by N. N. and V. N. Kharuzin (Moscow, 1901), p. 50.

Apart from his great efforts, which have been briefly noted, in the field of purely linguistic relationships (in which Max Müller differed from a great many "comparativist" philologists, who with passionate enthusiasm had devoted themselves to the comparative study of Indo-European languages), attention is drawn to the strange concept of Max Müller on the stages in the development of human thought. In his theorizing Max Müller sketched for himself the following stages in the history of human thought and language: the first period, the "thematic" (the period of the formation of roots, and of the grammatical forms of language); the "dialectic" period (the formation of the basic families of languages—Aryan, Semitic, Turkic); the "mythological" period (the formation of myths), and the "popular" period (the formation of the national languages). From this picture of human progress, drawn as it appeared to Max Müller, it follows that he relates the process of the formation of myths to a comparatively late stage of human culture. Besides, it is shown that primitive man looked quite soberly and realistically upon the phenomena of the world, and understood them quite clearly, and only later on, in the course of the "obscuring" of the original clear concepts, did he begin to form very vague explanations of natural phenomena, in the form of myths. The kind of history of human thought and culture which was outlined by Max Müller could not help but encounter decisive objections, as we also shall see below.

As regards the assertions of Max Müller on the "malady of language" as the cause of the formation of myths, no one will attempt to deny the well known facts that in the history of any given language, frequently a metaphor which has been understood literally or falsely, an interpretation of a common noun in the sense of a proper one, a confusion of synonymous expressions, or the presence of several words to designate the same object,[22] have produced, and even now can still produce, legends and fantastic tales. But to trace the roots of all myths to the phenomena of the so-called "popular etymology," of course, is a thing that no one would do at the present time.

Finally, it must be added that Max Müller, like both Kuhn and

---

[22] See, for example, in the theory of N. Y. Marr, the role which was assigned in the earliest stages of language to "semantic families."

Schwartz, assigned the majority of the myths to a very narrow range of natural phenomena; not to meteorological phenomena, however, as the above-mentioned scholars had done, but to the circle of phenomena connected with the sun and its activity. Therefore the branch of mythological theory introduced by Max Müller was called, in the history of science, "the solar theory" (from the Latin word *sol—*sun). But, as one may readily be convinced from what has been said above, it would be very erroneous to define under this term the whole complex, exceedingly erudite system of scientific views established by Max Müller. The theory of Max Müller is considerably broader, in spite of all its methodological unreliabilities.

The impasses, which the "mythological school" had begun to reach, soon were very clearly perceived in science, and evoked decisive criticism. It is interesting to notice that even the individual representatives of the theory themselves began to abandon it. In this connection it is curious to observe the scientific path which was followed by one of the outstanding scholars—Mannhardt.

Wilhelm Mannhardt (1831–1880) at first followed in the theoretical and methodological footsteps of Grimm, Kuhn, and Schwartz. Proof of this is given by his books, *German Myths,*[23] and *The World of the Gods of the German and Nordic Peoples.*[24]

But he was one of those representatives of the mythological school who themselves perceived its fallibility, and had the courage to acknowledge this openly. Mannhardt gave a detailed criticism of the methods of the mythological school in his celebrated work, *Cults of the Wood and Field.*[25] He shifted the center of attention of the mythologists from the problem of the restoration of lost ancient myths to the study of contemporary popular beliefs, successfully developing the picture of the "inferior mythology," which had already been projected by Schwartz. In the explanation of these phenomena he approximated to a considerable degree the principles of the so-called "anthropological school" of Tylor and Lang, which will be

---

[23] W. Mannhardt, *Germanische Mythen, Forschungen* (Berlin, 1858).

[24] *Die Götterwelt der deutschen und nordischen Völker* (Berlin, 1860), I.

[25] *Wald- und Feldkulte* (Pt. 2, Berlin, 1875–1877). The third volume appeared after the death of the author.

discussed farther on, in its proper place. Mannhardt, in particular, in the explanation of the myths, devoted some space to survivals of ancestor cults.

Up to this point we have spoken of the German representatives of the "mythological school." True, M. Müller worked in England, but in his education, and in the basic principles of his scientific work, he was very closely bound to the traditions of German scholarship.

The principles of Grimm's mythological school were taken up also by French scholars (Baudry, Darmesteter), Belgians (Van den Heyn), and Italians (Angelo de Gubernatis, author of the book *Zoological Mythology* [1872], which attached great significance to the figures of animals in the creation of mythological concepts).[26]

The work of the "mythologists" in folkloristics, in almost all cases, was combined with work in linguistics. The data of language served as the chief material for the explanation of the most ancient stages in the development of myths, religious and poetic concepts.

The "mythologists," beginning with Grimm, strove to reconstruct a picture of the most ancient mode of life of the Indo-Europeans.

A conspicuous place among these works was occupied by the book of the French philologist, A. Pictet (1799–1875), *The Origin of the Indo-Europeans, or, The Primitive Aryans*.[27] This book exerted a powerful influence upon the works of the Russian mythologist, A. N. Afanasyev.

In Russia the "mythological school" was also the first stage in the development of scientific folkloristics. As in the West, the scientific investigations were preceded by a period of the romantic collection of folk poetry, and the romantic utilization of it for artistic purposes. (We recall the folklore themes in Zhukovsky, Pushkin, the early Gogol, and others.) The passionate enthusiasm of Peter Vasilyevich Kireyevsky for collecting folk songs, in which he succeeded in interesting his numerous friends among literary men and historians, yielded

26 Among us in Russia, de Gubernatis' book had an influence on certain scholars—N. F. Sumtsov and L. Z. Kolmachevsky. This book received a detailed criticism by Acad. A. N. Veselovsky; see the *Collected Works of A. N. Veselovsky* (Academy of Sciences of the USSR, Vol. XVI, Moscow-Leningrad, 1938); L. Kolmačevsky, *Das Tierepos im Occident und bei den Haven*, pp. 204-207, 322-329.

27 *Les Origines indoeuropéennes ou les Arijas primitifs* (Paris, 1859).

tremendous results. Personal reasons—Kireyevsky's excessive dilatoriness and his minute care in preparing the text of the songs for printing—and chiefly causes of a public nature—the incredible captiousness of the censorship of Nicholas I toward the popular poetic materials which were being published—resulted in the fact that the grandiose collection, which had been made for the most part in the 1830's, began to appear in print only in the 1860's,[28] with the exception of a small collection of religious poems, which Kireyevsky himself managed—and that with difficulty—to publish in the year 1848.[29]

P. V. Kireyevsky was one of the most outstanding representatives of Slavophilism, a movement which in many ways corresponded to the nationalistic romanticism of western Europe. The idea of a "national spirit," a "popular soul," the idealization of national antiquity and its traditions in social life and modes of living, and finally, the direct influence of the Western romantic philosophy upon the Slavophilic conception (it must be borne in mind, for instance, that Kireyevsky and his brother I. V. Kireyevsky, in the 1820's, traveled to Germany, attended lectures by German philosophers and scholars, and were personally acquainted with many of them)—all this served as the basis for Kireyevsky's enthusiasm for collecting popular songs.

As it has now become clear,[30] Kireyevsky began to collect songs together with his close friend, the poet N. M. Yazykov, in the year 1831.

The beginning of the 1830's was a time of redoubled interest, on the part of Russian journalism and literature, in the questions of nationality; it was precisely in this period that the authors returned directly to the sources of popular life; in 1831 the tales of Pushkin began to appear, and in the same year Gogol's *Evenings on a Farm Near Dikanka* was published.

[28] *Songs Collected by P. V. Kireyevsky,* ed. P. A. Bessonov, Nos. I-X, 1860–1874; these are epic songs (*byliny* and historical songs). The ceremonial and lyric songs, however, were not published until the twentieth century, ed. M. N. Speransky: *Songs Collected by P. V. Kireyevsky,* new series (No. I, Moscow, 1911; No. II, Pt. 1, Moscow, 1918; No. III, Pt. 2, Moscow, 1929).

[29] P. V. Kireyevsky, *Russian Popular Poems: Lectures Before the Society of History and Russian Antiquities* (Moscow, 1848).

[30] See the article by M. K. Azadovsky, "Kireyevsky and Yazykov," in his book, *Literature and Folklore* (Moscow, 1938), pp. 138-153.

P. V. Kireyevsky, N. M. Yazykov, and other representatives of the Slavophilism which had just then begun, were caught up in the conflict with the ideas of the *Philosophical Letters* of Chaadayev, which were then widely circulated in manuscript. The young Slavophiles were especially agitated and infuriated by Chaadayev's assertion that the Russians had no proper historical past of their own.

Chaadayev asserted that we had "neither fascinating reminiscences, nor graceful images in memory of the people, nor powerful precepts in their legends." [31] But against these assertions, made by one of the founders of the movement of sympathy with Western ideas, war was waged by P. V. Kireyevsky, N. M. Yazykov, and their friends. In the traditional songs of the people, they saw the refutation of Chaadayev's thesis of the absence in the Russian people of "fascinating reminiscences" and instructive traditions. Hence the passionate collecting of *byliny* and various kinds of popular songs (historical, ceremonial, and lyrical).

Comparing the voluminous collection of Russian songs which he had presently unearthed with the printed collections of popular songs which were known at that time in western European countries, P. V. Kireyevsky justifiably considered his collection richer than all the foreign ones. [32]

Kireyevsky was not alone in his folklore activity. In the thirties and the forties of the last century, paralleling his collection of songs, a collection of tales and proverbs was made by V. I. Dal, but the publication of his materials did not begin until after the death of Nicholas I.

In the reign of Nicholas I the publication of folklore materials was possible only for scholars of the most reactionary, conservative tendency; the publication was accompanied by excessively biased com-

[31] M. Gershenson, *P. Y. Chaadayev: Life and Thought* (St. Petersburg, 1908), p. 209.

[32] On the activity of P. V. Kireyevsky in collecting popular songs, see the articles by M. N. Speransky, "P. V. Kireyevsky and His Collection of Songs" in *Songs Collected by P. V. Kireyevsky*, New Series (No. I, Moscow, 1911, and No. II, Pt. 2, containing the same "songs," Moscow, 1929). See also B. M. Sokolov, *Collectors of Popular Songs* (Moscow, 1923), and M. K. Azadovsky, *Letters of P. V. Kireyevsky to Yazykov* (Leningrad, 1935) and, by the same author, *Literature and Folklore* (Moscow, 1938).

mentaries in the spirit of the official doctrine of that time, with its three fundamentals: "Orthodoxy, autocracy, nationalism." In addition, even the very selection of the folklore material for publication was biased. Finally, as it has now been definitely established by investigators, even falsification of the oral poetic texts was permitted, so that the publications of these scholars must be employed with great caution. This is especially true of the publications of the self-taught scholar I. P. Sakharov. These include his *Russian Popular Tales*, Part I (1841), and also his well known publication of *Tales of the Russian People*, in two volumes (1849), containing proverbs, sayings, descriptions of popular agricultural and wedding ceremonies, songs, and so forth.

Still earlier, a Moscow professor, Latinist, and archaeologist, I. M. Snegirev, had begun to work on the collection and publication of national folklore. In the years 1831–1834 he published a vast collection of Russian popular proverbs: *The Russians in Their Proverbs*, revised in 1848 in the collection: *Russian Popular Proverbs and Parables*. In 1838 his large book on popular ceremonies (*Holidays and Ceremonies of the Plain Russian People*) appeared. Along with these publications of Sakharov and Snegirev, it is necessary to mention the great work of A. Tereschenko, *The Everyday Life of the Russian People* (St. Petersburg, 1848), containing, in addition to numerous ethnographic data, information on folk poetry.

Against the background of the collectors' work in the 1830's and 1840's, there stands out even more distinctly the research done by the first Russian scholars in the field of folklore. P. V. Kireyevsky, the Slavophiles, and the representatives of the "official nationalism" were not scholars in the real sense of the word; they were, above all, publicists, for whom folklore served as material for the basis of their political views and biases. The first genuine Russian scholar-folklorist was F. I. Buslayev.

The extent and character of the scientific activity of Fyodor Ivanovich Buslayev (born in 1818 in the city of Kerensk, in the province of Penza, the son of a minor official; died in 1897) recall to a great degree the activity of J. Grimm. Like him, Buslayev was a philologist, a historian of ancient national literature, and an investigator of folk poetry. Besides this, Buslayev was intensely interested in the history of the pictorial arts, and was—as in the case of philology, literary studies, and folkloristics—the founder in Russia of this science also. In his scholarly practice Buslayev was closely allied with the traditions of western European science.

In his first scientific work Buslayev emerged as a follower of Grimm. How deep this influence was, is shown by Buslayev's acknowledgement: "Of all contemporary scholars, I follow Jakob Grimm for the most part, considering his principles to be the most fundamental and the most fruitful, both in scholarship and in life." [33] Consequently, the teaching of Grimm was for him not only a scientific and theoretical guide, but also an expression of a *Weltanschauung* which they shared in common. In the study of the history of national culture (language, poetry, art) and in the popularization of its results (Buslayev was an excellent pedagogue), he saw a great social and educational work.

In the study of the Russian language [34] Buslayev was exactly what Grimm had been in the study of the German language.

He was interested not only in the formal side of the development of language, as became characteristic later on with many representatives of Indo-European comparative philology, but also in that which binds language to the ancient mode of life, to thought, poetry, mythology.

Buslayev derives the origin of poetry directly from the development of language itself, which in the early stages of its existence was distinguished by a vividly expressed imagery. Buslayev was convinced

[33] *On the Teaching of the Native Language*, composed by Fyodor Buslayev, senior teacher of the Third Realgymnasium, 1st ed. (Moscow, 1844), Pts. I, II. Later on, Buslayev, on the basis of these methodological principles, composed his *Textbook of Russian Grammar, Compared with the Church Slavonic* (Moscow, 1869), which went through a great number of editions, and likewise—also for use as a textbook—*A Russian Anthology: Landmarks of Ancient Russian Literature and Popular Letters* (Moscow, 1870).

[34] Buslayev's chief works on language, aside from those already mentioned, were: (*a*) *On the Influence of Christianity on the Slavonic Language* (Moscow, 1848); (*b*) *An Attempt at a Historical Grammar of the Russian Language* (Moscow, 1858; two parts, 2nd ed., 1863, under the title, *Historical Grammar of the Russian Language*); and (*c*) *Historical Anthology of the Church Slavonic and Ancient Russian Languages* (Moscow, 1861).

that the sustaining force in this process, the force which gave the content both to prose and to poetry, was religion.

In Chapter I, "Epic Poetry," of his monumental work, *Historical Essays*, which was made up of a collection of numerous articles on folklore and on the history of art, Buslayev formulates his basic views on the most ancient periods of national culture in this way:

In the earliest period of its existence, the people already possesses all the main ethical foundations of its nationality in language and mythology, which are closely connected with poetry, law, manners, and customs. The people does not remember that at one time it invented its mythology, its language, its laws, customs, and ceremonies. All these national foundations have already entered deeply into its ethical existence, as the very life which it lived through in the course of many prehistoric centuries, as the past, on which the present order of things firmly rests and the entire future development of life. Therefore all ethical ideas, for the people of the primitive period, constitute their hallowed tradition, the great past of our own country, the sacred legacy of the ancestors to their descendants.

The word is the main and most natural instrument of oral tradition. To it, as to a central point, there are joined together all the finest threads of the antiquity of our country, all that is great and sacred, all that serves to strengthen the ethical life of the people.

The beginning of poetic creation is lost in the dark depths of prehistory, when the language itself is being created, and the origin of language is the first, the most decisive and brilliant, effort of human creative power. The word is not a conventional sign for the expression of a thought, but an artistic form, called forth by a most lively sensation, which nature and life have awakened in man. The creative power of popular fantasy passes over directly from language to poetry. Religion is that dominant force which gives the most decisive impetus to this creative power, and the most ancient myths, accompanied by ceremonies, stand along the way of the creation of language and poetry, which embraces in itself all the spiritual interests of the people.[35]

Thus—not with absolute precision, but at any rate very insistently, in the spirit of the ideas of Grimm and of the mythological school— Buslayev binds together into one, language, poetry, and mythology.

[35] *Historical Essays on Russian Popular Literature and Art*, Vol. I (St. Petersburg, 1861), pp. 1-2.

In this same article in which he lays down his program, he also formulates the romantic ideas of popular literature as an impersonal creation of the whole people:

In the formation and structure of it [language] there is expressed, not the personal thought of one man, but the creation of the whole people. . . . The whole field of thought of our ancestors was bounded by language. It was not only an outward expression, but an essential, integral part of that indivisible ethical activity of the whole people, in which, though every individual takes a living part, he still does not rise out of the solid mass of the whole people. By that same power which created language, there were also fashioned the myths of the people, and their poetry.

Tradition, stability of concepts and forms, were characteristic of the popular creative works, as emphasized by Buslayev.

Everything went on as it should, as it had been established from time immemorial: the same tale was told, the same song was sung, and in the very same words, because you cannot take a word out of a song; even the transitory emotions of the heart, joy and sorrow, were expressed not so much as a personal outburst of passion, but as the customary outpourings of the feelings—at a wedding in the wedding songs, at funerals in lamentations, which had been composed once and forever in immemorial antiquity and always repeated practically without change. There was no outlet for individual personality from such a closed circle.[36]

As a supplement to this thesis of the "impersonality" of popular creative works, in other passages of his *Essays*, Buslayev often formulated a second proposition which is typical of the folkloristics of the romanticists, that of the "artlessness" of this popular creative work. Having described the merits of J. Grimm and his school, Buslayev concludes:

It can hardly be necessary to point out how much such a broad, impartial view of literature is indebted in its origin to the treatment of the properly so-called *popular artless literature*, which lives in the mouths of the simple people. It is precisely this literature which stands largely outside of all personal characteristics, which is chiefly

[36] *Ibid.*, pp. 6-7.

the word of the whole people, *the voice of the people,* as the well known proverb expresses it.[37]

These extracts from Buslayev's articles give an idea both of the bases of the theoretical position of Buslayev and of the character of their expression.

We see that Buslayev was altogether carried away by those ideas which are familiar to us through the statements of the western European romantic school of "mythologists"; but it would be altogether incorrect if we were to restrict the whole significance of Buslayev in the history of Russian science to the exposition of these general ideas. His special researches on the concrete problems of folkloristics, literary studies, and the study of art, by the interpretation of specific phenomena in the field of language and creative work, give an idea of the vigor of his scholarly endowments and of the significance of his scholarly activity. In explaining the concrete facts of language and poetry, he displayed great caution, discretion, and soberness of critical thought.

His great merit must be considered as the effort to survey the productions of oral poetry in comparison with the facts of written literature and literary art—with the phenomena of the imitative art.[38] Proof of the vigor of his mind, of his scientific keenness, is given by the fact that he later acknowledged the fallibility of the mythological theory, which he had upheld so long and with such enthusiasm,[39] and allied himself with the new movements in the field of scholarship—not, it is true, in the anthropological school, as was the case with

[37] *Ibid.,* p. 405.

[38] Besides the *Essays,* especially the second volume, where there are gathered many articles of Buslayev's on ancient Russian art, see "General Ideas of Russian Icon Painting," *Annals of the Society of Ancient Russian Art,* 1866; *Russian Illuminated Manuscripts of the Apocalypse: Index of Pictures from Illuminated Texts of the Apocalypse in Russian Manuscripts from the Sixteenth to the Nineteenth Centuries* (St. Petersburg, 1884), and others.

[39] In a more systematic form, the mythological views of Buslayev are presented in his course, *History of Russian Literature: Lectures Delivered Before the Tsarevich Nicholas Aleksandrovich, 1859–1860,* Nos. 1-3, Moscow, 1904–1907. The gradual changes in the theoretical views and methodological devices of Buslayev may be traced from his two books, *My Leisure Moments,* minor compositions collected from periodical publications, Vols. I and II (Moscow, 1886), and *Popular Poetry* (St. Petersburg, 1887).

Mannhardt, but to the Benfey school of "borrowing" (which will be discussed below).[40] Buslayev's delicate aesthetic taste and the stylistic excellence of his productions contributed much toward the success of his books and articles.

Another brilliant representative of the "mythological school" in Russia was Alexander Nikolayevich Afanasyev, who was born in 1826 in the city of Boguchar, in the province of Voronezh, like Buslayev, in the family of a district official; he died in 1871.

By his education Afanasyev was a jurist. He finished his studies in the faculty of law at the University of Moscow, where he came under the influence of certain professors—the historian of Russian law, K. D. Kavelin, and the historian S. M. Solovyov. After finishing his work at the university, Afanasyev served in the archives of the Ministry of Foreign Affairs; as the result of a denunciation he was, in 1862, deprived of this position, so well suited to scholarly activity, and was compelled to turn to work which had little interest for him. A. N. Afanasyev was distinguished by his exceptional capacity for work and his broad interests in various fields of historical science and literary study.

On finishing his work at the university, under the influence of Buslayev's works, A. N. Afanasyev was fascinated by the works of the "mythologists," and centered his basic scholarly interests in the field of folk beliefs and poetry.[41]

In Afanasyev's works on folklore, the "mythological" school in Russia found its fullest expression. Afanasyev did not have such a solid philological education as Buslayev, and he did not possess the scientific caution which was characteristic of the latter. Consequently, he was characterized, in a considerably greater degree than Buslayev, by all the enthusiasms for linguistic and mythological assimilations which led many of the European followers of Grimm to fantastic conclusions. Afanasyev brought together his numerous articles on my-

[40] Especially characteristic, in this connection, is the article "Beggars' Narratives" (1874), in *My Leisure Moments*, Vol. II, pp. 259-406.

[41] For biographical material on Afanasyev, and for the history of his scientific progress, see Y. M. Sokolov, "Life and Scientific Activity of A. N. Afanasyev," in *Popular Russian Tales* of A. N. Afanasyev, ed. M. K. Azadovsky, N. P. Andreyev, and Y. M. Sokolov (Moscow, Academia, 1936), Vol. I.

thology (written from the end of the 1840's to the middle of the 1860's), in a systematized and revised form, in his famous three-volume work, *The Poetic Attitudes of the Slavs on Nature.*[42]

Afanasyev assimilated the devices of the "mythologists" with all their methodological excellences and defects. With passionate fervor he accepted the teaching of Grimm, and especially of those who had continued his work—the "meteorologists" Kuhn, Schwartz, and Mannhardt in his early period. In the content of the Slavonic and Indo-European myths, Afanasyev, like them, saw most diverse forms of thunderstorms, tempests, clouds, the conflict of light with darkness. This "meteorological" theory he combined also with echoes of the "solar" theory of Max Müller. From the latter he took also the explanation of the actual process of the formation of myths from the waning primitive metaphors and other manifestations of the "malady of language."

Afanasyev formulated his basic theoretical and methodological aims in the first chapter ("The Origin of Myth: the Method and Means of Studying It") of this work. There are few works in which the principles of the "mythological school" (in its full development) have found such a clear and straightforward exposition, as in this chapter of Afanasyev's famous three-volume work. Here also is the teaching that the root both of poetry and of myth is in the word, and the belief in the possibility of a scientific reconstruction of the human (specifically, of the Indo-European) "parent language," and, on its foundation, of pictures of the ancient mode of life; and strange opinions, from the viewpoint of our contemporary linguistics, that the more ancient the language is, and the closer it is to the sources of human culture, the more clear and well ordered it will be; and a mistaken opinion to the effect that the history of language is a process of decline and decay, and not of gradual growth and enrichment— everything that has already become familiar to us from the romantic theories of the philologists and folklorists of the middle of the nineteenth century. In the epilogue to the first volume, Afanasyev himself

[42] A. N. Afanasyev, *The Poetic Attitudes of the Slavs on Nature: An Essay in the Comparative Study of Slavonic Traditions and Beliefs in Connection with the Mythical Legends of Other Related Peoples*, Vols. I-III (Moscow, 1865–1869).

candidly gives the names of those scholars whose works he has followed. "In the present edition," writes Afanasyev, "all these [his earlier.—Au.] articles have been newly revised, enlarged, and corrected, in accordance with those conclusions which have been reached in modern times by the combined efforts of European scholars: Max Müller, Kuhn, Mannhardt, Schwartz, Pictet, and others."

A few extracts from this first chapter may serve to characterize the theoretical positions of Afanasyev:

The rich and, it may be said, the only source of the various mythical representations is the living human word, with its metaphorical and harmonious expressions. In order to show how indispensably and naturally myths (fables) are created, it is necessary to turn to the history of language. The study of languages in the various eras of their development, from the surviving literary monuments, has led philologists to the justified conclusion that the material perfection of a language, which has been more or less highly developed, is found to be in inverse ratio to its historical destinies: the more ancient the period of language which is being studied, the richer will be its material and forms, and the better arranged will be its organism; the further you begin to advance into the later periods, the more perceptible will become those losses and mutilations which human speech undergoes in its development.[43]

Having described (with references to Max Müller) the picturesque character of primitive language, the role of metaphors and synonyms in it, the process of forgetfulness and confusion of the original meanings of words, Afanasyev continues:

In consequence of such long-continued losses in language, the transformation of sounds, and the modification of concepts inherent in the words, the initial sense of the ancient speech became constantly more obscure and enigmatic, and there began the inevitable process of mythical beguilements. . . .

It was only necessary to forget, to lose the original connections of ideas, for the metaphorical assimilation to take on, for the people, all the significance of an actual fact, and to serve as the occasion for the creation of a whole series of fabulous tales.[44]

In the further development of human speech and thought, in Afanasyev's opinion, there occurred a process (*a*) "of fissure of the

[43] *Ibid.*, Vol. I, p. 5.   [44] *Ibid.*, pp. 9-10.

mythical tales" and (*b*) "of bringing the myths down to earth and attaching them to a well known locale and to historical events." [45]

However, a comparative study of these fissured and altered myths can lead to the reconstruction of their original complete and well ordered form. The guiding medium for such work must be comparative philology.[46] The greater part of the mythical concepts of the Indo-European peoples goes back to the remote time of the Aryans; separating themselves from the general mass of the ancestral tribe and settling throughout distant lands, the peoples bore away with them, together with their richly evolved speech, their own opinions and beliefs. Hence it can be understood why the popular traditions, superstitions, and other fragments of antiquity must be studied comparatively. . . . The comparative method provides the means for restoring the original form of the traditions, and therefore imparts to the scholar's conclusions a special reliability, and serves as a necessary verification for them.[47]

Afanasyev deeply believed in the infallibility of the comparative study of mythology, after the pattern of comparative Indo-European philology; he was convinced that this method was an objective one, providing security against subjective interpretations and fantastic inventions. Afanasyev asserted:

Nothing is such a hindrance to the correct explanation of myths as the tendency to systematize, the desire to sum up the heterogeneous traditions and beliefs under an abstract philosophical rule. The earlier methods of interpretation of myths (methods which have now died out) chiefly suffered from this practice. Not having any reliable support, being guided only by their own conjectures, which had nothing to restrain them, scholars, influenced by the need inherent in man to perceive, in disconnected and enigmatic facts, some secret sense and order, explained the myths, every one according to his personal understanding; one system replaced another, every new philosophical doctrine produced also a new interpretation of the ancient tales, and all these systems, all these interpretations, died down again as quickly as they had arisen. . . .

The new method of interpreting myths is also particularly credible because it undertakes the task without previously formed conclusions, and bases all its assumptions upon the direct evidences of

[45] *Ibid.*, pp. 12-13.   [46] *Ibid.*, p. 15.   [47] *Ibid.*, pp. 17-18.

language: when correctly understood, these evidences have great value as a truthful and irrefutable memorial of antiquity.[48]

When Afanasyev was writing these arguments, he did not suspect that everything which he was saying with reference to earlier theories would also have to be applied, in a still greater degree, to the theory which he had developed. The "mythological school" "died down" primarily because it left too much scope for "personal reasoning," for the arbitrary workings of the scholarly fantasy of the investigator. Neither Afanasyev nor the "mythological school" was saved by that "support" on which they had relied—the testimony of language. "Correctly understood, these testimonies are of great value," Afanasyev had said. But the whole point of the matter lies precisely in the fact that these testimonies were incorrectly understood. The error of the "mythologists" was clear even to many of their contemporaries. It consisted in the arbitrary interpretation, above all, of linguistic phenomena. But even the methods of comparative thought, especially in the case of persons so poorly prepared, from the linguistic standpoint, as Afanasyev, were very unreliable. A wealth of imagination and completely unrestrained conjectures led to altogether fantastic conclusions.

The interpretation of myths by the "mythological school," especially by Afanasyev, later on became the subject of much talk. One must remember Afanasyev's effort "to sum up the heterogeneous traditions and beliefs under an abstract philosophical rule," which compelled him everywhere, in whatever legend, proverb, or song he dealt with, to perceive echoes of a myth about the thunderstorm, the clouds, the conflict of darkness with light.

To what lengths this persistent tendency of Afanasyev's went, is shown, for example, by such facts as these. The subject of a well known children's tale is as follows: The Witch wants to destroy Vanya; Vanya cleverly escapes from misfortune; having caused the Witch to sit down on the shovel, he then throws her into the fire. According to Afanasyev's "interpretation of myths," this signifies that the cloud (the Witch) wants to destroy the sun's light (Vanya), but

[48] *Ibid.*, pp. 11-12.

the sun's light frees itself from the power of the cloud and dispels it.

In another children's tale Afanasyev interpreted the figure of Sivushka-Burushka again as an image of the dark cloud, which is cloven by the lightning.

Or this is the way Afanasyev interprets the well known motif of the *bylina* of Elijah the Sedentary, and of his miraculous cure:

The beer, which Elijah of Murom drinks, is an ancient symbol of rain. Fettered by the winter cold, the heroic Thunderer sits sedentary, without moving (not revealing himself in the thunderstorm), until he slakes his thirst with living water, that is, until the warmth of spring breaks his icy fetters and transforms the snow clouds into rain clouds; only then does he gain the strength to lift his lightning-swift sword and to hurl it against the dark demons.[49]

At the present time Afanasyev's book, from the scientific and theoretical viewpoint, is obsolete; but it is valuable on account of its great mass of factual material. This book played its part not only as an awakener of scholarly thought. It also exerted an influence on scholarly literature.

Being possessed of a lively imagination and a wealth of fantasy, Afanasyev constructed such vivid "myths," he drew such fascinating figures and pictures of all kinds of folk beliefs, that Melnikov-Pechersky, for example, borrowed from the *Attitudes* of Afanasyev the material for the sketches of the superstitious concepts of the heroes of his famous novel *In the Woods*.[50] More recently Afanasyev's book yielded very rich material for the poetic images of Essenine.[51] (Essenine was fascinated not only by the examples of genuine folklore in the book, but also by the poetic reconstructions, the fantastic structures erected by the investigator himself.)

Great as was the influence of *The Poetic Attitudes of the Slavs on Nature* in its own time, it is not in this alone that Afanasyev's principal importance for the folkloristics of Russia and of the world consists. Afanasyev, as we have already said in connection with the work

[49] *Ibid.*, p. 305.
[50] G. Vinogradov, "An Attempt to Explain the Folklore Sources of Melnikov-Pechersky's Novel *In the Woods*," *Soviet Folklore*, Nos. 2-3, 1935.
[51] See B. V. Neumann, "Sources of the Eidolology of Essenine," *Artistic Folklore*, Nos. IV-V, Moscow, 1929.

of collection done by the Brothers Grimm, was the first scholarly collector of Russian folk tales. To him belongs the honor of being the scientific pioneer in this work. Basing his work on numerous collected records, but mainly on the materials which had been handed over to him by the Russian Geographical Society (organized in the 1840's) and on V. I. Dal's vast collection, and also arousing many other persons to the work of collection, Afanasyev published his *Tales* from 1855 to 1864, in eight parts.[52]

In working over the texts, and in his commentary on them, Afanasyev followed the principles of Grimm's famous collection of *German Tales*. In 1860 he published *Russian Popular Legends*,[53] which made a great noise, because they were banned by the ecclesiastical censor at the time of their appearance. In the 1860's, Afanasyev published his *Sacred Tales* abroad. This collection could not find its way into print in Russia, not only because it included some indecorous words, but mainly because these tales contained a biting satire on the lords and the nobility. Concerning these themes of social satire in the tales, Afanasyev manifested a great interest, in accordance with his democratic sympathies and the realistic elements in his general world concept, which had been intensified in the period of the 1860's.

One of the outstanding representatives of the "mythological school" in Russia was also a professor at the University of St. Petersburg, Orestes Fyodorovich Miller (1833–1889). In his enormously important book, *Elijah of Murom and the Kiev Knighthood*,[54] Orestes Miller applied to the interpretation of the Russian epos of the *byliny* the principles of the "mythological school," but with such literalness,

[52] *Russian Popular Tales* (1855–1864; 2nd ed., in 4 vols., 1873; 3rd ed., A. E. Gruzinsky, ed., in 2 vols., 1897; 4th ed., in 5 vols., Moscow, 1913; new 5th ed., in 3 vols., published by Academia, ed. M. K. Azadovsky, N. P. Andreyev, and Y. M. Sokolov. Vol. I appeared in 1936, Vol. II in 1938; Vol. III is now being printed).

[53] *Russian Popular Legends*, collected by A. Afanasyev (Moscow, 1860); republished, (1) under the editorship of I. P. Kochergin (Kazan, Young Forces, 1914); (2) under the editorship of S. K. Shambinago, in *Contemporary Problems* (Moscow, 1914).

[54] Orestes Miller, *Elijah of Murom and the Kiev Knighthood: Comparative Critical Investigations of Strata in the Composition of the Russian Popular Epos* (St. Petersburg, 1869).

and such a lack of critical judgment, that not only his adversaries, but even his supporters were obliged to point out the author's excessive enthusiasm. O. Miller had set himself a very interesting and necessary task—to distinguish the various strata in the epos, to divide the mythological elements from the later historical and social ones. He did not succeed in accomplishing this because of the lack of precision in his methodological devices.

The division, already projected by Buslayev and Afanasyev, of the heroes into older figures (such as Svyatogor), possibly including mythological figures, and younger (Elijah of Murom, Alyosha Popovich, Dobrynya Nikitich, and others), which, in Miller's opinion, constitute myths in themselves, but myths which have already been worked over into more real figures of historical personages—this division, in Miller's book, was reduced to a detailed, though very arbitrarily worked-out system, and from his lucky hand it was retained in the literature textbooks up to the twentieth century, creating incorrect ideas of the development of the epos.

The author did a great deal of harm, also, by introducing into his scholarly work the Slavophile journalistic bias, filling the book with moralistic opinions in the Slavophile spirit. With all this, Miller's book was valuable for its careful selection of a vast amount of material on the epos, for its attentive work on the compilation of variants, and because it was the first attempt at a philological reworking of the *byliny*.

The German mythological theory was powerfully set forth, also, in the works of the professor and student of Slavonic languages and literature, A. A. Kotlyarevsky (1837–1881),[55] who had the ability, however, more than anyone else among contemporary philologists, to maintain critical prudence in taking over the methods of the "mythological school," and who expressed many valuable critical observations on the *Poetic Attitudes* of Afanasyev.

In the spirit of the mythological theory, also, were written many of the works of the famous Kharkov scholar, Alexander Afanasyev

[55] His best known work is *On the Funeral Customs of the Heathen Slavs* (Moscow, 1868).

Potebnya,[56] who dedicated a series of his books on folklore to the disclosure of concrete poetic forms in folk songs. In the interpretation of the symbolic meanings of these forms, Potebnya proceeded from the theories of Max Müller as to the metaphorical character of the language which produced myth. Possessing a strong philosophical sense, A. A. Potebnya worked out an independent scientific system in linguistics and the theory of poetry, which was called "the psychological trend" or "Potebnyanism," but in folkloristics this system was not widely accepted.[57]

Potebnya proved in great detail the idea that in the creation of a myth, as of a poetic form, a vast role is played by speech itself. Potebnya does not agree, however, with the doctrine of M. Müller on the "malady of language," pointing out how unlikely it is that thought and speech at first should have an abstract character, and then should obtain a purely concrete and picturesque one.

The theory of Max Müller and A. N. Afanasyev leads, in Potebnya's opinion, to an incorrect idea of the presumably original elevation of human thought, and then of its fall in later times.

Upon the numerous other adherents of the "mythological school" we have no time to linger. It is enough for our purposes to characterize the works of its main representatives.

In the 1850's there occurs a great change in western European folkloristics. In it is reflected the general transition from the excessively idealistic, romantic attitudes to a more realistic, positivistic way of

56 For example his books: *On Certain Symbols in Slavonic Popular Poetry* (Kharkov, 1860; 2nd ed., Kharkov, 1914); "On the Mythical Significance of Certain Ceremonies and Beliefs," in *Lectures Before the Society of Russian History and Antiquities* (Moscow, 1865); *On St. John's Fire and Related Phenomena* (Moscow, 1867), published in the *Archaeological News* of the Moscow Archaeological Society; *The Passage Across Water as a Representation of Marriage* (1867); *A Little-Russian Folk Song, from a Version Made in the Sixteenth Century*, text and commentary (Voronezh, *Philological Memoirs*, 1877); *Explanation of Little-Russian and Related Folk Songs* (Warsaw, No. I, 1883; No. II, 1887).

57 General theoretical works: *Thought and Language*, a series of articles in the *Journal of the Ministry of Public Education*, 1862 (latest ed., Odessa, 1926); *From Notes on the Theory of Literature: Song, Proverb, Saying* (Pts. 1 and 2, Kharkov, 1894; 2nd ed., Kharkov, 1923; 3rd ed., Kharkov, 1930); *From Notes on Russian Grammar* (1st ed., 1874; 2nd ed., Pts. 1 and 2, Kharkov, 1889; Pt. 3, Kharkov, 1899).

thinking, which characterizes philosophy and the most diverse sciences in the middle of the nineteenth century.

The abstract, indistinct, hazy concepts of the "mythologists" ceased to satisfy scientific thought. In the field of folkloristics, as with related scientific disciplines, there were still circumstances which had extended the horizon of science.

Toward the middle of the nineteenth century in connection with the expansion of trade and industry in Europe, the study of the semi-colonial lands of the Near East, their material and spiritual culture, was widespread. The science of Orientalism, which had been developed at that time, revealed many phenomena in the field of language, religion, poetry, which afforded striking parallels with the corresponding phenomena in the life of western European peoples.

New materials were discovered, and the necessity arose of explaining the newly revealed facts. For example, it seemed completely impossible to explain the resemblance of subject in the tales of various peoples, in the old way, by the relationship of the peoples, by their descent from a common ancestor, according to the procedure of the "mythological school," following the methods of Indo-European comparative linguistics. It is clear that a new effort had to be made to explain the causes of this resemblance of subject.

Such an effort was made by the German scholar and Orientalist, Theodor Benfey. In 1859 he published a collection of Hindu tales, *Panchatantra* (The Five Books), composed in the third century of our era. Benfey provided his German translation of the collection with a long introduction, which is a turning point in the development of the science of folklore.

Benfey pointed out the striking resemblance of the Sanskrit (Hindu) tales to the European and to the tales of other non-European peoples.

Resemblance of subject, in Benfey's opinion, is caused, not by the relationship of peoples, but by the cultural-historical connections between them, by borrowing (hence arose also one of the names of Benfey's theory, as the "theory of borrowing"). Benfey indicates several periods of especially strong cultural influence of the East upon the European West, when this process also might be going on, of intensive borrowing of legends from the East. (The theory bears also the name of "eastern" or "Orientalistic".) There was, above all, the time of the campaigns of Alexander of Macedon, and the so-called Hellenistic Age which followed them (from the end of the fourth through the second centuries B.C.).

Another such period is the era at the end of the first thousand years before Christ, the era of the Arabian conquests and the era of the Crusades, including the period from the tenth to the twelfth centuries.

In addition, Benfey revealed several routes by which the Oriental influence had come into Europe. The first route was from the eastern shore of the Mediterranean Sea to the far West, to Spain, where the Arabs and Jews formed the Mauretanian state, which created its original composite, so-called Mauretanian culture; another route was, again, from the Orient through the Greek archipelago, into Sicily and Italy; the third route was the old route to eastern Europe—from Central Asia and Asia Minor through Byzantium and the Balkan Peninsula.

The basic reservoir from which the European peoples drew material for poetic creation was seen to be ancient India. From India legends traveled, both in oral and written form, to Persia, Arabia, Palestine, and thence, across the Mediterranean Sea—that great trade route— to the West, to Europe. A great role in the transmission of legends from East to West was played by the trading peoples: the Arabs and the Jews.

In Spain, Arabic and Hebrew scholars translated these legends into the literary language of medieval Europe—Latin; and the Latin texts were diffused through the whole of Catholic Europe and served as the basis for translations into the national European languages (French, Italian, German, Polish, and so forth).

The fate of the *Panchatantra* itself corroborated these general routes which Benfey revealed. Constituting in itself a revision, made around the sixth century, of certain Hindu tales which were considerably more ancient, the *Panchatantra* was translated in the sixth century, under the title *Kalila and Dimna*, into the Old Persian and Syriac languages; in the eighth century, from the Old Persian into the Arabic; in the twelfth century, from the Arabic into the Hebrew; in Spain, in the thirteenth century, from the Hebrew to the Latin; from the Latin into the French, the German, the Italian. Another translation from the Arabic was made, into the Greek language, in the fifteenth century (under the title *The Tale of Stephanis and Ikhnilata*); in the twelfth and thirteenth centuries, the collection was translated from the Greek into the Balkan Slavonic tongues, and thence it traveled to Russia and there produced a series of Russian tales.

Benfey's theory very quickly found numerous followers in all countries. It had an especially powerful influence on the study of tales. Among the French scholars it is necessary to mention Gaston Paris,[58] Cosquin;[59] among the English, Clouston;[60] among the German, Landau.[61]

The latter, following the principles of the school of Benfey, produced a very interesting book, *The Sources of the Decameron*, in which he adduced numerous parallels to the tales of Boccaccio from Eastern and Western oral and written productions, with attempts to trace the routes of the wanderings of the subjects.

In general, to trace the wanderings of this or that subject has become one of the favorite occupations of the folklorists (for this reason, also, the theory of Benfey sometimes bears also such designations as: "the theory of traveling or roving subjects," or "the theory of transient narratives," or, finally, "the migrational theory.")

In comparison with the arbitrary interpretation of folklore by the "mythologists," who carried their ideas back into the misty, uncertain past, the theory of borrowing placed folkloristics on more substantial ground. The conclusiveness of the new method, in comparison with the earlier one, was so obvious that even several major "mythol-

[58] Gaston Paris, *Les Contes orientaux dans la littérature du Moyen Age* (1875). There is an abridged Russian version, *Oriental Tales in Medieval Literature* (Odessa, 1886).

[59] E. Cosquin, *Les Contes populaires de Lorraine* (Paris, 1887). The introductory article to this book has been translated into Russian: E. Cosquin, *Investigation into the Origin and Diffusion of European Popular Tales*, transl. by Dmitriev (Kiev, 1907).

[60] A. Clouston, *Popular Tales and Fictions, Their Migrations and Transformations* (London, 1887). There is a Ukrainian translation: A. Clouston, *Popular Tales and Fictions, Their Migrations and Transformations* (Lvov, 1896).

[61] M. Landau, *Die Quellen des Dekameron* (Vienna, 1869; 2nd ed., 1884).

ogists" yielded to it. Max Müller himself acknowledged the victory of Benfey's school, and the fallibility of the "mythological school." In one of his articles, which he characteristically entitled "The Wandering of Legends," he took up the investigations which Benfey had made of one of the subjects, completed them, and made them more exact. From the theoretical side, great importance was to be attached to Müller's opinion on the point that the fact of the borrowing of a subject, in any kind of creative production, does not mean that the subject cannot be considered national, does not remove it from the field of national culture, since there is no borrowing without creative reworking.

In Russia Benfey's theory was not accepted at once, but on the other hand, it was taken up with excessive fervor. Its appearance in Russian science also was entirely in conformity to principle, just as in western Europe. Even before the appearance of Benfey's book in Russia, there had come out a remarkable production by the Russian scholar (who at that time was still very young) A. N. Pypin, *Survey of the Literary History of the Ancient Russian Narratives and Tales* (Petrograd, 1858). Pypin developed a broad picture of the connections of ancient Russian literature with the West and the East. It is true that, in his book, A. N. Pypin was speaking chiefly of written rather than oral productions; but the premises for the theory of borrowing had already been brought out with sufficient clearness. Especially influential, also, on the development of this theory in Russian folkloristics were the discoveries which had been made in the field of the study of the folklore of the Eastern peoples of Russia.

Russian Orientalistics (Turkology, Mongolian studies) was making vast progress at that time. In particular, the Academician Schiffner was producing a series of publications on eastern Mongolian folklore, the collection *Shiddi-Kur, The Wise Fool,* and others; in 1866 there appeared an enormous collection of tales of the Turkic peoples of southern Siberia, the Altaians, and others, by the Academician Radlov.[62] Having become acquainted with the poetic treasures of the

---

[62] Radlov, *Types of Popular Literature of the Turkic Tribes Living in Southern Siberia and the Djungarian Steppe* (Pt. 1, 1866; Pt. 2, 1868; Pt. 3, 1870; Pt. 4, 1872; Pt. 5, 1885; Pt. 6, 1886; Pt. 7, 1896; Pt. 8, 1899; Pt. 9, 1899; Pt. 10, 1904).

Near East, Russian scholars could not, like Benfey, fail to turn their attention to the sometimes striking resemblance of Turkic and Mongolian legends to Russian tales and *byliny*.

Schiffner, in publishing his collection, had already emphasized the coincidence of many narrative motifs of Russian *byliny* with Mongolian tales. These indications of Schiffner's were enthusiastically caught up, under the impression of Benfey's *Panchatantra*, which he had read, by the well known critic of art and music, Vladimir Vasilyevich Stasov. In *News of Europe*, in 1868, he published an extensive article, "The Origin of Russian *Byliny*." [63] This article was destined to become the object of violent conflict, in which many scholars took part (Buslayev, O. Miller, Schiffner, Bessonov, Vsevolod Miller, A. Veselovsky, and others), and to which a great deal of attention was attracted on the part of a much wider public.

Stasov's article produced such a powerful impression because it stated, in categorical form, a position which absolutely negated all the tendencies of the "mythological school," which had been so popular up to that time. And just as the national romanticism of the latter had been, in its aims, utilized by the champions of Slavophilism (O. Miller), so the conflict with Stasov also took on a clearly defined political character. Stasov, who had declared that the Russian *byliny* were not independent, but had borrowed their content from the East, was accused of lack of patriotism. Being a Western liberal, Stasov had bound up the special scientific question of the borrowing of the subjects of Russian tales and *byliny* with the general problem of the degree of originality of Russian national culture. The theory of Eastern borrowing gave Stasov and his partisans material for the utilization of folkloristics for journalistic aims: borrowing the subjects for tales and *byliny*, so to speak, destroyed one of the arguments both of the romanticist-mythologists and of the Slavophiles, who had fervently maintained the national originality of folklore.

Stasov took as an example the popular tale of Yeruslan Lazarevich,

[63] V. V. Stasov, "The Origin of Russian *Byliny*," *News of Europe*, 1868, January-April, June-July. Two years later he gave an answer to his opponents in the article, "A Criticism of My Critics," in the *News of Europe*, 1870, February and March. These articles of Stasov's have been reprinted in Vol. III of the *Works of V. V. Stasov* (St. Petersburg, 1894).

and by the method of comparison with the *Shah Namah* of Firdusi (episodes connected with Rustem) showed the borrowing of it from the Persian East; the tale of the Firebird he connected with the Hindu narratives of Somadeva (twelfth century), and for the Russian *byliny* he also found a multitude of parallels in the ancient Hindu tales and in the later Turkic and Mongolian renderings.

One of the most fervent opponents of Stasov was Orestes Miller, who, in fact, wrote the whole of his enormous book *Elijah of Murom and the Kiev Knighthood* (1869) on the plan of an answer to Stasov's theory.

Surveying now, after a few score years, that controversy which raged around Stasov's book, one must acknowledge that it was not, in the final analysis, concerned with essentials. Even the adherents of the school of borrowing itself were compelled to acknowledge that in his method, his mode of demonstration, his final conclusions, Stasov also was just as far from being right as his opponents, the adherents of the "mythological" nationalistic school.

As Max Müller had already shown (see above), borrowing a subject, or specific motifs, does not make a production non-national. Subsequent researches, applied to the poetry of all countries and all times, have established that there is no such thing as a subject which cannot be repeated. And for all that, who will undertake to deny the existence of national literatures? Stasov was not right when he assigned an exceptional significance to coincidence, and still more to general resemblance of schemes of subject matter or specific narrative motifs. As explained in subsequent scientific works, even by those who were representatives of that same school of borrowing, but who were distinguished by a sharper critical judgment and scientific caution, it is not a problem of schemes of subject matter and specific motifs, but of that content of ideas with which they are filled, and of those peculiarities of concrete artistic form in which they find their expression. Stasov did not reckon with this at all, and in this lay one of his basic errors.

A second major defect of his work (and also, to be sure, of that of many other comparativists, both Western and Russian, especially in the first stages of Benfeyism) consisted in the fact that the very method of the comparative theory was too feebly worked out. Coincidences of subject in the folklore and literature of many nationalities may be encountered with sufficient frequency. It would be necessary to make a detailed analysis of these coincidences, and to try to find substantial arguments in favor of borrowing from the particular source at hand and not from any other.

In the third place, Stasov was lacking in the proper analysis of the concrete historical conditions which made possible and necessary such an influence of one national culture upon another.

Later on, the works of another fervent adherent of the "Eastern theory," the well known traveler and explorer of Siberia, G. N. Potanin, also suffered from all of these methodological defects. Potanin traced not only the Russian, but even the western European epos, to a borrowing from Turko-Mongolian folklore.[64]

But, in spite of its obvious methodological shortcomings, Stasov's article had as great an influence in Russia as the *Panchatantra* of Benfey had in western Europe. No matter how much the "mythologists" might dispute and rage, still even they themselves began to feel the unsoundness of their positions. It is only necessary to reread the critical objections of Buslayev to Stasov's article,[65] in order to be convinced that, in making many correct critical comments on the weak points in Stasov's methodology, Buslayev is actually defending—if very indecisively—his own earlier opinions. His interests have obviously shifted from the questions of the most remote Aryan or general Slavonic antiquity to the phenomena of historical life which are closer to us in time. No longer does he deny foreign influences as the latest strata superimposed upon the original foundation; however, he demands a greater chronological and historico-cultural accuracy in determining these strata.

The Eastern or Asiatic element must necessarily be acknowledged as one of the superficial strata upon the primitive native soil of our *byliny*, and at the same time a rigid distinction must be made as to

[64] See the extensive work of G. N. Potanin, *Eastern Motifs in the Medieval European Epos* (Moscow, 1899).

[65] F. I. Buslayev, *Account of the Twelfth Award of Prizes from Count Uvarov* (St. Petersburg, 1870).

the routes by which this element entered into Russia, that is, whether it came at second hand, through Byzantium, and in general through literature that had been translated, or whether it came directly, from Asiatic nomads. . . . As regards the direct Asiatic influence on our *byliny,* ·in it we must distinguish two strata: the most ancient, from pre-Mongolian times and from the period of the Tartars, and the later one, added in recent times by Eastern nomads, through their proximity to the Russian population. But in order to decide the question of this twofold influence, it is necessary to follow a strict philological method, based on a knowledge of the Eastern languages. Therefore, along with the author of the work which I am analyzing, I cannot help expressing also the conviction that, in any event, the fate of the question of our own *byliny* is in the hands of our Orientalists, and that with them must lie the examination and decision of all matters concerning this subject.

Three years after making this criticism (in 1874), Buslayev, under the direct impression of Max Müller's article, "The Wanderings of Legends" (1873), which he had read, and following this western European authority, also acknowledged the victory of the theory of borrowing over the "mythological school." Developing and completing the article of Max Müller, F. I. Buslayev wrote a brilliant survey, "Wanderers' Narratives" (1874),[66] which reflects his philological skill and artistic sense.

But the most powerful representative of the theory of borrowing in Russia was the famous scholar A. N. Veselovsky, who was distinguished by his exceptional erudition in the history of ancient and modern literatures.

In 1872 his master's dissertation, *Legends of Solomon and Kitovras,*[67] appeared, revealing a broad picture of the "wanderings" of Eastern legendary tales (the first source being India) into Europe and across Europe. In the introduction to this book, he himself fixes exactly the role of the theory of borrowing in comparison with the mythological theory; he establishes a connection between the origin and confirmation of this theory in philological science and what could

[66] Later reprinted in the collection, *My Leisure Moments,* Vol. I, pp. 259-406.
[67] A. N. Veselovsky, *From the History of the Mutual Intercourse of the East and West: Slavonic Legends of Solomon and Kitovras, and Western Legends of Morolf and Merlin* (St. Petersburg, 1872), reprinted in the *Collected Works of A. N. Veselovsky* (Vol. VIII, Nos. I-II, 1921).

be observed also at that period in other fields of ideological life: "The return to a historical view, in appraising the phenomena of the popular literature of the past, may be a sign of the times, a return to realism. We have been groping so long in a romantic fog of primitive Aryan myths and beliefs, that it is a pleasure to come down to earth."

Another outstanding scholar, V. J. Miller, seized upon Benfey's theory with great enthusiasm. It is true that he, having taken part in the conflict with Stasov,[68] tried to restrain the ardor of a passionate neophyte for the idea of borrowing, pointing out the methodological hastiness of its conclusions; but, still, in a short time he stirred up no less tumult than Stasov, by the publication of his work, *An Opinion on the "Tale of Igor's Raid."* [69] In this book he demonstrated the lack of originality in this famous landmark of old Russian literature. He had to endure the most strenuous attacks on the part of E. V. Barsov. It cannot be said that Miller's conclusions were later confirmed by scholars, although this book too, like Stasov's article, caused the representatives of the extreme nationalist wing of philology to do some very hard thinking.

Along with his linguistic labors (comparative philology was his special field), Miller continued to occupy himself also with investigations in the field of popular folklore. In 1892 there appeared his famous *Excursus into the Field of the Russian Popular Epos.*[70] In these he again surveyed the question of the sources of the tale of Yeruslan Lazarevich and the *bylina* of the flight of Elijah of Murom with his son. Agreeing with Stasov's idea of their Eastern origin, he tried to define more accurately the route of the borrowing. In contrast to Stasov, who had defended the Turko-Mongolian influence, Miller showed the role which had been played by the Caucasian Iranians in the transmission of Eastern legends, through the agency of the Turks, into Russia.[71] The famous *bylina* about the flight of Elijah of Murom

[68] Vsevolod Miller, "On the Comparative Method of the Author of 'The Origin of the Russian *Byliny*,'" *Proceedings of the Society of Lovers of Russian Literature*, No. III, Moscow, 1871.

[69] Vsevolod Miller, *An Opinion on the "Tale of Igor's Raid"* (Moscow, 1877).

[70] Vsevolod Miller, *Excursus into the Field of the Russian Popular Epos* (Nos. I-VIII, Moscow, 1892).

[71] V. F. Miller, *Osetine Studies* (Nos. 1-3, Moscow, 1881-1887).

with his son, which O. Miller considered truly national, while Stasov regarded it as borrowed from the Persian East, was considered by V. F. Miller to have penetrated into the Russian epos by the route which has just been described—through the Caucasian Iranians and Turks. 'But, reading the *Excursus*, one sees that the author already senses the inadequacy of the method of Benfey's school, that he already acknowledges the necessity of a transfer to some kind of more solid ground; and in fact, as we shall see, V. F. Miller very soon found this ground in the new scientific trend created by him, in the "historical school."

Among the Russian followers of the theory of borrowing, it is necessary to mention also A. I. Kirpichnikov,[72] I. N. Zhdanov, [73] M. E. Khalansky,[74] I. Sazonovich,[75] A. M. Loboda,[76] and many others. The majority of them were occupied with questions on the connection of the Russian epos and legend with the Western and with the Byzantine ones. The "theory of borrowing," with the majority, was not presented in its pure form, but was complicated by other theories (mainly the product of the "historical school").

The theory of borrowing, at the end of the nineteenth century, was still the ruling theory on the European continent. However, it had already encountered not a few objections on the part of other rising scientific trends—the "anthropological" theory in the West and the "historical" theory in Russia.

[72] A. I. Kirpichnikov, *A Greek Romance in the New Literature: The Narrative of Barlaam and Josaphat* (Kharkov, 1876); *St. George and Egor the Brave: A Study of the Literary History of a Christian Legend* (St. Petersburg, 1879).

[73] I. N. Zhdanov, *Toward a Literary History of the Russian Epos of the Byliny* (St. Petersburg, 1895). Other works of his have been reprinted in the *Collected Works of I. N. Zhdanov* (St. Petersburg, 1904–1907).

[74] M. E. Khalansky, *Great-Russian Byliny of the Kiev Cycle* (Warsaw, 1885); here, it is true, there are also expressed ideas which were further developed in the so-called "historical school." By the same author: *Southern Slavonic Tales of Prince Mark, in Connection with the Productions of the Russian Epos of the Byliny: Comparative Researches in the Field of the Heroic Epos of the Southern Slavs and of the Russian People* (Warsaw, 1893). Both books were printed in installments in the *Russian Philological News*.

[75] I. Sazonovich, *Songs of a Maiden Warrior and Byliny about Stavr Godinovich: Sketches on the History of the Development of the Slavo-Russian Epos* (Warsaw, 1886).

[76] A. M. Loboda, *Russian Byliny on Matchmaking* (Kiev, 1904).

It called forth objections, also, on the part of the so-called "skeptical school" in France, in the person of the well known medievalist, Joseph Bédier. In his voluminous work, *Fabliaux,*[77] he expressed his doubt that, working by the comparative method, which had been adopted by the Benfeyists, it would in general be possible, eventually, to come to some kind of dependable conclusion as to the origin and routes of travel of this or that narrative subject. He called such exercises on the part of the comparativists nothing but a *jeu d'esprit,* a mental pastime, and summoned them all to abandon their study of fruitless comparisons of variations and to seek in an artistic production only that which connects it with the national poetry. This skeptical attitude found for itself (not all at once, it is true) great sympathy on the part of French students of literature and folklorists. It must be acknowledged that for the past thirty or forty years French scholars have taken hardly any part in the work on the study of the migration of subjects.

But the skepticism of the French scholar did not meet with approval in the majority of other countries. Thus, the Russian investigator of tales, the specialist in Sanskrit, and widely educated Orientalist, Academician S. F. Oldenburg, came forward with several articles directed against the skepticism of Bédier. Without disputing the excessive difficulties of the investigation, S. F. Oldenburg at the same time affirmed that in individual cases, when there was available a sufficient quantity of fully authenticated versions, coming from various times and various countries, it was possible, by the application of a strict comparative analysis, maintaining all the caution demanded by science, to establish even the starting points and the farthest routes in the wandering of a tale.[78] By several concrete examples S. F. Oldenburg proved that the subject foundation of a series of French *fabliaux,* beyond a doubt, must be traced to ancient India. The traditions of

[77] Joseph Bédier, *Les Fabliaux* (Paris, 1893).
[78] S. F. Oldenburg, "*Fabliaux* of Eastern Origin," *Journal of the Ministry of Public Education,* No. 4, 1903; No. 5, 1906; Nos. 8 and 10, 1907. On the works of Acad. S. F. Oldenburg, see the collection, *To S. F. Oldenburg, on the Fiftieth Anniversary of His Scientific and Public Activity, 1882–1932* (Leningrad, 1934), and the article by M. K. Azadovsky, "S. F. Oldenburg and Russian Folkloristics," *Soviet Ethnography,* No. 1, 1933, p. 15.

Benfeyism were still very clearly recognizable in the works of the Russian Orientalist.

With still greater insistence, the well known Czech folklorist, Professor Yury Polivka, continued to cling to the Benfey migration theory.

As an example of very detailed work in the spirit of the comparative school, one may point to his article, "A Woman Worse Than a Devil." [79] In it he gives a survey of European (especially Slavonic) versions of an anecdotal narrative, popular in the Middle Ages, to the effect that, if the devil could not succeed in causing people the evil which he had planned (he had to cause trouble between a man and his wife), then this task would be brilliantly performed for him by a woman. Polivka, adducing numerous parallels, ingeniously observes in them not only the elements of similarity, but even the features of national distinctions in social life. As if confirming the views of Benfey, he determines that the most ancient European version is a translation into the Latin language of an Eastern (Indian) tale of a designing wife. This translation was made in the twelfth century by a Spanish Jew. The Buddhist priesthood composed this lampoon on woman, which was taken up by the medieval Catholic and Orthodox clergy and, in many literary versions, diffused throughout Europe, penetrating deeply into European folklore.

Polivka remained faithful to the theory of borrowing to the end of his life. During the past few decades he has rightly been considered one of the leading connoisseurs of Slavonic folklore tales. During his long years of scientific work, he constructed a card index of "wandering subjects," which is widely known in the folkloristics of the world. There could not appear a single small and barely noticed collection of tales in any one of the Slavonic countries, without Polivka's publishing, in one of the international magazines of folkloristics, a most detailed list of "parallels" to the tales published in that collection.

In collaboration with the German folklorist, Johann Bolte, Poliv-

[79] Y. Polivka, "A Woman Worse Than a Devil," *Russian Philological News,* Nos. 1-2, 1910.

ka published a five-volume *Guide to the Tales of the Brothers Grimm*,[80] which became a reference book for all the folklorists in Europe. For each of the children's and family tales of the Brothers Grimm, Bolte and Polivka give lists of all the parallels which have been registered by world scholarship, together with an exact indication of the books and countries where these parallels have been published.

The work of surveying and systematizing the renderings of tales (versions, variants) was developed to a still greater degree in the Scandinavian countries—Finland, Sweden, Norway, Denmark. The initiator of the truly colossal work which is being carried on in Scandinavia on the comparative study of folklore was the Helsingfors professor Kaarle Krohn, who died in 1933 (1863–1933).[81] He created a scientific trend which received the name of "the Finnish school." In 1907, Krohn, together with the Swedish scholar Sidov and the Danish scholar Axel Olrik, founded an international federation of folklorists (Fellows of Folklore), which began to publish a series of *Folklore Fellows' Communications*, or, abbreviated, FFC.[82]

One of the main tasks of the federation was the study of the subjects of tales, and the determination of the starting points of their origin and the geographical routes of their diffusion.

Typical examples of the monograph works produced in the spirit of the "Finnish school" may be found in the works of Professor V. Anderson [83] and the early works of Professor N. P. Andreyev.[84] In them, there is given a scrupulous study of variations, a classification of them

---

[80] J. Bolte and Y. Polivka, *Anmerkungen zu den Kinder- und Hausmärchen der Brüder Grimm*, Vols. I-V (Leipzig 1913-1932).

[81] On the activity of Kaarle Krohn, see A. I. Nikiforov,"Kaarle Krohn," *Soviet Ethnography*, Nos. 1-2, 1934.

[82] By the year 1936, 39 volumes had appeared, including 117 numbers of research and indexes.

[83] V. Anderson, *The Romance of Apuleius and the Popular Tale* (Vol. I, Kazan, 1914), *The Emperor and the Abbot: History of a Popular Anecdote* (Vol. I, Kazan, 1916); later, the same study was published in German: *Kaiser und Abt: Die Geschichte eines Schwanks* (Helsinki, 1923), FFC No. 42; also, W. Anderson, *Novelline popolari summarinesi, publicate ed annotate* (I, Tartu [Dorpat], 1927), and *Der Schwanke vom alten Hildebrand* (Dorpat, 1931).

[84] N. P. Andrejew, *Die Legende von den zwei Erszündern* (Helsinki, 1924), FFC No. 54; *Die Legende vom Räuber Madej* (Helsinki, 1927), FFC No. 69.

according to groups (on the basis of the quantity and character of the coincident motifs), and a determination of the routes by which these variations wandered through the countries. Usually, also, there are appended to the research chronological diagrams and geographical maps, with straight and zigzag lines drawn on them, designating the route of travel of the subject. The Finnish school calls its method the "geographic-historical."

In 1913, one of the outstanding Finnish students of K. Krohn, Antti Aarne (1867–1925), published a methodological guide for the coordination of international work according to this method: *Guiding Principles of the Comparative Study of Tales*,[85] and in 1926, K. Krohn himself brought out a detailed account of his theory and method, under the title, *A Working Method of Folkloristics*.[86]

The theoretical and methodological theses of this Finnish school, since they were obviously dependent on Benfeyism, which had been reduced to a formalistic excess, called forth, and could not help calling forth, decisive expressions on the part of Soviet folkloristics. The purely technical aspect of the work of the Scandinavian folklorists was very highly valued. The aforementioned Antti Aarne compiled, in 1910, an *Index of the Subjects of Tales*,[87] which was destined soon to become the international model for the systematization of the outlines of subjects. It has many defects (too great subjectivity and conventionalism in the classification of subjects into groups, and in the indexing arrangement of the themes of the tales), but from the purely technical side it has already served to lighten the labors of the folklorists of the world, and has contributed to the unification of their efforts. It is made use of in the Scandinavian countries, in Germany, in England, in the United States of America (there is an English

85 Antti Aarne, *Leitfaden der vergleichenden Märchenforschung* (Helsinki, 1913), FFC No. 13. On the activity of Antti Aarne, see N. P. Andreyev, "Antti Aarne," *Artistic Folklore*, No. I, 1926.

86 *Die folkloristische Arbeitsmethode begründet von Julius Krohn und weiter geführt von nordischen Forschern, erläutert von Kaarle Krohn* (Oslo, 1926. For an account of this work of A. Aarne, in Russian, see R. O. Shor, "The Problem of Method in Folkloristics," *Artistic Folklore*, Nos. II-III, 1927, and the review by A. Nikiforov in *Ethnographic News* (Kiev, 1928), Bk. 7, pp. 228-229.

87 Antti Aarne, *Verzeichnis der Märchentypen* (Helsinki, 1910), FFC No. 3.

translation [88]), and in the USSR. It was translated into Russian, and revised in an appropriate manner, by N. P. Andreyev,[89] who included in this index all the Russian tales which had been published, up to 1929, in the large scientific collections of folklore. Now, in the collection and publication of new texts of tales, it is considered obligatory to designate the appropriate number in the index of Aarne and Andreyev.

And so, from the purely technical aspect, the initiative of the Scandinavian scholars and their united activity have yielded, beyond a doubt, valuable results. So far as the theoretical side is concerned, here the helplessness and lack of perspective of the "Finnish school" have been pointed out, not only by Soviet scholars,[90] but are beginning more and more to be acknowledged even by the representatives of that school itself. In August, 1932, in Sweden (at Lund), the Seventh Northern Congress of Philologists took place. The Swedish folklorist Sidov. mentioned above as an adherent of the "Finnish school," was obliged to acknowledge in his report that, from the viewpoint of theory, the school had reached an impasse.[91] Sidov establishes the connection of the "Finnish school" with the old theory of Benfrey, which also demanded the investigation of individual tales, and continues:

But if we are to evaluate the general result of the monographs by Antti Aarne on individual tales. and similar works written by the

[88] *The Types of the Folk Tale: A Classification and Bibliography*, Antti Aarne's Verzeichnis der Märchentypen, trans. and enlarged by S. Thompson (1928), FFC No. 74. Thompson compiled, according to this same pattern, an index, in several volumes, of the subjects of tales to be encountered in the folklore of the world: *Motif Index of Folk Literature: A Classification of Narrative Elements in Folk Tales, Ballads, Myths. Fables. Medieval Romances, Exempla, Fabliaux, Jest Books and Local Legends* (Bloomington, Ill., 1935–1936), FFC, Nos. 106-109, 116, 117.

[89] N. P. Andreyev, *Index of Subjects of Tales, After the System of Aarne* (Russian State Geographical Society, Leningrad, 1929).

[90] A. I. Nikiforov, "The Finnish School Faces a Crisis," *Soviet Ethnography*, No. 4, 1934, pp. 141-144.

[91] Sidov's report was published in the *Yearbook of the New Society of the Sciences in Lund* (Arsten, 1932) (*Yearbook of the New Society of Letters at Lund*). For a summary of the report, in Russian. see D. K. Zelenin, "The International Conference of Folklorists and Students of Tales. in Sweden," *Soviet Ethnography*," Nos. 1-2, 1934.

followers of the "Finnish school" in other countries, then it must be acknowledged that the study of tales has reached an impasse and can go no further along this road. The elaborately worked-out method of the "Finnish school" was somewhat schematic, and founded in part on unverified, and sometimes on obviously false, premises. The task of every monograph is to find the original historic form and first native land of a given tale; furthermore, all known variants of a tale are considered as of equal value, and the investigations of them become schematized and statistical. The investigation reveals, not that most simple primitive form of the tale, which could actually have been its starting point, but, on the contrary, a fuller and more integrated form of the tale, the end point of its development. And the supposed first native land of the tale is shown to be the country where the given tale approaches most closely to this supposed original form, which has been reestablished by fallacious methods.[92]

In other words, Sidov correctly discerns the methodological error of the "Finnish school" in its work toward the reconstruction of the original form of the tale. This error is analogous to that which was so characteristic of the old works in Indo-European linguistics, which strove to re-create the supposed parent form and the supposed parent language in its entirety.

Sidov urges investigators to concentrate on the study of the subjects of tales, first of all, on a national basis, where it is possible clearly to establish the connections of variations with one another, and to break them up more correctly into groups, and then only to compare the whole picture of the life of the national tale with the tales of neighboring peoples.

But the method which is recommended cannot provide a way out of the impasse, because, even if the comparative study is supposed to be carried on within the narrower national limits, still the character of the study, the very method of work on the variants, remains fundamentally the same—formal. But it is also important to note that bourgeois comparativist folkloristics acknowledges that "all is not well in the state of Denmark."

The defects of the migrational theory began to be perceived very long ago. In connection with the development of the colonial policy of England and the United States of America, there was accumulated

[92] See the article of D. K. Zelenin in *Soviet Ethnography*, Nos. 1-2, 1934, p. 223.

an ever greater and greater mass of material for comparative investigation.

Geographers, ethnographers, philologists, and folklorists undertook the study of near and distant lands, of the people who inhabit them, their economy, mode of life, customs, language, and creative productions. It was already impossible to limit the study to Europe and the nearer countries of the East—Central Asia and Asia Minor. It was necessary to include within the orbit of scientific investigation the peoples of all parts of the world; here the philologists and folklorists again encountered the striking facts of resemblance and coincidences. It was not possible to explain these facts of resemblance and coincidence either by the theory of inheritance of culture from a common ancestor, as the "mythological school" had done, or by the theory of cultural influences and borrowings, as the Benfeyists had done. In Africa, South America, in Australia, in eastern and southern Asia, on the islands of all the oceans, every year there have been uncovered such evidences of life as, on the one hand, very definitely recalled evidences in language and mode of life of European peoples, but which, on the other hand, could in no way be explained, either by relational or cultural ties with the Europeans. It was necessary to seek new explanations. And here appeared a new scientific theory, which in the history of science has received the not altogether exact designation of the "anthropological school." The founder of this theory must be considered to be the English scholar Tylor, and his follower, the Scotch scholar Andrew Lang.

Tylor already, toward the end of the 1860's, had published a book, *Researches into the Early History of Mankind*,[93] which by its very title indicates that Tylor was interested in the initial stages of the development of human culture. In 1871 Tylor published his famous book, *Primitive Culture*.[94] On the foundation of the vast amount of material which he had collected on the mode of life, views, and creative work of the most diverse peoples of the world, Tylor came to the conclusion that all peoples reveal a great resemblance in their

[93] Tylor, *Researches into the Early History of Mankind* (London, 1866; 2nd ed., 1870).

[94] *Primitive Culture* (London, 1871); Russian transl., *Primitive Culture*, Vols. I and II (St. Petersburg, 1896–1897).

mode of life, customs, and their creation of religious and poetic concepts. Tylor found the explanation for this in the essential community of human nature, mind, and thought, and in the identity of
the paths of development of human culture. In addition to this, he
discovered numerous coincidences between the evidences of culture
of primitive peoples and specific elements in the views of civilized
peoples, especially among the culturally retarded strata of the latter.

And Tylor formulated the idea of religious and cultural "survivals"
inherited by civilized peoples. He decisively rebelled against the doctrine of the "mythological school," which had assumed, at the early
stages of culture, the presence of well developed religious systems
(myths). Tylor demonstrated that in the primitive stages mankind
had worked out only exceedingly elementary religious concepts,
founded upon so-called "animism," that is, the naïve endowing with
a spirit of the natural phenomena surrounding man. In the conflict
with the pronouncements of the "mythological school," in his work
on the uncovering of animistic views among people of a low cultural
stage, and in the explanation of the survival aspects in the culture of
civilized nations, Tylor found for himself an enthusiastic comrade-
in-arms—Lang, the author of several monumental books on mythology.[95]

According as the problem of the resemblance of narrative subjects
among various nations was solved, the "anthropological theory" of
Tylor and Lang received also the name of "the theory of spontaneous
generation of subjects."

In comparison with the two preceding theories—the "mythological" and the "migrational"—the "anthropological theory" certainly
was a great step forward. It considerably enlarged the field of observation, surmounting the limits of ethnic relationship and direct
historical connection.

But however great a step forward the "anthropological theory" rep-

[95] A. Lang, *Myth, Ritual and Religion*, 2 vols. (1887); French transl., *Mythes,
cultes et religions* (Paris, 1896); *Custom and Myth* (London, 1884); *Modern
Mythology* (London, 1897), and the extensive article, "Mythology," in the 9th
ed. of the *Encyclopedia Britannica*. Vol. XVII, transl. into French under the editorship of Charles Michel, then from the French into the Russian: A. Lang, *Mythology*, transl. under N. N. and V. N. Kharuzin, eds. (Moscow, 1901).

resented in the movement of bourgeois science, its weak points are obvious for us. The doctrine of the oneness of the human mind, the oneness of the laws of development of human culture, of the single animistic essence of religious beliefs, of the presence of "cultural survivals" in the life and creative work of civilized peoples, seemed altogether too general a principle, and, in the main, devoid of a materialistic basis. What guides the regularity of human development, in what, concretely, this regularity consists, what is the nature of the sequence of stages in the cultural growth of mankind—this is not explained in Tylor's and Lang's theory. The most fruitful observations made by the representatives of the "anthropological" and "animistic school" could be clearly interpreted only when there was placed under them a firm foundation in the materialistic doctrine of Marxism on social-economic formations as the determining principle of human history from the most ancient eras down to our own time.

The English "anthropological theory" very soon found a lively response in other countries. In Germany, we have seen, its influence is shown on the works of the "mythologist" Mannhardt; in France the theory of the "palingenesis of tales," of Joseph Bédier, was also worked out under the influence of the "anthropological school"; this same school furnished materials also for the "evolutionary theory" of Brunetière and Letourneau.

Toward the end of the nineteenth century, in German science, the "anthropological theory" assumed quite another form. Tylor and Lang, in explaining the resemblance of religious and poetic phenomena among various nations, referred to the community of human psychology, but did not enter into an examination of the actual process of creation of myths and poetic motifs. But it was exactly on this aspect of the question that German scholars, headed by the well known psychologist Wilhelm Wundt, fixed their attention. In his *Psychology of Nations* [96] Wundt, analyzing the various myths and poetic tales of

[96] W. Wundt, *Mythos und Religion*, Pt. 2, Vol 5, of *Völkerpsychologie*, 3rd ed. (Leipzig, 1912). Only the first part was translated into Russian: *Myth and Religion*, ed. D. N. Ovsyanniko-Kulikovsky (Brockhaus and Efron, St. Petersburg, 1913). See also Lang's article "The Theory of Wundt on the Beginning of Myth," critical notes, *Memoirs of The Odessa Society of History and Antiquities*, Vol. XXX (Odessa, 1912), pp. 109-126.

the most diverse peoples, comes to the conclusion that many of the religious and poetic concepts were created under special conditions in the mind of man—in a state of dream and morbid hallucinations. This idea was developed with great enthusiasm by the German folklorists Laistner [97] and, later, von der Leyen.[98] Regardless of the point that individual facts, secured through the contemporary observations of folklorists, confirm the well known role of unconscious and semiconscious psychic states in the creation both of religious and of poetic concepts, still it is, of course, impossible for all folklore to be derived from this source. For this reason, also, the "psychological school" of Wundt did not attain a wide popularity.

Still greater narrowness distinguishes the Austrian variation of the "psychological school," represented by the well known physician and psychiatrist Freud, and his students. Freudianism in folkloristics (and in the study of literature) traced the origin of religious and poetic fantasy, in accordance with the general principles of Freudian doctrine, to factors of a sexual nature.

Desires connected with sex, repressed by conscience during the waking hours, but left unrestrained during sleep and the condition of hallucination, and also in the process of uncontrolled dreaming and fantasy, are objectified in concepts and images, where it is not hard to uncover the sexual symbolism.

Freud and his school interpreted the series of ancient myths, tales, and literary productions according to this psychoanalytic plan.[99] For example, in the subject of the Greek myth of Oedipus, as developed by Sophocles, Freud discerns the symbolism of a sexual attraction, which may frequently be encountered, between the child and the mother, and a hatred for the father (the so-called "Oedipus Complex").

[97] Laistner, *Die Rätsel der Sphinx* (1889).

[98] Von der Leyen, *Zur Entstehung des Märchens* (Leipzig, 1889), and *Das Märchen* (Leipzig, 1911), Chap. II. See also the article of E. N. Yeleonskaya, "On the Question of the Origin and Composition of Tales," *Ethnographic Review*, Bk. 72.

[99] Sigmund Freud, *Die Traumdeutung* (Leipzig und Wien, 1900); there is a Russian translation. See also S. Freud, "Psychological Studies," *Poet and Fantasy* (Moscow, 1912).

The "anthropological school" had had its origin in England. (The word "anthropological" is used here in the traditional English understanding of this term, in the sense of ethnography; it would be more accurate to call this school "ethnographic.") There, toward the end of the nineteenth century, it underwent its greatest development. Tylor, Lang, and their school had built up a theory on a vast mass of folklore and ethnographic material, gathered from all corners of the world. Their thought ran (and this is characteristic of English positivism) in a significant degree along the empirical and inductive channel, the channel of a vast accumulation and survey of material. Therefore, for many years to come, their works will serve as a very rich source of factual information. The same features distinguish also the works of the contemporary English folklorist and ethnographer, James Frazer.

In 1890 Frazer published his famous book, *The Golden Bough*,[100] in twelve huge volumes. This book occupies one of the most prominent places in contemporary world folkloristics. Around it, especially among us in the USSR, fervent discussions have been waged.

Frazer starts from the same premise as Tylor and Lang, that all mankind is the same in its mind, subject to identical laws of development, that everywhere it has passed through similar stages of culture, preserving in great numbers, in the later phases of its culture, the survivals of past stages. But one of the distinguishing peculiarities of Frazer's conception must be considered the significance which he assigns, in the life of primitive man, to the factor of magic.

On the basis of countless examples, chosen from the writings of contemporary ethnographers, contemporary and ancient travelers, and the landmarks of world literature, Frazer makes clear the nature of magic, and the role which it played, and plays, in the life of prim-

100 J. Frazer, *The Golden Bough: A Study in Magic and Religion*, 2 vols. (1890, 2nd ed., 1900). A final edition, in twelve volumes, appeared between 1911–1915. In 1922 there appeared an abridged edition. In 1924 there appeared a French translation, authorized and personally verified by Frazer, of this abridged edition, *Le rameau d'or*. From this edition the Russian translation was made: J. Frazer, *The Golden Bough*, Nos. I-IV, published by the scientific society, The Atheist (Moscow, 1928). In 1931 there appeared the first number of a new edition, ed. and with foreword by Prof. V. K. Nikolsky (Moscow-Leningrad, Unified State Publishing House, the Moscow Worker).

itive peoples, and also, in the character of survivals, in the culturally retarded strata of civilized peoples.

Many of the propositions of Frazer went deeply into contemporary bourgeois ethnography, folkloristics, the history of culture, and particularly the history of religion. Many of the propositions of Frazer are not disputed by Soviet science. Heated controversies, however, are being waged on the question as to whether magic appears as an aspect which precedes animism, or necessarily presupposes an already animistic world concept. This question is significant principally because it is closely bound up with the problem of the origin of religion.

Frazer defends the proposition that magic precedes animism (that is, the assigning of a spirit to nature—the primary form of religion). But, defending this point, separating magic from animism for the early periods, and considering magic as primordial for primitive society, Frazer, in the last analysis, thereby affirms also the primordial character of religion (no matter how much he may oppose magic, which he understood as an embryonic form of science, to the religious consciousness). Contemporary Marxist ethnographers, starting from the Marxist assumptions of the original nonreligious stage in primitive mankind, at the same time derive magic from the animistic world concept, and from this aspect they vigorously criticize the conception of Frazer.[101]

The unreliability of the nonmaterialistic, but positivist (in the last analysis, idealistic) world concept of Frazer constitutes the great weakness of his scientific positions. Objectively, by the many data of his exhaustive works, Frazer furnished very rich material for the scientific criticism of existing historical systems of religion (one need only mention that very solid volume, *Folklore in the Old Testament*,[102] or the chapters from the *Golden Bough* which are devoted to the theme of the "dying and rising god" or to the theme of "eating the god"), but subjectively he remains, in spite of the facts adduced by him personally, an adherent of the religious idea. He was very much vexed that

---

[101] See V. K. Nikolsky, "Religion and Magic," *The Antireligious*, No. 6, 1929.

[102] George James Frazer, *Folklore in the Old Testament: Studies in Comparative Religion*; Russian transl., J. Frazer, *Folklore in the Old Testament* (Moscow-Leningrad, State Social and Economic Publishing House, 1931).

his works were translated in the USSR as antireligious propaganda.

The whole of Frazer's book partakes of the basic error of the English "anthropological school" (as also of the majority of other bourgeois schools): it examines the development of superimposed phenomena immanently, in isolation from the development of social life on the whole, separated from the development of a material basis.

In prerevolutionary Russia the "anthropological theory" of Tylor and Lang did not have direct and immediate followers; but it was expressed in the works of Professor N. F. Sumtsov, who joined it with the "mythological theory," and also in certain works by Professor A. I. Kirpichnikov.[103]

However, the "anthropological theory" exerted its strongest influence in the capacity of one of the essential elements in A. N. Veselovsky's theory of "historical poetics."

Alexander Nikolayevich Veselovsky (1837–1906) belongs to that type of scholar who combines vast erudition with a propensity for deep theoretical thought, an ability to subject facts to a fine and detailed analysis, with a capacity for generalizing synthesis.

Veselovsky left a vast scientific heritage. In the *Bibliographical List of the Works of A. N. Veselovsky*, published by the Academy of Sciences (in 1921), 281 works are mentioned. Besides, it must be taken into consideration that certain of these works represent in themselves huge volumes of five or six hundred pages.

The tremendous productivity of Veselovsky's creative work is accompanied by the limitless diversity of themes of his historic and literary works. Veselovsky did a very great deal for the understanding of ancient (early Greek and Roman) traditions in the literature and culture of the Byzantine, western European, and Slavonic Middle Ages; Veselovsky did much for the understanding of the connections between the poetic work of the great writers of the Renaissance (Dante, Petrarch, Boccaccio) and the medieval literature which preceded them, and for the understanding of the world concept and art of the early European humanism; in addition, Veselovsky uncovered, be-

---

[103] See especially: A. Kirpichnikov, *An Essay in the Comparative Study of the Western and Russian Epos: Poems of the Lombard Cycle* (Moscow, 1873); *Kudruna, a National Poem of the Germans* (Moscow, 1874).

neath the strata of Christian legends, their forms and ideas, the traces of many centuries of tribal tradition or influence of Greco-Roman pre-Christian culture.

One of the favorite questions which occupied Veselovsky in the course of the decades of his activity in research, was the question of the reciprocal cultural and literary intercourse between the various peoples of the whole of Europe and the Near East. His doctoral dissertation, which has not lost its great scientific significance, even down to the present time (*Slavonic Legends of Solomon and Kitovras, and Western Legends of Morolf and Merlin* [1872]), had a characteristic subtitle, revealing the author's purposeful endeavor: "From the History of the Literary Intercourse of the East and West." In this literary intercourse Veselovsky disclosed the vast significance not only of Byzantium, but also of the Slavonic peoples, among them the Russian, establishing the very close connection between the culture of the Russian people and the culture of the lands surrounding them on the west and the east, and emphasizing the great complexity and richness both of Russian oral poetry and of Russian written literature.

He examined all these scientific problems, on the basis of a vast amount of factual material, in such monumental works of his (besides the doctoral dissertation already mentioned) as *Essays on the History of the Development of Christian Legend* (1875–1877), *Researches in the Field of Russian Religious Verse* (1879–1891), *From the History of Romance and Narrative* (1886–1888), *South Russian Byliny* (1884), and others.

In all these works A. N. Veselovsky followed, in the main, the comparative-historical or cultural-historical method, originally applying to material of the most diverse forms, which had very often been discovered by him personally, the methodological devices and theoretical principles of the representatives of western European positivism—Comte, Mill, Buckle, Taine, Benfey, and others.

Veselovsky broadened and deepened the methodology of the school of Benfey. He raised the question of literary influences and borrowings to a considerably wider extent than Benfey and his numerous followers in the West and in Russia had done (V. Stasov and others).

He put forward the problem of the influence of books upon oral poetry, and of oral poetry upon literature; he raised the question of the role of Christian legend and the creation of Christian myths which carried on the traditions of still older cultures; in his numerous works he disclosed the significance of Byzantium in the process of literary interchange; finally, by the analysis of an unlimited number of facts, he showed that the influences were ambivalent, that it was not only the East (as Benfey had maintained) which influenced the West, but that the West also influenced the East, and that, in particular, Russian folklore and Russian literature were found to be in extensive intercourse not only with the East, but also with the West.

It would be difficult to enumerate all the works of Veselovsky in which he touched upon these problems of cultural connections. Veselovsky's vast erudition and remarkable memory, which so impressed everyone, aided him in making completely unexpected comparisons, in adducing an unlimited number of parallels to every poetic fact, subject, and motif.

But Veselovsky did not confine himself to the establishment of concrete connections of specific literary phenomena one with another and with the general culture of this or that era. Subjecting to the most detailed analysis the concrete artistic productions and the literary life of every given people and of every given era, he always strove to establish conformity to established laws in literary development. Especially significant, in this connection, are his two famous historico-literary monographs: *Boccaccio, His Surroundings and Contemporaries*, in two volumes (1893–1894), and V. A. *Zhukovsky: Poetry of Sentiment and of Fervent Imagination* (1904). They go far beyond the bounds of an investigation of the individual work of a great author. Veselovsky attentively traces the connections of the writer he is studying with literary tradition and the literary and social currents of the preceding time and of the present era. The famous saying of Veselovsky (which will receive still further discussion below), "Petrarchism is older than Petrarch," vividly characterizes the great scholar's thinking. On the basis of numerous facts of the oral and written poetry of the world, Veselovsky was convinced of the dependence of the work of even the most highly gifted poets upon history.

All of Veselovsky's monographic historico-literary works written within a few decades, were to a considerable degree composed in the spirit of the comparative and historico-cultural schools. They established the national and foreign, the oral and the written sources of the works; they explained the connections of literary phenomena with other manifestations of spiritual culture—with philosophical, religious, and social-journalistic currents. Veselovsky combined the tradition of Benfeyism with the influences of the school which was supreme at that time in literary studies—the historico-cultural school of Hippolyte Taine and others.

But the fundamental, "leading" line in Veselovsky's theoretical investigations, which can be traced through all the decades of his scientific activity, from the beginning of the 1860's until the end of his life, was not Benfeyism or Taineism, but the *evolutionary principle* of the literary process, the establishment of general conformity to established principles in this literary development.

Alexander Veselovsky, from the very first years of his scholarly activity, had been under the very powerful influence of the scientific natural philosophy of the middle of the nineteenth century, especially under the sway of the ideas of Darwin, and also of those positivist scholars who had adapted (with varying degrees of clearness) the evolutionary method to the history of culture—Spencer, Tylor, Lang, and later Frazer and others.

Surveying the literary process as a whole, Veselovsky assigns an important place to folklore in the comparative theory of literature. He says:

It is beyond dispute that the science of folklore can be isolated; it has its special tasks, and a great deal of as yet undigested and unclassified material. Popular poetry—the main object of investigation of folklorists—is also the first phase of all poetic and literary development, which is subject to investigation in the comparative history of literature. In practice it is not always possible to separate one field from the other, in view of certain questions which arise in the field of poetics and can be settled only on the ground of popular poetry.[104]

[104] A. N. Veselovsky, *Collected Works*, Vol. I, p. 22 ("Note," 1887).

Working persistently on the problem of the development of poetry, Veselovsky calls the science which must concern itself with this problem, sometimes "the comparative history of literature," sometimes "inductive poetics," and sometimes, finally, "historical poetics." [105] He even stressed the latter designation, though, according to all the essentials of Veselovsky's theoretical pronouncements, it would have been more correct if this science, and the theory erected upon its foundation, had been called "evolutionary poetics."

Veselovsky was intensely interested in the origin of poetic genres (epic, lyric, dramatic) and their various aspects and forms; he was interested in the original rudimentary stage of poetry, the starting point of its further development; he was interested in the actual process of the progressive movement of poetry, the combination of that which is handed down by tradition with those new elements which are contributed by every period, by every creative individuality, the repetition or the gradual dying out of traditional subjects and motifs.

The primitive syncretistic stage in the development of poetry especially interested Veselovsky. As in the embryo, so in this stage there are closely interwoven elements which later become isolated, by means of a gradual separation from their syncretistic condition, into independent poetic genres and forms.

Veselovsky devotes the greater part of his *Three Chapters from Historical Poetics* to a detailed analysis of syncretism and to the process of separating from it the isolated poetic forms. Besides this, he makes use, to a very great degree, of information acquired by investigators who were representatives of the "anthropological school," at the same time frequently adducing examples from the folklore and way of life of the primitive peoples of Siberia, and also the culturally retarded strata of the peoples of Russia and western Europe.

Veselovsky wrestles with the remnants of normative aesthetics and

[105] Veselovsky called his basic theoretical work *Three Chapters from Historical Poetics* (I, "The Syncretism of the Very Early Poetry, and the Beginnings of Differentiation of Poetic Genres"; II, "From Singer to Poet: A Distinction in the Understanding of Poetry"; III, "The Language of Poetry and the Language of Prose"). Originally the *Three Chapters* was published in the *Journal of the Ministry of Public Education*, Nos. 4-5, 1898; then it appeared in 1899 as a separate book, and finally was reprinted in Vol. I of the *Collected Works of A. N. Veselovsky* (St. Petersburg, 1911).

poetics, strives for a broad historical synthesis, dreams of binding together in a single process all the developments of poetry, from the primitives of folklore to the productions of the world's geniuses; acknowledges a conformity to established principles in the development and change of forms, the succession of which is bound up with "the fixed and regular changes in social ideals."

In 1894 he defines the history of literature as "the history of social thought in picturesquely poetic experience, and in the forms which express it." [106]

In 1898, concluding the first chapter of his *Historical Poetics*, Veselovsky states that life has refuted the normative definitions of poetic productions, as given by Aristotle and Horace, and that, for the poetics of the future, broad prospects have been opened up.

Poetic revelations, not foreseen by Aristotle, hardly fitted into his framework; Shakespeare and the romanticists have made a great breach in it, the romanticists and the school of the Grimms have opened up the previously untouched field of popular song and saga. Then appeared the ethnographers, the folklorists; the material of comparative literature has been so much extended that it demands a new edifice, the poetics of the future. It will not standardize our tastes by one-sided propositions, but will leave our old gods on Olympus, reconciling, in a broad historical synthesis, Corneille with Shakespeare. It will teach us that in the forms of poetry which we inherited there is something which conforms to established principles, worked out by a social-psychological process, that the poetry of the word cannot be defined by an abstract conception of beauty, and that it is eternally being created by a continuous joining of these forms with social ideals which are undergoing alteration in conformity to established principles.[107]

The last of these propositions must especially hold our attention. Regardless of the meaning which Veselovsky assigns to the problems of artistic form, to the role of poetic tradition, which shackles the free beginnings of the author's individuality, it would still be altogether incorrect to consider Veselovsky as a kind of forerunner of the later formalism in the study of literature. External evidence for this can

---

[106] A. N. Veselovsky, *Collected Works*, Vol. I, p. 31.
[107] *Ibid.*, pp. 391-392.

be given by Veselovsky's articles, devoted to specific elements of poetics: "From the History of Epithet" (1895), "Epic Repetitions as a Chronological Factor" (1897), and "Psychological Parallelism and Its Forms in the Reflection of Poetic Style" (1898). But this would be erroneous, if only for the reason that these articles were being written in the period of Veselovsky's intensive work on his *Historical Poetics* as a whole, and that this work, as well as all Veselovsky's scientific activity—both in the treatment of concrete historico-literary and folklore phenomena, and in the raising and solving of theoretical problems of synthesis—always expressed his scientific thought on the question of the connections of poetic creations with the phenomena of social life. Not without reason does he insistently repeat that "the history of literature is the history of social thought," that the development of poetry [its forms and content] is an expression of "successive change in the mode of life, and the growth of a social and personal consciousness," that "it [poetry] is eternally being created by a continuous joining of forms with social ideals which are undergoing alteration in conformity to established principles."

It is true that these continually repeated references to "social ideals," to the "social consciousness," to "change in the mode of life," by virtue of their indistinctness and idealistic obscurity, of course, cannot completely satisfy us. But it is important that Veselovsky, analyzing a huge mass of factual material, directed scientific thought away from the field of purely immanent examination of a superstructure of phenomena, into the field of sociology, of the structure of society, of economic and social practice. In the process of development, broadly designated by him, from syncretism to an established cult, from song to poetry, from the singer to the poet, he repeatedly notices the role of social groups which are differentiated from the general mass—"ancestral groups, social classes, castes," [108] and so forth.

In specific, more informal statements, Veselovsky speaks of the class basis of the changes which are to be observed in poetry (for instance, of the bourgeois class nature of the Greek romance,[109] of the original reworking of chivalrous poetry by the bourgeoisie,[110] of the influence of the poetry of the cultured, that is, the ruling classes, on

[108] *Ibid.*, pp. 27, 93, 326, 354.   [109] *Ibid.*, p. 49.   [110] *Ibid.*, p. 353.

the popular creations),[111] "of the historical conditions, which prompt the selection and development of poetic manifestations." [112]

In the creative individuality at various stages of the development of poetry, Veselovsky sees, above all, the expression of group opinions, and he introduces the term, "group personality." [113]

With the

emergence of a cultured group, as the guiding one, the exponent of its mood will be some individual poet; the poet is born, but the materials and the mood of his poetry are prepared by the group. In this sense it may be said that Petrarchism is older than Petrarch. The individual poet, lyric or epic, always belongs to the group; the difference is one of degree and content of the evolution in modes of life which distinguishes his group.[114]

From an attentive reading of Veselovsky's works, especially on the concrete questions of the history of literature and folklore, it is possible to draw the following conclusion: the very character of the material, and the scientifically conscientious analysis of it, compelled Veselovsky more and more frequently to state that the fixed principles of literary development, which he strove all his life to find and determine, are based upon the fixed principles of the development of social life itself. Unfortunately—and this was Veselovsky's misfortune, as well as that of many other students of literature at that period—bourgeois literary studies, folkloristics, linguistics, and study of art were very far from a correct understanding of specifically social development, and of the material bases which determine it. Hence arose also the extreme diversity of sociological determinisms: all these "social" groups, "ancestral groups, social classes, castes"; hence arose also the free substitution of the concept of "the evolution in modes of life" for the conceptions of social-economic development and differentiation, and so forth.

But, noting the vagueness and precariousness of Veselovsky's concepts with regard to the established principles of social development, it is important to emphasize the fact that, in the course of his continually expanding work in research, Veselovsky was constantly obliged, more often and more vaguely, to raise again the question of

[111] *Ibid.*, p. 350.   [113] *Ibid.*, pp. 334-335.
[112] *Ibid.*, p. 399.   [114] *Ibid.*, p. 329.

the causal explanation of purely poetic facts. The purely immanent approach to poetry, and to its history, was absolutely alien to Veselovsky: one must remember his investigations of Boccaccio, Dante, Zhukovsky, Petrarch, of Russian *byliny*, religious verses, and tales.

Veselovsky did not bring the study of "historical poetics" to its conclusion. He was able to give a general sketch of the development of poetry only at its comparatively early stages. A complete building up of the whole structure which he had conceived, was hindered not only by the immensity of the task itself, which could hardly be carried out by the powers of one man; the fundamental cause was, as we have already said, Veselovsky's lack of a correct understanding of the connection between ideology and its material basis. Having his roots in bourgeois scholarship, Veselovsky was far from the one correct explanation of the history of social life, which is given by scientific Marxism.

But the attentive study of all the scholarly works of such giants of science of the past as Alexander Veselovsky, the critical mastery of his works on the poetic riches which he revived in Russia, western Europe, and the East, is one of the essential conditions of future progress.[115]

Along with the efforts of scientific thought to find a synthesis for the most diverse phenomena of world folklore—efforts which are most clearly expressed in A. N. Veselovsky's works—among Russian folklorists there could also be observed another effort—the effort to link Russian folk poetry with Russian history, to reveal the historical soil on which Russian folklore grew and developed.

Thus the "historical school" made its appearance. Its principal ex-

---

[115] A popular account of A. N. Veselovsky's *Historical Poetics* is given by E. Anichkov in the collection, *Questions of the Theory and Psychology of Creative Work*, Vol. I (Kharkov, 1911), and also by K. Tiander and F. Kartashev in the first number of the second volume of the same collection. See also the book by B. M. Engelhardt. *A. N. Veselovsky* (Moscow, 1924). The scientific activity of A. N. Veselovsky has been newly illuminated in the reports of V. F. Shishmarev, V. M. Zhirmunsky, V. A. Desnitsky, M. K. Azadovsky, and M. P. Alekseyev, read before the Academy of Sciences in connection with the 100th anniversary of the birth of Veselovsky (*Annals of the Academy of Sciences of the USSR* [Division of Social Sciences], No. 4, 1938). The articles of M. K. Azadovsky, "A. N. Veselovsky As an Investigator of Folklore," and of V. M. Zhirmunsky, "The 'Historical Poetics' of A. N. Veselovsky," are especially significant for folklorists.

ponent is usually—and we may say, rightly—considered to be Vsevolod Fyodorovich Miller (1848–1913), to whom its most systematic and detailed establishment must be credited. But the way to it was sought for a number of years before V. Miller established its positions in the middle 1890's, having for the sake of this abandoned the theory of borrowing, which he had so fervently defended.

Even at the beginning of the 1860's, when the "mythological school" of Grimm and Buslayev reigned almost undisputed in Russian folkloristics, when even the theory of borrowing had only come in from the West in echoes which as yet were far from clear—three years before the appearance of the sensational article of V. V. Stasov, "The Origin of the Russian *Byliny*," that manifesto of the Benfeyan theory in Russia—there appeared a work by L. N. Maykov, *On the Byliny of the Vladimir Cycle*.[116] The young author, as he was then, dismissing from his mind such problems—so much in vogue at that time—as the traces of primitive myths in the epos, placed the question on a more real ground, a historical one. He began to seek in the *byliny* the reflections of the history of manners and customs, and of the state, concentrating on the "specific" Kiev period of it, as it was then called. Maykov compares the names of the heroes of the *byliny* (Prince Vladimir, Dobrynya, and so forth) with the historical names which have been preserved in the chronicles; he compares the setting of manners and customs pictured in the *byliny* with what is known of the mode of life of the princes' *druzhiny*, from historical sources; he gathers facts dealing with the life of the state of Kiev and other principalities, and reaches the conclusion that the *byliny* of the "Kiev cycle" were composed during the period from the tenth to the thirteenth centuries. Here already may be noted, in essence, the characteristic features of the future "historical school" with its excellences (the search for the real historical basis of the epos) and defects (in particular the overrating of the *bylina* as a historical, rather than an artistic-poetic memorial). In Maykov's work, however, the criticism of historical sources was, of course, more crude than it was later on in the works of Miller and his followers; also, the comparative an-

---

116 L. Maykov, *On the Byliny of the Vladimir Cycle,* dissertation for the degree of Master of Russian Literature (St. Petersburg, 1863).

alysis (which later became compulsory) of the variants in the text of the *byliny* had hardly been developed.

One of the first to give a model of such critical analysis of the texts of the *byliny* was the "mythologist" Orestes Miller, of whom we have spoken above. He took as the chief task in his investigation of Elijah of Murom (1869) the disclosure of the most ancient mythological basis; but still he also occupied himself with the removal of the "historical strata" by means of a careful comparison of variants.

In 1883 the research study, *The Byliny of Alyosha Popovich*,[117] written by the Kiev professor, N. P. Dashkevich, appeared. Dashkevich makes a detailed comparison with the chronicles, and establishes the identity of the Alyosha Popovich of the *byliny* as the "brave Alexander Popovich," who is mentioned in the chronicles; and the same *bylina* which tells "how the knights became extinct in Old Russia," he sees as the battle of Kalka.

In the course of two years—in 1885—the Kharkov scholar, M. E. Khalansky, published an interesting investigation, *Great-Russian Byliny of the Kiev Cycle*,[118] in which, taking exception to L. Maykov and O. Miller, he advances the idea that the so-called "Kiev" *byliny* constitute in themselves the "Kiev cycle" only in name, but, in their origin, are to be assigned to a considerably later era—to the time of the Moscow centralization of the fifteenth and sixteenth centuries. He supports his idea by a comparison of the details as to history and modes of life in the *byliny* with the mode of life of the princes and boyars of the Muscovite Old Russia. This idea was at first greeted with skepticism, but presently found an enthusiastic echo in the later works of V. Miller, and especially of certain of his students (in particular, S. K. Shambinago).

Not breaking with the theory of borrowing, but, on the contrary, continuing to develop it in his numerous historico-literary and folkloristic works, A. N. Veselovsky repeatedly took issue with the trends of the newly created "historical school." For example, in his *South Russian Byliny*, particularly in the sketch of the *bylina* about Dyuk

---

[117] N. P. Dashkevich. *The Byliny of Alyosha Popovich, and How There Were No Knights Left in Old Russia* (1883).

[118] M. Khalansky, *Great-Russian Byliny of the Kiev Cycle* (Warsaw, 1883).

Stepanovich, having examined the literary and oral poetic sources of the *bylina*, Veselovsky also discloses the reflection in the *bylina* of history (the Galician-Volynian principality of the twelfth and thirteenth centuries); in the article "Tales of Ivan the Terrible" (1876), he pursues the problem of how the given subject is combined in the tale with the reflection of the real historical actualities of the sixteenth century, and so on. Such a combination of the "theory of borrowing" and the "historical school" is characteristic of A. N. Veselovsky's pupil, I. N. Zhdanov (1846–1901).[119]

In the general progress of historical development in Russia, the "historical school" was firmly entrenched in Russian folkloristics by the middle 1890's, and became the ruling school in it in the course of a quarter of a century. Its most outstanding exponent was V. Miller. He had gone over to it from the so-called "migrationary school," not without the influence of the works of Maykov, Dashkevich, Khalansky, and Veselovsky, which we have previously mentioned.

From the middle 1890's on, V. Miller began to reexamine and analyze, in succession, one *bylina* after another, trying in each to define mainly the "historical basis," that is, the agreement with historical facts. For a period of twenty years the slow but persistent work went on. His collected articles on specific subjects dealing with *byliny* made up the three volumes of the famous *Outlines of Russian Folk Literature*.[120] The last of these volumes appeared posthumously.

These three volumes of the *Outlines* constitute the fundamental work, reflecting all the characteristic peculiarities of the "historical school."

In the introduction to the first volume, V. Miller himself expounds in detail his theoretical purposes and method, and also gives a criticism of previous tendencies in scientific theory with regard to oral poetry:

[119] I. N. Zhdanov, *Russian Poetry in the Pre-Mongolian Era* (*Collected Works*, Vol. I [St. Petersburg, 1904]). By the same author: *Toward a Literary History of Russian Poetry of the Byliny* (St. Petersburg, 1881); *Songs of Prince Román* (St. Petersburg, 1890); *The Russian Epos of the Byliny* (St. Petersburg, 1895). With the exception of the last, all the works of Zhdanov have been reprinted in *Works of I. N. Zhdanov*, Vol. I (1904), Vol. II (1907).

[120] V. Miller, *Outlines of Russian Folk Literature: Byliny*, Vol. I (Moscow, 1897), Vol. II (Moscow, 1910), Vol. III (Moscow, 1924).

Contemporary scientific investigation of our epos of the *byliny* still does not give us, in my opinion, the ability to answer certain questions on its history, and to conduct a study which will satisfy all scientific requirements. The remote foundations of the epos are hidden from us by the thick veil of a long series of centuries, which, in the absence or the scantiness of written documents, hitherto has been lifted only by means of bold conjectures and hypotheses, which have not found universal acceptance. Neither the supposed mythological foundations of the epos, nor the theory of the prehistoric Indo-European and all-Slavonic heritage, nor the hypothesis of the Eastern origin of the subjects of our *byliny*, have explained satisfactorily the origins and the earliest period of development of the epos of the *byliny*. Greater progress in the correct evaluation of the *byliny* has been attained by indicating the historical strata and traces which are revealed in them, and the wandering subjects of tales, or the literary echoes, which have entered into the composition of the songs of the *byliny* by virtue of the processes of cyclization and historization. During the past decades, special attention has been turned to the study of the vast literature of European and Asiatic folklore, the collection of so-called "parallels" and the application of the comparative method to the study of the composition of our *byliny*. But it is impossible to rest too great hopes in these "parallels"; it is impossible to think that the detailed examination of the various wandering subjects of tales, establishing their genetic classification, can make clear in all instances, likewise, the routes of their transition from one people to another. . . .

A wandering oral tale is not like a letter sent from one country to another, preserving in its stamps the marks of all the states through which it has passed. To detect the routes of dissemination of an oral tale for the many centuries of its wandering, is exactly like trying to catch the wind in a field. . . .

Being doubtful of the success of such conjectures, which are unavoidable, if we do not have written literary sources for the *byliny*, I seldom make use of the comparative method in the *Outlines* for conclusions as to the route by which this or that subject of a *bylina* has penetrated into our epos of the *byliny*. I occupy myself more with the history of the *byliny* and the reflection of history in them, beginning the first of these studies, not from prehistoric times, not from the bottom, but from the top. These upper strata of the *bylina*, not possessing that enigmatic character which makes extreme antiquity so attractive to the investigator, are none the less interesting, because they can actually be explained, and can give, not a conjectural, but a more or less exact representation of a period in the life of the *bylina* which is nearer to us. Thus we often find in a *bylina* traces of the influence upon it of a cheaply printed folk tale or an old written narrative; sometimes we find clear traces of a burlesque adaptation, sometimes the presence of this or that proper name, making it possible for us to draw chronological conclusions. For the explanation of the history of the *bylina* I have tried, through the comparison of variants, to deduce its more archaic version and, examining the data as to history and modes of life given in this version, to fix, so far as possible, the period of its composition and the region of its origin.[121]

As we see, in these lines V. Miller very clearly and definitely formulated the bases of his methodology. His introduction, as well as his entire first volume, became the starting point for the works of the followers of V. Miller, who also occupied themselves mainly with the investigation of the epos: A. V. Markov,[122] S. K. Shambinago,[123] B. M. Sokolov,[124] and others. On specific private questions they differed. (For example, Markov defended the idea that the *byliny* had been composed at a comparatively early time—mainly in the era of the Tartar domination; Shambinago persistently affirms that the *byliny* could not possibly have been composed earlier than the sixteenth century, and so forth.) Certain investigators are distinguished for their well known methodological cautiousness; others, on the contrary, have given too great scope to subjective hypothetical constructions; but the starting points and the main features of the method were common to them all.

---

[121] *Ibid.*, Vol. I, pp. iii-v.

[122] A. V. Markov, "From the History of the Epos of the *Byliny*," *Ethnographic Review* (Moscow, 1905), Bks. 61, 62, 64, 70, 71, and separately published; "Features of the Mode of Life of the Russian Epos of the *Byliny*," *Ethnographic Review* (1904), Bks. 58, 59.

[123] S. K. Shambinago, *Songs of the Time of Tsar Ivan the Terrible* (Moscow, 1914); "On the Literary History of the *Byliny* of the Volga," *Journal of the Ministry of Public Education* (1905), Bk. XI; "The Early Russian Dwelling According to the *Byliny*," *Jubilee Collection in Honor of V. Miller* (Moscow, 1900).

[124] B. M. Sokolov, "*Byliny* about Danilo Lovchanin," *Russian Philological News*, 1910, XIV; "The Brother-in-Law of the Terrible, Mamstruk Temryukovich," *Journal of the Ministry of Public Education*, No. 7, 1913; "A History of Ancient Songs About the Forty Beggars and One," *Russian Philological News*, Nos. 1, 2, 1913; "*Byliny* of the Great Pagan Idol," *Journal of the Ministry of Public Education*, No. 5, 1916; "Germano-Russian Relations in the Field of the Epos: Epic Tales of the Marriage of Prince Vladimir," *Academic Annals of the Chernyshevsky State University at Saratov*, Vol. I, No. 3, Saratov, 1923.

As compared with the "mythological" school and the school of "borrowing," the "historical" school constituted a significant step forward in the general advance of scholarship. Folkloristics, out of the obscurities of mythology, out of the often fruitless search after the "wandering subjects," was striving to advance to the solid ground of historical facts.

But the misfortune lay in this, that the historical attitude itself was understood only superficially by the representatives of the "historical school."

The main questions which interested the representatives of the "historical school" were: *where* (that is, in what principality, city, and so forth), *when* (in what era, that is, in what century, decade, and even what year), on the basis of what *historical facts* (events of political and social life, foreign and internal wars, diplomatic life, incidents in the private life of the tsars, princes, boyars, and merchants); through the help of what poetic *sources* (oral and written, local and migratory) had the oral poetic production been put together? (This meant, however, not the concrete artistic production, but generally only the subject of the *bylina* or tale.)

Questions of geographical and chronological dating (*where, when*) were decided usually on the basis of an analysis of names and titles. For these, an effort was made to find, in chronicles and other historical documents, similar names and titles, and on the basis of the resemblance of their titles, an identification was effected of persons, cities, and territories.

There was plenty of room left for subjectivity of interpretations and conjectures; two, or sometimes several, investigators would differ in their reconstructions by a number of centuries and by vast distances: one would assign this or that *bylina* to Volynian Galich, one to Novgorod, one to Kiev, or one to Ryazan; one to Murom (near the city of Vladimir), one to Moroviisk (near Chernigov), and so on without end. Similarities in the sound of names and titles proved to be very unstable material, and made precarious the hypotheses which were constructed upon them.

Connections between details as to the subject and historic facts, were also made frequently on the basis of the most general motifs of social life and family modes of living (the assault of enemies, the burning of a city, treason, a quarrel, a domestic drama, and so on).

In the establishment of literary and oral poetic influences and borrowings, the "historical school" shared all the vicissitudes of the method of Benfeyism and its ramifications.

All this, on the whole, led to the crisis of the "historical school," which is still acknowledged by professional folklorists, including a number of its former adherents.

The infelicities in it were acknowledged by them, of course, even earlier. Not without reason were there so many disputes within the "historical school"; for example, concerning S. K. Shambinago's *Songs of the Time of Tsar Ivan the Terrible*, where the investigator sought to prove that Vaska Buslayev and Ivan the Terrible were the same person.

But, on the whole, the "historical school" was considered so reliable, so much the "last word in science," that even in 1917, in the year of the Great October Socialist Revolution, the author of a most extensive university course on *Russian Oral Poetry*, M. N. Speransky, wrote as follows concerning the method of the outlines of V. F. Miller: "It is beyond doubt that this method remains, up to the present time, the only correct one, and must be acknowledged as basic for the study of the history of our oral literature in general." [125]

Criticism of the "historical school" on the whole was first given in 1924 by the Saratov professor, A. P. Skaftymov, in his book, *Poetics and the Genesis of the Byliny*.[126] In spite of the (at times) very successfully demonstrated methodological instability in the use of proper names, titles, outward coincidences with historical facts, the inconsistency and extreme subjectivity of the structures of specific representatives of the "historical school," in spite of all its significance as an initial step, the criticism which A. P. Skaftymov made of the "historical school" still cannot be considered as fully successful. His criticism proceeded from half-formalistic, half-esthetic psychological

[125] Prof. M. N. Speransky, *Russian Oral Literature* (Moscow, 1917), p. 99. By this course, and by his well known two-volume collection of *Byliny* (published by the Sabashnikovs, 1916–1919), M. N. Speransky contributed substantially toward the dissemination of the views of the "historical school."

[126] A. P. Skaftymov, *Poetics and the Genesis of the Byliny* (Saratov, 1924).

theoretical positions, and also, it was frequently beside the point, since it was based on a selection of feeble works (frequently of such a kind that even their authors had later repudiated them), while it passed by in silence many works of the same authors which had arrived at definite positive results.

Apart from the precariousness of method described above, there was expressed in the "historical school" an incorrect theoretical tendency, which undervalued the productions of folklore as artistic and poetic works; and the distinction was too vaguely drawn between a historical document and a landmark of poetic creative art; though Khalansky still issued the warning that "a historical song is before all things a poetic production, and not prose, and, consequently, not history."[127]

The great defect of the "historical school" was at first an insufficient attention to the question of the social and class nature of the productions of oral poetry, and later on, when this question was raised, the incorrect solution of it.

In the first of his *Outlines*, written in the 1890's (see Volume I), V. Miller barely touched upon the problem under consideration. He established, by means of analysis, the content and forms of the *byliny*, and also, on the basis of the testimonies of the monuments of ancient Russian literature, showed that in the composition and diffusion of the *byliny* the professional singers and musicians of the Russian Middle Ages—the buffoons—must have played a great role. V. Miller noted that the "vagabond" buffoons served the most diverse classes of the people, but alongside of them were the so-called "settled" buffoons, who served wealthy and noble personages, and by their art satisfied their demands.

The problem of the class nature of folklore on the whole, and of the epos of the *byliny* in particular, was accentuated by a second book which came out in 1911, *A Course in the History of Russian Literature*, by V. A. Keltuyala.[128] He put forth the categorical assertion that not only the epos of the *byliny*, but also "all kinds and aspects of oral

---

127 M. Khalansky, *Great-Russian Byliny of the Kiev Cycle* (Warsaw, 1883).
128 V. A. Keltuyala, *A Course in the History of Russian Literature*, Pt. I (Moscow, 1911), Bk. 2.

creative work, had their origin, not in the masses of the people, but in their upper classes," and that, consequently, "the genuine creator of the ancient Russian national culture, of the ancient Russian literature, and of the ancient Russian concept of the world was not the 'people,' represented in their democratic and popular or peasant character, but a small part of the people; namely, its upper, ruling class." [129]

These opinions of Keltuyala's, in their turn, were not lacking in influence upon the ideas of V. Miller and other representatives of the "historical school" (for example, A. V. Markov, B. M. Sokolov, and others).

Thus V. Miller wrote of the most ancient heroic songs in the article, left unfinished at the time of his death, which summed up the results of his work of twenty years: [130]

In accordance with the historic character of these songs [the heroic tales—Au.], one must suppose that they were composed and diffused in a group which stood nearer in development and social position to the princely court and to the *druzhina*—which, according to modern conceptions, belonged to the "intellectual class." The songs were composed by singers of the princely court and the *druzhina* wherever there was a demand for them, or where the pulse of life beat stronger, or where there was prosperity and leisure, or, where the flower of the nation was centered, that is, in the wealthy cities, where life went on with more freedom and gaiety. Kiev, Novgorod (probably also Chernigov and Pereyaslav), before their destruction by the Polovtsy, could have been such, so to speak, centers of song, just as they were the centers of the written literature which had its birth in the eleventh century and attained its greatest development in the twelfth.

Celebrating the princes and the members of the *druzhina*, this poetry bore an aristocratic character; it was, so to speak, the elegant literature of the higher, more enlightened class, which, more than the other groups in the population, was permeated by a national consciousness, a feeling of the unity of the Russian land, and, in general, a sense of political interests.

If these epic poems, dealing with the princes and the *druzhina*, penetrated down to the lower class of the people—down to the farmers, bondmen and slaves—then they could only be distorted in

[129] *Ibid.*, pp. vi-viii.
[130] *Survey of the History of the Russian Epos of the Byliny*, written in 1912, first published in 1924; see V. Miller, *Outlines*, Vol. III (Moscow, 1924), pp. 27-28.

those ignorant surroundings, just as the contemporary *byliny* are distorted among the common people of Olonets and Archangel. . . . Surely the basic motif of these songs was the desire to celebrate this or that person of the upper class who was attractive to the composer of the song. It may be that the princely singers were even court poets (like the poets of the eighteenth century, who composed eulogies to order).[131]

Thus there was definitively formulated the fallacious idea of the origin of the epos of the *byliny* in the higher military surroundings of the *druzhina*, in the aristocratic surroundings of the early feudalism.

At that time V. Miller began to put forward similar thoughts with reference also to other aspects of folklore. So, in his introduction to the first volume of the new series of *Songs* collected by P. V. Kireyevsky,[132] he spoke of the powerful influence of the wedding ceremonial and of the wedding poetry of the ruling classes upon the wedding festivities of the peasants.

The problem of the class nature of folklore began to occupy other representatives of the "historical school" as well; it was solved by them with numerous variations, but basically in the same way; they all affirmed that this or that aspect, or in any case, this or that production of folklore, had been composed among the groups of the ruling classes.

The incorrectness of such "sociological" speculations had its roots, to a considerable degree, in the previously indicated methodological deficiency of the "historical school," in the failure to take into account the poetic nature of folklore productions, in the naïvely realistic approach to poetic forms, in the ignoring of modes of hyperbole, and other forms of poetic idealization which are typical of folklore, in the identification of the medium of representation with the setting that was being represented. If, let us say, in the epos of the *byliny*, the heroes are called princes, boyars, wealthy merchants; if in the tales the heroes are addressed as tsars and tsarevitches, kings or princes; if in the peasant wedding ceremonies and songs of tribute the bridegroom and bride are celebrated as prince and princess, while the

---

[131] Academician V. F. Miller, *Outlines of Russian Folk Literature*, Vol. III (Moscow, 1924), pp. 27-28.

[132] P. V. Kireycvsky, *Songs*, new series (No. I, Moscow, 1911).

"weddingers," that is, those who take part in the wedding procession, are called "commanders," boyars, merchants, then the representatives of the "historical school" would be inclined to see in all this, not the devices of poetization and idealization, but a proof of the aristocratic origin of the forms of folklore under consideration.

"Even the characters represented in the tales—tsars, tsarevitches, tsarevnas, kings, princes, princesses—and the luxurious setting in the midst of which they move, show that this kind of production, too, was composed in an artistocratic setting, and not 'in a popular one.' " [133]

These "sociological" speculations of the "historical school" seemed in their time "progressive movements," since they were dictated to a considerable degree by the desire to wage war with the remnants of the romantic, excessively idealistic views in folklore, the desire to transfer the study of folklore to more realistic grounds.

However, while waging war with the romantic and fantastic in scholarship, the "historical school" itself passed over, as we have seen, to excessively unreliable hypotheses, and fell into gross errors of common sociology.

These crude sociological errors continued to develop right ·down to the very recent past, until they were definitely and sharply exposed by Soviet social criticism (to be dealt with later).

This criticism was harsher by virtue of the fact that the conclusions of the "historical school" concerning the aristocratic origin of folklore as a whole (Keltuyala), or of the epos of the *byliny* only (V. Miller, Boris Sokolov, and others), later on, even in the period after the war, were echoed by one of the reactionary folklorists, Hans Naumann. In 1921 and 1922 Hans Naumann published two books, in which he set forth his theory of folklore.

Naumann perceives two contrasted beginnings in folklore: *gesunkenes Kulturgut* (sunken cultural values) and *die primitive Gemeinschaftskultur* (primitive communal culture). In the first category Naumann includes those manifestations of culture which were created among the ruling classes of the era of feudalism and the later eras, but

[133] V. A. Keltuyala, *Course in the History of Russian Literature*, Pt. I, Bk. 2, p. viii.

with the passing of time have been swept down from the cultural "heights" to the "lowest depths of the people." Thus the songs of the poets of the seventeenth and eighteenth centuries were transformed, in the nineteenth, into popular songs; the chivalrous poetry of the Middle Ages became the folk songs of the fourteenth to the sixteenth centuries.

Such arguments are directly contradicted by the facts, by the observations of numerous collectors of folklore since the end of the nineteenth century, including, especially, the Russian folklorists, all the way back to the time of Rybnikov and Hilferding, who have done so much for the explanation and demonstration of the creative character of the popular narrators, storytellers, singers, and other masters of the folk art.

Naumann personally did not occupy himself with the collection of folklore; he did not come into direct contact with the masters of popular poetry; he did not investigate either their life or their creative process.

Naumann did not perceive in popular poetry that which, among us, has been so finely observed by that wonderful connoisseur of popular life, Maxim Gorky, who emphasized, above all, the living creative beginning in the art of the working people, and the close connection of the popular creative work with labor, the basis of human culture.

The haughty preconceived attitude of Naumann toward the masses of the working people, and the denial of their creative power, of course, were not accidental, but were nourished by the general world view of Naumann, that typical representative of the bourgeois science of the era of decaying capitalism.

It is not surprising that the representatives of the more democratic section of German folkloristics should have discerned antidemocratic tendencies in these propositions of Naumann's theory. Through an attentive analysis of the "sociology" of Naumann, which is revealed in his books on folklore, it was possible to observe also the ripening of reactionary tendencies—the basis of the leading role of the "upper class" and the passive role of the masses of the people, who obediently and uncomplainingly follow them.

These tendencies began to be more and more strongly revealed in the later articles and books of Naumann, until at last he completely revealed his reactionary character in one of his books of the latest period.

Although the arguments of the representatives of the "historical school" as to the aristocratic origin of folklore, for example, the epos of the *byliny*, did not have the same origin as Naumann's theory, but had their own history based on Russian folkloristics, it is altogether natural that a connection between the views of Russian folklorists and Naumann's theory might easily suggest itself to readers. And this was in itself an indication of the fact that the folkloristic thought of the representatives of the "historical school" was proceeding along fallacious paths, and was leading to incorrect interpretations of the very nature of the folk creation and of its social significance. The errors of the "historical school" issued also from the separation of theory from practice, from a purely academic consideration of the phenomena of real active life, from a lack of attention to the living bearers of the popular creative work.

The "historical school" could have arrived at its conclusions concerning the aristocratic origin of the epos of the *byliny*, and of a number of other genres of folklore, only through a lack of appreciation of the *creative* factor in popular poetry, as a result of limiting the activity of the bearers of folklore (the narrators, storytellers, singers, wailers, and so forth) to the role of "custodians" of antiquity. For example, V. Miller evaluated this or that narrator of the *byliny* only with reference to his greater or lesser preservation of the ancient texts. The narrator as an independent master, as a creative artist, was ignored or even denied by Miller. This, in the last analysis, was the seignorial approach to the popular poets.

But it is curious to observe that, alongside such an attitude toward the masters of popular poetry, an attitude which was characteristic not only of the "historical school," but also of many representatives of the migration theory, who had interested themselves in the wandering of abstract subjects and had also ignored the creative individuality and that ideational content which was possessed by every work of folk poetry—alongside all this, in Russian folkloristics there existed also another tradition, which was opposed to it, and which emphasized the democratic factors in folklore.

V. G. Belinsky, in his opinions on questions dealing with popular creative work, had already expressed a number of thoughts which showed distinctly that he was interested not only in the echoes of the past in folklore—that which, above all, attracted the Slavophiles, the representatives of the "official nationalism"—and thereafter in "mythology," but was concerned chiefly with the reflection in folklore of the life and world concept of the contemporary peasantry. In the passionate conflict with the Slavophiles and the "official nationalism," Belinsky stood out against the idealization of antiquity, against the idealization of the ancient Russian mode of life. Therefore, also, in the old folk songs, the *byliny* and the tales, he did not treat everything sympathetically, but emphasized the presence in folklore of survivals of superstitions, family despotism, stagnation, and so on.

From time to time, in the heat of controversy, Belinsky erred in undervaluing the poetic and historic significance of this or that production of folklore; but on the whole his critical attitude toward traditional poetry was sound and productive of undoubted benefit to science and to the public. Especially important was the fact that he called attention to the real interests and longings of the popular masses as expressed in folklore. He particularly stressed the expressions in folklore of the factors of social protest and revolutionary tendencies.[134]

In the circles of liberal sympathy with Western ideas, in the 1840's and 1850's, a negative attitude toward folk poetry held sway. Such an attitude toward folklore, on the part of the liberal sympathizers with

[134] The most detailed expression of Belinsky's views on Russian folk poetry was given in a series of his articles in 1841, devoted to the selection of folklore materials in the collections of Kirsha Danilov (*Ancient Russian Poems* [St. Petersburg, 1840]), M. Sukharov, I. Sakharov (Tales of the Russian People [St. Petersburg, 1841], and the same authors' *Russian Popular Tales* [Pt. 1, St. Petersburg, 1841]); F. Studitsky (*Popular Songs of the Governments of Vologda and Olenets* [St. Petersburg, 1841]). All these surveys by Belinsky, and also his "General View of Popular Poetry and Its Significance," and a number of other articles dealing with popular creative work, are to be found in Vol. 6 of the *Complete Collected Works of V. G. Belinsky*, ed. S. A. Vengerov. Prof. A. P. Skaftymov has devoted his article, "Belinsky and Oral Popular Creative Works," *The Literary Critic*, No. 7, 1936, to the question of Belinsky's Views on Folklore.

Western ideas, proceeded from the frequent utilization of folklore by the Slavophiles, and by still more reactionary circles, for their own aims. A typical expression of such liberal tendencies, in sympathy with Western ideas, was A. P. Milyukov's book, *Outlines of the History of Russian Poetry* (1st ed., 1847; 2nd ed., 1858).

"Our tales," wrote Milyukov, "are distinguished by the very same character as the songs, with this distinction, that in them, as in epic poetry, which demands a greater social development, all deficiencies must be expressed more clearly, and there the barrenness and crudity of our life must be shown still more strikingly." In the Russian tales "there is to be seen only unrestrained fantasy, full of exaggerations and crudity."

The *byliny* show "only the aggrandizement of material force and the poverty of intellectual life." [135]

A different view was taken of folk creation by the representatives of revolutionary democracy, the first of these being N. A. Dobrolyubov and N. G. Chernyshevsky. Waging war, even more decisively and violently than the liberal sympathizers with Western ideas, with Slavophilism and the "official nationalism," revolutionary democracy made a different approach to folk creation than the liberal bourgeoisie had made. Dobrolyubov, Chernyshevsky, and Nekrasov saw in the folk creative works beauty, high ideals, a wealth of feeling, and genuine poetry.

"By old, inveterate habit," wrote Dobrolyubov, "we have hitherto looked upon the people with a certain prejudice. They always represent for us a rude crowd, incapable of elevated or noble or tender feeling. But meanwhile, on the contrary, in our society all these feelings have been much less highly developed. If poetry still exists in the world, then it must be sought for among the people." [136]

But Dobrolyubov is far from a wholesale idealization of all the many centuries of folklore. He perceives many dark aspects of it, he sees gross contradictions, he seeks historical explanations for them.

[135] A. P. Milyukov, *Outlines of the History of Russian Poetry* (St. Petersburg, 1847), pp. 40, 41, 46.
[136] N. A. Dobrolyubov, *Complete Collected Works*, ed. P. I. Lebedev-Polyansky (State Literary Press, 1934), Vol. I, p. 465.

Dobrolyubov acknowledges that there has been a great influence upon the ideology of the masses of the people on the part of the ruling classes, on the part of the Church and of ecclesiastical literature (for example, with especial clearness, in religious verses); he discloses the process of alterations which the popular creative works underwent in the course of the centuries of their development; finally, he emphasizes the differentiation of folklore in the social class system.

All these ideas were developed with especial clearness in his article, "On the Degree to Which the People Have Participated in the Development of Russian Literature" (*The Contemporary*, No. 2, 1858),[137] the basis of which is made up of a critical review by Dobrolyubov of A. P. Milyukov's *Outlines of the History of Russian Poetry*.

The main thing in folklore, for Dobrolyubov, is the expression in it of the folk world view, the self-consciousness of the people.

From this point of view, great interest is attached to Dobrolyubov's review of the first issues of the famous *Russian Folk Tales*, by A. N. Afanasyev.[138]

Dobrolyubov gives due credit to Afanasyev's industry and conscientiousness, to the fullness and exactness of the texts, to the copiousness of the variants; but Dobrolyubov is not satisfied with the academic, cold attitude toward the productions of the popular creative genius. Thus the main texts do not give an answer to those questions which naturally must arise with a man who is striving, through folklore, to understand the life, mode of living, world concept, and psychology of the popular masses. Dobrolyubov wrote:

One must not be limited in such work by the publication of productions which have been taken directly from the people. To preserve in one's version the White Russian *dz* and *tz*, and the Little-Russian *ehe* and *ho*, to point out that such a tale was written down in the Cherdyn district, and another in the province of Kharkov, and to add here and there variants found in different localities—this still is insufficient to give us an understanding as to what significance the tales have among the Russian people. . . . And you will not come to

137 Reprinted in Dobrolyubov's *Works*, Vol. I, p. 203.
138 Published in *The Contemporary*, Vol. 71, p. 70, 1858; reprinted in Dobrolyubov's *Works*, Vol. I, p. 429.

know the people from the tales which have been published by Mr. Afanasyev.

Dobrolyubov is eager to ascertain the historical and social meaning of the tales.

What of it, indeed, that among the people there are preserved tales of the friendship of the fox and the wolf, of the crafty intrigues of the fox against the wolf, of her relations to man, and so on? What of it, that in the Novogrud district there is a tale circulating about the Rolling Pea, while in the Novotorg district there is one about the seven Simeons, and so forth? Not one of the collectors and describers of data on the popular mode of life has explained to us what the relationship of the people was to the tales and legends which had been told to them. Was there a belief, for example, among the people, in that intelligent relationship among the beasts which is manifested in many of the tales? Or were such tales accepted by the people in much the same manner as we read Homer? . . . Thousands of such questions come into one's head on reading the popular tales, and only a living answer to them makes it possible to accept the folk tales as one of the means of ascertaining the degree of development to which the people had attained. . . . Therefore it seems to us that each one of those who write down and collect the productions of popular poetry would be doing a very useful thing if he would not confine himself to the mere writing down of the text of the tale or song, but would transmit the whole *setting*, both the purely external and, much more, the inner, the ethical setting, in which he happened to hear this song or tale.

Professor M. K. Azadovsky most correctly pointed out in connection with these lines—being the first of the investigators to give a review and characterization of the activity of Dobrolyubov as a folklorist [139]—"In essence, here is the program for further investigations, which will be taken in various ways by different compilers, but which, in one way or another, will exert an influence upon all of them." [140]

The prerevolutionary historiography of folklorists passed over in silence the vast role of a series of direct followers of Dobrolyubov's ideas, representatives of revolutionary democratism, who approached

[139] M. Azadovsky, "Dobrolyubov and Russian Folkloristics: Report to the Dobrolyubov Session of the Division of Social Sciences of the Academy of Sciences of the USSR, February 9, 1936," *Soviet Folklore*, Nos. 4-5, 1936, p. 21; reprinted in *Literature and Folklore*.
[140] M. Azadovsky, *Literature and Folklore* (Leningrad, 1938), p. 184.

folklore, not with abstract theories of an academic character, but from the viewpoint of social and political interests.

Such, for example, were the historian I. G. Pryzhov and the well known collector of folklore, I. A. Khudyakov.

Pryzhov, who occupied himself with the study of the social history of the masses of the people, who wrote, for example, the well known monographs, "Sketches of the History of Mendicancy in Old Russia," and "History of Public Houses in Russia," [141] was interested, above all, in folklore, in the reflection of the real life of the people, their struggle against the oppression of the Church, the landowners, the power of the tsars.

Pryzhov brought together a vast collection of satirical popular tales directed against the clergy, "Tales of Priests and Monks," which, unfortunately, was destroyed by him, as he himself acknowledged, on the eve of his arrest. He intended, on the basis of the rich material of folklore which he had collected, to write an investigation of "The History of the Institution of Serfdom, Based Chiefly on the Testimony of the People," and a "History of Freedom in Russia." His exile, however, and the difficult condition in which he was placed by the power of the tsars, did not permit him to complete these exceedingly valuable projects.

The other revolutionary democrat who worked in the field of the collection and study of folklore, I. A. Khudyakov, in his approach to folklore, maintained the same attitude, and was animated by the same idea—through folklore, to attain a deeper knowledge of the life of the people. He was also interested in the reflection in folklore of social protest, of class satire, of aspects of the revolutionary movements of the people. Exactly as Pryzhov had done, he collected a great number of anticlerical tales. (They perished at the time when he was searched and arrested.) Khudyakov's collection of *Russian Popular Tales* (Petrograd, 1861), his *Collection of Great-Russian Popular Historical Songs*, his historical essay *Ancient Russia* (a politically acute popular survey of Russian history), and his journalistic survey of the popular world concept on the basis of folklore and the

141 Both recently republished in I. G. Pryzhov's *Sketches, Articles, Letters* (Moscow, Academia, 1933).

landmarks of literature, are very widely known. Folklore was recognized by Khudyakov as being a powerful source of material for agitation.[142]

New and recently revealed data shed light on the activity of one of the best known folklorists of the 1860's—Paul Nikolayevich Rybnikov 1832–1885). His fascination with folk poetry and his enthusiasm as a collector of it have hitherto usually been explained as if due to the influence upon him of Slavophile ideas and personal acquaintance with specific Slavophiles. But, as Klevensky demonstrated convincingly not long ago, that circle of the 1850's, in which, as we already knew, Rybnikov took an active part, bore a definitely revolutionary-democratic character. In his very approach to the collection of folklore at the time of his exile to Petrozavodsk in the 1860's, Rybnikov followed the principles of Dobrolyubov. As Professor Azadovsky has correctly pointed out, Rybnikov, in his collection of folklore, was directly guided by those ideas which had been expressed by Dobrolyubov in his articles. Rybnikov's letters from Petrozavodsk reveal direct echoes of Dobrolyubov's articles.[143]

Rybnikov's introductory article to his collection of *byliny*,[144] and his notes to the texts which he had written down, show how deeply he was interested both in folklore itself and in contemporary life, and in the reflection of this life and of the popular world view in the folk poetry. From this, from the interest in the people, the creator and performer of folklore, there follows also Rybnikov's attention to each individual narrator, to his individual creative personality, to his repertory and style. Rybnikov once wrote to O. F. Miller on the subject of the projected publication of the *byliny* which he had collected:

Concerning this I would have only one request to make of you: everyone who wants to become fully acquainted with the Russian poetry of the *byliny*, must read all the *byliny* of every singer together.

[142] On the folkloristic activity of Pryzhov and Khudyakov in the spirit of revolutionary-democratic ideas, see M. Azadovsky, *Literature and Folklore*, pp. 175-180. See also M. Klevensky, *I. A. Khudyakov, Revolutionary and Scholar* (Moscow, 1921).

[143] See Azadovsky, *op. cit.*, pp. 188-190.

[144] *Songs Collected by P. N. Rybnikov* (1861), No. I, pp. i-xxiv.

There everything is presented to him that is common and characteristic of each narrator, not only as a representative of the people, but in his own particular capacity—on account of which the singer, from the ocean of songs, has chosen a certain wave of *byliny*.[145]

Unfortunately, the publication was carried out by the Slavophile P. A. Bessonov, and he disregarded this request of the collector; but soon this sound principle was, as we know, made an integral part of editorial practice by A. F. Hilferding. (The arrangement of Rybnikov's collection was reorganized according to this plan when the second edition came out in 1911.[146])

Alexander Fyodorovich Hilferding (1831–1872) made a name for himself in scholarship because of his works in the field of folklore. In 1871 he made a journey in search of *byliny*, the result of which was the recording of 318 texts; the care with which they were done and their philological accuracy have now been confirmed by new expeditions to the Olenets region. The great merit of A. F. Hilferding is that he was the first to apply the principle of arranging folklore material according to the narrator, and that he gave careful attention to every performer of the *byliny*. After Hilferding, the study of the repertory of the narrators, the gathering of information as to their biographies and the characteristics of the creative work of each of them, became one of the basic rules for folklorists. In the prefatory article to his collection, *The Province of Olenets and Its Popular Rhapsodists*, Hilferding pointed out the close connection between epic creations and the conditions of nature in the north, the peculiarities of social life, and, in particular, of the work of the northern peasantry.[147]

[145] See Azadovsky, *op. cit.*, p. 192.

[146] *Songs Collected bv P N. Rybnikov*, 2nd ed., A. E. Gruzinsky, ed., Vols. I-III (Moscow, 1909–1910).

[147] The majority of the works of Hilferding (with the exception of his philological treatises) has been reprinted in the four volumes of his *Collected Works* (1868–1874); the *Onega Byliny* were published twice: in one volume (St. Petersburg, 1873), and in three volumes (St. Petersburg, 1894–1900), appearing as Vols. LIX-LXI of the *Annals of the Division of Russian Language and Literature of the Academy of Sciences;* a detailed index, compiled by N. V. Vasilyev, is included in the second number of Vol. LXI. On the life and scientific activity of A. F. Hilferding, see the detailed index given by S. A. Vengerov, in *Sources for a*

And in general it must be said, that it is not only on this particular question that there is revealed the influence of principles which were introduced into folkloristics by the representatives of the revolutionary democracy of the 1860's. It is revealed in the whole practice of the collective work of the folklorists of the second half of the nineteenth century and the beginning of the twentieth.

The collective activity of the Russian folklorists took its course precisely according to this plan. And in the case of those collectors, who happened to be at the same time also investigators of folklore, there frequently arose a manifest divergence between the principles of their collective work, and theoretical and historical constructions, when a question arose concerning the elucidation of folklore.

The increases in the collection and publication of folklore are closely connected with the awakening and development of revolutionary-democratic tendencies in Russian public opinion.

If the first outburst of enthusiasm for the collection of the productions of popular creative art was closely linked, as we have seen, with the awakening of public interest in the problems of the people at the beginning of the 1830's (see above, in the discussion of romanticism and of the activity of P. V. Kireyevsky and N. M. Yazykov), then the second such period of deep public interest in folklore must be regarded as existing in the late 1850's and the 1860's.

The social revival of that time, the manifest development of democratic tendencies, in journalism, literature, and in science—all this, in the most beneficent manner, is expressed in the development of geographical, ethnographic, and folkloristic interests. The life of the country, the material and spiritual life of the popular masses, became the center of public attention. The Geographic Society, organized in 1846, soon opened branches at various points throughout the country.

The Geographic Society includes a Division of Ethnography, sends numerous scientific expeditions to various sites, publishes pro-

Lexicon of Russian Writers, Vol. I (St. Petersburg, 1900); Bestuzhev-Ryumin, introductory article to the 2nd ed. of the first volume of *Onega Byliny; Russian Antiquity*, No. 10, 1872, article by M. Semenovsky; *Russian Biographical Lexicon* (Moscow, 1916), article by Academician P. Lavrov; the magazine *Artistic Folklore* (Moscow, 1927), Bks. 2-3, article by Y. Sokolov.

grams for the collection of materials, preserves them in systematic order in its archives,[148] and publishes many of them in its various publications. A large place is assigned to folklore. A great deal of folklore material has been published in the *Annals of the Historical-Geographical Society for the Division of Ethnography*. When in 1858 A. N. Afanasyev undertook the publication of his tales, the Geographic Society turned over to him its collection, including the compilation made by V. I. Dal. In the 1860's extensive publishing activity in folklore began to be developed by the old Society of Lovers of Russian Literature in Moscow. In 1860–1874 it published, under the editorship of P. A. Bessonov, *Songs Collected by P. V. Kireyevsky* (ten issues); in 1861–1867 it published the *Songs Collected by P. N. Rybnikov*, which have been mentioned above. In 1861–1864 Bessonov was commissioned by the society to edit a collection of Russian religious verse (six issues), *Vagrant Beggars*.

In general, the 1860's and the 1870's are distinguished by a very large number of publications of folklore. This exceptionally powerful surge of interest in oral poetry reflected the revolutionary-democratic tendencies of the period. One of the outstanding figures among the collectors was P. I. Yakushkin (1820–1870).[149]

In the field of folklore, a series of remarkable discoveries was being made. The most important of these was the discovery by Rybnikov, soon confirmed by Hilferding, of a living epic tradition in the Olenets region. In the 1860's the work of collection was developed by a teacher in a theological seminary, E. V. Barsov (later the author of the extensive study, *The Tale of Igor's Raid as an Artistic Monument of the Kiev Druzhina Period in Old Russia*). He published the widely known *Laments of the Northern Region* (Vol. I, *Funeral Laments*, 1872; Vol. II, *Soldiers' Laments*, 1882; Vol. III, *Wedding Laments*, 1886); the greater part of the lamentations Barsov

---

[148] In 1914–1916 there appeared, in three volumes, a *Description of the MSS in the Scientific Archives of the Russian Geographical Society*, comp. by D. K. Zelenin.

[149] See *Works of P. I. Yakushkin*, with a portrait of the author, his biography by S. V. Maksimov, and personal recollections of him (St. Petersburg, 1884); also A. N. Pypin, *History of Russian Ethnography*, Vol. II (St. Petersburg, 1891), pp. 65-67; B. M. Sokolov, *Collectors of Russian Popular Songs* (Moscow, 1923).

wrote down from the famous wailing-woman, Orina Fedosovaya. The indefatigable collector and democrat (district teacher), P. V. Shein (1826–1900), began his work in this same period.[150] In 1859 his first small collection of songs appeared; in 1870, the large collection, *Russian Popular Songs, Collected by P. V. Shein* (published by the Society of Russian History and Antiquities at Moscow University). Later he occupied himself with the collection of White Russian * folklore, and toward the end of his life he published the well known collection, *The Great-Russian in His Ceremonies and Songs* (published by Academy of Sciences, St. Petersburg, 1900–1902, two parts in one volume).

In 1861 there was published the *Collection of Russian Religious Verse* of V. Varentsov; in 1869, the *Great-Russian Incantations*, by L. Maykov. In 1863 there appeared *Popular Russian Tales*, collected by the rural teachers of the province of Tula, under the editorship of A. Erlenvein.

In the ensuing decades the work of collection in the field of folklore was already being developed according to a national plan. There appeared *Tales and Traditions of the Samara Region*, by D. Sadovnikov (St. Petersburg, 1884); *Songs of the Russian People*, collected in the provinces of Archangel and Olonets, in 1886, by F. M. Istomin and T. O. Deutsch (St. Petersburg, 1894), and *Songs of the Russian People*, collected in 1893 in the Vologda, Vyatka, and Kostroma provinces by F. I. Istomin and S. M. Lyapunov (St. Petersburg, 1899).

At the very end of the nineteenth century and the beginning of the twentieth, the activities of the collectors were again renewed. But the collection was directed mainly toward that poetic genre which held the center of interest in the "historical school"—which was then supreme in folklore—namely, toward the *byliny*.

A. V. Markov, A. D. Gregoryev, and N. E. Onchukov started off on an expedition to the White Sea after *byliny*. The *byliny* which they had collected were published successively (by A. V. Markov

[150] See B. M. Sokolov, *Collectors of Russian Popular Songs* (1923).
* White Russian is used throughout for Byelorussian.—ED.

in 1901, by A. D. Gregoryev in 1904 and 1910, and by N. E. On-chukov in 1904).

If the main task of the collectors was the discovery of new texts which could be helpful in the work of the representatives of the "historical school," toward reconstructing the history of specific *byliny*, then the actual practice of collection was carried on accord-ing to the tradition established in the 1860's, the beginning of which was laid down by Rybnikov and Hilferding.

Thus the collections were prefaced by lengthy articles with a de-scription of the natural and economic conditions of life in the region, with biographies (which constantly grew more and more detailed) of individual narrators, with accounts of the characteristic repertory and poetic style of each of them, and so forth. The legacy of Dobrol-yubov had entered deeply into the practice of the collectors' work on folklore, in spite of the fact that in the investigations made, for ex-ample, by V. Miller and A. Veselovsky, these observations of the col-lectors as to the actual life of the epos of the *byliny*, and of its bear-ers, were utilized only to a relatively small degree. The result was that divergence between theory and practice of which we have al-ready spoken.

Still more detailed, fuller, and more thorough was the illumina-tion, in the works devoted to the collection and publication of the tales, of the popular life of the region which was being examined as a whole, and also the life and creative activity of individual masters of the popular art.

In 1909 there appeared *Northern Tales*, by Onchukov; in 1914, *Great-Russian Tales from the Province of Perm*, by D. K. Zelenin; in 1915, the same author's *Great-Russian Tales from the Province of Vyatka*; in 1915, *Tales and Songs of the Belo-Ozero Region*, by B. and Y. Sokolov. The last book is an attempt to embrace all the diverse aspects of folklore, all the oral poetic genres which existed at that time in the region chosen for study. The purpose of the col-lectors was to give, so far as possible, a full presentation of the popu-lar creative work and of the popular life which was reflected in it.

The very tasks—to see, through folklore, how the vast masses of the people live—were, in the last analysis, the same as those of the publishers of popular rhymes, that genre of folklore which, with the greatest detail and exactness, responded to contemporary life. In 1914 there appeared the large collection of *Great-Russian Folk Rhymes*, under the editorship of E. N. Yeleonskaya, and in 1913 the still larger collection of *Folk Rhymes* by V. I. Simakov.

Toward the revolutionary era, the collections of Russian folklore attain vast dimensions. I have mentioned only the most important collections, and besides, have dealt almost exclusively with Russian (Great-Russian) folklore. But a truly colossal work has also been accomplished in the collection of Ukrainian and White Russian folklore. Considerably more feeble has been the collection of the folklore of other nationalities of the former Russian Empire, but even of this, a great deal has been collected (though it is true that the distribution is unequal). It must not be forgotten, either, that the work of collection has been carried on at various places, and that, besides, not all of the material by far has been gathered into the central archives of folklore. Much of the folklore material has been published in local periodical publications: government reports, diocesan reports, in "notebooks" of the zemstvos, in government statistical annals.

The folklore materials flowed to the capitals (St. Petersburg and Moscow), not only into the already-mentioned Russian Geographic Society in St. Petersburg and the Society of Lovers of Russian Literature in Moscow, but also into the Ethnographic Division of the Society of Natural History, Anthropology, and Ethnography in Moscow and into the Division of Russian Language and Literature of the Academy of Sciences in St. Petersburg.

Folklore materials and researches appeared in the following publications: in the magazines *Ethnographic Review* in Moscow (1889–1916), *The Living Past* in St. Petersburg (1891–1916); in the *Annals of the Division of Russian Language and Literature of the Academy of Sciences* (since 1867), and in the *News* of the same division (since 1852); in *Reports of the Russian Geographic Society* of the Division of Ethnography (since 1867), and in the reports of the regional branches of the society; in the magazines *Russian Philological News* (1879–1917) in Warsaw, *Antiquities of Kiev* (1882–1906) in Kiev, *Philological Reports* (since 1860) in Voronezh, and elsewhere.

All this tremendous amount of folklore material, collected in the prerevolutionary period, had not been brought together. There was not even anything like a full bibliography of folklore. In reference to specific poetic genres, there had been attempts at unification. Thus, for the convenience of investigators, there had been republished from manuscripts and from provincial publications *Russian Byliny from Old and New Recordings*, under the editorship of N. S. Tikhonravov and V. F. Miller (Moscow, 1894); *Byliny from New and Recent Records*, under the editorship of V. F. Miller (Moscow, 1908). In 1915 there was published, also under Miller's editorship, a large volume, *Historical Songs of the Russian People of the Sixteenth and Seventeenth Centuries* (*Annals of the Division of Russian Language and Literature of the Academy of Sciences*, Vol. 93), which brought together all the versions of historical songs that had been written down until that time. In the years 1895 to 1902, Academician A. I. Sobolevsky published seven volumes of *Great-Russian Folk Songs*, reprinted from various kinds of songbooks, collections (with the exception of such large works as the *Great-Russian* of Shein, and so on), and provincial periodical publications. Such collections of the material which had formerly been scattered through various publications of course facilitate the work of the investigators; but on the whole, the number of such collections is still not nearly sufficient.

So we have arrived, in our survey of the development of prerevolutionary science, at the threshold of the Great October Socialist Revolution.

In the first years following the revolution, the folklorists' work of collection was to a certain degree suspended, but thereafter it was very widely developed, and in the past few years has attained previously unprecedented dimensions. In comparison with the prerevolutionary period, there has been a considerable broadening of the object of collecting. In addition to the peasant folklore, people began, in a much greater degree than before, to collect folklore of the factories and mills, folklore of the city; and expeditions began to be specially fitted out for the collection of craftsmen's folklore (the folklore of fishermen, and so forth); the collecting began to be handled so that it would reveal the dynamics of folklore, the changes which took place in it as a result of changes in the social-economic life; people began with great energy to conduct searches for folklore which reflected the revolutionary movements of the earlier time; great discoveries were made in the folklore of hitherto oppressed nationalities.

The institutions for scientific research, which have also directed methodical work in the collection of folklore, have been, during the past few years as follows: in Moscow, the Folklore Section of the State Academy of Fine Arts (from 1923 to 1930), which, under the direction of Professor Y. M. Sokolov, with the reorganization of the State Academy of Fine Arts into the State Academy of Artistic Studies, had its name changed to the Folklore Office of the State Academy of Artistic Studies (from 1930 to 1931). From 1932 to the present time the center, which has united the work of the folklorists in Moscow, has been the Folklore Section of the Union of Soviet Authors.

In Leningrad, from 1924 to 1926, the Section on Peasant Art, in the State Institute of the History of Arts, was active. From 1928 on, there was a broad development of the activity of the Folklore Section of the Institute for the Study of Nationalities * of the Academy of Sciences of the USSR, which was merged in 1933 with the Institute of Anthropology and Ethnography. In 1937 the Folklore Section was renamed the Folklore Commission, and is under the direction of Professor M. K. Azadovsky. In Leningrad, under the presidency of the Academician S. F. Oldenburg, the Commission on Tales of the Division of Ethnography of the Russian Geographic Society worked energetically. (See the *Commission on Tales: Survey of Works for 1924–1925, 1926–1927, 1927–1928.*)

Among provincial cities the work has been widely developed in Irkutsk, where it was under the direction of Professor M. K. Azadovsky (from 1923 to 1930); in Saratov, under Professor B. M. Sokolov (from

* The Russian letters IPIN are used as the abbreviation of this Institute.—ED.

1919 to 1924), and thereafter, since 1925, under Professor A. P. Shaf-tymov; in Kalinin (Tver), from 1919 to 1930, under Professor Y. M. Sokolov, then under Professor A. M. Smirnov-Kutachevsky; in Smo-lensk (since 1930), under Professor P. M. Sobolev. Important work in the collection and study of folklore is being carried on in the principal cities of the national provinces and republics.

News of the work of collection, and also researches and materials, have appeared in the following publications (the old ones, already mentioned, ceased publication soon after the revolution): *Artistic Folklore,* the organ of the Folklore Subsection of the Literary Section of the State Academy of Fine Arts, under the editorship of Y. M. Soko-lov, No. I, 1926; Nos. II-III, 1927; Nos. IV-V, 1929; *The Living Past of Siberia,* under the editorship of M. K. Azadovsky and G. S. Vino-gradov (from 1926 to 1929); *Ethnography* (from 1926 to 1929), under the editorship of Academician S. F. Oldenburg and of Professor B. M. Sokolov, reorganized in 1931 as *Soviet Ethnography,* which is still being published.

In 1934 the Folklore Section of the Academy of Sciences began to issue its annals, *Soviet Folklore,* with materials and researches, under the editorship of M. K. Azadovsky. The following numbers have ap-peared: No. I in 1934; Nos. II-III in 1936, Nos. IV-V in 1937.

Articles on folklore are to be found also in the magazines *Literature and Marxism* (1928–1930), *The Literary Critic* (since 1934); *The Star* (since 1935), *The Literary Review* (since 1936), *Studies in Liter-ature* (since 1936), *Folk Creation* (since 1936).

The vast accumulated materials of folklore for the Soviet period, which had been brought into the Folklore Section of the State Acad-emy of Arts and Sciences and the Folklore Office of the State Acad-emy of Fine Arts, have now been transferred to the Folklore Division of the State Literary Museum in Moscow. The Folklore Commission of the Institute of Ethnography of the Academy of Sciences possesses a very rich archive and library of records on folklore.

The Geographic Society also continues to accumulate materials on folklore in its archives.

The vast majority of the materials collected during the revolutionary period is still being classified. Only an insignificant part of these has as yet been published.[151]

In what direction has folkloristics developed during the twenty years of the Soviet regime?

At first the work in folkloristics continued to develop, following the line of least resistance, according to the same plan which it had followed in the prerevolutionary years. The ruling trend was, as formerly, that of the historical school. It is characteristic that in 1919 there appeared the second volume of *Russian Byliny*, published by Sabashnikov, with commentaries by Professor M. N. Speransky; in 1918 there appeared a collection of selected *byliny*, compiled by B. M. Sokolov. The commentaries were given in a spirit typical of the representatives of the historical school. The teaching in the higher educational

[151] M. K. Azadovsky has published a *Collection of Tales of the Upper Lena Region* (Irkutsk, 1924), which came out in a new edition in 1938, and also, under his editorship, there appeared a collection, *Tales from Various Parts of Siberia* (Irkutsk, 1926). We may mention also the Northern tales of O. E. Ozarovskaya, *The Five Rivers* (Leningrad, 1931); *Northern Tales*, by I. V. Karnaukhovaya (Moscow, Academia, 1934); *Tales of Kuprianikha*, written down by A. M. Novikovaya and I. A. Ossovetsky (Voronezh, 1937); *Tales of the White Sea, Told by Korguyev*, in the transcript of A. N. Nechavev (Leningrad, 1937). The State Literary Museum is preparing editions of the *Tales of I. F. Kovalev*, in the transcript of E. V. Hoffmann and S. I. Mintz; the Peasant Section of the State Institute of the History of Arts has published the results of its complex expeditions to the North in two issues of the annals, *Peasant Art* (Leningrad, Academia, 1927–1928). The State Literary Museum is preparing for publication *Byliny of the Onega Region*, collected by the expedition of the State Academy of Artistic Sciences in 1926–1928, under the direction of B. and Y. Sokolov; A. M. Astakhova is preparing an edition of *Northern Byliny*; the State Literary Museum is preparing for publication the *Byliny of M. S. Krukovaya*, in the transcript of R. S. Lipetz and E. G. Morozovaya. Of considerable significance are the publications on juvenile folklore: O. Kapitsa, *Juvenile Folklore* (Leningrad, *The Breakers*, 1928), and G. S. Vinogradov, *Juvenile Folklore and Modes of Life* (Irkutsk, 1925); G. S. Vinogradov, *Juvenile Satirical Tales* (Irkutsk, 1925). In late years there have begun to appear complex collections of the folklore of this or that territory. Such, for example, are *Folklore of the Volga* (Moscow, 1937), compiled by V. U. Krupyanskaya and V. M. Sidelnikov; *Prerevolutionary Folklore in the Urals*, collected and compiled by V. P. Biryukov (Sverdlovsk, 1936); *Songs of the Don Cossacks* (Stalingrad, Kravchenko, 1938). There are in preparation a collection of *Songs of the Voronezh Territory*, compiled by A. M. Novikovaya and Ossovetsky; *Folklore of the Yaroslav Territory*, V. Y. Krupyanskaya and V. M. Sidelnikov, eds.; *Folklore of the Gorky Territory*, by N. D. Komovskaya, and a number of other publications.

A great deal of attention has been paid to the popularization of the productions of folklore. With this aim, there has been published a series of collections with a

institutions also entered into this plan. Up to 1920, under wartime conditions, the folklorists could not undertake any expeditionary work. The new methods to be used in folk creation itself were only in the planning stage, and that not with sufficient clearness.

In the theoretical sphere, however, the impending crisis was already felt.

Voices were heard in criticism directed against the "historical school" of V. Miller, the "anthropological (ethnographical) school," and the "historical poetics" of A. Veselovsky.

The first blows were struck by the representatives of various degrees of formalism, which at that time played a very marked role in the study of literature. Thus V. Shklovsky criticized the explanation of the resemblance of subjects, which had been offered by the "anthropological school," and later by A. Veselovsky and V. Miller.[152]

The formalists, however, paid comparatively little attention to the questions of folklore. In addition to Shklovsky, mention must also be made of O. Brik, who analyzed the repetition of sounds in popular proverbs and riddles,[153] and especially of Professor V. M. Zhirmunsky, who worked out, from the principles of formalism, the specific prob-

---

reprinting of previously collected texts and a publication of new ones: thematic collections of tales, *The Priest and the Peasant* (1931), *The Nobleman and the Peasant* (1932), by Y. M. Sokolov; *Russian Popular Tales, Selected by a Craftsman*, 2 vols. (1932), by M. K. Azadovsky; *Riddles* (1932), by M. A. Rybnikovaya. In Saratov there appeared a book by A. N. Lozanovaya, *Songs of Stepan Razin* (1928), presenting an investigation and collection of all the songs hitherto known about Razin. In 1935 she issued, in the publication *Academia*, a collection of *Songs and Legends of Stepan Razin and of Pugachyov*. In various publications there have appeared many popular rhymes, recently taken down. A good deal of interest and controversy was called forth by the appearance of the book by S. Mirer and V. Borovik, *The Revolution*, tales of working people dealing with the citizens' war (Moscow, 1931). Another collection, compiled by the same authors, is *Tales of Working People Dealing with V. I. Lenin*, with a foreword by N. K. Krupskaya and an introductory article by Yemelian Yaroslavsky (Party Publishing House, Moscow, 1934).

The most outstanding publication of Soviet folklore, having the greatest social significance, is the collection, *Creative Works of the Peoples of the USSR*, published in 1937 by the editorial offices of *Pravda* to mark the completion of twenty years of Soviet power.

152 V. Shklovsky, "The Relationship Between Devices for the Development of Subjects and General Stylistic Devices, Ethnographic School," in the annals *Poetics*, No. II, St. Petersburg, 1919.

153 O. Brik, "Repetition of Sounds," in *Poetics*, No. I, St. Petersburg, 1919.

lems of the poetics of folklore—rhythm and versification.[154] In spite
of the fact that he started from formalistic principles, Professor Zhirmunsky still made a number of valuable observations in a field which
up to that time had been very slightly worked. It must surely be borne
in mind that the earlier works in the field of the poetics of Russian
folklore (the works of A. N. Veselovsky and A. A. Potebnya) had
dealt mainly with questions of subjects, motifs, composition, and
artistic forms, and had barely touched the problem of verse and sound
in folklore.

On a formalistic plan (but still with a profound difference from
the methods of A. N. Veselovsky) there were executed the works of
the Odessa scholar, R. M. Volkov,[155] and the Leningrad folklorist
V. Propp,[156] devoted to the question of the correlation of subject and
motifs in the popular tale. The influence of formal-artistic principles
was also expressed at that time, to a certain degree, in the works of
B. M. Sokolov, devoted to the poetics of folklore, but none the less,
rich in fresh and valuable observations on onomatopoeia in the *byliny*
and methods of composition in the popular lyric.[157]

However, I repeat, formalism did not attain a broad development
in folkloristics.

The basic line followed by the development of Soviet folkloristics
was the line of gradual mastery of the principles and methods of
Marxism-Leninism, though with frequent divergences, unevennesses,
and excesses.

Under the pressure of social life itself, investigations in folkloristics
passed beyond the limits of a narrow and impractical academism.

This was expressed, above all, in the awakening desire to study not
only the manifestations of the folklore of the remote past, but also
the manifestations of contemporary life; to observe the processes

[154] V. M. Zhirmunsky, "Rhythm in the *Bylina*," *Rhythm, Its History and
Theory* (1923); *Introduction to Metrics: The Theory of Verse* (Leningrad, 1925),
Par. 34; *Russian Popular Verse*.
[155] R. M. Volkov, The Tale. Researches on the *Development of Subjects of the
Popular Tale*, Vol. I (Odessa, 1924).
[156] V. Propp, *Morphology of the Tale* (Leningrad, 1928).
[157] B. M. Sokolov, "Excursus into the Field of the Poetics of Russian Folklore,"
Artistic Folklore, Vol. I, Moscow, 1926.

occurring in the poetic creative work of the Soviet countryside and the Soviet town; to mark the reflection in folklore of decisive changes in the popular self-consciousness, the mode of life, customs, and tastes, as the result of changes introduced by the socialist revolution into the economic structure of the country and into its social relationships.

Thus, gradually, the collection of folklore was developed from new points of view, and not only special staffs of scientific folklorists, but also students, teachers, regional students, writers, and members of literary circles on collective farms and factories or mills, took a great part in this work.[158]

There has been a great development of folklore expeditions, not only individual, but in particular collective undertakings, organized by research institutes and museums in Moscow (the State Academy of Fine Arts, the State Academy of Artistic Studies, the State Literary Museum, the Folklore Section of the Union of Soviet Writers, the Chair of Folklore of the State Institute of History, Philosophy, and Literature), in Leningrad (the State Historical Institute, the Folklore Section of the Academy of Sciences of the USSR), in the republics (Karelian, Mordvinian, Mari, Uzbek, Kazakh, Kirghiz), and by provincial publishing houses and other organizations (at Voronezh, Archangel, Azov on the Black Sea, and others).

The materials which have been collected have not only added to the store of the archives of folklore, but for the most part have swiftly become known (if only in their general features) to the whole Soviet public, thanks to the great cooperation in the work of folkloristics on the part of the central and local periodical press.

First in order, naturally, to attract the attention of the Soviet public has been that part of the collected materials which reflected Soviet

[158] See the detailed discussion of this point in the book by B. and Y. Sokolov, *Poetry of the Countryside: A Guide to the Collection of the Productions of Oral Literature* (Moscow, 1926). See also Y. M. Sokolov, "What Is Folklore?" *Library for Literary Circles on Collective Farms* (*The Peasant Gazette*, Moscow, 1935); Y. M. Sokolov, "Folklore and Regional Study," *Soviet Regional Study*, No. 1, 1933; V. M. Sidelnikov and V. U. Krupyanskaya, *The Folklorist's Companion*, Y. M. Sokolov (Moscow, State Literary Museum, 1938). The last-named book gives directions not only as to the collection of folklore material, but also as to the methods of classifying it, and a rational way of preserving it.

life, the reorganization of the consciousness of the people, the growth of socialist culture.

The folklorist-collectors, and also the folklorist-investigators, have isolated those productions of Soviet folklore which constituted an effective means of agitation and propaganda for Communist ideas.

Never, in all the history of Russia, has the oral poetic word served the social aims so broadly and powerfully as in the Soviet period. Soviet folkloristics has helped to reveal the agitational and propagandist significance of folklore. And thereby, Soviet folkloristics has firmly allied itself with the practical tasks of our social life. Here has come the full realization of those principles which, as we have seen, were already put forward by the representatives of the revolutionary democracy in the 1860's.

In Soviet folkloristics a great deal of attention has been devoted to such themes of contemporary folklore as the civil war (among other things, partisans' songs have been collected which are of great historical significance), the stages of development of the socialist organization, the collectivization of the rural economy, the new mode of life in its contrast with the old, the defense of the country, and the life of the Red Army; and the folklorists have studied with especial attention the figures of the great leaders of the socialist revolution—Lenin and Stalin—as depicted in the productions of popular oral creative work.[159]

With reference to the folklore of the past, there has come about in Soviet folkloristics a marked shifting of the center of attention, as compared with that of scholarship previous to the October Revolution.

There has been a wide development of the collection and study of those productions of the old folklore which for the most part were left in obscurity by the investigators of the prerevolutionary period; those in which, with the greatest clearness and vigor, there were reflected the revolutionary movements of the popular masses, the class conflict with their oppressors, and all kinds of popular protest against social injustice: songs and legends about Stepan Razin and Pu-

[159] For a more detailed discussion of all these points, see the chapter devoted to Soviet folklore.

gachyov,[160] tales, songs, stories about serfdom,[161] tales, songs, and proverbs of an anticlerical and antireligious character,[162] and so forth.

The work of Soviet folklorists on the study of the factory and mill, folklore of the period preceding the October Revolution, which had been almost completely ignored by the earlier investigators and collectors, should be considered one of the greatest contributions to the scholarship of folk creation.

At the present time, mainly by means of recordings made of veteran workers, it has been possible to fill in the gaps which previously existed in our material.

There has been a great enrichment of our information on the history of the revolutionary songs of the people, both those of folklore and also those of literary origin, and their influence on the song repertory of the people. Significant progress has been made in the treatment of the question of the mutual influences of folklore and artistic literature from the eighteenth to the twentieth century.

If in Soviet folkloristics the basic attention has been directed toward the manifestations of folklore in the contemporary period or in relatively recent times, nevertheless the field of the more ancient folklore has not been left outside the scope of study. The treatment of questions of the primary stages of development of oral poetry has been greatly influenced by the "new doctrine of language" of the Academician Nikolay Yakovlevich Marr. The method of "paleontological analysis," which Marr applied with such success to linguistic phenomena, he more than once adapted to the phenomena of the folklore of various nations.

In general, Marr, working mainly in the field of philology, at the

---

[160] See the above-mentioned publications by A. N. Lozanovaya, the article by Prof. N. K. Piksanov, "The Social-Political Destiny of the Songs About Stepan Razin," *Artistic Folklore*, Vol. I, 1926; M. Yakovlev, *Popular Songs about the Commander Stepan Razin* (Leningrad, 1924).

[161] See the publication of tales, *The Nobleman and the Peasant*, by Y. M. Sokolov; *Folklore of the Volga*, by V. U. Krupyanskaya and V. M. Sidelnikov, and many others.

[162] See the collection of tales, *The Priest and The Peasant*, by Y. M. Sokolov, the article by Prof. N. P. Andreyev, "Folklore and the Antireligious Conflict," *The Militant Atheist* (1931), Bk. 12, and also the numerous publications of anticlerical and antireligious folklore in the collections of folklore, in antireligious publications, and in general periodical literature.

same time made extensive use of the data of related sciences—archaeology, ethnography, and folkloristics—for the solution of many general theoretical and historico-linguistic problems.

This characteristic feature of Marr's scholarly activity is explained by the inherent peculiarities of his linguistic theory. His "new doctrine of Language" dealt a crushing blow to so-called "Indo-European" comparative linguistics. The blow was dealt against three things: Marr rebelled against the nationalistic narrowness of Indo-European studies, which were limited to the study of a comparatively small circle of the languages of Europe and of a certain portion of the Near East; he rebelled also against formalistic comparativism, that favorite method of Indo-European scholars, with their doctrine of the "parent language," artificially reinforced, mainly by the method of comparisons of phonetics and grammatical forms; he rebelled against the ignoring of the basic element in language—the aspect of its meaning, semantics.

An outstanding expert on the numerous languages and dialects of his native land, the Caucasus, and also on many languages of the West and the East, Marr was inspired by the idea of the establishment of a single linguistic, or, as he expressed it, "glottogonic" process. He was interested in the possibility of establishing general laws for the development of human speech since the most ancient times. In these searchings after conformity to some established principle in the development of human speech, there is something that connects Marr's doctrine with the theory of A. N. Veselovsky, who sought to establish a conformity to established principles in the development of the poetry of all mankind, without distinction as to race or tribe. It may be considered as definitely established, that we have here not an accidental coincidence, but, to a considerable degree, a reflection of the direct influence of Veselovsky's theory upon Marr's scholarly activity.[163] The latter, like Veselovsky, was first of all interested in problems of origin, the source of phenomena (with Marr, these were linguistic; with Veselovsky, poetic).

[163] See, on this point, the article by Prof. V. F. Shishmarev, "N. Y. Marr and A. N. Veselovsky," in the collection, *Language and Thought*, No. VIII (Moscow-Leningrad, Institute of Language and Thought, bearing the name of N. Y. Marr, Academy of Sciences of the USSR, 1937).

Centering his attention mainly on the semantic (meaningful) aspect of the word, Marr traced the origin and development of words, in the closest connection with the origin of concepts and ideas. But that which distinguishes Marr from Veselovsky, and especially from Potebnya, and furthermore from Afanasyev, M. Miller, the Grimms, and all the "mythologists," is the acknowledgment of the very close connection between the development of human language and thought (forms and ideas) and the development of the economic and social life of mankind.

After the Great October Socialist Revolution, a profound study of the works of Marx, Engels, Lenin, and Stalin equipped Marr with a clear, distinct understanding of the laws of development of human culture, and gave to his structures that materialistic basis, the absence of which had rendered so insecure the structures of very many of the prominent theorists in language and literature, who were still tied to bourgeois idealistic theories.

In the light of the ideas of a single glottogonic process and the principle of stages of progress, an altogether new appearance was given also to those "relicts," or "cultural survivals," which, as we have seen, were emphasized in human language and creative work even by the representatives of the English "anthropologial school." Already, it was not the reference to abstract generalizations of human psychology, but the connection of this or that word, and of the concepts expressed by them, with the concrete conditions of social life at various stages of its economic development, and with the state of thought corresponding to them, which constituted the basis of that scientific method, which Marr called "paleontological analysis." This paleontological analysis of the semantic phenomena of language, by its very nature, was interwoven in the closest manner, in Marr's works, with the attraction of the data of archaeology, ethnography, and folklore.

Exceedingly significant, in this connection, is Marr's noteworthy linguistic-mythological investigation, *Ishtar*, which has the characteristic subtitle: "From the Matriarchal Goddess Afrevrasia to the Romantic Heroine of Feudal Europe." [164] In this work, which, like many

[164] Originally published in Vol. V of the *Japhetic Collection*, and reprinted in Vol. III of the *Selected Works* of N. Y. Marr.

of Marr's other works, is striking for the incredible breadth of knowledge which it displays of the history of the most diverse languages and cultures, there is an examination of the process of gradual change of concepts and ideas, which have been expressed at various stages of human social thought, under the name of the Babylonian goddess Ishtar, the Egyptian Isis, the Kabardian and Ossetic Satanya, and finally of the heroine of the medieval legends of western Europe, Isolde.

No less curious and instructive are Marr's researches on the history of the myth of Prometheus, which, according to his opinion, appears significantly as a much later stage in the development of that figure which is known in more primitive forms in the Caucasian legends of Amiran. "For us the mythical Prometheus, with whom the Greeks connected the invention of fire, the stealing of it from heaven, is a very young man from the viewpoint of the evolution of human culture. He is not far from the time of origin of the so-called 'Indo-European' race itself, which in linguistic relationships is a very late formation." [165]

N. Y. Marr, by his paleontological analysis, penetrates into the most remote epochs of human consciousness, affirms the existence of an original period of nonreligious thought, and reveals the exceedingly protracted process of the formation of myths.

His scholarly legacy, by virtue of the extreme complexity of his method, which demands, moreover, the mobilization of a vast and many-sided linguistic material, and also by virtue of the boundless breadth of its theoretical and historical scope, has as yet been insufficiently studied and mastered, even by specialists in philology. Soviet folkloristics has as yet done very little toward the mastery and popularization of the ideas and methods of the great scholar in their application to its special tasks.[166] But the whole character of Marr's scientific and creative activity indicates that there are very broad horizons ex-

---

[165] N. Y. Marr, "On the Question of Primitive Thought in Connection with Language," *Selected Works*, Vol. III, p. 84.

[166] Of the articles devoted to the folkloristic interests of N. Y. Marr, I can mention only one, the article by Prof. M. K. Azadovsky, "To the Memory of N. Y. Marr," in the annals *Soviet Folklore*, Nos. 2-3, 1935.

tended before Soviet folkloristics through the extensive and deep mastery of the methodology of Marr.[167]

Several of Marr's students formed, in the Institute of Language and Thought (IYM) of the Academy of Sciences of the USSR, the Section of Semantics, Myth and Folklore, working under the guidance of Professor I. G. Frank-Kamenetsky. From 1929 to 1932 the section was working out the special problem of the origin of the subject on which is based the famous medieval French romance, *Tristan and Isolde*. As a result of the application of paleontological analysis, the scientific association of the section uncovered in this subject survivals of a cosmic myth of the union of the sun and water, and established in the folklore of a number of peoples the various stages of development of the myth under consideration. The results of these investigations were published in the book, *Tristan and Isolde*.[168]

But Marr's students were too one-sided in accepting the ideas of their famous teacher, who was distinguished, as is well known, by the exceptional breadth of his scholarly and social views; and they were so fascinated by the search for ancient "survivals," or "relicts," in the productions of literature and folklore, that they began, in general, to reduce the whole of folklore to these survivals of an ancient world concept, to "relicts," to "survivals." The majority of Soviet folklorists, however, decisively rebelled against such a narrow concept of folklore, a concept which ignored precisely that actual social significance which, as we have seen, was revealed with particular vividness by Soviet folkloristics. At a debate organized in Leningrad in 1932, the propositions defended by Professor I. G. Frank-Kamenetsky, Professor O. M. Freidenberg, and in part by Professor V. M. Zhirmunsky,[169] were opposed

[167] His scientific heritage has been assembled in the five volumes of his *Selected Works* (Moscow-Leningrad, 1933–1937).

[168] *Tristan and Isolde* (Works of the Institute of Language and Thought, collective work of the Section of Semantics, Myth and Folklore), Academician N. Y. Marr, ed. (Leningrad, Academy of Sciences of the USSR, 1932). Besides the works dealing with Tristan and Isolde, the members of the section have published a series of articles of the same type.

[169] These views have been set forth with great fullness by V. M. Zhirmunsky, in the article "The Problem of Folklore," in the collection in honor of the Academician S. F. Oldenburg (Leningrad, 1933).

by Professor M. K. Azadovsky, Professor N. P. Andreyev, A. M. Asta-khova, and others.[170]

According to the measure of development of Soviet folkloristics, other fallacious theories were also subjected to critical examination. Thus, as early as 1933, in a paper read by Y. M. Sokolov in the MOGAIMK (Moscow Division of the State Academy of the History of Material Culture) and in the Folklore Section of the Academy of Sciences of the USSR, in Leningrad, a drastic critical review was given of the "theory" of Hans Naumann on folklore as "degraded culture," and the reactionary tendencies of this "theory" were also revealed. At a scientific conference, convened in April, 1936, by the Folklore Section of the Academy of Sciences, in Leningrad, a number of papers were read in criticism of the theoretical fabrications of German and Italian bourgeois folklorists.[171]

In connection with the papers read by Professor N. P. Andreyev and Professor V. Y. Propp [172] at that same conference, there was extensive critical debate of the former theoretical and methodological errors of both the so-called "folklorists"—the aims of the "Finnish school" in the works of the former, and the formalistic principles in the works of the latter. And at that conference Professor V. M. Zhurminsky subjected to self-criticism his own earlier formalistic works, his theory of the nature of folklore as a "relict," and his former shortsighted attitude toward the "sociology" of Hans Naumann.

But the most widely prevalent and deeply entrenched theoretical

170 See a brief account of this debate in *Soviet Ethnography* 1932, Bk. 3, p. 12.

171 Papers were read by Y. M. Sokolov, E. V. Hofmann, Prof. E. G. Kagarov, Prof. V. P. Petrov, and others. For a concise account of these, see the annals, *Soviet Folklore*, Nos. 4-5, 1936, pp. 429-431.

172 In the works of Prof. N. P. Andreyev during recent years, there is definitely apparent a withdrawal from his former positions. See, for example, the anthology which he edited for institutions of higher education, *Russian Folklore* (1st ed., 1936; 2nd ed., 1938); the above-mentioned articles dealing with antireligious folklore, with the questions of the connections between folklore and artistic literature, and also *Folklore* (Moscow, 1933), a prospectus of a correspondence course; commentaries on the *Russian Popular Tales* of Afanasyev (Moscow, Academia, 1936–1938), Vol. I. Prof. Propp's withdrawal from formalism is spoken of in his articles, "On the Question of the Origin of the Fairy Tale," *Soviet Ethnography*, Nos. 1-2, 1934, and other works.

and methodological errors in Soviet folkloristics proved to be the errors of the so-called "vulgar sociologism."

The origin of these errors is fundamentally of the same kind as in Soviet literary study, though in folkloristics there were additional causes for them.

Like Soviet literary study as a whole, Soviet folkloristics directed its attention mainly to the reflection in artistic productions of the phenomena of social life, of class conflict, and considered it as one of its chief tasks to establish the social and class nature of every production, genre, style, and so forth.

In its movement, Soviet folkloristics, as we have already seen, also had to overcome the influence of formalism, the effects of the followers of the "migration theory" of the "Finnish school," and the especially powerful traditions of the "historical school." [173]

The conflict with the traditions of the "historical school," however, went on in quite a one-sided manner; and criticisms were made rather of the method of work, emphasizing the separation between form and content in the treatment by the "historical school" of the productions of folklore; while the "sociological" tendencies of the "historical school" were criticized, not so much in their essence, as along the line of reproaches for their failure to develop "sociological determinism" with sufficient breadth.

And the majority of Soviet folklorists have striven in every way to fill in the "gaps," quite boldly, decisively, and fully encompassing in their "sociological" interpretation all the phenomena of folklore, both past and present.

The main task which loomed up before Soviet folkloristics was acknowledged to be, so to speak, the "class passport system" of the productions of folklore.

[173] The paths followed by Soviet folkloristics, in the formulation of its principal purposes, can be clearly traced from the prospectus articles written by me in various years: "The Next Tasks in the Study of Russian Folklore," *Artistic Folklore*, No. 1, 1926; "On the Sociological Study of Folklore," *Literature and Marxism*, No. 2, 1928; "Folklore and Folkloristics in the Reconstruction Period," *ibid.*, Nos. 5 and 6, 1931; "The Nature of Folklore and the Problems of Folkloristics," *The Literary Critic*, No. 12, 1934; "The Russian Epos of the *Byliny*" (a problem of social origin), *ibid.*, No. 9. 1937; "Popular Poetry," *Pravda*, Dec. 29, 1937, No. 357.

These efforts of the folklorists were supported by the methods and theories of the school of M. N. Pokrovsky. In this "sociologization" the majority of folklorists were convinced that in their work they were traveling along the paths of genuine scientific Marxism. In reality, however, in the final accounting it was revealed that, both in their methodology and in their theoretical structures, these folklorists were repeating and pedantically elaborating that which, as we have said above, had been done by the "historical school" before the October Revolution—by Vsevolod Miller and, especially, by V. A. Keltuyala.

This tradition is very powerfully expressed in the works on the study of the epos of the *byliny*, which was acknowledged by all Soviet investigators, after Miller, as having been created mainly in the military surroundings of the *druzhina*. Such were the assertions of B. M. Sokolov, in his first issue of *Russian Folklore* (1929); my own, in the article "*Byliny*," in the *Great Soviet Encyclopedia*, Vol. VIII; those of N. P. Andreyev, of A. M. Astakhova, in the leading article and commentaries to *Epic Poetry*, published in 1935 under the editorship of M. K. Azadovsky, in the Minor Series of *The Poet's Library*; in the course of lectures by P. M. Solobev; in the chapters of the textbook on Russian literature for the eighth class, by Abramovich and Golovenchenko, and so forth.

Studying with enthusiasm the "class passport system" of the *byliny*, tales, and so on, the folklorists failed to notice that these hypotheses were in complete contradiction to the theses which they shared on folklore as the creation of the masses of the people, as the expression of the "expectations and longings of the people," and that, in essence, they harmonized with the tendencies introduced by the reactionary "folklorists" of the type of Hans Naumann.

The decisive blow to vulgar sociologism in folkloristics was dealt by the central organ of the Party—*Pravda*. In the newspaper for November 14, 1936, there was published a report of the Committee on Matters of Art, dealing with the play, *The Knights*, as presented by Tairov at the Chamber Theater. In this report it was pointed out that this play "undeservedly blackens the knights of the Russian epos of the *byliny* at that time when the major knights were the bearers of the heroic features of the Russian people."

In connection with the criticism of this play, there arose the question of the treatment of the epos of the *byliny* in Soviet folkloristics, and attention was directed to the vulgar sociological theory of the aristocratic, rather than popular, origin of the Russian *byliny*. *Pravda* (articles for November 15, 20, and especially 21), and also other organs of the press (*Izvestiya*, *The Literary Gazette*, *The Teacher's Gazette*, and many others) then exposed to keen criticism the works of B. M. Sokolov, my own, and those of other folklorists, written in the same spirit, concerning the social origin of the Russian epos of the *byliny*. The general criticism pointed to the fact that, independently of the subjective intentions of the authors, the vulgar sociological theory which they had developed of the aristocratic origin of the epos of the *byliny* leads to an echoing of the reactionary "theories" of the bourgeois "folklorists" of the type of Hans Naumann, and that there is a necessity for a decisive revision of fallacious and harmful conceptions.

This firm and at times very harsh general criticism was of great significance for the further development of Soviet folkloristics, evoking a wave of self-criticizing publications by folklorists, and compelling them to mark out new paths in research work.[174] Soviet folkloristics began to be impressed more deeply with those tasks with which science is faced in our time, tasks set for it by the Party and the government—to collaborate in the fostering of Soviet patriotism, love for one's socialist native land, for her cultural treasures; the fostering of genuine internationalism, based upon respect for the national culture of every fraternal nation; the revelation of that vast significance which the creations of workingmen have had in the development of world culture; for those ideational and artistic heights attained by the creative work of the people at the present time in the USSR.

The most outstanding events in the life of Soviet folkloristics were the appearances of A. M. Gorky at the first Congress of Soviet Writers, and his subsequent articles in the press; and also the appearance, in honor of the twentieth anniversary of the Soviet power, of the volume

---

174 A summary of my own self-criticizing statements will be found in the above-mentioned article, "The Russian Epos of the *Byliny*," in the *Literary Critic*, No. 9, 1937.

Creative Works of the Peoples of the USSR, published by the editorial offices of *Pravda*, and presenting summaries of the development of popular creative work during the twenty glorious years following the October Revolution.

The attention paid to the creative work of the people by the Party and the government; the constant concern of Comrade Stalin for conditions favoring the discovery and cultivation of the people's talents in the fields of poetry, music, the dance, and other aspects of folk art, and also for the disclosure of the rich artistic heritage, preserved in the memory of all the fraternal nations of the USSR—all this had great significance for the development of Soviet folkloristics.

The 750th jubilee of the great Georgian poet Rustaveli, the 750th jubilee of that most noteworthy landmark of ancient Russian poetry, *The Tale of Igor's Raid*, the poetic activity—supported by the leader of the peoples—of Suleyman Stalsky and of Dzhambul, and the ten-day celebrations in Moscow in honor of folk art—Ukrainian, Georgian, Uzbek, Kazakh, Azerbaijanian—powerfully aided an even greater flourishing of folk creation and of the science which deals with it.

The constantly increasing collection and study of the folklore of all the fraternal nations of the USSR must be acknowledged as an indisputable achievement of Soviet folkloristics. This collection and study of the poetry of the various types of peoples of our country does much for the understanding of a number of processes in Russian folklore, and opens up broad perspectives for the further development of Soviet folkloristics as a whole.[175]

[175] Not having the opportunity to sketch in detail all the work done in the collection and study of the folklore of the fraternal nationalities, both centrally and locally, I am appending only a bibliographical list of those collections of national folklore of the fraternal peoples of the USSR, which have been published during recent years *in the Russian language*. This list alone, which makes no pretensions toward exhaustive completeness, may give some idea of that vast interest of the general reader in the folk creations of the various nationalities, which has never been investigated to such a degree, and which could not be investigated earlier, in the pre-Soviet period. The bibliographical list offered herewith may prove useful in gaining a preliminary acquaintance with the folklore of other peoples, and for the general comparison of it with Russian folklore.

Anthologies of the folklore of various peoples are given first, then publications on the folklore of specific nationalities (in this order: the Caucasus, Central Asia, the Volga provinces, the North, Siberia).

[See pp. 153–155 for bibliography of National Folklore—Ed.]

A great deal of work, and that of the most fascinating kind, lies before us; but, for its successful completion, the personnel of the research staffs is very small. There is a keenly felt necessity for an influx of new young scholars, fully imbued with the theories of Marx, Engels, Lenin, and Stalin.

The successful development of folkloristics is possible only on the condition that Soviet folklorists will constantly remember that through their work they must bring real benefit to the people, by continually revealing more and more new riches of the poetry which has been created through the centuries, and is still being created; by making clear the historical and artistic values to be found in it; by cooperating in the collection, study, and popularization of the best productions of folklore, toward an ever greater enthusiasm for the socialist culture of the people.

The genuine science of folklore, of the creative work of the people, is only that which—in the words of Comrade Stalin—"does not separate itself from the people, does not hold itself aloof from the people, but is ready to serve the people, is ready to pass on to the people all the conquests of science, which serves the people not through compulsion, but voluntarily, with willingness."[176]

Folklore can develop only on the condition that it shall more and more attract new, youthful forces. The genuine science of folklore—again speaking in the words of Comrade Stalin—is that

which does not permit its old and acknowledged directors, in self-satisfaction, to shut themselves up in the shell of priests of science, in the shell of monopolists of science; but which understands the meaning, the significance, the omnipotence of a union of the old workers of science with the young workers, which voluntarily and willingly opens all the doors to the youthful forces of our country, and gives them the opportunity to conquer the heights of science; which recognizes that the future belongs to the youth.[177]

Genuine folkloristics can only be that science,

concerning which science the people, understanding the strength and significance of the established scientific traditions and knowing how

---

[176] J. V. Stalin, "Speech at the Reception in the Kremlin for the Workers of the Higher School," May 17, 1938; *Pravda*, No. 136, May 19, 1938.
[177] *Ibid.*

to make use of them in the interests of science, at the same time, do not want to be the slaves of these traditions; which has the boldness, and the resolution to break the old traditions, standards, and tendencies, when they become obsolete, when they become a brake that hinders the movement forward; and which knows how to create new traditions, new standards, new orientations.[178]

BIBLIOGRAPHY OF NATIONAL FOLKLORE

1. *Creative Works of the Peoples of the USSR* (Moscow, *Pravda*, 1937).
2. *Lenin and Stalin in the Poetry of the Peoples of the USSR* (Moscow, Literary Press, 1938).
3. *Verses and Songs of the Peoples of the East Concerning Stalin*, compiled by Chachikov (Moscow, 1935; library, The Light).
4. A. V. Pyaskovsky, *Lenin in the Russian Popular Tale and in Eastern Legend* (Moscow, The Young Guard, 1930).
5. A. M. Arsharuni, *Stalin in the Songs of the Peoples of the USSR* (Moscow, The Young Guard, 1936).
6. *Songs of the Kazakh Akyns Concerning Stalin* (Alma-Ata, 1937).
7. *Stalin's Constitution in the Poetry of the Peoples of the USSR*, ed. and with notes by V. Musaelyan (Moscow, Artistic Literature, State Publishing House, 1937).
8. *Creative Works of the Peoples of the USSR* (almanac) (Moscow, Artistic Literature, I, State Publishing House, 1937) (passages from translations of the Kazakh epic poem *Koblandi Batyr*, the Kirghiz epos *Manas*, the Kalmuck epos *Djangr*, the Kurdish epos *Zembyl-Frosh*).
9. Andrey Globa, *Songs of the Peoples of the USSR*, 2nd ed., enlarged (Moscow, Artistic Literature, State Publishing House, 1935).
10. *Choral Creative Work of the Peoples of the USSR*, No. 1, comp. and ed. by A. Gumennik and D. Zhitomirsky (Moscow, State Music Publishing House, 1936).
11. *Tales of the Peoples of the East* (Moscow-Leningrad, Institute of Eastern Studies of the Academy of Sciences of the USSR, 1938).
12. *Georgian Tales*, comp. by Nina Dolidze, Introduction by A. Arsharuni (Moscow, Artistic Literature, State Publishing House, 1937).
13. *Armenian Tales*, transl. by Y. Khachatryan, Introduction by Marietta Shaginyah (Moscow, Academia, 1st ed. 1930; 2nd ed. 1933).
14. G. Agayan, *Tales* (Tbilisi, Dawn in the East [publishing house], 1936).
15. Suleyman Stalsky, *Verses and Songs*, transl. from the Lezgian, ed. Effendi Kapiyev (Moscow, Artistic Literature, State Publishing House, 1938).
16. *Adygeian Legends and Tales*, literary adaptation by P. Maksimov, collected by Adygeian Scientific Investigation Institute for Cultural Organization (Rostov-on-the-Don, Adygeian-Circassian Publishing House, 1937).
17. P. Maksimov, *Mountaineers' Tales*, Introduction by M. Gorky (Rostov-on-the-Don, Adygeian-Circassian Publishing House, 1935; 2nd ed., Moscow, 1937).
18. *Kalmuck Tales*, ed., with Introductory Essay and Notes, by I. Kravchenko (Stalingrad, Regional Book Publications, 1936).

[178] *Ibid.*

19. *Anecdotes of Khodja Nasreddin and Akhmet Akha;* texts written down by the Folklore Brigade of the Alupkin Palace-Museum; text prepared for publication by S. D. Kotsyubinsky (Simferopol, Crimean Autonomous Soviet Socialist Republic, State Publishing House, 1937).

20. *Tales and Legends of the Crimean Tartars;* text written down by K. U. Useinov; preparation of text and Introductory Essay, by S. D. Kotsubinsky (Simferopol, Crimean Autonomous Soviet Socialist Republic, State Publishing House, 1936).

21. *Creative Work of the Peoples of Turkmenistan,* comp., transl., and annotated by G. I. Karpov and N. F. Lebedev (Moscow, Artistic Literature, State Publishing House, 1936).

22. *Dzhambul, The Folk Singer of Kazakhstan, Wearer of the Order: Songs and Poems* (Moscow, Artistic Literature, State Publishing House, 1938).

23. *Insurrection Songs of the Kazakhs of the Nineteenth Century,* transl. from the Kazakh by A. Nikolskaya (Alma-Ata, Kazakh Regional Publications, 1936).

24. *Songs of the Sixteenth Year,* transl. from the Kazakh by P. Kuznetsov and L. Archangelsk (Alma-Ata and Moscow, Kazakhstan Regional Publishing House, 1936).

25. Georgius Tveritin, *Song of Kozy-Korpech and Bayan-Slu: A Kazakh Legend;* Introduction and Notes by Smagul Sadvokasov (Kzyl-Orda, the Ministry of Popular Cultural Education of Kazakhstan, 1927).

26. *Kyz-zhibek, A Popular Kazakh Poem* (Alma-Ata and Moscow,.Kazakhstan Regional Publishing House, 1936).

27. *Baluchistan Tales,* collected by I. I. Zarubin (Leningrad, *Proceedings of the Institute of Eastern Studies of the Academy of Sciences of the USSR,* IV, 1932).

28. M. A. Vasilyev, *Landmarks of Tartar Folk Literature: Tales and Legends* (Kazan, Combined Editing and Publishing House of the Tartar Soviet Socialist Republic, 1924).

29. *Chuvash Tales,* the Chuvash Scientific Investigation Institute of Culture (Moscow, Artistic Literature, State Publishing House, 1937).

30. *Songs and Tales of the Udmurt People* (Kirov, Regional Publications, 1936).

31. Vyacheslav Tonkov, *Samoyed Tales,* Introduction by Prof. V. G. Tai-Bogoraz (Archangel, Northern Regional State Publishing House, 1936).

32. I. I. Avdeyev, *Songs of the People of Mansi,* ed. I. N. Popov (Omsk, Omsk Provincial State Publishing House, 1936).

33. *Ins-Khop: Khanteian Heroic Songs and Legends,* adapted by I. N. Yelantsev; Introduction and Commentaries by I. Popov; ed. E. Blinov (Sverdlovsk, Sverdlovsk Provincial State Publishing House, 1935).

34. *Materials on Evenkeian (Tungusic) Folklore,* No. 1; comp. by G. M. Vasilyevich (Leningrad, Institute of the Peoples of the North, Central Executive Committee, USSR, bearing the name of P. G. Smidovich, 1936).

35. *Dolgansky Folklore,* introductory article, texts, and transl. by A. A. Popov; literary adaptation by E. M. Tager: ed. M. A. Sergeyev (Leningrad, The Soviet Writer, 1937).

36. *Tales of the Altai,* literary adaptation by Anna Harf and Paul Kuchiyak (Novosibirsk, Novosibirsk Provincial Publishing House, 1937).

37. *Altaian Tales,* Introductory Essay by A. Koptelov (Novosibirsk, Novosibirsk Provincial Publishing House, 1937).

38. *Songs of Oirotia* (Novosibirsk, Novosibirsk State Publishing House, 1938).

39. S. Y. Yastremsky, *Types of Folk Literature Among the Yakutsk* (Leningrad, Proceedings of the Commission of the Academy of Sciences of the USSR for the Study of the Yakutsk Autonomous Soviet Socialist Republic, Vol. VII, 1929).

40. Adaniji Mergen, *The Buryat Epos*, transl. into verse by Ivan Novikov; Prefatory Essay and Commentaries by G. D. Sanzheyev; ed. Y. M. Sokolov (Moscow, Academia, 1936).

41. *The Mongolo-Oirotian Heroic Epos*, transl., Introductory Essay and Notes by B. Y. Vladimirtsov (Petrograd-Moscow, State Publishing House, 1923).

In addition to these, Russian translations of the folklore productions of the peoples of the USSR have been published in the magazines, *The New World, The Red Soil, The Star, October, Siberian Lights, The Literary Critic, The Literary Review, Popular Creative Work, Soviet Folklore,* and others, and in central and local newspapers.

FOLKLORE BEFORE THE
OCTOBER REVOLUTION

ON THE ORIGIN OF POETRY AND THE EARLY STAGES
OF ITS DEVELOPMENT

The questions of the origin of poetry, and of the earliest stages of its development, cannot be settled on the basis of the folklore of any one given nationality.

In solving the question of the rise of literary art, the same materials are drawn upon as in the solution of the broader question of the origin of art in general: historical and archaeological data concerning the primitive peoples of antiquity, ethnographic investigations of the life and folk creation of the peoples still on a low level of culture in modern times, and of the survivals of primitive culture in the folklore of civilized peoples.

Just as, according to the data of the materialistic teaching about language (see the statements of Engels on the origin of language, and the theory of Academician Marr), spoken language grew out of the process of the development of labor habits, utilizing the artificially created implements of labor, *literary art arose and developed in direct connection with laboring processes.*

The decisive factor in the rise and development of literary art, even in the era of primitive communism (the pretribal commune), was the rhythm of work, which evoked and subordinated to itself the rhythm of bodily movement, melody, and speech. This phenomenon has been revealed and explained in the well known book by the economist and sociologist K. Bücher, *Work and Rhythm.*[1]

[1] Karl Bücher, *Arbeit und Rhytmus* (Leipzig, 1896); Russian transl.: Karl Bücher, *Work and Rhythm*, transl. from the German by S. S. Zayaitsky (Moscow, 1923).

The simultaneous subordination of these rhythms to the governing rhythm of the laboring process formed the basis of the so-called "syncretism," that is, a nondifferentiated art, not divided into specific branches, but representing the indivisible coexistence of the elements out of which, in the further stages of their development, were crystallized the special aspects of art: the dance, music, and poetry.[2]

In the composition of this primitive syncretism, the semantic aspect of a word (its meaning and significance) originally played a secondary role. The dominating place was occupied by rhythm. The sounds of speech, in such a syncretism, were, originally, an imitation of sounds, and reproduced the sounds of work and of rhythmicized emotional exclamations. With the further development of culture and language, a literary text was also developed and became more complex; but for a very long time it remained, none the less, in a subordinate position as compared to rhythm and melody.

As indicated by the data of the folklore of primitive peoples, at the early stages of syncretism poetry does not have any kind of established text. The literary text is a variable improvisation, although with considerable stability of rhythm and melody, and also of the brief, repeated monotonous refrains.

Academician A. N. Veselovsky, in his famous work *Three Chapters from Historical Poetics* (1899), adduces a great number of examples of such poetic primitive improvisation. He says:

Such songs are not subject to tradition. The national song of the Kamchatkans consists of an endless repetition of one and the same word: *Bachiya!* Or they begin to sing thus: 'Darya is still dancing and singing!' This is repeated as many as eight times. The same phenomenon may be observed among the Australians, the Kaffirs; Arab women sing over five or six times the first two verses of a song, which are taken up by those present; but the third verse, in which the name of some illustrious knight-errant or other is mentioned, is repeated as many as fifty times.[3]

One need not think that improvisation in oral poetry is characteristic only of the very first stages of syncretism. As we have already said

[2] The problem of primitive syncretism has been illuminated in detail by Academician A. N. Veselovsky; see *Collected Works*, Vol. I (St. Petersburg, 1913).
[3] *Ibid.*, Vol. I, p. 232.

in the first chapter, the factor of improvisation is preserved in the folklore of all nations, at all times (it is true, in varying proportions) in relation to the established traditional text. As we shall see in later chapters, in almost all genres of Russian folklore, both in prose and in song, improvisation manifests itself, now in a less and now in a greater degree. And in fact it could not be otherwise, inasmuch as oral productions are preserved only in the memory of singers, narrators, storytellers, and other performers of folklore.

Characteristic of the primary stages in the development of folklore is its connection with the productive processes, which is frequently expressed also at considerably later periods, even down to our own time. Testimony to this is given by a great number of the so-called "workers' songs," that is, songs which grew up in the process of physical work. We need only remember the Russian *Dubinushka* in its different variations, depending on the differences in the character of the actual process of this or that kind of work.

Military, marching songs of all times and peoples reveal with especial vividness the role of the song as the regulator of physical movement and strain.

However, if we take poetry as a whole, and not isolated specific phenomena of it, then it is necessary to state that with the development of productive relationships, with the complexity of social-economic life, with the growth of social differentiation, literary art loses its direct connection with the laboring process, but still retains for a long time the traces of this connection. They are apparent, for instance, in magic games and ceremonies of a choral and choral-dancing character, utilized in various social structures for the purposes of religious worship, of which we shall speak farther on.

The subsequent process of the development of poetry goes on side by side with the development of choral song, and also of magic and religious choral dancing. In proportion to the degree of complexity of social life, the textual, literary part of the choral performance increases, falling mainly to the share of the soloist leader of the chorus (the coryphaeus); finally, the chorus is divided into halves, and the text is divided between the two leaders of these semichoruses. Such is the development of the epic and dialogue poetic speech; to the share of the chorus there remains, for the most part, only the performance of the lyrical refrains.

In such a way, out of the general syncretism there is isolated the role of the individual singer, combining in itself, in the course of a long period of time, the functions of poet, musician, and dancer.

The subsequent development of poetry moves in a direction away from the singer and toward the poet (the formula of A. Veselovsky), with the gradual separation of music from the dance, then of song from musical accompaniment, and finally of the literary text from the tune. However, traces of the original connection of these now disjoined elements are still preserved for a long time in the poetic use of words. (Compare, for example, the traditional representation, in poetry, of the poet in the form of a singer with a lyre.)

The syncretistic origin of poetry may be perceived even down to the present time in poetic creation, in so far as rhythm and melody play an important part in it; and in oral reproduction, where gesture and movement are also factors.[4]

According to the data of language and archaeology, the origin and infancy of the Slavs are assigned by contemporary science to the third and second millenniums before our era, but any kind of exact historical *information concerning the eastern Slavs* belongs to a considerably later period; the testimonies of Byzantine writers begin with the sixth century of our era; the testimonies of Arabian travelers are to be assigned to the eighth and ninth centuries, and the testimonies of actual eastern Slavonic (Old Russian) written literature begin with the landmarks of the eleventh century and form a chain of historical information only as far back as the events of the ninth century.

History knows the Slavs as early as the fifth century, on the shores of the Baltic Sea, along the Dnieper and the Danube, on the upper reaches of the Oka and the Volga. More or less definite historical information concerning them enables us to characterize their social

[4] Basic literature on the question of the origin of poetry: A. N. Veselovsky, *Three Chapters from Historical Poetics* (*Collected Works*, Vol. I [St. Petersburg, 1913]); Ernst Grosse, *Die Anfänge der Kunst* (The Origin of Art) (Freiburg, 1894); H. Werner, *Die Ursprünge der Lyrik* (The Origin of the Lyric) (München, 1924).

order from the eighth to the tenth centuries, as the order of the tribal commune in the period of its decline.[5]

The basic occupation of the eastern Slavs, with the passing of time, had come to be agriculture, which still bore a very primitive character.

But primitive agriculture, which demanded a vast expenditure of labor, of course, could not by itself feed the population. And, in fact, the eastern Slavs engaged also in the raising of cattle, though on a small scale; they bred the horned work cattle and work horses,[6] and, besides these, the smaller animals: the sheep, the goat, and the pig, and some of the domestic fowl—the chicken, goose, and duck.

The smoking out of wild bees and gathering of their honey played a large role in the economic mode of life of the eastern Slavs, who lived chiefly in wooded places; they also plied other forest crafts (the gathering of mushrooms and berries), and finally, fishing and hunting.

The tribal regime of the eastern Slavs in the last century of the first millennium of our era was strictly patriarchal, although in language and in certain specific aspects of its mode of life and outlook it preserved insignificant survivals of a former matriarchy.

The family life was completely regulated by the will of the head of the tribe, which was a "large family." He even determined the choice of wives for the younger members of the family. Marriage was for the most part monogamous, though it was permissible also to have several wives.

However, there still existed survivals of the forms of group marriage, preserved, as is typical of all peoples, in connection with religious ceremonies, for example, in the summer so-called "bathing" ceremonial, when an indiscriminate mingling of the sexes was permitted, or a ceremonial hetaerism (the terminology is that of the sociologist

[5] Prof. Dr. Lybor Niederle, *Život starých slovanů* (Life of the Ancient Slavs), Vol. 1 (Prague, 1912), Vol. 2 (Prague, 1913); Russian transl., L. Niederle, *Mode of Life and Culture of the Ancient Slavs* (Prague, 1924); also a brief account of the work of Niederle, by M. N. Speransky, "The New Work of L. G. Niederle on Slavonic Antiquities," *Ethnographic Review*, Bks. XCIV-XCV, p. 49.

[6] For a long time the earth was worked chiefly by hand, with the help of mattocks, which were used in specific instances of deforestation farming in the Russian North and in White Russia, even down to the time of the October Revolution. See the description of these in the book by D. K. Zelenin, *Russian (Eastern Slavonic) Ethnography* (Berlin, 1927), p. 13.

Bankhofen, adopted by A. Veselovsky and other historians of the ancient Slavonic culture). But, as a general rule, marriage was of a well regulated character.

The ancient Slavonic marriage had two forms: marriage by abduction and marriage by buying and selling; that is, either a carrying off, or marriage by ransom (eastern Slavonic *veno*, in the sense of the Oriental *kalym*). In the words of the chronicle, the Drevlyane, Radimichi, Vyatichi, Severyani, live after the fashion of beasts: "There are no marriages among them, but festivities among the villages; they come out to the festivities, to the dances, and to the demoniacal festivities, and there they carry off wives for themselves, after an agreement has been made; and they have as many as two and three wives apiece."

The religious survivals, preserved in the folklore of the Russian peasantry down to very recent times, also clearly reveal to us the religion of a specifically tribal order. But in a number of ceremonials, customs, and fantastic images it is possible, as it were, to perceive also the echoes of considerably earlier stages still, both in social development and also in the ideology corresponding to it: in them, though indeed in a very slight degree, are preserved the echoes of totemism.

Survivals of other religious phenomena of a pretribal order—animism and magic—of course, have been preserved in folklore in a considerably greater and a considerably clearer form, but they must have been so fused with elements of the religion of the tribal commune, that it no longer seems possible to separate them from it. Therefore we pass directly over to a characterization of the religion of the tribal order.

Every religion is a fantastic reflection in the conscience of the people of social relationships, in the form of faith in the existence of a supernatural world. Speaking of the precapitalistic social and productive organisms, Karl Marx writes:

The conditions of their existence are a low stage of development of the productive forces of labor, and a corresponding association of the relationships of people within the framework of the process which creates their material life; and along with this, a union of all their relationships with one another and with nature. This concrete association has its ideal reflection in the ancient nature religions and folk religions.[7]

From this viewpoint it is interesting to determine how the "connection of all the relationships with one another and with nature" is reflected in the religious ideology of the eastern Slavs in the period of the decline of the tribal order.

The basic features of the religion of the tribal order may be reduced to three points: animism, magic, and ancestor worship.

The "leading" factor of these three in the tribal society, so to speak, was ancestor worship, which had subordinated to itself both animism and magic; these were inheritances from the religious ideology of earlier stages of preclass formation. Animistic representations of the nature which surrounded man, the creation of spirits of fire, earth, vegetation, water, became fused with the representation of ancestors, who were the protectors of man in his activity in the field, in the forest, and on the water.

Typical of the agricultural tribal commune is the specific so-called "inferior mythology" (the term is Mannhardt's), which explains the life of nature, surrounding man, as the form and image of a "large family." The field, the forest, the river, and every dwelling, is under the direction of a "host" in the form of an "old man." That is why, in spite of all the individual distinctions in religious forms, corresponding to the peculiarities of each specific phenomenon of nature, these spirits are invariably represented in the aspect of "old men," "grandfathers," "grandpas." In the tribal commune everyone is subordinate to "the one," "the master," "the old men." Nature also, as represented by primitive man, is under the direction of old men, "grandfathers." Such are the forms of the *old man of the field* or *of the barley*, the *old man of the water*, the *old man of the woods* (frequently fused with the figure of the *old man of the frost*, Jack Frost). Such also is the figure, most popular both under the tribal order and in the form of survivals into later eras among the patriarchal peasantry, of an "old man of the house," with his various modifications according to the different divisions of the peasant economy, the

[7] Karl Marx, *Capital*, Vol. I (State Publishing House, 1920), p. 48.

old man of the bath, of the barn for drying crops, of the threshing floor, of the house, of the cattle shed, of the stable, of the drove of horses, of the cart shed, of the aviary, of the egg laying, and so forth.

These figures are not always sufficiently distinct in their outward aspect, but the connection of each with the sphere of natural or social phenomena which he represents is altogether beyond doubt. Thus, the "old man of the field" is frequently depicted in the aspect of "an old man working in the field," of the same height as the growing grain; and in autumn, after the harvest, he dwindles to the dimensions of the uncut portions of the stalk. The "old man of the woods" is sometimes tall, like a great tree, sometimes small, like a bush, depending on which kind of woods he is given charge of by the fancy of man. The "old man of the waters" is stout, bloated, like a man who has drunk too much, and green, like water. The "old man of the frost" (Jack Frost) has a white, fluffy beard. The "old man of the house" is warm, with soft paws, like the wool of a sheepskin coat.

Ancestor worship appeared also in other forms. Thus there is indisputably connected with it the worship of the hearth, of the domestic fire or the barn fire. Here, of course, it may be, there is preserved a deeper tradition of reverence for the fiery element as such, but it was interwoven in the closest manner with ancestor worship. For example, the well known ceremonial, preserved down to recent times, of transferring the coals from the old hearth to the new house must be interpreted as a symbolization of the passing over of the soul of the ancestor to a new dwelling place. Ancestor worship was more directly expressed in the reverence for the magic word *chur*, or *shchur*. (Compare the expression "*Chur* me!" * during a game of tag, when the player runs to "home," having recourse, as it were, to the safeguard of his ancestor-protector.)

Ancestor worship is perhaps also reflected in reverence for birth, and for women after childbirth, to which testimony is borne by several extant examples of ancient Russian literature. Sacrifices were brought for the birth, and for women who had given birth: "To the birth and the woman who has given birth they offer [that is, bring to the bed] loaves, cheese, and honey" ("Questions of Kirik Addressed

* "Don't touch me!"—Ed.

to Nifont, Archbishop of Novgorod," twelfth century). To the un-masking of this cult there was even devoted the whole of "The word of Isaiah the prophet, expounded by St. John Chrysostom, concerning those who set a second repast for the birth and for the women after childbirth" (a very ancient manuscript, of the fifteenth century, but the actual material is to be assigned to a considerably earlier era). However, in the latest period, a very recent investigator (Mansikka)[8] expresses his doubt that among the Russian people there was reverence for any kind of mythical beings of birth and of the women after childbirth.

But in addition to the animistic figures which have been described, typifying in themselves the worship of ancestors, the latter were also represented in the views of tribal society (and later, in the form of a survival in the views of the peasantry) in a more direct way. People turned to their ancestors, as such, with prayer and sacrifice. All funeral ceremonies are imbued with ancestor worship. From it arise many portions of the wedding ceremonies. It is seen more fully and distinctly in social recollections of the departed—the "parents." In ancient literary monuments there is described a most interesting custom of building a bathhouse for those recently deceased—the souls of the "parents."

In feudal Russia, and later, the peasants as well as the city dwellers dedicated special days to the remembrance of ancestors. The majority of these fell in the spring. Such days, hallowed by the Church and powerfully supported by it (since they brought in one of the largest revenues of the clergy), were: "Ancestors' Saturdays" (on the eve of Shrovetide), *Radunitsa* (Commemoration of the Dead, on Tuesday of the second week after Easter), Demetrius' Saturday (before the day of Demetrius of Thessalonica, October 26), *semik* (or Undine's Saturday, on the eve of Trinity Day).[9]

These ceremonies are described both in ancient literary monuments and, in later times, in scientific ethnographic literature: they were already, to a considerable degree, fused with Christian innovations,

[8] V. I. Mansikka, *Die Religion der Ostslaven: Quellen* (Helsinki, 1922), pp. 142-147.
[9] See D. Zelenin, *op. cit.*, p. 332.

but still their fundamental nature—the ancestor worship of the era of the tribal order—may be very clearly discerned. In a confessional question book the question is asked: "On Shrovetide Saturday and on Pentecost, when we make commemorations of the departed, have you not given orders for the bathhouse to be heated?" In the *Stoglav* (1551) there is mention of those who, on "the Holy Thursday, burn straw early in the morning, and call upon the dead," and "on the great days [that is, on the Easter days] of invocation, on *Radunitsa*, . . . sang the *vyunets* and gave rein to all sorts of mad deviltry," [10] that is, they followed the custom of invoking the departed and of singing wedding songs (*vyunets*) for newly-married couples. The latter recalls the ancient ceremonial of leading the young people to the water, and also is undoubtedly a survival of the worship of ancestors, whose blessing is, as it were, solicited for the marriage, that is, for the reception of a new member into the tribal commune.

Attention is drawn, in these public "wakes" for the departed, to the curious fact of a combination of funeral motifs, lamentations, wailings, and all other kinds of expression of grief for the deceased, with outbursts of unrestrained merriment, gluttony, drunkenness and debauchery. The departed ones are, as it were, present at the holiday, they are partakers at the table; those who are left alive want to bring them joy, to cheer them, but also to propitiate them. The Church, supporting the pagan survivals of the tribal cult in the ceremonial of the commemoration of the dead, at the same time strove to direct these commemorations into the channel of Christian views, of the conventional Christian devotion. In its official decrees and precepts it condemned the show of revelry, but, as is well known, in actual practice the clergy themselves took a direct part in this revelry, drunkenness, and gluttony. A vivid description of such "wakes," though it is true that they were not public, but individual, has been given by the famous seventeenth century traveler, Olearius.

Public "wakes" on Ancestors' Saturdays, on *Radunitsa*, during Undine's Week, and so on, were accompanied by even greater revelry. The *Stoglav* thus describes a "wake" on Trinity (Undine's) Saturday:

[10] Stoglav, ed. Kozhanchikov (St. Petersburg, 1863), pp. 23-27.

On Trinity Saturday, throughout the villages and throughout the churchyards, men and women go out on mourning ceremonies and lament at the graves of the dead, with a great crying. And when the buffoons begin to perform all kinds of demoniac games, then they cease from their weeping, and begin to leap and dance, and to clap their hands, and to sing satanic songs; at these same mourning ceremonies, there are swindlers and rogues.[11]

The same thing was done on *Radunitsa*. This custom even passed over into a characteristic proverb: "On *Radunitsa*, in the morning they plough, at dinner they weep, and in the evening they leap."

The customs described in the ancient literary monuments dedicated to the commemoration of ancestors fully correspond with what the most recent ethnographers have said of them. Here, for example, is what was written about the public commemoration of the departed, by the expert on the Saratov region, Minkh: throughout the whole province of Saratov there are celebrated by believers

days for general remembrance of the deceased; they are called ancestors' days, and occur several times in the year. The most important ancestors' day is considered to be the one after Easter, in St. Thomas' Week, on Tuesday. The second ancestors' day occurs on the Saturday before Trinity; others occur on the Saturday before Shrovetide, and on Saturday of the first week of the great Lenten fast.

On every ancestors' day the parishioners assemble for Mass, and present "names for memorial prayers," then a general office for the dead is said in the church, at which time a dish of porridge sweetened with honey is placed on the lectern, and around it on the floor are set pancakes, brought by everyone, which are then presented to the priest and his assistants, and also, by many, are distributed to the poor. Under the name of "ancestors" all relatives are commemorated, a custom that has been preserved from remote antiquity; in the seventeenth and eighteenth centuries "ancestors' wakes" were held even by whole parishes, and were concluded by carousing at the "ancestral cemeteries." The commemoration of ancestors at the cemeteries in Saratov is thus described by Minkh:

A great crowd of people gathers together, and all the priests from Saratov; on the graves they place pancakes, loaves or pretzels, a cup or glass of mead, sometimes sweetened cereal, and invariably one or two colored eggs apiece; while the office for the dead is being said,

[11] *Ibid.*, pp. 23-27.

they light wax candles, which are stuck into the graves or fastened to a saucer; all this the priests gather afterward into carts and take home with them; the villagers, for the most part women, by custom wail and weep, and then they disperse to their homes. Formerly, in these "wakes," at the cemetery they drank a great deal of vodka, and they had samovars, tea, and snacks.[12]

As may be seen from the descriptions of Minkh, the "commemoration of ancestors" had already been to a considerable extent Christianized; Christian motifs are closely interwoven with the traditional "pagan" ones, and, of course, must have overshadowed much of that which, in antiquity, constituted their inalienable characteristics. Therefore it is necessary to have recourse to a comparison with the customs of related or neighboring peoples.

So, for example, in a less Christianized, more archaic form, the worship of ancestors and the public commemoration of them was preserved among the White Russians, in a well known commemorative ceremonial, which bears the title of *dzyady*, that is, grandfathers, ancestors.

In considering the ceremonials of the commemoration of the departed—the "grandfathers," the "ancestors"—one cannot help observing that these public "wakes" are timed for the spring or for the fall. One cannot help connecting this fact with the household tools and tasks of the agriculturalist. It is true that, partly under the influence of the pressure of ecclesiastical ideology, the meaning of the ceremonials was being changed in the very peasant surroundings where these ceremonials were chiefly practiced. In part, the former ethnographer-collectors (especially those of the first half of the nineteenth century, when these ceremonies were still very much in vogue), voluntarily softened the obviously "pagan" features in them; finally, religious and secular censorship deleted much, even at times from specialized scientific works. Accordingly, the Russian commemorative ceremonials are known to us in a form which has already been greatly altered.

From the whole character of the commemorations (on *Radunitsa*, in Undine's Week, and so forth), however, it may be concluded that

12 A. N. Minkh, *Popular Customs, Ceremonials, Superstitions, and Prejudices of the Peasants in the Province of Saratov* (St. Petersburg, 1890), collected in the years 1861–1888.

the commemorative festivals were not limited to the expression of veneration, attention, and concern for deceased ancestors, but that their spirits were invoked (by means of prayer or magic) for the purpose of securing their aid in the everyday life of the family and the tribe, and in agricultural activities. So, the cult of ancestors was closely interwoven with the agricultural cults, which are exceptionally rich, as we shall see farther on, in the manifestation of all kinds of magic. Not without reason, as we have seen, on *Radunitsa*, at the cemeteries, did they sing wedding songs for the young people, invoking the blessing of ancestors upon the marriage; not without reason did they place their agricultural implements in order before the *dzyady*.

Scattered data confirm this conjecture. Thus, one of the teachers of White Russia (in the Osipov district, seventy versts from Minsk), A. S. Zmaginsky, has told me how the ceremonial of the *dzyady* used to be performed, only a very short while before the revolution. According to his account, the *dzyady* were celebrated according to "portages," that is, according to groups of territorially united households. (Apparently, at the basis of these unions there lay some kind of family connections.) At the general table the elder, before every dish, would appeal to the ancestors, at the same time putting a spoon into the food, with the words: "Let it bear, let it grow, let it live." In other words, in the consciousness of those who had charge of the commemoration, the departed were invoked with the specific purpose of having them give aid in the household and influence the harvest and fertility.

The direct connection of certain religious factors with productivity itself is entirely natural at the lower stages of social development. Only later does this connection become exceedingly complicated. However, even at the lower stages of the development of religion, there are reflected in it not only the productive life itself, but also the productive relationships. Thus, in our analysis of the commemorations of ancestors, and the seasonal ceremonials which are connected therewith, it is necessary to search for the reflections of those bonds among people which were characteristic of a fixed social-economic formation and of its individual stages.

In the White Russian *dzyady* and in the Russian *Radunitsa* ceremonials which are analogous to them, beyond all doubt, these bygone ties are reflected. In them it is not difficult to discover not only the cult of the veneration of deceased ancestors, but also survivals of the veneration of living elders, the guides of life in the tribal and communal organization. Here is a description of one of the spring ceremonials of commemoration, clearly illustrating this idea:

The consummation of the sacred feast at the graves of parents was formerly accompanied by family entertainments. The relatives assembled at the home of the eldest in the tribe, with their offerings—cakes, loaves and vodka—and then, in full train, started for the cemetery. The more numerous the train might be, the greater was the glory for the elders. The elders, as hosts, arranged the offerings upon the graves, and treated their relatives and acquaintances. The remains of the offering were distributed to the beggars. At every entertainment the elders recalled the lives of the departed, related accounts of their mode of existence upon earth, and expressed the hope that all the young people might live thus upon earth, leaving behind them honor and admiration.[13]

At this point we approach the question as to who were the leaders and organizers of the ancestor cult, the mediators between the living and deceased members of the tribe.

In the period of tribal organization, these were (it is natural to think, by analogy with what may be observed among peoples who are still in the stage of tribal development) the fathers of the tribe themselves, the old men, the grandfathers. But already, at the stage of decline of tribal organization, in the tribal commune there had begun to be distinguished professional groups of magicians, sorcerers, and wizards. Judging from the data of ancient literature and the more recent ethnographic observations, the magicians, sorcerers, and wizards, by the character of their activity, must be classified under the category of shamans, who have played such a vast role in the life, for example, of certain Siberian, Finnish, and Turkic nationalities, which have only in recent times begun to come out of the stage of tribal organization. The mention in ancient precepts of "whirling dances,"

---

[13] Sakharov, *Legends of the Russian People* (St. Petersburg, 1849), Bk. VII, p. 93.

that is, apparently a type of shamans' sorcery, and the account given in a chronicle of how "the wonder-worker lay and grew numb," that is, brought himself to a fainting condition, is exceedingly interesting.

On this point, E. Anichkov writes:

The resemblance of our ancient magicians to the shamans is to be found in the actual process of their sorcery. As the shamans allude to the spirits, so the magicians begin their predictions: "The gods have revealed to us" or "Five gods have revealed this to me." As the shaman falls into a stupor after his dance, so the magician, of whom Nikon [the chronicler.—Au.] tells, lies "benumbed." The strict prohibition of the "whirling dance," the declaration that, "of all games, by far the most accursèd is the whirling dance," leaves no doubt as to the fact that the magicians are like the shamans also in that method by which they brought themselves to the ecstatic condition.[14] D. K. Zelenin [15] also connects the Russian wizards with the shamans; a special work on this theme has been published by N. A. Nikitin,[16] adducing numerous parallels from the practice of Russian wizards and Eastern shamans.

The Church, throughout many centuries, waged a war against the magicians, wizards, and witches, but only strengthened its own belief in them still more by its persecutions of them, because, relegating the magicians—according to its custom—to the category of servants of the devil, the Church itself usually had no doubt of their power over nature.

The magicians, sorcerers, and wizards had, exactly like the shamans, two main functions—one, that of "cooperation" through their help in calling up spirits, their prayers and magical manipulations for production (the war with elemental calamities—drought, frost, famine, the lightening of agricultural labor, the foretelling of the weather, and so forth), and, on the other hand, their "healing" functions. The ma· gician was not only an augur and a sorcerer, but he was also a "medicine man." Later on, in the everyday life of the peasants, the functions of the wizard and the "medicine man" are often distin-

---

[14] E. V. Anichkov, *Paganism and Ancient Russia* (St. Petersburg, 1914), p. 271.
[15] *Op. cit.*, p. 395.
[16] N. A. Nikitin, *On the Question of Wizards* (*Annals of the Museum of Anthropology and Ethnography*, No. 7), (Leningrad, 1928), pp. 301-325.

guished, but very often they remain combined in the activity of one and the same person.

Such are the most important features of the religious ideology and practice of the eastern Slavs in the period of tribal organization and the era of its decay. It is not one of our tasks to give an exhaustive characterization of this religion. This can be done on the basis of special scientific literature; but it is necessary to emphasize the fact that, up to this time, we have no kind of fundamental work dealing with this question.[17]

We have already said more than once that survivals of the religion of the tribal society have come down to us in a greatly changed form, especially under the influence of the Greek Christian Church, which strove in every way, as we have seen, to adapt the old customs and concepts to its own. But the influence of the culture of the Greeks, and also of that of the Romans in a very powerful degree, told upon the culture of the Slavs, including the eastern Slavs, considerably earlier than the acceptance of Christianity by the latter. In many ceremonials and concepts obviously belonging to the period of tribal

---

[17] The most important works have already been indicated by us in the footnotes. These are either general works—Niederle, Zelenin, and also Prof. E. G. Kagarov, *The Religion of the Ancient Slavs* (Moscow, 1918)—or surveys of the sources—Anichkov, Mansikka. On the question of the ancestor cult, the factual materials may be drawn from the old works: Sakharov, *Tales of the Russian People* (St. Petersburg, 1849); Snegirev, *Russian Popular Holidays and Northern Ceremonials* (Moscow, 1837); Tereschenko, *The Social Life of the Russian People* (St. Petersburg, 1848). See also S. M. Solovyov, *Surveys of the Manners, Customs, and Religion of the Slavs, Chiefly the Eastern, in Pagan Times* (Archives of Historico-Juridical Information Relating to Russia, Moscow, Nikolay Kalachev, Bk. I, 1850); K. D. Kavelin, *Works*, Pt. 4 (Moscow, 1859); I. E. Zabelin, *History of Russian Life from the Most Ancient Times*, Pt. II (1st ed., 1879; 2nd ed., 1912), Chap. VI, "Pagan Beliefs of Ancient Russia"; A. N. Afanasyev, *The Poetic Attitudes of the Slavs on Nature*, Vols. I-III (Moscow, 1865–1869); A. N. Veselovsky, *Researches in the Field of Russian Religious Verse* (Annals of the Division of Russian Language and Literature of the Academy of Sciences, Vol. 46, No. 6, St. Petersburg, 1889), Essay XIII, "Fate and Destiny in the Popular Concepts of the Slavs"; A. Potebnya, *On Destiny and Related Concepts* (Antiquities: Proceedings of the Moscow Archaeological Society, Vol. II, Moscow, 1865); by the same author, *On Certain Symbols in Slavonic Popular Poetry* (Kharkov, 1914); E. Anichkov, *The Spring Ceremonial Song in the West and Among the Slavs* (Annals of the Division of Russian Language and Literature of the Academy of Sciences, Vol. LXXIV, No. 2, St. Petersburg, 1903), Pt. I, Chap. III, Sec., "The Spring Worship of Ancestors."

organization, one cannot help perceiving the influence of Greco-Roman pre-Christian religion, which truly did not change the essence of Slavonic tribal cults, of animistic concepts and magical ceremonies, but considerably complicated their outward manifestations.

By the labors of a series of investigators, chiefly of A. N. Veselovsky, the consequences of such Greco-Roman influence have been determined in no small degree.

Thus, the title *Radunitsa*, which designates the holiday of the commemoration of the dead, is convincingly derived by M. Marko from the name of the analogous Greek commemorative day, *rodonia*.[18]

We have mentioned above the *Rusaliae* (Undine's Week), against which the ancient Russian ecclesiastical preachers so revolted. The *Rusaliae* were later on known as Trinity Week, the time of the spring holiday, the holiday of the young vegetation. But with this holiday, as we already know, there was also joined the public remembrance of the departed. At the present time, certainly, no one disputes the derivation of the Slavonic term *Rusalia* from the name of the corresponding Latin spring holiday, *rosalia, dies rosarum* (days of roses).

From this same Latin name of the holiday is also derived the word *Rusalka*. The name of the holiday was carried over to the name of the mythical figure. Here Veselovsky, Anichkov, and a number of other investigators perceive a fusion of the form of *Rusalka* (Undine) with the concept of the dead in general; others, however, for example, D. K. Zelenin, see only the souls of those who died by an unnatural death (drowning, hanging, and so forth), and were left without ceremonial interment, bearing the title of "the unhallowed departed." [19] The opinion of Veselovsky should be considered the more correct. He says:

In the Little-Russian and White Russian traditional beliefs, the *Rusalki* are chiefly the drowned, and children who were born dead, or who died before they could be baptized; but this is only the individualizing of a more general conception, expressed in the names of the *Rusalki*: for example, Little-Russian *mavki* (that is, *navki, mayki,* among the Carpathians *boyki*); *navki* week—the week of Pentecost

[18] M. Marko, "Wörter und Sachen," *Grab als Tisch,* II (1910), p. 151.
[19] D. K. Zelenin, "Those Who Died by an Unnatural Death and the *Rusalki,*" *Outlines of Russian Mythology,* No. I (Petrograd, 1916).

(Whitsuntide); the Little-Russian word, *Rusalian,* or great day of the *navki,* is the designation of a *semik* (feast day).[20]

The name *kolyada,* which was used in ancient times for the holidays which were later adapted to the eve of Christmas, and the corresponding name for those who sang songs on that day (*kolyadki*), as it is now considered to be established beyond dispute, takes its origin from the name of the Greco-Roman New Year holiday—*kalanda, calendae.* The borrowing of the name was done by the Slavs a very long time before their acceptance of Christianity.

But the Greco-Roman, pre-Christian influence told not only upon the terminology, which began to be applied to the traditional cults and ceremonies that had been formed on the local soil of the agricultural tribal organization; to the eastern-Greco-Roman culture one must impute also some of the ceremonial details (for example, possibly, certain merrymakings at the time of the New Year holidays).

With the inculcation of Christianity among the masses, in the protracted process of the mutual adaptation of the traditional local ideology, which went back to tribal organization, to the Christian ideology, which was imposed in the feudal and capitalistic period from above, there developed the so-called *duality of belief,* a secondary religious syncretism.

That is why it is so difficult for the contemporary investigator to discern, under the Christian covering, the fundamental principle of a ceremony or a religious form. However, a great deal has been done by scholars in this respect. The work was considerably more widely developed after the revolution, when it became possible to carry on more boldly analytical work on the history of religion, and to uncover survivals of paganism in the Orthodox ceremonials.

With the figures of the Orthodox saints there were fused many concepts of the former religion and the former ancestor cult. Even in the old preachers one may find evidence that the cult of the Mother of God absorbed into itself the motifs of the ancestor cult. Just as a

[20] A. N. Veselovsky, *Researches in the Field of Russian Religious Verse,* No. V, Essay XIV, "January *Rusaliae* and Games of the Goths in Byzantium" (*Annals of the Division of Russian Language and Literature of the Academy of Sciences,* Vol. XLVI, St. Petersburg, 1889, p. 269).

"meal" had been set before the spirits of the ancestors, the "parents," so the custom was established, on the second day of the Christmas holidays, "of applying the hymn of praise to the Holy Mother of God, to the idolaters' meal," that is, of adapting to the pagan meal the hymn to the Mother of God. In the province of Kursk, in the 1880's, the second day of Christmas was called the "women's porridge." [21] Beyond all doubt, many elements of the ancestor cult were carried over to the revering of Nicholas the Miracle Worker, Florus and Laurus, George the Bearer of Victory, Vlas, Elijah the Prophet, and many others.

A fusion of ideas arose on the foundation of external coincidences— now as to the time of the worship (the springtime worship of Nikola, the springtime worship of Egor), now as to certain features of external resemblance: Egor, depicted on horseback, becomes the protector of horses, so to speak, the spirit of the horse tender, or the "god of the cattle." It is possible, however, that the agrarian cults of Elijah the Prophet, George, Florus and Laurus, and Vlas, go back even to the era which preceded the reception of Christianity in Russia. On the Greco-Roman soil they had already, in the course of several centuries, acquired those same features of the "duality of belief" by which they were also distinguished, later on, among the Orthodox Russian peasantry. Among other things, Vlas in the Greco-Roman world was considered the protector of the cattle. A very recent investigator— Mansikka—considers that Volos, or Veles, who is mentioned in ancient literary monuments in the capacity of a magic "god of the cattle," was in reality, so to speak, a Slavic version of the Greek St. Vlas, whose cult was accepted by the Slavonic masses before the official acceptance of Christianity. Volos is the Russian form of the name Vlasy, or Vlas.[22] It is possible that at that early period there had also penetrated onto Slavonic soil the agricultural cults of George, Florus and Laurus, and others. There is nothing surprising in this. Later on, an analogous phenomenon was observed among other peoples. For example, in the pagan region of the Udmurti and the Mordva, Florus and Laurus were included in the category of national gods, with the functions of "gods of the cattle." [23]

[21] Mansikka, *Die Religion der Ostslaven: Quellen* (Helsinki, 1922), p. 157.
[22] *Ibid.*, p. 391.   [23] *Ibid.*, p. 392.

But, in mentioning Volos, we must call to mind also other names of ancient Russian pagan divinities—Perun, Svarog, Khors, Dazhbog, Stribog, who are mentioned sometimes in a chronicle, sometimes in sermons, sometimes in the *Tale of Igor's Raid*. In speaking of pre-Christian religion, we have hitherto passed by in silence this Olympus of the eastern Slavs. The fact is that now we may regard the class character of this mythology as more or less authentic. Perun, Khors, Stribog, and the others are divinities, not of the popular masses, but of the princely circles.

They existed for only a short time in the consciousness and memory of the people, because they had penetrated but slightly into the depths of the population. Is it not strange that, with the exception of Perun, who at the acceptance of Christianity merged with the figure of Elijah the Prophet, and Volos, who was fused in the religious ideas of the masses with the tribal protectors of the cattle and the grain field (compare, for example, the custom of leaving in the field an unreaped sheaf, sometimes for the "god of the field," sometimes for "Volos"), the rest of the divinities enumerated are never encountered in the peasant folklore?

The story of the *Primary Chronicle* is well known: for several years before the acceptance of Christianity Prince Vladimir forcibly, with great persistence, disseminated the cult of a number of divinities, setting up idols in Kiev and Novgorod, and demanding worship of them on the part of the popular masses.

In the chronicle it is written: "And Vladimir began to rule Kiev alone, and he set up idols on a hill outside the palace court—a wooden figure of Perun, and his head was of silver and his mouth was of gold; Khors, and Dazhbog, and Stribog, and Simaregl, and Mokosh—and he and his people made sacrifice to the idols." Investigators (the Academician F. E. Korsh,[24] E. V. Anichkov[25]), turning their attention to the words, "outside the palace court," justly suppose that the

---

[24] Academician F. E. Korsh, *The Gods of Vladimir* (Kharkov, 1908); separately published also in Vol. XVIII of the *Annals of the Kharkov Historico-Philological Society*, in honor of Prof. N. F. Sumtsov.

[25] E. V. Anichkov, "The Gods of Vladimir According to the Testimony of the Chronicle," *Paganism and Ancient Russia* (St. Petersburg, 1914), Chap. XIII.

idols were intended for public worship. Simultaneously with this, "Vladimir also placed Dobrynya, his uncle, in Novgorod, and after Dobrynya came to Novgorod, he set up an idol of Perun above the river Volkhov, and the people of Novgorod revered him as a god."

But it is curious that both Vladimir in Kiev, and Dobrynya in Novgorod, overthrow the idols which have been set up by them, and with still greater energy propagated a new religion—Christianity. The setting up of the idols was the first attempt to establish a state religion. The religion of the royal family and of the *druzhina* was adopted as its basis. One cannot help turning one's attention to the "diversity of tribal origin" of Vladimir's gods, just as the royal *druzhina* also was of diverse tribal origin.

The name of Khors is derived by investigators from the Persian (Khores, Khor—the sun), Mokosh from the Finnish language (compare the tribe Moksha); the name Stribog hitherto has not been satisfactorily explained, though the majority of investigators assume its foreign origin; Simaregl (or, in other variants, Sim Regl) is most likely to be a name of literary origin—a distorted name of divinities mentioned in the Bible as Assyrian, Argel and Asimath (in Greek, Ergel and Asimath); Dazhbog is possibly a name designating the god as the bestower of good things (*deus dator*); Perun is a name which is apparently more constant, resting upon greater tradition, though certain investigators, connecting it with the Lithuanian god of thunder, Perkun (Perkunas), and the eastern Germanic Fiorgyn (from Perkunjos, the mother of Thor), presuppose the borrowing of this name from the Baltic peoples.[26] However that may have been, all this mythology, to which Afanasyev and other representatives of the "mythological school" have attributed a great, and at the same time an international, antiquity, must be acknowledged as being very

[26] A summary of all the interpretations of the names of the "gods of Vladimir" is given in a work which we have referred to more than once: Lybor Niederle, *Mode of Life and Culture of the Ancient Slavs*, 2nd ed. (Prague, 1924), Pt. II, No. I; see also Mansikka's book, *Die Religion der Ostslaven: Quellen* (Helsinki, 1922), pp. 379-397 (Über die Götter der Chronik). The feudal, class character of the "gods of Vladimir" is acknowledged also by D. K. Zelenin; see D. Zelenin, *Russische (Ostslavische) Volkskunde, pp.* 383-384.

diverse, belonging to a narrow class, having been current mainly in the circles of the prince's *druzhina* and in its literary usage.

This mythological system, diverse in its composition, and not having its roots among the masses of the people, naturally could' not long endure in the capacity of a means of political influence of the ruling upper classes upon the people of the lower classes, and was very soon obliged to give place to the Christian ideology, which had already been tested for many centuries in the practice of Byzantium. And Vladimir, who not long since had been a zealous pagan, a disseminator of princely idols, soon began persistently to inculcate Christianity. Easily accepted by the feudal upper classes, it waged war throughout a number of centuries, among the lower classes of the people, with the religion of the tribal organization, until it was joined with it in the compromise of the "duality of religion," which endured until recent times.

Now, having become acquainted with the bases of the religious ideology of the tribal organization, of the period of its decay, and of the beginning of feudalism, we shall be better able to understand all those productions of folklore which in their origin are linked with the culture of preclass formation, and which continued, as survivals, to exist during the course of the centuries in the life of the classes, preserving in their economic and social usage many of the features of this preclass culture.

Of all the forms of folklore, by far the greatest number of survivals of the preclass formation are preserved in the ceremonial poetry of the peasants. We now turn to a survey of this poetry.

CEREMONIAL POETRY
CONNECTED WITH THE CALENDAR

❦❦❦

The syncretistic condition of poetry is the starting point for the development of poetic forms. Russian ceremonials and songs, however, do not typify the ancient forms in their purest aspect; in this realm of oral poetry, as in that of magic spells, there is revealed with particular clearness the blending of the two cultures, pagan and Christian, that is, the "duality of religion." The primary agricultural mode of life and the primitive animistic world concept of the worker on the land had to yield gradually to the influence of Christianity, which was being persistently instilled from above, on the part of the ruling classes. But, in its turn, Christianity also, with its cults, ceremonials, and concepts, was constantly obliged to adapt itself to the traditional factors in the agrarian religion. In particular, the old agricultural heathen festivals had to be combined with the Christian holidays, while the ecclesiastical holidays were obliged to absorb into themselves the typical features of the agrarian animistic ceremonies. The pagan agricultural calendar of the eastern Slavs was merged with the Christian calendar—the Byzantine.

The rural ceremonies, sports, and choral songs, down to a very late period, were centered around the following holidays: the Nativity of Christ (December 25), St. Basil's Day (New Year's Day, January 1), the Baptism (January 6), Shrovetide, Easter, St. Thomas' Week, Trinity Sunday (the fiftieth day after Easter), and also the feasts of St. George the Bringer of Victory (April 23), St. Nikolay the Miracle Worker (May 9), St. John the Baptist (June 24), Elijah the Prophet (July 20), the Intercession of the Mother of God (October 1), and SS. Cosmo and Damianus (November 1).

In spite of this amalgamation with the Christian holidays, the general agrarian-religious character of the peasant ceremonies was preserved. At their foundation, as formerly, lay primitive magic, incantation, in the most diverse forms, not only for the purpose of

[179]

protection from some hostile "unclean" power (the so-called "prophylactic" magic), but also with the aim of securing for man certain positive values: fertility, wealth, love, and so forth (productive magic).[1]

The original division of agrarian ceremonies according to the seasons of the year, apparently based upon two fundamental cycles—those of the spring and autumn—was not strictly maintained.

Concerning ourselves chiefly with those aspects of the agrarian ceremonies which deal with songs and literary works, let us begin our survey with the Christmas holidays. These Christmas holidays, with reference to oral poetic productions, are characterized above all by the singing of *kolyadki*.

Kolyadki—the Christmas songs of the people—were widely diffused among the Ukrainians, and to a lesser degree among the White Russians and among the Russians. Among the latter they existed for the most part in the form of the so-called "vineyard songs," that is, in the form of songs of praise, with the traditional refrain: "O my vineyard, red and green." A parallel to the eastern Slavonic *kolyadki* exists in the folklore of all other Slavonic peoples, as well as in that of many other European nations. Especially allied, both in subject and in form, to the Slavonic *kolyady* are the Roumanian *kolyadki*, known as *colinda*. (Compare the Czech and Slovak name for such songs—*koleda*; the Slovenian *coleda*, the Serbian *koleda*, and the Albanian *kolendre*.) It is now considered as established beyond dispute that all the names of the songs which have been enumerated here have their origin in the name of the Greco-Roman New Year holiday, *kalanda* (*calendae*). The name of the New Year holiday, among many peoples, was transferred to the holiday of Christ's Nativity: Bulgarian —*kolada, kolyada, kolende;* French, *chalendes*, or the eve of the holiday; Russian, *kolyada*; Ukrainian, *kolyadj*, and White Russian, *kolyady*.

A detailed comparison between the New Year and Christmas festivals of the later European peoples, and the Greco-Roman winter holidays, reveals not only a resemblance in names, but also striking coin-

[1] See Prof. E. G. Kagarov, *On the Question of Classifying the Popular Ceremonies* (*Reports of the Academy of Sciences of the USSR*, 1928).

cidences as to individual factors in the ceremonies, entertainments, and so on.

In analyzing the intricate complex of ceremonies and songs connected with the newer European, and particularly with the eastern Slavonic Christmas holidays, ethnographers and folklorists (among whom, principally, must be mentioned the labors of the Academicians A. N. Veselovsky and A. A. Potebnya) have uncovered the following elements: (1) Those which go back, among many peoples, to the phenomena of the traditional agrarian magic and the local cults; (2) those which have been borrowed from the Greco-Roman culture, not only in the pre-Christian era, but also later on; (3) those which represent a fantastic blending of "pagan" and "Christian" elements.

Clear expressions of the primitive, so-called "productive" agrarian magic (though it is true that, in many cases, they were not recognized by the later peasantry) were the numerous ceremonies which, through the representation of fullness and satisfaction, were supposed to have the power of producing crops, children, happy marriage, and wealth. Such, for instance, were the customs, which were still widely diffused up to very recent times, of strewing the table and the floor of the hut with straw, the baking of ceremonial cakes and breads, called in the southern Slavonic lands *krachun* or *korochun*; the ceremonial eating of porridge (*kutya*) and of pork; the representation in games of sowing and other labors of the field; the carrying of a plow around the countryside, and the praising of it in songs; the singing in honor of Usen; the masquerading as a goat, mare, bull, bear, wolf, fox or crane; the giving of money, fortunetelling, and so forth. Many of these ceremonies, arising from the indigenous tradition of agrarian magic, and from the ancestor cults, may have been strengthened, supported, and complicated by borrowings from the higher and more complex Greco-Roman ceremonial culture. Besides, in the later ritualism connected with the *kolyadki* there must have been mingled ceremonies which in the Greco-Roman world had been appropriately assigned to holidays succeeding one another as follows: to the Brumalia (November 24 to December 17), to the vota (December 24 to January 1), and, finally, to the calends (January 1 to 5).

Many of these ceremonies had previously been so widely diffused that they were performed not only in the country villages, but also in the cities, and even in the capital. For example, in an imperial decree addressed to the provincial governors of Shuisk, in the year 1648, the following sketch is given of Christmas holiday ceremonies in Moscow: "It has come to our notice that in Moscow, first of all in the Kremlin, and in the Chinese City, and in the White City, and in the Earthen City, and outside the city, and along the byways, and in the Plebeian Quarter, and in the Coachmen's Quarter, along the streets and the byways, on Christmas Eve many people have invoked Kaleda and Usen, and on the eve before the Epiphany of Our Lord they have invoked the Plow," and so forth.[2] In the same year, 1648, in an imperial decree addressed to the provincial governor of the city of Dmitrov, mention is made of the same point.[3]

In the year 1928, A. B. Zernova wrote down, in the Dmitrovsky district, a song which accompanied the "invocation of the plow" at Christmas time (but the sense of the song and of the ceremony has been so largely lost that the word "plow" has been replaced by the meaningless word "meadow"):

Meadow after meadow. One after another.
The fires burn, the kettles boil.
Why do the kettles boil? To mend the scythe.
What is the scythe for? To cut the grass.
What is the grass for? To feed the cows.
Why do they feed the cows? To get the milk.
What is the milk for? For the pigs to drink.
Why should they drink it? To root up the hills.
Why should they root up the hills? To sow the grain.
Dear little cow, dear little cow with the sleek head,
She looks through the little window, she disappears inside the gate.[4]

The Church fought powerfully against the manifest remnants of paganism, not only by direct prohibitions, but also by the organiza-

[2] See Sakharov, *Legends of the Russian People* (*The People's Journal*, St. Petersburg, 1849, p. 99).

[3] *Ethnographic Review*, 1897, No. I, p. 147.

[4] A. B. Zernova, "Materials on Agricultural Magic in the Dmitrovsky Region," *Soviet Ethnography*, No. 3, 1932. Mention is made of the ceremonial pastries baked in the shape of a cow.

tion of its Christian celebrations and ceremonies, or by the infusion
of its own Christian meanings into the interpretation of the traditional popular ceremonies. In the fourth century, during the reign
of Justinian* the celebration of the calends of January was transferred by the Church to the full cycle of the Christmas holidays, ex-
tending from Christmas Day (December 25) to the Baptism (January 6). This circumstance must have contributed powerfully to the
mingling of ceremonies of the various cycles, and also of the songs
which accompanied these ceremonies. This process of the fusion of
Christian with agrarian-magic elements, and also especially the fusion
of the ceremonies of the calends (New Year) with those of Christmas, continued even later among many peoples who had been exposed to the influence of the Greco-Roman Christian culture. The
old pagan songs and games began to be replaced by the Following
of the Star and the Wise Men of the East; the agrarian-magic ceremonies of the scattering of straw, and so on, began to be interpreted
as the Church's way of commemorating the birth of Christ in the
manger, and so forth. The New Year ceremonies, fortunetelling and
songs, having as their purpose the securing of the harvest, began
with increasing frequency to be transferred from the New Year holiday, some to Christmas Eve, some to the eve of the Baptism. Hence
comes the absence of a strict dividing line between the Christmas
kolyadki and the New Year *shshchedrivki* † in Ukrainia, which were
originally distinct both in content and in form.

All these phenomena, in the field of the history of the fusion of
cults and ceremonies, told most fully upon the history of the development of ceremonial songs—the *kolyadki,* and the *shchedrivki* which
are related to them.

Naturally the ecclesiastical elements, in content and mode of life,
must originally have predominated in the Christmas songs, not in
those of the New Year. And indeed, A. N. Veselovsky has correctly
observed [5] that, for example, in Bulgaria the *kalyedari* (singers in

---

* Justinian, 483–565.—Ed.
† Originally Christmas songs but transferred to New Year's Day; sung by
choruses of young people to each farmer.—Ed.
[5] A. N. Veselovsky, *Researches,* No. VII, p. 106.

praise of Christ) are distinguished from the *vasilchari* (singers on New Year's Eve), just as in Ukrainia it was one thing to sing the *kolyady* and another to sing the *shchedrovi*; furthermore, in Ukrainia the *shchedrovi* were customarily sung by the young people, while the *kolyady* were frequently performed by groups comprising only the elderly parishioners, with the churchwarden at their head; and a similar distinction was observed also in Rumania. The Christian *kolyadki*, to a considerable degree, were nourished from ecclesiastical sources, approximating even in their melodies (for example, in Rumania) to the Church Psalms, and being chanted by the ecclesiastical brotherhoods, recalling the Christmas organizations of the Middle Ages in western Europe.

The *shchedrivka* was intended for performance on a "bountiful," that is, a rich evening; this term was applied to New Year's Eve, or to "St. Basil's Eve" (the eve of the holiday in honor of Basil the Great). But with the passing of time, as has already been said, many features of the New Year celebration were transferred also to the eves of Christmas and of the Baptism, and the distinction in principle between the *kolyadki* and the *shchedrivki* was lost.

What are the basic subject motifs of the *kolyadki*? A detailed analysis of the patterns of the Ukrainian *kolyadki* (which are, out of the repertory of all the peoples, by far the most diverse and numerous) has been made by A. A. Potebnya, and their connections with those of the Balkan peoples (the Rumanians, Greeks, and Serbs) have been established by A. N. Veselovsky.

In Russian folklore considerably fewer of the *kolyadki* are preserved than in the Ukrainian; but, judging from documentary evidences, one sees that in former times they were very widely diffused.

Very many of the *kolyadki* and *shchedrivki*, in full harmony with the original agrarian-magical significance of the New Year and Christmas ceremonies, have as their aim, by the aid of literary forms, to evoke the ideas of harvest, wealth, fertility, and marriage. The poetic word, as in many other instances in folklore, fulfills exactly the same magic function as the ceremony which it accompanies. Such, for example, is the following *kolyadka*, having a magical significance—the significance of an incantation for the harvest:

Where the she-goat walks,
 There the wheat springs up;
Where the she-goat turns tail,
 There the wheat grows thick;
Where the she-goat's foot passes,
 There the wheat is in a heap [in the shock];
Where the she-goat lifts her horn,
 There the wheat is in the stack.[6]

Or the *kolyadka* with an incantation for the increase of the family, the increase of the number of working hands in the household:

There are young singers
 In Ivanov's yard;
Of the tall Irene
 They bought a pot—
To boil the sweet porridge,
To feed their wives,
That they might bear children.
And let them plow the field,
And break up the fallow land.
 Bring on the pies! [7]

In view of the many centuries of life of the *kolyadki* and *shche-drivki* in the agricultural peasant surroundings, the majority of the forms in them are connected with the cares of the farm and the struggles of the peasantry. The majority of the forms are taken from the farming customs and from the nature of the countryside. Here again, however, in accordance with the magical function of the song, its performer sometimes strives for the creation of ideal forms, surpassing the actual living conditions of the peasantry. Hence, for example, when striving to express in their song the desire for wealth, or the incantation which would procure it, the peasant singers naturally are not satisfied with a description of the usual country modes of life, but draw pictures of the sumptuous life of the wealthy social groups: princes, boyars, merchants. In many of the *kolyadki*, therefore, we encounter figures and pictures of the mode of life of the prince's *druzhina* and the feudalistic boyar classes.

[6] Shein, *Materials* (St. Petersburg, 1887), Vol. I, Pt. 1, p. 91.
[7] Zernova, *op. cit.*, p. 17.

Finally, the elements of primitive agrarian magic, the historical and the real elements of social life, were interwoven with the figures and the stylistic features of the ecclesiastical singing and the ecclesiastical legendary creations in their popular reworking: here are also the motifs of the biblical and apocryphal legends, pictures of the birth of Christ, the Adoration of the Magi; the motifs of the journeyings of Christ, the Blessed Virgin, the apostles and the saints on earth; the search for the infant Christ, and his concealment by the Blessed Mother; the visitation by God and the saints of the householder for whom the song is being sung; the elements of apocryphal narratives of the wood of the Cross and its healing properties; apocryphal legends of the cursing by Christ or the Blessed Mother of an aspen and a thorn tree, and so forth.

In many of the *kolyadki* there is seen an obvious adaptation of Christian legends and myths to the requirements of agrarian magic. In one Ukrainian *kolyadka*, widely diffused in many variants, it is related "how the dear Lord Himself drives the bulls, the Most Holy Virgin causes springs to come forth, and St. Peter walks behind the plow." This song, by a device similar to that which is often observed in the charms (see below), introduces into its epic portion the figures of God and of the saints, in order to attach a still greater magical power to the poetic formula.

In some cases a comparative analysis of the variants reveals most clearly the gradual introduction of the ecclesiastical Christian elements into the primary traditional poetic forms. In many of the *kolyadki* there is an account of the visitation of the host by holy guests, on whom depends the future welfare of the man and his household. In other variants the "guests" are deprived of their Christian attributes: they are either the spirits of ancestors or the sun, moon, and rain, which bring joy both to nature and to man. The sun, moon, and rain enter into a dispute with one another, as to which of them is higher (more important) than the others; and the argument is settled in favor of the rain, the most longed-for guest of the agriculturalist.

The development of the epic portion of the *kolyadki* furthered the easy interpenetration into them of motifs drawn from other, very diverse genres of folklore: epic songs, particularly *byliny*, tales, religious verse, charms, riddles, lyrics, epithalamia, and other ceremonial songs. This endows the material of the *kolyadki* with an especially important significance for the investigations of folklorists.

Fortunetelling, masquerades, dances, songs—this is the content of the feasts and the evening gatherings in the earlier period, at the Christmas holidays. This holiday time (after all the work of the fall season has been finished, and before the beginning of the women's winter tasks of spinning and weaving), being fortunate so far as its outward circumstances were concerned, when the supplies had not yet begun to run low, was the favorite season of the peasant youth.

Following after the holidays of Christmas, New Year, and the Baptism, with ceremonials and songs related to one another, came the holiday of Shrovetide (the European carnival). The agrarian-magical significance of this holiday is not denied by anyone at the present time. Shrovetide, properly, is a spring holiday, but it has been drawn from the spring cycle and into the winter one, to a considerable extent, because of the Church's great Lenten fast, which forbade any kind of merrymaking in the course of the seven weeks preceding Easter.

Everyone is familiar with the Shrovetide revelry, the gluttony and drunkenness, the traditionally permitted license of conduct at that season. All this has a direct relationship to the primitive agrarian magic, as an example of its manifest survivals. Revelry and gluttony, in primitive culture, are not only an expression of fullness and satisfaction, but they also represent in themselves an incontrovertible example of the so-called "homeopathic" magic: the effort to attain the wished-for manifestation through a representation of it. The thought of the agriculturalist, from earliest spring, is directed toward the expectation of a good harvest, fruitfulness, and satisfaction. By the representation of fullness, satisfaction, merriment, the agriculturalist considered it possible to have an influence on nature and on his farm (both in the field and in the cattle stall). The sexual freedom permitted by tradition at the Shrovetide revels (in Europe at the carnivals) had a direct relationship to the incantations for fertility, both in the family and among the domestic animals. With the erotic aspects of the ceremonies there is connected also the eroticism of the words, amounting at times to a license which cannot be reproduced in print. The Shrovetide songs, ribald sayings, and jests are almost all of such a character as this.

The whole series of ceremonial aspects shows that the Shrovetide holidays were connected with charms to call out the warmth of the returning sun in spring. And here again the same ceremonial performances betoken the magical incantation. The primitive mind, as it were, does not believe that the sun will complete its revolution; it is necessary to help the sun, and the help of man is expressed through homeopathic magic—by the representation of a circle or of a circular motion. (They bake pancakes, make an uninterrupted circle on horseback around the village or around several country settlements, and walk out carrying a lighted wheel fastened to a tall pole.)

At first glance there may seem to be something strange in the interweaving into the merry Shrovetide revelry of motifs dealing with the dead. This, of course, is not an expression, as it was formerly thought to be, of the characteristic Russian national traits ("now bold revelry, now heartsick melancholy"). Here we have to do, as has been said above, with an inalienable part of all the spring ceremonies, with the commemoration of the dead, with departed ancestors and their cult. In the spring, when all nature comes to life once more, the man whose thinking ran along primitive lines naturally supposed that the dead kinsman would rise again; in any case, he supposed that it was precisely in spring, most easily of all, that the soul of the departed could commune with the living, in order to help them in their domestic affairs. But the possibility of an interview must be made easy for the departed; that is why magic is employed for them. People bring eggs to the cemetery, especially fried eggs (the symbol of life and of rebirth); and they also break eggs on the grave, or throw them behind their backs (the dead person will not appear before anyone face to face); after tearful lamentations they eat, drink, and make merry in the conviction that the departed will also do the same. It is true that, in the later period, the majority of the populace, who according to tradition performed these and other ceremonies, had already ceased to recognize their primitive magic significance; none the less, this significance may be considered as fully established. Here also the Church tried to adapt the pagan ceremony to its own purposes: the journey to the cemetery began to be interpreted as a leave-taking, that is, a prayer to the departed—to the "ancestors"—for the foregiveness of sins.

Still another ceremonial custom was in existence: the "burning" or "sending off of Shrovetide." On the "farewell" Sunday, while the older people are "saying farewell" at the cemetery, the young people will steal (it is absolutely necessary that it should be *stolen*) a peasant's sledge or a wooden harrow, placing it with the teeth upward; they lay firewood on it, thrust in bunches of straw, or a straw dummy, pour kerosene over it, and toward evening they draw this "Shrovetide" through the whole countryside and into a field of rye, shouting out the song: "Enough, O Winter, of wintertime," or such a song as this:

> Dear guest of ours, Shrovetide,
> Avdotyushka Izotyevna,
> White Dunya, rosy Dunya,
> With the long braid, three arshins long,
> With the scarlet ribbon adorned with silver coins,
> Snow-white kerchief of the latest mode,
> Black eyebrows so carefully groomed,
> Blue fur coat with red lapels,
> Finely woven bast shoes with big tops,
> White leg cloths, bleached snowy white.[8]

Then they begin to tease some person who is known for the quickness of his temper, provoking him to harsh language. Bidding farewell to Shrovetide, they sing such songs as these:

> Shrovetide, the deceiver, has deceived us,
> For the great fast she has given us the tail of a radish.[9]

> Dear guest, Shrovetide,
> Avdotya Izotyevna,
> Have you spent much substance,
> Have you drunk much wine, much beer? [10]

[8] *Ibid.*, p. 18.   [9] *Ibid.*, p. 18.   [10] *Ibid.*, p. 19.

Finally, they set fire to the "Shrovetide" with bunches of straw; they chase one another with firebrands; they toss them up into the air or scatter them through the field. The magical significance of such a rite is very easily revealed: the fire, the running with it—all this is related to the ceremonial magic of the springtime sun; the coarse language and the eroticism have been explained above. What, then, is the meaning of the "dummy" representing Shrovetide?

A comparative study of the agrarian cults, which has been made with especial brilliance in the works of Frazer (see his book, *The Golden Bough*), establishes the connection between the "dummy," made at the time of the spring and summer holidays among nearly all agricultural peoples, and the cult of the dying and rising divinity of vegetative nature. (Compare the cults which are homogeneous in character—that of Osiris in Egypt, Attis in Phrygia, Adonis in Syria, Dionysus, Hyacinthus, and Persephone in Greece.) The Russian agricultural pre-Christian religion lacked the ability for, or at least was not successful in, working out such complex religious-agrarian cults as these cults of the ancient peoples around the Mediterranean; however, in the Shrovetide and in many other peasant ceremonies we do constantly meet with elements of analogous cults.

As is well known, the Christian conception of the dying and rising god grew up in part on the soil of the religious traditions mentioned above. But on the Russian soil, as also in the case of many other Christian agricultural peoples, the individual features of the Christian myth, and the ecclesiastical ritualism corresponding to them (for example, the pre-Easter and the Easter rites: the adoration of the "Passion of Christ," the ceremony of the carrying out of the "shroud," the celebration of the resurrection of Christ, with the religious procession walking around the church, the consecration of the Easter cake, cheesecakes and eggs and many other things), easily acclimatized themselves, blending inseparably with the survivals of the tribal agricultural religion.

Usually, with the festival of the Annunciation (March 25), there begins the incantation of spring, that is, the magical ceremony which is an invocation for the swift coming of spring. The girls, as if representing the springtime hubbub of the birds, sing songs at opposite ends of the village, one chorus answering another; as soon as one finishes, another begins in the distance, and so on from village to village. Often the girls, besides, hold in their hands the branches of trees, with images of birds, made of cloth, placed on them, and they sing, "Larks, larks, come flying to us, bring the beautiful spring." There was a custom, throughout Russia, of baking cakes out of dough fashioned into the shape of larks, on March 9. At the foundation of this custom lies that very same homeopathic magic: the coming of the birds is one of the convincing signs of spring; by the representation of the birds it was thought possible to evoke their flight, and consequently, also, to evoke the arrival of spring. The confusion of cause-and-effect relationships is highly characteristic of the primitive mentality. There is a dialogue with Spring, reproduced in the spring songs of invocation:

Beautiful Spring,
What have you brought us?
The Summer beautiful.[11]

Beautiful Spring,
On what have you come?
On the rod, on the furrow,
On the ear of the oat,
On the wheaten cake.[12]

Spring, Spring,
On what have you come?
On the plow, on the harrow,
On the black mare;
O you larks,
Dear little larks,
Fly into the field,
Bring health:
First for the cows,
Second, the sheep,
Third, for man.[13]

[11] Sakharov, *Legends of the Russian People*, Bk. VII, p. 16.

[12] Shein, *The Great-Russian in His Songs, Ceremonies, Customs, Beliefs, Tales, Legends, etc.*, Vol. I, Pt. 1 (St. Petersburg, 1898), No. 1175.

[13] From MS materials preserved in the Central Museum of the Peoples of the USSR, in Moscow.

To meet the spring, the women went out of the village into the field, spread out on the meadow, so lately freed from snow, a white linen cloth, placed bread upon it, and gave the invocation: "This is for you, Mother Spring." [14]

In time the springtime holidays were linked to the festival of the Annunciation, to Maundy Thursday, to Easter, to St. Thomas' Week (the first week after Easter). Besides, St. Thomas' Sunday was called "The Hill of Beauty," Monday was called *Radunitsa* (ancestors' day), and Tuesday "The Day of the Dead." The last three days are closely connected with the customs of commemoration of the departed, of which we have spoken in detail above, when we were uncovering the survivals of the tribal ancestor cults.

Finally, as in the Christmas *kolyadki* and feasting songs, into the spring songs and games are interwoven the motifs of marriage, ravishing, or the choice of a bride by the youth. Great popularity was enjoyed by the well known springtime dancing and singing game, "The Sowing of the Millet": "And we have sown the millet, we have sown."

In the course of the seven weeks following Easter, the young people of the village made merry, performed choral dances, played games, and sang songs. But the merrymaking mounted with especial force toward Trinity Day. The week preceding it, the seventh after Easter (for which reason, the Thursday of that week bears the title of "The Seventh Day"), was called *Rusalia* week, and again was dedicated to the commemoration of ancestors (see above).

The motifs of agrarian magic in *Rusalia* week are sounded with particular power. With Trinity Day was connected the custom, which in its time was widely diffused throughout the country, of decorating the houses with fresh green branches, especially those of birch trees. According to the idea of the peasants, in these birch trees there dwelt the souls of deceased relatives. They decorated a birch tree with ribbons, walked with it through the countryside, and sang special songs in honor of it. Sometimes such a birch tree bore the name of the *Rusalka* (Undine) itself; sometimes one of the girls

[14] On this point see M. E. Sheremeteva, *The Agricultural Ceremony of the "Invocation of Spring" in the Kaluga Region* (Kaluga, 1930).

represented the *Rusalka*; sometimes, as at Shrovetide, a doll was made of cloth or straw.

Akin to this is a ceremony which at one time was widely diffused in the former province of Kaluga, of the "funeral of the *kukushka*," that is, of a doll, made of the roots of the plant called "the *kukushka's* teardrops."[15]

On the Wednesday before Trinity Day the girls started out to choose and "mark" the birches, and on the next day, on Thursday of the seventh week, or else on Saturday, with a fried egg yolk and beer, they went to garland the chosen birch trees. Each one brought with her a dish of fried eggs. After all the birch trees had been garlanded, the fried eggs were placed around one birch tree, and the girls, joining hands, performed a choral dance to the following song:

> To you the maidens have come,
> Birch tree, birch tree,
> Be garlanded, curly one!
> To you the fair ones have come,
> They have brought you cakes,
> With fried eggs.[16]

In the grove the girls in turn kissed each other through the garland on the birch tree, gave one another the oath of friendship and adoption, and along with this ceremony of adoption they sang songs:

> Let's adopt each other as sisters, let's adopt each other;
> Let us love each other, sisters, let us love each other,
> So that we will not wrangle with you for ever.[17]

Alexander Veselovsky sees in the custom of the adoption the survivals of a primitive hetaerism, that is, of a ceremonial seasonal mingling of the sexes, connected with the cult of spring.[18]

On Trinity Day the girls went to "ungarland" the birch trees. By the garlands which they had twined upon the birch tree, they fore-

[15] See R. E. Kedrina, "The Ceremonial of the Baptism and Funeral of the *Kukushka* in Connection with Popular Nepotism," *Ethnographic Review*, Nos. 1-2, XCII-XCIII, 1912. A review of this article was given by Y. M. Sokolov in *The Living Past*, 1913, Bks. 3-4.

[16] Zernova, *op. cit.*, p. 27.

[17] *Ibid.*, p. 17.

[18] A. N. Veselovsky, "Hetaerism, Brotherhood and Sisterhood in a Baptismal Ritual," *Journal of the Ministry of Public Education*, 1894, Bk. 2.

told their own fates: if the branches had withered, then the girl would either marry or die; but if they had not, then she would still remain among the maidens.

After ungarlanding the birch trees, the girls made garlands for themselves, adorned their heads with them, and then went, wearing them, to the river, and there again told their fortunes.

The garland is at one and the same time a symbol, a magical object (in the incantations for marriage, happiness, and fertility), and an object which is used for the divination of one's fate:

> I will go into the green garden to walk,
> I will pick from the plant the flower,
> I will weave a garland for my head.
> I will go to the River Volga.
> I will stand at the washing-place, on the raft,
> I will throw my little garland on the water;
> And I myself will walk on a little farther,
> I will watch my little garland:
> Does the garland sink, or not?
> Does my dear friend grieve, or not?—
> Ah, my little garland has sunk,
> I know my dear one has deceived me.[19]

The winding of the garlands was also utilized as a magical means for procuring the harvest. There is a song which gives clear evidence on this point:

> Let us go, girls,
> Into the grassy meadows,
> To weave garlands—
> We will weave garlands
> For the good years,
> For abundant grain,
> For full ears of barley,
> For dewy oats,
> For the black buckwheat,
> For the white cabbage.[20]

There is clearly revealed the connection of the *Rusaliae* with the cult of vegetation and with the ancestor cult, particularly in the cere-

[19] Shein, *The Great-Russian*, Vol. I, No. I (St. Petersburg, 1898), No. 1244, p. 362.
[20] Shein, *Materials*, Vol. I, Pt. 1, No. 178, pp. 185-186.

monies which are already familiar to us—the starting of camp fires, jumping through them, public bathing, and the making of a straw dummy. Such a straw doll was first carried in the choral dances, and then torn to pieces and the straw scattered in the air. Sometimes they let the doll or the decorated birch tree sink in the water.

We have already mentioned similar ceremonies in connection with other spring holidays. But these ceremonies are expressed most fully of all in the summer holiday of St. John the Bather, on the day of John the Baptist (June 24). In this holiday there has clearly taken place a blending of two ceremonial cycles: those of the spring and the autumn. The ecclesiastical calendar broke the sequence of the pre-Christian agricultural ritual. In this summer holiday there was also vividly manifested that "duality of religion" of which we have spoken above.

The popular epithet of John the Baptist—"The Bather"—was associated by the Russian peasant with the traditional custom of ceremonial ablution, bathing as a manifestation of "lustrational" (purificatory) magic. The "Bather" was very soon transformed into a personified representation of some kind of divinity, a natural vegetative object of worship. "The Bather," an epithet of a celebrated Christian saint, or the name of a holiday in his honor (compare again the *"kolyada"* and *"Rusalka"*), is treated, in some of the ancient Russian literary monuments, as a pagan divinity—consequently, for the Christian, as a demon. The Gustyn chronicle (seventeenth century) thus describes the holiday of the Bather:

The Bather was the god of abundance, as Ceres was among the Greeks; and to him the foolish ones rendered thanks for the abundance at that time when they had the harvest near. Even down to the present time, in certain lands, the foolish ones honor the remembrance of this demon, beginning with the 23rd day of June, on the eve of the birthday of John the Forerunner, even up to the harvest and beyond, in this precise manner: toward evening there gathers a simple crowd of both sexes, and they weave garlands for themselves from edible herbs, or roots, and girding themselves with grasses, they start the fire; or they set up a green tree, and joining hands, they circle around the fire, singing their songs, senselessly invoking the Bather; then they leap through that fire.

Frequently in later times the word "Kupala" or "Kupalo" (Bather) was understood as the name of a being of the female sex. This deity and John were paired together. Preserving the forms, already familiar to us, of the spring magical ceremonies (the bathing, the tossing of garlands, and so on), the holiday of John Kupala retained in full the customs of "sister adoption," lighting fires and jumping through them, and making ceremonial dummies. Besides, in the latter ceremony, in place of one dummy, there sometimes appeared two: (1) Kupala, Marena, Morena; (2) Yarilo, Kostroma, Kostrubonka. They either burned the doll, or drowned it, or tore it to pieces, and afterward buried it. The combination of merrymaking and lamentation, connected with the burial of the dolls, is a very clear analogy with the Oriental cults of the dying and rising god, Adonis and others. The survival of the cult of the dying and rising divinity is also preserved in the children's summer game: a woman among the children, called "Kostroma," pretends to be dead, but then suddenly springs up and frightens the children away. Frequently the ceremonial doll, the dummy, is replaced by a tree, a birch. Sometimes, it is true, chiefly in Ukrainia, in the bathing ritual, the central role is played by a girl adorned with a garland. Around her choral dances are performed, in her honor songs are sung. In such cases the girl was called a "poplar" or a "bush." Ceremonial trees or their living personifications, of course, are connected with the cult of the divinity of vegetation, familiar to us from the spring holidays.

On St. John's Night the young people went into the woods to search for miraculous flowers, most often for the fern, which was thought to bloom on that night. On the same night they sought for treasure. Many legends are connected with these traditional beliefs.

A high poetic quality distinguishes the Kupala songs, in which there is related the origin of the flower "John-and-Mary" (the cowwheat); a brother and a sister, ignorant of their relationship, were married, and were then transformed into a flower, consisting of yellow and blue petals.

Soon after the day of John Kupala, usually on St. Peter's Day (June 29), but in some places considerably earlier than St. John's Day, the triumphal "seeing-off of spring" took place. On that day all the maidens and youths, dressed in holiday attire, danced and sang songs, swaying on roomy swings. (Swaying is one of the devices of positive magic: it represents the rise and the growth of vegetation.) They sang songs, mostly of a cheerful nature, and tried as best they could to make merry on that day. Toward evening, at sunset, all the young people, with flowers and songs, started out, at first along the village, but then around it, and, finally, went to the farthest limits of the village fields. Here, as soon as the sun began to set, they all fell on their knees and bowed once to the ground, exclaiming: "Farewell, beautiful spring, farewell! Come quickly back again!" Then they went singing to the river, where they performed choral dances, played games of running and catching, and returned home; the songs were in one way or another concerned with spring and the springtime merrymaking. For example:

> Return again, beautiful Spring, come back—
> We will put up swings again,
> And we shall swing our dear friend, too.[21]

Having seen off the spring, the peasants went on to the haymaking and to other heavy tasks. Revelries were obliged to cease, and songs be silent for a time.

The approach to the harvest, and the conclusion of it, produced special feelings among the peasants and, of course, called forth their poetic creative powers. The beginning of the harvest is called *Zazhinki* (preharvesting), and the end *Dozhinki* (postharvesting). At the beginning of the harvest, the women and girls made garlands from the ears of rye, and with preharvest songs bore them home in triumph.

Dozhinki, or postharvest songs, are the songs performed at the end of the harvest, at the time of the holiday of the harvest home, the so-called *dozhinki, toloka,* or *taloka.* The postharvest songs were diffused among all agricultural peoples. Among the eastern Slavs they were preserved mainly by the White Russians, but they were found also among the Ukrainians and among the Russians. The basic mo-

---

[21] B. and Y. Sokolov, *Tales and Songs of the Belo-Ozero Region* (Moscow, 1915), No. 361, p. 404.

tifs of the eastern Slavonic postharvest songs are the portrayal of the
heavy work of reaping, praise of the masters, and allusions to regaling.
Basically, these motifs have their root in the conditions of the tribal
organization and of the "large family"; they are connected partly
with the general storing of the harvest—the "mutual help" or *toloka*
—and they are partly concerned with the work which a serf does for
his lord:

> Sound out then, you bells,
> Make glad the mistress' heart!
> For her we have reaped the harvest field clean.
> Yes, we have reaped and reaped,
> Yes, we have tended it carefully for her.
> But when we had reaped the field clean,
> We began to crave the fire drink.
> Our eyes perceive
> That the boundary is not far away.
> When we have reaped up to the boundary,
> Then we will drink our fill of the fire drink.
> We will eat our fill of pies,
> We will sing and sing our songs.[22]

The mistress—the mother of the large family—goes out into the
field and encourages her daughters and daughters-in-law, calling
them by caressing names:

> The little wife Petrochkova
> Went out very early
> Into her harvest field;
> With her she brought out
> Her daughters the swans,
> Her daughters-in-law the quail.
> "Reap, daughters-in-law,
> Reap, daughters!
> Daughters the swans,
> Daughters-in-law the quail;
> In the morning very early,
> In the evening very late,
> That we may have wherewith to live;
> Very well, yes, very good.[23]

[22] Shein, *The Great-Russian*, Vol. I, No. 1275.
[23] *Ibid.*, No. 1276.

In the field the tribal arrangement of places was strictly maintained. The mother-in-law reaps in front of all the others; beside her on the right hand is her eldest daughter, and only after the last daughter does the eldest daughter-in-law reap. At the end of the reaping they sang the songs indicated above, dealing with the harvest.

Other motifs of the postharvest songs are connected with archaic survivals of primitive agricultural ceremonies of a magical character: with the ceremonies of "curling the beard" of a he-goat or "god of the field," either Volos, or Elijah, or Egor, or Christ, that is, with the ceremonial reverence paid to the last sheaf in the field, with the making of a postharvest "grandfather sheaf" or a postharvest "woman," or of a postharvest garland, which is decorated and borne with songs to the master's house. The curling of the "beard" of a mythical he-goat (or of other creatures), and also the decoration of the sheaf, are variations of the numerous magical ceremonies among the agricultural peoples of the Mediterranean and of Europe, based on the view that the spirit of the harvest field is a he-goat, or a creature having the form of a goat (like Faunus or Silvanus), which is pursued by the reapers and hides itself in the last unreaped sheaf. This viewpoint has been expressed by Mannhardt, and was later developed in more detail by Frazer in *The Golden Bough*.

The curling of the "beard of the he-goat" is accompanied by the following song:

> The he-goat lies by the boundary line,
> And admires his beard;
> And whose is this beard,
> All dripping with honey,
> And all garlanded with silk? [24]

Or they sing a song, not to the he-goat, but to Egor:

> Egor, come,
> Leading your horse,
> And feed our horses,
> And feed the ewe lambs,
> And feed the little cow.[25]

[24] E. R. Romanov, *White Russian Annals*, VIII, p. 266.
[25] Zernova, *op. cit.*, p. 33.

Toward the end of the harvest the reapers roll or somersault across the harvest field, pronouncing the following incantations:

> Stubble of the summer grain,
> Give back my strength
> For the long winter.[26]

> Harvest field, harvest field, give back my strength,
> I have reaped you, I have lost my strength.[27]

Sometimes, with the same sentences, they drove across the field a pregnant woman or a priest in full vestments.[28]

The reaping songs complete the cycle of ceremonial poetry connected with the calendar of festivals. The Russian song, closely interwoven with a magical, or in any event with an agrarian-religious ceremony, clearly discloses the social nature of the ceremonial folklore; this song expressed the state of mind and the world concept of the peasant, the agriculturalist and plowman: both his thought and his feeling were directed toward the earth, to the plowland, to the field. From the beginning of the year, in the depths of winter, he started to dream of the future harvest; with joyful anticipation he greeted the spring; he was completely absorbed in heavy work during the summer, and only in the autumn, for a short time, did he find any satisfaction for himself; only in the autumn, for a short time, could he experience material prosperity. In the spring the young people, who were carefree and made merry, could be happy. But the peasant, the householder, speaks of spring unkindly: spring is "niggardly," she holds back all her stores, she sweeps out the bins to the last grain:

> Oh, the spring is beautiful!
> She has shaken out everything;
> From the grain bins
> She has scraped out everything;
> With her new broom
> She has swept out everything.[29]

[26] *Ibid.*   [27] *Ibid.*
[28] See D. K. Zelenin, "Related Slovenian Peasant Rituals of Tossing and Swaying on the Ground," *Ethnographic News*, 1927, Bk. 5.
[29] Shein, *The Great-Russian*, Vol. I (St. Petersburg, 1898), No. 1180.

BIBLIOGRAPHY

COLLECTIONS OF SONGS

Chubinskii, P. P., *Trudy etnografichesko-statisticheskoi ekspeditsii v Zapadno-russkii krai* (Proceedings of the Ethnographic-Statistical Expedition to the West Russian Region), Vol. III (St. Petersburg, 1872).

Golovatskii, L. F., "Narodnye pesni Galitskoi i Ugorskoi Rusi" (Popular Songs of Galician and Ugrian Old Russia,) *Obriadovye pesni* (Ceremonial Songs) (Moscow, 1878), Pt. 2.

Shein, P. V., *Materialy dlia izucheniia byta i iazyka russkogo naseleniia sev.-zap. kraia* (Materials for the Study of the Mode of Life and Language of the Russian Populace of the Northwestern Region, Vol. I, Pts. 1 and 2 (St. Petersburg, 1887) (*Sborn. otdeleniia russk. iaz. i slov.*) Akademii nauk (*Annals of the Division of Russian Language and Literature of the Academy of Sciences*, Vol. XLI).

——, *Velikoruss v svoikh pesniakh, obriadakh, obychaiakh, verovaniikh, skazkakh, legendakh i. t. d.* (The Great-Russian in His Songs, Ceremonies, Customs, Beliefs, Tales, Legends, etc.), Vol. I, No. I (St. Petersburg, 1898).

Kireyevskii, N. V., *Pesni, novaia seriia* (Songs, New Series), No. I, ed. Acad. V. F. Miller and Prof. M. N. Speransky (Moscow, 1911).

Sokolov, B. and Y., *Skazki i pesni Belozerskogo kraia* (Tales and Songs of the Belo-Ozero Region), Moscow, 1915.

RESEARCHES

Veselovskii, Aleksandr, *Razyskaniia v oblasti russkogo dukhovnogo stikha Rumynskie, slavianskie i grecheski koliadki* (Investigations in the Field of Russian Religious Verse: Rumanian, Slavonic and Greek Kolyady), VII (St. Petersburg, 1883) (*Annals of the Division of Russian Language and Literature of the Academy of Sciences*, Vol. XXXII).

——, *Razyskaniia . . . XIV, Genvarskie rusalii i gotskie igry v Vizantii* (Investigations . . . : January Rusalia and Games of the Goths in Byzantium, XIV) (St. Petersburg, 1890) (*Annals of the Division of Russian Language and Literature of the Academy of Sciences*, Vol. XLVI).

——, *Sobr. Soch.* (Collected Works), Vol. I (St. Petersburg, 1913), or *Tri glavy iz istoricheskoi poetiki* (Three Chapters from Historical Poetics) (St. Petersburg, 1899).

——, "Geterizm, pobratimstvo, i kumovstvo v kupal'noi obriadnosti" (Hetaerism, Brotherhood, and Adoption in a Baptismal Ritual), ZHMNP (Journal of the Ministry of Public Education), 1894, Bk. 2.

Potebnia, A. A., *Ob'iasneniia malorusskikh i srodnykh narodnykh pesen* (Explanations of Little-Russian and Related Popular Songs), Vol. III (Warsaw, 1887), *Russk. filologichesk. vestnik* (Russian Philological News, Vols. XI-XVII, 1884–1887).

Vladimirov, P. V., *Vvedenie v istoriiu russkoi slovesnosti* (Introduction to the History of Russian Literature) (Kiev, 1896).

Karskii, E. F., *Belorussy* (The White Russians), Vol. III, No. I (Moscow, 1916).

Miller, V. F., *Russkaia maslenitsa i zapodnoevropeiskii karnaval* (The Russian Shrovetide and the Western European Carnival) (Moscow, 1884).

Anichkov, E. V., *Vesenniaia obriadovaia pesnia na Zapade i u slavian* (The Springtime Ceremonial Song in the West and Among the Slavs), Pt. I (St. Petersburg, 1903), Pt. 2 (1905) (*Annals of the Division of Russian Language and Literature of the Academy of Sciences,* Vols. LXXIV and LXXVIII).

Kagarov, E. G., *Religiia drevnikh slavian* (Religion of the Ancient Slavs) (Moscow, 1918).

Zelenin, D. K., *Ocherki russkoi mifologii* (Outlines of Russian Mythology), No. I, *Umershie Neestestvennoi smert'iu i rusalki* (Those Who Have Died an Unnatural Death and the Rusalki) (Petrograd, 1918).

——, *Russische (ostslavische) Volkskunde* (Berlin und Leipzig, 1927).

Sheremeteva, M. E., *Zemledel'cheskii obriad "Zaklinanie vesny" v Kaluzhskom krae* (The Agricultural Ceremonial of the "Invocation of Spring" in the Kaluga Region) (Kaluga, 1930).

Zernova, A. B., "Materialy po sel'skokhoziaistvennoi magin v Dmitrovskom krae" (Materials on Agricultural Magic in the Dmitrovsky Region), *Sov. Etnografia* (Soviet Ethnography), No. 3, 1932.

WEDDING CEREMONIALS AND CHANTS

❧§❧

Wedding ceremonials and the songs, laments, storytellers' embellishments, and games connected with them are of particularly great importance for the understanding of the historical vicissitudes of folklore, the survivals in it of old points of view and poetics.

As in the ceremonial poetry connected with the calendar festivals, so also in the peasant wedding, there is often obvious an absolutely direct connection with the household mode of life which produced it. The wedding is, above all things, a definitely household proceeding: the reception into the family, into the household, of a new member—a worker and a continuer of the race. Therefore the wedding was considered by the peasant, who lived under a natural economy or had not definitively broken with it, as above all an economic necessity. In the large, patriarchal, undivided family the daughter-in-law is a worker who must perform the heaviest tasks (in the field, the yard, and the cottage). Therefore, in the choice of a daughter-in-law, they looked to this above all, that "she should be a terrific worker," that she should "have the strength of an animal, and the endurance of a horse," as it is expressed in one wedding chant. It was not outward beauty which was valued in the daughter-in-law, but strength, vigor, and health. These qualities were necessary so that the woman might be able to fulfill her second function in the family which was new to her—to produce a healthy and vigorous posterity, the future workers in that same household. By these two calculations, upon which the marriage was made, very many, or at any rate the basic, peculiarities of the traditional peasant "wedding game" are defined.

The sober, agricultural-economic aim of the traditional peasant wedding makes itself felt at every step of the wedding ritual, even in the most poetic ceremonies and songs, which are intended to further the attainment of the ends that are established for the bridegroom and the bride.

Here is the clue to the unproductive outlays of material resources on both sides, and the excessive waste of nerves and strength (for

example, at the beginning, in hysterical weepings and wailings, sometimes prolonged for the course of a week and even longer, and afterward in the unrestrained merrymaking, which often passed over into
wild revelry).

In analyzing these phenomena, it is necessary to bear in mind both
the altogether rational economic considerations, and also those which
are no longer acknowledged as such by us, but which seemed altogether rational for the man whose modes of thinking and feeling were
primitive, who had been nurtured on the animistic and magical concepts and traditions of a social order which was still tribal.

Apart from the fully tangible cares and troubles about the arrangement of the wedding and of a successful marriage, it was necessary
for the bridegroom, the bride, and both the families from which they
came, to take a multitude of measures for protection from the activity
of hostile spirits, or from the displeasure of their tribal domestic
spirits, from every kind of "unclean power," from the "evil eye," from
malevolent wizards and sorcerers. Besides this, it was necessary to
cooperate in every way toward the future good of the married couple,
toward the well-being and increase of their household, the fertility of
their "livestock," and finally, the propitious birth of children.

If we take all this into consideration, it will not be difficult for us
to understand what an enormous place in the wedding games must
have been occupied by the factors of *magic*, both prophylactic and
"productive." [1]

The hostile or "unclean" power can, according to the viewpoint of
the man whose thinking is primitive, be opposed by various methods:
(1) It is possible to drive out the unclean power, or to terrify him
(this is diversionary or apotropaic magic)—that is why they often
fire a gun at the time of the blessing of the bride and groom. At the
time when the wedding party starts for the altar, and so on, they drive
nails into the wall, they thrust pins and needles into the bride's dress,

---

[1] At the present time we project a detailed, systematic investigation of the
diverse forms of magic in the eastern Slavonic wedding ritual against the background of an extensive comparative study: see Prof. E. G. Kagarov, "The Composition and Origin of Wedding Ritualism" (*Annals of the Museum of Anthropology and Ethnography of the Academy of Sciences of the USSR*, Vol. VIII,
Leningrad, 1929).

especially needles without any eyes; they walk three times around the wedding party with an icon, or sweep around it three times with a whisk broom; the best man cracks his whip; they shout and make an uproar. (2) It is possible to deceive the evil power ("exapathetic," or dissimulatory, ceremonies)—hence come conversations with circumlocutions, and hints (especially characteristic are the allegorical conversations at the scene of the matchmaking): not calling the bride and groom by name for a long period of time, with the aim of leading the spirits astray; changes in the path, or the drive of the matchmakers and the wedding train, not going by the accustomed road, but by roundabout ways; the changing of the young people's clothes, the arraying of another girl in the bride's attire at the time of the arrival of the bridegroom for the bride (the custom of showing a pretended bride). (3) It is possible to conceal one's self from the evil spirits, to hide one's self (cryptic magic)—hence the custom of covering the head of the bride with a large kerchief from the moment of betrothal until the beginning or end of the wedding; the closing of doors, windows, and other apertures at various moments of the wedding ceremony; the surrounding of the bridegroom, or of the nuptial pair, by a large suite, the wedding procession, made up always of many "outriders," especially of "groomsmen," or "riders" (horsemen), with lashes in their hands, and little bells and sleigh bells on the necks of their horses. (4) One can get rid of the evil spirit by abstinence—from words (the silence of the bride and groom), from food (the fasting of the bride and groom before the wedding, the abstinence from food at the time of the general feast); sometimes by refraining from the sexual act on the first nuptial night; the avoidance of touching things—the threshold, the door; the avoidance of unlucky days for betrothal and marriage, and so on.

Among the ceremonies of productive magic, mention must be made, above all, of the fructiferous, or fecundatory, that is, those which secure fertility and wealth for the young people: the throwing of grain or hops on the young couple, and their licking up of salt; the placing of a boy on the knees of the young woman when she has just returned from the altar (so that she may bear sons, who are more useful for the peasant household than girls), the washing of the bride with wine, the strewing of straw or hay in the cottage, the deliberate profanity, the eroticism in the singing, the storytellers' elaborations, and the folk dances; the laying under their feet, or on their chairs, of a fur coat, with the fur turned upward (a symbol of wealth and of many children); the touching, or the blows, with a switch, branch, stick, or lash; the treats of eggs or scrambled eggs (the symbols of fertility and of vital power).

Other ceremonies were directed toward the securing of fertility among the cattle: the bed for the newly married couple was often made in the cattle shed, or not far away from the cattle shed, in the belief that the first sexual act of the young woman would exert a magical influence on the fertility of the cattle. A third group of ceremonies was directed toward securing fertility, wealth, and happiness for all those who took part in the wedding festivities: the sprinkling with water in which the bride had washed herself, and so on. A fourth group of ceremonies was directed toward strengthening the bond between the young couple ("syndiasmic," or uniting, ceremonies): the mingling of wine from the glasses of the young couple, their sharing of food and drink, the representation of a pair of doves on the wedding loaf, the simultaneous looking by the young people into the mirror, the stretching of a thread from a small fir tree, placed near the bride's house, to the house of the groom (the game of "telegraph" in the former province of Yaroslav), the treating of the bridegroom with a cake which has lain in the bosom of the bride, the tying together of the bride and groom with a handkerchief, the joining of the young people's hands, and so on.

A fifth group of magic ceremonies includes the rites denoting the bride's separation from the cult of the spirits of her own home: picking off a bit of the stove, or the touching of it by the bride at the time of betrothal and at her departure from the house to go to the altar. A sixth group includes the ceremonies of converse meaning, which signify the uniting of the bride to the cult of the spirits of her husband's family (initiation, or dedicatory, ceremonies): the father-in-law's removing the veil from the bride, the dividing of her braid into two, and the covering of her head with a headdress or headgear, the so-called "encircling" of the young woman, the young woman's walking around the stove, her taking off her husband's shoes in token of submissiveness (a ceremony to which testimony is given by the *Primary Chronicle*: see the words of Rogneda to the matchmakers of Prince Vladimir: "I do not wish to take off the shoes of a coward").

A seventh group includes the ceremonies of propitiation, for example, the bringing of a hen as a sacrifice to the stove (a rite of great antiquity), the throwing of money or bread down the well or into the nearby river, the preparation and distribution of a loaf as sacrificial bread. (Compare in the *Lay of a Certain Lover of Christ*, eleventh century, the expression "to sacrifice bread.") An eighth group includes the purificatory ceremonies, directed toward the cleansing from an unclean power: ablution, having water poured over one's self, the kindling of fires, for example, the riding of the wedding party through a camp fire built of straw, and many others.

The disclosure of the magical beginning of many wedding customs, which had been subjected by former scholars to mythological and esthetic interpretations, confirmed the very close connection of the wedding ritual with the economic life of the husbandman. The economic roots may without difficulty be disclosed also in other factors of the wedding which do not have a specifically magical significance. For example, attention is drawn by the fact of the exceedingly bountiful *distribution of gifts by the bride* to all the members of the numerous family, and sometimes also to all the relatives of the bridegroom.

If we remember, also, that the lion's share of the expenses fell to the lot of the bridegroom's side (which is certainly natural, since they obtained for themselves working strength and one who would prolong their race), then such a bountiful distribution of gifts by the bride would, as it were, seem to contradict this observation. But it is necessary to take into consideration the character of the bride's presents at the traditional peasant wedding: these are exclusively the work of the bride's own hands—shirts, handkerchiefs, and towels, woven and embroidered by her, with which, frequently, the whole cottage is ornamented at the time of the wedding feast, while the groomsmen are covered with them, and the shafts of the horses' harness in the wedding procession are adorned with them. All this is, as it were, an exhibition, for general inspection, of the proof that the bride is a good worker, one who can weave, spin, and embroider. Not without reason, at the arrival of the matchmakers with the first gifts from the bride, did almost all the women of the village, frequently, run together into the home of the bridegroom; they carefully examined and felt of the "gifts" and made a detailed criticism of them. But all this was characteristic, in the conditions of natural economy, in the localities which were the most patriarchal in their economic ways.

With the modification of the economic basis, there was a great change in very many of the factors of the wedding ritual. In particular, the *character of the dowry* of the bride was subject to decisive changes. In localities which had been more powerfully subjected to the penetration of capital and capitalistic relationships, the hand-made dowry quickly began to be replaced by the dowry of ready-made objects (ready-made clothing, domestic furniture of the urban type, mirrors, a gramophone, and other objects of urban culture). At that time, also, in the choice of a bride, according to the later plan, the concerns as to personal capacity for work and physical health begin to disappear; there began to be a great change in the very ideas of feminine beauty; the matchmaker no longer looked so much to the fact that the bride should be "a terrific worker," as to the fact that she should know how to "conduct and behave" herself, that she should be, as it was said in the song, "of good figure and manner." Very instructive are the folkloristic and ethnographic works devoted to the comparative study of weddings in adjacent, but economically differing regions (for example, the purely agricultural and the industrial), or of various periods in one and the same locality; such studies, conducted either according to the horizontal divisions of geography, or according to the vertical divisions of chronology, give a clear idea of the role of capitalism, which in various respects destroyed the patriarchal wedding ritual, which, as we have seen, had grown up on the foundation of many centuries of the natural peasant economy, and on the traditions of the tribal organization.

Besides the agrarian-magic survivals, which are to be discovered in great numbers in the traditional peasant wedding, there are also present in it no small number of historic and legal survivals. By a comparative study of the eastern Slavonic and other wedding rituals, and a comparison of these observations with the mode of life of primitive peoples, in the peasant wedding there are disclosed survivals of various forms of marriage which were peculiar to social-cultural formations that have long ago passed away. In certain details of the peasant wedding there may be perceived survivals of the very ancient *group marriage* of the pretribal commune, the echoes of which we have observed in the springtime ceremonial poetry; otherwise it is difficult to explain the custom which existed in many places, when the young people of the bridegroom's suite (groomsmen and guests) flung themselves upon the bed of the newly married couple before yielding it to them; or when, on the day of the party given for the girls, the youths passed the night with the maidens, the friends of the bride, and the groom with the bride.

In very many details of the "wedding festivities," investigators perceive the survival of another form of marriage, the so-called *abduction*, the kidnaping of the bride by the groom: the arrival of the wedding train, the performance of a carrying away of the bride by the groom by force, the overcoming of all kinds of obstacles. However, other investigators (for example, Professor E. G. Kagarov) treat these factors with caution, justly perceiving in them no less distinct echoes of magic. Apparently, in the many centuries of life of the peasant wedding ceremonial, many of its features must have become confused, blended, and entangled.

But there are facts in which one cannot possibly help seeing direct survivals of abduction. This is a special form of wedding, which even existed down to recent times in the north of Russia—the wedding by the "fiction" of elopement. As the basic cause for maintaining such a form of marriage, there were the direct economic considerations. If, on this side or that, the parties to the marriage were not in a position to sustain the great expenses customarily required by the wedding festivities (with the vast quantity of presents, of food and drink), then they made an agreement with each other for a fictitious abduction of the bride. The abduction freed them from the obligation of holding a sumptuous wedding. At a time agreed upon beforehand, generally when the bride was somewhere outside the house, at the common work (the so-called "mutual help"), the bridegroom, invariably mounted on his horse, rode up to the porch on which the bride was standing, placed her on the horse, and swiftly bore her off to his home. In the course of a day or two the young people went to make their avowal to the bride's parents, fell at their feet, and, having received forgiveness, discussed the material aspects of the marriage.

In the majority of the peasant wedding ceremonies which have been noted down by investigators, there are preserved, most fully of all, the survivals of another form of marriage, the marriage by "purchase and sale." The conversation of the matchmakers often assumes the character of a direct trading agreement, confirmed within a short time after the betrothal, formally, by an act—the striking of hands beneath the coat, as at a fair. Both forms—the abduction, and the purchase and sale—go back to very remote antiquity; in any event, in the period of the disintegration of the tribal structure, both forms of marriage were already in existence.[2]

Having grown up on the foundation of the rural natural economy, the peasant wedding ceremony, preserving many survivals of the tribal commune, and, it may be, in certain aspects, even of the pretribal (for example, the echoes of group marriage), as it continued its existence, was subjected to continual change. In particular, Christianity, which had been implanted from above, with its ecclesiastical rituals and ceremonies, introduced a multitude of its own elements, organizing its own mixed forms of the "duality of religion." Hence come the colossal number of signs of the cross and genuflections, of blessings, the lighting of candles before the images, the carrying of icons around and before the wedding train, and so on. As many investigators emphatically point out, however, among the peasantry, even at a late period, the rite of the church wedding was considered insufficient for an acknowledgment of the marriage as having been legally performed; for this it was necessary that there should be observed, in some degree or other, the popular wedding ceremonial.

[2] Prof. O. Schrader, *The Indo-Europeans* (St. Petersburg, 1913), pp. 112-114; L. Niederle, *Social Life and Culture of the Ancient Slavs* (Prague, 1924), Chap. III.

In studying the peasant "wedding ceremony," one cannot help paying attention to the similarity of very many of its aspects to the descriptions which have been preserved, from the fifteenth and sixteenth centuries, of the wedding celebrations of the grand princes, and later of the tsars.[3]

Many of these coincidences are explained by the depths of the general popular tradition. Such, for example, are the many magical ceremonies (the strewing of the young people with hops, the placing of baskets of grain and casks of beer in the bedroom of the newly married couple, arranging the sleeping room of the newly married couple "in the storeroom" near the horses' stall; the countless number of precautions of all kinds, and so forth). All these and similar ceremonies, beyond a doubt, go back to the depths of pre-Christian concepts of popular magic which had been worked out in agricultural surroundings.

But, on the other hand, even in the peasant wedding festivities (not only in the ceremonies, but also in the songs, the lamentations, the sayings of the groomsman, and so forth), a good deal of the color is drawn from the mode of life of the ruling classes. To see in this only a direct imitation of the ruling classes, as many of the folklorists at one time supposed, would be incorrect. This would be the same error which we have already had occasion to mention in connection with the characteristics of the so-called "historical school" of V. Miller, on the question of the social genesis of the Russian epos of the *byliny*.

Without rejecting individual cases of imitation and borrowing, one still must say that the basic factor at work here also was, above all, the striving for a poetic, creative idealization of the heroes (in the "wedding festivities," the bride and groom).

Most characteristic are the specific designations of the "wedding ranks" in the peasant ceremonies. The bridegroom is called the "prince," the bride, the "princess," the most honored guest a "chiliarch," the succeeding honored guests "senior boyar" (or "nobleman") and "junior boyar"; following the groomsmen and assistant groomsmen are the "sharers of the loaf," "wearers of the cap," and so forth.

[3] These descriptions have been published by N. I. Novikov in the eighth part of the *Ancient Russian Bibliotheca*, in 1775. (There is a republication, 1896.)

A detailed survey of such wedding ranks has been made by Professor P. S. Bogoslovsky.[4]

Besides the kingly, princely and boyar mode of life, the mode of life of the merchants, and later on, of the noblemen, lords, and country houses also served as material for poetic treatment.

On the foundation of the agrarian magic there were laid patterns in colors borrowed, at times, from a very far-off social setting. The wedding ritual, aiming at the poetization and idealization of the new-lyweds and their relatives, at times was colored in this idealization by the mode of life of the higher social classes and groups. But the basis of the peasant wedding poetry lay in a *Weltanschauung* prompted by the mode of life and the laboring activity of the husbandman-plow-man.

The wedding ritual, as we have already said, is customarily called the *wedding game* (and, in reality, it does represent such a game, in-cluding within itself elements of dramatic action, which will be dealt with in the chapter on the popular drama). It is characteristic that such a play does not have rigidly fixed texts: every person who takes part in the wedding is obliged to concern himself, as it were, with the scenic character, handed down by tradition, of that role which he performs at the wedding. The matchmakers must be emphatically courteous, ready of speech, diplomatic in negotiations; the parents of the bride, even in those cases when they are arranging their daughter's marriage against her will, must exhibit in their words and actions, at the time of the wedding play, their solicitude, attention, and bound-less love for their "dear little daughter"; the bride, in her turn, must express her humility, her gratitude to her parents because they "have nursed and reared her." Besides, tradition demands that, at the be-ginning of the wedding (from the moment of betrothal up to her ac-tual departure for the altar), the bride must weep bitterly for her maiden life in the parental home, and must express in every way her ill-will toward the groom—the "strange alien"—and toward his rela-tives—"strange, evil people." This had to be done even in those cases when the bride was marrying for love, following the inclination of

---

[4] P. Bogoslovsky, *On the Nomenclature, Topography, and Chronology of the Wedding Ranks* (Perm, 1927).

her own heart. Besides, the emotions themselves, in the traditional wedding ceremony, are strictly regulated as to time. Up to a fixed moment (the departure with the wedding train for the altar) the bride weeps (and it would be a bitter affront to her parents if she were to weep too little—she would be, as it were, demonstrating before the people her lack of respect and lack of love for her family); but from the moment of her departure with the bridegroom's train, not even the slightest tear must steal down from her eyes—the new relatives would be very angry.

One cannot think, however, that in the *wedding lamentations*, the so-called "howling," we are dealing with a pretense. On the bride herself, and particularly on the professional "weepers," "wailers," "criers," these singular poetess-improvisators, who were specially invited to the wedding, depends the ability to call forth in themselves, and in others, a definite mood—to awaken specific emotions and thoughts. Besides, we must consider the comparative homogeneity of the peasant mode of life, and consequently, the typicalness, for the whole setting, of the individual feeling of a specific girl, who was abandoning her family for the sake of another. To draw a line between genuine feeling and feeling that is demanded by ceremonial tradition in the wedding festivities, as well as in the other manifestations of syncretistic poetry, is exceedingly difficult. The real mode of life itself intrudes into the poetic play, constituting an organic, indissoluble part thereof. Unfortunately, anything like a detailed psychological analysis of the ceremonial wedding drama has not as yet been undertaken. Meanwhile, in the general theoretical and historico-social scheme, this analysis would have great significance.

It is interesting to consider the character of the creative work of the weepers, the composers of the lamentations. These were generally poor women, widows, and orphans. The composition of the wedding, funeral (and in earlier times also recruiting) chants constituted the profession of many of them. For a fixed remuneration (either in money or in the form of products: linens, kerchiefs, towels, and so forth) the weeper was invited to perform the chants. Her task was so to compose these chants as to reflect in the greatest detail and clarity the experiences of the person who had invited her—the bride, the widow who had just lost her husband, the orphaned children, or the young fellow who was being sent off to be a soldier. The wedding, funeral, and recruiting chants are distinguished from one another only in theme; their stylistic nature is absolutely identical; their creative processes are one and the same.

The wedding chants, and the other chants, represent in themselves a combination, which is characteristic of many genres of folklore, of improvisation with traditional poetics. Keeping in mind some kind of traditional plan of composition, possessing a rich store of stylistic *loci communes* (invocations, descriptive scenes), the talented weeper, having a retentive memory, with the aid of these poetic means, of this hereditary poetic stock in trade, can compose lamentations which are sometimes striking in their power, psychological fullness, and vast emotional infectiousness, and which are directly linked with the precise event in the peasant family life on account of which the weeper has been summoned. The skill of the weeper consists, of course, not in the mechanical combination of memorized and stereotyped formulas, but in the creative utilization of them for the attainment of the concrete artistic task which has been placed before her.

The wedding chants are not always performed by professional hired mourners. At least a certain number of chants must be known by the bride herself. In many localities the girls, when they are still small, learn the lamentations for their wedding, and after the betrothal they go specially to the weepers for instruction. It must be taken into consideration that the inviting of the professional wailer was attended with extra expenses; consequently, in the poor families they managed without her.

The wedding chants assumed very diverse forms. There are scenes, especially the "drinking bout" and the "girls' party," * when the conversations among the participating personages are conducted in the form of lamentations. The bride, with laments, turns now to her father, now to her mother, now to her brothers, sisters, attendants, and begs them all to intercede for her—"for the poor little orphan," "not to give her away to strange evil people," to permit her to play at liberty "but one more frosty winter, but one more beautiful spring,

---

* On the day before the wedding.—ED.

but one more warm summer," "to bar the way against the strange evil people, so that they may neither walk past, nor ride past." She reproaches her parents with their lack of compassion for her, she alludes to her youth and inexperience:

> I have little mind or reason,
> I am lacking in sense and understanding,
> I cannot in any way think out
> How I am going to live there among strange people.[5]

Even her older married sister cannot say anything consoling to her. In a striking lament the latter draws a disconsolate picture of the life of the young married woman in the strange house.

The married sister pictures the absolute inner solitude of a woman in a strange land—there one cannot provide one's self even with girl friends; they are kinsfolk of the "strange people," and will tell tales to them.

> You, little dove, my dear little sister,
> I, poor thing, do not know, in my bitterness,
> Whether I should speak, or should not speak.
> If I do not speak, then you will be angry,
> But if I do speak, then you will be terrified.
> Shall I speak, or not speak out,
> Shall I write with my pen, or not write out?
> If I tell you, dear sister,
> It will take three whole days,
> And as many long autumn nights.
> I cannot in any way think
> Of you, my dear sister;
> How will you live and be ruined?
> How will you live there among strange people,
> With a strange father and mother?
> There are three minds and three wisdoms,
> Three characters that are good-for-nothing.
> Listen, my dear sister,
> To what I say to you, my little dove!
> To live among malefactors and among strange people
> One needs a great deal of sense and wisdom,
> One needs a great deal of mind and understanding,

[5] B. and Y. Sokolov, *Tales and Songs of the Belo-Ozero Region*, pp. 338-339.

One needs a great deal of endurance and strength,
One needs the powerfulness of a beast,
And the endurance of a horse.
You will live, my dear sister,
With a strange father and mother.

Don't expect my dear sister,
That your father-in-law will wake you up gently,
That your mother-in-law will give orders nicely.
They will howl at you like wild beasts
And they will hiss at you like snakes.

And the sister touchingly instructs her:

It would be better for you to go out, dear sister,
Into the open country,
To wash away your sorrow and grief
With our mother the damp earth;
And fall down on the damp earth,
Upon the burning stones,
For surely you know, dear sister,
That our mother the damp earth will not betray you,
That the burning stones will not repeat it.
But you will go to strange people,
You will wipe off the burning tears.
Do not show your feelings to people.[6]

No less filled with dramatic effect are the laments at the time of the girls' party, that "last little evening," which the bride passes in the circle of her friends and relatives.

It is very curious that there is included as a subject for dramatization the bride's farewell, not only to her relatives and friends, but even to things: to her maiden headdress, the so-called "red beauty," to the ribbon which symbolized her virginity, to her maiden liberty, her "free will." In the name of the "red beauty" the laments are performed by the chorus of girls. The dramatic play with dialogues, conducted in the form of lamentations, very delicately and artistically renders the shades of feeling experienced by the bride: now the girl walks through the cottage, making her relatives admire her and the "red beauty" which has been placed upon her; now she begs her parents, one after the other, to remove from her the "red beauty," giving as her reason:

6 *Ibid.*, p. 341.

Though you do not take it off, father and benefactor,
Evil, strange people will take it off from me.[7]

But neither the father nor the mother will consent to remove from the daughter her maiden fillet:

I cannot lift up my white hands
Upon your willful little head.

Finally, the fillet is taken off by the youngest of the brothers. The girl, passing through the cottage without the "beauty," begins to implore it to return to her little head again. But the chorus of her friends, in the name of the "red beauty," answers with a refusal: now the girl "has not washed her white face," now she "has not combed her fair braid." The bride fulfills all the demands, the "red beauty" is again "yielded" to her "willful little head"; but the bride, when she has walked about a little in the "beauty," must acknowledge publicly that it is not her fate to wear the "beauty" any longer:

Look, my dear mother,
Look, my father and benefactor,
Upon me, upon the beautiful girl—
Though upon me is the red beauty,
Yet it does not become me, it does not beseem me,
Not in the old way, not in the former way,
Upon my willful little head.[8]

If the girl weeps hard, they begin persuading her to leave off weeping; but the old women advise her not to stop, since there is a sign: "If she does not have her cry out behind the table [at the girls' party], then she will have her cry out behind the post [in the cattle shed—in her husband's house]." In this way, even tears have a magical significance.

As a sharp contrast to the weeping of the bride and the weepers, there is the art of the other group of professionals invited to the wedding, the so-called "groomsmen."

The "groomsman" (*druzhka*, or *druzhko*) is one of the chief participants in the wedding ceremony. The name goes back to very an-

[7] *Ibid.*, p. 348.   [8] *Ibid.*, p. 349.

cient times. In popular usage the term *druzhka* is interpreted both as the close friend of the bridegroom and as a member of the prince's *druzhina*. (In the wedding ceremony the bridegroom is called a prince, and his suite—the "outriders"—may sometimes be called the *druzhina*.) This combination of the ideas of a friend, a warrior, and a wedding *druzhina* in one word is inherent in both the Slavonic and the Germanic languages: compare the Gothic *driugan*—to bear military service; Old High German *truht*—a military detachment, a guard; Anglo-Saxon *dryhtguma*—leader and friend of the bride.[9]

In the eastern Slavonic wedding ceremonies the functions of the wedding groomsman are very complex; by means of a comparative study of the folklorists' records of peasant wedding ceremonies, and a description of ancient Russian wedding ceremonies in royal, grand-princely, and boyars' surroundings, there may be revealed those basic elements out of which the role of the groomsman, in the free ceremonial "play," has been composed. First of all, he is the *druzhina* (one or several) of the bridegroom or the bride. Second, he is the main director, so to speak, the master of ceremonies at the wedding. Third, with the passing of time he took upon himself also the role of the medieval "buffoons," the "merry men," who were summoned to the wedding. Fourth, with the person of the groomsman there were blended the features and functions of the wizard, the sorcerer, who was obliged to protect the bridegroom and bride from "spells," from the "evil spirit," and so forth. Accordingly, in many localities the "groomsman" is called also the "watchman," the "knowing one," the "courteous one" (from the word to know, to be aware), and so forth. In the northern Great-Russian wedding ceremonies, the groomsman performs numerous ceremonies of magical significance (he walks around the wedding train with a whip, a rifle, a bell, and so forth), and in his sayings, or storyteller's exordia, which are of a jesting and obviously buffoonlike character, he includes a number of magic formulas of incantation.[10]

[9] O. Schrader, *op. cit.*, p. 118.

[10] An analysis of the traditional wedding storytellers' exordia is given in these articles: E. A. Blomquist, "Wedding Directions from the Rostov District," and A. K. Mareyevov, "Traditional Formulas in the Sayings of the Wedding Groomsmen," *Artistic Folklore*, Nos. II-III, Moscow, 1927.

It is curious that even after the revolution the genre of the wedding storyteller's exordia of the groomsman continued to develop, steadily losing more and more of the religious and magical elements, and greatly modernizing the jesting and merrymaking aspects. Thus, in the storyteller's exordia recorded at Lake Onega in 1926 by the expedition under our direction, sent out from the State Academy of Art, mention is made of motorboats, airplanes, aviators, and so forth, together with the ancient figures of the prince, the princely attendants, the falcons.

Here the groomsman-storyteller is Michael Kirillovich Ryabinin, grandson of the famous narrator of *byliny*, Trofim Gregoryevich Ryabinin. In the capacity of professional groomsman he must have taken part in nearly a hundred weddings. Michael Kirillovich related his storyteller's exordia to us for three hours; we recorded from him hundreds of these verses. He rendered the exordia both of the bridegroom's "groomsman" and of the "village elder" (also a species of groomsman) on the side of the bride.

Here is a dialogue, giving a rather clear idea of the blending of styles in the storyteller's exordia of our own time. The "village elder" delivers a poetic speech in the spirit of the traditional wedding poetics, and the "groomsman" answers in a speech which is already very much modernized:

> Elder: Our young princess
> Rose up in the morning very early,
> Washed herself snowy white,
> Prayed to God,
> From her father and her mother
> She received the blessing.
> She went out on the little porch,
> And her heart beat violently,
> She rose up on high,
> And flew far away;
> Beyond the woods, beyond the river,
> She has flown away forever.
>
> Groomsman: Do not be afraid of this,
> And do not be concerned about it.
> Our young prince

Has a great many servants:
He has bright falcons,
Swift eagles,
Hunting dogs,
Mounted Cossacks,
Leaping animals,
And birds that peck;
He has motorboats
And others that are submarines.
Of course there are airplanes
Given to you.
On them are fliers,
Ready answerers,
They will have much to tell,
If they come;
So they will find the princess.[11]

The breakdown of style is an evidence of the abandonment of the genre which is already in progress.

Finally, as regards those who sing the songs at the wedding, we should first of all notice the initial existence of a close organic bond between them and the ceremony itself. The songs at the wedding performed the same role which was fulfilled originally by the literary text of a charm: the song served as a literary explanation of the syncretistic ceremonial. In the most archaic variants of the wedding play, the song, performed by a chorus of girls, always has an established place, being organically connected with a specific aspect of the wedding.

This is obvious from the very content of many of the songs. So, when the bridegroom's train has arrived for the bride, and the grooms-man has overcome the various objections made to the bridegroom, solved the difficult problems which are presented to him, and purchased a place for the bridegroom and his suite at the table occupied by the bride and her friends, the chorus of maidens, coming out from behind the table, begins in song to reproach the bride:

Surely, Maryushka, this is not like you;
Surely, Maryushka, this should be a sorrow to you;
Your own family has abandoned you,

11 From unpublished materials in the State Literary Museum.

A strange family and circle have surrounded you,
Groomsman with bridesmaid, a strange matchmaker.[12]

At the time of the ceremonial walk taken by the bride, on the eve
of the wedding, to the bath, and during the braiding of her hair
there, the chorus of girls sings the famous song, "The Horn":

> The horn has made it known, early after the dawn,
> The beautiful girl has lamented for her fair braid—
> Soon they will divide my dear braid into two,
> They will wind my dear braid around my head,
> I am sorry, girls, for my fair braid.
> My heart begins to pine for the grave.
> Never in my life shall I forget my maiden freedom.[13]

The connection of the wedding songs with the ceremony which
they accompany is so strong that many of the *symbolic* aspects of the
wedding songs, many of the poetic forms, can be successfully interpreted only by the method of a comparative study of the variants of
the songs and ceremonies. This explains the apparent lack of meaning in some of the lyric songs. Divorced from the ceremony, they lose
their meaning, the sense of the symbolic forms becomes obscured, and
the song becomes increasingly distorted, blending with fragments of
other songs through accidental associations of sound and sense. As an
illustration, let us take one small example.

Known in many variant forms, printed in several of them by Sobolevsky in his *Great-Russian Folk Songs*, by Shein in his *The Great-
Russian*, and in the *Songs* of Kireyevsky, the song "On the little oak
tree sit two little doves" is often rendered, along with other lyric songs,
apart from any ceremony, simply at the country revels and the winter
evening gatherings of the women. Here is the song:

> When on the little oak tree sit two little doves,
> They coo and talk between themselves.
> They talk about the good young man,
> About Matthew Petrovich.
> He has trodden on thousands and thousands of rubles,
> Strewing the road with bank notes,

[12] B. and Y. Sokolov, *op. cit.*, p. 353.
[13] *Ibid.*, p. 344.

He has ransomed orphans out of bondage:
"Go home, dear orphans,
Pray to God for me,
As for a good young man." [14]

The song, in all the details of the images introduced into it, is understandable only if one makes a comparative study of a number of variants. We determine that this is a wedding song, sung at the moment when the young people, after the crowning, seated themselves on the oaken bench ("the little oak") before the table, but the guests had to purchase places for themselves from the girls ("ransoming orphans out of bondage") and load them with money ("strewing the road with bank notes").[15] At the same time this song is blended in its meaning with the category of the "songs of tribute," the purpose of which was to glorify and extol the guests; moreover, the extolling (as we know from the calendar-festival ceremonies, for example, from the *kolyadki*) included within itself aspects of "productive" magic: by the literary representation of wealth and good qualities for the person who was being extolled, by magic, as it were, these attributes were made secure.

The tone of the images of the "songs of tribute" was often taken from the mode of life and the poetry of the ruling classes; the wedding guests are represented now as princes, now as boyars, now as provincial governors, now as wealthy merchants. Their domestic and social life is drawn also with the features of the mode of life of the higher classes of the population. Here is one clear example, taken down by the late collector of folklore, the artist O. E. Ozarovskaya:

In the faceted halls of white stone,
The oaken tables did not shake,
The damask tablecloths did not rustle,
The wheaten loaves were not kneaded,
Nor were the pewter drinking vessels being fashioned,
Nor did the silver trays begin to jangle,
Nor did the crystal glasses tinkle;

[14] A. I. Sobolevsky, *Great-Russian Popular Songs*, Vol. IV, No. 94.
[15] For another example of the transformation of a wedding ceremonial song into a lyric, see M. I. Kostrovoy, "History of a Lyric Song," *Artistic Folklore*, IV-V (Moscow, 1929).

First, our Anna was fitted out,
Her face was whitened with a white cream,
Her cheeks were reddened with paint,
Before the princes and boyars she bowed down.[16]

But these aspects of the influences and imitations of the modes of life of other classes cannot conceal in themselves the original agrarian-magic nature of the wedding poetry—that clear poetic record of the mode of life of the peasant, especially of the peasant woman.

BIBLIOGRAPHY

Barsov, E. V., *Prichitaniia Severnogo kraia* (Lamentations of the Northern Region), Pt. III (Moscow, 1886), from *Chtenii v obshchestve Istorii i drevnostei rossiiskikh pri Moskovskom universetet* (Lectures Before the Society of Russian History and Antiquities at Moscow University, 1885), Bk. 3.

Pesni (Songs), collected by P. V. Kireyevskii, New Series, No. 1, *Pesni obriadovye* (Ceremonial Songs) (Moscow, 1911).

Shein, P. I. *Velikoruss v svoikh pesniakh, obriadakh, obychaiakh, verovaniiakh, skazkakh, legendakh* (The Great-Russian in His Songs, Ceremonies, Customs, Beliefs, Tales, and Legends), Vol. I, No. 2 (St. Petersburg, 1900).

Sokolov, B. and Y., *Skazki i pesni Belozerskogo kraia* (Tales and Songs of the Belo-Ozero Region) (Moscow, 1915).

Materialy po svad'be i semeino-rodovomu stroiu nadarov SSSR (Materials on the Wedding and on the Family-Tribal Organization of the Peoples of the USSR), Introduction by Prof. L. Y. Sternberg (Leningrad, 1926).

Vesclovskii, A. N., *Razyskaniia v oblasti russkogo dukhovnogo stikha, Rumynskie, slavianskie i grecheskie koliadki* (Researches in the Field of Russian Religious Verse: Rumanian, Slavonic, and Greek Kolyadki), Nos. VI-X (St. Petersburg, 1883), *Sborn. Otd. russk. iaz. i slov. Akademii nauk* (Annals of the Division of Russian Language and Literature of the Academy of Sciences, Vol. XXXII).

Zelenin, D., *Russische (ostslavische) Volkskunde* (Berlin, 1927).

Lafargue, N., "Narodnye svadebnye pesni i obriady" (Popular Wedding Songs and Ceremonies) collection of articles by Lafargue, under the title *Ocherki po istorii pervobytnoi kul'tury* (Outline of the History of Primitive Culture), Vol. II (Moscow, 1926).

---

[16] O. E. Ozarovskaya, "A Northern Wedding," *Artistic Folklore*, Nos. II-III, 1927.

FUNERAL CEREMONIES AND LAMENTS

◆§ફ◆

The traditional funeral ceremonies, and the poetry connected with them, originate in earliest antiquity. The basis of the funeral ceremonies, and of the weeping and songs which accompany them, is certainly to be traced to the immemorial times of the pretribal society. In them are clearly seen the attitudes toward the corpse, as toward an evil or, at any rate, a harmful power, from which it is necessary to protect one's self by all possible devices of magic. But still more powerfully there are expressed, in the funeral ritualism and in the literary folklore of the funeral, the traditions and outlook of the tribal organization and of the tribal religion, of which we have spoken in the chapter devoted to calendar-festival ritualism.

The further back we penetrate into antiquity, the more powerfully there are manifested in the mode of life the social, collective forms, both for the funeral of a deceased member of the tribal society and for the commemoration of him, along with the rest of the dead, on days established by tradition (especially, as we have seen, in the springtime "ancestors'" Saturdays and holidays, which in the course of time acquired a Christian veneer, but which undoubtedly originate in pre-Christian times and concepts).

With the gradual disintegration of the tribal structure, funerals and commemorations were transformed into factors of private, family life, but, like the wedding play, they retained many features which connected the ceremony of private social life with the survivals of the tribal structure and its ideology.

The attitude toward the deceased was twofold. On the one hand, they did not cease to fear him and to protect themselves from him by magic. On the other hand, they propitiated him, they placated him, they praised him, they tried to satisfy and honor him with offerings, with treats, they called upon him for help, they implored him not to forget his family, but to visit it, to preserve and defend it. Hence arise double meanings, and even downright contradictions, in the funeral ceremonies. In order to protect themselves from the return of the dead man, they would lay him out on a table or bench in the front corner, but invariably with his feet toward the outer door (with the aim of facilitating his departure from the house, and not giving him any possibility of delaying in the cottage). Very often they cut a special opening in the wall or the roof, and through this opening they carried the coffin out, and then stopped up the hole (so that the dead man might not find his way back into the house); sometimes they took the coffin out through a window, but at all events, not through the door. In carrying it out through the door and the gate, they avoided touching the coffin against the jamb, lest they attach the dead man to the house.

And along with these and similar customs, affording protection against the return of the dead man to the house, no less often there was performed a whole series of ceremonial acts, assuming the obligatory presence of the soul of the dead man in the house, or even invoking this presence. In the window, water was placed in some kind of vessel, and a towel was hung up, so that the soul of the dead man might wipe itself. At the wakes, after the return from the funeral, one place was left for the departed, and food was placed there, with full assurance that the dead man was taking his share at the table. After the funeral they heated the bath, brought linen for the dead man into the bathhouse, and in general conducted themselves as if the dead man were present in the bathhouse. In other words, many funeral and commemorative ceremonies show that the relatives of the dead man, those who remained alive, took all measures for honoring and appeasing the dead man in every way, no doubts whatever arising in their minds as to his invisible presence.

The *chants* (according to another folk terminology, the lamentations, weepings, wailings) which accompanied the funeral and commemorative ceremonies, to a considerable extent pursued these same aims, especially in antiquity.

The funeral laments were an invariable part of the funeral ceremony, exactly as the wedding chants were a part of the wedding ceremony. They, like speech in general in the ceremonial syncretism, were originally explanations of syncretistic activity. Just as specific aspects of the wedding ceremony were accompanied by chants or songs having a definite theme and mood, so specific aspects of the funeral ceremony were combined with chants of a definite character.

Good "weepers," "criers," "lamenters," "wailers" (the terminology is exceedingly diversified for these professional performers of funeral chants) generally knew well the "rank," or order, of the funeral or commemorative ceremony, being guided by the rules of tradition which had been handed down from generation to generation. At funerals which were conducted strictly, according to all the traditional rules, a certain sequence in the themes of the chants, especially a definite order of the appeals to the members of the family, the relatives, or of the lamentations in the person of each of them, was necessary. It must be borne in mind that the wailer at funerals, just as at a wedding, performed chants in the name of various persons who had taken part in the ceremony: for example, at the funeral of the head of a family, now in the name of the widow, now in the name of the orphaned children, now in the name of the mother, brother, and so forth.

Of course, along with the rendition of chants by professional wailers, who had been specially invited or had voluntarily appeared at the funeral, chants were also performed by each of the kinsmen, or, more accurately, by each of the kinswomen, since the chants, during the last few centuries, have been exclusively a genre of women's poetry, although previously, as we can judge from certain evidence, they were performed by men also. Every woman, old or young, had to know how to chant, and this was a comparatively easy thing to do, since in the composition of the funeral chant a large role was played by traditional devices, appeals and formulas, a store of which was inevitably lodged in the memory of every one who lived in the even tenor of the patriarchal mode of life.

There is a multitude of indications in the chronicles and in other landmarks of medieval literature of the existence of funeral and commemorative chants in ancient Russia, even in the most diverse classes of feudal society. Perhaps no one type of Russian folklore is recorded so frequently in ancient literature as this specific genre of the funeral chants. Besides, there are cited a great many—though it is true that they are very brief—fragments or versions of the laments. These fragments and versions, to a considerable degree, confirm us in the idea that the popular laments, taken down by folklorists in the second half of the nineteenth and the beginning of the twentieth century, fundamentally adhere very closely to the tradition which had been established from time immemorial.

Prince Gleb, according to the words of the ancient Russian biography, thus lamented his slain brother Boris: "It would be better to die with my brother, than to live in this world! . . . Where are your words, which were addressed to me, my beloved brother! Now I no more hear your quiet admonitions. . . ." Princess Eudocia, according to a poetic legend of the fifteenth century, thus lamented her husband, Demetrius of the Don:

O how is it that thou hast died, my dear life, and left me solitary, a widow? Why dost thou not speak to me! . . . My beautiful flower, why hast thou faded so early? . . . Why, my lord, dost thou not look upon me, dost thou not speak to me? Hast thou forgotten me? Why dost thou not look, even once, upon me, and upon thy children? . . . Agèd widows, console me, and young widows, weep with me, because the widow's grief is more bitter than that of all other people.

Many such literary laments, of course, have been subjected to considerable influence from the purely literary tradition of style, but still one cannot deny in them the connections with that which existed in the popular mode of life itself, in the oral creative productions of the people.

We were saying that, in the popular funeral laments, a great role is played by poetic tradition, which had worked out in the course of centuries a series of unchanging formulas, patterns, and compositional devices, which facilitated the memorizing of fragments of the lament, and improvisation within the limits of the established style—improvisation which often consisted only in a more or less free combination of the traditional formulas.

The stylistic traditions of the chants, as we shall see with reference to all genres of folklore, were diverse in various regions of the country; in any case, these divergences were observed by the folklorist-investigators at the end of the nineteenth and the beginning of the twentieth century. Without entering into the finer subdivisions, it is necessary to note the very sharp distinction between the lamentations of the South Russian and Central Russian provinces, and the lamentations of the North; the southern and central laments are comparatively brief productions of a purely lyrical character, filled with sorrowful cries, appeals, and ejaculations; while the northern lamentations—frequently of much greater dimensions—along with the expression of emotions, give extensive information as to how the death came, how it was received by the near relatives, how the life of the family had gone on previously, what sorrows have been brought to the family by the misfortune which has occurred. Besides, the composers of the lament are not sparing of detailed descriptions of the social setting, of the mutual relations which existed between the dead man and his family, the neighbors, society, and so forth.

In other words, the northern lament is a lyrico-epic production, even, at times, with prevalence of the epic aspects over the lyric, which on the whole approximates the northern lament, especially with talented performers, to the epic genre, to the *bylina;* whereas the laments of the southern and central provinces stand very close to the poetics of the usual lyric song. To these distinctions correspond also the distinctions in the character of the verse itself, of which the lament is composed: in the south it is quite a short seven- and eight-syllabled line; in the north it is a line which is very close to the line of the *byliny,* consisting of thirteen to sixteen syllables, with four accents, and an obligatory dactylic ending.

Free improvisation, allowed by the very nature of the lament, serving as an expression of the deep feeling called forth by the death of someone near, gave a broad field for the artistic creativeness of talented natures, especially in the North, where the very character of the lyrico-epic lament gave an opportunity to the gifted poetess-wailer fully to reveal her talent both in the expression of sorrow and in the description of real life.

And it is not surprising that, precisely in the forms of the northern lyrico-epic lament, the talent of a remarkable popular poetess, the famous wailer Irina Andreyevna Fedosova, found expression. To the collector of folklore, E. V. Barsov, who had encountered her, she related, on the whole, more than thirty thousand lines of wedding, funeral, and recruiting laments. Published in 1872, the first volume of Barsov's *Lamentations of the Northern Region* produced a great impression upon its readers. N. A. Nekrasov made use of Fedosova's laments for his poem, *Who Lives Happily in Russia?* (especially for the section, "The Peasant Woman"). He deeply valued, in the creative work of Fedosova, her ability to reflect in the lament all the depth of peasant sorrow, her realistic description of the outer and inner life of the country, and the power of the protest accumulated by the peasantry against social injustice.

I. A. Fedosova was striking in her ability to penetrate sensitively into another's grief, by her creative art to transform herself into the person in whose name she was performing the lament, and to find words for the expression of a whole complex of experiences. Exceedingly characteristic, in this connection, is the lament which she composed on "The Toper," that is, on a peasant who had died from hard drinking. Performing the lament in the name of the widow of the dead man, Fedosova, being guided by an inner feeling of truth, and, of course, by a surpassing knowledge of the old peasant mode of life, was able to give a moving picture of the contradictory experiences of the peasant woman, in whom the feeling of pity for her husband, "her legal master," struggles with the feeling of pity for herself and the children, who are left orphans; with reproaches to the dead man because he, by his drunkenness, "destroyed the whole peasant husbandry" (household), and finally, with a curse to the evil people, who have sent upon him "great misfortune." With all the individual quality of her descriptions of the life of a specific man or family, Fedosova knows how to give such characteristic, typical sketches of social life, to express such correct judgments, that her laments acquire vast significance as productions of a generalizing character; they are seen to be a wonderful artistic-historical record for the knowledge of peasant life in the middle of the last century.

Here, for example, is the realistic sketch given by Fedosova of the typical life of a woman who is married to a drunkard:

Do not grant, O God, anything like this, and, O Lord God,
I would not wish many good people
To live so long with hard drinkers
As I have lived, the sorrowful one,
With my brainless and hopeless master—
I have gone through the licensed taverns,
I have stood around by the public houses;
Looking at his spendings, I have trembled,
I have called upon him who should be my hope, I have
      humiliated myself,
I, miserable one, have heard enough of humiliation,
I have endured heavy beating;
He shamed me, he dishonored me before good people.[1]

In other laments of Irina Fedosova's, one is struck by the passionately expressed feeling of popular protest against the tsarist regime itself, which kept the countryside in poverty and injustice, degrading the human dignity of the peasant. In her creative work Fedosova often touches the motifs of the peasants' defense of their worth, a motif which is very characteristic, especially of the northern peasantry, who had not known the institution of serfdom, and who jealously guarded their feeling of self-respect. The researches of the ethnographers and folklorists also speak of this (see, for example, the characterization which the collectors Rybnikov and Hilferding have given of the best narrator of the *byliny* of the trans-Onega region, T. G. Ryabinin), as well as the ideals expressed in the *byliny*, which with great readiness describe the ability of the epic heroes to defend their honor from Prince Vladimir and the boyars (the figure of Elijah of Murom, Dobrynya Nikitich, Dyuk Stepanovich, and others).

An impression moving in its power is produced by Irina Fedosova's famous "Lament for the Village Elder." In it there is drawn the repulsive figure of the tsarist official, the magistrate, arriving in the village after his illegal extortions, but encountering a rebuff to his arbitrary will in the spirits and the speeches of the peasants, and the tactful conduct of the village elder. After a short time, this despot, again arriving at the village, found some pretext for avenging himself on the elder, arrested him, and thereby humiliated him be-

[1] E. V. Barsov, *Lamentations*, Vol. I, pp. 272-273.

fore the world. The old man could not endure the outrage, and soon he fell ill and died. At his funeral Irina Fedosova delivered the lament in the name of the elder's wife, and in her lamentations she gave a clear expression of the moods which had seized the village.

With what scorn the figure of the magistrate is drawn is seen even from the kind of words which Fedosova puts into the mouth of the village elder when he begins to make the rounds of the houses of the inhabitants of the village, with news of the official's arrival:

> When the unjust judge has arrived,
> And the magistrate stands at the prison,
> He is eager now for such a calamity;
> Come together, peasants, and you shall learn of it.
> With what news has he come:
> Has he come for the government taxes,
> Or has his boundless treasury given out,
> Or has his brightly colored suit worn out,
> Or are his goatskin shoes worn through? [2]

At the "prison" the peasants, for a long time, cannot pacify the angry magistrate.

> If there be sought out one man who is brave,
> And let him speak altogether of just affairs,
> Already so he begins to attack the man,
> And he will pounce like a beast in the dark woods;
> For with sportive feet he tramples down,
> As in the stalls a horse knocks with his hoof.

But the village elder will succeed, by his speech, sensible and full of dignity, as it is said, in putting the official in his place:

> The village elder begins to argue with the judge.
> "Do not take pride into your clever head,
> Nor do you take sternness into your eager heart.
> And do not exalt yourself because of your rank,
> For people have been made alike by God alone.
> Do not assail the peasants with your fists,
> Just sit down behind the oaken table;
> Hold back these little white hands of yours,
> And do not break your golden signet rings;

[2] *Ibid.*, pp. 283-284.

You cannot gain honor and praise
By attacking the Orthodox peasants.
For surely it is not for this that you are chosen judges!
Although you are eager, you magistrate, you will quiet down;
Although haughty, yet will you, commander, sit yourself
      down!" [3]

When Fedosova had further related the second arrival of the magistrate in the village, and the humiliation experienced by the village
elder, and his sickness and death, she concluded her lament with an
expression of passionate hatred for the tsarist official, and with a
curse, full of indignation, upon his head:

Fall then, you, my burning tears;
Do not fall into the water, nor upon the earth,
Nor upon the church of God, on the little building;
But do you fall, my burning tears,
Upon this hostile malefactor.
Do you penetrate straight to his eager heart!
And do Thou grant, O God the Lord,
That mold may come upon his colored garment,
As well as madness upon his furious head!
Further grant, O God the Lord,
That he may have in his house a wife who is not clever,
To produce children who have no sense!
Hear, O Lord, the prayers of a sinner!
Accept, O Lord, the tears of little children!

The poignancy and force of the experiences, the ability, by concrete figures and facts, to express the typical richness of poetic imagination, and also the astonishing command of verse and assonance—
these justify our considering the laments of Irina Andreyevna Fedosova as among the outstanding productions of Russian poetry.

The contagious power of the laments of Fedosova was enormous.

One cannot help recollecting the impressions of A. M. Gorky, described by him in the sketch "The Wailer," immediately after he
had been present at an appearance of Fedosova, with laments and
byliny, at the Nizhny Novgorod Fair in 1896. (Fedosova was then
in her nineties.)

[3] *Ibid.*, pp. 284-285.

But wails—wails of a Russian woman, weeping over her bitter fate —constantly burst forth from the dry lips of the poetess, they burst forth, and they awaken in the soul such poignant anguish, such pain, so close to the heart is every note of these motifs, truly Russian, sparing in their delineation, not distinguished by diversity of variations—yes!—but full of feeling, sincerity, power, and of all that, which now is no more, which you do not encounter in the poetry of the practitioners of the art and the theoreticians of it, which is not given by Figner and Merezhkovsky, nor by Fofanov, nor by Mikhailov, nor by any one of those people who utter sounds without content. . . . Fedosova was imbued with the Russian moaning; for about seventy years she lived by it, chanting the woe of life in the old Russian songs. . . . A Russian song is a Russian history, and the illiterate old woman Fedosova, whose memory contains thirty thousand verses, understands this much better than many very literate people.[4]

Among the popular wailers the folklorist-collectors have also uncovered other talents, for example, the magnificent wailer of the same trans-Onega region, who, exactly like Fedosova, is at the same time also a good narrator of *byliny*—Nastasya Stepanovna Bogdanova, from whom, in 1910, one of the collectors took down a series of laments, while in 1926 and following years the Moscow and Leningrad folklorists took down, besides the laments, many *byliny* and songs.

Unfortunately, in spite of the vast artistic and social significance of the laments, they have as yet been very little studied. Aside from the three-volume collection, *Lamentations of the Northern Region*, by E. V. Barsov (Vol. I, 1872; Vol. II, 1882; Vol. III, 1886), consisting in its greater part of the laments of I. A. Fedosova, and provided with copious introductory articles and commentaries, we have only one investigation by M. K. Azadovsky, *Lamentations of the Lena* (Chita, 1922), and the recently published anthology *Russian Mournings* (Lamentations) in the "Poet's Library" (Moscow, 1937), with an introductory article by N. P. Andreyev and G. S. Vinogradov. A detailed, monographic study of the lamentations, taking first of all the lamentations of Fedosova, is one of the immediate tasks of Soviet folkloristics.

[4] M. Gorky, "The Wailer," *Odessa News*, June 14, 1896.

The study of the prerevolutionary laments is all the more important because, as we shall see below, the laments are one of those genres of the traditional folklore which attained their fullest development in our Soviet popular creative work. (Compare, for example, the beautiful lament for Lenin, by the White Sea narrator M. S. Krukova, "The Stones of Moscow All Have Wept," and the "Lament for Kirov" by the Mordvinian narrator E. P. Krivosheyeva.)

BIBLIOGRAPHY

Barsov, E. V., *Prichitaniia Severnogo kraia* (Lamentations of the Northern Region), Vol. I (1872).

Azadovskii, M., *Lenskie prichitaniia* (Lamentations of the Lena) (Chita, 1922).

Russkie plachi (Russian Lamentations) ("Bolshaia seriia biblioteki poeta" [Major Series of the Poet's Library], Leningrad, 1937).

LAMENTS FOR RECRUITS
OR DEPARTING SOLDIERS

✦✦✦

Very close in their nature to the funeral lamentations are the *war-time or recruiting lamentations*. They are indisputably connected, if not with such antiquity as the funeral laments, then at any rate with a sufficiently ancient tradition of lamentations for seeing men off to war. Indeed, seeing a man off to war, in antiquity, was almost like seeing him off to certain death.

A special development, upon an older and undoubtedly traditional foundation, was given to these laments after the introduction of recruiting, in the time of Peter I, and the establishment of long terms of military service. Besides the continual danger of being driven away to war, the very conditions of the burdensome military service under the tsars, which tore the man, upon whom the lot fell in the levying of recruits, away from his own family for twenty-five whole years, created such a mood at the time of seeing the soldiers off, that these occasions were transformed, in their whole character, and in the power of their sorrowful experiences, almost into funerals. In the words of one of the laments, "This living separation is worse than death."

The recruiting laments were accompanied by a specific ceremonial of farewell of the new recruit to his family and friends, recalling the ceremonial of the farewell of the bride to her own home and her friends. The youthful recruit walked up and down in the middle of the hut, and took leave in turn of his father, mother, brothers, sisters, and other relatives; besides, a wailer, who had been invited or had offered her services voluntarily, performed appropriate laments in his name and in the names of his relatives.

Similar ceremonies were performed also at the seeing-off of soldiers who had come home on furlough and were again returning to service.

On the whole, all these laments for departing soldiers or recruits.

especially on the lips of the talented wailers and improvisers, give a moving picture of the people's sufferings occasioned by soldiering under the tsars.

A realistic sketch of the seeing-off of a recruit in the eighteenth century has been given by A. N. Radishchev in his famous *Journey from St. Petersburg to Moscow* (the chapter "City People"). There he has given examples of recruiting laments in what appear to be some of the most ancient records, and which therefore have great historical significance.

On going up to one of the groups, I learned that the levy of recruits was the cause of the sobbing and tears of the many who had thronged together. The recruits who were being sent off for enrollment had come from many settlements, both of state and manorial peasants.

In one crowd an old woman of fifty years, embracing the head of a youth of twenty-five, was wailing.

"My darling child, to whom will you abandon me? To whom will you entrust the parental home? Our fields will grow up to grass; our cabin will be overgrown with moss. I, your poor aged mother, must go wandering through the world. Who will warm my infirmity against the cold, who will shelter it from the heat? Who will give me food and drink? But all this is not so distressing to my heart; who will close my eyes when I breathe my last? Who will receive my parental blessing? Who will give my body to our common mother, the damp earth? Who will come to remember me at my grave? Your burning tears will not disappear upon it; I shall not have that consolation."

Beside the old woman stood a young girl, already full-grown. She also was wailing.

"Farewell, friend of my heart, farewell, my radiant sun. For me, your betrothed bride, there will be no more solace, no more joy. My friends will not envy me. The sun will not rise upon me for joy. You are forsaking me to my grief, neither a widow nor a wedded wife. If only our inhuman elders, if only they had given us permission to be married; if only you, my dear friend, if only you had slept for but one night, if only you had slept upon my white breast. Perhaps God would have forgiven me, and would have given me a little boy for my consolation." [1]

[1] A. N. Radishchev, *Journey from St. Petersburg to Moscow* (Academia, 1935), Vol. I, pp. 370-372.

Not a single work of Russian literature, even the "After the Ball" of L. Tolstoy, stand comparison with the representation of grief in the popular laments for the soldiers' service under the tsars, with the descriptions of the arbitrary dealing, the cruelties and injustices, which descended upon the soldiers' heads.

But the popular lament is not only a complaint, it is also a passionate, wrathful popular protest against a social evil.

Not without reason did V. I. Lenin, as I know from the reminiscences of V. D. Bonch-Bruevich, which will soon be published, out of all the productions of Russian folklore, devote his attention specifically to the recruiting laments, seeing in them the power of the popular wrath and hatred toward the enslavers, breaking through the complaints, the groans, and the efforts to find consolation in religion.

V. I. Lenin considered the laments for departing soldiers a most valuable record for the history of popular life and popular moods.

V. I. Lenin became acquainted with these laments from the second volume of the *Lamentations of the Northern Region* of E. V. Barsov, composed to a large extent of texts taken down from that same great popular poetess, I. A. Fedosova, of whom we have already spoken several times.

A harsh accusation against the accursèd regime of Nikolay Palkin is included in the hopeless complaint of the soldier in whose name the wailer appears:

Hear me further then, my parent, my mother:
And as the springtime streams pour forth,
Even so do our bitter tears flow down.
And to teach us, my parent, to torment us,
They even beat us, poor fellows, without our fault,
They even beat us to the point of wounds, my parent, to
   bloody wounds,
And to death they beat us, poor fellows,
And they make us run the gauntlet, us, poor unfortunate
   soldiers.
And when our feet will carry us no farther,
Then other unfortunate soldiers will drag us through to
   the end.
And here we fall, from the beatings, on the damp earth,

And here we lose our mind and sense.
And we do not feel the touch of any good people,
And we ourselves do not know ourselves from the beatings
    there,
And on our shoulders we do not feel any fine white shirts,
And we lie there, without knowing we have been beaten.
And so we are beaten, we poor fellows, and stabbed,
And to the damp earth we poor fellows are bent down.
And the soldiers raise us, and they say to us:
"And can you then, unfortunate soldier,
And can you raise your unfortunate head,
And can you lift yourself from your mother the damp earth,
And then stand up on your luckless and swift feet,
And still lift up your luckless little white hands?"

The feeling of despair is about to seize upon the physically and spiritually tormented soldier, he is ready to curse his parents for bringing him to the light:

And so much at that season, my parent, at that very time,
Will we remember our native land,
And we will curse our longed-for parents;
For why did you bear us, unfortunates that we are! [2]

The passing "through the gantlet," otherwise called in life and in the laments "the green street," and all the other numerous cruelties and humiliations have called forth not only curses against one's parents, but also others, better motivated and more just, curses against the whole tsarist regime, and chiefly against the cruel and evil military commanders.

In her laments Irina Fedosova puts into the mouth of the soldier's mother the most intimate, caressing words, with which she strives to console and encourage her son for his suffering:

Hear me now, my darling child,
For I cannot endure, sorrowful one. . . .
And you have told, poor darling child,
And you have told about your unfortunate adventures. . . .
And I also will lift up my unfortunate white hands

[2] Barsov, *Lamentations of the Northern Region,* II, pp. 220-221.

And lay them on my soldier's sorrowful head,
And on your shoulders, wearied by campaigns.
And I will press you to my eager heart,
And I will smooth my soldier's head:
And for me too, unhappy that I am,
Even without fire my heart also begins to burn.[3]

Brought to the highest pitch of suffering by her son's account of the injuries and affronts he has endured in service from his fierce commanders, the mother, who has just revealed such supreme tenderness for her son, flames out with an unrestrained wrath, and calls down curses upon the offenders—the commanders:

Be accursèd, you unkind malefactors! . . .
I would rip open the breast of these heathens,
And I would tear out the heart with the liver,
And I would spread out the heart into little pieces,
And I would dig a trough for the swine, in the filth,
And I would give the liver to the swine to eat.[4]

The number of military-service laments that have been taken down is unfortunately comparatively small, which is explained mainly by the conditions of folklorist work in the nineteenth century, by the difficulty of publishing those productions of folklore, in which the motifs of social protest were expressed with the greatest harshness and definiteness. There were left unwritten, for example, such productions as the laments for a girl or a lad who had been yielded up from the village into the manorial service. One of the examples of such a lament was taken down recently by A. M. Astakhova near Ryazan. This lament shows that the social thematics of the traditional genres were considerably wider than has been generally supposed. (See *Almanac*, "Year XX," Moscow, 1937, p. 384.)

The collection and study of prerevolutionary recruiting and martial laments have great significance in our time for the understanding of that deep contrast, which arises on a comparison of the accursed service of the soldier under the tsars, with the conditions of life and progress of that organization so beloved by the Soviet people, its own Red Army.

[3] *Ibid.*, p. 209.   [4] *Ibid.*, p. xxiv.

BIBLIOGRAPHY

Barsov, E. V., "Prichitaniia Severnogo kraia" (Lamentations of the Northern Region), Vol. II, 1882, *Russkie plachi* (*Russian Lamentations*) ("Bolshaia seriia Biblioteki poeta" [Major Series of the Poet's Library] Leningrad, 1937).

DIVINATIONS AND CHARMS

❧❧

1. DIVINATIONS

Divinations are those devices by the help of which the super-stitious man tries to find out the phenomena of life and nature which do not yield themselves to his intellect.

Divinations include, in the wider sense, occultism, under which one must understand magic, fortunetelling, and sorcery. But in distinction from magic and sorcery, which have, in the consciousness of those who make use of them, a character of coercion, with reference to nature and to supernatural powers, divinations are only the means of passively ascertaining secrets which are hidden from man. We shall dwell only on those aspects of divination which are connected with oral or written speech.

Divinations have been observed, and are still observed in our own times, definitely, among all peoples. A clear picture of the striking coincidences, the aspects and methods of divination among various peoples, is given in the well known book by Tylor, *Primitive Culture*. The basis of divination is hidden in the nature of primitive thinking. The man of little culture is convinced that the resemblance between two phenomena, which are in reality altogether diverse, denotes an inner connection between them. The determining of analogies between objects or phenomena observed at the time of the divination, and persons or facts in connection with which the divination takes place, creates a whole line of signs and symbols, combined among certain peoples at definite epochs into intricate systems of the prophetic art. The art of divination was widely diffused in Assyro-Babylonia, in Egypt, in ancient Greece and Rome. In the latter, divination played a great role in the life of the state. According to tradition, in the time of Tarquinius Superbus, an oracle of Asia Minor was brought to Rome from the city of Cumae, and furthermore it seemed that the then renowned Cumaean prophetic Sibyl brought some of the so-called "Sibylline Books," including a great

[241]

many aphorisms of a prophetic character. These books served for a long time as the basic source of the state divinations, which were conducted by a special college of augurs. Both in Greece and in Rome, such groups of augurs and priests must have exerted a great influence on the preservation of superstitious ideas among the masses of the people.

With the acceptance of Christianity as the official religion, divination, like many other manifestations of pagan culture, was subjected to condemnation and persecution on the part of the ecclesiastical and secular power; but, as in many other instances, condemnation by the Church did not repudiate the heritages of antiquity on principle, it only transferred them from the category of "sacred" phenomena to the category of "diabolical" and "unclean." Many Christian preachers and practical workers, bitterly attacking the fortunetellers, at the same time did not raise any doubt as to the reality of their "diabolical" proceedings. In some cases the possibility of acknowledging even an objective truthfulness for certain pagan oracles was admitted, if it were possible to interpret them in a sense which was desirable for Christianity. Thus, for example, the authoritativeness of certain chapters from the Sibylline Books was acknowledged, and not without reason did representations of the Sibyl frequently adorn the walls of Christian temples and the pages of religious manuscripts.

In the Middle Ages we observe the same dualism in the attitude of the Church and of literature toward divination. On the one hand, divination is treated as being identical with the sinful doings of the sorcerers; but on the other, the literature of divination is very highly developed, sometimes even consecrated by the Church. In the Middle Ages, as in the West, so also in Russia, many books of divination were very popular; for example, the translated "Moon Books," "Carol Books," "Books of Trembling," "Trowel Books," "Vessel Books," "Thunder Books," and also the various astrological books: "Planet Books" and others.

This literature, being diffused among the masses of the people, in the course of a number of centuries exerted a vast influence on the popular superstitions, supporting many of those which have their roots in primitive animism, and, on the other hand, implanting the false conclusions of the medieval secret sciences.

But even at a later time—in the eighteenth and nineteenth centuries—the less cultured strata of the population acquired a number of superstitious ideas from folk books. Thus, for example, an absolutely unparalleled popularity was attained among the bourgeoisie, the craftsmen, and the peasants, in the eighteenth century, by the famous Bruce Almanac, published in 1709, which, along with precise information on the calendar, gave a table of various predictions by the planets. Among the broadside publications of a divining character must be mentioned the so-called "Wheel," "The Wheel of Fortune," "Descriptions of Cases," and the "Wisdom of Solomon," which appeared, according to their type, to be continuations of medieval "Lotteries."

The principle of divination, according to all these manuscript and printed publications, is the casting of grain along ruled sheets of paper, on which, in squares, are designated the figures of aphorisms or the aphorisms themselves. One of the varieties of such divinations by aphorisms is the well known method of determining luck by a parrot, a goldfinch, or a mouse, from the boxes of wandering organ-grinders. By the help of broadside publications, an interest in the interpretation of dreams by means of "interpreters of dreams" (one of whom, Martyn Zadeka, is mentioned in *Eugene Onegin*) was strongly maintained. In a more cultivated society, divination was long ago transformed into a fashionable amusement, into a salon recreation. Interesting in this connection is a French book of the fifteenth century, published from the manuscript by A. Bobrinsky, and described by A. N. Veselovsky in the article, "Books of Divination in the West and in Our Country" (*European News*, April, 1886, pp. 895-898). Such was the fate, also, of many other divinations: from serious, though naïve efforts to come to know the world and fate, they passed to a cultural survival in the form of a trifling superstition, an amusement, a game.

The thematics of divinations were exceedingly diversified. We know of divinations concerning fate, marriage, domestic felicity, and so forth.

As regards the elements of oral poetic creation in the various forms of the so-called "popular" divinations, many of them are quite closely connected with certain related genres of folklore, first of all with charms.

Precisely as in charms, the oral formula often is only an explanation of the magic ceremony; the formula pronounced during the divinations (whether in prose or verse) frequently describes only the action which is being performed during the divinations. For example, during the weaving of garlands the girl says:

> I weave, I weave a circle for the lamb,
> Another circle for the mother,
> A third circle for myself,
> A fourth circle for my bridegroom.[1]

The so-called "Serving" songs, performed at the Christmas divinations with rings, drawn in turn out of a saucer covered with a handkerchief, also sometimes contain a description of the action. As in the charms, the oral formula, with the passing of time, being separated from the ceremony, becomes independent. For example, the original form of the divination demanded that the girl who wished to see her bridegroom in a dream should lock up the well with the words: "Promised one, masquerader, come to me for the key [of the well] to water your horse;" then they began to make, out of small fragments of wood, a model of a well, and to place it under her pillow; later on, the only requirement was that they should place some kind of key under the pillow; finally, the whole of the divination was reduced to the pronouncing of the appropriate oral formula. Thus, regularly, there is accomplished the transition from ceremonial syncretism to exclusively oral creative work.

In divination there are frequent appeals in prayer to a supernatural power, both to the Christian and also to the "unclean," for example: "Devils, devils, don't conceal him, but reveal my dear one to me." Many of the formulas of divination have a rhythmic structure and rhyme: "Give me, girdle, glimpses of the wedding train of my own

[1] Vasily Smirnov, *Popular Divinations in the Kostroma Region* (Kostroma, 1927).

love," or, "Little ring, little ring, My dear one's face you must bring," and so forth.

The thematics of a series of Serving songs and other formulas of divination contain in themselves clear indications of the direction of worldly longings, and the longings of that circle in which the divinations flourished. This circle was chiefly the peasantry, in all its classes and strata, and next the city bourgeoisie. Already, in the form only of a game or amusement, divinations were practiced also among wide classes of the noble and bourgeois intelligentsia, which essentially reproduced the traditional forms of the divinations.

Especially often, in the popular divinations, there is expressed the dream of wealth, household prosperity, and outward esteem. Hence the preservation, in the formulas of divination and the Serving songs, of the references to the wealthy boyars, trading merchants, and so on. Here, of course, we encounter, not a mechanical borrowing of phraseology and customs from circles which stood higher economically and culturally, but idealized figures, with social tendencies sketched in very high relief.

The vast majority of divinations and of oral formulas accompanying them, with their whole content, go back into the depths of the purely peasant mode of life, with the thoughts of harvest, fertility, and successful marriage. The ceremony itself is put into the form of activities conditioned by the manifestations of the peasant mode of life and economy: divinations at the well, at the barn for drying crops, at the shed, in the bathhouse, in the field, at the crossroads, at the boundary line, and so forth, with the drawing in of the domestic and the worker, of the living and dead stock of the peasant: the wooden plow, the harrow, the distaff, the hemp, the flax, the rooster, the hen, the cow, the horse, the sheep, and so on.

BIBLIOGRAPHY

Tylor, Edward B., *Pervobytnaia kul'tura, Issledovaniia razvitiia mifologii, filosofii, religii, iazyka, iskusstva i obychaev* (Primitive Culture: An Inquiry into the Development of Mythology, Philosophy, Religion, Language, Arts and Customs), 2nd ed., Vols. I-II (Petrograd, 1896–1897).

Bouché-Leclercq, *Iz istorii kul'tury, Istolkovanie chudesnogo v an-*

tichnom mire (From the History of Culture: An Interpretation of the Miraculous in the Ancient World) (Kiev, 1881).

Rovinskii, D., *Russkie narodnye kartinki* (Russian Popular Sketches), 5 books (St. Petersburg, 1881) *Sborn. Otd. Russk. iaz. i sl. Akademii nauk* (Annals of the Division of Russian Language and Literature of the Academy of Sciences, Vols. XXIII-XXVII).

All the Russian scientific literature is indicated in the work of Vasilii Smirnov, *Narodnye gadaniia v Kostromskom krae (Ocherki i teksty)* (Popular Divinations in the Kostroma Region [essays and texts]) (Kostroma, 1927).

2. CHARMS

A *charm* is an oral formula possessing magic significance. Russian charms are often designated also by other names, possessing a generic significance, such as: enchantments, precautions, incantations, charms for "drying up," charms for "falling off," whisperings, "words," and so forth. Among the Germans the most widely used terms are: *Beschwörungen, Besprechungen, Zauberformeln, Heilsprüche, Segen;* among the French, *incantations*

The exact definition of the concept "charm" presents great difficulties. The definitions best known among us—that of Krushevsky, who considered a charm as "a wish which must without fail be fulfilled," [2] and the definition, bordering upon this one, of Potebnya, that "a verbal representation of the comparison of a given or purposely produced phenomenon with one which is desired, having as its aim the production of the latter" [3]—cannot be considered as exhaustive, since not all aspects of charms can be fitted into the forms of a wish or comparison, but may include in themselves formulas of medical advice, prayer, magic lists, abracadabras (a collection of words which cannot be understood), commands, and so forth.

The widely diffused opinion that charms are based exclusively upon faith in the magical power of a word is not justified by an analysis of the origin of charms. Many charm formulas can be examined only in connection with the actions which accompanied

[2] Krushevsky, *Charms as an Aspect of Russian Folk Poetry* (Warsaw, 1876).
[3] Potebnya, *From Notes on the Theory of Literature* (Kharkov, 1905), p. 615.

them. Certain of the traditional charm formulas are nothing more than a descriptive explanation of the action. Such, for example, is the well known traditional beginning of many Russian charms: "I, the servant of God [name follows], will arise, blessing myself, and will go, crossing myself, out of the hut by the door, out of the yard by the gate, far out into the open country; there is, far off in the open country, the glorious River Nepr. As from that River Nepr," and so forth.[4]

Originally, it must be supposed, the whole power of the charm was contained in a ceremonial action of a sympathetic order: the magic was imputed to a thing or an act associatively linked with the object of the charm. It was supposed that the properties of the thing, into contact with which the object of the charm was brought, would pass over by that very means to the latter. A verbal interpretation was called forth by the desire to comprehend the action, which had begun to lose its intelligibility. The verbal formulas frequently, in fact, shed complete light on many magic ceremonials. At the pronouncing of a charm, which was noted down in the Pudozhsky district in 1914 by Professor Mansikka, it is prescribed: "That the cow may stand still—plane some shavings from a post in the shed, and put them into a bucket, and give it to her to drink," and the charm itself explains: "As this post stands, and does not sway or weave, and does not move from its place, so may my nice animal stand, without swaying or weaving. O my words, be strong and effective, henceforth and forever. Amen." [5]

With the passing of time, with the wide diffusion of the verbal charm formulas, these begin, in the consciousness of the persons who make use of the charms, to assume an increasingly independent significance with reference to the ceremonial action, gradually relegating the latter to the background, and taking on, in place of it, the quality of an autonomous magical device. So there is worked out a faith in the magical power of the word in the charm. However, even

[4] Nikolay Vinogradov, *Charms, Precautions and Apotropaic Prayers*, No. II (St. Petersburg, 1909), p. 35.
[5] V. Mansikka, *Charms from the Pudozhsky District of Olenets Province*, No. 207 (1916).

with the loss of the ceremonial activity, the oral charm, in the consciousness of those who make use of it, usually has power only if,
while it is being pronounced, certain conditions are fulfilled: the
charm must either be pronounced, without fail, by the glow of the
morning or the evening light, or at the crossing of the roads, or only
in a whisper, and so on. In this way a complete separation from the
syncretistic elements usually does not take place. The power of the
charm is thought of as being such that it can be broken or weak-
ened only by another charm, incantation, or spell.

Scientific thought has been interested in the role of rhythm in
the charms. Certain investigators have been inclined to elevate the
charm formulas to the forms of rhythm and song. But a comparative
analysis of Russian and western European charms leads inescapably
to the conclusion that poetic (rhythmic and frequently even
rhymed) charms, for example, the German, the French, and also
sometimes the Russian, are already indications of a later stage of
their literary development. In world folklore, and particularly also in
European folklore, there are, however, remnants of a *magic syncretism of songs*, so characteristic of all peoples at a low stage of culture (compare, among them, the hunting songs, and the martial folk
dances and songs); these are not yet charms in the proper sense of
the word, but varieties of ceremonial songs, explained in such detail,
even in the works of Alexander Veselovsky and Anichkov. But the
charms which we have examined have, properly speaking, no connection with the ceremonial songs, either in their form or in their
origin.

On the basis of their thematics, according to use, the charms are
divided into a series of groups. We know of love charms, charms
against illnesses, charms connected with the peasant economy, and a
whole series of others, even including charms the purpose of which
is to propitiate the judges.

Returning to the characteristics of the *composition* of charms, we
must bear in mind what has been said above as to the diversity of
the forms of charms. The charms do not possess one single plan of
composition, but specific elements of composition are encountered,
either in isolation or in combinations of types, in various forms of

charms. The greatest stability, with reference to composition, distinguishes the so-called "charms" with well developed formulas of comparison.

Let us enumerate the elements of composition. Many charms begin with the ecclesiastical introduction of prayer: "In the name of the Father, and of the Son, and of the Holy Ghost"; [6] among the Germans: "In dem Namen des Vaters, und des Sohns, und des heiligen Geists."

Next comes the *beginning*. I have previously cited one of the patterns. In the northern Russian charms the beginning is complicated or replaced by another formula, more poetically developed, but less ceremonially realistic: "I will arise, I the servant of God, Alexander, blessing myself, and will go, crossing myself, out of the hut by the door, out of the yard by the gate, I will go and bow myself down in the open field. . . . I shall be enveloped in a cloud, I shall be girded with the morning light, I shall bend myself like a new moon, I shall cover myself with crowded stars." [7] In the western European charms there are only remote parallels to such a formula: "Der Himmel ist mein Hut, die Erden sind meine Schuh'."

Next, very often, in the formula of the beginning, there comes the mention of some kind of stone: "In the open country there lies a white-burning stone; I will arise," and so forth. Many investigators of the mythological school were prepared to see here a reflection of certain very ancient myths; subsequent scholars, who worked mainly by the comparative method of the theory of borrowing, related this motif of the stone (often called the *Latyr*, altar stone) to the biblical legend of the Stone of Zion (Jagič,[8] Veselovsky,[9] Mansikka [10]); but it is most correct of all to explain the mention in the charm of a stone, on which someone usually stands or sits, as a description of

[6] See, for example, Mansikka, *op. cit.*, No. 18.

[7] Vinogradov, *op. cit.*, No. II, No. 16.

[8] Jagič, "Die christlich-mythologische Schicht in der russischen Volksepik," *Archiv für slav. Philologie*, I.

[9] A. N. Veselovsky, "The Altar Stone in Local Traditions of Palestine and Legends of the Grail," *Researches in the Field of Russian Religious Verse*, III-V (St. Petersburg, 1881).

[10] V. J. Mansikka, *Über russische Zauberformeln mit Berücksichtigung der Blut- und Verrenkungssegen* (Helsinki, 1909), pp. 163-213.

the sympathetic ceremonial action. Touching the stone transfers the properties of the stone to the sick or weak—its insensibility, solidity, and strength. Upon this image of the entirely real stone, gradually, according to the degree of literary development of the charms, there were superimposed the features of the Christian legends of the altar stone of Zion. The mention of the stone is found also in western European charms: "Es sitzen drei Jungfrauen an einem Marmorstein"; "Sainte Appoline étant assise sur la pierre de marbre."

After the beginning, and the mention of the stone, there follows, in many of the well developed charm formulas, the so-called *epic* portion, which usually relates the miracles that have taken place around this stone. The active agents are some kind of supernatural powers: the figures are taken either from primitive pagan mythology, or from the Christian, or else the figures are prompted by the magical purpose of the charm. In the charms to ward off the enemy's weapons there is metonymic mention of a certain "iron man"; in charms said over a wound or over blood, there is mention of a "red girl," and so forth. In this way the epithet itself is, as it were, a sympathetic expedient, and brings in its train the creation of new poetic forms which are characteristic only of the given genre of folklore. Certain of these epithets are "pervading," that is, they are applied to all the objects mentioned in a given charm.

How then are we to explain the origin of epic forms, independent of their social or literary sources? Apparently, the demand for these appeared at a time when the belief in the magical power of the charm formula had begun to grow even weaker. For the confirmation of the power of the charm, and the action which was joined with it, it was necessary to give proof, by authoritative substances, that the appropriate result was being attained. For example, blood must be stopped, since the Most Holy Mother of God, who sat on the stone, had sewn up the wound, or by some other means had checked the flow of the blood. It is clear that the well developed epic portion of the charm formulas—in its genesis a phenomenon of comparatively late origin—signifies a later stage in the development of the charms.

After the epic portion there frequently comes a detailed list of the symptoms of the given sickness, or of the parts of the body from which the sickness is being expelled. Such a list is called forth by the peculiarities of the exceedingly concrete thinking of the man of a low degree of culture, who supposes that the phenomenon which is not specifically noted may slip away from the magical influence. There follows, further, the *formula of expulsion* of the sickness or evil, whereby that sickness or evil is banished into some desert place. Here, for example, is a Byelo-Russian combined formula of enumeration and banishment: "Depart, ye monsters, from . . . the servant of God, go out of his bones, out of his strength, out of his veins and arteries, out of his joints and cartilages, out of his willful head, out of his swift eyes, and out of his ruddy face, out of his toiling hands, out of his swift feet, and out of all the inner parts of the man, over to the mosses, to the marshes, to the stagnant swamps." [11]

At the end of very many Russian charms there is placed the so-called *ratification*. Its most widely used form is: "Let my word be strong and good. The key and the lock upon my words." The mythologists have tried to find here, also, the echoes of very ancient myths. Mansikka, in conformity to his general theory of charms, perceives here a Christian symbolism; Poznansky [12] correctly traces the origin of this formula to a magic ceremony, which is practiced even at the present time, for example, by shepherds to protect their flocks: the flock is driven between a real lock and a key, and then the lock is locked with the key, and the key and the lock are thrown in opposite directions. By this ceremony, and its fixation in words, the strength and indissolubility of the charm are, as it were, confirmed. At the very end, both of Russian and of western European charms, comes the *solemn ratification* with the word "Amen."

We have spoken above of the so-called *pervasive epithets*, which in the charm have the significance of one of the sympathetic means, and we have also pointed out the persistent effort toward an exact concretization of phenomena, toward a fixation of shades and aspects

[11] V. N. Dobrovolsky, *Smolensk Ethnographic Collection* (St. Petersburg, 1891), p. 174.
[12] N. Poznansky, *Charms: An Essay in the Investigation of the Origin and Development of Charm Formulas* (Petrograd, 1917).

of one and the same object or fact. Hence comes the exceptional richness of epithets in the charms. But here there must be emphasized again, so to speak, the doubly practical use, prosaic in its purpose, of the epithets, which nevertheless give to the charms a vivid picturesqueness of speech; and this sheds light upon the process of the merely gradual working out of the esthetic functions of words, from the purely utilitarian, materialistic manifestations. We adduce as an example a passage from an old shepherd's charm:

I devote myself, the servant of God [name follows], with my cattle, with the peasant livestock, the cattle horned and hornless, large calves and small calves, work horses and mares, three-year-olds, two-year-olds and one-year-olds, sheep and rams and little lambs, and all the stock, the dear domestic animals, through all the beautiful summer, from season to season, until the white snow—with red and white hair, brown, gray and brindled colors, with the cloven hoof and the uncloven hoof, for preservation, for salvation, and at the same time for breeding, to the farmyard, for the multiplication of the peasant cattle, the dear animals, the cow with the cloven hoof, and the sheep, and the horse with the uncloven hoof. Wait, O Lord, health, ease, God's mercy upon the fruit and the cattle of the herd! From the black beast, the bear and the she-bear, from the one with the broad paws, from the beast that is inflicted, and the fat one, and from the anthill; from the inflicted gray wolf, and the she-wolf, and from their whelps; and from the brown animal with hair that is all one color, from the lynx, and from the she-lynx; from the task, from the gaze of the baleful eye of man, from the snake that crawls, and from the unclean powers of the evil spirit, from the pestilential wind, from the whirlwind, from the foreign infectious falling-sickness, from the wood spirit and the water spirit, demon and demoness and evil spirit of the field, and from shot-wounds, from heretics, male and female, from sorcerers and sorceresses, from the soothsayer and the soothsayeress, from the corrupter and the corruptress, from the evil eye and the evil thought of the wicked man, and all vile things of the woods and of the earth; from the black man and the black woman, from the fractured man and woman, from the white man and the white woman, from the priest and the priest's wife, with the evil eye, from the deacon and the deacon's wife, from the subdeacon and the subdeacon's wife, from the sexton and the sexton's wife, from the seller of altar bread, from the maid with her head bare, from the women with white heads and black heads and bald heads and blonde heads,

from the man who is a fornicator and the woman who is a forni-
catrix, from the man who has one tooth, two teeth and three teeth,
from the cattle which see and follow, from the man with the evil
eye who meets them and passes by, protect and defend, O Lord,
the servant of God [name follows], the shepherd, and my enumerated flock of cows and horses and sheep, by the mercy of God, by the
Archangel Michael, and by the brave St. George. And with these
prayers and words I make an enclosure. And as in the blue sea the
blue stone, and the stone of Oran in the Arian Sea, and the stone of
Ocean in the Ocean Sea, are strong, are not broken and are not
crumbled,—so strong be this passing around and this charm for my
cattle, the peasant's domestic animals—around the whole flock.[13]

As regards the *language* of the charms in general, it is made up,
both among the Russians and among the western European peoples,
of two fancifully interwoven elements: the clear, living, pointed popular speech, and elements from the ecclesiastical-literary language.
From much that has been said, it would already be possible to draw
a conclusion as to the significant role of the Church and of ecclesiastical literature in the matter of the oral formulation of many
charms. In fact, it must be supposed that the clergy, who performed,
in their activities, prayers and ceremonies of healing or of exorcism
like those used at baptism, composed, or at least in a definite manner stylized, the charms also; all the more so because it was difficult
to draw a sharp dividing line between those which were properly
prayers and those which were charms in the form of prayers.

An especially great influence upon the formation of charms was
exerted by the legendary apocryphal literature. In the chronicles, in
the materials contained in juridical archives, there is found a rather
large amount of information as to the existence of charms in ancient
times; furthermore, along with the other social classes which made
use of the charm literature, there is very frequent mention of priests,
deacons, and the rest of the clergy. One must keep in mind also the
nature of the medieval dualism of the Church, which made war
with the very harshest measures against "necromancy," "false letters,"
"heretical writings," but by these measures only deepened, among the
people, the belief in the real efficacy of spells, incantations, and

[13] L. Maykov, *White Russian Incantations* (Petrograd, 1869), pp. 114-115.

charms. In the legal affidavits of the seventeenth and eighteenth centuries, there are presented a great many facts on the use of charms, both those which were oral and also those which were written on leaves in a notebook, and even books, among the most diverse classes of the population, even at the royal court.

For example, in 1638, the court's "skilled embroideress in gold," Darya Lamanova, was accused of having "strewed ashes in the footsteps of the sovereign Tsarina," and saying, "Only let the hearts of the Tsar and the Tsarina be softened to me." At the examination she confessed that she had gone to a fortuneteller, and had been taught by her such sentences as: "As salt is beloved in nature, so may the husband love his wife;" "As quickly as soap is washed away, so quickly may my husband grow fond of me," and so on. In one case of the Preobrazhenskoe Chancery, it is related how "The wife of Peter of Volyn, the heretic Avdotya, when she was left a widow, walked to Preobrazhenskoe . . . and then she 'took out the footprints from the earth' * . . . before the first Azov campaign, according to the instructions from the Monastery of the Virgin, from the Tsarevna Sophia Alekseyevna." There are references to the use of charms by the children of boyars, by boyars' wives, by priests, peasants, musketeers, tradespeople, workers, herdsmen, and so forth. To the woman Daryitsa, of the village of Volodyatin, of the Dmitrovsky district, "Tsar Boris Fyodorovich, when he was among the rulers, and from him was sent a nobleman—they called him Mitrofan, but whose son he was, and what his surname was, one cannot recall—and this same nobleman posed the riddle, whether Boris Fyodorovich was to have the kingdom." [14] The diffusion of charms was concentrated mainly in the hands of professional specialists: sorcerers, sorceresses, fortunetellers, wizards, witches, "knowing" persons.

It may be said that charms were in demand among all classes of the population. But, of course, the specific texts of charms, and their

---

* Taking out footprints: an old method of sorcery. The footprint is taken out, and formulas are pronounced which bring bad luck to the one who left the footprints.—Ed.

14 See E. N. Yeleonskaya, Chap. I. "Charm Sorcery in Old Russia in the Seventeenth and Eighteenth Centuries," *On the Study of Charms and Sorcery in Russia*, No. I (Moscow, 1917).

variations, bear the features of a more definite social setting. The ones which are more simple in their structure, and less deliberately thought out, both in content and in language—such, for example, as the charm given above: "That the animal may stand still"—can be assigned entirely to purely peasant creative forms. Some charms, by their very content, being of an agricultural-economic character, betray, if not those who created them, at least those who used them: plowmen, hunters, military men, craftsmen, shepherds, servants, farm laborers, and so forth. In many charms there are very clearly revealed the social antagonisms of the earlier times. In the seventeenth century a certain landowner bowed very low before Tsar Alexis Mikhailovich, saying: "My man Ivashka the Red has boasted . . . 'Although my lord on some pretext may be angry with me, if I will speak [that is, pronounce the charm] while walking to the entrance, . . . he will do nothing to me' " [15] (that is, the lord accused his servant of making use of charms as a means of decreasing his master's wrath).

Great social-historical interest is to be found, for example, in a charm from an old manuscript, reprinted by L. Maykov in his remarkable collection, *Great-Russian Incantations*. The charm bears the title: "On the Approach to Rulers, or on the Appeasement of Judges." The text leads wonderfully to an understanding of the social relations of the old time in the period of the tsarist Russia of Moscow. A certain list of the rulers, whose unjust judgment was to be feared, sketches the mood of the man before whom one had to appear in court:

As the dark night rejoices at the bright new moon, and as the morning glow rejoices at the daylight, and as the daylight rejoices at the red sun,—so might they rejoice for me, the servant of God (name follows), at my arrival: tsars and tsarinas, princes and princesses, boyars and boyaresses, deacons and subdeacons, and all kinds of authorities, all government clerks, judges, and all ranks of people, who are my enemies; might they look upon me the servant of God, in the face or in the back, and from the side, as upon the red sun, and might they never be able to admire me sufficiently with their

[15] *Ibid.*, p. 72.

soul and body and eager heart, with their bright eyes, thoughts, and mind. Always, now and for ever and ever. Amen.

Unfortunately, from the point of view of class divisions and historico-social aspects, the charms have still been very inadequately studied.

BIBLIOGRAPHY

COLLECTIONS OF CHARMS

Maykov, L. N., *Velikorusskie zaklinaniia* (Great-Russian Incantations) (St. Petersburg, 1868), *Zapiski Russk. georg. ob-va po Otd. etnografii* (Proceedings of the Russian Geographical Society, Division of Ethnography), Vol. II, 1868.

Vinogradov, M. N., "Zagovory, oberegi i spasitel'nye molitvy" (Charms, Precautions and Apotropaic Prayers), *Zhivaia starina* (Living Antiquity), Bks. 1, 2, 1907; Bks. 1-4, 1908; Bk. 2, 1909.

Efimenko, P., "Narodnaia slovesnost" (Popular Literature), *Materialy po etnografii russkogo naseleniia Arkhangel'skoi gub.* (Materials on the Ethnography of the Russian Population of the Province of Archangel), Pt. 2 (*Trudy Etnogr. otd. Obshch. liub. est., antrop. i etn.*) (Proceedings of the Ethnographic Division of the Society of Lovers of Natural Science, Anthropology, and Ethnography), Bk. 5, No. 2, Moscow, 1878.

Mansikka, V., "Zagovory shenkurskogo uezda" (Charms from the District of Shenkura), *Zhivaia starina* (Living Antiquity) No. 1, 1911.

RESEARCHES

Pozanskii, N. F., *Zagovory: Opyt issledvaniia proiskhozhdeniia i razvitiia zagovornykh formul* (Charms: an Essay in the Investigation of the Origin and Development of Charm Formulas) (Petrograd, 1917).

Afansyev, A. N., *Poeticheskie vozzreniia slavian na prirodu* (Poetic Attitudes of the Slavs on Nature) (Moscow, 1865–1869), Vols. I-III, especially Vol. I, Chap. VII, and Vol. III, Chaps. XXVI and XXVII.

Kruzhevskii N., *Zagovor kak vid russkoi narodnoi poezii* (The Charm as an Aspect of Russian Popular Poetry) (Warsaw, 1876).

Potebnya, A., *Ob'iasneniia malorusskikh i srodnykh narodnykh pesen* (Explanations of Little-Russian and Related Popular Songs) (Warsaw, 1883), from *Iz zapisok po teorii slovesnosti* (Notes on the Theory of Literature) (Kharkov, 1905), and other works.

Veselovskii, A., *Sochineniia* (Works) (1913), Vols. I, II.

Sokolov, M. I., "Apokrificheskii material dlia ob'iasneniia amuletov nazyvaemykh emeevikami" (Apocryphal Material for the Explanation of Amulets, Called Snake Charms), ZHMNP (Journal of the Ministry of Popular Education), 1889, June.

Miller, V. F., "Assiriiskie zaklinaniia i russkie narodnye zagovory" (Assyrian Incantations and Russian Popular Charms), *Russkaia mysl'* (Russian Thought), Bk. 7, 1896.

Zelinskii, F., *O zagovorakh: Istoriia razvitiia zagovora i glavnye ego formal'nye chyorty* (On Charms: History of the Development of the Charm, and Its Main Formal Features) (Kharkov, 1897).

Yeleonskaia, E. N., *K izucheniiu zagovorov i koldovstva v Rossii, vyp. I* (On the Study of Charms and Witchcraft in Russia), No. I (Moscow, 1917).

Popov, G., *Russkaia narodno-bytovaia meditsina* (Russian Popular-Social Medicine) (Petrograd, 1903).

Novombergskii, N. Y., *Vrachebnoe stroenie dopetrovskoi Rusi* (The Medical Organization of Old Russia Before Peter the Great) (1907); *Koldovstvo v Moskovskoi Rusi XVII v.* (Witchcraft in the Moscow of the Seventeenth Century); *Materialy po istorii meditsiny v Rossii* (Materials on the History of Medicine in Russia), I-IV; *Slovo i delo gosudarevy* (Imperial Rescripts and Transactions), Vols. I-II.

Mansikka, V., *Über russische Zauberformeln mit Berücksichtigung der Blutund Verrenkungssegen* (Helsinki, 1909).

Wuttke, A., *Der deutsche Volksglaube der Gegenwart* (Berlin, 1869); rev. by E. Meyer, Berlin, 1900.

Ebermann, O., *Blut- und Wundsegen in ihrer Entwicklung dargestellt* (Berlin, 1903).

PROVERBS AND RIDDLES

1. PROVERBS

Proverbs [1] are brief aphorisms, applicable to various aspects of life, which have become turns of colloquial speech. In their origin, proverbs are exceedingly diverse. Their extensive diffusion, the anonymity of the majority of them, and the evidence of ancient monuments have created an illusion of the "universality" and archaic (primal-Slavonic and even primal-Indo-European) completeness of the whole body of proverbs. This illusion was fostered by the scholars of the mid-nineteenth century, who had been brought up either on openly chauvinistic, or else on philosophic-romantic theories (the Slavophiles, the "mythologists," and so forth). In reality the proverbs differ both in the time of their origin and in the nationalities which created them, and in the social setting in which they arose or, at any rate, were especially in demand, and also in the sources, which furnished material for the creation of this or that apothegm.

Very many proverbs have been produced as a conclusion from di-

---

[1] Very close to the proverb in its artistic nature (by its syntactical and rhythmic structure, by the peculiarities of its sound combinations, by the character of its images) stands the *adage*. The distinction between the adage and the proverb is seen by Dal as consisting chiefly in this, that the proverb represents in itself a fully expressed judgment, while the adage only hints at a conclusion, expressing itself by an allusion. Besides, the proverb, as will be seen below, is always expressed as a syntactical proposition, while an adage may be only one part of it. For instance, the expression, "to make someone draw your chestnuts out of the fire," is an adage, but if the full judgment were given: "It is easy to have someone draw your chestnuts out of the fire," then it would be a proverb. "To pass the buck" is an adage, but if we add to this adage the predicate, "It is easy," we obtain a proverb, a full parable. Sometimes, however, adages can represent in themselves, exactly like proverbs, a proposition (complete or incomplete, simple or complex), but the distinction consists in this, that the judgment expressed by the proverb has a generalizing, synthesizing sense, while the adage judges only concerning a given concrete instance: "He's not all there"; "The milk has not dried on his (or your) lips"; "It went in under his nose, but did not get into his brain" (referring to a certain individual). In view of the exceeding closeness of the proverbs and the adages to one another, both Dal and Illustrov, and in fact all collectors and investigators, always treat them together. It is necessary to follow this tradition also in the present course on folklore.

rect observations of real life (such, for example, is the vast majority
of proverbs reflecting the phenomena of the agricultural peasant
life), sometimes as echoes of an important historical occurrence, but
very many proverbs are linked in their origin with other genres of
oral poetry or with literature. A. A. Potebnya, in his *Lectures on the
Theory of Literature*, has adduced a large number of convincing examples of the origin of proverbs from fables, parables, morality or
satirical tales ("the beaten man carries the unbeaten man"), and
so on.

A proverb frequently appears as the conclusion of a whole story,
the tailpiece which sums up the fable, or in general as some kind
of pronouncement conveying the basic thought of the tale. Originat-
ing from such a tale, the proverb sometimes continues its independent life for many centuries, although the tale which gave rise to it
may long ago have vanished completely from the memory of the
people. Only by analogy with the aphorisms which are clearly connected with popular tales is it possible, with complete justification,
to assume such an origin for other proverbs as well. It is especially
natural to surmise such an origin for the proverbs which persist in
preserving certain proper names; compare the expression, "to drive
in [cattle] where Makar did not drive the calves." This aphorism
assumes some kind of tale, popular in its own time, it may be, a
story about a certain Makar. It may be that this Makar is the same
as that "poor Makar," upon whom "all the blows came down." The
proverb has been preserved, but, meanwhile, the tale corresponding
to it in the repertory of folk tales has not been finally determined.

Written literature, both native and foreign, was one of the sources
from which were drawn the proverbs which have passed into the
circulation of oral speech. Many proverbs which seemed to the earlier
investigators to be "indigenous," "Old Slavonic," have now, as a
result of the comparative study of Russian and other literatures, been
found to be of foreign origin (for example, such, it would seem, is
the national Russian proverb, "An affectionate calf sucks two mothers," * which is seen to be an exact translation from the Greek.)

* Kind words break no bones (Segal: Russian-English Dictionary).—Ed.

A significant influence on the composition of the Russian proverbs was exerted by ecclesiastical works, mainly by literature translated from the Greek. In Byzantium, as in the East in general, and also in medieval western Europe, moralizing aphoristic literature enjoyed wide popularity. As its models there may be regarded many books of the Bible, especially the Book of Jesus the son of Sirach, which served the especially practical purposes of instruction in respectable behavior—personal, in the family, and in general social life.

This book, among others, is powerfully reflected in the Russian "Household Rules" (Domostroy), an ethical and social codex for the ancient Russian boyars and merchant classes. Many proverbs clearly go back either directly to the sayings of the Bible (for example, the proverb, "God gave, and God has taken away," is a Russian translation of a saying from the biblical Book of Job, "The Lord gave, and the Lord hath taken away," 1:21), or else include within themselves only remote biblical elements, in imagery, lexicology, and so forth. No small influence upon the formation of Russian proverbs was exerted by the well known Byzantine collection of sayings, *Melissa* (The Bee), which had been translated into the Russian language as early as the eleventh century, and which enjoyed a wide circulation among the educated classes of the Russian people, and fostered and, in its turn, absorbed the Russian proverbs.[2]

The flow of bookish sayings into the oral proverbial speech, properly speaking, never ceased, and very many aphorisms, both in prose and poetry, which became popular, passed over into oral, spoken circulation. Especially great was the contribution to the repertory of proverbs on the part of those writers who formed their own poetic speech, to a considerable degree, after the pattern of the popular proverbs. Such was Krylov, who of all the Russian writers gave us the greatest number of sayings which have become proverbs in general use. In this connection a great role was played by the poetic genre favored by Krylov—the fable, which, like the parable and the compressed folk tale, verges upon the division of the proverb already described, which gives a resumé of the narrative: "And Vaska [the cat] listens and

---

[2] See the investigation of M. N. Speransky, "The Bees," *Translated Collections of Sayings in Slavonic-Russian Literature* (Moscow, 1904).

eats"; "Good for Moshka, she certainly is strong if she can bark at an elephant"; "You have been singing all the time, this is the way you work"; "And you, my friends, no matter what way you sit, won't be good as musicians, not one little bit." Through the school and children's books, the sayings of Krylov entered definitely into the colloquial speech of the most widely diffused and diverse classes of the people.

Into the proverbs and sayings there passed verses from *On the Misfortune of Being Clever* of Griboyedov: "To jest, and jest forever"; "Ah, my God, what will Princess Marya Alekseyevna say?" "What a task, O Creator, to be the father of a grown-up daughter!" "We make a noise, brother, we make a noise"; "I would be glad to serve; I scorn to be servile," and so forth. Into the proverbial sayings there have passed also many verses of Pushkin's: "All ages are submissive to love"; "Habit is given us from above."

From the examples which have been adduced it is seen how incorrect it would be, following the mythologists, to think that proverbs "were not composed, but born" (Dal), that they always originated, not as a form of a personal creation, but only as the result of collective work.

To establish a chronology of proverbs is exceedingly difficult, since the vast majority of them have lost their authors and have become anonymous. The only thing which can be helpful is an elaborate analysis, with literary and comparative-historical digressions, but because of the inexhaustible multitude of the proverbs and their relative changeability, the work of investigation is made incredibly difficult.

Some help may be rendered by the documentary testimonies of the monuments of ancient literature, but the store of proverbs encountered in them, in comparison with their general bulk, is far from great; though of all genres of folklore, except the lamentations, according to the correct observation of Professor P. V. Vladimirov (*Introduction to the History of Russian Literature*, page 132), "no genre of Russian folk literature was so fortunate in ancient Russian letters as the proverbs and sayings, which in antiquity were called parables." They are encountered in the chronicles. Famous, for example, is a proverb adduced in a chronicle: "for Rus, drinking is such fun—without it she can't get on" (*Hypatian Chronicle*, around A.D. 980); "Peace lasts till the army comes, and the army lasts till peace comes" (A.D. 1148); "Until you have smoked out the bees, you can't eat the honey" (A.D. 1231); "The situation does not fit itself to the head, but the head to the situation." Several proverbs were made use of by the author of the *Tale of Igor's Raid*; one of them, introduced by the author of the *Tale* as the "refrain" of Boyan, has been preserved in oral tradition down to our own time. (Compare "Neither the cunning nor the clever can escape the judgment of God," in the *Tale*, and "Neither the cunning nor the clever, neither the rich nor the poor, can escape the judgment of God," in Dal's collection of proverbs.) A literary work dating from the thirteenth century, *The Prayer of Daniel the Hermit*, is filled with proverbial sayings: actually, they are for the most part from books, partly borrowed from *The Bee*. In it there are quotations of "worldly parables," that is, popular proverbs.

Writers have had recourse to proverbs, as a stylistic factor, for the embellishment of literary speech, even in later times: to the sixteenth century, for example, are assigned the formal letters (reports) of the governor of Orsha, Kmita Chernobylsky, to the Polish king and the Lithuanian lords councilors (1573–1574). The letters are sprinkled with folkloric sayings and quotations, especially proverbs: "When you have burned yourself with hot milk, you had better blow on water"; "That woman was telling fortunes both ways"; "When they were drowning, they promised an ax [to their saviors]; but when they were saved, they would not give them even the handle." Proverbial expressions are encountered in the correspondence of Ivan the Terrible with Prince Kurbsky. Proverbs are used by the "Household Rules," by the journalist of the sixteenth century, Ivan Peresvetov, by the author of the *Tale of Peter and Fevronia*, Erasmus. Proverbs are very generally used, also, in the journalistic literature of a later period: the era of Peter the Great, at the end of the eighteenth century, and afterward.

The demand for proverbs in literary and oral speech was so great that from the seventeenth century there have come down to us specially compiled manuscript collections of proverbs. Part of these have been edited with great care by P. K. Simoni (*Annals of the*

Division of Russian Language and Literature of the Academy of Sciences, Vol. LXVI, St. Petersburg, 1899).

As we have said above, the impetus for the creation of this or that proverb was often some kind of far-reaching social-governmental, or, on the other hand, some local historical event. In laying bare the historical roots of proverbs, the work of investigation has not yet been carried forward to an adequate degree; but noteworthy results have already been attained. In a chronicle of A.D. 984, it is related how the army commander of Vladimir, Prince Tail-of-the-Wolf, overcame the tribe of the Radimichi at the river Pishchan, and a saying is quoted, with which people made fun of the Radimichi: "The people of the Pishchan run away from the tail of the wolf." The chronicle, relating the very ancient fortunes of the Slavs, the incursions upon the Slavs of the Obri (Avars), and, finally, the destruction of the latter, alludes to the "parable" (proverb) which was diffused throughout Old Russia: "They perished like the Obri, and there was left of them neither tribe nor heir." Many proverbs have been preserved in the memory of the people from the period of the Tartars: "A guest who comes inopportunely is worse than a Tartar"; "Empty, as if the Khan Mamai had passed by"; "As the Khan is, so his horde will be." An echo of the Northern War is seen in the proverb: "He perished like a Swede at Poltava." Many proverbs have been preserved from the period of the War of 1812: "Against the Frenchman, even a pitchfork is a rifle"; "A hungry Frenchman is glad even to see a crow"; "He was Neopalen [Napoleon], but he went out of Moscow *opalen* [singed]," based upon the popular etymology of the name Napoleon—Neopalen, "the unburnt one."

But it was not only military and historical events which were reflected in proverbs and sayings. The events of the internal cultural and social-economic life penetrated into proverbial expressions. Thus, the forcible implantation of Christianity in the Novgorod region is confirmed by a proverb, given in a chronicle "Dobrynya baptized with the sword, Putyata with fire." The abolition of St. George's Day, that is, the definitive binding of the peasant to the landowners as serfs under Boris Godunov, by the method of forbidding their free movement from one landowner to another at the conclusion of the working season (at the end of November), is reflected in a proverb, most directly rendering the mood of the deceived peasantry: "Here, grandmother, that's what St. George's Day does for you!"

There are proverbs which reflect the phenomena of a long-outmoded pattern of governmental institutions. Such, for example, is the proverb about the Vetche (popular assembly): "They are at the same Vetche, but not of the same speech." In the proverbs there is frequent mention of the administrative positions and state institutions of past centuries: "The princes' bailiffs are the tinder, and the private people are the sparks"; "Although the voevoda [governor] isn't worth the bark of a tree, yet you have to treat him like a grandee"; "The voevoda's request is a stern command"; "The horse loves oats; the earth, manure; and the governor, tribute"; "To be a voevoda is to live, not without money"; "A wise man is like the bailiff: everyone fears him" (the bailiff-magistrate had charge of criminal affairs, and was substitute to the governor); "The quill is not dangerous or frightful on the gander's skin, but only in the hand of the clerk"; "The scribe loves hot buns"; "The scribe is of dog's nature, the clerk is a fellow who slips through anything"; "God created two evils: the clerk and the he-goat." *

Proverbs give the richest material for the reconstruction of archaic beliefs and opinions. By virtue of their pungency and durable form, the proverbs, as we shall see later on, and the riddles have preserved a great number of religious and cultural survivals.

In the proverbs there is constant mention of the phenomena, objects and professions of a departed mode of life: "Misfortune produces coin [money]"; "Everyone dances, but not like a buffoon"; "The buffoon is glad of his balalaika"; "It is splendid to hear a buffoon on the psaltery, but when you begin to play yourself—that's another story." The territorial adaptations of specific folkways are interesting, in particular, for example, the assigning of the buffoons to Moscow, even to specific districts of the city: "A buffoon from Presnya strummed songs." Frequently, concrete local details or monuments (buildings, streets) are taken as a model; it is natural that they

---

* All of these proverbs are more forceful in Russian because they are based on clever rhymed puns.—ED.

frequently make use of the Moscow setting: "[The Tower of] Ivan the Great is marrying Sukhareva [Tower], and is taking as a dowry four watchtowers" (a jesting proverb in answer to the question, "Whose wedding is it?"). The idea of slowness or procrastination was expressed by such a purely Muscovite proverb as: "We came from the outskirts to the Kremlin on the ninth day."

Sometimes a citing of proper names, which seems to be only a play upon words, has not only a stylistic, but a cultural or historic significance. Thus, "There was truth with Peter and Paul"; "Truth came not from Peter and Paul"; "Truth has gone away to Peter and Paul, but falsehood has gone forth throughout the earth," are different variations in the meaning of an expression referring to a concrete historical fact—the torture chamber of the time of Peter the Great, at the Church of Peter and Paul, in the Preobrazhenskoe village. Another Moscow torture chamber (behind the church of the "great martyr Barbara," in St. Barbara's Quarter, near St. Barbara's Gate) is also reflected in proverbs and sayings: "Go to Barbara for retribution"; "As for St. Barbara's, there they took off my head"; "Barbara is my aunt, and the truth is my sister." From these same inquisitorial torture chambers comes the proverb: "You will not speak the truth, so you will speak secrets"; and also the proverbial expressions: "to speak the absolute truth"; "to find out the whole secret"; these are references to two methods of torture: tortures under the "long boy" (the horsewhip or rod), and tortures by means of driving iron or wooden nails under the fingernails.*

Through the centuries of Christianity, down to our own time, the proverb has carried the survivals of old concepts from the period of extinct paganism: "He took the god by the foot, and threw it on the floor"; "The god who gets wet will dry out again"; "Why should one pray to that god who shows no mercy?" There are very many proverbs which pass on the features of the primitive animistic beliefs, and of the elements of the so-called "lower mythology," that is, the concepts of goblins, wood goblins, water sprites, mermaids, and similar figures from popular demonology: "Though you may be brave and strong, yet

* Another case of puns in Russian.—ED.

still you cannot cope with a wood demon"; "In the woods a wood demon, and at home a stepmother"; "Don't drive the god into the woods if he has found his way into the cottage"; "If the goblin does not love [the cattle], it doesn't matter what you do" (that is, you will not be able to accomplish anything); "I could have spoken, but there's a stove in the house" (a reflection of the cult of the domestic hearth); "Not everything is a mermaid that dives into the water." A series of proverbs fixes ancient signs and divinations: "An old raven will not croak when he passes by"; "Let every raven caw down misfortune only on his own head." The proverbs reflect also a subsequent stage in the development of demonology—the replacement of the earlier spirits of vegetation and of the home by the synthesized figures of devils and demons: "If there can be a demon, there will also be a wood spirit"; "Mountains and ravines are the devil's dwelling place"; "In the still pool the devils dwell"; "A devil knows another devil by the horns, and a witch knows another witch by the tail," and so forth.

But there are many difficulties standing in the way of the historical study of proverbs: having arisen in a certain period, under the conditions of a definite social-economic structure, in a definite social setting, proverbs continue to live for centuries, becoming adapted to new social-economic conditions, adjusting themselves to a different class ideology, becoming filled with a new social content.

In addition, regardless of the relative stability of the verbal formula, every proverb inevitably undergoes some kind of change, with reference both to its sound and its lexicology. The majority of proverbs vary, and in the study of the historico-social fate of each proverb it is necessary to make a detailed comparison of the variants. This comparison of variants, as also in the study of other genres of folklore (*byliny*, religious verses, tales), makes it possible to establish frequently encountered alterations or changes in the original sense of the proverb. Thus, for example, it is discovered that the ironical proverb, "Here you are, Bozhe [God], take what we do not need," originally had a real and worldly sense: "Here you are, poor man [*ubozhe*, beggar], take what we do not need." The unintelligible proverb, "No time for Mass, if there is much nonsense," becomes understandable from its northern variants, preserving the original form of the ancient word: "No time for Mass, if there is much housework" (that is, domestic housekeeping cares, cooking, and so on).

Interesting are the variations of a proverb, which invest it with different meanings. Thus, Dal gives as an example four variants of one proverb, and gives their interpretation: "You must not call an old dog a wolf": because she has grown old, is no longer useful, you must not consider her as a wolf, you must not treat her as an enemy. "You must not call the priest's dog a wolf": no matter how much the priest has troubled you with his greed and with his oppressions, still you must not look upon his dog as upon a wolf, she is not guilty in any respect. "You must not call an old dog 'little father,' " that is, a father in answer to the demand to honor an old man, not according to his deserts; the dog is old, but you must not for that reason consider him as a father. "You must not call the priest's dog 'little father,' " that is, in answer to the demand for respect to people met by chance: no matter how much you may discourse about respect to the "little father," that is, to the priest, yet his dog is not a "little father"; in this form the proverb is applied to members of the gentry who are favorites of great nobles.[3]

Thus one and the same proverb, in its different variations, illuminates the mutual relationships, now among age groups, now among social groups, bringing us into the thick now of family, now of social conflicts.

The majority of the collectors of proverbs have sought to systematize the collected material, not according to social indications, but according to themes, either of an ethical or of a psychological order. For example, Dal classifies proverbs according to very conventional and subjective headings: Faith, Fate, Hope, Happiness, Sorrow, Misfortune, Truth, Falsehood, and so forth. Illustrov, approaching the study and systematization of proverbs from the viewpoint of a lawyer, classifies proverbs according to the headings of state, family, and criminal law, laboring activity, and conditions of property. Thus arranged, the material yields more for the understanding of the social nature of proverbs than it did in Dal's arrangement, but even such a

[3] Dal, *Proverbs of the Russian People* (Moscow, 1861), p. xv.

systematization is still very subjective, and—and this is the main difficulty—a great many proverbs are omitted.

It must be supposed that the vast majority of proverbs recorded by the collectors were expressions of the peasant ideology, which was superimposed upon the basis of the natural economy of the feudal era. The drawing power of the land, the direct dependence on the phenomena of nature, the patriarchal mode of life of a large indissoluble family, and the stability of the customary law, which was regulated by the rural *mir* (community)—here is the soil on which the proverbs grew up which have existed for centuries in conformity to the stability of the old peasant mode of life and the slowness of economic progress in the country in the prerevolutionary era.

All the interests of the peasant revolved around the land and its cultivation: "Peasant, prepare to die, plow your bit of earth"; "With fire, with water, with the wind, do not make friends, but make friends with the earth."

Direct dependence on the phenomena of nature, owing to the feebleness of agrarian technique, forced the peasants to the strict maintenance of the traditional observations on the weather, of knowing the signs, which were frequently expressed in the form of proverbs: "On St. Thecla's Day dig the beets"; "On St. Pud's Day take the bees out from under cover"; "Before St. Nikola's Day do not sow the buckwheat, but shear the ewe lambs," and so forth. Besides, the proverbs impressed upon the consciousness of the peasant the requirement to follow faithfully the age-old signs: "Without a sign, you can't get on"; "For him who does not believe in signs, there is no way to live in the world."

There are very many proverbs which characterize the economic stagnation of the old patriarchal countryside, the inertia, the fatalism, the resignation to the low level of agriculture: "If God does not bring it, the earth will not give it"; "It is not a calamity when there is pig-weed in the rye, but it is a calamity if there is neither rye nor pig-weed."

But there are proverbs which also reflect other, contrasting phenomena among the peasantry—the rudiments of cultural relationship to the earth and to the agricultural labor, characterizing the upheavals that occurred in various localities and on specific farms. Certain of these proverbs, even in our own days, can be utilized as watchwords for propagating rational agronomical measures: "If you have the *early fallow*, you need not go to the granary to draw on your resources"; "The *early fallow* brings the wheat, but the late fallow brings the broom"; "Lay the manure on thickly, and the granary will not be empty," and so on.

The proverbs which characterize the slow tempo of the former conservative economy are significant: "You can't do everything at once"; "If you hurry, you will make people laugh"; "The quieter you drive, the further you will get"; "A year is not a week, the Feast of Intercession is not now; it is more than two days until St. Peter's Day."

Even in the feudal countryside the peasantry was not altogether a homogeneous economic mass; with the penetration of capitalistic relations even into the country, the difference was constantly intensified and increased. "No one knows how the poor man dines"; "Bread and water, that is our peasant fare"; "Bread and kvas,* that is all we have"; "Before getting fat, we want to keep alive"; "I have one sheepskin, and that growing bare"—thus did the poor people of the countryside characterize their "well-being." Among them there grew up a social protest against the rich, the nobility, and the merchant class: "We look upon the same sun, but we do not eat the same food"; "The rye feeds everyone without exception, but the wheat makes distinctions." Naturally, reflections as to social inequality were awakened: "In the woods trees are not equal, nor in the world people." Telling observations were made upon the exploitation of peasant labor: "White hands love the labor of others"; "If there is no one to wear bast shoes, there will be no one to wear velvet"; "By the peasants' calluses the noblemen live well fed."

The dependence of the serfs on their secular and religious landowners is clearly reflected by proverbs from the beginning of the institution of serfdom to its point of highest development: "Into the boyar's yard the gates are wide, but the gates that lead out are narrow"; "Work done for a monastery is like work [*corvée*] done by a serf for his lord"; "You cannot fill either a duck's crop or a master's pocket"; "The gentleman said, 'I'll give you a sheepskin coat'; yes, his word was warm."

* Kvas: a Russian beverage made of dry rye bread and malt.—Ed.

Many proverbs deal with the gradual usurious enslavement of the poor peasantry by the wealthy men of the countryside: "You will take bast, but you will have to give back a belt for it"; "He took the devil's mat, but he'll pay him back with his skin"; "To hire is to sell yourself"; "It's fine to be on hire, but do not grant it, O God, to me"; "The wolf was sorry for the mare: he left her her tail and her mane"; "The hawk kissed the pullet, down to her last little feather."

No easier were the relations between the peasant and the state: "The treasury makes war, but the purse laments"; "A plow feeds, a spindle clothes, but taxes are elsewhere"; "The treasury is the first offender"; "The treasury is enriched by the peasants." *

The peasants' representation of the authorities, in proverbs, was of two kinds: on the one hand, in an idealized, somewhat abstract form, there was created the feudal figure of the tsar, though there was also a proverb at hand which gave a pessimistic evaluation of the supreme powers both of earth and of heaven: "God is high, and the tsar is far away"; on the other hand, there is the sharply negative relation to the local authorities, which came directly in contact with the peasant masses: the proverbs dealing with the governor, the clerks, and the scriveners have been given above. The most virulent satire is found in the proverbs dealing with the earlier courts and judges: "A judge's pocket is like a priest's belly"; "The pocket is empty, so the judge is deaf"; "Make a present to the judge, then he won't put you in jail," and so forth. The class oppression practiced by the courts drew after it, in the conscience of the masses, a pessimistic reasoning as to the very nature of the laws: "The law is a carriage shaft; whichever way you turn, that is the way it goes"; and also concerning the relativity and instability of legislation: "Necessity changes the law"; "Necessity knows no law, but strides through them all."

The attitude to the lord and master, as also in the tales, is mockingly half-contemptuous: "Undress me, take off my shoes, lay me down, cover me, and then go—I will fall asleep myself"; "The master's illness is the peasant's health."

---

* A rhymed play on words: in transliteration, "Kazennaia palata ot muzhikov bogata."—Ed.

Like the sketch drawn of the priests in the satirical tales, the attitude of the peasant proverbs toward the priests is sharply negative; there is emphasis on greed, avarice, envy—all those vices which, naturally, bore upon the peasantry in connection with economic interrelations: "The priest's belly is made of seven sheepskins"; "You are born, baptized, married, you die—for all these you have to pay the priest"; "Like a raven for bones, so the judge waits for the lavish robber, and the priest for the rich man who has died"; "The priest's eyes are envious, and his hands rake everything in"; "You can tell a priest even if he's dressed in matting: little father has his mannerisms"; "A priest never has any change, and a tailor never has any pay"; "The priest was not surprised that the peasant had been making beer, but he *was* surprised that he had not called him"; "The peasant twists the rope, but the priest casts the noose."

The proverbs reflect clearly and in a variety of ways the mode of life and psychology of the professional groups of craftsmen who separated themselves from the peasant masses, or of the groups who went away for seasonal work. In the proverbs, as well as in the tales, there is distinctly seen the complication of the basic class ideology by the specific additional features, produced by this or that craft, by the special conditions of labor and economic relationships. Only from the conditions of the [towpath] hauler's trade of an earlier period is it possible to understand such a proverb as this: "Necessity goes down [river], servitude comes up [river]"; the haulers, being subjected to the indescribable exploitation of the shipmasters, usually, before they had succeeded in reaching the lower reaches of the Volga, already found themselves entangled in debts to the master, and were obliged to enter into bondage to him when they started on the return journey up the Volga. "Toil and drudge, till they dig your grave," is an expression of the same hopeless social and economic status of the hauler of the earlier period.

If the collections of proverbs contain a vast amount of material characterizing the ideology of the various groups of the peasantry, and of the social classes connected with it, we find very few data on the other hand, concerning the proverbs of the privileged higher and middle classes—the noblemen and the merchant class.

However, there is some material, mainly from the milieu of the merchant trading class.

There are proverbs and sayings which reflect the actual trading process of an earlier time: "Goods are sold on looks"; "The price is according to the goods, the goods is according to the money"; "If you don't praise it, you won't sell it; if you don't find fault with it, you won't buy it"; "If you don't deceive, you can't sell." In the proverbs there is a good deal of expression also of neat, general observations on the laws of trade turnover: "Little in supply, much in demand"; "There is nothing freer than bargaining, but even there, necessity dwells"; "If you don't sell on credit, you'll never see any money"; "Goods that lie idle won't feed you"; "A good merchant has neither money nor goods" (that is, on hand). Of course, these proverbs, and others like them, can only conditionally be called "mercantile," since they can equally express the thoughts and observations both of the merchant class and of the group of the peasantry which was connected with the local market, fair, and bazaar.

We possess also proverbs which are purely aristocratic; though, as we said previously, we know relatively few of them, none the less they are exceedingly expressive in their clear, coarse class tendencies: "The peasants' bones are covered with dogs' flesh"; "Out of a boor you can't make a gentleman"; "A serf cannot argue against a gentleman"; and so forth.

As regarding proletarian proverbs, however, before the October Socialist Revolution they had hardly been recorded at all in scientific publications. This is to be explained mainly by the one-sided interest of the collectors and investigators, which was directed almost exclusively to the peasant folklore of the countryside. At present, the next task facing all folklorists is the systematic collection of the folklore, particularly the proverbs, of the factory and the mill. Efforts in this direction are already being made. In the vast collection of Illustrov one may find at most two or three proverbs which can be added to the number of those from the mill and the factory: "We wash the gold, but we ourselves wail aloud" (speaking of the workers in the gold-fields); "Little father Petersburg wore us out, our brothers the mills took away our years, and our mother the canal broke us utterly." (The proverb was composed under Nicholas I, at the time of the building of the so-called Mariinsky waterway system and the digging of the Belo-Ozero Canal.)

However, of course, there have been and still are very many proverbs current in the factories and mills. They are produced and exist in direct connection with manufacture. They can often be heard in the workshops themselves, during working hours: in order to take them down, it is not necessary to create those conditions which are necessary to the recording, for example, of tales or long songs. They fall easily from the lips of the workingman, and they can easily be caught up by the collector. F. P. Filin took down several proverbs and sayings of the factory and the mill: "He comes, with his iron heels he knocks the floor cracks" (a founder in the casting shop of the Dubnensky cast-iron foundry near Tula), and others.

If the proverb has hitherto been altogether insufficiently studied from the social and historical viewpoint, Russian folkloristics cannot boast, either, of anything like a detailed study of its artistic aspects. The investigators usually emphasize the fact that "the proverb generally appears in a rhythmic or harmonious form," [4] or that "the form of the proverb is a more or less brief aphorism, often expressed in harmonious, rhythmic speech, frequently in metaphorical (poetic) language," [5] but on the question as to precisely what this "harmony and rhythm" consists of, we have up to the present time no detailed investigations.

In a few words, "harmony and rhythm" are attained: by the compositional structure of the proverb (in particular, by the syntactical construction), by rhythmic patterns, repetitions of sounds (various forms of reiterations of sounds and internal rhymes), and also by a wealth of imagery, with the use of different tropes and figures and, finally, often by original lexicology.

Proverbs, in the majority of cases, are composed of two members; but there is frequently encountered also the division into three members, and even into many. It is important that the rhythmic division

[4] Dal, *op. cit.*, p. xxix.
[5] Vladimirov, *Introduction to the History of Russian Literature* (Kiev, 1896), p. 13.

into members should be sharply felt. Based on the syntactical construction, the measure of the proverb is maintained by rhythm, rhyme, and other forms of connection of sounds.

Every member of a proverb constitutes a certain integral part of a simple or complex sentence. This contributes very substantially toward one of the main requirements of a proverb—clearness of thought. The most characteristic and basic type of construction of proverbs is the relation of the first part to the second, as that of subject to predicate: "To live your life is not so easy as to cross a field"; "One man in a field is not a warrior"; "It's not always Shrovetide for the cat"; "A priest's belly is made of seven sheepskins." Such a twofold form, repeating itself, is also the basis of many complex proverbs, each part of which is formed according to this elementary type: "Little father Petersburg wore us out, our brothers the mills took away our years, and our mother the canal broke us utterly."

The relationship of the parts of the proverb, as that of subject and predicate, is not obligatory; in the proverbs there is only observed a striving to have every part represent, in its syntactical relationship, something complete in itself. Thus, in proverbs which represent in themselves a complex sentence, it is permissible that the first member should be joined to the second according to the principle of conjunction of a conditional sentence ("Once you've started a job, don't say that you can't finish it"; "If there is no one to wear bast shoes, there will be no one to wear velvet"; "If the pocket is empty, then the judge is deaf"); a contradictory sentence ("You will take the bast, but you will have to give back a belt for it"; "The treasury makes war, but the purse laments"); a comparative sentence ("A judge's pocket is like a priest's belly"); an explanatory sentence ("Spread the manure thickly, and the granary won't be empty"; "The law is a carriage shaft; whichever way you turn, that is the way it goes"); a provisional sentence ("Toil and drudge, till they dig your grave"), and so forth.

In simple sentences, to a given member of the proverb complements can be added ("You must not call a priest's dog 'little father' "), and definitions, and so forth.

And so, clearness of syntactical structure is the reason for the division of the proverb into parts. In this lies the beginning of the "harmony" of the proverb. This harmony is often maintained by the similar structure of each member, by a syntactical parallelism; compare the proverb, "Little father Petersburg . . . "; "If you don't praise it, you won't sell it; if you don't find fault with it, you won't buy it"; "God is high, and the tsar is far away"; "You can't fill either a duck's crop or a master's pocket."

The same clearly marked composition is maintained by rhythmic structure, though it is not possible to establish strict meters in the proverb: in their rhythmic structure, proverbs are very diverse. In them we can, perhaps, notice a prevalence of three-syllabled feet (dactylic, amphibrachic, and anapestic), frequently in fanciful conjunction with two-syllabled feet (trochaics and iambics) and four-syllabled feet (paeonic). This corresponds to the colloquial Russian speech, consisting of many-syllabled words, which consequently, it is obvious, will not fit into the close framework of the trochee or the iamb. Besides, it is necessary to keep in view here, as indeed for every oral creative work, that much depends on the musical aspect of speech: on the lengthening or, on the contrary, the shortening of the length of a sound in its pronunciation.

As in the other forms of folklore, the proverb demands not only a phonetic, but also a musical recording. Only then will it be possible to make exact deductions as to the rhythmic structure of the proverb. It is important to note, in the meanwhile, that the proverb strives to maintain the rhythmic balance of its members, and to reinforce by rhythm the content which it sets forth, to attain a rhythmic picturesqueness. Dal [6] has correctly emphasized the amazing rhythmic pattern, and its striking correspondence to the content, in the following multimembered proverb:

> He beat down, he knocked together—and there was a wheel!
> He mounted and rode off—ah, that was good!
> He looked around behind him—
> Only the spokes were left lying there!

[6] Dal, *op. cit.*, p. xxxi.

In this four-membered proverb we perceive a great rhythmical exactness: the first two members consist of eight or nine syllables apiece,* and besides, each half of the first member is rhythmically constructed in almost exactly the same way as the corresponding half of the second: between the two accents there are, in each case, two unaccented syllables; the two last members consist of six syllables apiece, and are constructed anapestically (with the accent on the last syllable of a three-syllabled foot). This original rhythmic structure of the proverb fully corresponds to the development of the subject: the unexpected transition after the second member to an altogether different structure, with a lesser number of syllables, compels us to make an expressive pause, and to retard the tempo of the narration, beautifully emphasizing the astonishment which is depicted.

Very often, in the symmetrical rhythmic construction of the members of a proverb, the combining parts of speech (conjunctions and so forth) do not enter into the rhythmic accent, but, breaking the rhythm, clearly emphasize the meaning of the proverb as a pronouncement, and not an outward embellishment of speech: "If the pocket is empty, [so then] the judge is deaf"; "If there is no one to wear bast shoes, there won't be anyone to wear velvet [either]." The words which are contrasted according to the sense of the proverb are placed at symmetrical points in the proverb; the rhythm is deliberately broken, so that the lack of concurrence, either in the number of syllables or else in the accent, may make the contrast clearer and more acute: "You will take the bast, [but] give back the belt"; "You can't fill a duck's crop, [and] you can't fill a master's pocket."

Repetitions of sounds play a vast role in the proverbs. Here, most often of all, we have to do with end rhymes and assonances at the end of a line or a half-line, emphasizing and strengthening the arrangement of the proverb in members: the syntactical structure, reinforced by the rhythmic symmetry, finds new support in the correspondence of sounds. This may easily be seen from the vast majority of proverbs. In order not to multiply examples, we revert again to the complex three-membered proverb which we have already

* In the original Russian.—ED.

cited more than once, which is divided by its rhythms still further, into half-lines: "Little father Petersburg wore us out, our brothers the mills took away our years, and our mother the canal broke us utterly," or, "The horse loves oats, the earth loves manure, and the governor loves gifts," and so forth. Besides, in proverbs, as in all folklore, there are permissible not only exact and marked rhymes, but the so-called "rhymoids"—approximate rhymes, assonances. So, in the example which has just been given, on the one hand we see rhymes: "*Peter—vyter* (Petersburg wore out); *zavody—gody* (mills, years)"; but on the other, we see assonances: "*kanava—dokanala* (the canal broke us utterly)."

The play of sounds in the proverb is not restricted to the limits of end rhymes and "rhymoids". The sonant connections among the words which enter into it go considerably further—in proverbs there are repeatedly encountered, alongside of the end rhymes, inner rhymes, that is, those which connect by their consonance, not the ends of lines or half-lines, but also the middle and the beginning: "*Tolkuy, Fetinya Savishna, pro botvinyu davishnyu*" (Chatter, Fetinya Savishna, about the cold beet soup of long ago); "*Salo bylo, stalo mylo*" (It was fat, it became soap); "*Kushay varyono, slushay govoryono*" (Eat what is cooked, listen to what is said).

Along with the end rhymes, the initial and inner rhymes, very many proverbs are strengthened by persistent internal repetitions of sound, that is, by sounds which are repeated in various words of the proverb. These repetitions of sound may be included in the so-called "assonances" (repetitions of vowels), "consonances" (repetitions of consonants), and frequently in the complex repetition of groups both of vowels and of consonants. Besides, the sounds which are repeated may be encountered in one and the same order, but they may also be in an order that is reversed or confused. A great number of examples may be cited, showing various forms of repetitions of sounds.

It is necessary, however, in studying the play of sounds, to take into account the living, not bookish, pronunciation, which, besides, is frequently in the local dialect. For example, the "orchestration of sound" on the *o* in the proverb, "*BOdlivuyu kOrOvu s pOlya dOlOy*" (Drive the butting cow out of the field), was especially striking in the ancient Russian language (before the pronunciation of unaccented *o* as *a*), and is striking also at the present time in the northern Russian dialects where the pronunciation of *o* is retained: the *o* should be heard not only in accented, but also in unaccented syllables; conversely, the proverb, "*Ne zAmAkhivAysA pAlkoy i so-bAkA ne zAlAet*" (Don't raise your stick and the dog won't bark at you), with reference to its sounds, is much more expressive in the Moscow dialect where unaccented *o* is pronounced as *a*, since in the word *sobáka* (dog) the *o* in the syllable standing before the accent must also be sounded as an *a*. It is clear, therefore, that in the course of many centuries, many proverbs, in conforming themselves to changes in the language, have lost no small degree of their beauty of sound.

I cite a further series of examples of the repetition of vowels: (*i*) "*u FIlI bYlI, FIlyu zhe I pobIlI*" (They were visiting Filya, and they beat Filya); (*e*) "*i chEst' nE v chEst', koli nEchEvo yEst'*" (Even honor is not an honor, if there is nothing to eat); repetitions of consonants: (*pr, t*) "*PRoTiv PRiTchi ne posPoRish'*" (Against a parable you cannot argue); (*sh*) "*Skupomu duSHa deSHēvle groSHa*" (To the miser, a soul is worth less than a half-kopek); (*zl, z*) "*SkaZaL, shto uZLom ZaviaZaL*" (His word is as good as a tied knot); (*g*) "*Ne Goditsa boGu molit'sia, Goditsa Gorshki pokryvat'*" (He's not fit to pray to God, he's only fit to paint pots); (*st, r*) "*STaRost' ne RadoST', a smeRt' ne koRySt'*" (Old age is not a joy, but death is not a gain); (*r, t, m, b*) "*VReMeneM i sMeRd Ba-Ryshnyu BeRet*" (Sometimes even the peasant carries off the young lady); (*vs, kr, t*) "*VSyo na SVete KRyTo KoRyTom*" (Everything in the world is covered with a trough); complex repetitions of groups of vowels: (*lop*)"*KhoLOP na boiarina ne POsLukh*" (A bondsman cannot be witness against a boyar); (*ach*) "*Vsyak pod'iACHy lyubit kalACH goryACHy*" (Every scrivener loves a hot loaf); (*rak, sh*) "*VRAKi, SHto kaSHliayut RAKi, to SHaliat RybAKi*" (That's idle talk, that the crawfish cough; that's the fishermen playing pranks!); (*mel, yel*) "*MELi EMELia, tvoia nedElia*" (Go on, Emelian, it's your day); (*sv, vi*) "*SVetu VIdal: so SVin'iami korni yedal*" (I have seen the world; I have eaten roots with the pigs); (*kra*) "*Gore od-*

novo tol'ko RAKa KRAsit" (It's only the crawfish that turns red [beautiful] from grief); *(ra)* *"BRAn' dRAkoy kRAsna"* (An argument is fine only when there's a fight); *(by)* *"BYl BY BYk, a miaso BUdet"* (If there was a steer, there will be meat).

In particular, the last proverb is also an example of onomatopoeia (the bellowing of the bull: *by-by-by-bu*). Onomatopoetic proverbs, in comparison with the whole repertory of proverbs, are few, but still they are encountered frequently, and contribute powerfully to the vitalization of the form.

As Buslayev [7] has already noted correctly, "The proverb was the creation of the reciprocal powers of sound and thought." A word frequently attracted to itself a word of similar sound: *"Nevinno vino, vinovato pyanstvo"* (There's no harm in wine, it's drunkenness that is at fault). The choice of one word from a series of synonyms is prompted by the striving toward a connection and strengthening of sound: *"Mila vorona, da rot shirok"* (The crow is nice, but her mouth is wide) mouth, *rot*, and not beak, *klyuv*, because the word *rot* is connected by the repetition of sounds with the word *shirok*, wide); *"S toboi nado govorit' gorokhu nayevshis"* (I can talk with you only when I have eaten plenty of peas), has a variant, *"kashi nayevshis"* (when I have eaten plenty of porridge), but has no variant, *"khleba nayevshis"* (eaten plenty of bread), because in the first variant a part is played by the repetition of the sounds *"gor,"* in the second, by the repetition of the sounds *"shi,"* while in the third example there would be no connection of sounds at all.

The introduction of proper names (a form of synecdoche) serves as one of the favorite figurative devices. Owing to the introduction of proper names, the proverb gains in its picturesque concreteness. The choice of this or that name is conditioned either by a poetic source (a fable, narrative, or tale), or again by the striving for a play of sound (compare the proverbs above, *"U Fili byli, Filyu zhe i pobili"* (They were visiting Filya, and they beat Filya); *"Tolkuy, Fetinya Savishna, pro botvinyu davishnyu"* (Chatter, Fetinya Savishna, about the cold beet soup of long ago).

[7] F. I. Buslayev, *Historical Sketches*, Vol. I (St. Petersburg, 1864).

It goes without saying that the proverb, constructed with an eye to especially vivid expression, repeatedly has recourse to the use of metaphors, metonymy, synecdoche, and variations of them.

Many proverbs are of an ironical turn: "Lord, forgive us, let us get into someone else's storeroom, help us to load it up and to carry it out"; "The cartload went out and carried off the horse"; "I have seen the world, I have eaten roots with the swine."

In its urge to concreteness for the expression of general pronouncements about the world, nature, and human conduct, consequently, in its whole figurative composition, and also in its striving to work out established and pointed formulas, easy to memorize and to pass on traditionally (with the use of clear syntax, rhythmic symmetry, and connections of sounds), the proverb provides a model of the closest possible bond between content and artistic form. The laconic quality and expressiveness of the popular proverbs have called forth the admiration of Pushkin: "What gold the Russian proverbs are! But it does not just give itself into your hands—no!" To master the wealth of the popular proverb was Pushkin's ardent desire. A. M. Gorky, also, advised writers to study the compactness and expressiveness of speech found in folk proverbs.

BIBLIOGRAPHY

COLLECTIONS OF PROVERBS

Dal', V., *Poslovitsy russkogo naroda* (Proverbs of the Russian People) (Moscow, 1861; 2nd ed., Moscow, 1879).

Illustrov, I. I., *Zhizn' russkogo naroda v ego poslovitsakh i pogovorkakh* (Life of the Russian People in Their Proverbs and Sayings), 3rd. ed. (Moscow, 1915).

Snegirev, I., *Russkie narodnye poslovitsy i pritchi* (Russian Popular Proverbs and Parables) (Moscow, 1848).

Novyi sbornik poslovits i pritchei (New Collection of Proverbs and Parables (Moscow, 1857).

Simoni, P., *Starinnye sborniki russkikh poslovits, pogovorok, zagadok i pr. XVII-XIX* (Ancient Collections of Russian Proverbs, Sayings, Riddles, etc., from the Seventeenth to the Nineteenth Centuries), Nos. I-II (St. Petersburg, 1899), *Sborn. Otd. Russk. iaz. i slov. Akademii nauk* (Annals of the Division of Russian Language and Literature of the Academy of Sciences, Vol. LXVI, 7).

RESEARCHES

Dal', V., *Predislovie k sborniku "Poslovitsy russkogo naroda"* (Preface to the Collection, Proverbs of the Russian People).

Buslaev, F. I., *Istoricheskie ocherki* (Historical Essays), Vol. I (St. Petersburg, 1864), or (Works of F. I. Buslayev) Vol. II (1913).

Potebnia, A. A., *Iz lektsii po teorii slovesnosti* (From Lectures on the Theory of Literature) (1894), X.

Vladimirov, P. V., *Vvedenie v istoriiu russkoi slovesnosti* (Introduction to the History of Russian Literature) (Kiev, 1896).

Liatskii, E. A., *Neskol'ko zamechanii k voprosu o poslovitsakh i pogovorkakh* (Some Observations on the Question of Proverbs and Sayings), *Annals of the Division of Russian Language and Literature of the Academy of Sciences*, Vol. II, Bk. 3 (St. Petersburg, 1897).

Voznesenskii, *O sklade ili ritme i metre kratkikh izrechenii russkogo naroda; poslovits, pogovorok, zagadok, priskagok i dr.* (On the Order or Rhythm and Meter of the Brief Aphorisms of the Russian People: Proverbs, Sayings, Riddles, Storytellers' Exordia, and Others) (Kostroma, 1908).

Timoshenko, I. E., *Literaturnye pervoistochniki i prototipy trekhsot russkikh poslovits i pogovorok* (Literary Primary Sources and Prototypes of Three Hundred Russian Proverbs and Sayings) (Kiev, 1897).

Perets, V. P., *Iz istorii poslovitsy: Istoriko-literaturnye zametki i materialy* (From the History of the Proverb: Historico-Literary Notes and Materials) (St. Petersburg, 1898).

Kuznetsov, Y., "Kharakteristika obshchestvennykh klassov po narodnym poslovitsam i pogovorkam" (Characterization of Social Classes in Popular Proverbs and Sayings), *Zhivaia starina* (Living Antiquity), No. III, 1903.

Nezdorov, A., *Torgovyi oborot v poslovitsakh russkogo naroda* (Trade Turnover in the Proverbs of the Russian People) (St. Petersburg, 1906).

Sheidlin, B., *Moskva v poslovitsakh i pogovorkakh* (Moscow in Proverbs and Sayings) (Moscow, 1929).

Mikhel'son, M. I., *Khodiachie i netkie slova* (Current and Pointed Expressions), 2nd ed. (St. Petersburg, 1896).

——, *Russkaia mysl' i rech'* (Russian Thought and Speech), Vols. I-II, Shakhnovich, M., "Kratkaia istoriia sobraniia i izucheniia poslovits i pogovorok" (A Brief History of the Collection and Study of Proverbs and Sayings), *Sov. fol'klor* (Soviet Folklore) Nos. 4-5, 1936.

2. RIDDLES

A *riddle* may be defined as an ingenious question, expressed usually in the form of a metaphor.

According to Aristotle, a riddle is a well composed metaphor. A. N. Veselovsky examines the riddle in connection with formulas of parallelism, and is inclined to see in it a parallelism having only one member, with a transfer of certain features from the suppressed portion of the parallel, for example, "A beautiful maiden walks across the sky."

The metaphorical character of the riddle, however, does not appear to be altogether obligatory. We encounter riddles in the form of a direct question, without any figurative meaning of the words which enter into it. Frequently, even, complicated arithmetical problems are included under riddles.

Riddles now are only a means of amusement; in children's games they are adapted to educational purposes, and because of their pedagogical importance they are encouraged by the school.

But in earlier times they played a considerably more important role, partly entering into the repertory of cult ceremonials. This cult role of riddles in Russian folklore ended long ago, but it was still extant, not so very far back in the mode of life of many other nations. Up to a recent time there was preserved among the Udmurts the custom of propounding riddles at a fixed period of the year: from the end of the field labors in the autumn to the beginning of spring, especially at the time of the Christmas holidays. Besides, in the huts there were arranged special "evenings of riddles," and the material was disposed according to thematic cycles (riddles about mankind, about the cattle, about the field, and so forth).

Many riddles possessed a clearly magical character.

The riddle in antiquity served a cult, appearing as the revelation of a religious mystery, or as one of the forms of transmission of the religious concepts—the myths. This can be seen even in the legends of the Sphinx, in the references to the role of riddles in the practice of oracles.

Apart from this religious significance, the riddle served in antiquity, and among certain nations even until recent times, as one of the means of making a trial of wisdom, frequently appearing as one of the forms of the so-called "judgment of God," when the fate of the accused depended on his readiness of mind.

In the Russian chronicle there are interesting evidences that the form of the riddle sometimes served as one of the aspects of secret diplomatic language; compare, for example, the conversation of Yaroslav the Wise, through the spy, with his partisan in the enemy camp, when the orders for battle were conveyed in the metaphorical words: "Give some honey to the druzhina." The trial of wisdom was preserved in rudimentary form in the wedding rituals both of the Russians and of other nations. Thus, for example, the bridegroom received the right to sit beside the bride only in the event that he, with his groomsmen, solved the riddles which were propounded to him.[8]

A great place was occupied by riddles not so long ago in the Christmas merrymakings of the peasantry, and they were also quite often interwoven into the magic *Rusalia* and *Kolyadi* songs.[9]

The motif of riddles is diffused in the epic forms of world folklore (see, for example, the legends of Oedipus, the motif of the contests of Odin with the giant Waftrudir in the *Edda*, and numerous episodes of the *Kalevala*). In the dramatic genres, in the medieval ceremonial performances, for example, in the Christmas mystery plays, the riddle served as one of the formative elements.[10]

In the medieval productions, both of the West and of Russia, written in the question-and-answer form, the riddle occupies a very prominent place. One need only refer to the "Colloquy of the Three Holy Men," on which is based the well known religious verse about the Book of Wisdom; the greater part of this work, and in fact the whole scheme of it, is built upon wise questions and answers. Riddles are encountered in the medieval collections of aphorisms of the type of the Byzantine and Old Russian *Melissa* (The Bee). They are

[8] A. N. Veselovsky, *Collected Works*, Vol. I, pp. 271 ff.
[9] E. F. Karsky, *The White Russians*, Vol. III, No. I (Moscow, 1916), p. 176.
[10] Veselovsky, *op. cit.*, Vol. I, p. 101.

frequent also in the medieval popular narratives, for example, in the legends of Solomon and the Queen of Sheba, based on the biblical tale of the contests between the keen-witted queen and the most wise Solomon, and also in the narratives of Akir the Most Wise, of Alexander of Macedon, of Apollonius of Tyre, of the merchant Basarga, and, finally, in the famous narrative of Prince Peter and the wise maiden Fevronia. In the last-named production the author makes use of riddles which are clearly derived from folklore.

In general, the mutual influence of book literature and of folklore has very graphically told upon the fate of riddles. In their time such books as the abecedaria contributed to the diffusion of riddles.

The riddle is interpolated also into the rich genre of the tales of folklore. Generally the riddles serve only as introductory episodes in the tales, but sometimes they form the whole fabric of the narrative.[11]

As regards the *structure* of the riddle, however, as has been indicated above, it generally includes within itself a metaphor, and rests upon parallelism. Sometimes it is constructed upon a "switching-off,"[12] and then it approximates to a negative parallelism: "She is red [pretty], but she is not a maid; she is green, but she is not a grove of trees" (a carrot); "It is spotted, but it is not a dog; it is green, but it is not an onion; it whirls around like a demon, and its direction is into the woods" (a magpie). Frequently, under riddles there are included complicated problems in number: "Four cats are sitting, opposite each cat there are three cats—how many are there of them?" Often the riddle is built on a play of homonyms: "Why [from what] does the goose swim?" (Answer: from the shore.)

In their stylistic construction the riddles are exceedingly close to the proverbs and sayings. For example, in the famous collection by V. Dal, *Proverbs of the Russian People*, there is included a considerable number of riddles, which later on were borrowed by D. Sadovnikov for his special collection, *Riddles of the Russian People*; this is, for completeness and systematic arrangement, the best

11 See the special investigation by E. N. Yeleonskaya, "Certain Notes on the Role of the Riddle in the Tale," *Ethnographic Review*, No. 1, 1907.
12 Veselovsky, *op. cit.*, Vol. I, p. 206.

collection of Russian riddles. Sometimes, only by means of a single change of intonation, a proverb is transformed into a riddle: "Nothing hurts it, but it groans all the time." In the proverb they are speaking of a hypocrite and a beggar, but in the riddle, by those very same words, a swine is meant.[13]

For the *artistic semantics* of the riddles, a very characteristic feature—as, however, for the proverbs also—is the use of proper names in the capacity of common nouns (the principle of metonymy): "Darya and Marya see each other, but they do not come together" (the floor and the ceiling); "Churilo stands with his snout all smeared" (a candle); "Two Onisims, four Maxims, the seventh is Sophie" (a chair); "Arina sits with her mouth hanging open" (a trumpet).[14]

Great subtlety is added to the riddles by the possibility of their two-fold solution, the plays of double meanings; moreover, the greater part of such riddles bear a definitely erotic character. This is characteristic of the folklore of all peoples. V. Shklovsky, in the collection *Poetics*, speaks of such riddles as a special form of "sublimation."

Riddles are very rich in alliterations: *"Mat' Soph'ia den' i noch' sokhnet, utro nastanet, proch' otstanet"* (Mother Sophie day and night dries away, morning comes, she stands aside) (the oven door), and in other forms of repetitions of sounds and consonances; besides, sometimes the answer has a sound similar to that of the basic word of the riddle: "Katyukha and Palakha, Samson and Fefel" (a muffler, a sleeping platform, a table, and old clothes) (rags). As the ultimate development of the latter type, there serve the riddles in which assonance appears as the sole basis for the replacement of certain words by others, sometimes even by those which are almost meaningless: "Kutchka [Kut] and Laika [Lavka] and Pipupochek [Pristupochek]" (a muffler, a bench, and a little step). The degree of assonance in the riddles is not identical—there are encountered assonances which are very remote, approximate, but exact rhymes are also frequent. Sometimes the play of sounds is connected with an onomatopoeia

[13] Dal, *op. cit.*, p. xxvi.
[14] On the correlation of proverbs and riddles, see Buslayev, *Essays*, Vol. I, p. 24.

corresponding with the idea of the answer to the riddle: "The priests fought, the priests finished their fight, they injured each other, the priests went away and hanged themselves" (the threshing).

With reference to syntactical construction, however, in spite of the question which is contained in the riddle, the interrogative form is not obligatory. Because of the brevity of its form, the riddle usually consists of one, two, or three clauses, which are frequently incomplete.

The *thematics* of riddles are exceedingly diversified, with reference both to the question and to the answer.

In view of their aphoristic form, riddles are suitable for easy memorization and for sustained retention in the memory of generations. Accordingly, it is not surprising that in them we find a series of concepts and patterns connected with very ancient, long outmoded forms of life and thought. In riddles the animistic world concept finds clear expression. A great number of riddles are devoted to the description and interpretation of the phenomena of nature (thunder, day and night, fire, snow, frost, water).

In the riddles may be found an expression of the successive stages in the development of the people. In Russian riddles there are survivals of the pastoral mode of life, which, it is true, were later adapted to new conditions. The thunder is represented as a roaring bullock: "The bullock roared upon a hundred lakes." Day is represented in the form of a bull or a white cow, night in the form of a black one: "The white bull poked its nose in at the window"; "The black cow knocked down all the people, but the white one arose and raised them all up again"; "The blue-gray bull drank up the waters of the dale" (frost).

To the same category are to be assigned the riddles dealing with the shepherd, and so on. The night sky, the stars, the moon are represented in the forms of a flock and a shepherd: "The field is immeasurable, the sheep cannot be counted, and the shepherd has horns."

Rural life, peasant labor, the peasant economy were fully reflected, down to the last detail, in the riddles. Both the answers to the riddles and the forms of the metaphorical riddles exhaustively describe the household inventory, the objects of domestic utility, the peasants' buildings, the clothing, all the aspects of farm work (sowing, plowing, mowing, reaping, threshing, the cultivation of flax, spinning, weaving, and so forth).

In these riddles reflecting the life of the peasantry, there is developed with especial power a distinctive feature of the poetic thought of the peasant: realistic concretization. The phenomena of nature, the sky, the air are filled with figures drawn from the everyday life of the countryside: "Over the old woman's hut hangs a crust of bread; the dog barks, but cannot reach it" (the moon); "Whenever I look in at the little window, I unfold the matting, I sow the peas, I put in a crust of bread, everyone sees it, but not everyone will tell: for one it is light, for another it is dark, but for me it is blue" (the sky, stars, and moon); "The oven is overheated, the oven is full of pies, among the pies is a loaf" (the same); "A woman's head warmer slipped into the space by the gate" (a snowdrift); "A bald gelding looks under the gate" (the moon); "Sweet milk is poured upon the floor, and neither with a knife nor with the teeth can one scrape it off" (the sunlight); "Father has a stallion—not all the world can hold him back; mother has a box—not all the world can pick it up; brother has a belt—not all the world can measure it; sister has a towel—not all the world can roll it up" (the wind, the earth, the stars, the road).

Thoughts concerning man, concerning his structure and outward form, are accompanied by the associations of the peasant economy: "A wet calf lies in the vegetable garden" (the tongue); "The sheepcote is full of white sheep" (the teeth), or the variants: "The space under the stove is full of little white sheep"; "Two perches full of white hens are sitting there."

Owing to the aphoristic form of the riddles, which are confirmed in this by assonances, their vocabulary is fitted to preserve, in the course of centuries, elements of an outmoded way of life and thought. Because of this, in the riddles which are still used by the peasantry at the present time, one may frequently encounter forms which no longer find any real counterparts in contemporary life. For the historian of everyday life they possess an indisputably great interest: "A gray cloth is spread over the window" (the smoke in a chimneyless hut), or the variant: "On the stove is a lout, on the sleeping platform is a lout, on the benches is a lout, on the floor is a lout, the lout went out of the little window"; "Winter and summer they ride on one runner" (a movable window through which smoke escapes). Sometimes the riddles give an exact description of objects of the old domestic furniture, and may possess an interest for the historians of material culture: "Four ears, the fifth is the belly, the sixth is the paw of an awkward bear" (a candlestick); "The field is of water, the vegetable gardens are of leather" (a looking glass in a leather frame); or, "The little threshing floor is of gold, the little border is of oats" (apparently, a metal mirror); "The young hen has a light under her tail" (meaning, a woman's coiffure with brocaded ornaments); "It makes a noise, it laughs, it yearns for the maiden" (a silk *sarafan*); "Under the woods hang many-colored wheels, they adorn the lasses, they tease the young lads" (ring-shaped earrings)

The riddles expressed with precision the traditional bases of the patriarchal, conservative family life of the countryside: the family hierarchy, the respect for elders, the difficult position of the bride, the authority of the father-in-law and mother-in-law.

The majority of the riddles expressed, as it were, a fatalistic resignation to the traditional family and social way of life. Only sleep and death make men equal: "Who is it that neither the tsar, nor the dog whippers, nor the prince's hound, can overcome?" (sleep); "On the Volynian mountain stands an Ordynian oak, on it sits a bird, repetitious as a spinning wheel; she sits and says, 'I am not afraid of anyone, neither the tsar in Moscow, nor the king in Lithuania" (death); "An owl sits on the trough, she cannot be satisfied, neither with priests, nor with clerks, nor with the world, nor with good people, nor with elders" (the same).

In analyzing the thematics of the riddles, it is necessary, however, to take account of the external conditions which determined the composition of the folklorists' collections, of the significant role of tsarist censorship, which indisputably told upon the selection of the riddles, both in Dal's collection and in that of Sadovnik.

In riddles, as in proverbs, class differentiation also found expression. In the riddles there is expressed, for example, class satire on wealth: "With the rich man it's thin, with the poor man it's thick; it's always on them" (a shirt); "What the peasant casts on the ground, the master puts into his pocket" (nasal mucus).

Like the other genres of folklore (especially the tales), the riddle reveals an exceedingly caustic attitude toward the clergy, endowing them with the same satirical features as in the tales about priests: "Who fleeces both the living and the dead?" (the priest); "What is it in the church that bleats?" (the deacon); "In the dense fir wood, in the thick birch grove, he often wags his tail" (the priest offers incense); "A man in front, but a woman from behind" (a priest); "Someone went out who was not a woman, nor an old woman, nor a Mordvinian; not wearing a dress, nor a *sarafan*, nor a caftan; holding in his hands neither pancakes nor flat cakes" (the same).

We have spoken above of the mutual influence of the oral riddle and of written literature in ancient times. Artistic literature made use of oral riddles for its own purposes at all times, interpolating the riddles into a large-scale work, or sometimes even constructing upon the riddle an entire composition. Sometimes, even, the riddle became a literary fashion, for example, in the seventeenth century in France (Fénelon, Boileau.). Riddles were used by Rousseau, Schiller, Hebel, and among the Russian writers, by Zhukovsky, while in recent times an exceedingly rich use was made of the folk riddle by Esenin.

BIBLIOGRAPHY

COLLECTIONS OF RIDDLES

Sadovnikov, D., *Zagadki russkogo naroda* (Riddles of the Russian People) (St. Petersburg, 1901).

Dal', V., *Poslovitsy russkogo naroda* (Proverbs of the Russian People) (Moscow, 1861; 2nd ed., Moscow, 1879).

Rybnikova, M. A., *Zagadky* (Riddles) (Moscow, Academia, 1932).

RESEARCHES

Vladimirov, P. V., *Vvedenie v istoriiu russkoi slovesnosti* (Introduction to the History of Russian Literature) (Kiev, 1896).

Speranskii, M. N., *Russkaia ustnaia slovesnost'* (Russian Oral Literature) (Moscow, 1916).

Veselovskii, A. N., *Sochineniia* (Works), Vol. I (St. Petersburg, 1913).

Potebnia, A. A., *Ob'iasneniia malorusskikh i srodnykh narodnykh pesen* (Explanations of Little-Russian and Related Folk Songs), Vol. II (Warsaw, 1887) (*Russkii filologicheskii vestnik* [Russian Philological News], 1885, Vol. XVIII).

Buslayev, F. I. *Istoricheskie ocherki russkoi narodnoi slovesnosti i iskusstva* (Historical Surveys of Russian Popular Literature and Art) Vol. I (1861).

Yeleonskaia, E. N., "Nekotorye zamechaniia o roli zagadki v skazke" (Certain Observations on the Role of the Riddle in the Tale), *Etnograficheskoe obozrenie* (Ethnographic Review), No. 1, 1907.

Kapitsa, O. I., *Detskii fol'klor* (Children's Folklore) (Leningrad, 1928).

THE BYLINY

❦

Among the endlessly diversified productions of the Russian popular creative art (folklore), one of the most prominent and honored places belongs to the ancient epic songs, called by the peasant narrators *"stáriny"* or *"starinki"* (old tales), but known in scholarship as *"byliny."* *

The term *"bylina"* is an invented one, introduced into scientific use in the 1830's by the scholar-dilettante Sakharov, on the basis of a well known expression from the *Tale of Igor's Raid*—"the *byliny* of this time."

The significance of the *byliny* in the history of Russian national culture is exceedingly great. In these ancient songs are very clearly and fully reflected the most diverse aspects of the historical and everyday life of the Russian people; they appear as wonderful landmarks of the original folk art. The *byliny* are striking in the wealth of their narrative subjects and motifs; in the generalizing force and monumental character of their artistic figures, which incarnate in themselves the heroic features of the Russian people, their dreams and hopes; in the perfection of poetic forms, which have been worked out by many generations of popular singers; in the richness and expressiveness of their folk language.

The monumental character of the epic figures, and the full poetic value of the Russian *byliny*, make them not only the national pride of Russia, but place them rightfully in the ranks of such celebrated productions of the epos of other nations, as the Greek *Iliad* and *Odyssey*, the French *Chanson de Roland*, the German *Niebelungenlied*, the Scandinavian sagas, and also—for though they have been worked over by individual writers, still they are based on ancient traditional popular songs—the Iranian *Shah Namah* of Firdusi, the Georgian poem "The Knight in the Tiger's Skin," by Rustaveli, and the Karelian *Kalevala*.

* Plural of *bylina*.—ED.

Not without reason have the Russian *byliny* attracted the attention not only of scholarly investigators (both Russian and foreign), but also of great poets, musicians, and artists, giving them many stimuli for their creative work. The *byliny*, known to Pushkin in the collection of Kirsha Danilov, contributed much, as it has now been sufficiently established, to the impregnation of Pushkin's poetry with the figures and the poetic riches of the popular speech. The *byliny* inspired Rimsky-Korsakov to the creation of his famous opera, *Sadko*. From the *byliny* Vasnetsov took the figures of the "Three Knights." The *byliny* are regarded as being the inspiration of poets, musicians, and artists, both in our own time and for the future.

In the Russian epos there are reckoned to be about a hundred subjects of the *byliny*. About two thousand records of the texts of *byliny* have been accumulated. Regardless of the fact that many of the *byliny* can be traced to remote antiquity, the recording of Russian epic poetry began at a comparatively late period. The oldest records are dated in the seventeenth century; the most ancient of those which have come down to us are assigned to the years 1619–1620. In those years, for Richard James, an Englishman who had traveled to Russia, there were written down several historical songs, relating the events of the end of the sixteenth and the beginning of the seventeenth century.[1]

From the seventeenth and eighteenth centuries there are known to scholarship, in all, twenty-four records of *byliny*; of these, only five can be assigned to the seventeenth century.[2] The old records set forth seven different subjects of *byliny*. With especial frequency we encounter in them the *bylina* of Elijah of Murom and Solovey the Robber. These records of *byliny* were made, not with a scientific aim, but in order to produce interesting reading matter. Not without reason do their titles contain the names which are characteristic of the written literature of the seventeenth and eighteenth centuries:

[1] P. K. Simoni, "Great-Russian Songs, Written Down in the Years 1619–1620 for Richard James in the Far North of the Kingdom of Moscow," *Annals of the Division of Russian Language and Literature of the Academy of Sciences*, Vol. LXXXII, No. 7.

[2] See B. M. Sokolov, "Records of the Ancient *Bylina*," *Ethnography*, Nos. 1-2, 1936.

"Lay," "Legend," "History"; for example, "The Legend of the Knights of Kiev: How They Went to Constantinople."

From the middle of the eighteenth century there has come down to us a famous collection of *byliny*, compiled by the Cossack Kirsha Danilov for the rich man of the Urals, Demidov. It includes more than seventy texts.

This collection appeared in its first (incomplete) edition in 1804; it was republished in 1818, in a fuller and more scholarly form, under the title, *Ancient Russian Poems*. The complete scientific edition of this collection did not appear before the beginning of the twentieth century (edition of 1901, under the editorship of P. N. Sheffer).

In the first half of the nineteenth century the *byliny* were collected at various places in Russia and were sent to the famous connoisseur and collector of folklore, P. V. Kireyevsky; they were published in the ten issues of *Songs Collected by Kireyevsky*, in the years 1862–1874, after his death.

A great deal of collecting of Russian *byliny* epos was achieved in the 1860's and 1870's. From that time there have come down to us two large and valuable collections of *byliny*: (1) *Songs, Collected by P. N. Rybnikov* (1861–1867); (2) *Onega Byliny*, by A. F. Hilferding (1873). Rybnikov wrote down 224 texts of *byliny* in the Onega region, and Hilferding, in the course of several years, wrote down 318 texts in the same region.

During the whole course of the second half of the nineteenth century, there were partial records made of *byliny*, also, in other areas of the European part of Russia and in Siberia. These records were later brought together in two collections: *Records of the Old and New Bylina*, by N. S. Tikhonravov and V. F. Miller (Moscow, 1894, 85 numbers), and *Byliny of the New and Newest Recording*, by V. F. Miller (Moscow, 1908, 108 numbers).

On the very verge of the twentieth century, the work on the collection of the epos of the *byliny* was being advanced in the remote areas of northern European Russia, where new treasures of *byliny* were discovered. In 1901 the large collection, *White Sea Byliny* (116 numbers) appeared as the result of the records made by A. V. Markov on the shore of the White Sea. After this, A. D. Grigoryev issued a collection of *Archangel Byliny* (Vol. I, Moscow, 1904, and Vol. III, Moscow, 1910, 424 numbers in all), written down along the seacoast and on the Mezen and Pinega rivers. In 1904, in St. Petersburg, there appeared a collection of *Pechora Byliny* (101 numbers), written down by N. E. Onchukov on the Pechora River.

These collections, in the technique of their recordings and the principle of their publication, came up to the highest standard of scholarly requirements of that time; fundamentally, they were based upon the principles which had been established by Hilferding.

Byliny were partially recorded in other places also. In the Belo-Ozero region, B. and Y. Sokolov wrote down twenty-eight numbers of *byliny*, and in the Saratov region twenty-four numbers were taken down (by M. Sokolov, B. Sokolov, and others). In Siberia, V. G. Tan-Bogoraz and others wrote down twenty-seven numbers. A considerable amount of *bylina* material, in original variations, different from the northern texts, was written down at the beginning of the twentieth century among the Don, Terek, Ural and Orenburg Cossacks (records made by Listopadov, Arefin, Zheleznov, Myakushin, and others).[3]

After the Great October Socialist Revolution, the work of collection in the field of the epos was developed still more widely, and, what is especially important, received a new direction in the USSR. Regardless of all the value of the work of the prerevolutionary collectors, their activity suffered from this great deficiency, that in the process of their work they gave information only about the static aspect of the epos, and did not collect sufficient materials for a judgment of the changes in the epos of a definite locality.

The three-year scientific expedition of the Moscow folklorists to the north, which took place, under the direction of B. and Y. Sokolov, in 1926–1928 was of especial importance in the work of studying the Russian epos in the years following the October Revolution.

According to a plan which had been worked out long before, this

[3] Information concerning these records of Cossack *byliny* has been brought together in an article by V. F. Miller, "Cossack Epic Songs of the Sixteenth and Seventeenth Centuries," in *Surveys of Popular Literature*, Vol. III, (Moscow, 1924).

expedition studied in detail the contemporary state of the epos of the *byliny* in various districts of the former provinces of Olonetsk and Vologda (now the Karelian Autonomous Soviet Socialist Republic, and in the regions of Archangel and Vologda), the regions beyond Lake Onega, the Pudoga shore, Vodlo Lake, and Keno Lake, visiting exactly those places where, several decades before, the records of *byliny* had been made by Rybnikov and Hilferding.

This expedition "In the steps of Rybnikov and Hilferding" wrote down 370 texts of *byliny*, and made a series of important observations on the state of the tradition of the *byliny* among three or four generations of narrators, and determined the character of the changes which had taken place in the creation of the *byliny* during the preceding sixty years.[4]

A great work was carried on also in the collection of the epos in the north of the Russian Soviet Federative Socialist Republic, in the years following the October Revolution, by the Leningrad folklorists, especially by A. M. Astakhova.[5]

The observations of the geographical distribution of the *byliny* show that the chief custodian of the epos of the *byliny* was the Far North of the Russian Soviet Federative Socialist Republic—the former province of Archangel (the present *oblast* [region] of Archangel), the shore of the White Sea, the basin of the Mezen, Pinega, and Pechora rivers; the former province of Olonets (a part of the present Karelian Autonomous Soviet Socialist Republic), and chiefly the islands and shores of Lake Onega. As indicated by observations made in the nineteenth and at the beginning of the twentieth century, the *byliny* were partially preserved, also, in a number of other provinces and regions. Many of the *byliny* were written down in Siberia, and there are records from the Central and Lower Volga provinces (the provinces of Nizhny Novgorod, Saratov, Simbirsk, and Samara), and from the central Russian provinces: Novgorod, Vladi-

[4] Concerning this expedition, see the article by Y. M. Sokolov, "In the Steps of Rybnikov and Hilferding," *Artistic Folklore*, Nos. II-III, Moscow, 1927.

[5] See her article, *"Byliny* in the Trans-Onega Region," in the collection, *Peasant Art of the North*, No. I, Leningrad, 1927, and "The Tradition of the *Byliny* in the Contemporary North," in the *Collection of Articles Dedicated to the Academician A. S. Orlov* (Leningrad, 1934).

mir, Moscow, St. Petersburg, Smolensk, Kaluga, Tula, Orlov, Voronezh, and others. The *byliny* have been preserved long and steadfastly
in the Russian Cossack districts on the Don, the Terek, and in the
Urals.

In Ukrainia no *byliny*, in the genuine sense of the word, have been
written down.

In White Russia they have been written down in small numbers
and in a greatly altered form. But the existence of similar subjects in
the tales and songs, the presence of the names of a number of heroes
of the *byliny* in Ukrainian and White Russian folklore, the mention
of these same names in certain written remains (for example, in the
letter of the elder Orsha Kmita Chernobylsky, 1574), and other indirect data testify to the fact that the *byliny* in ancient times were
known within considerably wider boundaries than those within which
they have been preserved in the nineteenth and twentieth centuries.

But why have the *byliny*, for the past two and a half centuries, been
preserved only within a comparatively narrow portion of the Russian
territory, mainly in the far North of European Russia, while in other
localities they have either disappeared altogether, or have been preserved in disjointed and scanty fragments? The causes for this must
be sought in the specific historical conditions of the life of the
peasantry of the northern region.

In the sixteenth and seventeenth centuries, when the creation of
byliny, according to all the data, was diffused among the Russian
populace of the whole country, the northern region was one of its
most active districts.

From the middle of the sixteenth century to the first decades of the
eighteenth, the North, with its rivers and lakes, constituted in itself
a busy transit route, which joined the center of the Russian state with
its frontiers.

This trade route, so full of life at that time, attracted a multitude
of people: the summer travel on boats and barges, with the trans-
shipment of goods over portages and on estuaries; the hauling of
goods along the frozen rivers in winter, demanding a great number of
loaders, drivers, barge haulers, boatmen, and so on. The northern
region lived a tumultuous life, being connected with all the culture

of the trading and administrative centers of the old Russia of Moscow and Novgorod.

This was reflected in the artistic culture of the peasant North: the remarkable peasant cottages with their delicate, elegant carving, the ancient wooden tentlike churches with their many cupolas, for example the famous Kizhsky Cathedral of the region across the Onega, with its twenty-two cupolas; the astonishing beauty of the brocaded and silken costumes and the pearl-studded headdresses of the northern peasant women, the various kinds of embroidery of towels, tablecloths and linen, known to all the world—all this bears witness to the activity and high level of the artistic culture of the peasant North in ancient times.

From the beginning of the eighteenth century, however, the fortunes of the region underwent a decisive change. With the conquest of the Baltic region (in the times of Peter I) the northern trade route rapidly began to dwindle to nothing, the region gradually became deserted, and the rich artistic past was, as it were, brought to a standstill and preserved.

The loss of contact with the cultural centers, the feeble influx of the ideas of the new culture, contributed to the result that the peasantry of the North, more strongly than in the other regions, clung to the traditions of the past, through the course of two centuries and more. The preservation of this antiquity was facilitated, also, by the peculiarities of the northern environment and the primitive forms of rural economy. The northern soil, covered with stones and with forest, demanding a vast expenditure of toil from the tiller of the land, still did not give him the means for sustaining life. The northern peasant was obliged, usually, to turn to additional sources of income: to fishing, hunting, the felling and rafting of timber. The caprices of the weather, which often compelled the fishermen to wait a long time for the storms and bad weather to pass, the work at weaving nets in the course of many weeks, or sometimes even months, in the circle of one's family and neighbors, the companionship of the woodcutters in their associations, with the long winter evenings in their mud huts in the forest—all this must have disposed the people to the relating and hearing of the long and epically tranquil "tales of antiquity."

Also highly significant for the folk art of the North was the fact that the northern peasantry had been less oppressed by serfdom, and possessed more self-sufficiency and independence than the peasantry of the provinces of the central and "fertile-soil zone," which had experienced all the weight of the dependence of serfdom.

The North proved to be—by virtue of the historic and natural conditions which we have indicated above—the living preserver of the artistic past. The old popular poetry, which had disappeared in many of its manifestations in the center and in the south of Russia, was preserved in its living forms in the North, and owing to the retentive memory and creative work of the northern narrators, we have been able to judge the poetic creations of antiquity, creations which so vividly reflect all the diversity of the life of the Russian people through the centuries.

Who then brought to the far North the ancient *byliny*, which speak to us also of the southern steppes, and of the Dnieper, of Kiev, of Volynian Galich, of Novgorod the Great, of Ryazan and Moscow? As we were saying, the North attracted masses of people from all the far corners and regions of ancient Russia. To the North came boatmen, barge haulers, carters; also stonemasons and carpenters, builders of churches and decorated huts, and artist-painters of icons (we recall the remarkable frescoes of the St. Therapontus and St. Cyril monasteries); hither came also the artists of the word—the creators of the landmarks of folklore.

The *byliny*, these songs which are so diverse in their historical content, penetrated into the North through the medieval popular poets and musicians, the so-called "buffoons" and clowns, analogous to the French *jongleurs*, the German *Spielmänner*, the Caucasian *ashugi*, the Central Asiatic *bakhshi* and *akyny*.

Buffoons, "vagabonds" or "wanderers," were the itinerant artists of the Russian Middle Ages, appearing with songs and games in the city squares and the village streets. They were the bearers of the popular art, who at times introduced into their creative work a very marked element of social satire and protest against the ruling classes.

Hence it is easy to understand the many centuries of hatred toward the buffoons and their art on the part of the Church. This hatred reached its climax during the years of the reign of Tsar Alexis Mikhailovich. Relying upon temporal power, the obscurantism of the Church executed its fierce judgment upon the buffoons. Their wonderful musical instruments, which the ecclesiastics abusively called "the vessels of demons," were confiscated and burned, while the buffoons themselves were caught and sent away to the distant "borderlands." But there these remarkable folk artists and poets were fully able to develop their art freely, finding appreciative listeners and followers among the local population. Many of them settled down and became fully identified with the northern peasantry, others continued their professional artistic work.

As the exponents of the interests of the toiling masses of the people, the buffoons, in their productions, sometimes expressed a very sharp protest against the persecution of folk art by the Church and the tsarist government.

In many of the *byliny*, in counterbalance to the effort of the religious preachers and the tsarist officials to defame the art of the buffoons in the eyes of the people, the buffoons lovingly depicted the figures of the "daring buffoonery," the "merry people," the "celebrated psaltery players."

According to the *byliny*, there is clearly established a twofold attitude toward the buffoons on the part of the ruling classes of ancient Russia. Under the influence of the Church, and also from class motives, the circles of the boyars, the grand princes and the tsars could not help treating the democratic art of the buffoons with suspicion and hostility. But, on the other hand, the art of the popular singers, musicians, and artists was so alluring that the buffoons were admitted even into the palaces of the tsars and grand princes, and the mansions of the boyars and merchants. It is true that the very last place was always assigned to the folk artist.

Here speaks the bold buffoonery:
Ah, you, Vladimir, our sun of the capital city of Kiev,
Where then is our buffoons' place?
Vladimir of the capital city of Kiev replies to him:

Your buffoons' place
Is somewhere by the stove and the space behind the stove.[6]

The buffoons, in their protest against the persecution which they endured at the hands of the Church and the autocrats, did not limit themselves to satirical thrusts against the princes, the boyars, and the priests, but even created whole productions that magnified and celebrated the art of the buffoons.

Delineated with exceptional sympathy is the figure of the Novgorod zither player Sadko, saddened by his temporary unemployment:

And here is how it happened now to Sadko,
They do not call Sadko the whole day long to the feast of honor,
And they do not call him on the next day to the feast of honor,
And on the third day they do not call him to the feast of honor.
And now Sadko felt exceedingly melancholy,
And Sadko went to Lake Ilmen,
And he sat down on a blue and burning stone,
And there he began to play on his zither,
And he played from the morning all through the day, until the evening.[7]

As is known, the *bylina* relates that Sadko by his playing was able to charm even the king of the sea.

An absolutely exceptional apologia for the popular art of the buffoons is found in the unique *bylina* of Vavila the Buffoon, written down from the remarkable northern narrator, Marya Dimitryevna Krivopolenova, the direct inheritor of the masterly skill of the buffoons. In this *bylina* the buffoons are delineated as saints who perform genuine miracles by their art. Not without reason were the people who met the buffoons compelled to acknowledge:

These people who have come are not common,
Not common people—these are saints.[8]

In the *bylina* it is related that, being exalted to the position of saints, "the merry people, the buffoons," went to "another kingdom" to "compete with the dog of a tsar," and not only attained the aims

[6] A. F. Hilferding, *Onega Byliny*, No. 5.
[7] *Ibid.*, No. 70.
[8] O. E. Ozarovsky, *Old Wives' Tales*, p. 66.

which they had set before themselves, "surpassing" the tsar, but even deprived him of his kingdom, placing on the throne the peasant-buffoon Vavila. The basic antigovernmental meaning of this *bylina*, clearly emphasizing the popular democratic tendencies of the buffoons' art, is obvious. It is fully understandable that the art of the buffoons was profoundly perceived and developed by the northern peasantry, who brought forward, from among their own people, brilliant and talented inheritors and continuers of the masterly skill of the medieval folk artists.

The art of telling *byliny* among the northern peasantry, however, is not a common possession: it always demands special artistic endowments and training. In the North the *byliny* are performed by "narrators," for whom, however, the telling of the *byliny* does not generally serve as a means of livelihood, as was formerly the case with the buffoons. It is known, however, that narrators, who generally speaking were not professionals, still at times were specially invited to take part—as narrators—in one or another branch of northern industry, for example, in fishing or lumbering; furthermore, that the narrator, who went out for the fishing or lumbering, received wages on a par with those of the other members of the fishing and lumbering artel,* and sometimes even greater. Not infrequently, among the narrators, there were persons who followed the tailor's, shoemaker's or fuller's trade, since these occupations, by their very character, were well adapted to the telling of long, slowly chanted *byliny*.

For the memorizing and performing of the *byliny*, according to the acknowledgment of the northern peasantry itself, there is necessary the possession of a "special talent," and several of the narrators enjoyed great honor among the populace.

Good narrators devote themselves seriously to the performance of their *byliny*. They profoundly immerse themselves in the content of the *byliny*, and sensitively observe their "ritualism," that is, the peculiarities of the poetic form which are inherent in the *byliny*. In spite of the fact that they devote themselves with great attention to the

* Artel: Workmen's (cooperative) association.—ED.

preservation of the texts which they have assimilated from their teachers, every narrator always manifests his special, individual creative manner of constructing the *bylina*, and frequently also makes significant changes in its form and content. This is to be explained by the fact that the performance of the *byliny* is never a mechanical reproduction of a fixed text, but is always an independent act of creative artistry. In imitating the *bylina*, the narrator, according to the observation of the investigators, never learns it by heart. He fills it in with the descriptions or narrative passages which are customary for the epos of the *bylina*, the so-called *loci communes*, the invariable epithets and comparisons and other traditional peculiarities of the poetics of the *bylina*.

The genuine master narrator is not the one who mechanically memorizes extensive texts, but the one who fully possesses the art of narrating the *byliny*. The good narrator is, above all, the good judge of the traditional poetics of the epos. He knows the peculiarities of structure of the *bylina*. With him, the *bylina* consists of the "introductory verse," the "beginning," the basic narrative parts of the *bylina*, and the "exode" or conclusion.

The "introductory verse" in the *bylina* performs a definite artistic function: not having in its content any direct connection with the *bylina* which is to be set forth, it usually tries by its melody, rhythm, its unexpected poetic form, to draw the attention of the hearers to the performance of the *bylina*. Characteristic is the famous "introductory verse" in the *bylina* about Solovey Budimirovich, utilized by Rimsky-Korsakov for the opera *Sadko*:

> O height, height that reaches up to heaven,
> Depth, depth of the Ocean-sea,
> Wide expanse, throughout all the earth,
> Deep still pools of the Dnieper.[9]

This poetic introductory verse, creating the concept of vast, boundless spaces, in combination with the major melody, is calculated at once to awaken in the hearers a lively interest in the *byliny*, and to dispose them to listen to the long epic narrative. There are also intro-

[9] K. Danilov, *Ancient Russian Poems*, No. 1.

ductory verses of another character, clearly reflecting the wandering manner of life of the medieval composers of tales, their experience, their merry profession. In such introductory verses there are enumerated the various localities in which the performers of the *byliny* have chanced to sojourn during the period of their wanderings. These introductory verses usually contain a playful mockery or a mirthful satire on the various cities, villages, and their inhabitants. Such, for example, is the introductory verse:

Ah, there is open country at Pskov,
And there are broad open spaces at Kiev,
And high hills at Sorochinsk,
And church buildings in Moscow the city of stone,
And the ringing of bells in Novgorod,
Ah, there are sly rogues in the Valdai Hills,
Ah, there are fine fellows and dandies in the city of Yaroslav,
And easy kisses in the Belo-Ozero country,
And sweet drinks in St. Petersburg,
And mosses and swamps by the blue sea,
And skirts with wide hems in Pudoga,
Ah, the *sarafans* are tanned with the wool inside along the river Onega,
And the women of Leshmozersk are fruitful,
And the women of Poshezersk have bulging eyes,
Ah, the Danube, the Danube, the Danube,
And beyond that I know of no more regions to sing.[10]

Several of the "exodes," also, are distinguished by a similar comic character. In them hints are frequently encountered as to a reward and a treat for the performance of the *byliny*. But in the "exodes" which were composed among the peasant narrator-fishermen, there is frequently sounded the motif of an incantation, based on a belief in the power of the poetic word and melody over nature itself. Sometimes both these types of "exodes" are joined into one general formula:

Such was the ancient time, and such were the deeds,
As if for the calming of the blue sea,
And glory to the swift rivers till they reach the sea,
As if for good people to listen,
For young fellows to imitate,

[10] Hilferding, *op. cit.*, No. 60.

And for us, the merry young fellows, for a diversion,
Sitting quietly in conversation,
Drinking down the mead and the green wine.
And where we drink beer, there also we render honor
To that great boyar,
And to our kindly host.[11]

After the introductory verse, in the well composed *bylina*, follows the "beginning." The "beginning" is again a traditional form, giving the start of the narrative. In the heroic *byliny* the beginning often consists of descriptions of a feast at Prince Vladimir's palace. The plot, in a number of the *byliny*, is revealed in this beginning: the boasting of a knight at the feast, or the task which Prince Vladimir gives the knights, is the starting point of the action which constitutes the content of the whole *bylina*.

Here is a typical formula for the beginning, with the description of a princely feast:

When in the glorious city of Kiev,
When at the palace of the gracious Prince Vladimir
A banquet was given, a splendid feast.
And everyone was drinking his fill at the feast,
And everyone was eating his fill at the splendid feast,
And surely everyone was boasting of himself at the
      splendid feast.[12]

The description of the boasting, in the developed formula, is given as follows:

When everyone there at the feast had drunk his fill,
When everyone at the feast had eaten his fill,
They all fell to boasting and bragging.
One boasts of one thing, another brags of that:
One boasts of his countless purse of gold,
Another boasts of his strength and daring good luck,
Another boasts of his good horse,
Another boasts of his illustrious fatherland,
Another of his youthful courage,

[11] Danilov, *op. cit.*, No. 27.
[12] Beginning of the *bylina* of Mikhail Denilovich, Rybnikov, *Songs*, 2nd ed., Vol. III, p. 41.

The clever and sensible man boasts
Of his old father and his old mother,
And the brainless fool boasts of his young wife.[13]

As regards the *narrative* itself, here the experienced narrator strives to maintain strictly the traditional device of a threefold repetition of every episode. Besides, the repetitions often do not prove to be altogether identical, but there is permitted a slight variation, which gives great liveliness to the story.

The majority of the narrators, not only in the introductory verses, in the beginnings and the exodes, but in the narrative also, make use of the *traditional formulas* (*loci communes*). For every typical episode encountered in the various *byliny*, each narrator has his poetic formula, cast in a more or less complete form. Such is the formula for the saddling of a horse, or the formula representing the description of the arrival of a knight at the prince's court, and his entrance into the royal palace. The narrative formulas of the selection by the knight of his horse and his weapons, of his equipment for a journey, of his encounter with an adversary in the field, and so forth, are of the same type.

The other stylistic and compositional devices of the *byliny* are also in full agreement with the traditional form of the beginnings, and the typical formulas of the conclusions.

To this is to be ascribed the abundance of every possible kind of *repetitions*. The poetics of the *bylina* is not disturbed by the literal or nearly literal repetition of entire motifs or episodes of the *byliny*, which are of considerable length, and produce a slowing down of the narrative, the so-called *retardation*. For example, the commands of a prince to his ambassador are repeated with literal exactness when the ambassador reports these instructions to the tsar of another country. Especial favorites are the threefold repetitions of episodes—with a certain tendency, it is true, toward the accumulation of new material. This same principle of repetitions is clearly felt in the literary style of the *byliny*. Such are the simple repetitions of words ("Wonder of wonders," "marvel of marvels," "it was out of the wood, the dark

[13] From the *bylina* of Duk Stepanovich, Rybnikov, *op. cit.*, Vol. I, No. 30.

wood"); the repetition of prepositions, the repetition of one and the same word in two or several verses which follow after one another ("of that same sable from overseas, that sable from overseas with the long ears, that long-eared sable which was so soft"); the repetition of contrasts by way of negation ("But I walk as a single man, I do not go around as a married man"; "That is no small affair, it is a great one"); the use of synonyms ("Without fighting, without a brawl or bloodshed"; "You do not know, you have no knowledge of it"); the joining of etymologically related words ("Small brooks she crossed by a ford, deep rivers she swam by swimming"; "The rain rains"; "I serve a long-continued service"); to the same phenomenon belongs the increase of a number in every new verse: "There they collect tributes and dues, for twelve years, yes, for thirteen years, yes, for thirteen years and a half."

To the crystallized traditional devices of the *byliny* belong also the so-called *constant epithets*, attached to various objects: white (birch tree, breast, day, gerfalcon, swan, ermine, hand, light, snow, tent), high (table, salon, gate, and others), red (sun, gold), gray (wolf, goose, drake), broad (yard, steppe, road, portion, expanse), knightly (voice, steed, horse, strength, dream, plunder). Many of these epithets give an idea of the esthetic tastes and partialities of the Russian *byliny*. The majority of the constant epithets are applied only to one or two words: open country, blue sea, little pearl, moving cloud, rich guests, tightly-drawn bow, and others. Epithets often give important indications as to historical situations (the illustrious and wealthy city of Volyn, the heathen Tartar, brave Lithuania, a Circassian saddle); or to mode of life (women's apartments with golden roofs, little gates, "like a precious narwhal's tusk," a glazed stove); and to social characteristics (Vladimir of the capital city of Kiev, the old Cossack Elijah of Murom, the councilor-boyars) of previous periods in the life of the Russian *byliny*.

Very frequent in the Russian epos of the *byliny* are *comparisons*, such, for example, as: "Again day after day, as sure as the rain rains, Week after week, as the grass grows, And year after year, as the river runs." Or in the *bylina* of the Great Idol: "Great eyes, like bowls, A

great hand, like a rake"; still more often, similes are encountered
("Vladimir the glowing sun"; "Black brows of sable").

Parallelisms, especially negative ones, are also frequent in the *byliny*,
for example: "It was not a bright falcon that flew out there, It was
not a black raven that fluttered out there, There rode out an evil
Tartar."

The traditional character of the style of the *bylina* produced as its
consequence, in certain instances, an insensibility to the meaning of
some expressions, words, and turns of phrase. For example, the *"petri-
fied" epithets* (clichés) that is, those epithets which, dictated by custom, sometimes appear out of place in the *bylina*. For example, Prince
Vladimir is called "kindly" even at a time when, according to the action of the *bylina*, he is, on the contrary, very unkind; Tsar Kalin calls
his Tartar subordinate "vile," while the Tartar, transmitting a threatening command to Prince Vladimir in the name of his sovereign,
calls the latter "that dog, Tsar Kalin."

The methods of *composition* of the *byliny* have been treated considerably less than those of its outward technique and stylistics. Both
in the design itself of the internal composition, and in the forms of
the action of the story, the *byliny* are very far from being all of the
same kind. Above all, in these respects the knightly *byliny* must be
set apart from the story *byliny*, as V. F. Miller long ago distinguished
them on the basis of content. In the knightly *byliny* the movement is
distinguished by a centripetal attraction to the main character of the
action—the knightly hero. This does not always progress in a straight
line, but very often with sudden spurts of movement in the opposite
direction. A favorite device of the knightly *bylina* is the method of
antithesis. (Elijah, contrary to the warning inscription at a place
where three roads meet, goes along them, and by his actions refutes
these warnings; Dobrynya does not heed the instructions of his
mother, and bathes in the river Puchay, and so forth.)

Analogous to the device of antitheses in the development of the
action in the knightly *byliny*, we see the same device of *contrast* also
in the organization of the figures of the heroes of the *byliny*. At the
beginning of the *bylina* the hero is not highly appraised, he is even
held in disrepute, his enemy seems more important and stronger than

he; later, all this is at once refuted by the further, and in particular by the final, development of the knightly *bylina*. (The knightly hero alone avenges himself upon a force of many thousands of the enemy.) In contrast, for example, there are sketched such pairs as Elijah and the Great Idol, Potanya and Kostruk, Dobrynya and the Dragon, and others.

Very characteristic, for the delineation of the knightly heroes, are the various forms of *hyperbolization*, both of the outward aspect of the heroes of the *byliny* and of their attributes, and also of their acts and exploits.

The story *byliny* (Churila and Katerina, Alyosha and Dobrynya, Khoten Bludovich, and others), in distinction from the knightly *byliny*, include considerably more elements of purely dramatic action. No small role is played, in the poetics of the *byliny*, by the various forms of *dialogue*; however, in the martial, knightly *bylina*, dialogue, or direct speech in general, is less used than in the story *bylina*, for which the dialogue form of exposition, to a considerable degree, is the formal mark of this particular genre of the *bylina*. Dialogue performs an essential, dogmatic function in the construction of the *byliny*; to a considerable degree, it moves the action.

With reference to prosody, it is only comparatively recently that the *byliny* have begun to be subjected to scientific analysis. This, for example, is true of the matter of *rhyme*. If formerly it was universally accepted that the *bylina* verse is to be unrhymed "blank" verse, yet now, according to the new investigations (Zhirmunsky), on the contrary, an undoubted role is assigned to the end rhyme in the metrical structure of the *bylina*. It is true that, in the majority of instances, this rhyme of the *bylina* appears to be an involuntary consequence of the rhythmic and syntactical parallelism of successive verses or half-verses, which is characteristic of the *bylina*, and therefore there predominate in it harmonies of morphologically identical terminations (suffixes or inflections): *podlygaeshsa—nasmekhaeshsa* (you flatter, but it is only a mockery); *kushati—rushati* (to eat, to destroy); *stolovym—dubovym* (with the table, made of oak).

Moreover, our usual concept of rhyme in the verse of the *bylina* is complicated by the circumstances that in this verse, in singing, it is necessary to assume every final syllable as stressed, independently of the phonetic accent of this syllable (Korsh). From this point of view, in the *bylina*, such words as the following must be regarded as rhymed: *po solnyshku, po mesyatsu* (by the sun, by the moon); *Nikitinich, Ivanovich.* However, the usual harmony of rhyme in the *bylina* extends as far back as the third syllable from the end (antepenult), acquiring the character of dactylic rhyme, with the metrical thesis on the last syllable, or ultima: *soloviny, zveriny* (nightingale's, beast's); the end harmonies which are quite frequent in the *bylina* bear the character of complete rhymes, owing to the parallelism of·sentences: *prizadumalis—prizaslukhalis* (they became thoughtful, and began to listen).

As seen from the last example, for purposes of rhyme in the *bylina*, no great importance is attached to the lack of identity of the consonants between the accented vowel of the third syllable from the end, and the final syllable. Compare, further, *poskakivat', pomakhivat'* (to have jumped, to have swung); *khorobroey, klenovoey* (with the brave; made of maple). In general, in the *bylina*, inexact rhymes predominate, those which are approximate, or even simply assonances; therefore it is better to speak, not of rhymes, in the *bylina*, but of "rhymoids" (Zhirmunsky).

Nevertheless, these end harmonies give a certain character of articulateness to the verses of the *byliny*, to the uneven and inconsequent compositional rhythmico-syntactical units (not strophes, but "strophemes"). Usually the rhyme in the *bylina* joins together two or three verses following one another: "But the plowman plows in the field, he shouts at the horse, and the plowman's share creaks a little (*poskripyvaet*) and the teeth of the share scrape against the stones (*pochirkivayut*)."

Sometimes we encounter more spacious *strophic unisons* in one rhyme, usually in the exode of the *bylina* or at the effective height of the action. Usually, in the *byliny*, the successive joining of the verses by various rhymes takes the form aa-bb-cccx; here the x designates the final unrhymed verse, which in itself concludes such a stropheme. By an approximate calculation, about one-third of the verses in a *bylina* are, in one form or another, connected by the rhyme, in the form of a "rhymoid." The qualitative and quantitative distinction in their use frequently depends on the artistic manner and practices of the individual narrators. Besides the end rhymes, there are frequently found, in the verse of the *bylina*, rhymes at the beginnings and in the middles of words (based on the same rhythmico-syntactical parallelism). "*Poshipi zmey po-zmeinomu, Zaryavkay zver po-turinomu*" (Let the dragon hiss like a dragon, Let the beast roar like a bull); and also the rhyming of hemistichs and the "picking up" of the second hemistich at the beginning of the following verse: "*A kto stoya stoit, tot i sidya sidit, ·A kto sidya sidit, tot i lezha lezhit*" (And he who standing stands, he also sitting sits; and he who sitting sits, he also lying lies).

In general, we personally are inclined, in the verse of the *bylina*, to assign the greatest significance, not to the end rhymes, but to the other forms and devices of prosody, such as the various forms of *assonances*, *alliterations*, and *repetitions of sound*, which frequently organize whole phases of the *byliny*. Upon these devices, for example, is based the introductory verse which has been cited above: "Ah, there is open country at Pskov, Ah, there are broad expanses at Kiev," and so forth. In this introductory verse, the striking attributes of each locality are selected, not according to the principle of meaning alone, but also according to the attraction of sound. Examples of the construction of whole verses of the *byliny* by means of alliteration are quite frequent: "*Poveli Ilyu, da po chistu polyu, A ko tym polatam polotnyanyim, Provodili ko palatke polotnyanoey, Priveli yevo k sobake tsaryu-Kalinu*" (They led Elijah, yes, across the open country, and to those tents of linen, They brought him to the linen tent, They brought him to the dog, Tsar Kalin). Sound also plays a large part in the forming of the constant epithets: *Lyuto lokhalischo* (fierce, shaggy hair), *Vykhody vysokie* (high exits), *Pivo pyanoe* (exhilarating beer), and others. A vast number of the constant epithets, in our opinion, have been formed by the mutual attraction of the liquid consonants *r* and *l*: *syra zemlya* (damp earth), *strelochka kalenaya* (tempered arrow), *stremya bulatnoe* (steel stirrup), and others.[14]

The versification of the *byliny* has been treated by the well known

[14] For further details see B. M. Sokolov, "An Excursus into the Field of the Poetics of Russian Folklore," *Artistic Folklore*, No. 1, 1926.

scholar, F. E. Korsh. The rhythmic turn of the verse of the *bylina* is surveyed by Korsh in connection with its melody. The verse of the *bylina* is characterized by the presence of four dominant accents, the last of which constitutes the metrical thesis, and in the melody it is frequently accompanied by a musical lengthening (a long note). In the verse of the *bylina* the musical accent can be not only the accent of a word, but also the accent of a whole phrase group (the good young *man*, the *gold*en Horde, the *fal*con bird).

Unimportant, for the verse of the *bylina*, is the number of unaccented syllables in the verse. The number of syllables sometimes runs as high as fourteen or fifteen, but one frequently encounters also a verse of eight syllables. The caesura in the *bylina* verse can be very mobile. It can be feminine: *"U velikovo knyazya* || *vecherinka byla* (The great prince had an evening party), or masculine (*"A sideli na piru* || *chestný vdový* (And the honorable widows were sitting at the feast), and dactylic (*"I sidela tut* || *Dobrynina matushka* (And the mother of Dobrynya was sitting there), and, as may be seen from the last example, it does not require a logical pause.

The tunes of the *byliny*—exactly like the subjects—and the style have undergone a long series of changes. The *bylina* has several types of tune. Among them may be distinguished two melodies: the tranquil, even stately, and the swift, gay tune—suggestive of the buffoons. The *byliny* are performed leisurely, smoothly, with few changes of tempo. The long-drawn monotony of the melody not only does not draw the attention away from the content of the *bylina* by any kind of musical effects, but, on the contrary, it soothes the listeners, harmonizing exceedingly well with the tranquil, measured account of events of distant times.

On the whole, these compositional devices, combined with threefold or manifold repetitions, with the steady, so-called "constant" epithets, with figures that have been forged in the course of centuries, with the slow melody, give the epos of the *bylina* an original poetic integrity, a monumental quality, a stateliness.

Within the limits of this traditional poetics, however, there lies open a vast scope for the individual creative initiative of talented narrators. In the ability to arrange the *bylina* compositionally, in the combination of the descriptive elements of traditional poetics and of its poetic formulas, in the preference for certain of these, depending on their personal tastes, there is expressed the original poetic manner of every performer of the *bylina*—of every *narrator*.

The creative individuality of every narrator manifests itself very prominently, both in the selection of his repertory and in his original treatment of the figure of the bylina's hero, and sometimes in the change of this or that detail in the content and in the poetics.

The dependence of the *byliny* on the world concept and spiritual character of the narrators expresses itself in the most various directions. In the performance of a pious narrator, the heroes of his *bylina* themselves become pious, they are constantly making reverences and crossing themselves. With a narrator who is fond of reading books, involuntarily, even the text of the *byliny* is permeated with bookish turns of phrase, or with specific words taken from literature. As an example of such a performer may be mentioned the White Sea narrator Agrafena Matveyevna Krukova, whose *byliny* were written down by the collector A. V. Markov.

Certain details of the text of the *byliny*, also, are to be explained as individual peculiarities of the narrators. It is fully understandable why, with one of the narrators, a tailor by profession, the head of the Great Heathen Idol, at the stroke of Elijah of Murom, "flies off like a button."

For the narrator of the *byliny*, a great deal of receptivity was required. Usually people "came to understand" the *bylina* in their early years, although they rarely performed it in public before they were forty years of age. Thus, for example, one of the best narrators, from whom *byliny* were being written down in 1926, the extremely old man Myakishev, used to tell how he well remembered the visit to his village in 1871 of the collector A. F. Hilferding. When the narrator was asked why he had not sung some *byliny* for A. F. Hilferding, Myakishev replied that at that time he was still a very young man, and though he knew the *byliny*, indeed, yet the thought could never have entered his head of coming forward with his *byliny* at that time, when all around were aged and famous narrators, from whom he was learning his art.

The narration of *byliny* is found to be chiefly the work of people of a "sedate" age (usually around sixty, seventy, and sometimes even ninety or a hundred years of age). The best narrators possess a remarkable memory, and often know tens of thousands of verses by heart. Such, at the present time, are M. S. Krukova, of the White Sea area, or G. A. Yakushov, from Lake Onega, who died recently. The custom was to transmit the art of narrating the *byliny*, by inheritance, from father to son. An example of such a family tradition was the famous Ryabinin family of narrators, in the Onega region, among whom the art of the narration of *byliny* can be traced from the eighteenth century to our own days.

The first famous classic narrator who is known to us from this family was Trofim Gregoryevich Ryabinin, from whom Rybnikov and Hilferding wrote down *byliny* on twenty-three different subjects. This is how P. N. Rybnikov describes his meeting with T. G. Ryabinin: "Across the threshold of the hut there stepped an old man of medium height, sturdily built, with a small gray beard and yellow hair. In his stern look, deportment and greeting, gait, and in his whole appearance, from the first glance, there was to be noted a tranquil strength and reserve." [15] In describing how he sang, Rybnikov wrote:

The tune of the *byliny* was very monotonous, the voice of Ryabinin, by virtue of his sixty-five years, was not very loud, but his wonderful ability as a storyteller gave a special meaning to every verse. More than once I was compelled to throw down my pen, and I eagerly listened to the flow of the narrative, then begged Ryabinin to repeat the refrain, and he reluctantly set himself to fill in what I had omitted. And where had Ryabinin learned such masterly diction! Every object, with him, stood out in clear light, every word had its own significance! [16]

This narrator passed his art on to his son, Ivan Trofimovich, no less famous as a master of the tale. The fame of his art spread throughout Russia. After the death of his father he appeared, in the 1890's, as a narrator of *byliny* in many cities, and was even taken abroad. An eyewitness describes in these words the method of creative work used by this remarkable narrator:

[15] P. N. Rybnikov, *op. cit.*, 2nd ed., Vol. I, p. lxxvi.
[16] *Ibid.*

When I. T. Ryabinin sings his *byliny*, usually after work, teaching them also to his children, there is very clearly perceptible in him the manifestation of a personal creative art. Preserving, in the majority of cases, only the general content of the *bylina* which at some time had become imprinted on his memory, the singer adapts various ready-made poetic pictures and expressions, and he creates new ones. In one place he heightens the colors, in another he omits two or three details, sometimes because he has forgotten them, and sometimes because they are not worthy of his interest or attention; and harmoniously, beautifully, there unfolds itself before the hearer an old song, to a new mode.[17]

I. T. Ryabinin was not pleased when, on the occasion of his numerous appearances in schools, some of the teachers required of him the omission of this or that "indecent" verse in the *bylina*.

"But how can I help singing it? Would you take away a word from the song? Because it is an ancient one, and as the men of old used to sing it, so must we sing it. You know yourself, it was not composed by us, and it will not end with us."

Neither did he hold with the performance of the *byliny* not in their entirety, but in parts and fragments: "But it is possible that the best words will be spoken just at the very end," he used to say.

The art of the narration of *byliny* was absorbed from Ivan Trofimovich by his stepson, Ivan Gerasimovich Ryabinin-Andreyev, who, in the years preceding the revolution, made an appearance at St. Petersburg; and, finally, as the representative of the latest generation of narrators in the family of the Ryabinins, there appears the son of Ivan Gerasimovich, a young peasant and collective farmer, who lives at the present time in the native place of the Ryabinins, in the village of Garnitsy, of the Kizhsk region, on Lake Onega—Peter Ivanovich Ryabinin-Andreyev. In his creative work is evident the splendid family tradition which has been handed down from generation to generation. However, a survey of the repertory of the *byliny* among the narrators of one family, over the space of four generations, leads to definite conclusions regarding the gradual extinction of the creative art of the *byliny*. With every new generation there is a diminution in the num-

[17] E. Lyatsky, "I. T. Ryabinin and His *Byliny*," *Ethnographic Review*, Bk. XXIII, Moscow, 1894.

ber of *byliny* that are performed. Thus, for example, from Trofim Gregoryevich there were twenty-three subjects taken down (though it is quite possible that he knew even more than that), while the contemporary narrator P. I. Ryabinin-Andreyev knows in all only eight subjects.

Beyond a doubt, losses also occur in the poetic methods of narration. The contemporary narrators are forgetting and losing the various musical motifs, and whereas T. G. and I. T. Ryabinin performed their *byliny* to several (as many as ten) different motifs, their great-grandson, on the other hand, sings all the *byliny* to only two musical motifs.[18]

During the entire period of the recording of *byliny*, the folklorist-collectors heard numerous tales and legends concerning many outstanding narrators, the memory of whom had lived for more than a century, and had been diffused throughout a large region. The outstanding narrators were the teachers of a number of generations. In the manner of narrating the *byliny*, in the subjects and devices back of the literary and also of the musical system, one can definitely perceive whole schools of narrators, going back to individuals who were the best masters. In addition to the Ryabinins in the Onega region, a well known narrator was V. P. Shchegolenok, whom L. N. Tolstoy knew personally, and from whom he borrowed a number of subjects for his works (especially for the tale "What Men Live By").[19] In 1926 the *byliny* were taken down from his two daughters—very old women. At Kenozero (in the former province of Vologda), in the second half of the nineteenth century, there lived the famous narrator Sivtsev-Poromsky, who founded his own "school" of narrators, the last representatives of which are still living at the present time.

[18] See Y. Sokolov, "In the Steps of Rybnikov and Hilferding," *Artistic Folklore*, Bks. II-III, 1927.
[19] On V. P. Shchegolenok, see: N. V. Vasilyev, "Some Observations on the Reflection of the Personality of the Narrator in the *Byliny*," *Annals of the Division of Russian Language and Literature of the Academy of Sciences*, 1907, Bk. II; V. I. Sreznevsky, "Language and Legend in the Records of L. N. Tolstoy," *Collection to S. F. Oldenburg* (Leningrad, 1934), and also the Commentaries to the 25th volume of the *Complete Collected Works of L. N. Tolstoy*, Moscow, State Literary Press, 1937.

A great interest, from the point of view of theory, attaches to the creative work of the above-mentioned narrator Gregory Alekseyevich Yakushov, from the eastern bank of Lake Onega. The expeditions of 1926 and 1928 took down, from him, *byliny* on thirty-seven different subjects. As it turned out, Yakushov is a pupil of three talented narrators of the period of Rybnikov and Hilferding: Ivan Feponov, Nikifor Prokhorov (called Utitsa), and Potap Antonov. A comparative study of the texts of Yakushov with the corresponding texts of his teachers (according to the collections of Rybnikov and Hilferding) reveals that he did not follow them mechanically, but that he worked out an independent, individual style, which bears witness to the great creative work of this fine narrator.[20]

Of the women performers of *byliny*, the ones who have enjoyed the greatest fame are the celebrated White Sea narrator A. M. Krukova, whose repertory included more than two-thirds of all the subjects known in the Russian epos, and the no less remarkable narrator, the poor peasant woman from the river Pinega, M. D. Krivopolenova. For the greater part of her life, Krivopolenova was supported by charity. In the seventy-second year of her life, the artist O. E. Ozarovskaya brought her to Moscow, and Krivopolenova appeared at numerous public gatherings, astonishing many audiences by her marvelous art. B. M. Sokolov, recalling the impression produced by this remarkable narrator, wrote:

Truly, Krivopolenova was a genuine artist. When she was singing her *byliny*, she became excited before her appearance, revealing the agitation characteristic of artists. But she needed only to begin the singing of her beloved *byliny*, when, in spite of the fact that she was singing before an audience of thousands, the narrator swiftly caught the attention of all, and felt herself altogether free. Krivopolenova took her *byliny* close to her heart, she lived in them, she treasured them.

When Krivopolenova was singing her favorite cheerful *byliny*, of the "buffoon" type, she became especially lively, her eyes sparkled with genuine rapture and infectious mirth. At certain points in the

[20] The texts of the *byliny* of G. A. Yakushov, like all the texts written down by the expeditions of the State Academy of Artistic Sciences in 1926–1928, have been prepared for publication, and will be published by the State Museum of Literature in the book, *Byliny of the Onega Region*, by B. and Y. Sokolov.

cheerful *byliny*, for the sake of greater animation, she began to represent specific episodes by gestures. *Byliny* of serious content she sang in an altogether different way. Tears of agitation repeatedly hindered her in singing one of the dramatic *byliny* on the subject, "How Prince Román Lost His Wife." [21]

At the present time, as indicated by the latest researches of contemporary folklorists, the ancient *byliny* are clearly passing into oblivion among the northern peasantry. Certain talented and expert narrators are still living, as, for example, the Onega narrator Fyodor Andreyevich Konashkov, the White Sea narrator Krukova,[22] Martha Semyonovna (the daughter of A. M. Krukova), Peter Ivanovich Ryabinin-Andreyev, and others; but these are mostly either direct descendants (grandchildren and children) of well known narrators of the second half of the nineteenth century, or else their "students." At the present time there is to be observed, among the majority of narrators, an obvious shrinking of the repertory of the ancient *byliny*; the narration of *byliny* is losing its significance as a special skill. The character of the popularity of specific subjects has essentially changed: the fantastic-legendary *byliny* are the quickest to disappear, and the *byliny* which are stories of a romantic character, with subjects taken from everyday life, are preserved the longest. If Hilferding wrote, for example, that "at Kenozero it seems as if the very air is permeated with the poetry of the *byliny*," yet at the time of the expedition of 1927 they were able, with difficulty, to discover only a few old men and women who were expert in the art.

This is perfectly natural, since, as Hilferding himself noted, the most important condition of the natural, spontaneous life of "epic poetry" is faith in the miraculous, in myth.[23]

The current fate of the Russian epos of the *byliny* confirms the words of Karl Marx, in the Introduction to the *Critique of Political Economy*.

---

[21] B. M. Sokolov, *Narrators* (Moscow, 1924), pp. 110-112. On the creative work of M. D. Krivopolenova, see also O. E. Ozarovskaya, *Old Wives' Tales*, 2nd ed. (Moscow, 1923).

[22] A. M. Astakhova and V. P. Chuzhimov, "On New Records of the *Byliny* Along the Seashore," *Soviet Folklore*, Nos. 2-3, Leningrad, 1935.

[23] Hilferding, *op. cit.*, introductory article.

Is it possible that the way of looking at nature and at social relationships, which lies at the basis of Greek fantasy, and therefore also of Greek [art], could have existed in the presence of "self-acting [textile] mules," railways, locomotives, and the electric telegraph? . . . Every mythology overcomes, subjugates, and shapes the forces of nature, in imagination and with the help of imagination; mythology disappears, consequently, with the actual mastery over these forces of nature.[24]

The ancient traditional epos of the *byliny* is obviously disappearing from the memory of the people. The number of narrators who know the *byliny* dealing with the events of the tenth to the sixteenth centuries, and who believe in the mythical figures created by the imagination of the singers of the former time, is constantly being more and more reduced. Among the young people of the northern regions, even those most saturated with the traditions of the *byliny*, there are hardly any narrators. (Ryabinin-Andreyev or the twelve-year-old boy Artemyev, who had assimilated a number of *byliny* from his grandmother, the narrator A. T. Artemyeva, from the village of Pershlakhta, are exceptions.) And this is exactly as could be expected. So much the more energetically must the work of collecting the monuments of the old popular epos be developed.[25]

But this does not mean that the epic creative folk art, itself, is disappearing.

On the contrary, we in our time, in the remarkable epoch of the creation of the new socialist culture, are assisting at the birth and development of new poetic forms in folk creation. In place of the old traditional epos of the ancient Russian knights, there is growing up the new Soviet epos. This epos speaks of our own time, of the Soviet country, of the heroes of our great era. And this new epos, reflecting the new life and expressing the new realistic world con-

---

[24] K. Marx, *On the Critique of Political Economy* (Party Publishing House, 1935), p. 32.

[25] On the contemporary state of the traditional epos of the *byliny* in the North, see the above-mentioned article by Y. M. Sokolov, "In the Steps of Rybnikov and Hilferding," also Boris and Yury Sokolov, "A la recherche des bylines," *Revue des études slaves*, Vol. XII, Nos. 3, 4, Paris, 1932, and A. M. Astakhova, "The Tradition of the *Byliny* in the Contemporary North," *Collection of Articles for the Fortieth Anniversary of the Scholarly Activity of the Academician A. S. Orlov* (Leningrad, 1934).

cept, far from the mythological world concept of the past, is naturally being created in new artistic forms. It is true that with certain narrators, for example, with P. I. Ryabinin-Andreyev, whom we have mentioned, there are attempts to speak of the new life in the style of the old *bylina* (Ryabinin-Andreyev has composed a *bylina* about Chapayev), but the break between the old form and the new content is very noticeable, and such a creation seems rather a stylization. Among other narrators, however, we observe a more sensitive attitude toward the stylistic unity of form and content.

Thus, that excellent connoisseur of the ancient *byliny*, the narrator F. A. Konashkov (from the Pudoga bank of Lake Onega), creates new songs, working over with originality the poetics of the various old popular genres (*byliny*, wedding songs of praise, storytellers' exordia); and the famous narrator from the White Sea, M. S. Krukova, from whom, not long ago, there were written down more than a hundred ancient *byliny*, creates altogether new productions dealing with contemporary life; in them are elements of the *byliny* and the lamentation and the tale, and there is lyric poetry in them, but on the whole they constitute a kind of new genre.

It may be called a story, a poem, or a tale that is sung. Such are her "Stories of Lenin," "Of Chapayev," "Beard to the Knees" (a poem about O. U. Schmidt and about the crew of the steamer *Cheluskin*), the poem "Papanin's Expedition." These facts attest that the new life and the new world concept are seeking for new forms of narrative, while the tranquil, even, imperturbable style of the ancient *byliny* which have survived through the centuries is being replaced by the lyrico-epic style. The contemporary narrator cannot speak without agitation of those great events and of those heroic exploits which are going on before his eyes. Soviet folklore, including also the Soviet epos, is being created anew, and in this new creative work the ancient *bylina*, like the other ancient traditional genres of popular poetry, is utilized in the capacity of a rich cultural heritage. (These new phenomena of the epic creative art will be discussed in more detail below, in the section on "Soviet Folklore.")

The *history of the Russian epos*, like the history of the epos of any people, is very complex. The study of the history of Russian *byliny* is complicated, furthermore, by a whole series of circumstances. In the first place, by the fact that in Russia the epos existed, and exists, in the form of separate songs, treating this or that relatively small subject, and not combined into magnificent poems like the Greek *Iliad* and *Odyssey*, the Persian *Shah Namah*, or the German *Niebelungen*; secondly, by the fact that, as we have already indicated, the records which we possess of the texts of the *byliny* belong to a very late period; and finally, by the fact that we have hardly any testimony concerning the Russian epos—the monuments of the ancient literature—earlier than the seventeenth century.

None the less, following scattered casual, mostly indirect references, encountered in the ancient manuscripts, but mainly on the basis of a scientific analysis of the actual texts of the *byliny*, with verification by historical facts, it has been possible to examine the history of the epos, and to arrive at more or less well established conclusions.

As we have previously pointed out, the assertion of the historical school and of the vulgar "sociologists,* " that the heroic epos arose originally, in the period of the formation of feudalism, among the upper-class surroundings of the military *druzhina*, is obviously incorrect. This assertion was based upon the fact that in the *byliny* there are scenes depicting the life and customs of the princes and the boyars. It is incorrect, because of the military themes of many of the knightly *byliny*, and their concern with the *druzhina*, to consider the *byliny* as the product of the creative work of the aristocracy and not of the people.

In the first place the military heroic epos was created, for the greater part, not by the feudal upper class—the princes and boyars— but by the singers of the *druzhina*, the representatives of the democratic classes of the *druzhina*. (An analogous phenomenon is observed also in the life of the epos among peoples who have only comparatively recently emerged from feudalism, for example, in Central Asia and in the Caucasus, and among a number of the peoples of Siberia.) In the second place, also in those comparatively few in-

---

* "Vulgar sociologists": those who, in Marxist parlance, "are apologists for the capitalist system." *Ushakov.*—Ed.

stances when the heroic song was perhaps composed by some singer-poet from the upper class of the *druzhina,* one cannot consider this a production which did not come from the people. The Princes and other leaders of the early feudal *druzhina* could compose songs which expressed the ideas of the whole people, for example, the ideas of conflict and victory over the nomads, who by their incursions had ruined the whole Russian population. In any event, the popular memory could retain, in the course of centuries, only those creations of the poetic art which did not contain antipopular, exploiting tendencies. And, in fact, in the Russian epos of the *byliny* one cannot point to a single *bylina* which expresses such tendencies, hostile or alien to the people.

In the third place, whoever may have been the original composer of this or that heroic song—whether he were a private soldier of the *druzhina* or a representative of the upper class—in his poetics, language, and artistic forms he was compelled to rely upon the traditions of popular poetry, which had its roots going far back, even into preclass society.

It would also be incorrect to see in the vagabond as well as in the permanently settled professional singers of succeeding eras—in the buffoons—only the performers of the "social demands" of the ruling classes (the princes, the boyars, and the rich merchants). As we have already said above, the buffoons were authentic singers of the people. To maintain, however, that the creators and performers of the *byliny* in ancient Russia were only peasant tillers of the soil, that the *bylina* was from beginning to end the product only of peasant creative art, would be incorrect, since the vast majority of the *byliny* speak of events which took place in the cities (Kiev, Novgorod the Great, Volynian Galich, and so forth), and since they contain details historically correct of city life (of the military, the princes and boyars, and the merchants). In any event, the composers of the *byliny* were people of varied experience, people who had a good knowledge of the land, and of the everyday and social life of the various classes of the population.

The knowledge of the diverse material and spiritual life of ancient Russia, of the various phenomena of national culture, also gave the composers of the popular *byliny* an opportunity to express with poetic vividness, in the figures of the knights, the heroic features of the Russian people, and equipped them with that wealth of colors and poetic devices by the aid of which they delineated the favorite *figures* of the *byliny*. The creative imagination of the folk singers, with all its hyperbole in the description of events and the delineation of heroes, was nevertheless based on a true understanding of historical reality, of typical characteristics of the Russian people, of their hopes and expectations.

We remember, for example, the striking figure of the ideal peasant, the plowman Mikula Selyaninovich, who had plowed vast tracts of land:

> But the plowman plows in the field, he drives ahead,
> From one edge to the other he turns back the furrows,
> He goes far off to the one edge—he cannot see the other,
> Now he digs out the roots and stones,
> And the great stones he throws off to one side.[26]

With exceptional power there are expressed, in the figure of the miraculous plowman, both the creative, productive power of the people, and also their dreams of the mastery of the earth by human toil, of the subjugation of the forces of nature, of easy and joyful work. Radically wrong are the reasonings of those investigators who, emphasizing the vast tracts of land plowed by Mikula, were inclined to see in him, not the poetized figure of a peasant-plowman, but a landowner with property of his own, or even a kulak, though the *bylina* does not give any kind of data which could lead us to attribute to Mikula any of the features of these social groups.

The representatives of the "historical school," and the "sociologists," have also, to a considerable degree, reduced and degraded the heroic figure of the chief knight of the Russian *byliny*—Elijah of Murom. The historical fate of this remarkable figure in the Russian epos is very complicated; but at the same time one cannot help perceiving that monumental quality which it attained during the course of many centuries. Elijah of Murom, in spite of all the changes to which his figure was subjected at various periods, remained the ex-

[26] Hilferding, *op. cit.*, No. 73.

ponent of truth, patriotism, love of mankind, not only of the physical, but also of the moral strength of the people.

Elijah of Murom is the favorite hero of the epos of the *bylina*. He is delineated by the narrators of the *byliny* as a son of the peasantry. He knows how to speak the truth to princes, to their faces. With sympathy the *byliny* tell of the wrath of the peasant knight when he encountered an inattentive and disrespectful attitude toward himself on the part of the prince, the princess, and the "fat-bellied boyars." Elijah of Murom is the exponent of genuine popular patriotism. When enemies attack, he finds in himself the strength to rise above the insults and offenses which have been inflicted upon him by the prince. Touchingly (in the *bylina* about Tsar Kalin) he exhorts the other knights to go against the enemy:

> Not for the sake of Prince Vladimir
> Nor for Princess Apraxa the king's daughter. . . .
> But for the sake of our mother, the holy land of Rus.[27]

Elijah is the defender of orphans, widows, and the poor. He is not a marauder, thirsting for conquest and blood; he is the convinced bearer of the idea of defending his native land, and in this conviction he is strong. Elijah is free from avarice, from the desire for personal enrichment; this is the ideal figure of a man who has dedicated himself to the general good. With what indignation he hurls the reproach upon the mendicant wanderer Ivanishche, that the latter has not stood up for those who were oppressed by the Tartar ravager, the Great Idol! In bidding the wandering knight good-bye, Elijah says to him:

> Goodbye now to you, great and powerful Ivanishche!
> Henceforth you are to do nothing more,
> Except to rescue old Rus from the unclean ones.[28]

The figure of Dobrynya Nikitich is, according to popular notions, the figure of an ideal knightly "diplomat," who, in addition to his exploits of bravery, by his courtly manners, his knowledge of people, life and foreign customs, his courtesy, his clever speech, and his adroitness knows how to win success in dealing with his enemies.

---

[27] Rybnikov, *op. cit.*, No. 57.   [28] Hilferding, *op. cit.*, No. 48.

The popular narrators have endowed Dobrynya not only with a subtle mind, with education and with knowledge of people, but also with a complex mind, with aesthetic tastes (skill in playing on the zither, and in composing and singing songs), and with deep feelings.

The figure of Alyosha Popovich is more complex, since in the course of time it has sustained considerable changes. At the beginning it was the figure of a knight, a "brave man," distinguished both for boldness and for adroitness. Not without reason is the epithet "the Bold" attached to Aloysha. But his nickname "Popovich" could not help having an ironical, mocking, satirical influence on the subsequent treatment of this figure. In folk creative art (in the songs, tales, and proverbs), the priests (*popy*) and priests' sons (*popovichi*) endure a great deal of popular derision. Such a negative attitude toward persons connected with the clerical class is the result of many centuries of oppression of the people on the part of the Church and Clergy. Therefore the *byliny* sometimes endow Alyosha also with the traits of jealousy, greed, arrogance, and boastfulness. However, these later additions to the character of Alyosha Popovich cannot overshadow the primary significance of his figure as one of the powerful knights (bogatyrs) standing on the "heroic outposts" and preserving Rus from external enemies.

In addition to these three most popular knights—Elijah of Murom, Dobrynya Nikitich, and Alyosha Popovich—the *byliny* gave sketches also of many other figures, less complex, but possessing both individual characteristics and typical features: such, for example, as the figure of the brave knight, the youthful Michael Danilovich; the tragic figure of the enterprising and supremely brave Sukhman, whose honesty and patriotism Prince Vladimir could not discern, and humiliated him by his distrust.

The motif of the knight's defense of his outraged honor, this motif of the defense of his own human dignity before the prince, is very frequently encountered in the epos of the *byliny*. The later peasant narrators dwelt with great sympathy on the development of this motif, at times still further intensifying the antimonarchical tendencies which it contained.

Typical in this respect is the ending of certain variants of the *by-*

lina about Duk Stepanovich. Prince Vladimir did not believe the
words of Duk, and imprisoned him in the deep cellars. But when,
according to the investigation conducted by Dobrynya Nikitich, the
words of Duk had been confirmed, Prince Vladimir began to en-
treat Duk to remain in service at the court of Kiev. But the affronted
Duk Stepanovich answered the prince with bitterness:

Vladimir, thou prince of the capital of Kiev!
As surely as the sun does not parch anyone in the morning,
And the sun does not warm toward the evening,
So thou tookest no part in greeting the young knight when he came,
And now at his going away thou needst not bid him farewell,
But be thou a hairless swine! [29]

To the peasant narrator the retort of the knight to the prince
seemed inadequate, and he added on his own initiative the out-
spoken characterization of the prince in the last verse.

The figure of Duk Stepanovich, the princeling, a rich man and
a dandy—a figure depicted in the *bylina* with obvious sympathy—
was utilized in recent vulgar sociological rationalizations as an argument in favor of the aristocratic origin of the *byliny*. But in reality
the figure of the knight, possessing incalculable riches, is a figure related to the fabulous "Ivan Tsareviches" and the other fantastic heroes, who gained possession of authority and riches. In these figures
and pictures (in both tales and legends and in the *byliny*) there is
expressed the common dream of a toiling people, for a rich and
happy life. And consequently there are no grounds for assuming the
creation of the *bylina* about Duk among the upper classes of feudal
society.

Absolutely in the folk genre, on this same plane, is also the figure
of Sadko, who from a poor zither player, with the aid of miraculous
powers, was transformed into a "rich guest," who even dared to enter
into a contest with the whole of Novgorod. The figure of Sadko, the
poet and musician, is drawn in the *byliny*, as we have seen, with
great warmth and affection.

Contradictory, in the *byliny*, is the figure of another hero of the
Novgorod *byliny*—Vaska Buslayev. In the content of the *bylina*

[29] *Ibid.*, No. 230.

about him ("The Combat of Vaska Buslayev with the Peasants of Novgorod") it is not difficult to perceive the original tendency of the *bylina*—to condemn this reckless hero, the son of a boyar, whose undisciplined conduct is obviously contrasted to the life of his father, the sedate, universally respected Novgorod mayor Buslay, who

> Lived with all the city of Novgorod, he lived without a quarrel.
> Nor to the Novgorod peasants ever spoke a cross word.[30]

But Buslay's son, Vasily, is the ringleader of all the lawlessness in Novgorod, he violates the established social customs and without cause quarrels with and insults the Novgorod citizens, "the peasants of Novgorod" (that is, the small merchant class and the craftsmen). Another *bylina* about Vasily Buslayev (the *bylina* entitled, "How Vasily Buslayev Rode Out to Pray") was also created originally with the inclination to condemn Vasily for his lawlessness, for his brigandage, for his violation of religious customs; not without reason does Vasily, according to this *bylina*, find retribution in a tragic death.

And yet, closely observing the figure of Vasily Buslayev, as it is given in the different variants of the *byliny*, one sees that, in contradiction to the original tendency of the *byliny* themselves, the figure of Vasily is delineated in them with great sympathy for his expansive nature, his boundless daring, bravery, and boldness with reference to all that was hallowed by the traditions of religious life and folkways. The popular narrators of the *byliny* obviously admire the character and conduct of Vasily. In distinction from the original conception, the figure of Vasily was endowed with democratic features, he was made the exponent of social protest, and was allied with the "public-house rabble" so frequently encountered in the *byliny*, with whom both Elijah of Murom and Vaska the Drunkard are on friendly terms, as well as other heroes of the emphatically democratic tendency.

Without enumerating other diverse types of the heroes of the *byliny*, let me only comment on the women characters. The *bylina*

30 Danilov, *op. cit.*, No. 9.

has given splendid delineations of several types of the women of ancient Rus.

Such, for example, are the figures of the staid, commanding types of mothers, imbued with the consciousness of their own worth: Amelfa Timofeyevna, the mother of Vasily Buslayevich; Malfa Timofeyevna, the mother of Duk Stepanovich; Afimya Aleksandrovna. the mother of Dobrynya Nikitich. Such is the touching figure of Nastasia Mikulichna, the faithful, devoted wife of Dobrynya Nikitich. Such, again, is the figure of Vasilisa Mikulichna, the intelligent, resourceful, and brave wife of Stavr Godinovich, whom she rescues from misfortune. Such, finally, is the figure of the heroic woman, "the bold woman of the glade," Nastasia Korolevichna, the wife of the knight Dunay.

But, alongside of these positive types of Russian womanhood, the wife and mother, there is also depicted in the *byliny* the type of the dissolute woman; this is, above all, the figure of the wife of Prince Vladimir, Princess Apraxa, and the figure of the unfaithful wife of Tsar Solóman.

Finally, everything evil which the imagination of the ancient Russian could find in woman was concentrated in the figure of the crafty sorceress Marinka, the historical prototype of whom, by the general acknowledgment of the investigators, appears to be the wife of the pretender Gregory Otrepiyev—the Polish adventuress Marina Mnishek.

The general ideological significance of the popular epos, the artistically and socially educative function of the *byliny* and of the heroic figures of the *byliny*, have attracted too little attention from scholars, both in the prerevolutionary period and thereafter.

The disclosure of the artistic-ideological significance of the *byliny*, and of its figures, should be the chief object of the researches of Soviet folkloristics in the next few years. This, of course, does not detract from other, no less important tasks, and above all, from the task of studying the chronology and the historical basis of every *bylina*.

The chronological assignment of the texts of the *byliny* is exceptionally difficult. The *byliny*, which have come down to us in records dating from the seventeenth to the twentieth centuries, being transmitted from mouth to mouth in the course of centuries, could not help being subject to the most diverse changes, both in content and in form. These changes were not of an outward character, but brought about a profound organic reworking of the *bylina*, its content and its poetics. This circumstance makes it extremely difficult to determine the date of origin of the *byliny*.

The Russian *byliny* originally arose, it is probable, as early as the tenth century, and certainly in any case not later than the eleventh. The definite narrative motifs—which, it is true, had already been to a great extent reworked—the historical names, the outward details of social life, the moral and social views introduced in the *byliny* testify to the fact that the basic group of martial and heroic *byliny* belongs to the period of the formation of the principality of Kiev. Thus, for example, very many investigators are inclined to see in the name and figure of the hunter-prince of the *byliny*, Volga, a modification of the names of Oleg the prophet and Princess Olga (tenth century), who engaged in "catching" (hunting) and rode "on an expedition" (for the collection of tribute).

To the transition period from the tenth to the eleventh centuries belongs a creation which later became the traditional picture of the description of the feasts of Prince Vladimir. To the period of this same prince should be assigned the creation of the *bylina* about Dobrynya (in its variants, about Dunay), who made the match for the bride of Prince Vladimir. Investigators connect this *bylina* with the account in the chronicle of the marriage of Prince Vladimir to the Polovtsian princess Rogneda. According to Lyashchenko's research, the artistic *bylina* about Solovya Budimirovich, who espoused the niece of the prince of Kiev, reproduces the history of the marriage of the Norwegian king Harald the Bold to Elizabeth, the daughter of Yaroslav the Wise (middle of the eleventh century). To the eleventh century belongs also the famous *bylina* of the battle of Dobrynya with the snake. In this subject the investigators perceive a legendary narrative, cast in the religious and symbolical forms which were customary for that time, of the baptism of ancient Rus, in which a great part was taken by Dobrynya, the uncle of Prince

Vladimir. (See in the chronicle the story which relates how "Do-brynya baptized with the sword, Putyata with fire.") At the basis both of this *bylina* and the *bylina* about the river Dnieper and the Don, lie ancient cosmic beliefs, connected with the productive proc-esses of the preclass society; these traditions, with their religious-historical interpretation, clothed themselves in the form of song and epic in the eleventh century.

The era of strife between the South Russian feudal principalities and the nomads of the steppes (the Pechenegi and the Polovtsi) left its traces both upon the subjects of the *byliny,* and also upon the individual names and figures in them. For example, the names of Konchak and Atrak are those of Polovtsian khans of the twelfth cen-tury, and Tugor-kan, of the end of the eleventh century and the be-ginning of the twelfth. Tugor-kan became in the *bylina* the monster Tugarin Zmievich, who is conquered by the Rostov knight Alyosha Popovich. Alexander, the "Brave," of Rostov (an ancient Russian title of a knight), is mentioned also in the chronicle.

In a great number of *byliny* the original figure of Prince Vladimir (end of the tenth and beginning of the eleventh century) is overlaid with the features of another, no less famous prince of Kiev, Vladi-mir Monomakh (end of the eleventh and beginning of the twelfth century).

Along with the epos of Kiev, one may speak definitely of the de-velopment of the creative art of the epos in Galician-Volynian Rus, although at a somewhat later epoch, in the twelfth and thirteenth centuries. At this period there was observed a social and economic flowering of the Galician-Volynian principality, which had entered into constant trade and political relations with the neighboring Eu-ropean states (Byzantium, Bulgaria, Hungary, Poland, Lithuania), and had preserved itself from the Tartar devastation. A Galician-Volynian origin has been established (by Veselovsky, Vsevolod Mil-ler, Lyaschenko) for the *byliny* about the visiting wealthy foreigner, Duk Stepanovich (in this *bylina* there is revealed also the influence of the book which was contemporary with it, *Tales of Wealthy In-dia*); and about Michael Potyka (beginning of the twelfth century), founded on the legend of the Bulgarian saint, Michael of Potuka.

According to the opinion of V. F. Miller, Vladimir the Volynian, like Vladimir Monomakh, also bestowed certain of his features upon the figure of Prince Vladimir in the *byliny*. Of Galician-Volynian origin also, apparently, is the *bylina* about Michael Kazarinov (twelfth to thirteenth centuries). In the realm of the western principalities there arose, also, the *bylina* about "Prince Román and the Livik Brothers," in the subject of which, according to Markov's researches, there was reflected the clash of Prince Román Mikhailovich of Bryansk with the Lithuanians in the year 1263. Of the same origin, also, is the *bylina* of "The Princes of Kryakov."

Events connected with the strife of the Russians with the Tartar invasions have left very powerful traces on the epos of the *byliny*. In the *byliny* all the earlier enemies from the steppes (the Pechenegi and the Polovtsi) have been replaced by the Tartars. The battle of the Kalka, in the year 1224, is described as a legend in the *bylina* "About the Massacre of the Kama" and in the *bylina* "About Tsar Kalin." The epithet "of the Kama" and the name Kalin are distortions of the name "Kalkan" (V. F. Miller). The incursion of Batiya (1237–1240) and his destruction of Kiev are reproduced in the *bylina* "On the Bulls," or "Vasily the Drunkard and Batyga" (a distortion of the name Batiya). In the *bylina* "About the Massacre of the Kama," particularly in the episode of the boasting of the "Suzdalian brothers," one may presuppose also an echo of a somewhat earlier event; namely, of the Battle of Lipitsk in 1216, which was lost by the Suzdalian princes Urey and Yaroslav, the descendants of Vsevolod. The old figure of the knight of the *byliny*, Dobrynya, clearly showed the influence of local Ryazan legends of the period of the Tartar domination. The Battle of Kulikovo Field, through the medium of literary narratives about the Slaughter of Mamay, found a reflection in the *byliny* about Sukhman.

The main attention in the majority of these *byliny*, which originated in the period of early feudalism, is centered on the description of martial exploits, on service in guarding the frontiers of the state, to standing "on the heroic outposts," and to service at the court of the grand prince.

Another portion of the *byliny* of that time is devoted mainly to the description of the peaceful city life of various classes under the early feudalism. Typical in this respect is the *bylina* about Duk Stepanovich. This *bylina* can serve, at the same time, as an example of the concrete political significance of the *byliny* for their own time: in it is clearly expressed the tendency of the Galician-Volynian principality of the end of the twelfth century to minimize the significance of Kiev as the cultural-economic center of Russia, and to emphasize its own power.

To the *byliny* having the character of a short novel of everyday life one must also assign those of Novgorod *byliny*.

Novgorod the Great, situated far from the conflict with the nomads of the steppe, who had assailed the Russian land, played an exceedingly great role in the development of the Russian epos. In Novgorod there was created a series of famous *byliny* of folkways, clearly depicting the life of the commercial city: the *bylina* about the rich guest Sadko (this name is mentioned in the *Novgorod Chronicle* for the year 1167), reflecting the mode of life of Novgorod from the twelfth to the fourteenth centuries, and the two *byliny* about Vaska Buslayev, the typical Novgorod river pirate, were composed, apparently, in the fourteenth and fifteenth centuries. To the thirteenth and fourteenth centuries is assigned the *bylina*, which is of Novgorod origin, but included in the Kiev cycle, "about the nobleman Stavr Godinovich," who was thrown into prison by Prince Vladimir, but saved by his resourceful wife.

Of Novgorod origin, also, is the *bylina* "about Ivan the merchant's son," who won out over Prince Vladimir in a dispute about horses. There also, apparently, was created the remarkable *bylina* "about Khoten Bludovich," depicting the family and social relationships among the wealthy Novgorod merchant class and the noblemen. The series of the novel-like Novgorod *byliny* is completed by the *bylina* "About Tsar Solóman," which very interestingly combined in itself the elements of the medieval legends of Solomon, not only with the features of the Novgorod commercial mode of life, but also with allusions to political events and to historical personages of the end of the fifteenth and beginning of the sixteenth centuries (allusions to the unsuccessful marriage of Vasily III to his first wife Solomoniya, and the portrayal of the Novgorod mercantile overseer Vasily Tarakanov under the name of Vasily Torokashka). With Novgorod is connected also the origin of the rather isolated *bylina* about the "Forty Beggars and One." This *bylina* had its origin, it is true, among the pilgrims to holy places: at that time (the fourteenth and fifteenth centuries) pilgrimage was a very characteristic phenomenon of everyday life. Vsevolod Miller, and after him also a series of other investigators, assign to Novgorod or, in any case, to the North-Russian provinces the *bylina* of "The Volga and Mikula." This *bylina* constitutes in itself a combination of the ancient Kiev *bylina* about the prince who collected tributes from the Volga, with a local northern song about a wonderful peasant-plowman.

We have spoken of those *byliny* which, with greater or less probability, can be assigned to this or that region or to a definite period, at least so far as their origin is concerned. But there are in the Russian epos those songs which have come down to us in a form so greatly reworked that it is almost impossible to get back to their sources. Thus the *byliny* about the most outstanding knight of the Russian epos—Elijah of Murom—yield themselves to historical analysis with very great difficulty.

The figure of this most popular knight, in the course of time, was subjected to very substantial changes, in accordance with historical development. According to the conjectures of scholars (Veselovsky, Khalansky), Elijah is a Russified adaptation of the name of Prince Oleg. Later on, Elijah of Murom was transformed into an "old Cossack" (at the transition from the sixteenth to the seventeenth century, in the era of confusion, when the Cossacks played such a significant role in the political life of the country). And still later (with the end of the seventeenth and beginning of the eighteenth century) Elijah of Murom was transformed into a heroic peasant. In almost all records of the *byliny* in which there is mention made of the youth of Elijah of Murom, he is derived from the city of Murom, from the village of Karacharov. But at the present time the majority of investigators (following Vsevolod Miller) see in these geographical designations a later replacement of cities of the principality of Chernigov—Moroviysk, or Morovsk, and Karachev, which, in their opinion, originally figured as the birthplace of Elijah of Murom. Not without reason, in one of the landmarks of the sixteenth century (in the above-mentioned memoirs of the governor of Orsha, Kmita Chernobylsky), is Elijah called the man of Muravl. In the same locality there is a river, Smorodinnaya, which by its name greatly recalls the River Smorodinka, which is spoken of in the *bylina* about Elijah and Solovey the Brigand.

It is difficult to establish the exact chronology of the *bylina* about Elijah of Murom and Solovey the Brigand; one can only say that it was created not later than the fourteenth century. The *bylina* "Elijah and the Falconer" also yields itself with difficulty to an exact dating; all the more so because at its basis there lies a very widely diffused, international, migratory subject of the fight of a father with his son (see, for example, the Iranian epic songs about Rustem and Zorab, the German legends of Hildebrand and Hadubrand, and others). Inasmuch as, according to the latest researches, this Russian *bylina* exerted an influence on one of the fourteenth century German versions of the legends of Hildebrand and Hadubrand, one must assume that it was composed before the fourteenth century.

In later times all the *byliny* were subject to gradual adaptations and alterations. A powerful impression upon the pictures of social life, and upon individual figures, was exerted by Muscovite Rus.

In especial detail there were worked out, in Muscovite Rus, the pictures of the setting of everyday life (old houses, utensils, clothing), and scenes of domestic and social life: feasts, fist fights, the boasting of the nobles, haughtiness, conflict over precedence, and so forth. The individual traditional figures of the epos also underwent great changes. Thus, for example, the figure of the "kindly Prince Vladimir," often timid and powerless even before his own *druzhina*, takes on the features of a menacing and cruel dictatorial tsar, who has as one of his favorite occupations "to execute and hang people." At times the figure of Prince Vladimir takes on features which are characteristic of Ivan the Terrible. Thus, on the basis of events in the time of Ivan the Terrible in Moscow, there arose the *byliny* about "Danilo Lovchanin," who was slain at the order of Prince Vladimir, who wished to marry his widow. B. M.

Sokolov is altogether correct in perceiving in this *bylina* the tale, somewhat obscured by the aid of the traditional subject, of the marriage of Ivan the Terrible to Vasilisa Melentyeva, whose husband had been slain by the tsar's *oprichnina*.*

From the middle of the sixteenth century (with very slight exceptions) the creation of new *byliny* ceases. Almost all the *byliny* fundamentally reflect the events of earlier centuries. But precisely from that period, when the composition of new *byliny* ceased, there began to arise a new epic genre, for which the scholarly term is "the historical song" (see below).

The perceptional and esthetic value of the Russian epos of the *byliny* is very great. It clearly inculcated, in poetic figures, the history of the Russian people, its heroic features; it reflected in a lofty artistic form the dreams and expectations of the masses of the people. The interest of the wide Soviet public in the ancient national epos is not diminishing, but on the contrary, it is possible to affirm a constantly increasing striving of the Soviet reader and listener toward a deep knowledge of the history of the poetic folk creation both in its ideational content and in its artistic skill.

Generations of folk singers and poets have lovingly worked over the finishing and polishing of the monumental figures, which are distinguished, according to the correct observation of Aleksis Maksimovich Gorky, for their unique power as generalized folk types. The especial vitality of the productions of folklore, including the epos, is explained by their close connection with the activities of toil. In the creation of folklore there are revealed the many centuries of experience of the laboring people. In his report at the Congress of Soviet Writers, A. M. Gorky said on this point:

I draw your attention once more, comrades, to this fact, that the most profound and striking, the most artistically perfected types of heroes are created by folklore, by the oral creative work of the laboring people. The perfection of such figures as Hercules, Prometheus, Mikula Selyaninovich, Svyatogor, and further, Dr. Faustus, Vasilisa the All-Wise, the ironical ne'er-do-well Ivan the Fool, and finally,

---

* Term applied only to Ivan the Terrible's personal guard.—ED.

of Petrushka, who vanquished the doctor, the priest, the policeman, and even death itself—these are all figures in the creation of which reason and intuition, thought and feeling are harmoniously blended. Such a combination is possible only by the direct participation of the creator in the creative work of actual life, in the conflict for the main-tenance of life.[31]

Love for the fatherland, honor for those who stood guard at the borders of the native soil, who dedicated their lives to the service of their own people, who aimed at the care of the unfortunate and the oppressed, who knew how to keep the word they had given, who were strong in spirit, bold, brave, who gave a fierce repulse to the enemies of the country and the people, who knew how to speak the truth directly to one's face, who struggled against the violence of the tsars, princes, and nobles—all this constitutes the pathos of many of the heroic *byliny*. This pathos of the ancient popular pro-ductions is transmitted to new readers, who cannot help yielding to the artistic power of the characters, the poetic cast and the majestic melodies of the *byliny*.

BIBLIOGRAPHY

COLLECTIONS

Pamiatniki starinnogo russkogo iazyka i slovesnosti XV-XVIII *sto-letii, Prigotovil k pechati Pavel Simoni: Skazanie o kievskikh boga-tyriakh kak khodili v Tsar'grad* (Landmarks of Ancient Russian Language and Literature of the Fifteenth to the Eighteenth Cen-turies, prepared for publication by Paul Simoni: The Legend of the Knights of Kiev, How They Went to Constantinople) (Petrograd, 1922), *Sborn. otd. russk. iaz. i slov. Akademii Nauk* (Annals of the Division of Russian-Language and Literature of the Academy of Sci-ences, Vol. C, No. 1).

Drevnie rossiiskie stikhotvoreniia, sobrannye Kirshei Danilovym (Ancient Russian Poems, Collected by Kirsha Danilov) (St. Peters-burg, 1818); popular-priced republication (Suvorin, St. Petersburg, 1893); scholarly edition, ed. Sheffer (St. Petersburg, 1901); latest edition, ed. S. K. Shambinago (Moscow, 1938).

Pesni, sobrannye P. N. Rybanikovym v.4 tomakh v. 1861–1867 gg. Izd. 2-e, pod red. A. E. Gruzinskogo (Songs Collected by P. N.

[31] M. Gorky, *Articles and Speeches on Literature, 1928–1936* (Moscow, 1937), p. 450.

Rybnikov, in 4 vols., 1861–1867; 2nd ed. A. E. Gruzinsky) (Vols. I-III, 1909).

Hilferding, A. F., *Onezhskie byliny* (Onega Byliny) (St. Petersburg, 1873); 2nd ed., 3 vols. (St. Petersburg, Academy of Sciences, 1895); 3rd ed., Vol. II (Academy of Sciences, Leningrad, 1938).

Pesni, sobrannye P. V. Kireevskym, desiat' vypuskov, (Songs Collected by P. V. Kireevsky: Ten Parts) (Moscow, 1860–1874).

Markov, A. V., *Belomorskie byliny* (White Sea *Byliny*) (1901). Grigor'ev, A. D., *Arkhangel'skie byliny* (Archangel *Byliny*), Vol. I (Moscow, 1904); Vol. III (St. Petersburg, 1910); Vol. II has not been published.

Onchukov, N. E., *Pechorskie byliny* (Pechora *Byliny*) (St. Petersburg, 1904).

Miller, V. F., *Byliny novoi i noveishei zapisi* (*Byliny* of the New and Newest Recordings) (Moscow, 1908). N. S. Tikhonravov and V. F. Miller, *Byliny staroi i novoi zapisi* (*Byliny* of Old and New Recordings) (Moscow, 1894).

The following popularly scientific collections have been published:
Sokolov, B. M., *Byliny* (Moscow, 1918).

Byliny pod. red. M. N. Speranskogo (*Byliny*, Under the Editorship of M. N. Speransky) (published by the Sabashnikovs, Vol. I, 1916; Vol. II, 1919).

Astakhova, A., and Andreev, N., *Epicheskaia poeziia* (Epic Poetry), "The Poet's Library: Minor Series" (The Soviet Writer, 1935).

Sokolov, Y. M., *Byliny*, State Pedagogical Publications for Teachers (Moscow, 1938).

Byliny, collection comp. with commentary by A. V. Hofmann, Y. A. Samarin, V. I. Chicherov; ed. Prof. Y. M. Sokolov (Moscow, State Literary Press, 1938).

Byliny, ed. and with introductory article by Prof. N. P. Andreev, "The Poet's Library: Major Series" (Leningrad, 1938).

RESEARCHES

1. General Critico-Biographical Surveys

Vladimirov, P. V., *Vvedenie v istoriiu russkoi slovesnosti* (Introduction to the History of Russian Literature) (Kiev, 1896).

Loboda, A. M., *Russkii bogatyrskii epos* (The Russian Knightly Epos) (Kiev, 1896).

Skaftymov, A. P., *Poetika i genezis bylin* (Poetics and the Genesis of the *Byliny*) Saratov, 1924 (Chap. IV).

"Materialy i issledovaniia po izucheniiu bylin c 1896 po 1923 gg." (Materials and Researches for the Study of the *Byliny* from

1896 to 1923). Both these books, of which the second is a continuation of the first, give a full survey of materials and literature on the *byliny*.

Speranskii, M. N., "Russkaia ustnaia slovesnost' " (Russian Oral Literature) *Vvedenie v istoriiu ustenoi slovesnosti, Ustnaia poeziia povestnovatel'nogo kharaktera* (Introduction to the History of Oral Literature, Oral Poetry of a Narrative Character) (Moscow, 1917).

Archangelskii, A. S., *Vvedenie v istoriiu russkoi literatury* (Introduction to the History of Russian Literature), Vol. I (Petrograd, 1916).

Borozdin, A. K., *Istoriia russkoi literatury* (History of Russian Literature), Vol. I, (Moscow, Mir Corporation, 1908).

Sakulin, P. N., *Russkaia literatura* (Russian Literature), Pt. I (Moscow, 1928).

2. On the Narrators of the *Byliny*, and the Conditions of Existence of the *Byliny*, see notes of collectors and introductory essays in the collections of Rybnikov, Hilferding, Markov, Onchukov, Grigorev, and the brothers Sokolov. Also:

Sokolov, B., *Skazateli* (Narrators) (Moscow, State Publishing House, 1924).

Kharuzina, V. N., *Na severe* (In the North) (Moscow, 1890).

Vasil'ev, N. V., "Iz nabliudenii nad otrazheniem lichnosti skazitelia v bylinakh" (Some Observations on the Reflection of the Narrator's Personality in the *Byliny*) (*Annals of the Division of Russian Language and Literature of the Academy of Sciences*, 1907, Bk. 2).

Miller, V. F., *Ocherki russkoi narodnoi slovesnosti* (Sketches of Russian Popular Literature), Vol. I, the first three sketches.

Liatskii, E., "I. T. Riabinin i ego byliny" (I. T. Ryabinin and His *Byliny*), *Etn. Obzor* (Ethnographic Survey), Bk. XIII, 1894.

Ozarovskaia, O. E., *Babushkiny stariny* (Old Wives' Tales) (Moscow, 1917; 2nd ed., 1923).

Miller, V. F., "Kazatskie epicheskie pesni XVI-XVII vv." (Cossack Epic Songs of the Sixteenth and Seventeenth Centuries), ZHMNP (Journal of the Ministry of Public Education), 1914, Bks. V and VI, reprinted in *Ocherki* (Sketches), of V. F. Miller, Vol. III (Moscow, 1924). In this article, a survey is given of all the collections and individual records of *byliny* and historical songs among the Cossacks.

Azadovskii, M., *Epicheskaia traditsiia v Sibiri* (Epic Tradition in Siberia) (Chita, 1921).

Sokolov, B. M., *O bylinakh zapisannykh v Saratovskoi gub.* (On the *Byliny* Written Down in the Province of Saratov) (Saratov, 1922).

Sokolov, Y. M., "Po sledam Rybinkova i Gil'ferdinga" (In the Steps of Rybnikov and Hilferding) (Expedition of the Folklore Subsection of the State Academy of Artistic Sciences to the Olonets Region in 1926 and 1927), *Khudozh Fol'klor* (Artistic Folklore), Vols. II-III, Moscow, 1927.

Sokolov, B. M., "Byliny starinnoi zapisi" (*Byliny* of Old Recordings) (seven unpublished texts), *Etnografiia* (Ethnography), Nos. 1-2, 1926; No. 1 and No. 2, 1927. Here a survey is given of all the texts of old recordings.

3. The Mode of Life According to the *Byliny*.

Markov, A. V., "Bytovye chërty russkogo bylinnogo eposa" (The Features of Everyday Life in the Russian Epos of the *Byliny*), *Ethnographic Survey*, 1904, Vols. 58-59.

Shambinago, S. K., "Drevnerusskoe zhilishche po bylinam" (The Ancient Russian Dwelling According to the *Byliny*), *Iubileinyi sbornik v chest' V. F. Millera* (Jubilee Collection in Honor of V. F. Miller) (Moscow, 1900).

4. Style, Versification, Musical Tunes.

Mikloshich, Fr., "Izobrazitelnye sredstva slavianskogo eposa" (Descriptive Methods in the Slavonic Epos), *Trudy slavianskoi komissii M. Arkh. obshch.* (Proceedings of the Slavonic Commission of the Moscow Archaeological Society), Vol. I (Moscow, 1895).

Sirotinin, N., *Besedy o russkoi slovesnosti* (Talks About Russian Literature) (St. Petersburg, 1913).

Korsh, F. E., *O russkom narodnom stikhoslozhenii* (On Russian Popular Versification) I (St. Petersburg, 1897).

[Annals of the Division of Russian Language and Literature of the Academy of Sciences], 1896, Vol. I, Bk. 1; 1897, Vol. II, Bk. 2).

Veselovskii, A. N., *So'br. soch.* (Collected Works), Vol. I.

Maslov, A. L., "Byliny, ikh proiskhozhdenie i melodicheskii sklad" (*Byliny*, Their Origin and Melodic Cast), *Izv. obshch. liub. estestvozn. antrop. i etnografii* (Annals of the Society of Lovers of Natural Science, Anthropology and Ethnography), XIV, Moscow, 1911.

Notes to the *byliny* are found in the collections of Kirsha Danilov, Grigoriev, and also in the *Trudakh muzykal'noi komissii obshchestva estestvozn. antropol. i etnogr.* (Proceedings of the Musical Commission of the Society of Natural Sciences, Anthropology and Ethnography.)

Skaftymov, A. P., *Poetika i genezis bylin* (Poetics and the Genesis of the *Byliny*); *Ocherki* (Essays) (Saratov, 1924).

Gabel', M. O., "Forma dialoga v bylinakh" (The Form of Dialogue in the Byliny), *Zbirn. na. poshanu akad. D. Bagaleia* (Collection in Honor of the Academician D. Bagaley) (Kharkov, 1928).

——, "K voprosu o tekhnike russkogo bylinnogo eposa" (On the Question of the Technique of the Russian Epos of the *Byliny*), *Nauchkov zapisi nauchno-issled. kafedry* (Scientific Reports of the Chair of Scientific Investigation), Vol. X (Kharkov, 1927).

Zhirmunskii, V., *Rifma eë istoriia i teoriia* (Rhyme, Its History and Theory) (Petrograd, 1923).

——, *Vvedenie v metriku* (Introduction to Metrics) (Leningrad, 1925).

Sokolov, B., "Ekskursy v oblast' poetiki russkogo fol'klora" (Excursus in the Field of the Poetics of Russian Folklore), *Artistic Folklore*, No. 1, 1926.

5. On the Eastern Origin of the Russian *Byliny*.

Stasov, V. V., "Proiskhozhdenie russkikh bylin" (The Origin of the Russian *Byliny*), *Sobr. soch.* (Collected Works), Vol. I.

Miller, V. F., *Ekskursy v oblast' Russkogo narodnogo eposa* (Excursus in the Field of the Russian Popular Epos) (Moscow, 1892).

Potanin, G. N., *Vostochnye motivy v srednevekovom evropeiskom epose* (Eastern Motifs in the Medieval European Epos) (Moscow, 1899).

6. The Mythological Theory.

Miller, O. F., *Il'ia Muromets i bogatyrstvo kievskoe* (Ilya Muromets and the Kiev Knighthood) (St. Petersburg, 1869).

Buslaev, F. I., *Rysskii bogatyrskii epos* (The Russian Knightly Epos), 1862; *Bytovye sloi russkogo eposa* (The Social Strata of the Russian Epos) (1871). Both works have been reprinted in Buslaev's book *Narodnaia poeziia* (Popular Poetry) (St. Petersburg, 1887).

7. The connections of the Russian epos with the European and the literary sources of the *byliny* are surveyed especially in the following works:

Veselovskii, A. N. "Iuzhnorusskie byliny" (South Russian *Byliny*), *Annals of the Division of Russian Language and Literature of the Academy of Sciences*, Vols. XXII and XXVI, St. Petersburg, 1884.

——"Melkie zametki" (Minor Notes), *Journal of the Ministry of Public Education*, No. 12, 1885; No. 5, 1888; No. 5, 1898; No. 8, 1896.

Zhdanov, I. N., *K literaturnoi istorii russkoi bylinoi poezii* (On the Literary History of the Russian Poetry of the *Byliny*) (1881), also in *Works*, Vol. I.

Zhdanov, I. N., *Russkii bylevoi epos* (The Russian Epos of the Byliny) (St. Petersburg, 1895).

Sazonovich, I. I., *Pesni o devushke-voine i byliny o Stavre Godinoviche* (Songs of the Maiden Warrior and *Byliny* about Stavr Godinoviche) (Warsaw, 1886).

Khalanskii, M. E., *Iozhno-slavianskie skazaniia o kraleviche Marke v sviazi s proiskhozhdeniem russkogo bylinnogo eposa* (Southern Slavonic Legends of Prince Mark, in Connection with the Origin of the Russian Epos of the *Byliny*) (Warsaw, 1893–1896).

Loboda, A. M. *Russkie byliny o svatovstve* (Russian *Byliny* About Matchmaking) (Kiev, 1904).

Kirpichnikov, A. I., *Opyt sravnitel'nogo izucheniia zapadnogo i russkogo eposa* (Essay on the Comparative Study of the Western and the Russian Epos: Poems of the Lombard Cycle) (Moscow, 1873).

Veselovskii, A. N., "Russkie i vil'tiny v sage o Tidreke Bernskom" (Russians and Viltiny in the Saga of Tidrek of Bern), *Annals of the Division of Russian Language and Literature of the Academy of Sciences,* 1906, Bk. 3.

8. Historical Reflections in the *Byliny*. (The researches which are presented here draw attention chiefly to the historical basis and the latest strata in the *byliny*, not failing to consider, however, in the majority of cases, the questions of the literary sources of the *byliny*.)

Maikov, L. N., *O bylinakh Vladimirova tsikla* (On the *Byliny* of the Vladimir Cycle) (St. Petersburg, 1863).

Kvashnin-Samarin, N. D., "O russkikh bylinakh v istoriko-geograficheskom otnoshenii" (On the Russian *Byliny* in Their Historico-Geographic Relationship), *Beseda* (Conservation), 1871.

Kostomarov, N. I., "Predaniia pervonachal'noi russkoi letopisi" (Traditions of the Primitive Russian Chronicle) *Vestnik Evropy* (The European Messenger), Nos. 1-3, 1873.

Dashkevich, N. P., *K voprosu o proiskhozhdenii russkikh bylin* (On the Question of the Origin of the Russian *Byliny*) (Kiev, 1883).

Khalanskii, M. E., *Velikorusskie byliny kievskogo tsikla* (Great-Russian *Byliny* of the Kiev Cycle) (Warsaw, 1886).

Miller, V. F., "Ocherki russkoi narodnoi slovesnosti" (Outlines of Russian Popular Literature), *Byliny*, Vols. I (Moscow, 1897), II (Moscow, 1910), III (Moscow, 1924).

Shambinago, S. K., *Pesni vremen tsaria Ivana Groznogo* (Songs of the Times of Tsar Ivan the Terrible) (Moscow, 1914).

Markov, A. V., "Iz istorii bylinnogo eposa" (From the History of the Epos of the *Byliny*), *Etn. Obozr.* (Ethnographic Review), Bks. 61, 62, 67, 70, 71.

Shambinago, S. K., "K literaturnoi istorii starin o Volge" (On the Literary History of the Ancient Tales of the Volga), *ZHMNP* (Journal of the Ministry of Public Education) 1905, No. 11.

Sokolov, B. M., "K byline of Danile Lovchanine" (On the *Bylina* About Danilo Sovchanin), *Russk. fil. vestn.* (Russian Philological News), 1910, XIV.

——, "Shurin Groznogo, Mamstriuk Temriukovich" (The Brother-in-Law of the Terrible, Mamstruk Temrukovich), *Journal of the Ministry of Public Education*, 1913, No. 7.

——, "Istoriia starin o soroka kalikakh so kalikoiu" (History of the Ancient Tales About the Forty Beggars and One), *Russian Philological News*, 1913, Vol. LXIX.

——, "Byliny ob Idolishche Poganom" (*Byliny* About the Great Pagan Idol), *Journal of the Ministry of Public Education*, May, 1916.

——, "Germano-russkie otnosheniia v oblasti eposa: Epicheskie skazaniia o zhenit'be kn. Vladimira" (Germano-Russian Relations in the Field of the Epos: Epic Legends of the Marriage of Prince Vladimir), *Uch. zap. Sar. universiteta* (Scholarly Annals of the University of Saratov), Vol. I, No. 3, 1923.

Iarkho, B. I., "Il'ia-Ilias-Khil'tebrant" (Elijah-Elias-Hildebrand), *Annals of the Division of Russian Language and Literature of the Academy of Sciences*, 1917, No. 1.

——, "Epicheskie elementy, priurochennye k imeni Mikhaila Potyka" (Epic Elements, Adapted to the Name of Michael Potyk), *Ethnographic Review*, 1910.

Liashchenko, A. I., "Byliny o Solov'e Bydimiroviche i saga o Garal'de" (*Byliny* About Solovya Budimirovich and the Saga of Harald), *Sbornik v chest' prof. P. Maleina "Sertum biblologicum"* (Collection in Honor of Professor P. Malein, Sertum Bibliologicum) (1922).

——, "Byliny o Diuke Stepanoviche" (*Byliny* about Duk Stepanovich), *Annals of the Division of Russian Language and Literature of the Academy of Sciences*, Vol. 30, 1925.

Sidorov, N. P., "Zametka k bylinam o Dobrine-Emeebortse" (A Note on the *Byliny* of Dobrynya the Snake Fighter), *Sbornik statei pamidti P. N. Sakulina* (Collection of Articles In Memory of P. N. Sakulin) (Moscow, 1931).

HISTORICAL SONGS

❧❧❧

Very close to the *byliny* as an epic genre of Russian folklore are the so-called *historical songs*.

This term, just as the term "*bylina*," is not of popular origin, but was introduced by the investigators of folklore to designate those productions which border upon the epos of the *byliny*, but still are distinguished from it both in content and in form. In popular usage, on the lips of peasant narrators, the historical songs usually are not divided into a special genre group, but are called, like the *byliny*, "old songs," "ancient songs."

But for the investigators and collectors of folklore, the distinctions in genre between the historical song and the *bylina* are basically quite clear, though in specific instances one infrequently encounters texts of an intermediate type: historical songs which shade off into the *bylina* and, less frequently, *byliny* which have been transformed into a historical song. These will be spoken of further on.

In its general features the historical song, as a specific genre of folklore, may be defined (when placed alongside the *bylina*) as an epic song which, by comparison with the *bylina*, is of shorter dimensions, with a less strict adherence to the epic "ceremonialism" (that is, with less consistent methods of retardation, repetitions, and traditional epic formulas), with less strict adherence to the order of the traditional epic verse; in its content more distinctly and nearer to real life than the *bylina*, transmitting historical facts (events and names of personages).

By virtue of their whole character, the historical songs constitute a later genre formation than the *bylina*, formation in a considerable degree having grown up on the basis of the rich *bylina* tradition, and in their further existence having been exposed in the creative work of the narrators to the *bylina's* artistic influence.

In defining the date of origin of the historical songs as a specific genre, one's attention is involuntarily drawn to the fact that the era which is represented in many of the historical songs has reference to the second half of the sixteenth century, or to the beginning of the seventeenth century, or (with certain changes in the style of the songs) to the end of the seventeenth century. The events which are sung in the historical songs are the events of the reign of Ivan the Terrible, or the events of the peasant movement and the Polish intervention, the so-called "Time of Troubles" of the beginning of the seventeenth century, or else the peasant movement of Stepan Razin, half a century later.

According to the data collected by the folklorists, it is possible to assume that the historical song, as a new epic genre, distinguished from the *bylina*, had its origin from the beginning of the sixteenth century, and in Moscow. One of the earliest songs of the sixteenth century is the song about the taking of Kazan by Ivan the Terrible in 1552.

Against such a supposition it would have been possible to put forward the song about Shchelkan Dudentyevich, which mentions the events of a considerably earlier period; namely, an event which occurred in Tver in 1327. But, as one of the recent investigators of this song has convincingly proved,[1] this song in reality originated in the second half of the sixteenth century, and constitutes, under the guise of a narrative about an ancient event, a political pamphlet on the occurrences of the reign of Ivan the Terrible. Another historical song, referring to the era of Tartar domination—"Avdotya of Ryazan"— must be included by virtue of all its features, not in the category of historical songs, but in that of the *bylina* ballads (like the *byliny* about Prince Mikhaylo and his wife whom he killed, about Prince Román and his wife, who was worried to death by her mother-in-law, and about the sister and brothers who were brigands) which treat predominantly the themes of family relationships, and often, in their variants, pass over into typical family and folkway songs of peasant lyric poetry.[2]

[1] A. D. Sedelnikov, "A Song of Shchelkan and Others of Related Origin," *Artistic Folklore*, IV-V, Moscow, 1929.

[2] See *The Russian Ballad*, ed., with foreword and notes, by V. I. Chernyshev, with introductory article by Prof. N. P. Andreyev ("The Poet's Library," Leningrad, 1936), also in the book *Epic Poetry* ("The Poet's Library," Minor Series,

Thus the historical songs as a special epic genre arose during the reign of Ivan the Terrible. One who examines the content of the historical songs of that period will be convinced that they are deeply fraught with political meaning. The historical songs were not only productions of poetic art, they had at the same time an emphatic social significance; they had an agitational-political function. Furthermore, it is exceedingly characteristic that the majority of them were at that time devoted to the activity and personality of Ivan the Terrible, expressing a definitely sympathetic attitude toward him, interpreting his political and military activity as an activity which was carried on for the good of the people. The historical songs repeatedly describe the irascibility, wrath, and cruelties of the Terrible, but they do not condemn the tsar for this. In the series of historical songs there is perceptible a tendency toward the idealization of Ivan the Terrible, because the people saw in him a tsar who was waging a violent struggle against the nobles, and who consequently was the defender of the popular interests. The figure of Ivan the Terrible, as delineated in the historical songs, is basically the same as that presented to us in the historical tales and legends, as will be discussed below (in the chapter on "Tales"). The publicistic trend in the historical songs of the period of Ivan the Terrible very closely resembles that of the literature of the second half of the sixteenth century, for example in the works of the propagandist of the ideas of Ivan the Terrible, Ivashka Peresvetov.

It may be assumed that the historical songs had their origin among those who had taken part in the military campaigns of the Terrible, among the masses of the people, who sympathized with his struggle against the Tartars, and shared with the tsar a distrust and hatred of the treacherous noblemen.

In only one historical song can one detect a negative attitude toward the policy of the Terrible; namely, in the above-mentioned song about Shchelkan Dudentyevich, that secret pamphlet, which was apparently composed by the people of Tver. They were opposed

---

No. 1, Leningrad, 1935). Such *bylina* ballads were formerly called, infelicitously, "inferior epic songs," and under such a designation they were published in Vol. I of *Great-Russian Popular Songs* of A. I. Sobolevsky.

to the centralizing policy of Tsar Ivan, but they did not dare to attack him directly, and therefore they filled this supposedly historical song about the events at Tver, which had happened two and a half centuries earlier, with stinging allusions to the Terrible and to the period contemporary with him.

A song which adheres quite closely to history (as we know it from the chronicles) describes the event of the uprising of the people of Tver, headed by their prince (in history this is Prince Alexander Mikhailovich, but in the song there are two princes, the brothers Borisovich—an echo of the life of Tver as late as the fifteenth century, when Prince Boris Aleksandrovich ruled in Tver—), against the Tartar viceroy, Shevkala, the son of Dedenya (in the song, Shchelkan Dudentyevich), who had been appointed to Tver by the Ordynian Khan Uzbek (called in the song Azvyak). In the song it is related that for the mob violence against Shchelkan no one received any punishment, "nor was any search made for anyone." According to historical testimonies, it is known that Uzbek, with the help of the Moscow prince Ivan Kalita, pillaged the principality of Tver, and forced Prince Alexander Mikhailovich to flee.

Under the guise of Azvyak, who dispensed cities to his favorites and relatives for the cruel deeds they had performed, the composer of the song pamphlet has represented Ivan the Terrible and his *oprichnina:*

> Tsar Azvyak spoke out the sentence,
> Azvyak Tavrulovich:
> "Ho there, my brother-in-law,
> Shchelkan Dudentyevich!
> Slaughter then your own son,
> Your beloved son,
> Fill a cup with his blood,
> Drink this blood, which is your own,
> The hot blood:
> And then I will bestow upon you
> The ancient city of Tver,
> The rich city of Tver." [3]

[3] K. Danilov, *Ancient Russian Poems*, No. 4.

Alongside such an exaggerated picture of the cruelties of Ivan the Terrible, the composers of the song, in an ironic-satirical tone, have satirized—keeping close to the historical facts—the dispensation by Tsar Ivan (in the song, Azvyak) of "important cities" to his relatives (by which one must understand, the *oprichnina*):

> The Tsar Azvyak Tavrulovich
> Rewarded his brother-in-law
> With important cities:
> Vasily he appointed to Ples,
> Gordey to Vologda,
> Akhramey to Kostroma.[4]

The cities indicated, as is well known, were among the first to be assigned by Tsar Ivan to his *oprichnina*. The burlesque verse of this song is very close to the burlesque verse of a series of songs which indisputably belong to the sixteenth century, for example to the burlesque "Kostruk," which will be spoken of further on. It is also known that the epic genre was used for a political pamphlet with veiled allusions to Ivan the Terrible and his *oprichnina*. As we have said in the chapter on the *byliny*, we must consider as such a pamphlet on the Terrible the *bylina* about Danila Lovchanin, introduced by its composers into the cycle of the Kiev *byliny*, but, in the figure of Prince Vladimir, reproducing very obviously the features of the personality of Ivan the Terrible, with a manifest condemnation of his despotism and cruelty.

However, the negative attitude toward the Terrible is revealed only in very rare cases. The popular view of Tsar Ivan, so far as it is expressed in folklore (in tales, legends, and especially in historical songs), is usually well disposed. In the folk creations there is noticeable an obvious effort to emphasize the positive value of the political and national activity of the Terrible, to justify even his cruelty by the inevitability of struggle against the power of the nobles, to explain his arbitrariness and despotism as only the manifestation of his zeal and irascibility, to discern in his spiritual type the features of the patriot, filled with the feeling of national pride.

4 *Ibid.*

Although in the specific details of the historical songs or the popular legends and tales about Ivan the Terrible there are permitted inexactnesses in the transmission of concrete historic facts, yet these works of oral popular poetry give excellent material for ascertaining the popular historical opinions on the phenomena of our nation's history, and on its statesmen, as M. Gorky has correctly pointed out:

From remote antiquity, folklore persistently and with originality attends upon history. It has its own opinion of the doings of Louis XI, of Ivan the Terrible, and this opinion differs sharply from the evaluation made by history, which is written by specialists who are not very much interested in the question of what the conflict between the monarchs and the feudal lords actually contributed to the life of the laboring people.[5]

The historical song about the taking of Kazan describes, with a sufficiently close adherence to historic fact, the event of the year 1552, when Kazan was taken by the troops of Ivan the Terrible, with the help of a successfully placed mine and an explosion. The song, in accordance with the general tendency of the folklore dealing with the Terrible, introduced an episode depicting the tsar's irascibility, but also his freedom from malice, when he suspected that perhaps the gunners, who were preparing the explosion, were traitors. In accordance with that love for sharply characterized figures and for direct contradictions which is typical of the popular epos, in the historical song the master of Kazan, the Tartar tsar Simeon, for his pride and audacity to the Terrible, perishes, whereas the historical tsar of Kazan, Ediger, as is well known, was taken captive, carried off to Moscow, and baptized, receiving at his baptism the name of Simeon. But, in spite of all these and similar minor deviations from the historical facts, what is important is that the general political and governmental sense of the subjugation of Kazan is very accurately caught and illuminated by the historical song. The new victory won by Moscow over the Tartars is explained as one of the major factors which led to the founding and consolidation of the kingdom of Moscow:

[5] M. Gorky, *On Literature*, 3rd ed. (1937), p. 456.

And he [the Terrible] took away from him [Simeon] the royal
crown,
And he took away the royal purple,
He received the royal staff into his hands.
And at that time the prince became Tsar
And was established in the kingdom of Moscow,
And at that very time Moscow was founded,
And great is the glory of those times.[6]

There are data which lead us to assume that there existed also a
song about the subjugation of the Tartar khanate of Astrakhan. In
the record made for the Englishman James (1619) is preserved a
brief but expressive song about the repulse of a raid made by the
Crimean khan (reference is to the raid of the khan Devlet-Girey on
Moscow in 1572). In the preceding year Devlet-Girey had succeeded
in burning Moscow and taking a great many prisoners, but in 1572
he was decisively routed by the troops of Ivan the Terrible, under
the leadership of the famous commander, Prince M. V. Vorotynsky.
In the song there is again expressed the idea of the strength and soli-
darity of the consolidated kingdom of Moscow.

The beginning and end of the song are contrastingly set off against
each other:

But it was not the heavy cloud that lowered,
But it was not the loud thunderclaps that rolled:
Where is this dog going, the Crimean Tsar?
Why, he is going against the powerful kingdom of Moscow:
"But now then, let us ride to Moscow the city of stone,
And then we will ride back, and take Ryazan!" . . .
You have fled, you dog, you Crimean Tsar,
You are not on the way, nor on the road,
You are not following your banner, your black banner! [7]

In the light of this decisive conflict with the Kazan and the Crimean Tartars, so successfully waged by Ivan the Terrible, and recognized in the consciousness of the people as the final stage in the
freeing of ancient Russia from the many centuries of the Tartar

[6] Danilov, *op. cit.*, No. 28.
[7] P. K. Simoni, "Great-Russian Songs, Recorded in the Years 1619–1620."
*Annals of the Division of Russian Language and Literature of the Academy of
Sciences,* Vol. LXXXII, No. 7, St. Petersburg, 1907.

yoke, there becomes intelligible also the popular dissatisfaction with
Tsar Ivan, when, after the death of his first wife Anastasia Roma-
novna (1559), he married the Circassian (Kabardan) princess, Marya
Temrukovna (in 1561). The song about the death of Tsarina
Anastasia, composed, apparently, several years after the event, puts
into the mouth of the dying tsarina a warning to the tsar not to
marry a wife from the "vile horde," Marya Temrukovna.

The Kabardans, who were at that time in constant relations with
the Crimeans, now fighting against them, now going out with them
in the capacity of allies, and who besides, at that time, had already
become Mohammedans to a very considerable extent, were thought
of as "infidels," as "Tartars," and did not evoke any kindly feelings
or sympathy for themselves. And even Ivan the Terrible himself
had a dual attitude toward the relatives of his non-Russian wife. His
younger brother-in-law, Michael Temrukovich, he would at times
exalt, then would extort money from him by beatings, then would
appoint him leader of his army, then would punish him mercilessly,
and at the very end, tortured him. The Terrible behaved more
benevolently toward his other brother-in-law, Mastruk Temrukovich,
valuing him for his bravery, boldness, stateliness, and cunning. But,
apparently, in making concessions to the moods of the people of
Moscow, he did not refrain from mockery of him also, as related in
detail by the historical song "Mastruk Temrukovich" (in the majority of variants, "Kostruk Temrukovich"), which is composed in
the style of a gay "burlesque."

From the historical documents it is known that Mastruk arrived
in Moscow in the third year after the marriage of Ivan the Terrible
and Marya Temrukovna. In the variants of the song it is also said
that Mastruk "in the third year had a drinking bout, and came to the
Tsar for a feast." But in the historical testimonies nothing is said
about the fight of Mastruk with the Moscow fist-fighters. The basic
content of the song consists of a description of how the boastful
Circassian was humiliated and disgraced with the tsar's permission
and the approval of the Muscovite boxers. The sense of the song is
expressed with sufficient clearness in the words of the Terrible,
spoken by him in reply to the reproaches of the tsarina, that a

"country bumpkin" is committing an outrage on the tsar's "favorite brother-in-law":

> Up spoke the sovereign Tsar:
> "You there, Tsarina in Moscow,
> Yes, you, Marya Temrukovna!
> But this is not my honor in Moscow,
> That the Tartars are fighting;
> But this is my honor in Moscow,
> That the Russian people are amusing themselves!" [8]

In the majority of the historical songs about Ivan the Terrible may be observed the effort to justify the actions of the tsar, relating them to a fixed political idea (as, for example, in the instance just given), or at least to soften the cruelty and arbitrariness which they reveal, at times even to reject a perfectly well established historical fact.

Characteristic, in the latter respect, is the historical song "On the Attempt of Ivan the Terrible to Murder His Son." It is well known historically that, in the year 1581, Ivan the Terrible, in a fit of wrath, murdered his elder son Ivan, who on essential points had supported the policy of his father, but who apparently had reproached him for the surrender of Pskov to the Polish king Stefan Batory. The historical song, which preserves a great many of the real circumstances, and describes among other things the reproaches of the tsarevich Ivan because the tsar has not completed the tasks he had begun (as the song has it, "he could not root out the treachery from Pskov" and other cities), introduces, however, a curious substitution: the Terrible vents his wrath, not on the tsarevich Ivan, but on the younger tsarevich, Fyodor, who had been accused by his brother of treachery; and he orders the execution of Fyodor.

Further on, it is related how the brother-in-law of the Terrible, the nobleman Nikita Romanovich, manages to snatch the tsarevich from the hands of the executioner, Malyuta Skuratov, and at that moment when the tsar, having repented of his fury, is torn with grief for the loss of his son, he brings the young man into the presence of the tsar. In this manner the historical folk song, in its sym-

[8] Danilov, *op. cit.*, No. 5.

pathetic tendency to illumine the figure of Ivan the Terrible, has removed from him the charge of the murder of his son. This manifest departure from historical fact, together with the tendency to idealize the figure of the Terrible, gives a clear conception of the popular moods and the popular understanding of the historical significance of tsar Ivan's activities.

The historical folk songs interpret in their own way, also, the activity of one of the favorites of song folklore, the Cossack commander Ermak Timofeyevich, the conqueror of Siberia. His Siberian expeditions and conquests are treated, in accordance with the basic theme of many of the martial *byliny* and historical songs, as the final chord in the conflict, which had lasted for centuries, against the rule of the Tartars. For the victory over the Tartar tsar Kuchum, Ivan the Terrible forgives Ermak and his Cossack free troops all their offenses against the representatives of the royal power:

> And for this the sovereign Tsar did not grow angry,
> Rather he showed supreme mercy,
> He ordered them to spare Ermak.[9]

In a spirit of deep patriotism, it is related in the song how successfully the Cossacks, under the leadership of Ermak Timofeyevich, beat the Tartars:

> The Cossacks slew no small number of the Tartars,
> And the Tartars were astonished at this,
> How strong the Russian people were,
> So that they, all together, could not overwhelm them;
> And they were shot full of tempered arrows, as in sheaves,
> But the Cossacks stand unharmed.[10]

The figure of Ermak Timofeyevich, which is depicted in the popular historical songs as that of a brave hero and a clever ataman,* entered deeply into the folklore of songs, legends, and tales. Violating, according to the laws of their creation, the chronological limits, many songs, traditions, and legends make Ermak Timofeyevich also

[9] *Ibid.*, No. 13. [10] *Ibid.*
* Ataman: Cossack leader or chief.—ED.

a participant in the expedition against Kazan and against Astrakhan, but later transformed him into a contemporary and participant in the exploits of the popular favorites Stepan Razin and Emelyan Pugachov.

Following after the period of Ivan the Terrible, there is reflected in the historical songs, with great distinctness, the period of the peasant movement and of the Polish intervention, the so-called "troubles" of the beginning of the seventeenth century. In the song, a stern condemnation is passed upon the pretender Gregory Otrepyev, who brought foreign troops into ancient Russia. With particular hatred there is delineated in this song "About Grishka Otrepyev," his Polish wife, Marina Mnishek, who is contemptuously called Marishka or Marinka. Her figure was so completely hateful to the masses of the people, that in the popular poetry it was identified with the figure of a sorceress, an evil enchantress, and in this guise it penetrated not only into the historical songs, but also, as we have seen, even into the *byliny* (see the *bylina* "About Dobrynya and Marinka").

From the historico-literary side, no small interest is attached to the historical song about one of the active figures of the period of "troubles" the talented military leader and diplomat who gained a brilliant victory over the Polish interventionists in the year 1610, the young prince Michael Vasilyevich Skopin-Shuysky. The young general aroused envy, however, on the part of his uncle, Prince Dmitry Ivanovich Shuysky, the brother of Tsar Vasily; and the wife of Dmitry Shuysky, Marya, the daughter of the famous executioner of the era of the Terrible, Malyuta Skuratov, poisoned Michael Vasilyevich at a feast in the palace of Prince I. M. Vorotynsky, to which she had been invited, along with Skopin-Shuysky, for the baptism of a child.

This event, which greatly disturbed the people of Moscow, who had loved Skopin-Shuysky very much and had rested in him their great hopes in the struggle with the Poles, served as the basis for several historical songs. One of these, rather of a lyrico-epic than of a strictly epic character, was composed, apparently, very soon after the tragic death of Skopin, since as early as the year 1618 it was written down for Richard James. Another, more extensive, also originated soon after the event, since the echoes of it are to be heard distinctly in a most interesting literary narrative, the first part of which is entitled, "On the Birth of the Commander, Prince Michael Vasilyevich Shuysky-Skopin," and the second part, "Account of the Death and Burial of Prince Michael Vasilyevich Shuysky, Called Skopin." This narrative was written, according to the opinion of investigators, about the year 1612.[11]

The historical song about Skopin (aside from that which was written down for Richard James) is known in a number of variants of the eighteenth and nineteenth centuries; the most ancient of these, the variant of Kirsha Danilov, reproduces with the greatest fullness the original type of the song, setting forth in detail the struggle of Skopin against the Poles, with the help of Swedish warriors, and the poisoning and death of Skopin. Other texts, in later records, either reproduce only the episodes of the struggle of Skopin with the Poles, or else, on the contrary, dwell only on the scenes of the poisoning and death; furthermore, they gradually lose the features of the concrete historical facts and are transformed into typical *byliny* (with inclusion in the Kiev cycle and with reference to the time of Prince Vladimir, with the traditional motifs of the boasting at the fast and the disobedience of the mother). Especially characteristic, in the scheme of the reworking of the historical song into the *bylina*, are the variants which were written down at the beginning of the twentieth century, in the province of Archangel, by A. V. Markov, and especially by N. E. Onchukov. There was a corresponding kind of change, not only in the subject matter of the song, but also in the whole of its poetics: the historical song as a genre, in these instances, was transformed into a *bylina*, overgrown with the devices, so typical of the *bylina*, of retardations, repetitions, traditional poetic formulas and figures. The study of the historical songs, *byliny*, and narratives about Skopin-Shuysky is of great importance with reference to method, since in the given instance we have the original

[11] See the detailed investigation by V. F. Rzhiga, "Narrative and Songs About Michael Skopin-Shuysky," *Annals of the Division of Russian Language and Literature of the Academy of Sciences of the USSR*, Vol. I, Bk. 1, 1928.

facts on which the song is based, and quite a long series of folklore records (from the beginning of the seventeenth to the beginning of the twentieth century), giving us the opportunity to trace graphically the evolution of artistic forms and of the ideas contained in them.

From the end of the sixteenth century, and certainly very definitely from the beginning of the seventeenth, the majority of the historical songs are composed among the Cossacks, and reflect the events which were connected with the political life of the free Cossack troops. We are already familiar with the reflection of Cossack motifs in the historical song, from the song about Ermak Timofeyevich. Throughout the course of the whole seventeenth century there extends a long series of songs, making up the vast popular cycle of the songs about Stepan Razin.

In the chapter on the *byliny* we have seen that the Cossack life and the motifs of Cossack creative work began to resound clearly in the epos of the *byliny*, and also from the beginning of the seventeenth century. We recall the introduction into the figure of the beloved popular knight, Elijah of Murom, of Cossack features: the constant designation of him as "the old Cossack"; the reworking of the epos of the *byliny* so as to depict Elijah of Murom as the leader of the public-house poor folk; and the sharpening of the theme of class conflict, as, for example, in the *bylina* about the quarrel of Elijah of Murom with Prince Vladimir. Long ago, research scholars began to perceive in all this a reflection of the stormy events of the beginning of the seventeenth century, with which the movement of the peasant masses against the oppression of the tsar and the landowners began. In this revolutionary peasant movement the Cossacks played a major organizing role, as is well known. The combination in the historical songs of the figures of Cossacks with the themes of social protest is very characteristic, and fully justified historically.

The relations of the Cossacks with the tsarist government of Moscow were highly contradictory. The tsarist government frequently had recourse to the military aid of the Cossacks, but at the same time clearly aimed at the full subjugation of the Cossacks to its own authority. This subjugation was not achieved by the tsarist government for a very long time, because of the remoteness of the Cossack settlements, and because of the fixed habits which had been developed among the Cossacks, who defended their "freedom" and forms of self-government. Frequently the Cossacks developed their own independent policy with reference to the neighboring peoples. Hence arose numerous instances of misunderstandings and conflicts, which sometimes turned out well for the Cossacks, and sometimes brought in their train the tsar's disfavor and retribution.

An echo of one of these misunderstandings of the Cossacks with tsarist Moscow is seen in the song "On the Murder of Prince Karamyshev." In 1630 the tsar sent Prince Ivan Karamyshev to the Cossacks on the Don, with the purpose of persuading them to fight, together with the Turks, with whom the tsar's government had at that time concluded a military agreement, against the Poles. But the Cossacks, in the first place, did not want to go on a military campaign under the leadership of their age-long enemies, the Turks, and in the second place they were disturbed by the rumors which were being circulated, that Prince Karamyshev wanted not only to exhort the Cossacks, but even by force to make them consent to the government's proposition. The song describes the fierce retribution which the Cossacks visited upon Karamyshev, whom they killed and threw into the Don.

Closely approximating the historical facts, though also introducing legendary motifs (for example, the motif of the taking of the city by a ruse—by means of hiding the Cossacks in carts along with merchandise), a historical song relates the taking of Azov by the Cossacks. Of the three known captures of Azov (in 1590, 1637, and in 1697), the song, according to the opinion of investigators,[12] refers to the independent capture of Azov by the Cossacks in 1637, when they encountered no support on the part of Moscow, which at that time was trying to avoid a dispute with Turkey. After six years, not obtaining the support of Moscow, the Cossacks were compelled to abandon the fortress. This fact is also reflected in the song, but with that alteration in chronology and motivation which is typical of the epos. The song about the capture of Azov in 1637, was

[12] See the research of Acad. A. S. Orlov, *Legendary Songs about Azov* (Moscow, 1906).

readapted later on, in different variants, particularly as regards the expedition of Peter I against Azov.

In the series of historical songs of the seventeenth century, there should be noted one which stands somewhat apart from the majority of those dealing with the events which are connected with the Cossacks and the peasant revolutionary movement, a song about the great historic event of the middle of the century—the *restitution of Smolensk* to the tsardom of Moscow. The long and stubborn conflict with the Poles for the restitution of the old Russian city of Smolensk came to an end in 1654, when it again became part of the Russian state. The song also reflected this event, changing the outward circumstances, ascribing the settlement of this question to an assembly of the zemstvo, summoned by the tsar, which did not actually take place.

However, in this historical song also, as we have seen in others, the alterations of specific, relatively minor details do not distort the basic political idea which is expressed by the song. The idea of the song is deeply patriotic—the consciousness that Smolensk is an inalienable part of ancient Russia and must belong to the Russian state. Two lords who are introduced into the song—an Astrakhan prince and a Bokharan prince—propose to give up Smolensk to the enemy, and in return for it to accept some vaguely defined land of Khina, offered to them by the enemy. The tsar does not agree with these counsels, but, on the contrary, expresses great joy when Prince Miloslavsky, who then came forward (in reality two Miloslavsky princes took part in the conclusion of the peace), began to insist on the incorporation of Smolensk into the Russian territory:

> "Thou, O sovereign, our hope, our sovereign Tsar,
> Alexis Mikhailovich, sovereign of Moscow!
> Graciously allow me, sovereign, to utter a word:
> That Smolensk was not built by the Lithuanians,
> But Smolensk is the work of the people of Moscow. . . .
> We will not give up to them the city of Smolensk,
> And we will not take for ourselves the land of Khina!
> And these words were well pleasing to the sovereign." [18]

[18] A. F. Hilferding, *Onega Byliny*, No. 154.

The same idea of guarding the boundaries of one's state, the idea of a decisive repulse of the solicitations of the enemy with regard to the ancient Russian lands, and the very reserved attitude toward the ideas of the seizure of foreign lands, expressed in this historical song of the middle of the seventeenth century, as we have seen it earlier, in the ancient *byliny* and from the historical songs of the sixteenth century, long ago entered deeply into the consciousness of the Russian people.

The songs about Stepan Razin and the peasant revolutionary movement which he headed were among the leading Russian historical songs.

The figure of Razin himself, and also the folklore about Razin, have attracted the attention of many investigators, writers, and artists. A general sketch of the interest of the Russian political, scientific, and artistic intelligentsia, in Razin and the Razin movement, is given in the work of Professor N. K. Piksanov.[14] It is widely known how greatly interested Pushkin was both in Razin and in the poetic folk reaction to his activity. Pushkin, in his enthusiasm, even considered Razin "the only poetic character in Russian history." Pushkin, both personally and through his friends, collected popular songs about Razin, and proposed to bring out a collection of them, which he had compiled, but through Benckendorff his request was refused. Benckendorff, reflecting the opinion of the tsar, wrote to the poet: "The songs about Stenka Razin, in spite of all their poetic worth, are in their content improper for publication. Besides, the Church execrates Razin, just as she does Pugachov." [15] The songs which had been collected by Pushkin were finally published by Annenkov, in 1881.

All the information concerning the collected songs and the other folklore about Razin, as well as the results of a great many researches on the Razin folklore, have been summed up in the two detailed books on Soviet folkloristics, by A. N. Lozanova.[16]

[14] See N. K. Piksanov, "The Social-Political Destinies of the Songs About Stepan Razin," *Artistic Folklore*, No. I, 1926.

[15] Letter of Benckendorff to Pushkin, dated April 22, 1827, *Correspondence of Pushkin*, ed. V. I. Saitov, Vol. II (St. Petersburg, Academy of Sciences, 1908).

[16] See A. N. Lozanova, *Popular Songs About Stepan Razin, Historico-Literary Investigation and Texts* (Saratov, 1928), and *Songs and Legends of Razin and Pugachov* (Moscow, Academia, 1935).

The songs about Razin circulated over a vast area, passing far beyond the boundaries of those localities where the Razin movement proper had spread. This testifies to the exceedingly great popularity both of Razin himself and of his movement, among the masses of the people, not only in the 1660's and 1670's, when the actual events were taking place, but also a good deal later. These songs lived on in the memory of the people for a period of two centuries and a half. It is true that many of the songs, and also of the legends, about Stepan Razin were subjected to various reworkings which frequently lost that directness with which the songs originally echoed the events of the time of Razin; many of them were subjected to censorship (especially on the part of the officers, since the songs about Razin enjoyed great popularity also among the masses of the Cossacks and of the soldiers), but still it is possible to establish the basic character of the original popular songs about Razin.

As A. N. Lozanova has rightly remarked, the distinguishing characteristic of the folklore about the Razin movement is the diversity of its subjects. In the Russian folklore of the prerevolutionary period, there is undoubtedly not a single hero, either of the histories or of the *byliny*, around whom there has grown up such a multitude of songs, narratives, traditions, and legends. "This affords the strongest possible proof as to how vividly the memory of the Razin movement lives among the masses." [17]

The basic idea which permeates the songs and legends about Razin is that of the social conflict with the landowning boyars and with the tsarist administrative officials, who, by an anachronism, in the songs are usually called governors. All the cruelties of Razin are justified in the popular songs by the feeling of class vengeance for the oppression, the arbitrariness, and the cruelties which had been perpetrated by the ruling classes. The songs about Stepan Razin are songs of the people's wrath.

In the historical songs there are frequently described, with historical fidelity, the scenes of retribution wreaked upon the tsarist authorities by the followers of Razin:

[17] *Ibid., Songs and Legends*, p. iv.

After a swift attack, they came straight to the governor,
    to the court.
But the governor had hardly met Stenka,
When Stenka Razin put the governor into prison.
And what is more, he hung him on the gallows.[18]

In the song about the capture of Astrakhan by Razin it is sung:

Stenka Razin rushed to the corner tower,
And with a great roll he threw the governor down,
And all his little children he hung up by the feet.[19]

But this atrocious cruelty of Razin is justified in the songs as a response to the similar cruelties of the tsarist authorities:

Surely you, O good governor, were very severe to us,
Surely you beat us, you destroyed us, you sent us into
    exile,
At the gates you shot down our wives and children.[20]

The songs about Razin and the Razin movement are an evidence of the power of the people's wrath, which was stored up through the long years of feudalism. The songs and legends about Razin are mainly the voice of the peasant and Cossack poor, of those countless masses of the peasants who had borne upon themselves the full weight of serfdom.

The poor, the "public-house rabble," that is, the ruined and unfortunate peasants, were the faithful and unswerving companions of Razin, his comrades and advisers. Razin relied upon them above all.

My good sirs, brothers, the public-house rabble,
Let us go, brothers, to sport upon the blue sea,
Let us, brothers, destroy the ships of the infidels,
Let us, brothers, take their treasures, as much as we need,
Let us go, brothers, to Moscow the city of stone,
Let us, brothers, buy garments of many colors,
And when we have bought garments of many colors, let us
    sail away downstream.[21]

The songs about Stepan Razin, as all the Razin folklore, are striking in their fanciful combination of vivid realism, strict adherence to

---

[18] Hilferding, *op. cit.*, No. 274.
[19] P. V. Kireyevsky, *Songs*, No. 7, p. 148.
[20] *Ibid.*, pp. 149-150.
[21] Lozanova, *op. cit.*, p. 38.

historical facts, and sometimes even minuteness in the description of specific events, with the quality of fantasy in the delineation of the figure of Stepan Razin himself.

Razin is represented as a sorcerer, a magician. He is able to divine his own fate and that of his fellow champions. He can easily transport himself from place to place, all that he needs to do is to draw the outline of a boat on the sand. He knows how to charm away bullets, to cast a spell over snakes, to open locks by magic.

In one of the songs about the taking of Astrakhan (1670) Stepan Razin, in answer to the governor's command to the gunners to load the cannon and to fire on Stenka, remarks:

> Don't waste your powder and don't spoil your shells;
> The kindly bullet will not touch me, the friendly
>   cannon ball will not take me off.[22]

In another song, which was very widely diffused and exceedingly realistic in its character—"On the Little Son of Stepan Razin"— there are also present elements of the legendary and fantastic in the delineation of the figure of Razin.

In Astrakhan "there appeared a stalwart fellow, a man unknown." By his dandified array, his haughty and independent conduct ("he bowed to no one, neither princes nor boyars, and to the Astrakhan merchants' wives he did not bow himself down, the fine lad; nor did he go under trial to the governor of Astrakhan, the fine lad"), he attracted general attention. The governor personally summoned him and questioned him as to who he was. The boy called himself the son of Stepan Razin. (In the song this word is interpreted as meaning "son" by blood relationship, since the term "sons" of Razin was in fact applied to his agents and agitators, whom he sent about through the cities, before conquering them.) The son advises the governor to give a fitting reception to his "papa," who must soon come to visit Astrakhan. The governor sends the young man to jail. At that time Razin, sailing on his boat, begins to feel that something is going wrong:

[22] Kireyevsky, *op. cit.*, p. 148.

"Still for some reason, my brothers, my children, I feel
    sick, very sick,
Something makes me feel sick, very sick, and exceedingly sick,
Do you give me now some water from under the right hand."
And over that water Senka uttered a charm, and poured the
    water back again:
"I can see, surely here is my dear son, and he is lying in a
    prison of white stone.
Pull in closer, my children, to the steep bank.
Surely we will break down the wall, and we will scatter the
    prison also, stone by stone,
And we will take the governor of Astrakhan prisoner among
    ourselves,
And we will take the wife of the governor of Astrakhan to be
    our concubine." [23]

The songs which depict the relations of Razin to the Cossack
"circle," to the higher classes among the Cossacks, are of especial
historical interest. In the songs, in accordance with historical reality,
Razin is depicted as the leader of "the poor," with whom "he also
meditated sound judgments." The songs about the relations of Razin
to the Cossack circle, and also the tragic songs about the treacherous
betrayal of Razin to the tsarist authorities, and about the execution
of Razin, are valuable historical evidences of the social differentiation and class conflict which existed among the Cossacks.

The masses of the people were so deeply devoted to Razin, and
believed in him to such an extent, that even after his execution the
conviction was rooted among the people that he had not perished,
that he was still alive, and that, at a critical moment for the people,
he would come to help them.

The wealth which he had taken from the boyars and the rich
men, according to popular legends, Razin hid for the poor. All along
the Volga there were spread traditions as to the supposed treasures
left by Razin. These traditions, attached to specific regions, are num-
bered by the hundreds.

The rich folklore about Razin, in song and legend, has had a vast
influence upon oral poetic creative work (not only upon the Russian,

[23] Hilferding, *op. cit.*, No. 208.

indeed, but upon the creations of a number of peoples along the Volga). The songs about Stepan Razin had their fullest development later on. Many of them, losing their connection with the name of Razin, passed over into the vast cycle of the so-called "bandits' songs." Many of the songs and legends of Razin, in the course of a century, became attached to the name of the leader of another peasant uprising—to the name of Pugachov.

Here is a specimen of the felicitous reworking of the songs about Razin (of a song about the son of Razin) into a song about Pugachov:

When in the renowned city of Astrakhan
The bold youth appeared,
The bold youth, Emelyan Pugach;
He was dressed in a caftan worth a hundred rubles.
His scarf was worth fifty rubles.
He wears his cap on one side,
And in his right hand is a silver walking stick,
And on the walking stick is a flowered ribbon.
He walks all through the town,
And leans on his staff, and shows off his ribbon.
He does not bow to the princes and the boyars,
He does not make any agreement with the governor of
        Astrakhan.
The governor of Astrakhan became thoughtful;
He saw him through his crystal windowpane;
He sends after him faithful servants,
To examine him at an oral interview.
The faithful servants pursued him,
They questioned him by word of mouth,
"Of what race and tribe are you,
Are you a Tsar, or the son of a Tsar?"
And thereupon he said to them:
"I am not a Tsar nor the son of a Tsar.
By birth, I am Emelyan Pugach.
I have hanged many lords and princes,
Throughout Russia I have hanged also the unjust judges." [24]

[24] Recorded in the province of Saratov, first printed in *Russian Antiquity*, Bk. XII, 1874; reprinted in Lozanova's *Songs and Legends of Razin and Pugachov*, pp. 187-188.

The songs about Pugachov have a still more realistic character than the songs about Razin. There is hardly any fantastic element in them. The political and social trend of this series of the songs is very definitely expressed, as we have seen in the text given just above, or in the following brief song about the meeting of Pugachov with Count Panin:

Thereupon Count Panin tried the robber Pugachov:
"Tell me, tell me, Emelyan Ivanych Pugachonka,
 Have you hung many of the princes and the boyars?"
"I have hung, of your brothers, seven hundred and seven
      thousand,
And you may be thankful, Panin, that you never came into
     my hands:
I would have promoted you, I would have straightened out
   , your back,
And upon your neck I would have placed the thief's reins.
And for your desserts I would have hung you higher still."
And Count Panin was terrified, he struck his hands
      together.
"You, my faithful servants, take the robber Pugachov,
Lead him, conduct him to the fine city of Nizhny Novgorod.
Announce it in Nizhny Novgorod, tell it in Moscow,
All the Moscow senators cannot judge him." [25]

This song is a popular echo of an actual talk between Count Panin, the suppressor of the followers of Pugachov, and Pugachov himself, when the latter had been captured and put into an iron cage (October 2, 1774, in Simbirsk). From Panin's own letters and from much other evidence, it is apparent that Pugachov conducted himself with Panin very haughtily and with deliberate insolence. According to the accounts of eyewitnesses, Panin struck Pugachov for this several times on the cheek, and, according to the information presented by Pushkin in his *History of the Pugachov Rebellion*, even pulled a tuft out of Pugachov's beard. But popular feeling could not be reconciled to such a degradation of the leader of the uprising, and in their song the people have represented the whole episode otherwise: in the song it is shown how Panin was reduced

[25] Recorded by A. M. Yazykov in the province of Simbirsk, published in Kireyevsky's *Songs*, No. 9, p. 248.

to terror by Pugachov's bold words, and decided not to try him himself; furthermore, in the song, even all the "Moscow senators" did not dare to try Pugachov, being convinced of his truly royal origin (thus, by implication, the historical song speaks of this, and the popular legends are much more definite on this point).

Few songs about Pugachov have been written down, as compared with the songs about Razin. This is explained, to a very great degree, by the fact that it was dangerous not only to write down, but even to perform songs about Pugachov, for almost a whole century after his death. The tsarist government of the landowners rigorously fought against the displays of sympathy toward the Pugachov movement; the folk singers cautiously and unwittingly imparted songs and legends to the collectors, at times deliberately distorting the meaning of the songs. The external and internal censorship, which had been exercised in the case of the folklore concerning Razin, was still more apparent in the case of the Pugachov folklore. For this reason, among the transcripts of songs and legends about Pugachov, there is quite a large percentage of material which either has a double meaning, or expresses ill will toward Pugachov, calling him "thief," "dog," "bandit," and so forth. The folklore about Pugachov has been comparatively little studied, and the great task still remains before the investigators of making an appraisal of all the existing material and analyzing the history of the texts and their revisions. It is necessary to note that substantial additions to our knowledge of the Pugachov folklore have been made in our own time by a number of Soviet folklorist-collectors and investigators (A. N. Lozanova, B. M. Sokolov, V. M. Sidelnikov, V. U. Krupyanska, and others).

Among the historical songs about the Pugachov movement, one is particularly noteworthy because of its own peculiar fate, showing over what complicated paths a popular poetic work sometimes travels.

P. V. Shein wrote down a song which told how "the bold youth, Zachary Gregoryevich Chernyshov," was thrown into a dungeon in the village of Lyskovo.[26] This song, in its content, is quite different

---

[26] This song was included in the ninth number of the *Songs* of P. V. Kireyevsky, pp. 145-146.

from the historical song, known in many variants, about the participant in the Seven Years' Prussian War (1756–1763), the close friend of Peter III, who later on became a magnate in the reign of Catherine—Count Zachary Gregoryevich Chernyshov. At the time of the Prussian War, Chernyshov was captured, imprisoned in the fortress of Kyustrin, and then, under an exchange of prisoners, was returned to Russia. The song depicts Chernyshov as a stanch patriot, who did not consent to go over to the service of the Prussian emperor.

Recorded by P. V. Shein, and related in origin, as A. N. Lozanova has well shown,[27] to the songs about Count Chernyshov, the associate of Peter III, this song is about the close collaborator of Pugachov, Zarubin-Chika, who was also called, among the followers of Pugachov, Count Zachary Gregoryevich Chernyshov. Chika was seized by the tsarist troops even before the capture of Pugachov, and executed; furthermore, as is known from historical sources, he was taken to his execution by a roundabout route, through Lyskovo, so that the people might be convinced that Chika had really been caught.

This song about the Chernyshov of the Pugachov movement has been revised in the spirit of the popular songs about Razin and the traditional "robbers'" and "prison" songs, once more confirming the close connection between the Pugachov and the Razin folklore.

We have dwelt upon the songs about Pugachov in direct connection with the songs about Stepan Razin, inasmuch as the cycle of songs about Pugachov carries on the tradition of the historical songs about Razin, with clearly expressed tendencies toward social protest.

But the historical songs of the end of the seventeenth and of the eighteenth century touched also, as may be seen in the song about Z. G. Chernyshov, upon other historical phenomena, in addition to those which have a direct relation to the movement of Razin and Pugachov.

The songs about Peter I deserve particular mention among historical songs. Ivan the Terrible and Peter I are the two figures among

---

[27] A. N. Lozanova, "Social Interpretations of Songs about Chernyshov," *Soviet Folklore*, Nos. 2-3, 1935, pp. 278-292, and also A. N. Lozanova, *Songs and Legends of Razin and Pugachov*, pp. 388-389.

the tsars who merit the greatest attention in Russian folklore. However, in the delineation of the figures of both tsars, along with the similar motives, there is also a substantial difference. The songs about Ivan the Terrible, as we have seen, express a sympathy for his general activity as sovereign, and for his military campaigns, in which he finished the struggle with the Tartars and consolidated the kingdom of Moscow. Peter's general activity as sovereign, his military campaigns, specific episodes from the great Northern War (the capture of Schlüsselburg, the siege of Vyborg, Riga, Revel, and other places, and especially the Battle of Poltava), also evoke the sympathy and approval of the masses of the people, who understood the vast significance of all this for the consolidation of the might of the Russian state. Not without reason does the song, "The Birth of Peter I," which certainly was composed in the very years of the triumphs and glory of Peter, laud him as the "first Emperor on earth." A great and unfeigned sincerity emanates from the songs of lamentation which were composed, apparently, among the soldiers, on the death of Peter. Here is a passage from one of these songs:

It was at that palace of the sovereign,
It was at the painted porch,
A young sergeant stood on guard.
His swift feet were chilled, down to his very boots,
And his white hands, down to the very bone.
Standing so, he became thoughtful,
And when he had become thoughtful, he began to weep bitterly.
And he weeps, as a river flows,
And he lets fall the tears, like flowing streams.
He began to sigh, like the murmuring of the woods,
And he broke into violent sobbing, as the thunder rolls.
And having burst into sobs, he began to speak:
"Blow ye from the mountains, O winds of tempest,
Bear down from the skies the white snowflakes,
Push aside, O winds, the white-hot stone,
Shake ye loose our mother the damp earth
In all four directions.
Break, O winds, the coffin lid,
Push aside the golden brocade,
Open wide the fine white shroud!

And do thou arise, awaken, Orthodox Tsar,
Orthodox Tsar, Peter Alekseyevich!
Raise up thine indomitable head,
Look upon thy force:
Thy force stands in order,
It stands in order—it does not move,
It is learning the arts of war;
It is departing for the war." [28]

The people, as may be seen from the historical songs, and especially from the numerous legends and anecdotes about Peter, liked his simplicity, his affability toward the working people, and they also liked the fact that the tsar himself was no stranger to physical labor; and they were impressed, finally, by his stalwart and powerful figure.

Very characteristic, for the understanding of the popular attitudes toward the personality of Peter, is the historical song "Peter I and the Dragoon," the subject of which is that the tsar offered to wrestle with a private soldier of the dragoons, and when the latter overcame him, the tsar praised the soldier.

Peter is endowed with justice and, like Tsar Ivan, with freedom from malice in his wrath. But the whole distinction between the songs about Peter and the songs about Ivan the Terrible consists in the fact that in the former there is lacking the motif which was so typical of the songs about the Terrible—the motif of the conflict with the princes and the boyars, the motif which is so close to the popular consciousness, and which is present, as an outstanding feature, through the most diverse poetic genres of the traditional folk creation. Of the two well known songs about the revolt of the Streltsy * and about the execution of the Streltsy by Peter, one obviously expresses attitudes which do not favor Peter, and the other bears a certain vague, indistinct character with reference to politics.[29]

The historical song of the post-Petrine era (with the exception of the songs about Pugachov, which, as we have said, are closely connected with the traditional songs about Razin) deteriorates strik-

---

[28] Kireyevsky, *Songs*, No. 8, pp. 279-280.

* *Streltsy* (plural of *strelets*): Musketeers who mutinied under Peter the Great. —ED.

[29] *Ibid.*, No. 8, pp. 18, 520.

ingly, both in its form, and in its ideational and political content. It records, with inadequate detail as to subject and lack of fullness of ideas, isolated facts of history which are not always significant. In its structure the historical song of the eighteenth and the beginning of the nineteenth century is departing more and more from its former epic character, and approximating in its genre to the so-called "soldiers' ", Cossacks'; and folkway songs. Such are the songs about the Swedish War (1741–1743), about the first Turkish War (composed about 1769), the song about Count Rumyantsev (circa 1779), about the death of Catherine II (an imitation of the above-mentioned songs on the death of Peter I), and so forth.

Of the historical songs of the first half of the nineteenth century, one should be noted which has a soldierly cast, and which was exceedingly popular for a century, about the hero of 1812, General Platov, who disguised himself as a Frenchman and seemingly appeared, unrecognized, in the camp of Napoleon. Also the song "Nicholas I and His Brother," recorded in several variants, which in a confused form relates the rumors that were diffused among the people about the events of December 14, 1825, and about Constantine's abdication from the throne.

On the whole, the historical song, as it flourished in the sixteenth and seventeenth centuries, had by the eighteenth century and the beginning of the nineteenth been greatly transformed both in content and in form, and by the end of the nineteenth century it had, so to speak, outlived itself, continuing to be preserved only in the memory of the narrators of the peasant North or of the Cossack Southeast, in order that it might be reborn with new strength, in new forms, after the Great October Socialist Revolution, reflecting all the events of the Soviet era.

BIBLIOGRAPHY

COLLECTIONS

Simoni, P. K., *Velikorusskie pesni, zapisannye v 1619–20 gg. dlia Richarda Dzhensa na krainem severe Moskovskogo tsarstva* (Great-Russian Songs, Written Down in the Years 1619–20 for Richard James in the Far North of the Kingdom of Moscow) (St. Petersburg, 1907), *Sborn. Otd. Russk. iaz. i Slov Akad. nauk* (Annals of the

Division of Russian Language and Literature of the Academy of Sciences, Vol. LXXXII, No. 7).

A large number of historical songs, arranged in chronological order, have been printed in *Pesni* (Songs) collected by P. V. Kire. ..ky, Nos. VI-X (Moscow, 1862–1874), and also in the basic collections of *byliny* (by Rybnikov, Hilferding, Markov, Gregoryev, Onchukov); in the collection of *Skazok i pesen Belozerskogo kraia* (Tales and Songs of the Belo-Ozero Region) by B. and Y. Sokolov; in the collections of Cossack songs: A. I. Miakutin, *Pesni orenburgskikh kazakov* (Songs of the Orenburg Cossacks) (Orenburg, 1904); N. G. Miakutin, *Sbornik ural'skikh kazach'ikh pesen* (Collection of Songs of the Ural Cossacks) (St. Petersburg, 1890); Listopadov and Arefin, *Pesni donskikh kazakov, sobrannye v 1902–1903 gg.* (Songs of the Don Cossacks, Collected in 1902–1903) (Moscow, 1911); I. I. Zheleznov, *Pesni ural'skikh kazakov* (Songs of the Ural Cossacks) (St. Petersburg, 1893); P. Kravchenko, *Pesni donskikh kazakov* (Songs of the Don Cossacks) (Stalingrad, 1938).

Variants of the historical songs of the sixteenth and seventeenth centuries have been reprinted with great fullness, from various publications, by the Academician Vsevolod F. Miller, in one volume: V. F. Miller, *Istoricheskie pesni russkogo naroda XVI i XVII vv.* (Historical Songs of the Russian People in the Sixteenth and Seventeenth Centuries) (Annals of the Division of Russian Language and Literature of the Academy of Sciences, Vol. XCIII, Petrograd, 1915).

All the variants known to science of the songs about Stepan Razin have been published in the book by A. N. Lozanova, *Narodnye pesni o Stepane Razine* (Popular Songs about Stepan Razin) (Saratov, 1928). New folklore materials about Razin and Pugachyov are presented in the book by V. M. Sidelnikov and V. U. Krupianskaia, *Volzhskii fol'klor* (Folklore of the Volga) (Moscow, 1937).

For collections of historical songs, see the following publications:

Byliny, Istoricheskie pesni (*Byliny*, Historical Songs), Vol. II, ed., with introductory essays, by M. N. Speranskii (published by the Sabashnikovs, Moscow, 1919).

"Russkii fol'klor, Epicheskaia poeziia" (Russian Folklore, Epic Poetry), *Biblioteka poeta* (The Poet's Library: Minor Series), under the general editorship of M. Azadovskii; introductory essay, editing, and notes by A. Astakhova and N. Andreyev (Leningrad, 1935).

Pesni i skazaniia o Razine i Pugacheve (Songs and Legends of Razin and Pugachov), introductory essay, editing, and notes by A. N. Lozanova (Moscow, 1935).

Veinberg, P. I., *Russkie narodnye pesni ob Ivane Vasil'eviche*

Groznom (Russian Popular Songs about Ivan Vasilyevich, the Terrible) (Warsaw, 1872; 2nd ed., Petrograd, 1904).

Aristov, *Ob istoricheskom znachenii russkikh razboinich'ikh pesen* (On the Historical Significance of the Russian Robber Songs) (Voronezh, 1875).

Shambinago, S. K., *Pesni vremeni tsaria Ivana Groznogo* (Songs of the Time of Tsar Ivan the Terrible) (Moscow, 1914).

Miller, V. F., "Kazatskie epicheskie pesni XVI-XVII vv." (Cossack Epic Songs of the Sixteenth and Seventeenth Centuries), ZHMNP (Journal of the Ministry of Public Education), Nos. 5 and 6, 1914, reprinted in Vol. III of *Ocherki russkoi narodnoi slovesnosti* (Outlines of Russian Popular Literature) (Moscow-Leningrad, 1924).

Sokolov, B. M., "Shurin Groznogo, udaloi boets Kostriuk Temnukovich" (The Brother-in-Law of the Terrible, the Daring Warrior Kostruk Temrukovich), *Journal of the Ministry of Public Education*, No. 7, 1913.

Alborov, V. A., "Pesni o Mikhaile Vasil'eviche Skopine-Shuiskom" (Songs About Michael Vasilyevich Skopin-Shuysky), *Izvestiia kavkazskogo pedagogicheskogo instituta* (Annals of the Pedagogical Institute of the Caucasus), 11, Vladikavkaz, 1924.

Rzhiga, V. F., "Povest' i pesni o Mikhaile Vasil'eviche Skopine-Shuiskom" (Narrative and Songs About Michael Skopin-Shuysky), *Annals of the Division of Russian Language and Literature of the Academy of Sciences*, Vol. I, Bk. 1, 1928.

Iakovlev, M. A., *Narodnoe pesnetvorchestvo ob atamane Stepane Razine* (The Creation of Popular Songs About Commander Stepan Razin) (Leningrad, 1924).

The two previously mentioned books by A. N. Lozanova.

Piksanov, N. K., "Sotsial'no-politicheskie syd'by pesen o Stepane Razine" (The Social-Political Destinies of the Songs about Stepan Razin), *Khudozhestvennyi fol'klor* (Artistic Folklore), No. 1, 1926.

Lozanova A. N., "Sotsial'noe pereosmyslenie pesen o gr. Z. G. Chernysheve" (The Social Interpretations of the Songs About Count Zachary Gregoryevich Chernyshov), *Sovetskii fol'klor*, (Soviet Folklore), Nos. 2-3, Leningrad, 1936.

Onchukov, N. E., "Pesni o dekabristakh" (Songs of the Decembrists), in the collection *Links*, No. VI, Moscow, 1935.

RELIGIOUS VERSES

Religious verses are epic, lyrico-epic, or purely lyric songs having a religious content. Religious verses were generally sung by blind beggars—the "itinerant beggars." However, in the living speech of daily life, those of the religious verses which were of an epic cast (for example, those about the Profound Book, about Egor the Brave, about Fyodor Tiron, about Anik the Warrior, and others) were not separated from the *byliny*; they went under the general designation of "ancient songs," and were not always the exclusive property of the professional beggar singers. In ancient times the carriers and, probably, the composers of many of the religious verses were the "beggars"—pilgrims, travelers to the "holy places." Pilgrimages to Jerusalem, Constantinople (Tsargrad), and other "holy places," in the Russian Middle Ages, took on at times a spontaneous mass character, so that the ecclesiastical and secular authorities were compelled to take a number of prohibitory measures against them.

It was not only people of the lower classes who became pilgrims. On the contrary, the leaders of the mendicant troops were generally representatives of the higher, ruling classes, both lay and clerical. Such were, for instance, almost all the famous Russian pilgrims, who have left their manuscript notes of their journeyings, the so-called "progresses"; as the Abbot Daniel (circa 1118), Dobrynya Yadreykovich (circa 1200); the future Archbishop of Novgorod, Antonius; Gregory the Lame (1321–1323); another future Archbishop of Novgorod, the monk Stefan of Novgorod (1350), who in his origin was undoubtedly a rich Novgorod boyar, and others. Such pilgrims traveled with their own vast retinue, had considerable means to pay for offices for the dead and services of prayer, and employed, for pay, the services of a "leader," a guide.

One of the *byliny* which has come down to us, a religious verse "About the Forty Beggars and One," gives an excellent description of the ancient mode of life of the beggars—it clearly depicts the organization of the pilgrims' retinue, "the beggars' circle," describes in detail the beggars' dress, refers to the existence of their own special beggars' court for transgressors, speaks of the vows of the beggars, and reflects in detail the ideas and mode of life of the beggar troop. This *bylina*, as well as a series of others, which speak of the beggars or "old pilgrims," represents the beggars as singing religious, particularly Byzantine-Greek, songs or verses. In their historical development the religious verses later became the property mainly of the professional beggar singers, most of whom were blind, and the very word "*kalika*" (from the name of the pilgrims' shoes—*caligae*) was understood as referring to a new group of singers—the "mendicant beggars."

In the Ukraine the singers of religious verses assumed, under the influence of the Magdeburg Law, the form of "guilds" of artel * associations. Such associations—"flocks" of beggar singers—had, even at the end of the nineteenth century, their own regulations, worked out in detail; they possessed a common treasury, they had chosen persons to govern them, their craft was hereditary, they had special rules and a ritual for the reception of new members. They had teachers—"master craftsmen" and their students—they had special forms for teaching and giving examinations, they had a division among the singers on the basis of territorial regions, and so on. The Ukrainian and White Russian singers usually sang their religious verses to the accompaniment of the lyre, and sometimes of the bandore; since among the (Great) Russian singers of religious verses the use of a musical accompaniment was rare, the information we have about the presence of such factors is all the more interesting. But, aside from the professional beggar singers, among the Russian populace the religious verses entered into the usual repertory of the peasantry, chiefly the old men and women, particularly into the repertory of the narrators of the *byliny*. The religious verses were widely used among the Old Believers and the dissenters.

So far as geographical distribution is concerned, the religious verses were not all of one and the same provenience. There are religious verses which were equally well known, among the Russian, the Ukrainian, and the White Russian population. But even the purely Russian religious verses were unevenly diffused: some were known only in the

* Artel: a cooperative craft society.—Ed.

Russian North, others only in the central Russian regions, and a third group only in the southern part of the Russian population. There are religious verses which were written down only in the Ukraine or only in White Russia.

With regard to their form and style, the religious verses are divided into two basic groups—*epic* religious verses, and *lyric* religious verses. At a point midway between them are the lyrico-epic religious verses, approximating more closely in character to the latter group. This division as to form constitutes at the same time, to a great extent, a chronological classification. The epic religious verses, the greater part of them, are more ancient in point of time, while the lyric religious verses are newer (mostly of the seventeenth and eighteenth centuries) and are subject to the influence of specific factors in the Russian literary life of that late period. In general, however, for all the diverse kinds of religious verses, there is apparent an undoubted dependence on literary sources.

In this genre of Russian folklore, more than in any other, is revealed the influence of literature upon oral creative art. This is also readily understandable, if we take into account the religious and ecclesiastical character of almost the whole of medieval Russian literature and culture. For almost all the religious verses there has been established, if not a direct, then in any case a related literary source. But at the same time there is hardly a single example of religious verse which would seem to have slavishly followed this literary source. This bears testimony to the fact that the religious verse is indisputably a product of poetic creative power, which not only clothed a borrowed theme or subject in an original poetic form, but often made very substantial transformations, both poetically and ideationally, in its original.

One of the most ancient epic religious verses is the famous poem about the Profound Book, which contained the questions of King Volotoman Volotomanovich and the answers of King David, the son of Jesse, read off by him from an enormous ("forty sazhens in length, twenty sazhens in width") "deep" (that is, depths of wisdom) book. The questions and answers deal with the origin of the world and its phenomena, and of the chief objects on earth (as to which object is the "father" or "mother" of all things), of living creatures and holy relics. The sources of the medieval wisdom expressed in this religious verse were the apocryphal works: "The Colloquy of the Three Holy Men"; "Of How Many Parts Was Adam Created?"; "Questions of St. John the Divine upon Mount Tabor." Social concepts were expressed with a good deal of clearness, even in the answers to the questions about the creation of the various social strata: "The Tsars and Tsarinas were engendered from the honored head of Adam; the princes and the boyars were engendered from the honored remains of Adam; the Orthodox peasants were produced from Adam's knees." The end of the poem sets forth in symbolic forms the struggle between Truth and Falsehood, and the victory of the latter: "Now Falsehood has put Truth to rout, and Truth has passed into the heights of heaven, but Falsehood has remained on the damp earth— she has entered into our eager hearts."

The mention, in several variants of the religious verses, of the victory of Falsehood over Truth ("This shall be for the latter time, it shall be for the eighth thousand years") enables us to see the reflection in religious verses of the pessimistic attitudes which were characteristic of the period around the year 1492, when there came to an end the apocalyptic seven thousand years from the creation of the world, and when there was widely diffused the superstitious expectation of a "terrible judgment." Here is reflected also the social-political conflict, which was especially aggravated in the region of Pskov and Novgorod in the period of the overthrow of the independence of Novgorod and Pskov. A number of other data in the poem itself argue in favor of the composition of the poem in that precise region.

Great popularity was enjoyed by the epic religious poem about Egor the Brave. Two subjects are known concerning this "holy warrior," who in the reworking of the religious poem acquired a good many of the general features of the figures of the knights of the *byliny*. One so-called "great" poem about Egor speaks of his tortures by the evil tsar Deklianische (the emperor Diocletian), about Egor's miraculous escape from a deep cellar, and of his journey throughout "holy ancient Russia" with the book of the Gospel in his hands, with the purpose of organizing Old Russia and confirming her in the "holy faith." If the subject of the torture of Egor arises entirely from the apocryphal writings on this theme, then the whole second part of the poem, about the exploits of Egor in Old Russia, can be explained as a song *bylina*, which at one time had existed in an independent form, about the propagation of the Orthodox faith in Old Russia in the eleventh century by the Grand Prince George—Yaroslav (the Wise), son of Vladimir. The second poem—the "small" one—about the rescue, by Egor the Brave, of a maiden from a snake, originates in a literary legend "about the miracle which George wrought upon the snake," which made use of the ancient myth about the struggle with a snake.

From this same type of legend about the struggle with the snake, there is derived also the popular religious poem, which acquired a purely *bylina* form, about Fyodor Tiron, who rescued his mother from a snake; the source of this poem, also, was an apocryphal legend of St. Fyodor Tiron. A religious poem about the warrior Demetrius of Thessalonica, which was connected with a corresponding literary legend about him, took on a purely Russian historical and social adaptation—Demetrius of Thessalonica does not defeat the tsar Koloyan (as in the literary legend), but the Tartar tsar Mamay, and he delivers two Russian women from captivity. As the subject of the poem about Anika the Warrior, there serves the fight which Anika the Warrior had with death, the source of which was the "Contest of Life with Death," which has passed over to us from the West, in a form which is not earlier than the sixteenth century. The very name "Anika" is to be explained from the Byzantine legends and songs about the Greek epic hero Digenis Akritas, the Invincible; the epithet "invincible" was understood as a proper name. Of the other epic religious poems we may mention the religious poem about Nikolay the Miracle Worker, and his saving of Basil, the son of Agrik (the source being the "Miracles" of Nikolay). These old epic religious poems, in their thematics as well as in their plot and in their dominating figures, are closely connected with the heroic *byliny* of the warriors.

Quite different is another series of verses. There was a very widely diffused religious poem about "Alexis, the Man of God," composed in the seventeenth century, based on the "Life" of this saint. The patronage of Tsar Alexis Mikhailovich, which he showed to his "sovereign beggars" who lived at the palace (in contrast to his cruel persecution of the buffoons), possibly gave a special impetus to the praise of the "holy" royal patron. To speak more definitely, in real life and in the poem, Alexis, in the character of an unknown beggar, lived, through the kindness of his father the tsar, in the latter's house. This poem, by its ideology, obviously reflects the psychology of the "fraternity of beggars." Only through an analysis of this psychology is it possible to come to a full knowledge, also, of the meaning of two other religious poems which were very popular among the beggar singers, "On Lazarus," and on "The Ascension of Our Lord." "To sing the 'Lazarus'" became a synonym for the beggars' singing of religious verses, and for their soliciting alms.

The religious poem "On Lazarus" was based on the corresponding parable in the Gospels; however, the religious poem supplemented it with the motifs of a happy and an unhappy death (compare on this theme the religious poem "On the Parting of the Soul with the Body"), and complicated the dramatic effect of the parable by making the rich man and the poor man blood brothers. In the religious poems, among other things, there is reference to the medieval concepts that the means of the salvation of the soul are to be found in the giving of alms, in bequests to monasteries for the commemoration of the soul: "I have the wherewithal, being a rich man, to enter into Paradise; I have the wherewithal, being a rich man, to save my soul: a rich man has many estates and possessions, much bread and salt, much gold and silver"; the poor man, on the contrary, "has no means of entering into Paradise, no means, in his poverty, of saving his soul."

The religious poem "On the Ascension of Christ" relates how Christ, before His Ascension, wanted to leave to the fraternity of beggars a golden mountain, but St. John the Divine opposed this, because, he said, the rich men and the boyar princes would get possession of this wealth, and would not let the beggars have access to it: "The princes and the boyars will find out the mountain, the pastors and the authorities will find out the mountain, the traveling merchants will find out the mountain; they will take away from them the golden mountain, they will divide the mountain among themselves, they will apportion the mountain among the princes, and will not let the fraternity of beggars have access to it." St. John Chrysostom advises Christ to give the beggars, in place of the golden mountain, his own name of Christ, whereby they will collect alms. For this, Christ gives St. John the "golden mouth." V. F. Rzhiga [1] dates the composition of this religious poem to the sixteenth century, in connection with the ideational and social conflict centering around the question of the monastery properties as the possession of the beggars, when "there were present all the real historical data for the motifs of the golden mountain, which was intended for the beggars, which became the object of a general conflict, and which the beggars did not obtain."

A special category is made up of the numerous religious verses of a lyrico-epic character on the themes: "Of the Last Judgment," "The Sinful Soul," "On the Parting of Soul and Body," "On the Kind or Hallelujah-Singing Wife," and so on. Some of them are very old: for example, there are the religious poems about the "repentance for the earth," which the researchers, quite justifiably, have connected with the well known heresy of the "Strigolniki," [*] in the fourteenth century; there is the religious poem "The Lament of Adam," fixed in one manuscript as early as the fifteenth century, with the characteristic note, "The poem is an ancient drinking song."

But the golden age of lyrico-epic, and especially of lyric, religious verses falls in the seventeenth and later centuries, in connection with the spread of the Old Believers and of sectarianism. In their form these religious verses resemble the doggerel rhymes which were diffused among us under the influence of southwestern literature, and bear the characteristic designations of "psalms" and "canticles." These religious verses, along with the oral tradition, were widely diffused as early as the seventeenth century, both in manuscript notebooks and even in whole collections.

[1] V. F. Rzhiga, "A Poem About the Fraternity of Beggars," *Annals of the Division of Russian Language and Literature of the Academy of Sciences of the USSR*, Vol. XXXI, Leningrad, 1926, pp. 177-188.

[*] "The shorn," i.e., "short-haired": a sect "who believed that priests were unnecessary, that laymen might preach, and that prayers for the dead were of no avail" (Pares).—ED.

A great number of the *Old Believers' verses* (of various sects, particularly the "Netovtsy," "Stranniki," "Morelschiki," and others) deal with the coming of Antichrist and the end of the world, with the temptations of the world, with flight into the "desert" for salvation; they praise a desert abode and the beneficent meaning of death; they summon people to it (particularly in certain sects, in connection with the custom of burning one's self to death). A special group of the Old Believers' religious verses is made up of poems with a historical content, taken from the life of the Old Believers and their sects: on the siege of the Solovetsky monastery, on the destruction of the hermitages, on the persecution of the Old Believers, on specific "teachers" among the Old Believers (for example, on Andrey Denisov, and others), on the ideas which served as the object of dissension among the separate sects (for example, the question of marriage and celibacy). The whole cycle of the Old Believers' religious poems has a satirical, accusing character: the accusation of the deficiencies of life, of customs, of the social order, and all kinds of "innovations" by the ruling Church, and also accusations of the deficiencies of the Old Believers' everyday life. Finally, there are the numerous religious verses on religious-historic and moralizing themes: on the judgment, on prayer, on the world beyond the grave, and so on.

A great store of religious songs, verses, "chants," was possessed by the Russian mystical sects (the "Flagellants," the "God's People," the "New Israel," the "Eunuchs," and others). Many of these verses were improvised, and therefore the variants of the sectarian verses are often sharply distinguished from one another in content and in form. Many of these songs speak of the various representatives of sectarianism (the "Christs," "Mothers of God," "archangels," "prophets," "saints," and other ranks of the sectarian hierarchy; of their fates, persecutions, imprisonments, "meetings," prayerful appeals of sectarians to their own sectarian "fathers" and "mothers," and so on).

Many of the verses are devoted to allegorical representations of the sectarian Church in the form of a garden with cypress trees, with rivers and mountains located in it, with birds that inhabit it: in the form of a ship sailing over the sea of life, and so on. Other sectarian verses are devoted to general religious and moral themes, particularly to the mortification of the flesh, the relations between sectarians and the nonsectarian world, the appeal for patience, and so on. A historical and psychological interest centers in the sectarian songs, together with the cult, ceremonies, and vigils (the longing for the vigil and the summons to it, the specific prayers, the representation of the vigil, and so on). The researches as to the exhilarating effect of the sectarian religious verses on those who take part in the vigil (compare the sectarian expression, "A song is a ladder up to God") are also interesting.

At the present time, under the influence of antireligious propaganda, owing to the general cultural development and the progress of the Soviet organization, the soil for the existence of religious verses is being destroyed, and they are gradually disappearing.

BIBLIOGRAPHY

COLLECTIONS

Bessonov, P., *Kaliky-perekhozhie* (Vagrant Beggars), a collection of verses, Nos. 1-6, 1861–1864.

Varentsov, V., *Sbornik russkikh dukhovnykh stikhov* (Collection of Russian Religious Verses) (Petrograd, 1860).

Liatskii, E., *Stikhy dukhovnye* (Religious Verses) (Petrograd, 1912).

Rozhdestvenskii, T. S., "Pamiatniki staroobriadcheskoi poezii" (Monuments of the Poetry of the Old Believers), *Zapiski Mosk. arkheol. instituta* (Reports of the Moscow Archaeological Institute), Vol. VI, Moscow, 1910.

Rozhdestvenskii, T., and M. Uspenskii, *Pesni russkikh sektantovmistikov* (Songs of the Russian Sectarians and Mystics) (Petrograd, 1912).

Bonch-Bruevich, V. D., *Materialy k istorii i izucheniiu russkogo sektantstva i raskola* (Materials for the History and Study of Russian Sectarianism and Schisms), Nos. III-IV, No. VII, Petrograd, 1909–1916.

RESEARCHES

For a bibliographical review of the researches, see the book by V. P. Adrianova, *Zhitie Alekseia, cheloveka bozhiia, v drevnerusskoi literature i naradnoi slovesnosti* (The Life of Alexis, Man of God, in Ancient Russian Literature and Popular Productions) (Petrograd, 1917).

Kirpichnikov, A. I., "Dukhovnye stikhi" (Religious Verses) in

Galakhov's *Istoriia russkoi slovesnosti* (History of Russian Literature) (Moscow, 1894).

Speranskii, M. N., *Russkaia ustnaia slovesnost'* (Russian Oral Literature) (Moscow, 1917).

Veselovskii, A., "Kaliki perekhozhie i bogumil'skie stranniki" (Wandering Beggars and Bogumily Pilgrims), *Vestnik Evropy* (The News of Europe), 1872, IV, pp. 682-722.

—— *Razyskaniia v oblasti russkikh dukhovnykh stikhov* (Researches in the Field of Russian Religious Verses) (St. Petersburg, 1879–1891).

Maksimov, S. V., *Brodiachaia Rus' Khrista padi* (Ancient Russia a Wanderer for the Sake of Christ) (Petrograd, 1877), or in the *Sobr. soch.* (Collected Works), Vol. V, Pt. I.

Speranskii, M. N., "Iuzhnorusskaia pesnia i ёё sovremennye nositeli" (The South Russian Song and Its Contemporary Carriers), *Sborn. Ist. fil. obshoh. pri Institute Bezborodko v Nezhine* (Annals of the Historical and Philological Society at the Bezborodko Institute in Nezhin), Vol. V, Kiev, 1904.

—— "Dukhovnye stikhi iz Kurskoi gub." (Religious Verses from the Province of Kura), *Etnograficheskoe Obozrenie* (Ethnographic Review), Bk. L, 1901, No. 3.

TALES

❦

By the folk *tale*, in the broad sense of the word, we understand an oral poetic narrative of a fantastic, adventurous, storylike character based on folkways. We derive this definition from observations of the development of the tale on the lips of the people. These narrative "tales" include, as we shall see, a whole series of genres and forms, each one of which must be studied separately.

The ancient designation for the tales was the word *basen'*, from the verb *bayat'* to speak, and so the storytellers in ancient Russia were called *bakhari*, and, it may be, *bayany*. The designation "tale," in the contemporary meaning of the word, is encountered from the seventeenth century on.

In spite of the fact that the existence of tales in ancient Russia is a fact beyond dispute, the actual *records of the tales* are very late in appearing. This is to be explained by the general ecclesiastical trend of the ancient Russian literature, which had been the property of the ruling classes, who in every way resisted the appearance of a book of secular productions, and especially of oral literature. But the very accusations of the stern preachers against the "fables of the demons" speak of the presence of the latter in the life of the people. As early as the precepts of the twelfth century it is forbidden "to tell fables." Serapion Vladimirsky (thirteenth century) implores his congregation not to listen to "the fables of men," but to turn to "the divine Scriptures." This attitude of the ecclesiastics continued until the very end of the long-continuing Russian Middle Ages. When, under the influence of the Church, Tsar Alexis Mikhailovich instituted a massacre of the buffoons, and in general began a persecution against secular art and poetry, his "disfavor" did not spare even the tales. In the famous royal rescript to the governors, of the year 1649, it is said that "many men senselessly believe in dreams, in encounters, and in the evil eye, and in the calling of birds, and they propound riddles and tell tales of things unheard-of, and by idle talk and merrymaking, in blasphemy they destroy their souls with such benighted

[381]

deeds." For all this the "most serene" tsar commands the governors to impose the severest penalties.

However, in spite of all this, the art of storytelling, widely diffused throughout ancient Rus, in one form or another, managed to surmount all kinds of obstacles, and to penetrate into literature. In the chronicles, in various legends, in the narratives, in the biographies, one may find a great many echoes and reworkings of oral narrative material. It will be sufficient if we merely refer to the well known *Life of Peter and Fevronia of Murom* (sixteenth century), which makes use of the storytelling motif of the "wise maiden"—the diviner and counselor.

In the sixteenth and seventeenth centuries, in manuscripts, there begin to be widely diffused, under the form of narratives, Eastern and Western tales, which had come into Old Rus partly by the oral, partly by the written route.[1] Such are the well known narrative tales of Eruslan Lazarevich [2] (a tale coming from the East, reflecting the well known theme of Rustem and Zorab, which goes back to the poem by Firdusi, *Shahnama*), of Bova the Prince (a medieval Italian romance, coming in through White Russia in the sixteenth century),[3] the narrative of the Judgment of Shemyaka [4] (of Eastern origin, received through oral transmission), the narrative of the seventeenth century about Karp Sutulov [5] (probably of Eastern origin and also coming through oral tradition), and others.

All these tales were highly Russified, and even in their written form they took on the appearance of the purely Russian oral storytelling style. But even so, these are not records of oral tales in the full sense

[1] See Acad. A. S. Orlov, *Translated Narratives of Feudal Russia and of the Kingdom of Moscow, from the Twelfth to the Seventeenth Centuries* (Leningrad, 1934). A historiographic and bibliographic survey is given in the book by Prof. N. K. Piksanov, *The Old Russian Narrative* (Moscow-Leningrad, 1923).

[2] See Piksanov, *op. cit.*, pp. 59-60.

[3] See A. N. Veselovsky, *From the History of the Romance and the Narrative*, No. II (St. Petersburg, 1888).

A new investigation, including all the oral variants of the narrative of Bova the Prince, written by V. D. Kuzmina, is being prepared for publication.

[4] F. I. Buslayev, "Wanderers' Narratives," *My Leisure Moments*, Vol. II (St. Petersburg, 1874).

[5] Y. M. Sokolov, *The Narrative of Karp Sutulov: Text and Researches in the Field of the Subject* (Moscow, 1914).

of the word. The first records of oral Russian tales, just as in the case of the first Russian epic songs, belong to an inquiring foreigner. The Englishman Collins, who traveled in the Russia of Tsar Alexis Mikhailovich [1629–76], wrote down ten tales, two of which were connected with the name of Ivan the Terrible. One of the tales relates how a certain commoner made the tsar a present of a pair of bast shoes and a big turnip, and how the tsar ordered all the boyars to buy bast shoes from the peasant; while to the envious boyar, who had decided to make the tsar a present of a horse, the tsar gave the peasant's turnip. Another tale, also opposed to the boyars in its attitude, tells of the encounter of Ivan the Terrible with a clever thief, who refused to rob the royal treasury but expressed his readiness to rob an eminent boyar.[6]

The eighteenth century, with the mannered pseudoclassical literature of its upper classes, was not a favorable period for the introduction of the oral tale; but educated persons among the urban artisan class and the peasantry were very fond of reading, and diligently copied productions of a storytelling character. These were mainly the tales which have already been mentioned above, of Eruslan, Bova the Prince, of the Tsarevich Peter of the Golden Keys, and others; that is, they were mainly tales and narratives which had originated in other countries. They were disseminated also in cheap popular editions. Other Russian tales, however, were seldom encountered in the manuscripts of the eighteenth century.

In the middle of the eighteenth century, mainly in the 1760's, the storytelling genre, as it were, began to flourish. Under the influence of the wide popularity in western Europe of the knightly romance of adventure, and of the "fairy tale" (like the well known French collection of Perrault (1697),[7] and the vast collections of the end of the eighteenth century—*Cabinet des fées, La Bibliothèque bleue,* and others), Russian writers began to compile similar collections of

[6] On these subjects, see the interesting article of A. N. Veselovsky, "Tales of Ivan the Terrible," *Old and New Russia,* Bk. 4, 1876; recently reprinted in Vol. XVI of the *Collected Works of A. N. Veselovsky* (Leningrad, 1938).

[7] See Charles Perrault, *Tales,* transl. and ed. M. Petrovsky, introductory article and commentaries by N. P. Andreyev (Moscow-Leningrad, Academia, 1936).

"knightly" tales of gallantry, in which were preserved from the Russian tales and *byliny* only the names and certain details; but the popular storytelling style had faded away, and frequently the subject of the tale had been altogether changed. Such are the collections of M. D. Chulkov, *The Scoffer, or, Slovenian Tales* four parts (Moscow, 1766–1768); and of V. Levshin, *Russian Tales, Comprising the Most Ancient Narratives of the Renowned Knights, Popular Tales, and Other Adventures, Which Through Retelling Have Remained in the Memory*, in ten parts (Moscow, 1780–1783).[8] In the eighteenth century there were a great many of these collections of pseudotales.[9] However, there were hardly any genuine Russian tales in them. This was due not only to the compilers of the collection, but also to the literary tastes of the readers of that time.

Characteristic, for example, is the following fact. Into the colleclection *Russian Tales*, Levshin introduced three really genuine popular tales; but at once this inclusion of authentic popular tales called for a sharp protest from his contemporary critics:

Of the new tales which have been added by the editor, certain ones, such as that of the thief Timokha, of the gypsy, and others, might with great benefit to this book have been left for the most common taverns and public houses, for the most thoughtless peasant could without difficulty invent dozens of others like them, and if all of these were to be put into print, it would be a sorry day for the paper, the pens, the ink, and the typesetting, to say nothing of the labor of the esteemed authors.[10]

In spite of the extremely conventional nature of the storytelling material given in the numerous collections of the end of the eighteenth and beginning of the nineteenth century, still, for the investigator of the Russian folk tale, they are all valuable in that they are pervaded, in greater or lesser degree, with the records of genuine tales, as for example in the collection, *Russian Tales*, compiled and edited by P. Timofeyev (Moscow, 1787). Moreover, they accustomed people

[8] See V. Shklovsky, *Chulkov and Levshin* (Moscow, 1933).
[9] A detailed survey of them is given in the important work of V. V. Sipovsky, *Surveys of the History of the Russian Romance*, Vol. I (eighteenth century) (St. Petersburg, 1909–1910).
[10] *Ibid.*, p. 236.

to treat the Russian folk tale with tolerance, who, swayed by the conventional tastes of classicism, would otherwise have turned away from it with contempt. The collections had this effect, because, in the magical romances, the reader very often met with the same story-telling motifs, which were already known to him from oral tradition, and, naturally, this imperceptibly linked the folk tale, in his eyes, with formal literary productions, and brought the former close to the level of the latter.[11]

The awakening of a living interest in the popular tale manifests itself at the end of the first decade, and especially during the third decade, of the nineteenth century, in connection with the establishment of romantic moods and ideas in the fields of literature, philosophy, and history; with the cultivation of "nationalism," and with the growth of interest in the remote past.

As is well known, the writers Zhukovsky, Pushkin, and Gogol not only concerned themselves with the literary reworking of the tales, but were themselves among the first collectors. Soon persons made their appearance who devoted themselves intensively to the collection of tales. Such was the well known collector of folklore, V. I. Dal, who wrote down as many as a thousand tales.

In 1838 there appeared the first attempt (within a very small compass, it is true) at a collection of genuine folk tales, the *Russian Folk Tales* of Bogdan Bronitsyn. In the collection were published five tales, which had been taken down, as it is said in the preface, "from the words of an itinerant storyteller, a peasant from the region of Moscow, to whom they had been related by an old man, his father: in them the form of the story is noteworthy, presenting generally a series of verses all having the same meter." Later on these tales were reprinted by Afanasyev. In 1841 the collection, *Russian Folk Tales*, by I. P. Sakharov appeared. But a very close examination, by recent critics, of the make-up of this "compiler's" collection, as well as of his various other collections on folklore, leads to the regrettable conclusion that Sakharov was frequently a falsifier of folklore; he published texts which were not genuine, and reworked in a sickly-sweet national-

[11] S. V. Savchenko, *The Russian Folk Tale: History of Its Collection and Study* (Kiev, 1914), p. 89.

istic style various materials which had been well known prior to his time, for example, the *byliny* from the collection of Kirsha Danilov, the cheaply printed popular tales, the tales from Chulkov's collection and others.

The first important collection of folk tales (still unsurpassed, so far as quantity is concerned) is the famous collection, *Russian Folk Tales*, by A. N. Afanasyev, which appeared in eight issues in the years 1855–1866, and which included as many as 640 specimens of tales. The tales which were actually taken down by Afanasyev do not number more than ten; the whole vast amount of material which entered into his collection was compiled from the records of other persons who had preceded him, from Dal and Yakushkin, from the numerous records accumulated in the archives of the Geographical Society, which was founded in 1848, and from other sources.

Afanasyev's adherence to the "mythological school" is reflected in his collection of tales, not only in the extensive commentaries, in the spirit of the mythological school, which are appended to every tale (where the vast comparative material is presented, primarily from the collections of the Brothers Grimm and from tales of the Slavonic and other Indo-European peoples), but also in Afanasyev's very attitude toward the tales which he was editing, and in the arrangement of the narrative material itself.

Searching in the tales, as all the romanticist-mythologists did, primarily for the deep foundations of ancestral times, Afanasyev attached no value whatever to the information concerning the vicissitudes of the tales in his own time, or to the storytellers from whom the tales had been written down, as a reflection of the real-life relationships in the tale. Afanasyev saw nothing blameworthy in the stylistic revision of a tale, in the working-up of its style, and in the composition of collated texts from several variants; [12] furthermore, he did not always indicate the place where the tales had been written down. This, how-

---

[12] Such a method of editing the tales had been to a very great degree influenced by A. N. Pypin. See, on this point, the article of Y. M. Sokolov, "Life and Activities of A. N. Afanasyev," in Vol. I of the latest edition of the *Popular Russian Tales* of A. N. Afanasyev (Moscow, 1936).

ever, sometimes was not his fault, since in this respect the sources for his collection were frequently faulty; such was the condition of the science of folkloristics at that time. Despite all this, Afanasyev's collection is very important, even now, for the science of collecting Russian tales. It served as the source of numerous scientific researches by Russian and foreign folklorists.

Many of the tales in the collection have been translated into various foreign languages, and the entire work has been translated into the German. In the Russian language the collection has gone through five editions. Beginning with the third edition in 1897, the collection was provided with detailed indexes, and a biography of the investigator and collector of Russian folklore, prepared by A. E. Gruzinsky. The fifth edition (in three volumes) is appearing under the editorship of M. K. Azadovsky, N. P. Andreyev, and Y. M. Sokolov. Vol. I (1936) and Vol. II (1938) have already appeared; Vol. III is in process of publication. Afanasyev was not alone in the collection and publication of tales. In the 1860's, in the period of heightened interest in the life and social customs of the peasantry, there appeared the collections of tales by I. A. Khudyakov, *Great-Russian Tales*, in three sections (Moscow, 1860–1862, 125 numbers); in 1863 there appeared *Folk Tales, Collected by Rural Teachers*, edited by A. A. Erlenwein (41 numbers); these tales had been written down in the province of Tula. After this collection came the *Russian Folk Tales, Facetious Sayings, and Tales*, of E. A. Chudinsky (Moscow, 1864, fifty-four numbers in all); the tales had been written down mainly in the central Russian provinces. Passing over a number of excellent but minor collections (by Efimenko, Kolosov, Ivanitsky —all from the northern provinces), we may mention the remarkable collection of D. N. Sadovnikov, *Tales and Legends of the Samara Region* (St. Petersburg, 1884), containing 183 tales. It is a matter of very great regret that Sadovnikov's death prevented him from supplying the work with indices, and particularly with information about the storytellers from whom he had derived his records of the tales. Following Sadovnikov's collection there was a considerable interval—almost twenty-five years—in which no major work appeared.

The real rise and, it may be said, the flourishing of the collection and study of the Russian tale fall within the last decades of the twentieth century, and especially within our contemporary Soviet era. At the same time this period is the time of the application of a strictly scientific method to the collection of folklore. The collectors struggle against any kind of manifestation of subjectivity in the selection of the material which has been written down, or in the recording itself. The effort toward collecting, and toward exactness and fullness, along with the application of the principle of examination of each separate region, become their binding slogan.[13]

The collectors, in the majority of cases, are at the same time scientific investigators. In writing down the texts of the tales, they strive to maintain absolute accuracy, preserving all the peculiarities of dialect and all the trifling details of the personal style of the storyteller. They attentively study and describe the real conditions of the existence of the tales, they intently study every storyteller, they compile his biography, they give his characteristics; the collector strives to exhaust the repertory of every storyteller, to study the sources from which he has drawn the records of his tales. They study the surroundings, the setting, the conditions of cultural-economic and everyday life.[14] The collections of tales themselves are accompanied by various indexes, lists of themes, glossaries, and so on.

The first collection of this type was the extensive work of N. E. Onchukov, which came out in 1909, *Northern Tales*, comprising 303 tales from the provinces of Olonets and Archangel (the seacoast and the Pechora). But not all the tales were recorded by Onchukov himself. A valuable inclusion in his collection were the records, ideal in their exactness, of Olonets tales, by the famous linguist and Academician, A. A. Shakhmatov (seventy-one numbers); part of the records belong to the well known author, M. M. Prishvin. Onchukov's contributions consisted in the collection and communication of information about the storytellers whom he had met. It was an exceedingly happy thought of his to arrange the story material, not by

---

13 See B. and Y. Sokolov, *Poetry of the Countryside* (Moscow, 1926), Chap. III.
14 Here are undoubtedly reflected the scientific traditions established by the views of N. A. Dobrolyubov, who, as we have said in the historiographic survey, exerted a great influence upon succeeding generations of collectors of folklore.

subjects, but according to storytellers, with the addition of their biographies and characterizations, that is, to apply to the arrangement of the tales the same principle which, in his time, A. F. Hilferding had made use of in editing the *Onega Byliny*. All the succeeding editors of Russian tales began to follow this fruitful principle. Onchukov's collection was provided with a detailed article on the life of the tale in the North, and with observations on the storytellers.

In 1908–1909 the brothers B. and Y. Sokolov published records of the productions of folklore in the Belo-Ozero region (the Belo-Ozero and Kirillov districts, the former province of Novgorod). The larger part of the material of their collection, which appeared as a publication of the Academy of Sciences, *Tales and Songs of the Belo-Ozero Region* (Moscow, 1915), proved to consist of tales (163 numbers).

Contemporaneously with this collection, the Geographic Society published extensive collections of tales, made by the well known ethnographer, Professor D. K. Zelenin, *Great-Russian Tales from the Province of Perm* (St. Petersburg, 1914), and *Great-Russian Tales from the Province of Vyatka* (St. Petersburg, 1915). The first of these included 110 and the second, 139 tales. Zelenin's collections are furnished with interesting articles on the life of the tale in the given regions, and on the storytellers, and also with an account of the subjects, and with references to similar variants in other collections. These collections dealt exclusively with tales of the Russian population in the North of the European part of the Soviet Union. Even later, the collectors of tales continued to turn chiefly to the North. Thus, with great artistic taste, if with some stylization, O. E. Ozarovskaya, the well known performer of folk tales, collected Northern tales [15] during her frequent trips to the North from 1915 on. (Ozarovskaya died in 1936.) In the North also (in the years 1926–1929) tales were collected by the Leningrad folklorist and performer of tales I. V. Karnaukhova.[16] In 1935, in the Karelian White Sea region, A. N. Nechayev discovered the outstanding master of the

[15] *The Five Rivers* (Leningrad, 1931).
[16] *Tales and Legends of the Northern Region*, text, introductory article and commentaries by I. V. Karnaukhova, foreword by Y. M. Sokolov (Academia, 1934).

tale, M. M. Korguyev, from whom he succeeded in writing down 115 tales. Selected tales were published by A. N. Nechayev in the book *White Sea Tales, Related by M. M. Korguyev* (Leningrad, 1938).

In the central provinces of European Russia, in the period before the revolution, comparatively few tales had been collected. It is true that excellent records had been made in Orlov Province by I. F. Kalinnikov, and in Tambova Province by N. F. Poznansky. However, these records have not as yet been published. A multitude of facts testify to the great wealth of tale material not only in the North, but also in the central and South Russian provinces. Thus in 1925 the Leningrad folklorist and ethnographer, N. P. Grinkova, discovered the wonderful storyteller A. K. Baryshnikova (known by the name of Kupryanikha) in the Zemlyansky raíon of the province of Voronezh; but she has not been able to publish her records up to the present time, limiting herself to a characterization of Kupryanikha's creative work. (See the article, "Tales of Kúpryanikha," in the magazine *Artistic Folklore*, No. I, 1926.) Selected *Tales of Kupryanikha* (75 numbers) were newly written down by two young Voronezh folklorists, and published by the Voronezh Provincial Press in 1937, as a separate volume.[17] Tales from the province of Saratov have been published in new recordings.[18] A number of excellent tales from the province of Kuibyshev have been collected and published by V. M. Sidelnikov and V. U. Krupyanskaya.[19]

In this manner the gap keenly felt in the publication of tales from the central, southern, and Volga provinces began gradually to be filled. In Siberia a series of important and interesting collections of Russian tales was also published. This is the collection of tales printed in the *Reports of the Krasnoyarsk Subsection of the Eastern Siberian Division of the Russian Geographic Society*, No. I, 1901, and No. II, 1905, containing 155 tales. In the years immediately

[17] *Tales of Kupryanikha*, text of the tales, articles on the creative work of Kupryanikha, and commentaries, by A. M. Novikova and I. A. Ossovetsky; introductory article and general editing by Prof. I. P. Plotnikov (Voronezh, 1937).

[18] T. M. Akimov and P. D. Stepanov, *Tales of the Province of Saratov* (Saratov Provincial Press, 1937).

[19] *Volga Folklore*, comp. by V. M. Sidelnikov and V. U. Krupyanskaya, with foreword and ed. Prof. Y. M. Sokolov (Moscow, The Soviet Writer, 1937).

following the October Revolution, there had appeared two collections by the well known folklorist, Professor M. K. Azadovsky, *Tales of the Upper Lena Region,* No. I (Irkutsk, 1924, twenty-two tales),[20] and *Tales from Various Places in Siberia,* under the editorship of Azado`·sky (20 tales). Both of these collections have been compiled in accorc ance with all the rules of contemporary scientific collection and editing, and provide valuable information about the storytellers of Siberia and about their poetic creative work. In the past year (1937) there appeared, under the editorship of M. K. Azadovsky and N. P. Andreyev, the wonderful collection of *Tales of the Krasnoyarsk Region,* collected by M. V. Krasnozhenova from 1909 to 1932. The collections are supplied with introductory articles by the editors. It must be noted, also, that the publication of tales from the northern Urals has begun.[21]

However, the catalogue of the most extensive collections of tales during the past few decades is not limited to these printed publications. In the archives of the Geographic Society in Leningrad there lie, ready for publication, very extensive collections of unpublished tales; in addition to the above-mentioned collections by Kalinnikov and Poznansky, there are also the collections of Vologda tales by M. B. Edemsky, of Pskov tales by N. G. Kozirev, of tales from various parts of Russia by V. I. Chernyshev, and others. A great number of tales are preserved in the manuscripts of the archives of the Folklore Commission of the Institute of Ethnography of the Academy of Sciences in Leningrad, and in the archive of the Folklore Division of the State Literary Museum in Moscow (among others, a great collection of tales written down by E. V. Hofmann and E. I. Mintz, from the storyteller of the Gorkov province, I. F. Kovalev, and a collection of various productions of folklore, including the tales which were written down by the students of the Moscow Institute of Philological and Literary Research in the Belo-Ozero region in 1937 and 1938).

The extensive materials in the archives of the scientific societies

[20] There recently appeared a new edition of *Tales of the Upper Lena,* by M. K. Azadovsky (Irkutsk, 1938).

[21] *Prerevolutionary Folklore in the Urals,* coll. and comp. by V. P. Biryukov (Sverdlovsk, Sverdlovsk Provincial Press, 1936).

and academies preserve the most valuable of the unpublished tales. The publication of the tales in the archives of the Geographic Society, which were not made use of by Afanasyev in his time, and which have accumulated chiefly since his work appeared, made up the imposing two-volume collection by A. M. Smirnov, *Collection of Great-Russian Tales from the Archive of the Russian Geographic Society* (Petrograd, 1917), containing 367 specimens of tales from various parts of Russia. Unfortunately, this collection was published without the proper indexes and references, and the material could not be arranged according to storytellers.

Much of the unpublished story material lies in the various societies and museums of regional studies. There has not been brought together into one place the very vast store of material published in the various provincial and regional-study publications, annuals, memorial volumes, newspapers, proceedings, and collections. Nor has there been compiled, as yet, a full bibliography of Russian tales. Our science, especially during the last few decades, has uncovered vast amounts of story material, which are in need of summarizing.

The material to be found in the separate large printed collections of Russian tales includes more than three thousand items; and there is an equally great number of tales scattered through the various small publications; an amount of material almost as great, if not greater, is still lying in manuscripts which have not yet been published.[22]

And yet, under no circumstances, must one suggest that it is time to stop collecting tales. That is absolutely untrue. The study of tales, especially in their world-wide connotation, requires a considerably greater accumulation. Nor are we even speaking here of the fact that the increased stature of the science of folklore is constantly making greater and greater demands upon the collectors, and constantly setting new tasks before them.

[22] Here we are confining ourselves to the Russian tales alone, inasmuch as our whole course is devoted to Russian folklore. The Ukrainians and the White Russians possess a colossal amount of material in the field of the tales. A survey of the history of the collection of Russian, Ukrainian and White Russian tales, as well as a history of the study of them (up to 1914), is given in the work of S. V. Savchenko, *The Russian Folk Tale*.

The vast quantity of Russian tales, however, by no means indicates that there is an equal number of types or subjects of these tales. Their number, as we shall see, is many times less. The fact is that many of the tales which have been written down are only variants of one and the same story subject. As we have already said, and as we shall see farther on, for scholarship it is not of absolute importance to have a record of a new, unknown subject. For the folklorist, every individual variant is of importance: it is important in its concreteness, in its style, in its peculiarities; moreover, it is the reflection of the poetic creative work of each individual storyteller. The resemblance among the subjects of the tales, not only in Europe and Asia, but among almost all peoples over the whole surface of the earth, has led to the necessity of a classification of the tales according to genres and types, and to the compilation of surveys and indexes of story subjects and patterns. Among the earlier efforts along this line, we may refer to the work of the German scholar Hahn (*Griechische und Albanische Märchen*), which reduced a wealth of story material to forty patterns for tales.

The Russian scholar P. V. Vladimirov [23] has divided the tales into three basic groups, or genres—the animal epos, the myths, and the tales of everyday life, and within the limits of these groups he has enumerated forty-one types. However, neither Hahn nor Vladimirov was able to achieve a unity as to the principle of classification; they confused subjects with motifs and exalted certain incidental details of the tale into a generalized type. Nor was there much favor found among us by the later attempt of A. N. Smirnov toward a classification of the tales—*A Systematic Index of the Themes and Variants of the Russian Folk Tales*. His system, even apart from the fact that he applied it only to the animal tales, is distinguished by excessive complexity, and is little suited to rapid orientation. [24]

The Finnish folklorist Antti Aarne made a survey of the basic story

[23] P. V. Vladimirov, *Introduction to the History of Russian Literature* (Kiev, 1926), pp. 155 ff.

[24] A. M. Smirnov, "A Systematic Index of the Themes and Variants of the Russian Popular Tales," *Annals of the Division of Russian Language and Literature of the Academy of Sciences*, 1911, Vol. XVI; 1912, Vol. XVII, Bk. 4; 1914, Vol. XIX, Bk. 4.

types, which has won international recognition. In 1911, in the *Proceedings of the International Federation of Folklorists* (which had originated in 1907), issued in Finland, Aarne published, in German, an index of the types of tales.[25] Aarne, availing himself of the immense collections of Finnish tales, and of the most important European collections, including that of Afanasyev, gave a brief exposition of all the subjects known to him, that is, of the more or less well established narratives, composed of well defined basic episodes. Aarne divided the whole rich treasure of story subjects into three basic groups, typifying, from the viewpoint of subject, three main genres of tales: (1) animal tales; (2) tales, properly so called; and (3) anecdotes. The most complex in its make-up seems to be the second group—"tales, properly so-called"; it naturally was in need of a further classification. Aarne subdivided this group, again, into four divisions: (A) magical tales; (B) legendary tales; (C) romantic tales; (D) tales of the foolish devil.

The subjects of the tales, within the groups and divisions, are arranged according to special groups, or thematic families; the related subjects follow one after another; the thematic groups, for example, in the division "magical tales," are given by Aarne as follows: "The Miraculous Adversary," "The Miraculous Consort" (spouse), "The Miraculous Task," "The Miraculous Helper," "The Miraculous Object," "The Miraculous Strength or Skill."

In Aarne's index were included two thousand specimens of subjects of tales, but the actual number of subjects fixed by Aarne totaled not more than 540 in all. This is to be explained by the fact that Aarne, anticipating the opportunity (and his expectation was soon justified) of finding new subject types, left within every thematic family a whole series of blank numbers, so that he could insert under them the newly discovered subjects. In spite of the numerous deficiencies of Aarne's catalogue (the lack, at times, of a

---

[25] Antti Aarne, *Verzeichnis der Märchentypen* (Helsinki, 1911) FFC No. 3. A new and revised edition of Aarne's index has appeared recently in English: *The Types of the Folk Tale: A Classification and Bibliography*, Antti Aarne's *Verzeichnis der Märchentypen*, transl. and enlarged by S. Thompson (Helsinki, 1928), FFC No. 74.

clear formulation, the possibility of transferring certain subjects into other groups, and so on), it proved exceedingly convenient, and quickly passed into international scientific usage. According to Aarne's catalogue, he himself, and many of the folklorists of other lands, soon began to compile indexes of the tales of various nationalities: Finnish, Swedish, Estonian, Norwegian, Laplandic, Czech, and so on.

Stith Thompson, who has been mentioned previously, compiled a vast index (in six volumes) of the motifs which are encountered in the folklore of the world.[26]

In the interests of international scholarship, both for the inclusion of Russian materials in its sources, and also for the practical purposes of Russian folklorists, especially in connection with the vast accumulated wealth of recordings of tales already mentioned; and because of the necessity of orientation and of selecting subjects necessary to the investigator, with their variants, there arose the urgent task of putting into practice among Russian folklorists Aarne's system, which had become international.

This task was performed by the Leningrad professor N. P. Andreyev. He translated Aarne's catalogue and completed it, on the basis of a study of all the most important and recent collections of Russian tales, by adding those subjects which were lacking in Aarne's work. To facilitate its use, he made references under every subject to the texts which were known to him from the Russian collections which have been indicated, and he altered somewhat the actual formulation of the subjects of the tales. Aarne's sequence and numbering have been preserved, however.[27] The custom has only now come into use of accompanying every new recording of a tale by a reference to the corresponding number in the index of Aarne and Andreyev.

To facilitate an understanding of the principles which govern the

[26] Smith Thompson, *Motif Index of Folk-Literature: A Classification of Narrative Elements in Folk-Tales, Ballads, Myths, Fables, etc.* (Bloomington, Ill., 1932–1936), Vols. I-VI.

[27] N. P. Andreyev, *Index of Subjects of Tales According to the System of Aarne* (Leningrad, State Russian Geographic Society, 1929).

catalogue, and the method of their use, we present one or two examples of the exposition of a subject according to the Russian catalogue of Aarne and Andreyev.

No. 315. The Milk of Wild Beasts. A sister (mother), by the advice of a serpent (devil, and so on), pretends to be ill, and asks her brother to bring her the milk of a wild beast; she wishes to destroy her brother, but the caged beasts free themselves and save him. (The tale is assigned to the number of the "magic tales," to the family of "The Miraculous Adversary.")

No. 1525. The Clever Thief. A. A clever thief steals a bull, horse, casket, or ring from a gentleman, a sheet from the bed, a lady, a priest. (He dresses himself as an angel and promises to raise people in a sack up to heaven.)

D. (One of the variations.) The hero tricks the thieves, steals the bull or goat and so on, throws down on the road first one shoe, then the other, his clothing (tempting them to bathe), cries "Not I, but others did it," the thieves run, abandoning their treasures. (The tale is assigned to the group of anecdotes, to the family of anecdotes about "crafty fellows.")

In all, the catalogue of Aarne and Andreyev contains actually 915 types of subjects, but if we take into consideration the breakdown of several types into two or three variations (not to be confused with variants), the aggregate number of subjects and basic variations in European folklore, so far as it can be estimated from the materials known to scholarship, mounts up to 1,021 numbers.

The profitableness of a combined international index of tales goes far beyond the limits of the purely practical, subsidiary tasks of investigation. This index afforded the opportunity to draw a whole series of very important theoretical scientific conclusions. Among other things, it enabled us to give a characterization—though, to be sure, it is preliminary, and perhaps not altogether accurate—of the composition of the repertories of tales among the various peoples. N. P. Andreyev made a curious and important attempt to characterize the Russian repertory of tales, in its resemblance to, and its difference from, that of western Europe, utilizing for this purpose the index which has been analyzed above.[28] He brought together for his comparisons 2,136 recordings of Russian tales, from the very extensive collections of Russian folk tales which have been enumerated above.

The comparison of the list of subjects of Russian tales with the index of Aarne and Andreyev led first of all to the conclusion that of 915 types (or 1,021 variations), 613 types (683 variations) are found in Russian folk-tale material. One-third of all the types found in the international catalogue prove to be common to the Russian material and to the western European (317 types, 327 including variants); one-third of the subjects (302 types, 338 including variants) are not met with at all in the Russian material; conversely, one-third of the subjects (296 types, 356 including variants) prove to be the specific property of the Russian repertory of tales, and are absolutely unknown to western Europe.

A further examination of the question under consideration leads to the conclusion that the subjects which are common to the Russian and western European repertory are found in the largest number among the magical tales (out of the 192 types in the catalogue, 106 are present in the Russian repertory). This testifies to their considerable antiquity; they constitute 21 per cent of all the known Russian subjects (variations); they are, furthermore, characterized by the greatest traditionalism and repetition (nearly half of the magical subjects were encountered in more than five recordings).

The smallest group of all in the Russian repertory, by comparison with the western European, is found to be that of the tales about animals and about the stupid devil. Out of 192 variations, 73 tales of animals are lacking in Russian folklore, and out of 116 about the devil, 71 variations are not encountered. This is explained by the historico-cultural conditions of the West, where these genres were particularly cultivated during the Catholic Middle Ages. Conversely, the realistic genres—the anecdotes and the romantic tales (tales of everyday life)—proved to be exceedingly rich in the Russian repertory. Of the common store of 404 anecdotes, the Russians possess 297, of which 197 are specifically Russian, not encountered in west-

[28] N. P. Andreyev, "Toward a Survey of the Subjects of Russian Tales," *Artistic Folklore*, II-III, 1927, pp. 59-70.

ern Europe. Of the 94 types (variations) of the romantic tales, the Russians possess 74, and 43 of these occur only in the Russian repertory. This fact, in spite of the tentative nature of such a calculation, is, in our opinion, exceedingly characteristic. With absolute objectivity it destroys the romantic and Slavophilic concept of the peculiar dreaminess of the Russian people, their detachment from worldly interests. On the contrary, as we see, their creative power is manifested to its fullest extent, not in the magical (fairy) tale or in the tale about animals, but in the everyday, realistic tale and the pointed anecdote.

Of course the repertory of tales is far from being identical throughout the whole expanse of territory where the Russians live. All the diversity of the natural, economic, social, and everyday living conditions of the Russian people testifies to the indubitable *differentiation* of the repertory of tales according to the various regional and provincial *districts*. This is perfectly obvious to everyone, even on the basis of a cursory acquaintance with the collections of tales which have been compiled on the basis of provenience. (Compare the Belo-Ozero, Olonets, Vyatka, Perm, Samara, and other tales.)

Making use of the subject catalogue of tales by Aarne and Andreyev, the Leningrad folklorist A. I. Nikiforov showed this with sufficient exactness, and graphically.[29] He took for comparison two northern regions: one was the trans-Onega region, in the former province of Olonets; the other was the Pinega region, in the former province of Archangel. In both of these regions, as we have indicated above, he made detailed records of tales, in 1926 and 1927. It is important to notice that Professor Nikiforov was collecting tales with complete objectivity, trying to write down all the tales which he encountered, and that he did not make a choice of storytellers. In this way he acquired a rather complete knowledge of the whole repertory of tales in the regions which he studied. We shall not touch upon many of the interesting details; we will only adduce some of the final conclusions made from his observations.

Out of 122 types of tales in the Pinega region and 162 types in

[29] Alexander Nikiforov, "The Modern Pinega Tale: Certain Problems of Story Lore in the Light of Local Materials," *Ethnographic News*, Bk. 8, Kiev, 1929.

the trans-Onega region, only 68 types were found to be common to both regions. The Pinega tales are significantly poorer than the Onega in the realistic genres of everyday life. In the trans-Onega region the folkway tales and anecdotal tales make up half of the whole trans-Onega repertory of tales, whereas with the Pinega tales, in this respect, hardly one-third is devoted to these realistic subjects. On the other hand, the Pinega tales are distinguished by a more archaic quality, by a "ceremonialism" and severity of narrative style. These regions are distinguished also by the special popularity of certain subjects of tales. Professor Nikiforov also makes interesting observations on the diversity of the tales, in the regions under comparison, with reference to structure, form, and style, in the types of narrators, in the manner of the telling, and so on. Professor Nikiforov correctly explains the marked distinction in the repertory of tales and the form of tales, in these two regions, by the difference in social-economic conditions, the extreme remoteness of the Pinega region from urban culture, the lack of seasonal work in cities, the difficulty of communications at the very time when the trans-Onega people were occupied with seasonal work and trade away from home, and were closely connected with Leningrad. All this has its reflection on the everyday life and psychological type of the population, and consequently, also upon the artistic creative work, particularly upon the tradition of storytelling.[30]

There is no doubt whatever that the collecting of tales which is practiced by Russian folklorists, and also the arrangement of specific subjects and variations of tales according to the provincial and regional principle, are proving to be very productive. The tale, in all its vital significance, can be understood and studied only on the actual soil where it grows, in all its concrete social, economic, cultural, and natural surroundings. The use of a cartographic representation of the repertories of tales, and of specific subjects of tales, according to provenience,[31] is exceedingly helpful.

[30] *Ibid.*, p. 52.

[31] See A. I. Nikiforov, "On the Question of a Cartographic Representation of the Tales," *The Commission on Tales, in 1926* (Survey of Works, Leningrad, 1927), pp. 60 ff; A. M. Smirnov-Kutachevsky, "On the Folklore Map," *Artistic Folklore*, IV-V, Moscow, 1929, p. 218.

The tale is a fact of deep social significance. If a song can be sung for one's self, a tale, on the other hand, a living narrative, inevitably presupposes an audience of listeners for whom it is related. The study of the *real conditions of the folk life of the tale* leads to the irrevocable conclusion that the tale fulfills a very important social function, being indissolubly connected with the social, collective work, often helping and lightening this work, or giving a well deserved, healthful rest, so necessary for highest productivity. This one thing alone makes the investigators of the life of the people treat the tale with great seriousness and attention. Its existence in the popular mode of life is conditioned by the very life of the working people and by the various aspects of their working activity.

From the wealth of literature on this question, which has accumulated at the present time in the Russian scholarship of folklore, we present some characteristic information, given by the collectors of the tales themselves.

Thus, in the Belo-Ozero region, where we made our recordings in 1908–1909, we found it necessary to make the following observations on the local conditions of life of the tale. We wrote:

The tale here lives a full life. Above all, it satisfies the demands for diversion. And here, as soon as the peasants have any leisure, and the appropriate conditions are created, the storyteller appears on the scene, and with his artless, but often truly poetic speech, dominates the minds of the peasants, who eagerly listen to what he says.

A special condition of the development and life of the tale, in those places where we have been making our records, is found to be the character of the peasants' work. First, the cutting of wood: in the winter, in the depths of the forest, far from any habitation, there is often a whole village gathered together—peasants, and women, and children. By day there is the heavy work, but when it begins to grow dark, there is the well deserved repose by the blazing hearth. In the woods they construct a "camp," that is, a spacious mud hut with a hearth in the middle. The people are packed in here in a crowd. And here, when they have warmed their chilled limbs, and satisfied their hunger and thirst, the workers begin to while away the long winter evening. What a wished-for person, then, does the storyteller prove to be! Among the dense forests, the trees which are crackling from the frost, to the accompaniment of the howling of the wolves, besides the blazing fire—what an appropriate setting, what a favorable soil for the magical narrative, filled with all possible kinds of terrors! The working people, wearied by their labor, when they have heard their fill of this deviltry, and of unparalleled exploits "in a faraway kingdom," seek for still greater repose, diversion; they thirst for the wholesome laughter which will restore their physical and spiritual powers. There appear on the scene the storyteller, the jester, the merry fellow—the witticisms and mockeries are poured out as from a horn of plenty; the whole audience is attuned to a merry, joyful harmony, and unanimously and sympathetically acclaims his merry, laughter-provoking speech.

In general we must say, that if it had been possible to write down the tales with complete stenographic accuracy, recording on paper all the exclamations made by the public, then, beyond a doubt, the record of the popular tale would have gained a great deal in the liveliness and freshness of the impression which it produces. . . . No less than the common "associative" life in the woods, in the camp, during the time of the forest labors, the fishing also furthers the maintenance of the life of the tales in the Belo-Ozero region. The fishermen, going away onto the lakes for a long period, when they had cast their nets there, or while they were waiting for a favorable wind, had to pass a good deal of time in forced inactivity, and for this reason they were especially well disposed toward the storyteller. We recall, for example, how the fishermen utilized the record of the tales which we were making for their own purposes; they came to us, into the hut, listened to the storytellers, and concluded a kind of bargain with the storyteller who pleased them most particularly. They promised the storyteller a certain portion of their catch, if only he would not refuse to go with them when they plied their craft. In the same way, all kinds of narratives flourish in the original rural club—the mill. Many peasants assemble at the mill, and while waiting for their turn, they are sometimes obliged to spend several days there. Here, too, the tale is the best and most attractive means of whiling away the time. People contribute a great deal toward the diffusion of the tales, who because of their profession have to pass from one place to another, who have the opportunity of seeing much, and who have many people to listen to, such as "painters of God" [icon painters], tailors, soldiers, beggars, and other kinds of wandering people.[32]

[32] B. and Y. Sokolov, *Tales and Songs of the Belo-Ozero Region* (Moscow, 1915), pp. v-vi.

Similar observations upon the conditions of diffusion and assimilation of the tales have been made by N. E. Onchukov in the Pechora region, and by Professor D. K. Zelenin in the Perm and Vyatka regions.

Interesting information as to the conditions of existence of the tale in the trans-Onega region is given by I. Karnaukhova, on the basis of observations made in 1926.[33]

Nikiforov stresses the circumstances which have contributed to the cultivation of the tale on the Pinega, in the former province of Archangel.[34]

The great significance of the common, associative work, as a condition which is especially favorable for the existence of the tale, is confirmed by information from Siberia. Professor M. K. Azadovsky, speaking of the life of the folk tale on the Upper Lena, especially stresses this aspect.[35]

Also, exceedingly curious information on the conditions of the contemporary condition of the tale on Lake Baikal is given by A. V. Gurevich, who wrote down tales there in 1926 and 1927.[36]

The information that has been given indicates how vital the tale still is, even at the present time, among the working people, how closely it is connected with their labor and their common origin, how highly valued, and even necessary in their daily life, a good and expert storyteller is. There is no doubt that the conditions of development of the tale merit the sharpest attention, not only of scholars and specialists, but of educators in general, of teachers, village librarians, and workers in political education. Following the track of the tale to the lumber camp, to the rafts, to the fishermen's cooperatives, to the mills—there branch libraries, along with readers and workers for political education, must go. The living tale, and reading aloud, will there find proper application, a favorable setting, and, with an expert approach will meet with a wonderful reception on

---

[33] I. V. Karnaukhova, "The Storyteller and the Tale in the Trans-Onega Region," *Peasant Art of the USSR, I, The Art of the North: The Trans-Onega Region* (Leningrad, Academia, 1927), pp. 105-106.

[34] A. Nikiforov, *The Contemporary Pinega Tale*, p. 56.

[35] M. Azadovsky, *Tales of the Upper Lena Region* (Irkutsk, 1925), p. xii.

[36] *Tales from Various Places in Siberia*, ed. M. K. Azadovsky (Irkutsk, 1928).

the part of the listeners who have gathered there, thirsting for the living word.

The task of the Russian folklorists is, as we have indicated above, the study of the "carriers" of the creative work of folklore, particularly the storytellers.

The material which has already been accumulated and published at the present time gives biographical information and characterizations of a whole gallery of Russian storytellers. The arrangement of the texts of the stories, in collections of tales, according to storytellers, has given exceptionally valuable sources for the formulation and solution of the question of the *reflection of the creative personality of the storyteller in his tales*. Russian scholarship even possesses, at the present time, whole investigations devoted to the personality and the creative work of separate outstanding storytellers.[37]

Profoundly anachronistic are the words of the Academician A. N. Pypin, spoken by him at the beginning of his activity, when he himself was under the influence of mythological tendencies: "The tale, in and for itself, does not at all require this setting [that is, interlarding of its speech, as Pypin incorrectly defined it, 'by supposed popular jesting']. It even rejects it, because it belongs not to one, and not to many well known narrators, but to the whole people, or, at least, to the whole region; it is obvious, that there must be removed from its exposition everything which expresses the arbitrary manner of one man." [38]

It is precisely in the exact recording of individual peculiarities, of all the fine points of the text of the story, of every variant of the tale; precisely in the attentive study of the "arbitrary manner" of one storyteller, of his style, and in the elucidation of every concrete fact of the tale's development that the basic requirement of contempor-

---

[37] *Cf.* Mark Asadowsky, *Eine sibirische Märchenerzählerin* (Helsinki, 1928), FFC, No. 68; M. K. Azadovsky, *Russian Tales* (Moscow, *Academia*, 1932); N. P. Grinkova, "Tales of Kuprianikha," *Artistic Folklore*, I, Moscow, 1926; E. V. Hofman, "On the Question of the Individual Style of the Storyteller," *Artistic Folklore*, IV-V, Moscow, 1929; S. I. Mintz, "Kuprianikha," *The Literary Critic*, No. 4, 1936, and others.

[38] A. N. Pypin, *Russian Folk Tales: Records of the Fatherland*, No. 4, 1856. See also the article previously mentioned, by Y. Sokolov, in the first volume of the *Popular Russian Tales* of A. N. Afanasyev.

ary collection and study lies, especially in revealing the social nature of the tale. Observations upon the storytellers have led to the definite conclusion that storytelling is not an easily accessible occupation which is identical and easy for everyone. The telling of a tale is primarily an art, a special skill, accessible to the artists of the poetic word, to persons who are especially gifted for this kind of work.

Of course, as in every art, so also in the creation of the tale, there are great masters, but there are also mediocre artists and people altogether lacking in talent; but this only emphasizes the necessity of special mastery, of excellence in the telling of tales.

The storytellers' repertories vary greatly with reference to the quantity of tales. The majority of storytellers know from five to ten, and very many know only two or three tales in all. On the other hand, there are storytellers who are exceptionally rich in their store of subjects for tales. Such, for example, was the Samara storyteller Novopoltsev, from whom Sadovnikov wrote down seventy-two tales; such was the Voronezh storyteller Kuprianikha, who related fifty-six tales to N. I. Grinkova, and in 1936 related 120 tales to A. M. Novikova and I. A. Ossovetsky. From I. F. Kovalev, a storyteller of the Gorky province, E. V. Hofmann and S. I. Mintz wrote down forty-six tales. More than one hundred tales were written down by A. N. Nechayev from Korguyev, a storyteller of the Karelian Autonomous Soviet Socialist Republic. The Perm storyteller Lomtev imparted twenty-seven tales to Zelenin. There are also a number of storytellers known who are familiar with as many as fifteen tales and more. In the literature about the tale there are many references to certain storytellers who are able to relate tales not only the whole night through, but for several days together.

But the peculiarity of the repertory of every storyteller is found to be not so much with respect to quantity, as to quality. Every storyteller takes, adopts, and creatively reworks only those tales, those subjects and motifs of tales, which correspond to his tastes, interests, general view of the world, and psychology. Between the storyteller and the tales which he adopts, there is a special "meeting of moods." Every repertory is as a rule exceedingly characteristic of this or that storyteller.

The chief and most important feature for the understanding and elucidation of the mutual relation of the tale and of the storyteller is found to be the style of his tales. We wrote in our collection, *Tales and Songs of the Belo-Ozero Region:*

As a source for the judgment of the reflection of the storyteller's personality in the tales, there can serve the actual manner of narration, the artistic devices and peculiarities of phrasing—in a word, all that constitutes the "style" of the storyteller. The folk tale, in this respect, confirms in the best possible way the well known saying: "Style is the man." The style of the storyteller, above all, is manifested in the devices of composition of the tale, in the choice or elimination or modification of the sequence of motifs in specific episodes, in the peculiar characterization, according to his own taste, of the persons in the tale, in the intensification or the softening of specific details. Moreover, with regard to style in the narrower sense of the word, an especially important feature, depending to a great extent on the individual inclinations and tastes of the narrator, consists in his utilization of the traditional story formulas (*loci communes*), in the varying degree to which he utilized them, in his choice of those for which he has the greatest fondness, and also in his original utilization of the word material, without even speaking of the great distinctions which are to be observed among the narrators in the very manner of narration, in the intonation, in the utilization of mimetics, of gestures, exclamations, and a number of other purely dramatic devices.[39]

The bond between the storyteller and his tales is exceedingly profound and intimate. Often, without noticing it himself, the storyteller introduces into his tale all his practical knowledge of life, his moral philosophy, his experiences.

Among the storytellers we find tranquil, measured epic poets, presenting a sedate and detailed narrative of knightly exploits, battles, and the adventures of the heroes of the tales; we shall find also fantastic dreamers, living in a world of fancifully created magic reveries, in a far-away kingdom, in a realm at the world's end; many times we meet also with storytellers who are moralists, searching after truth, but there are still more storytellers of another type.

[39] B. and Y. Sokolov, *Tales and Songs of the Belo-Ozero Region*, p. lxiii.

In contrast to the types which have been indicated, these story-tellers prefer to a wonderful, imaginary land their own real life, the mode of living which surrounds them, and the real human interre-lationships. We may call these storytellers realists specializing in daily life; the romantic tale dealing with everyday life, the anecdotal tale—these are their favorite genres. There are storytellers who are jokers, jesters, humorists without malice; they love, and in fact, know almost nothing except cheerful banterings, facetious sayings, little "narrations" and comparatively harmless anecdotes. On the other hand, we have, and encounter frequently, bitter, sarcastic, satirical storytellers, with no small share of venom, and sometimes with exceedingly malicious and pointed social satire. There is also a considerable number of storytellers who relate chiefly "shameful," that is, indecent, or even downright cynical erotic tales. To a con-siderable degree, one can isolate the storyteller-dramaturgists, for whom the center of interest and artistic invention lies in the drama-tization of the tale, in a purely theatrical manner of narration, in the skill and animation of the handling of the dialogue.

There exists a type of storytellers whom we might call the bookish storytellers; [40] in the prerevolutionary period these were in the ma-jority of cases literate or partly literate people, who had read plenty of cheap popular works or other novels of excitement and adventure, who were exceedingly avid for the "educated" bookish speech, and at times overzealous in transmitting it. There can be classified sep-arately the storytellers, and chiefly the women who told stories, for children. They usually know mainly children's amusing sayings, nurs-ery tales, and particularly tales of animals. The special social and everyday conditions of the life of the women, of the peasant woman's heavy lot, have placed their imprint on the tales which were related by women.

From the vast gallery of storytellers, both men and women, now known in the scientific literature of the tales, lack of space permits us to dwell only on a few of the more or less characteristic types.

[40] M. K. Azadovsky, *Russian Tales* (Moscow, Academia, 1932); "The Narra-tive and the Book," in the collection *Language and Literature*, Vol. VIII (Acad-emy of Sciences of the USSR. 1932).

The storyteller A. M. Ganin, encountered by us in 1908 in the Belo-Ozero region, can serve as an example of the epic storyteller. Ganin was one of the few preservers of the fragments of the epos of the *byliny* in his region, and at the same time a good judge of tales. His knowledge of the *byliny* was not accidental, but derived from his general interest in productions of that kind. This is obvious from his repertory of tales: out of fourteen tales imparted by Ganin, which undoubtedly constituted, in all, only a portion of his store, a good half approximate in their content to the motifs and subjects that are closest to the Russian knightly epos. Such is his "legend" of the marriage of Prince Vladimir, which undoubtedly represented one of the reworkings of an ancient version of the Russian legends, and it may be also of the songs on this theme. In a later form it was carried over to the *byliny* that are sung down to the present time, the "ancient tales" "of the marriage of Prince Vladimir," usually known as the ancient tales "of the Danube." [41] The following legendary tales: on the boy Daniel, and on his fight with the heathen idol; on King Solomon (a tale which has its parallel also in the reworking of the subject in the *byliny*), on Bova the Prince, and on Eruslan Lazarevich, indicate by their titles the knightly character of their content.

The remaining tales imparted by Ganin (we use this term in the broad sense of the word) have to do with a class of legends which stands very close to another aspect of the folk-song epos—the religious verses. There are several short *byliny*; one tale belongs to the realm of the fantastic, and in all, only one bears the character of a *fabliau*, and clearly testifies by its form that it is not the genre of Ganin; in his treatment it came out to a great extent as cynical, and lacking in skill. On the other hand, if we turn to the study of the peculiarities of form in the basic tales of Ganin, we shall be compelled to acknowledge his great perfection and artistry. It is evident that here is an expert storyteller, with an excellent mastery of the traditional poetics of the tale and the *bylina*. One is struck first of all, especially

---

[41] The scientific significance of this legend of Ganin has been illuminated in detail in the work of B. M. Sokolov, "Epic Legends of the Marriage of Prince Vladimir," *Scholarly Annals of the State Chernyshevsky University at Saratov*, Vol. I, No. 3, 1923.

in the category of the knightly tales, by the great abundance of *loci communes* inherent in the Russian epos of the *bylina*. Besides, it must be observed that many of these circulating formulas are literally identical with those which are present in the ancient tales imparted by Ganin himself. From this it becomes evident how great a role in the process of assimilation of the popular poetics, even of an extraneous and bookish subject, can be played by the individual personality of the narrator.

As a typical representative of the narrators of magical, miraculous tales, and a master of the "ritualism" of the storyteller's style, we consider another storyteller of Belo-Ozero, Elijah Semyonov (who was fifty-seven years of age in 1908), a man of wide experience, who had worked as a sawyer and had gone to earn money in distant places, for example, in the province of Tula. His tales are almost all of a fantastic character; they include many diverse, often rhythmic, storytelling formulas, inserted expressions, proverbs: "Ah," he would say, "the cat is scratching her back; but the little bird would have begun to sing early, if the little cat had not eaten her up." "One person is never poor; but even if he *is* poor, he's only one." "If you're a lord you'll have a pair of heels, you'll have no taxes." "But the farther you go into the woods, the more you will have to cut your way," and others.

As with Ganin, we notice a considerable number of the *loci communes* of the epos of the *byliny*, which indicates, it seems to us, either an acquaintance with the ancient tales on the part of Semyonov himself (however, we have not succeeded in obtaining definite information on this point), or else his inheritance of the story material from someone who was an expert in the *byliny*. But especially striking and well formed in the work of Semyonov are the introductory and concluding embellishments of the storyteller, in which there are undoubtedly expressed the "ritualism" of the tales and the proficiency of the storyteller. The "ritualism" of the tales of Semyonov is also revealed in the continued grouping of the episodes by threes, and in the literal repetitions.

In all probability the features of Semyonov's personal interpolations are to be discerned in certain new words, in a knowledge of urban culture. For example, one of his heroes plays "in the club," while living water is to be found "at such and such a street number," and an adversary makes his appearance "with a mine."

The Samara storyteller Novopoltsev, mentioned above (in the collection of Sadovnikov), obviously also belongs to this type of storyteller. His tales (seventy-two in number), including some of the longest and best, are distinguished by originality of structure, by the combination of subjects, and by masterliness in transmission. The "mythical" tales, with Novopoltsev, are related with due observance of the ritualism.[42] In this same division of epic poets, who are experts in the miraculous tale, belongs the best storyteller in Onchukov's collection—the blind old man, A. M. Chuprov.[43]

As an example of the moralist-storyteller there may serve the aged storyteller Sozont Kuzmich Petrushichev, a retired sexton, and whom we have already encountered.

In 1908 he was sixty-six years old. Earlier he had worked as a peasant, but then, for twenty-one years, had served as sexton in the village of Ramenye, and here he was living out his days in retirement. In the 1870's Sozont Kuzmich had had to work for a time on the railroad, and he had been engaged also in the floating of wood along the river. He had had considerable experience of life. Sozont Kuzmich lived his whole life as an illiterate. In appearance Petrushichev was a little, insignificant-looking old man. He was very good-natured, and in general was not averse to having a laugh at his own expense. The latter trait was also apparent in the tales which he told. In the tale of Ivan the Fool he good-naturedly acknowledged, in speaking of the three sons of the peasant: "But there was a peasant, and he had three sons: two of them clever, but the third a fool, like me, Sozont."

A man with a well defined code of ethics, in general admiring sedateness and piety, Sozont Kuzmich dwelt with especial pleasure on "ethical" themes, and the questions of the triumph of virtue touched him so closely that he was sincerely agitated by them, even to the

[42] Savchenko, *The Russian Folk Tale*, p. 155.
[43] Onchukov, *Northern Tales* (St. Petersburg, 1909), p. 1, and Savchenko, *op. cit.*, p. 164.

point of tears. The tale of Ivan the Fool brings forward, in the figure of Ivan, who was neglected by men and outraged by fortune, a hidden power of discrimination, which makes him wiser and loftier than kings. In the tale of Prince Ivan there is reestablished a truth which had perhaps been violated. It is curious to observe that, in harmony with the mildness which is inherent in our storyteller, there is nothing said in his tales about any kind of punishments.

This love of Sozont's for "integrity," for "honorableness," is reflected in the very style of his speech. Thus he repeats several times one of his favorite expressions, by which, obviously, there is determined the very high degree of his taste: "fairly and honorably"—even a ship, with him, went "fairly and honorably," and even Ivan the Fool, when he laughed at the queen and the princess who were lacking in uprightness, did so "fairly and honorably." The moralizing tendency and the peaceful, benign temper of Petrushevich do not keep him from a deliberate emphasis of the social inequality prevailing in the world, and several times he contrasts the poverty of the people with the prosperity and wealth of the kings. The well known type of impressibility and responsiveness, which are characteristic of the narrator, are expressed in the tale by frequent exclamations of a lyrical nature, especially when conveying to the listeners some kind of striking phenomena or events. We may note, besides, the general inclination of Petrushevich toward abrupt, yet expressive speech. The unusual liveliness with which the dialogue is carried on in the tales of Petrushevich, also, cannot possibly give that tranquility, that measured quality, which are inherent in the genuine epic speech.

Quite a number of storytellers are encountered to whom the realm of the fantastic is altogether alien, and who are not inwardly interested in the magic tale. When they try to relate it, it comes out in such a pale, dry, schematized form, that it produces no impression whatever. On the other hand, the tales of everyday life, all kinds of "true-to-life" stories, "miniature *byliny*," and so on, prove to be their element. In our collection, *Tales and Songs of the Belo-Ozero Region*, a whole gallery of these types is given. Of these, we may mention the old man V. S. Suslov, a man who was rich in the experience of life, of powerful spirit and physique, in spite of his seventy years. Suslov had an excellent understanding of the era of serfdom, and one may even be so bold as to call him the local historian of the end of that era. This fact is expressed also in the "ancient tales" imparted by him. For example, the ancient tale about Serega and Mitya, the two local peasants, delineates with uncommon vividness a genre picture of the era of serfdom, its corporal violence and contemptuous treatment of the peasantry.

We consider the Belo-Ozero storyteller V. S. Sharashov, a typical storyteller of the facetious and jesting type. He was a popular favorite in the neighborhood as a groomsman, that is, master of ceremonies at country weddings. He was a cheerful, sprightly old man. His genre is that of the good-natured, cheerful exordia of the storyteller, the brief narratives, the little rhythmic narratives.

The satirical storytellers, in whose tales the cheerful tone by no means bears the character of careless and good-natured jesting, also merit great attention. In their tales, as we have said, there is a good deal of venom and biting social satire. As one of the striking examples of such a type, there may serve a storyteller whom we encountered at that same time in the Belo-Ozero region—the junior sexton Vasily Vasilyevich Bogdanov. He was a small, reddish-haired man, about thirty years of age, rather foolish in appearance, but hiding under this mask a great deal of resourcefulness and cunning. He was everlastingly winking at his listeners, teasing them. In his railleries he would not leave unnoticed the members of the local clergy—of course, behind their backs.

In his life Vasily Vasilyevich had seen a great deal, had tried a number of professions, and had even been in St. Petersburg. All this, in one way or another, is reflected in his narratives. He knew how to make them unusually lively, to give them the color of real life. In their content all the four "tales" imparted by him belonged to the type of the humorous *fabliau*. But in his transmission these tales received a strikingly satirical, at times even unusually sharp character, far removed from the tone of good-natured humor. One narrative (No. 86, Kapsirko) aimed its satirical barbs against the noblemen; the others dealt with the village clergy, who were intimately known to Bogdanov. They all ridiculed the priests (No. 84, The Priest, the

Deacon and the Subdeacon; No. 85, The Priest's Girl Was Put to Shame, and No. 87, The Little Old Man Osip and the Three Priests). By this knowledge of the everyday life of the clergy is explained the prominent description of their weak sides, which we find in the tales of Bogdanov. Greed, avarice, the demand for "offerings," the utilization of "holy things" for purposes of gain, at times even blasphemy, lasciviousness, envy, and petty animosities, drunkenness, boasting—these are the features of the representatives of the clergy who are described in Bogdanov's narratives.

If certain of these features belong to the story motif itself, and are characteristic of all the Russian tales about priests, still, on the other hand, many details of the narrative, the specific striking minor features in the characterization of the persons who are active participants, are found to be the personal interpolations of Bogdanov himself. This becomes particularly clear after a collation of the tales of Bogdanov with their other Russian variants. Bogdanov knew how to fascinate the listener with his tale, he knew how to introduce him into its contents. He was greatly helped here by constant allusions, by winking or simply pointing out local persons who were well known to his listeners, with whom he connects the heroes of the tale.

Bogdanov handled his narrative in an unusually lively way, never being in the least at a loss in his choice of words; he loaded the tale with favorite expressions, of which the most frequent were: "I mean, really," "Well, all right, good," "So then, all right, good," "So it was, really, at that precise moment." Very often, in the transmission of the speeches of others, there was felt the irony, which was distinctly brought out by the intonation or by special expressions that had been interpolated. In general, the dialogue in Bogdanov's tales is lively and clever. Especially curious is the fact that the tales in Bogdanov's exposition, under the constantly increasing enthusiasm of the narrator, without his perceiving it himself, began to take on a rhythmic and even a rhyming form, the more, and the more strikingly, the mockery and the jesting were emphasized.

In Bogdanov we see how important gesture, pantomime, ejaculations, retorts, acting, and so on are in the "telling" of a narrative. Characteristic of the comic storytellers is not only the content of their tales, but also the method of exposition. The contemporary collectors of tales, who have studied them in their realistic setting and have attentively examined the actual manner of their transmission, are assigning more and more significance to the dramatic aspect, and the almost theatrical art of the storytellers. Certain of the storytellers attain great virtuosity in this respect, particularly in the narration qf tales of everyday life, and especially in the handling of dialogue. How conscious at times the attitude toward this art is, on the part of the storytellers themselves, is shown by their own comments on this point. Thus, the Siberian storyteller F. I. Zykov (seventy-nine years of age) is exceedingly clever at dialogue. "Conversation" (dialogue), in the opinion of this old man, is the most important and the most difficult thing in the tale. "There one word is somehow wrong, and no results can be attained. There you have to do everything swiftly." And the persons who take part in the tale with him, actually do both speak, and weep, and grow angry in a natural way, just as living persons do.[44]

Making a special study of questions concerning the art of "storytelling," I. V. Karnaukhova emphasizes the fact that in studying the manner of narration of the story, one must take into consideration: (*a*) the storyteller; (*b*) the material (the story itself); (*c*) the performance, and (*d*) the audience.[45]

Of the above-noted special group of "bookish" storytellers we may mention one whom we encountered in 1909, the Belo-Ozero storyteller A. O. Ershov (thirty-five years old). Ershov indisputably belonged to the transitional types to be found in our prerevolutionary countryside. This was a man who had already, in part, come in contact with culture. In the first place, he was literate; in the second place, he was a genuine lover of reading. His one sister was a student in the Kirillov Gymnasium, and was preparing herself to be a teacher of an elementary public school. His mother was a very intelligent, energetic woman, a *sinelshchitsa* (weaver). Ershov himself managed the Zemstvo station and the post office. Even his outward appearance,

---

[44] M. K. Azadovsky, *Tales from Various Places in Siberia*, p. 52.
[45] I. V. Karnaukhova, *Tales and Legends of the Northern Region* (Moscow, 1933).

particularly his eyes, set him apart from the ranks of the inhabitants of the same village. The amount of contact which Ershov had had with "education" could not fail to be reflected also in his language—in the style of his conversation and narrative speech. We used to notice in him a striving for "educated" words, which he often used naïvely and not in the proper place; for a strange, half-literary, half-colloquial, intricate construction of phrases. It may be that this necessarily reflects the poorly assimilated influence of books. Beyond a doubt it is to this influence that we must ascribe the presence, in Ershov's tales, of sentimental love tendencies, which are somewhat alien to the folk tale, and which have found expression in certain details of the narrative.

Ershov had certain storytelling formulas, but in his transmission they have been greatly modernized. As an example there may appear the very last closing formula of the tale. "And when his parents had looked upon the knight, they also recognized him, and such was the joy, that I, the narrator, cannot estimate it, nor tell it in my tale, nor write it in a book, nor relate it with my pen. And a feast was made for everybody at once, and various kinds of drinks were, there. And I, the narrator, was there; I drank the mead, it flowed over my lips, but not one drop came into my mouth. Thus, respected listeners, my pleasing tale has come to an end."

As we have noted above, there is a peculiar, special kind of impression, all their own, produced by the tales that are related by women. N. E. Onchukov, in his introductory article to the collection, *Northern Tales*, wrote:

P. N. Rybnikov asserts that the women have their own "womanish" ancient tales, which they sing with special fondness, but the men not nearly so willingly. Hilferding confirms the correctness of this observation with reference to the trans-Onega region. There are no purely feminine tales, with the exception perhaps of those which are purely for children, and of the tales of the animal world, which are also especially beloved by children, and which the women know especially. But in relating any tale, a woman involuntarily reflects in it that which especially interests her, everything that touches her everyday mode of life. The woman storyteller, relating a folk tale, among other things, always describes in detail and with special fondness the everyday life that she knows so well, and the life of a woman.[46]

Marimyana Ivanovna Medvedeva, from Terekhova in the Belo-Ozero district, occupied an honored place among the women storytellers. She was at that time still a young woman (thirty-two years of age), healthy, full of strength and energy. But on her whole face lay the shadow of sorrow. The cause of this was a too early marriage, which had not been in accordance with her own will; the burden of a large family, poverty, the general conditions of the hard life of womankind.

Medvedeva was an excellent "wailer," known throughout the district. In the lamentations, especially those for marriages, she undoubtedly embodied the genuineness of her own experiences. How hard she cried when she was married, how she went out on the street several times to call her dear father—of this, she herself used to speak. To write down songs and lamentations from her—thanks to her wonderful voice and her veracity of tone—was a great delight. A considerable share of her subjective moods and tastes can be observed also in the tales. She knew a remarkable number of tales; her memory was wonderful, and her curiosity was so great that it led her to reading and writing, which she mastered by teaching herself. In this manner the assimilation of the tales came easily to her. In her tales Medvedeva manifestly avoided anything indecorous or cynical. Fantastic tales she would relate with an observance of "ceremonial" stylistics, at times not avoiding considerable repetitions. Besides this, however, in her tales there was perceptible a certain emotional excitement: for emphasis, she liked to have recourse to the heightening of an impression by means of literal repetition of this, that, or the other word, or by means of tautological repetitions: "A deep, deep ditch"; "The girls cry, it is terrible, how they cry"; "He was grieved, he was sorrowful, and he shed some tears"; "He seized him, he shook him and shook him, he shook him all to pieces."

Another of Medvedeva's peculiarities was a marked inclination to give explanations as she went along. The positive characteristics of

[46] N. E. Onchukov, *Northern Tales* (St. Petersburg, 1909), p. xxxvi.

the heroes of her tales are given in soft, womanly outlines. With reference to women, her sympathy is on the side of the "noble," the "good," and the "faithful." A certain delicacy is added to her heroes by the use of the respectful second person plural in personal address, especially when the young are speaking to their elders.

The recent collectors of tales have made us acquainted with two remarkable representatives of the women storytellers, and have even devoted special research articles to them. Such is the Voronezh storyteller "Kupryanikha," whom we mentioned previously—one of those who possess an exceptionally rich repertory of tales (120 numbers). "Kupryanikha" is the nickname of a peasant woman of the village of Great Vereika, of the Zemlyansky region, in the province of Voronezh, Anna Kupryanovna Baryshnikova. She is illiterate. "Kupryanikha," Grinkova writes concerning her, "is a very lively, cheerful, affable, and sociable old woman. In her enormous village (of 4,500 inhabitants) she is regarded as the best narrator and expert on songs. After two weeks of association with Kupryanikha, her love for tales and songs became prefectly understandable. In all the circumstances of life her artistic nature manifests itself, looking with far from indifferent eyes upon everything that is beautiful." [47]

Her fondness for beauty of words and tune is revealed both in the singing of a song and in the telling of a tale. Toward the narration of tales, this storyteller had a very serious attitude. First she recollects each tale to herself in brief, and then she relates it. The repertory of her tales is varied: she knows a considerable number of animal tales, also miraculous tales, everyday tales, especially about priests, and she also passes on the content of literary productions. She herself values above all the long magical tales, noting always that the given tale is especially good, especially interesting.

Kupryanikha relates her tales with an observation of all "ceremonialism"; she understands narration as the artistic transmission of a subject that is well known to her. Every personage who participates in the tale speaks with his own voice; it is always possible to distinguish whether it is the bass rumble of Ivan the Fool, or whether Ivan the tsarevich is speaking with feeling, with meaning, with deliberation,

[47] N. P. Grinkova, "Tales of Kupryanikha," *Artistic Folklore*, I, 1926, p. 82.

or whether it is some other hero, and so on. Without any kind of cues, by the intonation in the dialogues alone, one can tell where, in the transcription, to place quotation marks. Certain passages of the tale are sung. Characteristic of Kupryanikha are the remarkable rhymed exordia. They are alive, harmonious, rhythmic. Her tales are ancient and traditional, not only in subject, but also by virtue of the style of the narration. In them we encounter all the accessories which are well known and necessary for an ancient tale, and the typical storytelling formulas. The style of her tales is distinguished by measured and rhymed speech. Sometimes the whole of the tale is permeated with this peculiarity. This is, again, a characteristic peculiarity of her artistic manner.

In the winter of 1935–1936, Kupryanikha traveled to Voronezh and to Moscow, where, with invariable success, she repeatedly made public appearances with her tales. (For the literature on Kupryanikha, see page 390.)

Exceptional in her talent and her striking individuality is the Siberian storyteller Vinokurova, discovered by M. K. Azadovsky, who wrote a series of articles about her. (See p. 403.)

Every tale, as we have already become convinced, is important for all its concrete qualities of content and of form, which have been created by the storyteller. Only through this concrete quality do we perceive and comprehend the breath of genuine life, and recognize the power and perfection of the artistic craftsmanship. Therefore, for an investigation of the tale, every variant or rendering of it is valuable and important. Only in such variants do we have a concrete oral artistic production, endowed with flesh and blood. But at the same time we are convinced that every tale bears within itself a considerable element of traditional legend, which has existed for many years, which sometimes goes back into the depths of the centuries, and which is the property of the international heritage of oral literature. This has to do both with content and with form. From this point of view, for the comparative study of the tale, within the limits either of the Russian repertory alone, or in its broad international existence, we have to establish its general traditional bases. It is altogether natural that every establishment of such a similarity leads to a certain abstraction, generalization, and schematization. Categories created in such a manner will possess a varying degree of general validity.

Above all, we see that the tales are classified according to basic categories—according to the peculiarities of content and form which are dominant in them. With certain reservations, these categories bear the character of specific *genres of tales*. Such are the tales of animals, the miraculous tales, the tales of everyday life, the anecdotal tales. These categories, in their turn, are divided into their groups and subgroups.

The usual classification of the actual recordings of tales is their division according to subjects, and within the subjects, according to motifs. Thus, the concepts of "subject" and "motif" are seen to be correlative.

According to the definition of the Academician A. N. Veselovsky, "subjects [plots] are a complex of motifs," or "a series of motifs." [48] Speaking more accurately, the subject is determined by the presence of a more or less stable group of motifs. If one or another group of texts of tales have a series of similar motifs, proceeding in a relatively well established sequence, and permeated with a general artistic trend (theme), then these tales may be related to one subject, which serves as their framework. The motifs are seen to be an integral part of the plot. By "motifs" Veselovsky means "the simplest narrative unit." Genetically, such a narrative unit "picturesquely answered the various inquiries of the primitive mind or of everyday observation." [49] But the question of the origin of the tale motif, as of the tale in general, will be dealt with below.

Our immediate interest is in the definition of the actual concept of the motif as a basic component of the tale. Veselovsky, emphasizing the fact that the motif is "the simplest narrative unit" (for example, the representation of the sun and moon as brother and sister, the motif of the ravishing of a maiden or a wife, the motif of the transformation of a man into a beast, and so forth), is ready to assign to the motif a character of indivisibility. "The characteristic of the

---

[48] A. N. Veselovsky, "The Poetics of Subjects, and Its Problems," *Collected Works*, Vol. II, No. I (St. Petersburg, 1913), pp. 3, 11.
[49] *Loc. cit.*

motif is its figurative unimembral schematism; such are the elements, which cannot be resolved any further, of the lower mythology and of the tale." [50] In this definition there is, of course, a striking incorrectness. With such an understanding of the motif, it would be impossible to speak of its variation, but this actually arises precisely from the resolution of the motif into parts—elements. These elements of the "simplest narrative unit," of the motif, expressed even in one proposition, include in themselves the characters who take part in the story, and the action itself which is performed by them.

In this connection an apt comment is made by V. Propp, though in certain places, as we have indicated above, his work is not free from gross errors:

Let us take the motif, "A dragon carries off the Tsar's daughter." This motif resolves itself into four elements, each of which, in itself, may vary. The dragon may be replaced by Kaschey, by a whirlwind, a devil, a falcon, or a wizard. The abduction may be replaced by vampirism, and by various doings, through which, in the tale, the disappearance is brought about. The daughter may be replaced by a sister, bride, wife, or mother. The Tsar may be replaced by the Tsar's son, by a peasant, or by a priest.[51] In this way all the categories which we have indicated—the classes (or genres) of tales, the story subjects, motifs, and elements—prove to be a kind of scientific convention, though exceedingly necessary for scientific research, and above all for the classification and systematization of a very vast number of tales: for purposes of their comparison and study; and for the determination of their origin and of their complicated, but at times very capricious, life on the lips of mankind, of peoples, tribes, and specific social groups. The further questions of composition, as well as of the poetics of the tale in general, will be dealt with in our subsequent survey of the tales according to genres, or basic categories.

Miraculous or magical tales, according to a calculation made on the basis of the printed materials, occupy one-fifth of the whole Russian repertory of tales. At the same time the Russian miraculous tales, according to their subjects, appear to be international. Out of 192 magical subjects, 144 are known to the Russians, of which 106 are

50 *Loc. cit.*
51 V. Propp, *Morphology of the Tale* (Leningrad, 1928), p. 22.

found to be shared in common with western Europe, 48 are lacking, but on the other hand, 38 are found to be unknown in the west. This fact bears testimony that the vast majority of the subjects of miraculous tales must go back in their origins to remote antiquity. The miraculous tales constitute one of the most traditional genres of folklore. It is not without reason that the motifs and elements of the miraculous tales, most of all, provide material for determining the survivals of the beliefs, customs, and concepts of primitive culture.

One may form for one's self a concept of the basic attributes of the magical repertory of the Russian tale from an inventory of the most popular ones, that is, those which have been written down by the collectors in the greatest number of variants of the story subjects.[52] The most popular tale in Russian oral tradition proves to be the tale "Three Kingdoms": the golden, the silver, and the copper, where the heroes are going in search of the tsar's daughters who have disappeared, and take turns in preparing dinner. There appears a little man of the height of a finger, but his beard is a cubit long; one of the heroes descends underground and saves the tsar's daughters from the dragon, and so forth; his companions, having drawn up the tsar's daughters on a rope, will not draw the true preserver of the tsar's daughters out of the pit, but at the very end he is saved. The tale has been recorded in forty-five Russian variants.

Next to it in respect of the number of copies (forty-one) comes the tale "The Miraculous Flight" (the fugitives are transformed into various animals and objects), in several variations. Then follows the tale "Ivashka and the Witch": having enticed a boy to her house, the latter wants to burn him up, but the boy by his cleverness brings it about that the witch's daughter falls into the stove, and later the witch herself. (One of the variations of this subject is "The Boy as Tall as a Finger, at the Man-Eater's House.") There follow also the tale of "The Magic Ring," a ring which is stolen from the tsar's daughter and returned to the hero by the grateful animals (the cat,

---

[52] See N. P. Andreyev, "Toward a Survey of the Russian Story Subjects," *Artistic Folklore*, II-III, 1927, p. 66. See also the most recent characterization of the magical, or miraculous, tales in the detailed commentaries of N. P. Andreyev on Vol. I of the latest edition (Moscow, 1936), of *Popular Russian Tales* by A. N. Afanasyev, pp. 558-573.

dog, and others); and the tale "About the Tsar Saltan," which was made famous by Pushkin.

Next in degree of popularity come the well known story subjects of the hero who conquers the dragon, and of his liberation of the tsar's daughter; of the tsar's daughter who rose from the grave, and of the fearless hero who guarded her tomb (the same theme used by N. V. Gogol in his *Viy*); the tale of the milk of wild animals, which the wicked sister sends her brother to fetch; the tale of the search made by the husband for his wife who has been carried off, her liberation with the help of miraculous objects or animals; the tales of the stepmother and the stepdaughter (or "Morozko"), of the little sea horse, of the apples of perpetual youth, which are procured by the youngest of three sons, but which the older sons get possession of, by casting the younger son into a pit, from which he is nevertheless miraculously saved. There are also the tales "of the horns that grow out of berries" (with the help of these, the hero regains possession of miraculous objects, which had been seized by the tsar's daughter); of the miraculous bird, after eating of which, one brother becomes a tsar, the other a rich man; the tales of truth and falsehood, of the girl without hands, who had had her hands cut off by her brother (she became the tsar's wife, was slandered, exiled, but later healed and returned again to her husband); the tales of the "hero's fight with the dragon at the Kalinovsky Bridge" and of the hero's transformation of the dragon into a mare.

Well known are the tales of Kashchey's death in the egg, which the hero procures by the method of transforming himself into various animals, or else with their aid; of Ivan the Son of a Mare; of the birth of heroes from fish that has been eaten, water that has been drunk, and so on. There are the tales of "the science of cunning," which a father sent his son to a wizard to learn; by the help of this science (of making transformations) the son saves himself from persecution; of Helen the Fair, from whom her future bridegroom hides himself three times (in plants and animals); the tale on the theme, "Go thither, I know not whither; bring with you that, no one knows what," where the girl-bird, having become the wife of the hero, helps him to perform these tasks.

Then there are the tales of the Brazen Face, in which the tsar's son liberates a miraculous captive, who becomes his faithful servant and helper; the tales of the gray chestnut, who becomes the property of the youngest brother (the fool); on this steed he gallops to the tsar's daughter and becomes her husband; the tales of know-nothings, where the hero, by the advice of his horse, makes answer to all questions, "I don't know," vanquishes his enemies, and wins the hand of the tsar's daughter; the tales of the animal brothers-in-law, who help the hero to gain a beautiful bride; the tales of Ivan the Bear's Ear, the hero who was a man of unusual strength, and finally, the tales about the dead daughter of the tsar, who came to life in the tomb, and was received by the tsar's son into his own house. These are the most popular magical tales in Russian folklore, which have been encountered in the recordings of scholars in more than ten variants.

It is of interest, following Andreyev, to note the subjects of magical tales, which appear to be, as it were, the peculiar property of Russian folklore, inasmuch as they are not encountered in western Europe, or else are very uncommon there (they number thirty-eight). Of the most popular, the following should be mentioned at this point: "The Battle at the Kalinovsky Bridge," "Ivashka and the Witch," "Morozko," "The Tsar's Dog," and "Troubles." On the other hand, as we have already said, there are forty-eight types of miraculous tales, native to western Europe, which are unknown in Russian folklore; such, for example, are the subjects of "The Kingdom Turned to Stone," of "The Enchanted Prince in the Wood," of "The Miraculous Mill," and others.

Even the very thematics, the subjects and motifs of the magical tales characterize these tales, with sufficient clearness, as constituting a special genre. The magical tale has also its characteristic *personages*, who are native to it. They may be broken up into several groups. These are the heroes themselves, who perform the exploits, or the persons who are liberated or rescued by the heroes—mostly women (brides, wives, sisters, mothers, and so on), and then the miraculous helpers or good counselors, who make the hero's exploits easy for him. Opposed to the hero are his enemies and those who help his enemies. The contrast of the figures of the tale (the heroes and their enemies) results from the very thematics of the magical tale (combat, exploits, rescues). Hyperbolism of representation is an attribute of the very genre of the wonderful, magical tale. Although the personages who take part in the motifs and subjects of the tales may very often vary, still this variation occurs within fixed limits: the personages who take part in the magical tale have their traditional type, they assume the definite coloring of the type. These personages are endowed with their own characteristics in the tale, and the representation of them proceeds according to specific methods.

The wondrous heroes of the tales are mostly Ivan the tsar's son, Vasily the king's son, and so forth. Often they are of miraculous origin, and this fact is emphasized by their nicknames: Ivan the Bear's Ear, Ivan the Son of a Mare, Ivan the Son of a Bitch, or simply without any name: the Tsarevich, the king's son, the tsar's son. He is generally handsome: "a picture of beauty, his glance is that of a falcon, he rises up like the lion among beasts, you cannot take your eyes from him." But often, for purposes of the contrast of types which has been emphasized above, this true hero, at the beginning of the tale, is represented as the traditional Ivanushka the Fool, Ivanushka Sit-by-the Stove, who "was sitting on the stove, winding the mucus from his nose into a ball." Such he seems to all those who are about him, but still he, recognized by no one, under a miraculously changed aspect performs his exploits, prevailing over his clever brothers and his other rivals. Much less frequently, in the miraculous tale, the chief hero is the son of a merchant or a peasant. These personages are chiefly the heroes of another genre of tales—the tales of everyday life. Somewhat more often, the hero of the miraculous tale is a soldier, but even he still has to be acknowledged as a personage appearing in the main type of everyday tale, the legendary tale (the conflict with an unclean power) or anecdote.

The heroines in the miraculous tales are mostly either "wise virgins," or "pictures of beauty" who are saved by the heroes, and are endowed with all the virtues and beauty which are native to the tale. There are Helen the Fair; Martha, Anna, and Vasilissa, who are all-wise; Nastasia the king's daughter, Marya Morevna, the girl tsar, the tsar's daughter "the golden stream," "the golden-haired maiden from beyond the sea," "Lena the beauty, with her golden braid." The heroine of the tale is usually "such a beautiful girl, that everyone who catches sight of her stands still," "such as cannot be told in a tale, nor described with the pen." Some of these heroines of the tales are warrior maidens. "A maiden, and her glance was that of the bright falcon, her brows were of the black sable, her little face was white, her cheeks were scarlet; she was an exceedingly handsome girl." The character of such a martial maiden is clear from the epithets which are applied to her in such cases: "the all-powerful princess," "the powerful enchantress," "the valiant maiden," "she who is valiant," "the valiant one." On the other hand, modesty, simplicity, and lyric tenderness are the distinguishing marks of the suffering heroines, such as Zolushka, the Ice Maiden, Little Sister Alenushka, and others.

The characters of the miraculous helpers of the hero, and their functions, are often depicted in their very names: such, for example, are the well known figures in the tales, Obyedalo (the Great Eater), Opivalo (the Great Drinker), Gorynya (the Great Mountain), Dubynya (the Great Cudgel), Usynya (the Big Whiskers), the knights, Gorokat (the Mountain Roller) with the Nine Drinks, "Usynets (the Mustached) the knight—with his mustaches he blocks up the river, with his mouth he catches the fish," Break-the-Iron, Pull-Down-the-Wall, and others. As miraculous helpers of the hero there appear the "tutors" Nikita Koltoma, or Mishka the Knapsack, or the Stormy Knight, or the Story Valiant, Mishka the Water Carrier, or "Matthew the Hunchback, with his multiangular helmet, his accurately aiming arm, his swift foot, his powerful shoulder—he can do many things." Among the kind helpers of the hero in the tales there appear often the "old women of the household," enchantresses, or even sometimes the witch Baba-Yaga. But most frequently of all, it is the animals who come to the aid of the hero: among these miraculous helpers the first place must be assigned to "the gray chestnut, the prophetic chestnut mare," "the golden-maned and golden-hoofed steed." One must mention also the little goldfish, and the pike ("at the bidding of the pike"), and the "little gold bristly pig," and the lion among beasts, and the little fish from the brook, and the wasp from the wasp's nest, and the gray wolf, and the eagle, raven, and the miraculous bird, which feeds with its own flesh the hero who is flying upon it, and others.

With the greatest clearness, at times with all the boldness of sculpture, there are delineated the story types of the enemies of the hero, of the miraculous hostile forces. A typical example of the magical tale is afforded by the witch Baba-Yaga. She is the favorite character of the Russian miraculous tale. Her characteristics are set forth in a special rhymed form: "Baba-Yaga has a long foot, she goes riding in a mortar, she chases people with her broom." She sits in the hut: "In front is her head, in one corner is one of her feet, in the other is the other." Another representative of the hostile forces in the Russian tale is Kashchey (or Kosh, or Koshchuy) the Immortal, who often takes on the appearance of a dragon. The most constant type, in the Russian miraculous tale, is the dragon (the Serpent, the Great Serpent of the Mountains), which is endowed with three, six, nine, twelve or more heads, the Flying Dragon, the Fiery Dragon. He carries off beautiful girls and devours people. We may further mention the wicked enchanters and enchantresses—the Evil One with the one eye, the One-Eyed Woe, the Great Pagan Idol, and others.

Magical objects and prodigies perform essential functions in the miraculous tale. Essentially, they are the same personages who are active in the tale: the miraculous objects in the tale live and are active. Here also the tradition of the tale has worked out standard formulary figures. The figures of "inexhaustible" miraculous objects are very popular in the Russian magical tale. Here we have, above all, the famous "tablecloth that spreads itself," or the miraculous "little table" which sets itself at the command of the hero, or the "little pitcher with the forty spouts" or "horns," from which appear various kinds of drinks and viands, or the "purse that shakes itself," or the "decanter that does the catering": it fills itself, and does the serving itself. Closely related to it are the miraculous "self-acting" objects of the type of the "magic carpet," or the "carpet that flies." Such also are the "swiftly running shoes" of the tale. Here belongs also the "self-sounding psaltery," or "self-singing psaltery," which dances itself, sings songs, and causes everyone involuntarily to dance.

The list of variations includes the figure of the miraculous self-acting weapons: "the sword that cuts by itself," "the cudgel that fights by itself," "the hatchet that chops by itself," and others. We may note especially the miraculous objects which conceal the brave young warriors, and at the proper moment allow them to issue forth again. The magical tale often speaks of the miraculous coffer, box, egg, and other objects, out of which there can appear both a garden and a palace, and even whole kingdoms. No small role in the Russian miraculous tale is played also by the "cap of invisibility," which confers upon its wearer the power to remain invisible to other people. Typical of the miraculous tale are the concepts of living and dead water, of the water which increases or diminishes strength, and also the concepts of the "soporific draft" or of other "sleep-inducing" objects, such as the "sleeping herbs," the "sleeping drops," the pins, ring, comb, and other articles, which also possess the properties of inducing sleep.

Very frequent in the miraculous tales are the enchanted objects which have the magical power to transform themselves into powerful barriers, in order to save the fleeing heroes from their pursuers. Such are the little comb, out of which a forest grows or a mountain is formed; the handkerchief or short towel which transforms itself into a lake, a river or a sea, and so on. Characteristic of the Russian miraculous tale are the magical objects which possess the property of revealing, at a great distance, what has happened to the hero. These are, as it were, "prophetic objects." They may be a handkerchief, a towel, a pair of gloves, a shirt from which blood must appear in case any misfortune has overtaken the hero; a glass filled with blood, which will turn black in case of any accident to the hero, and so on. Very rich, in the magical tale, is the stock of miraculous natural wonders employed in the storytelling: the firebird, the silver saucer with the juicy apples, the miraculous singing tree with the golden foliage, the gold and silver apples; the "apples of youth," the stag with the golden horns, and many others. In the storyteller's understanding, all these objects, without exception, are thought of as endowed with life and the power of action.

No matter how characteristic of the tale its heroes and objects may be—the living or animated bearers of the *action of the tale*—still the most important thing, and the most characteristic of the tale as a genre, is the action itself. For the miraculous tale, this action determines the magical and adventurous character of that tale as a specific narrative genre. The acting personages, in the variants of the tale, are less well established than their functions, that is, the action itself. The sequence of this action, its combination in the miraculous tale, are subject to a definite and established law. This determines a certain stability in the inner composition of the miraculous tales.

In very recent years there has appeared, in our folklorists, a series of works concerned with the study of precisely this aspect of the miraculous tales.

The effort of R. M. Volkov to treat the study of the "subject composition of the popular tale" in his book [53] is based upon a selection of Russian, Ukrainian, and White Russian variants of the tales of the persecuted innocents. These are tales of the type of the stepmother and stepdaughter, about the substitute wife, about the unjustly persecuted wife, about the calumniated sister (with the short arm), and others. The author has made an effort to determine the major and minor motifs of which the subjects of this series of magical tales are composed, and to reduce them to certain formulas. The author, having, as we have said, put his book together on an exceedingly formalistic plan, has at the same time failed to show sufficient precision in his method, and in the concept of "motifs" he has included both the "simplest narrative units" (motifs) and also those immanent details which we have referred to above as "elements."

It is A. N. Nikiforov who places us upon the firm ground of principle in the study of the morphology of the tale, with particular reference, above all, to the functions (that is, the actions) of the persons who take part in the tale.

Starting from the altogether correct idea that the concrete personages of the tale do not appear to be to any extent stabilized, that they are endlessly changing in the variants, and that, on the other hand, the only things that are found to be constant are the functions of the personages, he proposes to take as the basis of study precisely these

[53] R. M. Volkov, *The Tale: Researches on the Subject Composition of the Folk Tale*, Vol. I (Odessa, 1924).

functions of the persons, and their classification, through which he will be able to study the picture of the actions in the tale. He shows that the range of the functions of each type of personage (he distinguishes two types: the hero and the secondary personages—his helpers or his enemies) is very limited.

The main personage, the hero, assumes functions, so to speak, of a biographical kind (miraculous birth, swift development, the test of his powers, the acquiring of his weapons, his horse, his helpers, the choice of an aim, the journeying, the dream, the solution of difficult problems, the attaining of something or other, and so on). The secondary personages assume functions of a kind which, so to speak, "complicate the adventure" (helping or hindering the hero), or serve as the object that is to be sought (for example, a bride, or miraculous objects).

Furthermore, it is the grouping of the particular functions of the main personage and of the secondary personages into a certain number of combinations, according to the principle of very (but not absolutely) free conjunctions, that constitutes the mainspring of the tale's plot structure.[54]

It is precisely to the task of studying the *functions* of the persons who are active in the magical tale, and their combination, that the above-mentioned book by V. Propp is devoted.[55] According to his opinion, for the study of the tale "the important question is, what the personages of the tale do; but the questions of who does it, and how he does it—these are questions requiring only incidental study." In these words, beyond a doubt, is expressed the formalistic approach to the tale; for a full study, of course, all these functions are very important. But for the study of the structure of the tale, the actions, the behavior, or, as the author expresses it, "the functions of the persons who take part in the action," as the best established components of the tale, have an unspeakably greater significance. The author, analyzing these functions (he worked over 110 magical tales from

[54] A. N. Nikiforov, "On the Question of the Morphological Study of the Folk Tale," *Annals of the Division of Russian Language and Literature of the Academy of Sciences*, Vol. CI, No. 8, Leningrad, 1928, pp. 173-177.
[55] *The Morphology of the Tale.*

Afanasyev's vast collection, tale by tale), came to the conclusion that the number of functions known to the magical tale is limited, that the sequence of the functions is always identical, and that, in the last analysis, all the magical tales are uniform in their structure. In the tales which he studied, Propp counted altogether thirty-one basic functions (apart from their variations).

Personages who are typical of the stories, typical magical objects, and finally, typical behavior, the "functions" of the heroes of the tales, and of the personages in general, by themselves define the particular character of the miraculous tale as a specific narrative genre. Still more helpful in the isolation of this genre is an examination of the internal devices, the structure, the composition of the tale, by the use of correct, alternating sequences of the actual events of the tale, coming in sequence one after another

The miraculous tale has also a specific method of systematizing its literary material. To put it briefly, the miraculous tale is characterized by the peculiarities of its stylistics. The wealth of carefully worked out, original literary formulas, passing by tradition from mouth to mouth, with their variations of one kind or another—this is what constitutes the striking peculiarity of the style of the miraculous tale.

The stylistically sustained Russian miraculous tale has its typical formulas for the beginning and the end of the tale, the so-called "storytellers' exordia" (embellishments) (compare the proem of the *bylina*) and "conclusions." Recently a well known Czech scholar, the folklorist Professor J. Polivka, compared these opening and closing formulas of the Russian tales with the formulas used in the tales of other nations, and the conclusions of the Russian tales proved to be especially rich and very artistically varied on the lips of individual storytellers, within the limits of the traditional formula.[56]

The storytellers themselves call the approach to the tale the "storyteller's exordium," contrasting it to the tale itself. The purpose of the storyteller's exordium is to focus the attention of the listener. The

[56] See "Jiři Polivka, Úvodni a záverečne formule slovanskych pohádek (Formules initiales et finales des contes slaves), *Národnopisny českoslovansky Vistnik* (Czechoslovak News of Popular Literature), XIX-XX, Praha, 1926–1927. The stylistics of the Russian tales has been analyzed in detail by Prof. Polivka in his book *Slovanské pohádky*. I úvod. Východoslovanské pohádky (Prague, 1932).

exordium usually is not connected with the content of the tale. It is generally rhythmic in form. It is usually spoken in a dashing manner, and, as we shall see from the examples, it is customarily humorous in content. Here are typical storytellers' exordia:

The tale begins with the gray chestnut, with the nag, with the prophetic steed. By the sea, by the ocean, on the island of Buyan, there is a roast bull, beside it is a crushed onion, and three young fellows are going along, they stop and have lunch, and they go on farther and start boasting, and they are amusing themselves: we are really brothers at such a place, and we eat our fill, more than a peasant woman, of dough. This is the exordium, the tale lies before us (Afanasyev, No. 79).

Or the exordium which is used in part by Pushkin:

This affair takes place on the sea, on the ocean, on the island of Kidan; there stands a tree, with a golden top; along this tree walks a tomcat, purring, and when he goes up, he sings a song, and when he comes down, he tells stories. There would be something curious and amusing to look at! This is not the tale, but it's still the exordium that is going on, and the whole tale lies before us. This will be a tale to be told from the morning until after dinnertime, when we have eaten some soft bread. And here we will introduce the tale (the Sokolovs, No. 139).

Other storytellers' exordia designate the place of the action; but in distinction from the *bylina*, which, as we have seen, usually has a historical basis, the designations of place in the tale prove to be vague, and definitely "fantastic." "In a certain kingdom, in a certain realm, there once lived a prince, a tsar, a merchant, and so on."

Frequently such a formula takes on a certain, actually ironical coloring, emphasizing the fabulous unreality of the kingdom: "Here in a certain kingdom, in a certain realm, in that very one where we are living now, there once lived Ondron the Unfortunate" (the Sokolovs). In certain of the exordia this irony is further developed: "In a certain kingdom, in a certain realm, in that precise one in which we are living, on a place that was smooth, as if on a harrow, there lived a Tsar and a Tsarina" (the Sokolovs, Onchukov, and others). Widely diffused in the Russian tales are the simple formulas of the beginning: "There lived—there was," which is undoubtedly an ar-

chaic verb form (the pluperfect) from the verb "to live," which has
disappeared from the living language but has been preserved in the
tale: "there lived—there was," "there lived—there were," "there was
existing and living," and so on.

In a fashion similar to that of the exordia and the beginnings, the
Russian miraculous tale worked out its typical formulas for the *endings*, the conclusions of the tale. These also often bear the stamp of
humor. The function of the ending is to release the attention of
the hearer, to call forth in him a smile or even a laugh, and sometimes also to turn the attention upon the storyteller himself, with
the aim of receiving thanks, a treat, or a present. The ending is
usually rhythmic, is spoken with a rapid "tongue twisting," and sometimes has rhyme. A typical formula is the indication: "And I was
there, I drank the mead and beer, it flowed over my mustache, but
missed my mouth." But this formula has a further expansion, worked
out by various storytellers in a whole series of variations.

The appeal to the listeners, with an allusion to a treat as a reward,
is manifest in endings of this type: "For you the tale, but for me the
little wallet of money" (the Sokolovs); "Here is the tale for you,
but for me a string of baked dough rings," or: "Here the tale comes
to an end, a fine fellow told it"; "For us, the fine fellows, a little
glass of beer apiece, at the ending of the tale a little wine glass full
of wine" (Afanasyev). Or such brief endings as these: "This is all
the story, well, there are no more lies to tell" (the Sokolovs); "That's
the whole story" (Onchukov); "Well, that's all"; "And this is the
end of the story." Especially popular in the Russian tales are the concluding formulas: "They lived happily ever after, in the enjoyment
of their property" (Afanasyev); "Now they live there and eat their
bread" (the Sokolovs), and so on.

From the characteristics of the storytellers, we have seen that certain of them make particularly frequent use of the storytellers' exordia, and work them up artistically. We need only mention the
Voronezh narrator Kupryanikha, in whose tales there are a great
many of these exordia.[57]

---

[57] They have been cited by N. P. Grinkova in *Artistic Folklore*, No. I, 1926.

The whole wealth of stylistic formulas in the tales is by no means exhausted by the initial and final exordia. Every typical situation, action, and figure is expressed by *its own typical storytelling formula,* has its own *locus communis.* We cannot exhaust these formulas here. We may note only those that are most frequently used.[58]

Such, for example, are the transitional phrases, "The story is soon told, but the business is not soon done." Such are the typical speeches of individual personages in the story, for example, the words of the miraculous helper: "Do not grieve, lie down and sleep, morning is wiser than evening"; or the words of the hostile creature (a dragon, the witch Baba-Yaga, Kashchey, and so on): "Phew, phew, it smells of Russians"; or the appeal of the masters, who have come to their deserted house, to the strange woman who has hidden herself from them: "If you are an old person, you shall be to us as a mother; if you are a beautiful girl, you shall be to us as our own sister," and so on. Also typical is the address of the hero, Ivanushka the Fool, to his miraculous steed: "My grayish chestnut * my prophetic Ka-vurko, stand before me, quivering, like a leaf before the grass." By a typical formula, there is depicted, in greater or lesser detail, the actual running of the little grayish chestnut horse: "The horse runs, the earth trembles, from his nostrils there comes smoke, and out of his ears there issues flame."

By a traditional formula there is depicted also the fabulous beauty of the hero, "which cannot be told in a tale, nor described with the pen." The customary formula depicts the climactic moment of the majority of tales—the wedding of the hero: "Let us gather, not to brew beer, not to distill spirits, but at a fine pleasant feast, and for a wedding." Upon the skill and artistic sense in the utilization of this kind of story formulas depends the stylization, or "ritualism," of the tale. The best storytellers, as we have seen, usually devote the most attention to the stylistic adornment of the

---

[58] For a more detailed exposition see S. V. Savchenko, *The Russian Folk Tale,* Chap. I; R. M. Volkov, "Devices of the Storytelling Style," *The Tale,* Chap. I, and the above-mentioned works of Prof. Y. Polivka.

* *Sivka-burka:* Standard form of fond address to horses in Russian fairy tales. Literally translated as "grayish chestnut," it is actually a general, endearing address for a faithful horse.—Ed.

magical tale. A characteristic and exceedingly essential feature of the storytelling style, and specifically of the style of the miraculous tale, is the *device of repetition*, or *retardation*. A characteristic type of the repetitions is the triad. In the tale, whole motifs are repeated, episodes with slight variations. An essential device is repetition with a constantly greater and greater heightening of effect. The *heightening of effect* is often expressed in numerical relationships: at first the hero fights with a dragon that has one head, then with one that has three heads, then with one that has nine heads. The same kind of increase will be shown also in the heightening of the quality and value of the miraculous objects or phenomena, and in the gradual increase of the difficulty of the tasks or obstacles, and so on. The device of the triad and of the heightening of effect can be discovered in any variant of the miraculous tale.

Tales of animals constitute approximately 10 per cent of the entire Russian repertory of tales, as known to scholarship. In western Europe this genre of the tale, as we have already said above, is a good deal more widely diffused; this is to be explained by the special character of the medieval literature of western Europe, where the animal epos was very popular. Out of sixty-seven subjects in the Russian tales of animals, half of these subjects are common with the western European, while half belong only to the Russian repertory. On the other hand, seventy-two subjects encountered in western Europe are totally unknown to the Russian tale. The best known and most popular Russian animal tales are the tales on a well known subject, such as the fox who pretended to be dead, and stole fish from the cart. Also popular is the subject of the wolf who had his tail cut off: the wolf's tail is freezing, but the women attack the wolf with yokes; he manages to save himself, although he is deprived of his tail.

A third, especially popular subject, is also connected with the fox. It relates how the fox eats up the butter (or honey), pretending that she is invited to a delivery, or a christening (the subject of the fox midwife). Further down the scale of waning popularity come the subjects of the quarrel between the mouse and the sparrow, who had set up a common household; from this quarrel arises a war between the birds and the beasts. We may mention a subject, known by the title "The Mansion of the Fly," where the fly, the hare, the fox, and the wolf crawl in, and the bear crushes them all; the subject of the cat, the cock, and the fox, the latter having, in the absence of the cat, carried off the cock; but the cat, having caught up with her, takes the cock away from her. The subject of the fox and her tail is popular. The fox, having saved herself from the dog by flight, has a talk with the members of her own body, as to who has done what, and thrusts out her tail from her lair for the dogs, because it has hindered her in her flight.

Then there is the subject of the beasts in the sledge at the fox's, which relates how these beasts, during their journey, eat up the steer which has been yoked to the sledge. There is known, not only in oral transmission, but also in popular print and in manuscripts, the tale of Ersha the Fish's Son, who is judged on the complaint of the bream, but the elusive defendant laughs at the court and the judges. In a somewhat smaller number there are encountered records of the tale of "The Winter Lodge of the Beasts," who drive away the enemy that is trying to penetrate into their house; the tale of the wolf who by his hypocritical song entices away from the old man the various animals, and then his little granddaughter and his aged wife.

Closely akin to this is the subject of "a goose for a rolling pin." In the morning the fox, on the pretext that she has lost her rolling pin, demands of the owners, in whose house she has spent the night, a goose, and after the goose a ewe lamb, and so forth. The subject of the hut of ice and bast again speaks of the fox, who in winter built a hut of ice, and then intended to drive the bear, the hare, and the other animals out of their bast hut. Also popular is the tale of the she-goat who does not come out of the woods with the nuts: after the she-goat they send a wolf, after the wolves a bear, and so forth ("The She-Goat with the Nuts"). Typical of the animal tales of the world is the figure of the fox, appearing in the tales of the fox nurse or wailer who eats up the children, the bear, or the dead old woman, and of the fox confessor, who confesses the cock and then seizes him. Also famous are the subjects of the judgment of the eagle upon the crow, and of the death of the cockerel: the cockerel is choking, the pullet goes to the stream for water, the stream sends to the little linden tree for a leaf, the linden tree sends to the girl for a thread, and so forth; when help does arrive at last, the cockerel is found to be dead. The list given here of the most popular subjects of the Russian animal tales has already characterized the latter to a sufficient extent.

It is not without interest to point out that of the tales enumerated, those which are typically Russian—in any event, those which are unknown in western Europe—are found to be "The Fox Midwife," "The Cat, the Cock, and the Fox," "The Singing of the Wolf," "The Cockerel Was Choked," and "The Mansion of the Fly." On the other hand, in the Russian Folk tales of animals, such western European tales as "The Crow and the Fox," "The War of the Wild and the Domestic Animals," "The Crow and the Frog," "The Bear on the Cart" (compare the "General Toptygin" of Nekrasov, and others) are unknown.

The animal tales developed their own *typical figures*. Their typical-ness is often manifested even in those attributes and epithets which the animal tale assigns to its heroes. The chief heroine of the animal tales is the crafty fox, the fox Patrikeyevna, the handsome fox, the beautiful fox, the fox with the oily lips, the wonderful beauty, the raspberry-colored one, the godmother-fox, the gossip, Godmother Lisafiya, little sister the fox (her brother is the wolf or the cock), the little fox; this crafty fox is often represented as a smooth-tongued seller of holy bread, a wily confessor, or a deceiving midwife. Her speeches are invariably sweet, studiedly caressing, and flattering. Not without reason is she called: "the fox with the caressing words," "the most wise princess," or "the fox who is a beautiful talker."

A direct contrast to the crafty fox is the simple-minded wolf. The "fool of a wolf," "the stupid old wolf," "the gray fool," is the very one upon whom the fox generally plays her tricks. In the animal tale the bear is shown as clumsy and sluggish—"Mikhaylo Ivanych," "Mishka," "Mishka the uprooter of trees, he came to uproot the trees, he lies around at his den," "the forest crusher," "the gray good peasant." All the sluggishness of this denizen of the woods is expressed not only in the literary image, but even in the very rhythm of the little song which is sung by the bear "with the linden paw":

> *Ker-thump, ker-thump, ker-thump.*
> On a linden foot,
> On a birchen staff,
> On a fine stick.
> In the villages people sleep,
> In the countryside they sleep,
> Only a woman does not sleep,
> She sits upon my skin,
> She spins my hair,
> She boils my flesh,
> She dries my skin.[59]

As a type of the cowardly animal in the tales, there is introduced the hare, "the little gray fellow" or "the little white fellow," "the hare who runs away," "the rascally hare," "the hare, Peter Rabbit," "his legs are very slender, he himself is very light." The cat, represented either as the "purring cat" (the storyteller), or in the form of a "zither player," "the nice purring cat, the gray forehead," "the handsome cat," Kotofey Ivanych. The she-goat is usually an unscrupulous creature; her character is clearly represented in the tale of the she-goat who has been beaten, the tale which relates how she took the hare's house away from him; here the she-goat is described: "the she-goat who is crumbling, half her side is beaten."

There is a whole series of tales which give a neat characterization of the various animals: the definitions themselves, the names of the animals, their very sound and form, are dictated by visual, motor, and especially by aural impressions and observations upon the life of animals.[60] Thus in the well known tale "The Mansion of the Fly," all of the ill fated inhabitants of that mansion are characterized by precise epithets. At the end comes the heavy-footed bear: "Who, who, who is in the mansion? Who, who, who is in the lofty room?" "I am the fly, the unfortunate one"; "I am the louse, the crawling

---

[59] K. Avdeyeva, *Russian Tales for Children* (St. Petersburg, 1879), p. 37.

[60] See a more detailed discussion of this point in the article by A. M. Smirnov-Kutachevsky, "The Creation of a Word in the Folk Tale," *Artistic Folklore*, II-III, Moscow, 1927.

one"; "I am the flea, the jumping one"; "I am the mosquito, the long-legged one"; "I am the little mouse, the squeaking one"; "I am the little lizard, who makes the leaves rustle"; "I am the fox, Patrikeyevna"; "I am the little hare, from under the little bush"; "I am the great big wolf, with the big gray tail." Then they all cry out from the mansion: "But who are *you?*" The bear says, "I am the reckless fellow who crushes everyone," and he puts his paw down across the mansion and crushes it. Of course every variant of the tale has its peculiarities. Here, in fact, there is revealed the story-teller's rich narrative ability in the creation of words.

Let us take another variant of this same tale of the "mansion." Here several other animals are enumerated, and several other defini-tions are given for the animals that we have already encountered, though it is curious that the general character of each figure is pre-served: "Here is the bear coming toward us: 'Mansion, little man-sion, who is living in the mansion?' 'The little mouse who lives in the hole, the frog that croaks, he who runs on the mountain [the hare], she who leaps and bounds everywhere [the fox], and he who springs out from behind the bushes and catches you' [the wolf]. 'But I am he who crushes all of you.' He sat on their heads and crushed them all." A great gallery of representatives of the animal world is given in the tales of trials, such as that of Ersha, Son of the Fish, of the "Trial of the Crow," and also in the poetic *bylina* tale of "The Birds."

A majority of Russian animal tales are distinguished by a particular *style* of their own. With reference to their composition, these tales are set apart from many others by virtue of the fact that, from the viewpoint of their composition, the majority of them are constructed upon the *motif of a meeting*. In fact, the tales of the "little mansion" are based on a meeting of the beasts, the tales of "the speckled pul-let" on meetings of human beings; the tale "The Cockerel Was Choked," on meetings of the pullets; "The She-Goat Who Was Beaten," on meetings with a she-goat; "The Linden Paw," on meet-ings with a bear, and so on. The specific peculiarity of this genre is seen to be the manifold *repetitiousness* of the same subject element, which has been reduced to a specific form: the pullet many times repeats the request for water for the cock; the hare, driven by the fox out of the little bast hut, makes his complaint in precisely the same words, in turn, to the dogs, to the bear, the ox, the cock, and so on.

There is a change in the first responsive onomatopoetic phrase used by the animals, but the text of the dialogue is basically unaltered. "A dear little hare is going along and weeping, and the dogs meet him and say: 'Tyaf, tyaf, tyaf. Why are you crying, little hare?' And the hare says: 'Wait a minute, dogs. Why should I not cry? I had a fine hut of bast, and the fox had one made of ice. She invited herself in, and drove me out of my house.' 'Do not cry, little hare,' say the dogs, 'we will drive her out.' 'No, do not drive her out.' 'No, we will drive her out.' They went up to the fine mansion. 'Tyaf, tyaf, tyaf! Come out here, fox.' But she answered them from the stove: 'When I spring out, when I jump out, the fur will fly, through all the furthest corners.'" The dogs were terrified and fled. When the hare complains to the cock, he repeats his complaint word for word, while the cock crows in answer. "Cock-a-doodle-doo!"

The form of the animal tales is that of a *dialogue*; furthermore, the dialogue may be in prose (as in the example given above), or in the form of a poetic song. The latter form of dialogue is an especial favorite in this genre. Compare the little song sung by the fox under the window of the cock's house ("Cockerel, cockerel, with your comb all of gold" and so forth); the little song of the small round loaf of bread ("I am scraped from the basket, swept from the floor, mixed with the sour cream, and mingled with the butter, chilled at the window; I avoided the grandfather, I avoided the grandmother, but as for you, hare, it doesn't take any great cleverness to avoid you"). Compare the little song, cited above, of the bear with the linden paw, the songs of "The She-Goat Who Was Beaten," "The She-Goat and the Young Goats," and others. All this, especially in conjunction with the theatrical quality imparted to the tale itself (the singing of little songs, the imitation by the voice of the sounds of animals, the representation by action, pantomime, gesticulation, and so on), compels us to add the genre of animal tales to the genre of dramatic tales, as A. I. Nikiforov has done with absolute correctness. The animal tales are now mainly found to be children's tales, that is, they are related either by children or for them. In their scope the animal tales are usually rather short; they are never long.[61]

A part of the animal tales must be, according to their composition, related to the cumulative tales, that is, to the tales which are chainlike, with an increase in the action, like the famous tale of the "turnip." Of the animal tales, those which belong completely to this type are the tales of "The She-Goat with the Nuts," "The Little Round Loaf," and others. The she-goat went out nutting and did not return home; the he-goat sends the wolves out to look for her, the wolves refuse to come; after the wolves they send men, after the men they send bears, after the bears they send the butt end of an ax, and so on, until the time when someone refuses to perform what is asked, after which "the geese went to pick worms, the worms went to gnaw the butt end of the ax, the butt end of the ax went to throw down the bulls, the bulls went to drink water," and so forth. The final outcome was that the she-goat returned home with the nuts.

As we have already said above, the realistic tales (the short stories, or those dealing with everyday life) and anecdotes undoubtedly occupy the dominant place in the repertory of the Russian tales. They constitute in the aggregate more than 60 per cent of all the Russian tale material. In these genres the Russian tale has yielded the greatest number of subjects which are unknown in western Europe: the short-story subjects which we have in common with those of western Europe constitute 41.9 per cent of our total, and those which are original with us, 58.1 per cent; of the anecdotes, those which we have in common with those of western Europe constitute 33.7 per cent, and the original, 66.3 per cent.

The *themes* of the short stories dealing with everyday life fall into the following basic groups: the marriage of a hero, the correction by a husband of a refractory or lazy wife, the themes of good, prudent counsels, of the clever youth or maiden, the themes of fate ("There is no escaping destiny") and good fortune, of brigands

[61] Cf. A. I. Nikiforov, "The Popular Children's Tale of Dramatic Genre," *The Storytelling Commission in the Year 1927* (Leningrad, 1928).

and thieves, and others. The inner themes, the basic "ideational problems" of these tales, are found to be questions of social inequality,
the contrast between wealth and poverty, personal independence and
fate, good fortune and ill fortune, good and bad, cleverness and
stupidity, questions dealing with marriage (fidelity, faithlessness, deceit). *Contrast*, opposition, are basic to the composition of these
tales and to the delineation of the heroes. But, in contradistinction
to the magical tales, this conflict of two principles takes place in the
sphere of real social and everyday relationships.

The most popular, those which are encountered most frequently
of all in the Russian records, are the following subjects from everyday life, the tales of good counsels, "of the three words": A husband,
at the advice of his wife, sells her wares for three counsels: "Finish
what you have begun," "Raise your hand, but do not strike," "Iron
is more precious than gold," and so on. With the help of these
counsels he attains good fortune. The most popular tale is that of
fate ("There is no escaping destiny"—compare also "Marko the Rich
Man"). To a poor man's son it is foretold that he will be the heir of
a rich man; the rich man buys him, wants to destroy him, abandons
him in the woods (or throws him into the sea, and so on); the boy is
brought up by a miller (in a monastery, and so on), the rich man
again meets him, takes him into his house, and sends him to his
wife with a letter; another letter is substituted for this one, the youth
marries the daughter of the rich man, the rich man gives orders that
he shall be destroyed in a tar pit (or something of that kind), but
perishes himself.

Further along comes the subject of the wise little girl, "the seven-
year-old." She answers the difficult questions of the tsar (or a gentleman), "What is swifter than anything else?" She herself throws him
into embarrassment by her doings and sayings ("Father rode away
to sow a thunderclap," or, "In order to hatch the chicks out of boiled
eggs, you have to raise boiled peas," and so on); she becomes his
wife, the tsar grows angry at her and orders her to go away; she takes
with her the sleeping tsar, as that which is the most precious to her.

Equally popular is the subject of a wife's faithfulness: the hero
has an argument with a merchant (or someone like that) as to the

faithfulness of his wife, the merchant by a ruse obtains proof of her infidelity (for example, a ring), the husband abandons his native land, his wife follows him in male attire, and finally everything is straightened out. Connected with this is the subject of the slandered girl; at the time of her father's departure the uncle wants to seduce the girl; not succeeding in this, he calumniates her; the father commissions his son to kill his sister, she is saved, and marries the tsarevich; a servant (an officer, and so on) tries to seduce her, she flees in male attire, and the final outcome is a happy ending.

Especially popular as a theme of short stories, among the Russian tales, is the subject of the monastery that was free from care. The tsar puts questions to the abbot: (1) Is it far to the sky? (2) How much am I worth? (3) What am I thinking, and so on. In place of the abbot a miller answers, or else a soldier, speaking for himself in his own person, answers the tsar: how high is the sky, how wide is the world, and how deep is the earth; and then he sells these answers for money to the courtiers. This subject is permeated with a great number of everyday and social elements of Russian life. Closely related to it is the also popular subject of the pot: a potter astonishes the tsar by his clever answers, the tsar orders the noblemen to buy his wares, the potter compels the nobleman to carry him on his shoulders (and so on). Realistically worked out, in the Russian tales, is the subject of the tokens of the tsarevna; with the help of a fife and three swine which dance to its tune, the hero finds out the distinctive marks of the tsarevna (to whom she will turn in the night, and so on).

The subject of the son of the tsar (Solomon) and the son of the blacksmith (or shepherd) is also popular. The children are changed; in the children's games, Solomon takes upon himself the role of the tsar, and reveals his wisdom. A short-story theme is the subject of Vasilisa Popovna, who changed her clothes, putting on male attire, and by cunning avoided the discovery of her sex. A wise woman is described also in the subject which follows next in popularity among the everyday tales, the theme of the purchased wife: a young man complains, "I've got a mind, but no money"; he buys a wife for money, who teaches him to block up precious stones into bricks (and so on), and to take these bricks as a present to the tsar; the young man receives a reward. Of the tales on the contrasting themes of shrewish or lazy women, in the Russian repertory there is often encountered the subject of the taming of the shrew: a husband tames a shrewish wife by the device of shooting a dog or a horse for disobedience, before her eyes; he breaks the dishes, and so on; the final result is that the wife becomes obedient, and at a subsequent trial by the husbands, to see whose wife is the most obedient of all, this wife is awarded the first place. Among other short-story subjects, the tales of "The Clever Thief," "The Brigand's Bride," who fled from him by cunning, and others, are popular.

Closely related to the short stories dealing with everyday life are the *anecdotes*; the distinction between them and the tales is conventional and to a great extent formal. So far as thematics is concerned, they have this entirely in common, except that in the anecdote there is a still greater dominance of realism and the quality of everyday life, and one feels more keenly the social, class accentuation and satire. There is no opportunity of enumerating here the 297 anecdotal subjects which are known in Russian records. Availing ourselves of the calculations of Andreyev, we may point out merely the most popular of these, that is, those which are encountered in the greatest number of Russian recordings. The most popular has proved to be the subject of the clever thief who steals an ox, a horse, a casket or a ring from a gentleman, a sheet from the bed, a young lady, a priest (in the latter case, by the device of dressing himself like an angel and promising the priest to lift him in a sack up to heaven). There are a great many subjects dealing with "clever thieves" among the Russian tales.

Another subject, no less popular, deals with the cunning jester (usually a peasant) who fools everybody: he sells a cow for a she-goat, he has a reputedly miraculous hat, which is supposed to "pay for everything"; a stick which reputedly has the power to raise the dead; a pot which cooks the food all by itself; a horse that will go and bring him money, and so on. As a final climax, the hero allows himself to be buried alive, and digs his way out of the grave with a knife. Upon the theme of a similar kind of cunning there is based the plot of "the dead body": the corpse of a murdered man is placed at someone else's window, or mounted on a horse, placed in a sledge, a boat, and so on, and each time a new person declares himself to be the cause of the man's death, while the real murderer gets paid off. Whereas this subject deals with a clever murderer, another subject, which vies with this one in popularity, tells of the murderer who is a fool. His brothers put a goat into the place where the corpse was, and in this way they keep the fool from being suspected of murder.

The subject, known widely, if not indeed throughout the world, of the man who became a diviner by accident is very popular in its Russian adaptation. The sorcerer Zhuchok guesses where a stolen horse will be found, or something of that kind (he has hidden it himself). Having gained renown as a diviner, he is called upon to find the tsar's seal ring, which has disappeared (he wants to run away, and says, "I have already got one," and so on). He must guess what the tsar has either in his hand (and he says in addition, "Zhuchok has fallen into the hands of the Tsar"), or in a tureen (he says, "The crow has flown away into the high mansions").

The anecdotes of impossibilities are very popular: a man climbs up into heaven by a tree, he lets himself down from there on leather straps, the straps are not long enough to reach down to the ground, he weaves ropes out of chaff, and so on, and in the end he falls. Or the impossible tale of how the wolf draws the man out of the marsh: on the man's head the duck builds a nest, the wolf comes to have a feast on the eggs, the man catches him by the tail, and in this manner he is freed from the marsh. Also popular are the impossible tales on the theme of a contest in lying, or a lie on a bet, especially the following variation: three brothers come to an old man's camp fire, asking for a light; he requires them to tell him an impossible tale; two of the brothers cannot comply with this request, and for this the old man cuts off from them, by previous agreement, the straps from their backs. The youngest brother compels the old man to cry out, "That's not true!" and thereby to lose the wager. The old man shouts, "That's not true!" at the words of the youngest brother, that "your grandfather carried my grandfather mounted on his back." Very well known, also, among the Russians is the subject dealing with the theme of luck by accident, about Thomas Berennikov, the burlesque knight, who kills seven flies at one blow, and accidentally, while blindfolded, kills his chief antagonist.

The subjects of wedded life, of infidelity, of the punishment of lovers, occupy a large place in the anecdotal tales and short stories. Of these, aside from the examples which have been cited above, those that are especially widely diffused among us are the following: "Nikola of the Hollow Tree," in which an unfaithful wife asks a tree how she can get rid of her husband; the husband, who has hidden himself in the hollow of the tree, answers her from there, playing the role of Nikola of the Hollow Tree; he advises her to feed her husband on pancakes with plenty of butter, in order to blind him. He pretends to be blinded, and then kills the lover. Widely diffused is the subject which was made use of by Gogol, dealing with the lovers of a beautiful woman (a priest, a deacon and a subdeacon), whom she conceals by turns in a trunk; her husband then draws them away to be sold in the bazaar. (The subject was also utilized in a literary narrative of the seventeenth century, the story of Karp Sutulov.) Closely akin to this is the no less popular subject of the expulsion of the lover in the form of a demon. A passer-by is accidentally shut up along with the lover of a woman, he threatens to sing out, and receives from the lover money and clothing; he is let out instead of the lover, then he proposes to the husband that he will drive the unclean power out of his house, and drives the lover out, after coating him with soot. The subject of the guest Terentieshch, which has been worked up in the form of a burlesque *bylina*, exists also in the guise of a popular tale. A wife sends her husband to fetch medicine, while she herself makes merry with her lover; a passer-by conceals the husband in a sack of straw, and begs permission of the wife to pass the night there; the wife sings a song about her husband, but the passer-by, in a song, gives him the advice that he should avenge himself upon his wife.

Very popular is a whole group of anecdotal subjects dealing with half-wits. There is the very well known subject of the absolute fool or simpleton, who speaks inopportunely: at a funeral—"Bear them out, and keep bearing them out"; at a wedding—"The vigil and the funeral incense." In another popular subject is set forth how a fool makes purchases: in town he buys cups, meat, butter, and so forth; he smashes the cups because they rattle, he breaks the spoons, and gives the meat to the dogs. Many other subjects exist concerning the fool. Closely related is an extensive group of anecdotes dealing with slow-witted provincial characters, with the stupid devil, priest, and so on. Among the anecdotal tales of the stupid devil, one which is encountered with special frequency, and which has been immortalized by Pushkin, is that of the workman Balda, who "threatened the devil that he would beat up the lake into waves with a rope"; other tales are about those who can throw the cudgel the farthest (a man threatens to throw it over a cloud); the flight from the workman who had climbed into a sack of provisions, the running contest with the hare, the struggle of the devil with his brother or grandfather, the bear-man, and many others.

The tale in the form of a short story from everyday life, and the anecdote tale, have their own *heroes* who are generally very different from the dignified heroes of the magical tale—the tsars, the princely knights, or potentates of the magical world—such figures as Vikhor * the Son of the Whirlwind, Kashchey the Deathless One, Likh the One-Eyed, and so on. The heroes of these tales are more real, more lifelike and close to us. As we have said already, both the tale of everyday life and the anecdote also are based upon contrasts. Contrasted also are the persons who take part in them: heroes and their enemies. But the "heroism" of these heroes consists neither in the accomplishment of difficult exploits, in the surmounting of enchanters' obstacles, nor in knightly combat with supernatural powers, but in the struggle of life—by cunning, by cleverness, by skill—against real social enemies. The "positive" persons who take part in the action are found to be chiefly the clever or cunning common man, who is generally a poor peasant, a workman, soldier, barge hauler, potter, tailor, shepherd, son of a merchant, a simple country woman or girl, a cunning thief, a jester; while, on the other hand, the "negative" element includes the nobleman or noblewoman, the general or the general's wife, the priest or the priest's wife, the rich

* Wind (or storm).—ED.

merchant, the rich peasant kulak, the miser or stupid provincial person, the absolute fool, and his kinsman the peasant, or the devil, but stripped of every vestige of his miraculous quality, and what is more, of grandeur.

Both the tsars and the tsarinas of the magical tale are brought in here, sometimes into the one, sometimes into the other category, but they are mainly abstract personages, feebly endowed with the real features of everyday life. Frequently the persons taking part in the action of the everyday tales are the members of the peasant family: the husband, wife, the clever and foolish brothers, the rich and poor brothers, father-in-law and daughter-in-law, uncle and niece, son-in-law and mother-in-law, father and children. The positive and negative qualities of these types are assigned in accordance with the subject of the tale.

In distinction from the miraculous tales, the outward delineation of the positive and negative heroes is not so picturesque as that of the heroes of the miraculous magical tales. The persons who play a part in the everyday tales are characterized mainly by their behavior and speech; the verbal characterization of them, however, is given in one or two epithets, chiefly of an emotional nature. Their social-economic status is defined with especial frequency: "a poor wretch of a Cossack," "a fellow who was poor to the last degree," "Ondron the unfortunate." With characteristic frequency, their positive character is expressed by the application of endearing suffixes to the name of the hero (dear little soldier, dear little peasant, dear little old man, dear little old woman, Vanyushka, and so on), or by the method of expressing a kindly irony (for example: "Ivan the Ill Fated, luckless peasant, there's no use laying down your money, there's no need to buy a bag," or "the last of the scum—a poor beggar of a peasant"). The negative characterization is more frequent: "a greedy priest, a fat belly, with envious eyes, and hands that seize everything"; "an illiterate priest, an illiterate deacon, an illiterate subdeacon"; "In a little parish lived a priest, he lived in good circumstances, he had no anxiety whatever, and so he grew fat, exceedingly so"; "At a certain parish church there lived a priest and a deacon, and they were terrific drunkards"; "In the country house was the mistress, and she was so cross, there was no living there for anybody;" "There was a merchant who was rich, and respected, and a successful trader. And he was impious to such a degree, that he would not let anyone pass the night there; neither travelers on foot nor riders on horseback."

The realistic genres of the tale—the short stories and the anecdotes—are in a very essential manner distinguished from the *style* of the magical, fantastic tale. Here there is none of that stylistically developed "ceremonialism," of which we have spoken in characterizing the fantastic tale. The initial storyteller's exordium is generally lacking. And this is perfectly understandable: the effective purpose of the exordium consists, as we have seen, in the effort to draw the listeners away from real, actual life, to absorb them in a world of fantasy and fiction; in the tale of everyday life this function, by virtue of the very nature of the realistic genre, disappears from the exordium. For this same reason, the tale of everyday life usually does not have the traditional beginning which has been referred to above: "In a certain kingdom, in a certain realm."

The story of everyday life and the anecdote usually have reference, in their action, to the real activity of life, and to a time which is quite close to our own. It is curious that the tale of everyday life rarely makes use of the traditional form of a long-past period, "Once upon a time." The tale of everyday life shows a predilection for indicating exactly the place and time of the action: the realistic storytellers like to connect the place of the action with their own locale, and relate it to their own time. The listener is at once introduced into the world of real relationships, and from the first words of the tale, there is given quite a precise definition of the setting in social, economic, and practical life, in which the further unfolding of the fable is to take place. This social characterization, given at the beginning of the tale of everyday life, or anecdote, lends it its basic tone as a genre with clearly expressed social and class implications. As an example we may cite the typical beginnings of such tales. "There was a rich merchant. They had a son, Vanyushka. And now the father and the mother are talking" (the Sokolovs, No. 97, "The Faithful Wife"). "There was a peasant who was very poor. He struggled and strove so that he sweat blood, but he did not have good luck in anything" (*ibid.*, No. 9). Even so, some of the realist storytellers sometimes prefix an exordium even to the tales of everyday life; but in such a case it bears a character that is chiefly realistic and satirical, or humorous in nature, and very often indecent (compare, in the Sokolovs' work, the exordium to Tale No. 147, "The Priest and the Cossack").

Quite another matter is the conclusion, or *epilogue*; the realistic tale and the anecdote are very partial to this. Usually such an epilogue is rhymed; it has a swift, "crowded" rhythm, and it serves the purpose of breaking off the realistic, usually even satirical tale with a laugh. In characterizing the styles of the individual storytellers who are realists and satirists, we have adduced several examples of this. In particular, this constitutes a characteristic feature of the tales of the Voronezh storyteller Kupryanikha. Here is the end of her anecdote tale, "Cowardly Vanya":

The bread turned out badly, they rolled it under the benches, they put it on the ovens in the corner, they raked it together into boxes. When they had not raked it together into boxes, they did not carry it to town. No one wanted to buy the bread, no one would carry it away for nothing. The swine Ustinya came up, she began to trade in the bread, she traded and traded, and soiled her whole snout. Three weeks she lay ill, the fourth week the swine began to writhe, and in the fifth week she died altogether.

The tale of everyday life, the realistic tale, and even more the humorous and satirical tale, in general have a very distinctive rhymed, *rhythmic speech*. We have seen this in the case of a whole series of storytellers (Bogdanov, Kupryanikha, and others). Usually the concentration of the rhyme and the quickening of the rhythmic tempo come toward the end of the tale. There are whole tales, "tongue twisters," "facetious sayings," "humorous apothegms," "narratives," where this device permeates the whole tale from beginning to end. (There are a great many of these in Onchukov's collection, in some parts of that of the Sokolovs, and others.) This formal device is very rare in the "earnest," sedate magical tale, and appears to be the peculiar property of the realistic—especially of the humorous and satirical—forms of the tale. In distinction from the miraculous tale, the realistic tale has hardly any recourse to the stylistic *loci communes*, and in it there is far less use of the device of retardation; very often it is completely lacking. The tale of real life, in the vast majority of cases, is built exclusively upon living, elaborated dialogue.

Very many of the tales of everyday life, especially the anecdotes, consist of uninterrupted dialogue. Here is an example of such a tale —No. 51 in Onchukov's collection:

A man was going out of the city of Rostov, and there met him a fellow who was coming into the town of Rostov. They met and greeted each other.

"Where are you from, brother?"

"I am from the city of Rostov."

"Is there anything good happening among you in Rostov?"

"Well, they've hanged Vanka Kocherin there."

"And by what [reason] did they hang him, the dear fellow?"

"Why, by the neck."

"Confound you, brother, what a stupid you are! . . . His fault [vina] * was of what kind?"

"No wine at all, sir, he wasn't a drinking man."

"Confound you, what a stupid you are! but what had he done?"

"But what had he done?—He stole St. Nikola's hollow rolls,† he stole the crown ‡ from the head of the Mother of God."

"Alas, poor dear Vanya! That fault of his was a trifling one, and yet they hanged him for it."

This is an anecdote tale. But in actual fact, on the whole, it is very difficult to draw a line between the tale which is a realistic short story, and the popular anecdote. Here the difference is chiefly one of dimension—the anecdote is distinguished by its brevity and condensation, it has a greater humorous or satirical acuteness, and the whole center of attention is carried over to the climax of the action, which is to be found at the very end of the narration, where also the dénouement of the whole situation occurs.

Furthermore, in the anecdote tale a poetically concrete form is

---

* Pun understandable only in Russian, based on *vina* (fault), *vina* (of wine), etc.—Ed.

† *Podkovki:* (also) horseshoes.—Ed.

‡ Wreath of flowers, or of silver or gold on an icon.—Ed.

given to some kind of general concept, proposition, or bit of "popular wisdom." Not without reason is the anecdote so often compressed into a single proverb; or, on the other hand, not without reason does it serve as a concrete application of a current proverb: "The thief's cap burns him"; "I'll sell it for what I paid for it"; "They sell fools down the river"; "The crow chanced to another's mansion"; "Foreordained from birth," and others. Characteristic of the anecdote, with reference especially to its composition, is the emphatic contrast between the persons who take part in the action (the priest and the workman, the peasant and the gentleman, the clever and the stupid man, the German and the Russian), and their behavior and speeches; and also the principle of unexpectedness, particularly at the "climactic" moment of the action.

Especially significant in the structure of the anecdote is the device of the "play upon words," the use of words in various senses: hence arise the "inopportune" answers (for example, in the instance which has just been cited, the anecdote of what happened at Rostov). Pointedness of language and the trenchant quality of expressions serve also as a characteristic feature of the anecdote. Unfortunately, in Russian folkloristics (and to a considerable extent in western Europe also), hardly any attention has been devoted to the study of the composition, and of the poetics in general, of the realistic genres of tales. The works which we have of Russian scholarship, dealing with popular anecdotes, treat exclusively the questions of origin, the sources of the anecdotes, which lie at the basis of the "migratory motifs." [62] Accordingly, there is not even a single work devoted to the composition and style of the realistic tales of everyday life.

The *legendary tales* may be divided into the following three groups: (*a*) brief legendary tales, legends, with a reflection of the popular beliefs in wood spirits, goblins, ghosts, and so on; (*b*) traditional tales, historical tales; and (*c*) legendary tales of a moralizing

[62] Cf. A. Peltzer, *The Origin of the Anecdote in Russian Folk Literature* (Kharkov, 1898); N. F. Sumtsov, *Researches in the Field of Anecdotal Literature* (Kharkov, 1898); A. A. Potebnya, *Some Notes Dealing with the Theory of Literature* (Kharkov, 1905).

character, tales of "divinity," imbued with the ideas and imagery of the Christian mythology.

The brief legendary tales bear also other similar designations: "legends," "brief legends," "happenings," and so on. These terms indicate that the narrator, and the group which listens to these narratives, attach to them a character of authenticity, they believe in the actuality of the encounters with wood spirits, goblins, spirits of the field, spirits of the bath, water goblins, witches, undines, werewolves, ghosts, wizards, necromancers, semipagans, "heretics," and other representatives of the vast world of the supernatural. These narratives are transmitted as "truthful" histories, they are related in the name of the storyteller who was an eyewitness or a participant in the encounters with these "unclean" powers. This type of story was especially popular among hunters, fishermen, pilgrims—in other words, among persons who most often found themselves in the midst of conditions where any kind of vision, hallucination, or dream could easily arise.

Conditions favoring such phenomena include weariness from long walking, constant strain, expressing itself even in dreams, a great accumulation of impressions during the day, the horror and mysteriousness of surrounding nature, nervous excitement, and so on. On being related thereafter, as a legend, such a brief legendary tale is transformed into an "archaic legend"; this term indicates that the affair, people say, was long ago, "in antiquity," "ages" ago. Arising by chance, under the influence of concrete conditions, the brief narrative tale, passing over into an archaic legend, becomes interesting in and for itself, and, becoming overlaid with story details, gradually passes over into a miraculous, fantastic tale. The "brief legendary tales" and "archaic legends" are usually very short; the narrative is filled with references to the place where the incidents occurred, there are names of villages and natural boundaries, there is mention of the first names and family names of those persons among whom "the affair took place," or of those persons who have handed down the account of what happened. For an understanding of the psychology of the creative work of the tale, for the solution of the fundamental questions of the actual origin of the "miraculous" in the tales, and of the rise of the tale in general, the genre which is now being analyzed has a great deal to contribute. In our own times this genre of tales is disappearing with exceptional rapidity.

The *historical legends* and *traditions* are usually referred to by the German folklorists under the term *Sage*, in distinction from the tale in the strict sense of the word. These traditions are usually connected with some place or other, with cities, country villages, natural boundaries, lakes, and burial mounds. Very often they serve as the explanation of the name of some district or settlement, which cannot be understood at the first glance. In the Russian narratives and traditions there is mention made chiefly of treasures, bandits, Tartars, "gentlemen" (Poles of the era of the Time of Troubles), of Swedes, of the first settlers of the region, and others. One of the contemporary researchers in the field of regional studies says:

Treasure, in the popular legends, is not simply money hidden in the earth, in a cave, in a well, or under a stone; it is, because of the spell which has been laid upon it, something which has come alive, something which lives its own mysterious, enchanted life. At times it comes out to warm itself in the sun, to dry itself out; at night it burns like a candle, it is menacing, and it groans when it is obliged to hide itself again.[63]

In the traditions there is frequent mention of sunken cities, churches, bells, of mysterious footsteps on the rocks, of golden-horned reindeer which come running at fixed times, and of many other things.

Many traditions deal with actual historical personages: these traditions, imbibing migratory subjects and motifs, and also bookish legends and narratives, expand to very considerable dimensions, and become transformed into "historical" legends and tales. It will suffice to mention such facts as the following: the famous tale on the international subject of the unjust judgment has, among us, become linked with a historical personage of the fifteenth century—with Prince Dmitry Shemyaka. From this comes also the name that is generally used for the tale, "The Judgment of Shemyaka." We have referred above to the tales in the records of the seventeenth century,

[63] V. I. Smirnov, "Treasures, Gentlemen and Bandits," *Ethnographic Surveys of the Kostroma Region* (Kostroma, 1921).

connected with the name of Ivan the Terrible.[64] With a whole series of historical names and details of this period of Ivan the Terrible there is connected the legendary tale of Barma the Clerk, founded upon the well known narrative of the kingdom of Babylon, which in the Russian texts clearly expresses the idea of the derivation of the authority of the Russian grand princes and tsars from Byzantium and the East. The oral tale has basically preserved this tendency.[65]

With the name of Peter I is connected an extensive cycle of oral legends, traditions, and tales.[66] Everyone is familiar with the extensive round of legends and traditions concerning the leader of the peasant movement of the end of the seventeenth century, Stepan Razin.[67] From these we derive various legends, "true stories," and traditions about the institution of serfdom, about the work done by the serf for his lord, about landowners who were especially odious.[68]

The *religious legends* constitute a narrative genre which, in its thematics, is akin to the type of song epos that has been analyzed by us above—the "religious verses." They both have common sources, chiefly bookish and oral legends, apocrypha, lives of the saints, which have come down to us from Byzantium, through the Bulgarians, or directly by means of translations.

As in the religious verses, there is in the legends a whole division of cosmogonic traditions, chiefly of a dualistic character, dealing with the creation of the world, and the fashioning—by God and the Devil—of man and the animals. But the most widely diffused themes

[64] A. N. Veselovsky, "Tales of Ivan the Terrible," *The Old and New Russia*, 1876, No. 4 (reprinted in Vol. XVI of the *Collected Works* of Veselovsky).

[65] V. F. Miller, "On the Tales of Ivan the Terrible," *Annals of the Division of Russian Language and Literature of the Academy of Sciences*, XIV, Bk. 2, 1909.

[66] E. V. Barsov, "Peter the Great in the Popular Legends of the Northern Region," *Proceedings*, Bk. V, 1872.

[67] A. N. Lozanova, "Popular Legends and Traditions of Stepan Razin," *Artistic Folklore*, IV-V, Moscow, 1929; A. N. Lozanova, *Songs of Stepan Razin* (Saratov, 1928); A. N. Lozanova, *Songs and Legends of Razin and Pugachov* (Academia, 1935).

[68] N. L. Brodsky, "The Institution of Serfdom in Popular Poetry," *The Great Reform*, Vol. V (Moscow, 1911); N. L. Brodsky, "Toward Liberty: The Institution of Serfdom in Popular Poetry," Collection No. 5067, "The Universal Library" (Moscow, Benefit, 1911). See also the collection of tales by Y. M. Sokolov, *Master and Peasant* (Moscow, 1932).

of the "divine" tales or legends were, in Russian folklore, the themes of Christ and the saints. Especially widespread were the traditions of the "pilgrimages" of Christ with the Apostles, or with specific saints, up and down the earth, of their disclosure of human "untruthfulness," of the punishment of the proud, the greedy, the wealthy, and the reward of the poor and unfortunate. Especially frequent are the subjects of the punishments meted out by Christ, by God, or by one of the saints—appearing in the guise of a wandering beggar—to the parsimonious householders who are inhospitable to guests. Also widely diffused is the theme of sin and forgiveness. For example, the theme of "the two great sinners": the great sinner (a bandit) repents, receives a penance which cannot possibly be performed (to pasture black sheep until they become white; to pour water over firebrands until they burst into bloom, and so on); but he kills a still greater sinner (in a series of variants he kills a cruel steward of the master's) and receives forgiveness.[69] This subject was utilized by N. A. Nekrasov in his poem, *Who Lives Happily in Russia?*

The subject of the Satan's friend's bed is popular: a child has been sold to the Devil; for help he turns to the friend of Satan, procures the bill of sale in hell, whereupon Satan's friend finds out about the terrible bed which is awaiting him, and as a result he repents and obtains forgiveness.[70] Widely diffused is the subject of Christ (sometimes replaced by a devil) and the blacksmith. Christ cuts off the horse's legs in order to shoe him, reshoes an old woman and changes her into a young one, but the blacksmith, in spite of all his efforts, is not able to do this. There is a widely disseminated subject of the punishment of the "greedy priest," who because of his greed was constrained, against his will, to tell the truth. This is a tale on the theme, "Who Ate Up the Holy Wafer?" St. Nicholas (or Peter and others) is making a journey with a priest, who on the sly eats up all the wafers

[69] This subject has served as the theme of an investigation by N. P. Andreyev, *Die Legende von den zwei Erzsündern* (Helsinki, 1924), FFC No. 54. A brief summary is given in *Annals of the Herzen Teachers' Training Institute in Leningrad*, 1924, Bk. 1.

[70] See another work by N. P. Andreyev, *Die Legende vom Räuber Madej* (Helsinki, 1927), FFC No. 69.

and does not acknowledge it to Nicholas. The saint heals the tsarevna (the priest cannot do this), and divides the money into three parts; at the division he announces that the third part is intended for the one who ate up the wafers. The priest then hastens to say that he was the one who ate them.

Widely diffused also are the subjects on the theme of the journey of man "into that other world." The most popular of the Russian legends is found to be the tale of "The Little Brother of Christ": Christ's brother by baptism is going to visit him; along the road he sees a picture of various torments and receives questions from various persons, to which he then gives the answers; he sees a place in Paradise, which has been prepared for him, and the future torments of his parents. After all this he returns to earth and relates what he has seen and heard "in that world." Very widely diffused are the legends of children who "have been sold to the Devil," "cursed" by their parents. The best known of these is the legend of "the accursèd daughter," who was carried off by the Devil in consequence of an imprudent word (the oath, "The Devil take you!") spoken by her mother.

The majority of the legends clearly expressed the ideology of the peasant tiller of the soil, the poor farmer. Such "saints" as Nikola the Merciful, Elijah the Terrible, Egor the Brave, became in the Russian oral legend, as also in the popular agrarian ritual and the popular calendar of the village economy, the helpers and patrons of agriculture. Their aspect took on, in the oral legend, a purely peasant character. The peasant legend deals with them on a basis of goodfellowship. If the "saint" does not satisfy the wants of the peasant, the latter punishes him—smashes his icon or deprives him of his candles, public services of prayer, and holidays. On the other hand, those saints who gratify his desires are rewarded with offerings, prayers, and public services.

Very characteristic, from this point of view, is the legend of the contest of Elijah and Nikola. Elijah wants to punish a peasant (he sends hail upon his harvest-field, promises a poor yield of grain, and so on), but Nikola informs the peasant as to the other's plans, and puts matters right. The legends of Nikola and Cassianus are also interesting. The latter, meeting on the highroad a man with a loaded cart stuck in the mud, does not want to help him, being afraid of soiling his sacerdotal vestments, which he is wearing to go to God in Paradise; but Nikola helps the peasant. For this reason, God assigns Cassianus one holiday in every four years (the festival of Cassianus is celebrated on February 29), while Nikola has two holidays every year.

It must be noted that in the peasants' oral legends the saints are contrasted to the members of the clergy—the priests; the attitude toward the latter, as we have already pointed out more than once, both in the tales and in the legends, is sharply negative. In its style and composition the legend stands closer to the tales of everyday life than it does to the miraculous and magical tales: not without reason is it, in its content, closely packed with everyday details, having a socio-ideological tendency.[71]

Everything that we have made clear above concerning the Russian tale—the conditions of its existence, the role of the storytellers, its thematics, the systematizing of its style—all this confirms its profound and fundamental connection with social life. If, indeed, we take into account the considerable prevalence in the Russian tale of the realistic genres, of those dealing with everyday life, and even more of the humorous and satirical genres, then the solid social content of the Russian tale comes before us with still greater definitiveness and indisputability.

If in the nineteenth and twentieth centuries the tale has its locale, to a very great extent, in the countryside among the peasantry, this does not mean that such was always the case, even in the earlier period. On the contrary, we know that the tale existed from very remote times, and in the daily life of the most diverse classes.

In Russian antiquity the telling of tales was a daily adjunct to life

---

[71] The chief collection of Russian legends, which remained for a long time under the ban of the censorship, is the work of A. N. Afanasyev, *Popular Russian Legends* (Moscow, 1860). New editions appeared as early as 1914, in Moscow and in Kazan; *Popular Russian Legends*, ed. I. P. Kochergin (Kazan, Youthful Powers, 1914); and *Popular Russian Legends*, ed. with Introduction by S. K. Shambinago (Moscow, Contemporary Problems, 1914). Many legends have been printed in the latest collections of Russian tales, by Onchukov, the brothers Sokolov, Zelenin, Smirnova, and others.

in all classes of society. In a certain ecclesiastical discourse of the twelfth century, a most vivid description is given of the rich man's retiring to sleep: "When he lies down and cannot fall asleep, his friends rub his feet, others stroke his hips, others scratch him across the shoulders, some play a tune, others fabulize and tell blasphemous tales."

We have already said that the word "fabulize" means the telling of tales or fables, just as the word *bakhar* signifies a storyteller. All of these popular narrators and *bakhary* were an inalienable adjunct of the everyday life of peasants, tradespeople, the merchant class, the noblemen, and even of the princely and royal court of the Old Russian principality of Moscow. Tsar Ivan the Terrible could not fall asleep without hearing stories; at his bedside there were always to be found three blind old men, to whose stories he listened until sleep overtook him. There have been preserved in the documents even the given names and family names of the storytellers of the succeeding tsars, such as Vasil Shuysky, Michael Romanov, and others. Both these tsars and Tsar Aleksis Mikhailovich rewarded their storytellers with cloth, caftans, and other gratuities. This tradition survived for a long time, even at the "Europeanized" imperial court of the eighteenth century. Empress Anna Iannovna, being fond of all kinds of diversions, kept jesters and storytellers about her person. Empress Elizabeth had an expert in tales, an old man, a court footman, who "frequently told stories to the empress in her leisure hours of rest."

The practice of making use of the art of the storytellers was current also among the other representatives of the nobility, the higher and middle aristocracy. Prince Nikita Volkonsky, in the eighteenth century, laid out money on storytellers and hangers-on. Among the minor landed nobility, the employment of storytellers was a typical feature of their life. A contributor to *The Universal Miscellany*—a satirical magazine of the eighteenth century—describes how he went to visit his elderly aunt. Among the necessary "appurtenances" which surrounded this old woman in her sleeping chamber, he includes the peasant storyteller.

According to Lev Tolstoy, his grandmother had a storyteller who had been bought because of his proficiency in the art of telling tales.

All these facts show that in ancient Russia, and later on, the professional storyteller existed as a type. According to the data which have been given above, tales were included in the repertory of the typical professional artists of medieval Russia—the buffoons. Investigators see in the artistic manner of the storytelling style, in the elaborately developed stylistic devices, the tokens of mastery on the part of an extinct professionalism. Many tales, written down in the nineteenth and twentieth centuries from the lips of peasants, bear the obvious traces of this professionalism—of the *bakhary*, buffoons and other masters of the popular narrative art.[72]

"Ah, do you want to be amused with a story? Then here is a miraculous tale: it contains wonders of wonders, miracles of miracles, and the farm hand Shobarsha, the cheat of cheats: for as soon as he took hold and began to pull, there was nothing to be said, he was strong enough for anything." This is the beginning of one of the stories (Afanasyev, No. 88), which by this beginning betrays the fact that it was formerly that of a professional storyteller. Another story (Afanasyev, No. 232) finishes off with the following exceedingly burlesque epilogue, in which it is definitely mentioned that its authors are "we fine young fellows," that is, the buffoons:

> Whoever is rich and parsimonious: he does not brew beer,
> To us, the fine fellows, he does not give food or drink,
> To him God will give a cat's breathing,
> A dog's gasping.
> But to a poor man who is capable,
> Who brews his beer, and treats us, the fine fellows, with drink,
> God will give issue of the cattle on the field,
> Abundance on the threshing floor,
> Success in the rising of the bread,
> Plenty on the table.
> Of his beer the peasant drank his fill,
> When he had drunk his fill, he lay down in the shed,
> About his mouth are crumbs enough to fill a nightcap and a half.

Similar traditional concluding formulas, connected with obvious hints as to the necessity of a reward, are frequent in the tales; and in

[72] N. L. Brodsky, "Traces of the Professional Storytellers in the Russian Tales," *Ethnographic Review*, No. 2, 1904.

their traditional form they testify to their origin from the earlier remarks of the professionals.

The storyteller Novopoltsev (in the collection of Sadovnikov) ends his tale thus: "Here the tale is ending too, a fine young fellow told it through, *and for us, the fine young fellows,* let there be a little glass of beer apiece, at the ending of the tale let there be a little glass full of wine [spirits] apiece." It is clear that the words "for us, the fine young fellows," on the lips of a single storyteller, are the result of an old, now crystallized formula used by the storytellers and buffoons.

The deep-seated vitality of the tale, in so far as it appears still to be a factor in its oral existence, depends on the *creative*, and not on the mechanical character of the transmission of the tale by the storytellers. The vital spring of this form of poetic art is the social life which conditions it. The tale is seen to be a clear expression of the whole psychological and social way of life to be found in those surroundings, which are represented by this or that storyteller. The tale, in all its diverse genres which we have surveyed, deeply absorbs the quintessence of the social life which surrounds it. As a visible proof of this, we have the observations of the researchers, who have taken down the tale direct from the lips of the people, as to the close connection of the tale with the life of that region where that tale was recorded. The tale, in spite of all the many centuries of traditionalism of its subject, invariably and unavoidably transmutes into poetic form the impressions received from the immediate surroundings and activities of the world in which lives the storyteller who is unfolding the tale. Let us give some examples.

The unique and fabulous setting of the Ural Mountains found abundant reflection in the tales of the Perm region:

The dense and boundless forests of the Urals, often still untouched, even today, by the ax of the woodcutter; the deep valleys, rocky summits and crags, and all the rich abundance of the animal kingdom, especially snakes, lizards, and insects, the life of which is totally unknown to man; finally, the abundance of large and small lakes, with their reed-grown banks and their rocky little uninhabited islands—all of this could not fail to produce, upon the man who dwells here, an impression of some mysterious and magical power; all this must surely have directed the imagination of the inhabitant of that region to the mysterious world of the unknown and the miraculous, it must have powerfully nurtured his faith in the nearness of that miraculous and mysterious world. Not without reason is the scene of the action, in the greater part of the tales which have been taken down in the Perm region, none other than the Urals.[73]

In the Urals, in the dark forests, was born Ivan, the peasant's son, the hero of the tale of know-nothing; and it was on the Urals that he came upon the vast house of the man-eating monster, who took him in among his children. . . . It is in the Urals that the complete action of the tale "The Milk of Wild Beasts" transpires. . . . Along the Urals, through the wild places, where there is no path or road, Ivan the Tsarevich sets out on his search for Helen the Fair. . . . On the Urals he works as a servant in the house of Yaga-Yagishna: "Not by the path and not by the road, but through the thickets and the holes." Through the Urals goes Vasily the Tsarevich, and encounters the vast droves of horses of Voron Voronevich. Among the first inhabitants of the Urals were the very rich millowners; they lived in sumptuous castles, surrounded by all kinds of conveniences, inventions, and rare objects known to the culture of those times. Far removed from the capital, among the lawless peasantry (the serfs and those bound to work in the foundries), among the venal minor officials, the life of these earlier "kings of the Urals" was singular and bizarre. . . . Popular report, of course, has exaggerated and elaborated the magnificence of the local plutocrats, so that actuality has here become intermingled with the tale. The reflection of the traditions concerning this magnificence may be seen also in the local tales: for example, in a narrow room in an old man's house "there are immured all kinds and conditions of birds, they sing in various voices" (that is, something like a menagerie); "in the first room the sea at once [immediately] is represented, and ships. In the second room are a garden, ducks, swans, fountains, apples. In the third room they are having a battle: there is a war in progress, and they are firing off cannon. In the fourth room is a crystal palace, and music. In the fifth are mountains, so high that you cannot see their summits," and so forth.

In the tales of Perm are reflected the originality and diversity of the local population: they had been conveyed thither to the ironworks from various places in Russia, and had become intermingled

[73] D. K. Zelenin, *Great-Russian Tales of the Province of Perm* (1914), p. xx.

with the various non-Russian populations, such as the Bashkirs, the Tartars, and others. Also the occupations of the people had become blended, both the agricultural and the factory work. The geographical names which are introduced into the tales of Perm characterize the scope of the geographical knowledge of the storyteller, as being limited to the environment to which he belonged, and from which he drew his knowledge. The road leading from the center of Russia into Siberia has given names to the tales of the Perm region: Petrograd (Leningrad), Nikolayevsk, Petropavlovsk, the Urals, Siberia.[74]

The tales which have been written down in Siberia are deeply imbued with the conditions of Siberian life and customs. Especially powerful in these tales is the expression of the "wanderer" element which is so typical of Siberia, and which is obviously revealed in a great number of the "migratory" motifs. The collector and researcher M. K. Azadovsky states:

Very often, in the various difficult circumstances of life, when it is necessary to save themselves from unjust persecution, the heroes go away into the woods, into the vast Siberian forests, to wander or to roam. The king's daughter, who has been calumniated, sits in a tower of stone. The compassionate keeper helps her to escape. "When your husband comes back, you will not be alive anyway, so go and lead a wandering existence with your son," the keeper says to her. "But here's what it is—I helped her to escape from there, and she went with the help of God to wander away from this tower." The king comes home. His minister, a landowner, on account of whose slander she was placed in the tower, reports: "What then, she's gone off as a wanderer—your wife—I couldn't keep her in the prison." [75]

This example is not an isolated one. By a life of wandering, also, the chambermaid saves herself in the tale "The Enchanted Garden," when she also has been put into a stone tower, because she did not keep the tsar's daughters safe. "She went all alone to wander through the woods, through the mountains, through the marshes." Later in

---

[74] E. N. Yeleonskaya, "Influence of the Locality upon the Tale: Apropos of Zelenin's Collection of the Tales of Perm," *Ethnographic Review*, 1915, Bk. I, pp. 18-36.

[75] M. Azadovsky, *Tales of the Upper Lena Region* (Irkutsk, 1925), No. 1, p. xvi.

this same tale we see her, now a wealthy woman, with her three knightly sons, keeping an inn on the highroad. "Behold, at a certain time, in the night, wayfarers knocked at their door. The sons asked their mother what to do. 'Ah, my dear children, let them in, if they are wayfarers; I myself was long a wanderer, I am sorry for them all.'"

"In the last example given," Azadovsky correctly observes, "there is perceptible an altogether different motif, which might be defined as the motif of 'sheltering the wayfarer,' for settlements which were located along the great highroad, or at any rate were in one way or another connected with the highroad. This motif is exceedingly characteristic, and discloses one of the typical features of the local mode of life." It is very frequently encountered in the Siberian tales. Abundant reflection is found also in the Siberian tales of another side of the life of those who had been deported to Siberia—the life of the prison and of convicts.

In the creative work of the best of the Siberian storytellers, Vinokurova, there is diffused a vast wave of the "Siberian" element. Now it is reflected in some detail of daily life, now it peeps through a certain characteristic of the dialogue, now it is unfolded in the broad, typical picture of Siberian daily life. The son of Oryol the Tsarevich, dressed as a girl, fascinates Kashchey by his playing. The latter sends his servant to invite the supposed musician for the evening. "The servant puts the question to the girl, but she [that same Vasya] replies: 'I cannot play for your master, however—I am one of the common people. A common servant girl.'"

In the tales of Vinokurova were reflected nearly all the most important aspects of the trading life of the Upper Lena region: the rafting, the transport of goods, the hunting, and so forth. . . . A typically Lena picture of the hiring of workmen for the mines or for rafting is encountered in the tale of "The Clever Wife": "Here, Vanya, is a memorandum book for you: go and hire a hundred workmen, write down the name and surname of each one, and send them to me, and for each one advance a hundred rubles." Very often there is mention also of hunting and of the "tradesmen" [hunters]. It is characteristic that the hunter's little winter lodge in the woods has altogether crowded out of the stories the little Russian "hut on wobbly legs." [76]

[76] *Ibid.*, pp. xx ff.

The characteristic peculiarities of natural and social conditions, which are typical of one region or another, are expressed in unchanged form in the tales. Significant, for example, in this connection is the distinction between the conditions of life in the Pechora and Onega regions. The former was entirely connected with the sea, the latter was drawn toward the city, to "Petersburg." "Just as there was not a single family in the Pechora region which did not have some connection with the sea, especially with the Pechora [River], so there was not a family in the Olonets region, especially in the districts beyond the Onega, which would not have some connection with St. Petersburg (going there to earn money)," N. E. Onchukov, the collector of tales, wrote in 1908. He comments:

Need it be stated that this could not have remained unexpressed in the tales. In the Pechora tales, Moscow not only does not figure at all, there is not even mention of it, much less of St. Petersburg; while in the recordings made in the province of Olonets, Moscow is mentioned four times, and St. Petersburg figures continually; and not only the capital itself, but also its environs, reflecting that connection of the trans-Onega region with St. Petersburg, which exists in actuality.[77]

For example, a peasant lives in the village with his wife, he goes away to St. Petersburg, dies there, and rides back dead to his village. Or his wife is living in the village without her husband, and her husband is living in St. Petersburg, and she takes it into her head to be unfaithful to her husband. Or an old man and woman have three sons and a daughter; the sons go away to St. Petersburg, and there they hire a working woman, a "destroyer," who would almost have destroyed their sister, when the brothers sent for their sister to come to Petersburg. Or, for example, a country thief goes to do his thieving in St. Petersburg where there is more money. In St. Petersburg he walks, among other places, along the Street of Millions, and robs first a bank, then the royal palace. A plenipotentiary and a colonel undertake, at the request of the tsar, to catch the thief, but the thief invites them to come and see him, at his house on the Nevsky Pros-

[77] N. E. Onchukov, *Northern Tales* (Petrograd, 1909), p. xxv.

pekt, and entertains them, after which they start off for Tsarskoe Selo. It is possible to cite a very large number of similar examples.[78]

With reference to the mention, in the tales, of the capitals St. Petersburg and Moscow, while reading through the collection of tales by A. M. Smirnov,[79] from various parts of Russia, we made the following observations: In reality, the tales from the northern provinces, the former provinces of Olonets and Archangel, make mention of, and transfer the place of the action to, the northern capital; but the farther east, and especially the farther south one goes, the more St. Petersburg is replaced, and at last totally eclipsed, by Moscow. For example, in the Vyatka tales, "In Moscow I bought up a great stock of goods" (Zelenin, No. 122), "the Moscow merchant" (*ibid.*, No. 143), or in the Tver tales, "a capital like Moscow"; in the Kaluga tale, again, there figures the "Moscow merchant." In a word, in the tales there is manifested the economic attraction of the region toward one center or the other.

In other respects the tales of the Olonets region have a great deal in common with those of the Pechora region: the same forests, rivers, lakes, and sea figure, in the common picture of natural conditions, in the tales of the Olonets as in those of the Pechora region. But the tales of the Summer Shore are distinguished from those of both regions, at least by the fact that the sea stands out in them in bold relief, with all its special qualities, and the toilsome lives of the people who live on it and on its shores.

The tales of the southern provinces have their own specific local coloring. Thus, in the Voronezh tales, according to N. P. Grinkova,

there stands out in especially bold relief what it might be possible to call the *couleur locale* in the tale. Thus, in the tales there often figure the Kuban and the Caucasus—the points of departure for the earnings of the local populace; in the field, ancient mounds are encountered, of which there are many in the local steppes; along the sides of the road, in the steppe, "willows" are found, osiers, of which there are so many here. The scene of the action is usually in the field,

[78] *Cf.*, in confirmation of this point, I. V. Karnaukhova, "Storytellers and Stories in the Trans-Onega Region," *Peasant Art*, No. I (Leningrad, 1927), p. 119.

[79] A. M. Smirnov, *Collection of Great-Russian Tales from the Archive of the Russian Geographical Society*, Nos. I and II (Petrograd, 1917).

where there are ravines, while the village of Mastuchino, where the tales were written down, stands on a high place, all around are ravines, gulleys and chalk cliffs, and near the houses are stone passageways. The place of the famous provincials is here taken by the "Tsukany" (a special group of the populace of the Voronezh province, contrasted to the freeholders, to whom the storyteller belongs), living in the neighboring "volost" (administrative district).[80]

Since the great majority of the tales have been written down from the lips of the peasantry, it is perfectly clear that our tales have reflected, in exceedingly minute detail, the whole agricultural mode of life and work of the populace, in all their local variations. In the Novgorod tales there is mirrored the heavy northern work of "deforestation," clearing the land. "The poor brother cut down the branches, burned them, and plowed the land, but he had nothing to sow" (Smirnov, No. 54). In another Novgorod tale (No. 56) in the same collection, it is said directly "to clear the land." In our collection of Belo-Ozero tales, this form of agriculture also found expression many times. In a Smolensk tale (Smirnov, No. 185) the conditions of the local plowland are described: "And he [the peasant] planned that on his plot of land he would clear the ground for wheat. He has a poor worthless horse; there he grubs out the trees, scratches the surface a little, and begins to sow." [81]

We will not multiply examples. From what has already been said, it is clear with what organic closeness the Russian tale, whether it be a realistic story of everyday life, or whether it be "miraculous" and "fantastic," is linked with the social life of the people, with the methods of work, with all the real surroundings of life. It is altogether natural that the folk tale should be shot through with the psychology and ideology of the social setting which has created it.

This refers, as we have said, not only to the tales of everyday life, which in itself is perfectly obvious, but also to the miraculous tales, the magical and legendary ones. The storytelling fantasy itself, the

[80] N. P. Grinkova, "On the Record of Tales in the Voronezh Province in 1926"; *Storytelling Commission in the Year 1926* (Leningrad, 1927), pp. 41-42.
[81] B. M. Sokolov, "A Little Corner of the Russian Storytelling World," *Scientific Annals*, No. II, Moscow, 1922.

"miraculous" invention, are conditioned by the social nature of the peasantry, by their mode of life.

The magical tales, taken as a whole, are not something that stands outside of ordinary life; on the contrary, they are something that is contained within it, in all that surrounds a man, that makes up his customs, his mode of life. Such a stable, inseparable union of the natural and the miraculous is the result of a well defined view of the world, which is manifested not in one tale alone, but yet is especially noticeable in it.[82]

The very representation of that which is miraculous and, in its essence, far removed from the peasant world, such as the world of miraculous, magical beings, of tsars and princelings, of rich noblemen and merchants, is presented within the limits of the peasant concepts and views. The very character of the "miraculous" details is limited at times by the exceedingly modest scale of the country village and its boundaries: the peasant carries over into this world his own longings and ideals, which at times are very modest and naïve, but for him are seemingly unattainable, and therefore "miraculous," out of the ordinary.

Here, for example, is the way in which the mode of life of kings is represented in the tales, in forms which, in their essence, are purely of the peasantry. "The 'Tsar-necromancer' slept all the night through, arose early in the morning, washed his face with water from the spring, wiped it with a short towel, lighted his stove, took his book of magic, and sat down on a woven leather chair" (Onchukov, No. 2). As if the matter under discussion were a representation of the peasant mode of life, there is a description of the following details of a tsar's mode of life, in the tales. The tsar's daughter was going through the yard, and "she sees, there stands a bedstead made of yew, on the bedstead is a downy feather bed and a silken pillow, and she asks: 'What is this, my maidens?' 'That is the yew bedstead of your father, in the summertime he goes out walking, and on this bed he rests and takes his repose'" (Onchukov, No. 4).

Even the Tsars' pleasures are of a simple kind: "And Fyodor Vodo-

82 E. N. Yeleonskaya, "Influence of the Locality upon the Tale," *Ethnographic Review*, 1915, Bks. 1-2.

vich steamed himself in his steam bath, and he went with his working people to the lake, to bathe" (Onchukov, No. 4). The royal etiquette is not complex, but of a very simple kind: "Once upon a time there was a Tsar, and he had a maidservant, and the Tsar ordered the maidservant to buy a pike. They boiled this pike, the Tsar with the Tsarina and the maidservant ate it up, and then they brought some for the ox" (Onchukov, No. 27). Or in the tsar's kitchen they buy a loaf for a hundred rubles. The "Sovereign Emperor" gives audiences in the kitchen. Ivan Roguyen, when he appears in "Petersburg itself," asks a certain "drinking man," whom he meets at an inn, to conduct him to the sovereign emperor: "The sovereign was busy with his affairs. He waited for half an hour. The sovereign was going out to the kitchen. He kept questioning this peasant, and then a little peasant made his appearance" (Onchukov, No. 72). The very notion of "ruling" is developed by analogy with the peasant relationships. "There were seven brothers, six of them were Tsars, and the seventh worked as a servant in their houses, and he served with each brother for three years. His brothers did not give him anything to live on" (Onchukov, No. 57).

For a tsar to forget his crown is exactly the same thing as for a peasant to leave his cap at home. "A Tsar with his troops had marched far away from his kingdom, and when all the Tsars assembled for a meeting, they were all wearing their crowns, but our Tsar alone was without his crown, he had forgotten his crown at home, and they would not let him into the meeting without his crown" (Onchukov, No. 156). The tsar's son takes to the road in peasant fashion. "He could not choose himself a bride suited to his taste. For the third time the Tsar made a feast for the daughters of all classes of men, and for the third time he could not make up his mind. In the morning he rises and says: 'Dear Papa and Mamma, bake for me whatever I shall need on the road, I am going to seek my promised one'—and he started off" (Onchukov, No. 97). The magnificence of a tsar's way of living consists in this, that the servant places the samovar before the Tsar on the table: "The sovereign came home, and the servant Fedka was there before him. He brought him the samovar, and he asks: 'Your Royal Majesty, what did your bride say to you?' " (the Sokolovs,

No. 7). The Tsar's daughter, having purchased a miraculous berry, will not eat it at once: "When they bring the samovar, I will drink my tea, and then I shall eat it." [83]

In the tales, the tsar's or king's feast is not so very different from a country feast on a large scale.

Egor the unfortunate returns home, and he sees that at home the stove has not been heated, the house is cold. When a little time has passed, his wife makes her appearance. She lights the stove. The sovereign, as soon as he sees that the stove had been lighted, comes running home (he had been across the way from the palace), and he asks: "Well, now what? You went thither, I know not where, and you brought something, I know not what?" "I brought it," she says. "Well, then, give it to me here." "No," she says, "I will not give it. Let us first make out a schedule, let us hold feasts, first you, and then I, and if you make a better entertainment than mine, then I will lay my head on the block, but if I do the best, then you will lay down yours."

So then they made such a schedule. And the sovereign gathered together all the carpenters from the whole city. The carpenters began to build tables and benches on the streets. Then they brought the people together, from the whole city and from all the near-by towns, and so the entertainments went on at the sovereign's palace. Then the feast at the Sovereign's was over, and the feast began at the house of Egor the unfortunate. Again the people began to gather. But when the party was in full swing, then everyone's table was overturned, the chairs, and everyone's knife, fork, and spoon, and they all got drunk to such an extent that it was terrible to see (the Sokolovs No. 59).

Even a royal wedding, in the tale, is performed in purely peasant fashion, and the incidents at the wedding are those of the peasant mode of life.

The Tsar did not have to brew beer or to distill brandy, but went straight to a splendid feast, and for a wedding. They appointed Mishka as groomsman in charge of the whole ceremony. And Mishka the water carrier gives instructions to Ivan the Tsarevich: "They will bring you from the nuptial ceremony, they will place you at the king's table—then I will drink a little, and will begin to play pranks and go out of my head. I will begin to smash and break things, and no one

[83] D. K. Zelenin, *Great-Russian Tales from the Province of Perm*, No. 23, p. 206.

will be able to quiet me. But you, then, you say to me: 'You, Mishka, listen to me, or I'll lead you away to bed.' And lead me to that sleeping room, to which they will conduct you, to the storeroom" (the Sokolovs, No. 143).

"To the storeroom——" after the wedding feast, the tsar is invariably led away, in the tales, according to the rules of the peasant wedding ritual. When he was married, "they led the new Tsar Ivan off to the storeroom" (Onchukov, No. 66, and others).

The powers of fancy, in representing the wealth and magnificence of other, privileged classes, are conditioned in general by the not-too-fastidious tastes of the peasant mode of life. From a tree, a soldier saw a light, and went out into the field.

And there stands a huge house, three stories high, all made of crystal. And in the very top story there is a light. He went into that house, and in the house there was no one at all. And he went through those rooms, from room to room, and in none of them was there any-one at all. In this room, also, there was a collection of drinks. The soldier sat down—he drank and ate his fill—the supply did not de-crease at all. Also there were hanging on the wall a great many musical instruments; he sat down, and began to sing songs. The house turned out to belong to a "lady-in-waiting" (the Sokolovs, No. 57).

Also in accordance with peasant concepts is the description of the attire and the mode of life of wealthy people—generals, noblemen, merchants. The distinction from the peasant mode of life is more in quantity than in quality, and at times is only a matter of literary terms. "And there was a ball going on at the merchant's house," one story-teller related her tale to the Academician Shakhmatov, adding also this explanation: "What is called a name day in our speech; in yours, a ball" (Onchukov, p. 239).

Likewise in the spirit of the peasant psychology is the representa-tion of the "miraculous world" of all kinds of supernatural beings found in the magical tale—Kashchey, the witch Baba-Yaga, Satan, and so on. Characteristic also is the representation, in the peasant tales, of the world "on the other side," of heaven, and the blessedness of Paradise. Paradise is a fine, clean room with a big, downy feather bed in it.

Mikola the Merciful One let the old man Savely in at the door: "Lie down, there you will find rest." And how splendidly that room was furnished: it was clean and large, and the bed was a large one, and the pillows were of down. And he locked him in. So then the old man walks up and down the room, and he says: "O Lord, the true Christ, this is what the kingdom of heaven is like." Mikola then explains to the pious Savely: "This is your place for eternity" (the Sokolovs, No. 8).

In the same spirit is the description of Paradise in another legendary tale. "The old man (Christ) led him off to sleep. He conducted him into a room. He feeds him nothing but essence of manna. And the bed was so soft that he thought he would never go out of that room. And the night appeared to him to be only one hour long" (the Sokolovs, No. 117). We have already pointed out that the legendary mode of life of those who dwell in heaven—of Christ and the other "peasant saints"—is delineated with purely peasant features: Christ sleeps on the warming place by the stove, Mikola goes about in the guise of a peasant pilgrim, and even the formidable Elijah walks the earth in the form of a peasant. Not without reason does the stingy Marko, a rich merchant, shout at the "heavenly pilgrims: 'Ah, it is the Evil One who brings you, with your dirty feet and your bast shoes. I,' he says, 'am waiting for God, and here you are with your dirt. Be off with you into the rear hut by the back gate, and you can spend the night there.' " Also in the peasant spirit is the description of the "mode of life" of an "evil spirit." Satan in his realm, thinking up difficult tasks, at last gives Ivan the Tsarevich the heaviest labor of all, which reflects essentially the forms of the peasant agriculture: "Here opposite my window, to clear this tract of land: what is good, thick logs, to pile up; and that which is worse, to burn it in the fire; to grub out the stumps, to plow up the land, to harrow it, reap it, grind the meal and bake the cake, and on the ninth morning to serve it to me for tea (breakfast), with fish" (the Sokolovs, No. 66).

In this way the peasant psychology permeated the tales which existed among the peasantry, regardless of their sources and without reference to the genres of the tales. But since the peasantry itself was socially and economically differentiated, naturally also in the peasant tales themselves one expects to find the expression of this differentiation. This can be seen most clearly of all by a study of the social motifs of the tales which have been written down from the lips of the peasantry.

The peasant psychology and ideology are especially clearly expressed in those tales of everyday life in which the theme itself is posed as that of the peasant in contrast or comparison with the representatives of other classes. From this point of view these tales may be brought together, so to speak, into a "social trilogy": they include tales on the themes of: (1) the peasant and the lord, (2) the peasant and the priest, (3) the peasant and the merchant. In the old collections of tales, for example, that of Afanasyev, these subjects are far from being represented in that fullness in which they undoubtedly existed among the people in the nineteenth century. The causes of this are found to be the direct suppression by the censor, and also the character of the scientific tendencies which were dominant in Russian folkloristics at that time. The collections made in the twentieth century (those of Onchukov, Zelenin, the brothers Sokolov, and others), on the other hand, presented a vast amount of material of social significance, which we also shall chiefly make use of in the future.

The relationship of *the peasant to his lord*, almost without exception in the tales, is decisively negative, even going as far as deep hatred and enmity.[84] Here it is impossible to perceive any kind of stratification in the attitude of the peasants with reference to their lords. The age-long feudal dependence of the peasant upon his master has developed in the peasantry a sharp feeling of class hostility: every tale on this theme is found to be an expression of protest against the lords, of hatred and contempt for them. The peasant in his tale finds an outlet for this class spirit; the class conflict of the peasantry with the lords and landowners is ever present in the tales.

According to the stylistic design of the tale, the victor in this conflict is invariably the peasant: he, the "ignorant peasant," makes a fool out of the "clever" master, makes fun of his seeming wisdom, takes advantage of his "weaknesses"—greed and envy—catches him

[84] See a more detailed discussion in the foreword by Y. M. Sokolov to the collection of tales, *Master and Peasant* (Academia, 1932).

up on his excessive ambition and boasting, shows up his slothfulness, his laziness, his thoughtless life at the expense of the peasants' labor, laughs at his unfitness for work, ridicules his seignioral conceit and his contempt for the peasant. The whole setting of the nobleman's life, his attire, his manners, his language, are depicted in the tale in amusing outlines. But this laughter is far from always being the laughter of amusement; back of this laughter there are often apparent hatred and fierce hostility. Now and then, in the tale, there occurs some decisive violence against the master. Certain popular titles for the tales of the nobleman are sufficiently characteristic, and speak for themselves. We need mention only the titles on this theme which are found in the collection made by the brothers Sokolov (*Tales and Songs of the Belo-Ozero Region*): "The Master and His Workman Luke," "How the Peasant Made Fools of the Lords," "The Angry Mistress," "The Young Lady, the Cavalier, and the Soldier," "The Master and the Peasant," "How the Master Bore a Calf," "The Cunning Peasant," and others.

The most widespread tales and anecdotes of everyday life, in connection with the noblemen, have been noted by us previously, when we were speaking of the everyday tales. Many of these subjects are found to be the property of tales the world over—to be among the "migratory" subjects. But it is important for our purposes that in the Russian peasant tale these migratory subjects were adapted to the class psychology and world concept of the Russian peasantry, being utilized by them for the expression of their attitudes toward the representatives of the hostile exploiting class. Without concerning ourselves with a survey of the actual content and subjects of the tales concerning the noblemen, we may merely cite a few examples which give a concrete characterization of what has just been said regarding the expression of the class consciousness of the peasants in the tales on this theme. This tendency in the peasant tales is by no means the product only of the last decades preceding the revolution. It existed also in ancient times, and, of course, grew stronger with the constantly increasing enslavement of the peasantry.

Such tales of satire as that of the Perch, Son of the Perch, of the birds, of the trial of the crow, carry us back, at the very least, to the period of the seventeenth century, and some of them to an even earlier time. The tales of Ivan the Terrible are directed against the nobility. In tales which were written down considerably later than the seventeenth century, the antinobility sentiments of the peasantry of the Old Russia of the principality of Moscow live among the peasantry as tradition. In a tale from Onchukov's collection, No. 7, "The Tsar and Cherepan," the Tsar asks the other: "Well, Cherepan, is our sovereign fierce?" "Well, this is how fierce the sovereign is: the noblemen have whole cellars lying full of gold, yet all the while he favors them, but from the man in need, the poor man, he takes the very skin of his teeth, and he collects taxes for everything. . . ." The Tsar asks again: "Cherepan, there are people who say, 'That man is the dearest of all, who has a lot of money.' " "But those who say that are the nobleman or the nobleman's son; they are fat-bellied and fond of money."

But it is natural that in the recorded tales about noblemen, there is also a reflection of the later period, of the *barshchina* * (eighteenth and nineteenth centuries). The proverbs: "Necessity teaches, but work done for one's lord tortures"; "The soul belongs to God, the life belongs to the Tsar, the back belongs to the master," express the tone of the tales and legends about the *barshchina*. The tale of "The Angry Mistress" (the Sokolovs, No. 45), regardless of the possibly foreign origin of the subject itself, in its Russian adaptation is full of the motifs of the period of serfdom, and of the class animosity between the peasantry and the landowners.[85]

In certain tales, as we have said, the animosity is not confined to ridicule and contempt: the tale speaks of a harsher "mockery" of the masters by the peasants, in the form of murder and the burning of the country houses. The bailiff comes to the mistress of the estate, and to her question whether everything is going on well in the mansion, answers:

[85] Y. M. Sokolov, "On the Sociological Study of Folklore," *Literature and Marxism*, Bk. 2, 1928.
    * *Barshchina:* rent in the form of labor.—ED.

"Everything, mistress, thank God; only your favorite raven has eaten too much carrion."

"But where in the world did he find it?"

"Well, the black stallion is done for."

"How did that happen?"

"The manor house got on fire, so we used him to haul water and drove him to death."

"But how did the fire start?"

"Well, when they were burying your mother with lights [torches], then they inadvertently set it on fire." [86]

The peasant makes fun of his master; under the pretense of being a simpleton, he develops his speech in such a way that the master can take no exception to its form, but in its real essence, the master is compelled to listen to a number of bitter truths. The master asks the bailiff:

"But have you collected the flour from the peasants?"

"I've collected it, I've collected it, my lord and master."

"And how did you lay it out?"

"For you and for the pigs, fifty *chetverts;* * for the black dog, and for your dear father, forty *chetverts;* for the ducks and chickens, and for your silly sisters, twenty *chetverts.*"

"What kind of names are you calling there, you fool?"

"My lord and master, it's only a proverb that runs that way." [87]

Or the peasant handles the matter so cunningly, that he himself remains, as it were, quite extraneous to it. A peasant, going after a treasure he has found, and having his talkative wife with him, passes close by the master's yard and hears the goat bleating. His wife says: "Good heavens, husbandman, who in the world's that?" He says, "Oh, my, let's get out, it's certainly the master—the devils are holding him down." Rumors have come to the master's ears that the peasant woman has been boasting about a treasure which her husband has found. The master summons them before him. To the master's ques-

[86] N. L. Brodsky, "Serfdom in Popular Poetry," *The Great Reform*, Vol. IV, Moscow, 1911.

* Chetvert (literally "quarter"): a grain measure approximately equal to 8 bushels.—Ed.

[87] *Op. cit.;* *cf.* also the collection by N. K. Brodsky, *Toward Freedom*, "University Library" (Moscow, 1911), p. 81.

tions the woman gives absurd answers. Finally the master asks her: "At what time, then, were you going [after the treasure]?"

"At the very time, at the very same time we were going, when the devils were strangling you."

"Get out with you, fool that you are!" The master seizes her by the neck. "When were the devils holding me down? Get out, get out!" He begins to stamp his feet. Then the peasant says: "There, there, Your Excellency, that's the way my wife talks. She doesn't do a thing but lie, and I've been living with her like that my whole life long."

"Well, my poor peasant, go home, and God be with you—it's all a pack of lies." In this way he kept the treasure for himself (the Sokolovs, No. 14).

There is also a well known motif, very popular in the Russian tales, of how the peasant made the master keep watch, under his cap, on apples and nightingales, but in reality it was dung. Meanwhile the cunning peasant was driving off the master's team of three horses.

The majority of the tales about the masters are conditioned by the mode of life of the peasant serfs. But many of these subjects have passed over into a much later period, after the "emancipation of the peasants." The economic dependence upon the landowners remained. Nor did the class hostility diminish in the slightest degree. The tales have carried this attitude down to our own days.

In the tales about the masters, as we have pointed out, a part is very frequently played by the peasant laborer, the workman, the domestic servant. The direct association with the masters, and the daily sensation of one's dependence upon them, produced in such tales a still greater heightening of the class hatred and hostility. The boldness of the protest against the masters was increased among those classes of the peasantry which participated in the working life of the (urban) proletariat. The tale served to inculcate this. A nobleman, riding along, asked a carpenter whom he met, what village he was coming from. "From Raikova" (Paradise Valley). "And where am I going?" "To Adkova" (Hell's Corner). "Ah, you fool! You're a peasant, but you're from Paradise Valley; and I'm a lord, and yet I'm going to Hell's Corner." A footman, at his master's orders, gave the peasant a stiff beating. Well, thought the carpenter, you won't get away with that. And sure enough, the carpenter found a pretext, three times, for beating the master almost to death. It is characteristic that at each flogging the carpenter pronounced the sentence; the first time: "I'll give it to you, you son of a bitch, two times more: don't insult a workingman"; the second "Well, still once more you have to be beaten by me, to learn this lesson: don't insult a workingman without cause"; and finally, the third time: "Now, master, remember, understand that you cannot insult a workingman without paying for it" (Onchukov, No. 223).

In this tale we already have a distinct expression of class consciousness. It is not an accidental fact that this tale was written down soon after the revolution of 1905.

A sharp class antagonism permeates the tales on the *theme of priest and peasant*.[88] The tales on this theme could not, for a long time, make their way into print: to the prohibition of the secular censorship there were added the interdictions of the ecclesiastical censorship. There was a reason why the first collection of these tales (compiled by Afanasyev), under the title, *Sacred Tales*, was published abroad, in secret, with fictitious bibliographical data, for example, "*Balaam*, by the Typographical Art of the Monastic Fraternity, the Year of Obscurantism." The preface says:

Our book is appearing as an accidental and simple collection of that aspect of Russian folk humor for which there has hitherto been no room in print. Under the extreme conditions of Russian censorship, its distorted understanding of ethics and morals, our book has been quietly printed in that cloister, far removed from the disturbances of the world, into which there still has not penetrated the sacrilegious hand of any kind of censorship.

A large place in this collection is occupied by stories of priests. "The division of the tales dealing with the popularly so-called 'breed of foals' [colts], of which at present we are giving only a small portion, clearly illuminates both the relationships of our peasant to his spiritual shepherds, and the correct understanding of them."

The newer collections of tales, especially those of Onchukov and

[88] See a more detailed account in the foreword by Y. M. Sokolov to the collection of tales *Priest and Peasant* (Moscow, Academia, 1931).

the brothers Sokolov, were able to print the works representing this aspect of the tale. However, the latest collection which appeared in 1915, published by the Academy of Sciences, did not escape the punitive hand of the old censorship. The Academy of Sciences was compelled at once, immediately after its appearance, to withdraw the collection from sale. It was not possible to purchase the book until after the revolution. The majority of the tales about priests are of a coarsely erotic character. Of course the choice of a priest as the leading personage who takes part in such an erotic tale is dictated by the very character of the anecdote: a "sacred" person in the capacity of a lover endows the anecdote with an exceptional piquancy, it makes the situation unusually comical and ludicrous. But the significance of this purely literary factor must not be exaggerated. The Russian popular anecdote tale concerning priests, almost without exception, develops this subject from the class aspect; it invariably places the priest in a setting of class conflict between the peasantry and the exploiting class, the clergy also being found among the ranks of the latter. Even the erotic motifs are subordinated to this purpose. The priest's wife and daughter, in the tales, most frequently appear as the objects of the "attentions" of crafty peasant Don Juans, mostly from among the priest's workmen, the hired hands.

The conflict between the peasant and the priest, as we have said, has its origin according to the tale (just as it originated also in actual life) on the ground of economic relationships. Accordingly, in the peasant tale, the primary emphasis is placed on the greed of the priest, so much celebrated in folklore, his concern for the increase of his revenues by means of a collection of "donations" from the peasants, and his maximum exploitation of the hired laborer, with the minimum payment for his labor, both in money and in "maintenance." Hence comes the popularity of tale subjects with such characteristic titles as: "The Greedy Priest," "How the Priest Starved the Workers," "A Maiden Put a Priest to Shame," "The Jealous Priest and Nikolay the Miracle-Worker," "The Priest and the Cossack," "The Priest and the Three Bandit Brothers," "The Priest's Wife, the Deacon and the Workman," and so on. The characteristics of the tales of priests have already been touched upon sufficiently above, when we were speaking of the individual storytellers (for example, of Bogdanova), and when we were enumerating the basic subjects of the tales of priests.

Here we may emphasize, by several concrete examples, the manifestation of the class conflict between the peasantry and the priests, upon economic grounds. The sons of a poor peasant were obliged to go out as workmen. First the lot fell upon the eldest brother. The eldest became one of the priest's workmen. The priest gave him hardly anything to eat, and he suffered all the winter through. The eldest went away. In the following year, the second brother went to the priest's, and he, too, nearly died of hunger. The youngest brother proved to be more cunning; he devised a way not only to give the priest a good lesson, but also to get more money from him. In a strange village, where they both happened to be spending the night, he warned the innkeepers: "But please, I beg you, don't give the priest any supper: if you feed him well, he will only get much crazier than ever." The consequence is that the priest is thereupon left hungry. At the end, having learned his lesson, "the priest became such a good man that he began to feel sorry for the working people. When he himself sits down to drink tea, then he makes a workingman sit down with him" (the Sokolovs, No. 53). But this is a comparatively mild punishment vented by the workingman upon the priest.

Very popular in the tales is the motif of the murder of the priest, and then the sinking of his body in a river or a lake. For example, this is the way this motif is developed in the tale of "The Old Man Osip and the Three Priests" (the Sokolovs, No. 87): The greedy priest, having secretly eaten up Nikola's wafer, and having been discovered only later on, when it was said that he who had eaten the wafer would also receive a third part of all the money, was not able to profit by the wealth which he had received: "The priest hid the money and went home. And he got as far as his own field. And the path lay before him, straight up to the house. And he had to climb over the fence. So he climbed over the fence. And the sack flew out from behind his back, and fell beyond the vegetable garden. And he remained on this side of the vegetable garden, but the sack had fallen on the other side. And there he was trampled down" (the Sokolovs, No. 101).

The motif of the tricks played by the priests, with the aim of increasing the "donations" of the parishioners, and thereby enlarging their own revenues, is worked out in a great number of different ways in the Russian peasant tales. The priest, from the pulpit, is delivering his sermon. "For every contribution God will render you six times as much. Bring in a cow, and God will send you six cows." The peasant and his wife obeyed the priest, and then, when the priest's cows wandered into their yard, they took them as having been sent by God, and would not give them back to the priest (the Sokolovs, page xvii). This greed of the priests for revenues becomes perfectly candid and open: the priest, the deacon, the subdeacon turn the whole of the divine service into a dialogue, as to what each person is bringing into the church.

Here is a characteristic anecdote tale:

The deacon comes out, he takes his place on the pulpit, and then the priest says: "Deacon, deacon, look out of the little window, isn't there anyone coming, isn't he bringing anything?" And the deacon replies: "An old woman is coming, and she is carrying a measure of oil." And the deacon sings the Mass: "Give us, O Lord." And again the deacon proclaims: "An old woman is coming, she is carrying a *chetvert* of rye"; and to the third inquiry of the priest, the deacon replies: "A peasant is coming, he is carrying a cudgel for the priest's back." The priest and the deacon chant: "Unto Thee, O Lord" (Onchukov, No. 262).

In the same tone are cast the well known tales of the priest Pakhomius. The frankly cynical attitude of the clergy toward the objects of the religious cult, their consideration of them only as instruments of their trade and a means of profit, have found expression in a great number of the tales about priests. An icon is important and valuable for the priest only in so far as it gives him profit. A priest carried a pail of sour cream into the church "for Mikola to protect." A workingman ate up the sour cream, took the mustache of the sacred image and smeared it with cream, poured some drops of it on the image's beard, poured some drops on its breast, locked up the church, and went away. A holiday came, the priest went into the church, he walked over, glanced at the image, and saw that it was smeared with sour cream and that the basket was empty. "And here I have wrongly accused one and another, and look who it is that has eaten up the sour cream!" He took the image and threw it on the floor; the image was shattered. He seized the bucket and ran home. "Priest's-wife, I have shattered Mikola the Sanctifier—he eats the sour cream, I caught him, he only had time to close his mouth, he couldn't turn around, he was all covered with the sour cream" (Onchukov, No. 41).

Without exception, in all the tales the priest is shown in sharply satirical, negative outlines. Beyond a doubt this expresses the class hostility of the peasantry to the clerical estate as the representative of those classes which were antagonistic to him. The cause, as it is not difficult to discover in any given tale, lies in the economic relationships between them.

However, one must not fail to emphasize that the majority of the tales about priests, in their subjects, thematics, and their very treatment, express above all the attitudes of the poorer masses of the peasantry, the peasant laborers. An indirect confirmation of this is found in the circumstance that the bearers of these tales about priests—the storytellers—judging by their biographies, appear to have been poor laboring men. (Compare what we have said above of the storyteller Bogdanova, in the collection made by the brothers Sokolov; in the collection by Onchukov, the poor storyteller Shisholov devoted almost all his tales to the theme of the priests and their workmen; another specialist in tales about priests, in the collection of Onchukov, the storyteller Gregory Kashin, was also a poor man.)

The *figure of the merchant*, in the prerevolutionary Russian peasant tale, is sharply distinguished from the other two social types which have been surveyed above—the nobleman and the priest. If both the latter are appraised in the tale as having sharply negative features, from the point of view of the peasantry, the merchant, on the other hand, is depicted in altogether different colors. Quite often, the merchant was presented in the tales as a positive type. The cause for this lies in the petty bourgeois organization of considerable groups of the prerevolutionary peasantry, in any case, of its well-to-do classes, and of those middle-class masses who, in their individualistic economy, also expressed with considerable clearness their petty bourgeois nature. The sharply negative figure of the merchant serves usually, in the tale, as an indication of the creative work of the poor part of the peasantry; however, as we shall see, even here the center of attention is still directed, not so much to the delineation of the figure of the merchant, as such, as to that of the rich man in general, or, most frequently of all, to that of the peasant kulak.* Thus, in the tales of merchants and rich men we may clearly discern the social stratification which had arisen within the peasantry, and the distinction which had been conditioned thereby in the actual psychology and ideology of these class groups, as this has been expressed in the creation of the tale.

Some of the tales about merchants completely and clearly express the merchant world view and attitude. The narrative, in these tales, revolves around the successfulness of the trade itself, the fortunate accumulation of wealth, the increase of profits and revenues, the positive results of foreign trade and the merchant's safe arrival home. In these tales, there is depicted with great affection the actual process of trade, the buying and selling, and there is an affectionate drawing out of the display of the merchant's staidness, the business economy, and, on the other hand, of his great capacity at times for feasting and merrymaking. The very character of adventurousness, in the tales of merchants, is closely connected with the themes of the peasant mode of life—the unexpected receipt of money, of wealth, the successful trading operations, the choice of a wealthy bride, the receiving of an inheritance, and so on. There is no doubt that many of the popular tales about journeys abroad, on shipboard, for trade, especially in the North which was connected with the sea trade routes, have been composed in the setting of overseas trade.

It is curious that many of the tales on this theme present Mikola as the patron saint of trade and the preserver of those who travel by water; this is also precisely the function performed by Mikola in the *byliny* about Sadko. In these tales Mikola, in the form of an old man, works among the salesmen of a pious merchant who has preserved from insult the image of Mikola the Miracle-Worker, and thus functions directly as a partner and good adviser in overseas trade. In full

* Kulak (literally, a fist): a well-to-do peasant, able to hire workers.—Ed.

detail these tales describe the selection of a ship, the loading of it, the sea voyage, the mooring at the ship landing, the presentation of gifts to the city authorities, the contracts for free trade, the journey back, the safe arrival home, and the distribution of the goods which have been brought, in warehouses and shops. (Compare the tales: "Nikolay the Miracle-Worker and Ivan the Merchant's Son," the Sokolovs, Nos. 77 and 38, Onchukov, No. 281, and others.)

But, of course, many of the tales of a merchant cast are to be assigned to a later epoch, to a period of time which is nearer to our own. As we have said, there is a detailed description of the actual process of trade. The composer of the tale and the storyteller, as it were, personally experience, along with the heroes of the tale, the mercantile mentality.

There lived a famous merchant. He had a son, Ivanushka. When he was fifteen years of age, his father and mother appointed him to engage in trade in their store. When he began his splendid work, the business went better than before, when it had been handled by his father. The young ladies, especially, tried most of all to patronize that store. And now, on a certain beautiful day, Ivanushka concluded a very profitable transaction. Every evening he would give the accounts to his father. And thus a considerable time went by with these profits. His father loved him for these transactions. . . . Now another day comes, and already the people, the customers, are waiting for the young man at the store, for him to open the store. When he opened it, his trade went on at such a rate, that there was no such thing as taking up just an arshin * of cloth in his hands, but he sold it by whole bolts and pieces (the Sokolovs, No. 129, "Ivanushka, the Merchant's Son, and the Little Old Man").

This is quite a detailed and thorough description of a trading transaction.

In the tale "The Merchant Skorobogaty" (Get-Rich-Quick) (the Sokolovs, No. 94), the hero of the tale buys the home of a "bankrupt" count. He went out into the city, and in the city they were having a meeting of all the merchants, and the gentlemen were there —a great company. "How much," he says, "are you asking for the house? The stores are intact, everything is for sale." "We are asking

* Arshin: 28 inches.—Ed.

three hundred thousand for it." And so he says: "By your leave, let us pray to God, I am willing to take it all, and tomorrow I will bring the money, I haven't any money with me now." And so they let him go home. There is a detailed description in the tale also of the competition among the merchants, the deliberate lowering of prices on the part of some of them, with the purpose of beating the competition of the others.

Having gone abroad in the dress of a salesman, a merchant's daughter went into trade on her own.

And she bought herself a small store, and in this store she began to trade in bark mats, and she hung out a sign saying: "I sell a pair for cash, and a dozen on credit." And the people came flocking to her from all directions, so that they couldn't supply them with bark mats fast enough. And now for a year's time they had been going into debt to her for these, and her brother, Ivan Vasilyevich, comes into the shop, and he asks: "Why do you sell the bark mats so cheap?" "This is why I sell the bark mats so cheap, because I want to take away the profits from Ivan Vasilyevich" (the Sokolovs, No. 26, "The Merchant Serogor and His Two Children").

It is very significant that such tales as these, with their clearly expressed merchant attitudes, have been written down by the collectors mostly from the lips of storytellers who were wealthy men, engaged in trade or some kind of profitable enterprises. The above-mentioned tale of "Ivanushka, the Merchant's Son, and the Little Old Man" (the Sokolovs, No. 129) was taken down from the Belo-Ozero storyteller Ershov (see the Sokolovs, p. 43); the tale of "The Merchant Skorobogaty" (the Sokolovs, No. 94) was taken down from the well-to-do peasant Kuzmin; the tale of the merchant's pious son who built a church for Nikolay the Miracle-Worker, a helper in his trade, a tale with a distinctively peasant ideology, was written down by Onchukov in one of the northern suburbs, from the church elder Moshnakov (Onchukov, No. 281); a series of tales of similar type (Onchukov, No. 13, No. 15), where definite trading proclivities are revealed, was taken down from Chuprov, an "efficient" peasant who occasionally did some trading. All this serves to confirm the conclusion, which we have drawn previously, that through the creative personality of the storyteller there is revealed, in his tales, the nature of that social group to which he belongs. This serves to confirm also the similarity between the psychology of the merchant class and that of the well-to-do trading group among the peasantry. The tale itself repeatedly shows how close the connection is between this group and the merchant class; the trading North, especially, drew from the upper classes of the village its representatives in the merchant class of the capital and of the cities in general. In the tale "The Calumniated Sister" (Onchukov, No. 80), the rich peasant, who has a shop in the village, represents essentially this same merchant type.

The expression of the poor man's psychology in the tales is found, not so much in the delineation of the merchant as such, as in the representation of the rich man, or the rich peasant, and his opposite, the poor peasant. The Russian tale has even intensified the dramatic quality of this kind of tales by making the rich man and the poor man blood brothers. From the artistic point of view this results in a heightening of the negative qualities of the rich man in relation to the poor one: his boundless greed, his cruelty, and his disdain even of natural family feelings.

The tales on the theme "*of the rich and poor brothers*" set forth in sharp relief the problems of economic inequality within one's own family, and are sometimes blended with the themes of the tales of truth and falsehood, of good and evil fortune, of fate. The thematics and the actual treatment are conditioned by the surroundings of the poor peasantry.

The numerous tales on this theme show—so well that it could not be better done—the social-economic conditioning, among the poor peasantry, of the conceptions of "destiny." The chief persons who take part in them are found to be two peasant brothers, rich and poor, a kulak and a poor peasant. The principal figure in them is the poor peasant; the tales are seen to be an expression specifically of the poorer part of the countryside. A well known tale from the collection of Afanasyev, No. 172, "Two Destinies," reflects the mood and the ideology of the poor man, but the tendency of the poor peasant as reflected in this tale (the theme of personal enrichment, the receiving of the "destiny" of a rich man) reveals the pressure of the bourgeois ideology, which was typical of the peasant in the prerevolutionary period, in the era of proprietary economy and capitalistic influence.

The representation of destiny in Russian folklore, as Veselovsky has with perfect correctness observed, is "complex," being a combination of heterogeneous elements of heredity and chance, inevitability and free will which can change destiny.[89] The above-mentioned tale of the two destinies serves as an example of the exertion even of a certain power by man over his destiny. But very many tales, developed according to the plan which is so characteristic of the Russian peasant tale, of setting the poor man against the rich one, give obvious examples of the primary form of the idea of destiny, as of something which is inborn in a man from his first coming into the world. Such are the tales of Marko, the rich merchant, of Ivan the Luckless, Ondron the Unfortunate, and many others.

In speaking of the tales of the "two brothers," we wish to emphasize how thoroughly and clearly the tale, among the poor peasant classes, depicted the mutual relationships of the rich man and the poor man in the country village, the various forms of dependence of the poor man upon the kulak, and so on. Already, in the above-mentioned example from Afanasyev's collection, we have emphasized the indebtedness and obligations of the poor man with reference to the kulak, the dependence of the poor man upon the kulak with regard to the implements of production, stock, and so on. In other tales there is shown the form of the economic enslavement of the poor peasant; the poor man asks the rich man for bread: " 'Work for me this week, and then I will help you.' What was to be done? The poor man sets about his work; he cleans the yard and feeds the horses and carries water and chops wood. At the end of the week the rich man gives him a loaf of bread: 'This is for your work.' 'I thank you even for that much,' said the poor man; he bowed, and wanted to go home" (Afanasyev, No. 171, "Woe"). In another tale (Zelenin, *Great-Russian Tales of the Province of Vyatka*, No. 85), the rich brother, at the market, hires his

---

[89] A. N. Veselovsky, "Fate and Destiny As Popularly Represented among the Slavs," *Researches in the Field of Russian Religious Verse*, No. V (St. Petersburg, 1889), Chap. XVII. See also, on the same theme, the works of A. A. Potebnya, *On Destiny and Its Related Concepts*, 2nd ed. (Kharkov, 1914).

own brother to be one of his workmen, and the latter plows the rich man's land.

The tales, employing the device of contrast, delineate with precision the figures of the kulak and the poor peasant. The tale, as developed among the poor, is not sparing in its vivid description of the coarse proprietary psychology of the kulak. The poor brother, Petrusha, plows the earth with the horses of his rich brother Peter. "Peter had three fine horses, but Petrusha had only one mare. All through the week, Petrusha fed Peter's horses, and Peter went out riding; but Peter fed the horses on Sunday, and that day Petrusha went out riding. Once Peter went to Mass, and Petrusha was plowing, and he shouted to the horses: 'Ah, there, my horses, my dear good horses!' And Peter didn't like this. 'Why, Petrusha, do you address the horses as though you owned them, when surely all you've got is one mare?' Petrusha says: 'Well, brother, forgive me, I won't do it any more.'" But on the following Sunday the same thing was repeated again. "The rich brother flew into a rage, returned home, took an ax and cut off the head of Petrusha's mare: 'There now, you won't make yourself so familiar with another man's horses'" (Onchukov, No. 83). The tale specially emphasizes the unbounded greed and the haughty swaggering of the kulak in his relations to the poor peasant. The poor brother asks the rich one for "a measure of rye." "Take the icon as a pledge," says the poor peasant to his rich brother, "and give me a measure of rye." The poor brother died without having paid back the debt. When the rich man heard of this, he went out onto the street: "I will chop up," he says, "the image of Nikolay the Miracle-Worker; let my measure of rye be a loss!" (the Sokolovs, No. 38). Usually the rich brother refuses to give the poor one any kind of help, he does not believe him, and has no compassion upon him.

"There were two brothers, one rich, the other poor. This poor man's family weighed heavily upon him. The poor brother comes to the rich man: 'Help me,' he says, 'I have nothing today.' He had a cow. 'I will sell the cow, and pay my debts to you.' But his brother did not believe him" (the Sokolovs, No. 91). The poor man, by chance, finds some gold, he tempts fate by trying to return the gold (which had been hidden in a tree by the father of the rich man) to his brother.

He sends him the money, baked in a fish pie. But the angry, jealous rich man will not accept the pie: "Let my brother not think I have fallen so low that I have need of his pies" (Onchukov, No. 159).

In all these tales of the two brothers, of destiny, of truth and falsehood, there are considerable variations in the degree of hostility toward the rich man; some of them even emphasize the mildness of the poor peasant, as in the tale just referred to; in others the poor brother helps the rich man to build up another fortune, but the majority of the tales end by having the rich man become poor, and the poor man rich. But in many of the tales the attitude and the punishment of the rich man are very severe. Marko, the rich man, plots the death of his heir who has been designated by fate; but he himself perishes in the boiling kettle. But some of the tales, as, for example, the tale of "The Two Brothers—the Rich Man and the Poor Man" (Zelenin, *Great-Russian Tales of the Province of Vyatka*, No. 109), bring down a harsh vengeance upon the wealthy brother. In this tale the poor man, the "naked wretch," pours boiling water on the greedy wife of his brother, who had hidden herself in a trunk, in order to find out whether the poor brother had slaughtered the swine.

The most active and clear manifestations of class conflict and of class antagonism in the tales are mostly connected with the rural classes who are becoming proletarianized. We have already seen this in the tales about noblemen and priests. The fatalistic ideas of destiny are replaced by active conflict, boldness, resourcefulness. The heroes of these tales usually include a hired laborer, a workman, a "Cossack." Already the psychology of this group of landless farm laborers is not in such dependence upon the "powers of the earth," and is not so closely connected with the proprietary psychology, which is characteristic of the peasantry, conditioned as it is by individual ownership, even if only of a small farm. This psychology of the poor laboring peasants is not so characterized by the moods of reconciliation and fatalism. Of the laborers' tales, and of the laborer as the "hero of the tale," we have already spoken at sufficient length above, and a considerable number of examples have been given. Therefore we shall not dwell upon these any further.

Closely connected with the tales of the poor laboring peasants, both in subject, and in the character of the figures appearing in them, as well as in their general trend, are the tales of certain other groups of people in the countryside. Such, according to our views, are the tales of barge haulers, small craftsmen, seasonal workers, and other representatives of the working people of the old countryside. The rigorous struggle for existence, the complete or partial detachment from the traditional peasant economy, the perpetual wandering in search of work, the beggarlike existence, the dependence on the employer—all these created social-economic prerequisites which were akin to the conditions of life among the farm laborers. Hence arises the common psychology, hence comes also the common character (or in any case the kinship) of the figures in their tales; of the subjects (in particular, their adventurous nature, their anecdotal character, their poetizing treatment of craftiness, boldness, and resourcefulness); and of the ideological tendencies (the intensification of hostility toward the wealthy, property-holding classes, the derisive, satirical attitude toward them, and so on).

The barge haulers' tales, as we have already had occasion to observe, are quite a noteworthy segment of the Russian folklore of the tale. The laborious life of the barge hauler found expression in the folklore of the barge haulers' productions in various genres. But the barge hauler, as distinguished from the agriculturalist who stayed at home, had from ancient times enjoyed, in the countryside, the reputation of being a "free" young man (compare the ancient song, "The Free Downriver Barge Hauler"). According to the testimony of the author of an early work on the barge haulers, "For our simple folk, the barge hauler's trade, because of its vagabond character, has precisely the same attraction which the life of the ancient Cossacks had. It represents a certain type of revelry and personal freedom, not restrained by domestic bondage." [90] In the Russian tales the barge hauler is frequently introduced as an active participant; the diffusion of the tales, precisely by the barge haulers, is confirmed by the collectors of tales even in the twentieth century (Onchukov, Zelenin, Azadovsky, and others). D. K. Zelenin is altogether correct in draw-

[90] I. Kornilov, "The Barge Haulers of the Volga," *The Sea Collection* (1862), No. 7, p. 7.

ing the conclusion, on the basis of his study of the Russian tale material with this end in view, that "the barge haulers took a noteworthy part both in the diffusion and also in the alteration (the editing, and sometimes, it may be, even in the creation) of the Russian folk tales." [91] The figure of the barge hauler, who is accustomed to everything and can endure everything, is splendidly delineated in the Vyatka tale "The Barge Hauler's Contest with the Frost." Here the barge hauler proves to be the conqueror of the frost; the nobleman, in his bearskin coat, is easily chilled by the frost, but the barge hauler, in his short peasant coat, cannot be chilled by the frost; the barge hauler even in time of frost took off his mittens and cap. The Volga barge hauler is represented as a powerful hero, in the legendary tale of Nikitushka Lomov. "Along the Volga, in the thirties of the last century, went to and fro the powerful barge hauler Nikitushka Lomov; he was born in the province of Penza. The masters of the vessels valued him for his formidable strength: he did four men's work, and received also the allowance of four. Concerning his strength, wonders have been related on the Volga, and he is remembered also on the Caspian Sea."

One episode in the tale of that barge hauler, Elijah of Murom, is very significant. He grew angry at a merchant, who had paid the barge haulers one ruble for drawing up a twenty-pood * anchor, instead of the three rubles that had been agreed upon, because they had been helped by Lomov, with whom the merchant had made no bargain.

The barge haulers felt resentful toward the merchant. But Lomov says: "Don't distress yourselves, I'll play a trick on him; only, after you have received your money, set out a bottle of vodka for me." He took the anchor on his shoulder and tramped off to the hill. He came to the merchant's house and hung the anchor on the gate. He returned to the peasants, and he said: "Well, brothers, now he won't get off even with three rubles, and you shall take it [the anchor] away. See to it that you don't do it cheap." The peasants thanked

[91] D. K. Zelenin, "Barge-Haulers' Tales," *Great-Russian Tales of the Province of Vyatka* (Petrograd, 1915), Chap. IV.
* A pood is equal to 36 pounds.—ED.

him, and afterward they took a great deal of money from the merchant.[92]

Characteristic are the tales about the barge hauler who "conjured" the hosts with whom he asked permission to spend the night. The barge hauler lets in "the spell" that is, he makes the host see that which in reality does not exist; in the given instance he persuaded the host that the latter was a bear and he himself a wolf (Afanasyev, No. 214, "Witchcraft"). At the same time, in these tales, the barge hauler is introduced as a clever storyteller, for which also he has a night's lodging given him. Various other tale subjects, connected with the barge hauler, place him in a position analogous to that of the subjects we have previously surveyed, about the farm laborer, the workingman ("The Priest and the Workman," and others). It is very significant that, in the different variants of these tales and others like them, in place of the barge hauler there is introduced either a workingman or a soldier, or simply a vagabond. This fact once more emphasizes the similarity of the figures in these social groups of the peasant poor.

The burdensome realities of the Russian soldier's service, especially before the Reform,* have created in the tale the characteristic *figure of the buck private.* The soldier's barracks, the soldier's campaign and military life, were the setting where his own soldier story was created and recreated. Soldiers, from remote times, have been celebrated as excellent storytellers, and they are introduced in the tale itself in that capacity. Both the old and the newer collections of tales, in the nineteenth and twentieth centuries, give an abundant quantity of information about the soldier storytellers. By the telling of stories the soldiers, like many other representatives of the "vagabonds of ancient Russia," gained for themselves the chance for a night's shelter and sustenance. The hungry, homeless soldier, "discharged after his difficult service, going on furlough, weary and chilled, was occupied above all with thoughts of the satisfying of his simplest needs:

---

[92] D. N. Sadovnikov, *Tales of the Samara Region* (Petrograd, 1884), No. 121.
* 1872 reform of military service. Prior to the Reform, recruits were taken only from among peasants and the lower classes, and military service lasted 25 years.—ED.

to warm himself by the stove, to allay his hunger, and to fall peacefully asleep. On the basis of these simple, but exceedingly acute experiences and strivings of the poor peasant wanderers, there was created also the simple "framework" of subjects of the soldier's tale. The soldier's tale confirms the proverb which was composed during the centuries: "The poor man is quick to find ways." Developed by the exceedingly difficult struggle for existence, the soldier's cunning and resourcefulness help him, in the tale, to attain the satisfaction of his desires: he knows how to win for himself both a night's lodging and a dinner. The majority of the subjects of the soldier's tale, and their renderings, are different variations of this theme, giving various examples of the soldier's resourcefulness, the soldier's quick wit, and the soldier's endurance.

The soldier is used to seeing all kinds of people, he is not surprised at anything, he displays an astonishing coolness—it is true, only so long as no one infringes upon his soldier's predilections—to smoke or to take snuff. The soldier is not afraid of anybody; he has endured so much from the government of the land, that dead bodies, devils, witches, wizards, and such "uncleanness," and even death itself, do not produce any fear whatever in him. On the contrary, he himself mercilessly thrashes them, puts them into his old knapsack or bag, and takes out on them everything he has had to stand. The soldier's tale (and it almost always proves at the same time to be a tale about a soldier) not only developed its own imagery and types, but it also has, in its vocabulary, as well as in its style and rhythm, its own "soldier-tale" poetics. We may dwell for an example upon a certain very popular story theme, "The Soldier and Death." We will make use of the detailed text published by E. V. Barsov, as a supplement to his collection of recruiting laments, presenting it in brief summary, and with exact quotations from the text itself.[93]

Dismissed at the end of his service "to go wherever he wished," the soldier, first of all, on his meager pittance, entertained his comrades who remained behind, and gave away his last five kopeks to an old beggar woman. The old woman gave him an old knapsack;

[93] E. V. Barsov, *Laments of the Northern Region*, Vol. II (Moscow, 1882).

the knapsack proved to be a "magic wallet." The soldier, in order to try out its miraculous properties, first of all ordered that "there should immediately be a bunk, a table, a snack, vodka, and a pipeful of tobacco." In his further journeying he came upon a manorial country house, and asked the master to put him up for the night. He entertained the master from his "magic wallet." The master, even though he was a rich man, had never had such delicacies in his house before. They began to eat something, and the master stole a gold spoon. . . . The soldier searched the master, gave the spoon to a footman (who had sprung out of the wallet), and he himself began to thank the master for the night's lodging, and got him so ruffled up that the master, out of anger, went to work and locked all the doors. "At midnight the devils pounced upon the soldier, and the soldier kept making the sign of the cross all around him." The devils raised such an outcry that it would make you stop your ears. Thereupon one of them cried: "Attack him, attack him," and another shouted back at him: "And how can I attack him, with crosses everywhere?" The soldier put the devils into an empty sack and made the sign of the cross over it, took a twenty-pound weight, and went to beating on the sack. He beats, and he beats, and he feels of it, to see whether it is getting soft. Presently the soldier saw that at last it has become soft; he opened the window, untied the sack, and shook out the devils, outside. "The master rewarded him with money for the deliverance from the devils."

Farther along on his way, when he had walked three days' journey from the house, the soldier met an old woman—"and this old woman was so gaunt and terrible, and she was carrying a knapsack full of knives and saws, and of various kinds of hatchets, and she was leaning on a scythe." She blocked the soldier's pathway, "and the soldier would not have this, so he drew out his cutlass, and he cried: 'What do you want of me, old woman? Do you want me to split your skull?' " The old woman was called Death, and she had been sent by the Lord, to take his soul. She gave the soldier no time at all, she swung her scythe, and killed the soldier.

The soldier found himself in the other world. He would have gone to Paradise—but they would not let him in there: "It is because you have been unworthy." He landed in Hell; the devils were going to draw him into the fire. The soldier said to them: "What do you want of me? Ah, you barefoot rascals, have you then so soon forgotten the nobleman's bathhouse, hey?" The devils all ran away. "Oy, Father," they cried, "Satan, that very same soldier is here." Satan himself also ran away into the fire. "The soldier walked and walked all through hell, and he grew bored. He went straight to the Lord, and asked him for some kind of work. And the Lord said: 'Go, my servant, and ask Michael the Archangel for a gun, and take your stand as sentry at the doors of Paradise.' So the soldier stood on guard. Death came along. The soldier would not let her in: 'The Lord will not receive anyone who is not announced by me.' He found out from her that she had come to the Lord for instructions as to which people He would order her to slay that year."

The soldier gave Death his gun to hold, and went and put her question to the Lord, and then took the words of His answer and changed them. In place of His command, "Let her slay the oldest," out of compassion for his own aged relatives ("if my father is still living, and she slays him, as she did me, then I dare say, I shall never see him again") he transmitted instructions to Death, as if they came from the Lord, that that year she was to gnaw the old oak trees. The next year the same thing happened, and out of consideration for his brothers he changed the Lord's command "to slay the most mature," and so forth. Finally, in the third year, the soldier said to her: "Now as for you, old one, go, if you must, yourself, but I will not go, I am sick of you, you have bothered me enough." The Lord found out from Death about the soldier's tricks: "Angels, go bring the soldier to me." The Lord commanded them to let the soldier go into the wide world, and gave orders that he was to "fatten up Death for three years." The soldier put her into his sack, along with stones and sticks. "And when he marched off in soldier fashion, then the old woman's bones rattled." He left the sack with a tapster. The soldier came home, and his father was still living; he rejoiced that he had safely reached his home, and his relatives rejoiced still more.

After a year, he let Death out of the sack; she was there, "almost suffocated." The soldier bought a snuffbox with snuff, he smelled of it, and he sneezed. And Death said: "Veteran, give me some." She always asked for everything that she saw in the soldier's possession. So the soldier said: "What then, Death, surely you see there is hardly one little pinch of it; but go sit in the snuffbox, and smell of it as much as you like." As soon as Death had taken her place in the snuffbox, the soldier banged the lid shut, and carried her around again for a whole year. At the end of the year, he let Death out. "Oh," says Death, "that was bad." He began to feed her, and she ate enough for seven. He carried her off to the cemetery, and dug a pit and put her into it. The Lord commanded that Death should be found; the soldier showed the angels where he had hidden her. They brought her to the Lord. "Why, Death, are you so thin?" Death told the whole story. And the Lord says: "It is plain to see, Death, you are not going to get any food from that soldier, so go and feed yourself." Death again went forth through the world, only that soldier she did not dare to slay any more. He lived a whole hundred years, and then he went to war, and there he was killed.

The figure of the fearless, cheerful, and resourceful veteran, with his simple habits and whimsies, repeats itself in many other soldier tales. There are well known anecdotal tales about the soldier: of how he boasted to the master that he sleeps on his overcoat, puts the overcoat under his head, and covers himself with that same overcoat; but the master, who bought the overcoat from him, cannot get along with it at all; of how he replaced a roast chicken with a bast shoe; how he made soup out of an ax; how he guessed the peasant's riddles and answered with a riddle; of how to the old woman's riddle, "Does Kurukhan Kurukhanovich [Chicken Son-of-Chicken] prosper in the city of Pechinsk?" * he made answer with a laconic riddle in similar vein, "He has been transferred to the city of Sumin" (Knapsack) † how he cut off the leg of a corpse, shoved it onto the sleeping platform ‡ where he was spending the night, and his comrade began to demand of the landlord a compensation for the soldier who had, as it seemed, been murdered while staying at the inn. But the sol-

---

* "Stove-ville," pun on Russian *pech* (stove).—Ed.
† I.e., he has stolen the chicken and transferred it to his knapsack.—Ed.
‡ Usually, directly over the brick stove in a peasant hut.

dier in the tale specialized particularly in the expulsion of devils, the reading of prayers over the bodies of dead women, the punishment of witches and cross ladies, and in the art of magic. The soldier also plays an active part in certain other "magic" tales: he rescues tsarevnas, fights with a dragon, and so on. But even in these tales his figure, created on the basis of real life, remains on the whole exactly the same as in the tales of everyday life.

Besides the laborers', barge haulers', and soldiers' tales, in Russian folklore there are tales composed (or revised, which with reference to folklore is essentially one and the same thing), among other classes in the setting of the poor peasantry. The tale was composed and diffused by the representatives of various *minor wandering handicrafts* (fullers, shoemakers, tailors, stove setters, and so forth), and by other representatives of the "seasonal trades," in particular, the seasonal workers from the countryside. Such forms of the tale as those written down by us during our time spent in the Belo-Ozero region, the tales of happenings "to one's self," "How I went to Petersburg," and so forth, serve as a confirmation of this. Many of the tales were composed and diffused by the representatives of the country "*lumpen*-proletariat," *—beggars, tramps—the more so since, as we have indicated, the narration of tales often served as the means of their subsistence. On the motif of "vagabondage" in the Siberian tales we have dwelt above.

Along with the reflection of the character of the storytellers, as we have written in the collection *Songs and Tales of the Belo-Ozero Region*, in the tales it is frequently possible to find a reflection of their profession, special occupations, and experience of the world. This is expressed in the selection of the subjects of the tales, in the details as to character, in the choice of words and expressions. With the beggar Peshekhonov, in the tale there figure the beggar "who has no passport" and the "police," while with the sexton Bogdanov, this type is introduced into the list of persons taking part in the action. The tales deal, above all, with the world which was known to

---

* *Lumpen* (German, "ragamuffin"): used in Marxist parlance to denote that section of the proletariat outside the framework of socially useful production— beggars, criminals, etc.—ED.

the storyteller, the world of the clergy—the majority of his tales being "about priests"; but, with the storytellers who are soldiers (Mezalev, Lazarev), the soldier, in turn, occupies a worthy place, and the soldier's characteristics are indicated in the style, expressions, and content. The experience of the storyteller, his acquaintance with other places, especially with the city, with the capital, are expressed essentially in the tale, in its details, selection of words, in the impressions of the city, which are often naïve in their perceptions.

From the survey which we have made of the diverse types, subjects, motifs, figures, ideas, and stylistic peculiarities of the Russian folk tale, it is obvious how broadly and clearly there are reflected in it folk life, the popular folkways, and the people's dreams.

Not without reason did V. I. Lenin, in reviewing the collections of folklore, give the greatest attention, as we have already said, to the popular tales, finding in them the expression "of the hopes and expectations of the people," and also to the significance of the tales for an understanding of the popular psychology, while he also insistently pointed out the necessity of studying them "from the social-political point of view."

A. M. Gorky attributed great importance to the tales in the artistic and social education of the people, since the tales lift the mind above the pettiness and coarseness of everyday existence, and make the people think of a better life.

Back of the tales, back of the thoughts, I have sensed a certain miraculous entity which creates all the tales and songs. This is, as it were, a force, not powerful, but clever, farsighted, bold, stubborn, conquering everything and everybody by its persistence. I call it an entity because the heroes of the tales, passing over from one story to another, repeating themselves, have become blended in my thoughts into one person, into one figure.

This entity is altogether unlike the people among whom I have lived, and the older I have become, the more sharply and clearly I have seen the distinctions between the tale and the tedious, pitiably moaning, trivial life of the insatiably grasping, envious people. In the tales people have flown through the air on a "magic carpet," they have walked in "seven-league boots," they have raised the dead, sprinkling them with the water of life and of death; in a single night

they have built palaces, and in general the tales have opened before
me a vista into another life, where some free and fearless power existed and wrought, in the dream of a better life. And, it goes without saying, the oral poetry of the working people of that time, when
the poet and the workingman were blended together in one person
—that deathless poetry, the progenitor of book literature—has greatly
helped me to familiarize myself with the fascinating beauty and
wealth of our language.[94]

BIBLIOGRAPHY

COLLECTIONS

Afanas'ev, A. N., *Narodnye russkie skazki* (Popular Russian
Tales), 1855–1864; 2nd ed., in 4 volumes, 1873; 3rd ed., in 2 volumes, ed. A. E. Gruzinskii, 1897; 4th ed., in 5 volumes, Moscow,
1912. A new edition, in three volumes, is being published by Academia, ed. M. K. Azadovskii, N. P. Andreev, and Y. M. Sokolov (Vol.
I, 1936, Vol. II, 1938).

Sadovnikov, D. N., *Skazki i predaniia Samarskogo kraia* (Tales
and Legends of the Samara Region) (St. Petersburg, 1884).

Onchukov, N. E., *Severnye skazki* (Northern Tales) (Petrograd,
1909).

Zelenin, D. K., *Velikorusskie skazki Permskoi gub.* (Great-Russian Tales of the Province of Viatka) (St. Petersburg, 1915).

Sokolov, B. and Y., *Skazki i pesni Belozerskogo kraia* (Tales and
Songs of the Belo-Ozero Region) (St. Petersburg, 1915).

Smirnov, A. M., *Sbornik velikorusskikh skazok arkhiva Russkogo
geograficheskogo obshchesta* (Collection of Great-Russian Tales from
the Archive of the Russian Geographic Society), Nos. I-II, 1917.

Azadovskii, M. K., *Skazki verkhnelenskogo kraia* (Tales of the Upper Lena Region) (Irkutsk, 1924; 2nd ed., Leningrad, 1938).

Karnaukhova, I. V., *Skazki i predaniia Severnogo kraia* (Tales and
Legends of the Northern Region) (Moscow, 1934).

"Skazki Kupriianikhi" (Tales of Kupriyanikha), transcript of the
tales, introductory article, and commentaries by A. M. Novikova and
I. A. Ossovetskii (Voronezh, 1936).

Akimova, T. M., and Stepanov, P., *Skazki Saratovskoi oblasti*
(Tales of the Region of Saratov) (Saratov, 1937).

Sidelnikov, V. M., and Krupianskaia, V. IU., *Volzhskii fol'klor*
(Folklore of the Volga) (Moscow, 1937).

Belomorskie skazki, rasskazannye M. M. Korguevym (White Sea

[94] Gorky, A. M., *On Literature* (Moscow, 1937), p. 174

tales, Related by M. M. Korguev), ed. A. N. Nechaev (Leningrad, 1938).

Krasnozhenova, M. V., *Skazki Krasnoiarskogo kraia*. (Tales of the Krasnoyarsk Region) (Leningrad, 1938).

Ozarovskaia, O. E., *Piatirech'e* (The Five Rivers) (Leningrad, 1931).

ANTHOLOGIES OF RUSSIAN TALES

Kapitsa, O. I., "Russkie narodnye skazki" (Russian Popular Tales), introductory article by A. I. Nikiforov, *Skazka, eë bytovanie i nositeli* (The Tale, Its Mode of Existence and Its Carriers) (Leningrad, 1930).

Azadovskii, M. K., *Russkaia skazka* (The Russian Tale), 2 vols. (Moscow, Academia, 1932).

Sokolov, Y. M., *Pop i muzhik, sbornik russkikh skazok* (Priest and Peasant: A collection of Russian Tales) (Moscow, Academia, 1931).

Sokolov, Y. M., *Barin i muzhik, sborn. russkikh skazok* (Master and Peasant: A collection of Russian Tales) (Moscow, Academia, 1932).

RESEARCHES

Savchenko, S. V., *Russkaia narodnaia skazka* (The Russian Folk Tale), history of its collection and study (Kiev, 1914).

Vladimirov, *Vvedenie v istoriiu russkoi slovesnosti* (Introduction to the History of Russian Literature) (Kiev, 1896).

Speranskii, M. N., *Kurs russkoi ustno islovesnosti* (Course in Russian Oral Literature) (Moscow, 1916).

Andreev, N. P., *Ukazatel' skazochnykh siuzhetov po sisteme Aarne* (Index of Tale Subjects According to the System of Aarne) (Leningrad, Russian Geographic Society, 1929).

Andreev, N. P., "K obrozu russkikh skazochnykh siuzhetov" (Toward a Survey of Russian Tale Subjects), Khudozhestvennyi Fol'klor (Artistic Folklore), Nos. II-III, Moscow, 1927.

Veselovskii, A. N., *Sobr. soch.* (Collected Works), Vol. XVI (Leningrad, 1938).

Buslaev, F. I., "Perekhozhie povesti" (Migratory Narratives), in the collection *Moi dosugi* (My Leisure Hours), Pt. II (1884).

Rovinskii, D., "Russkie narodnye kartinki" (Russian Popular Scenes), *Sborn. Otd. Russk. Iaz. i Slov. Akad. Nauk* (Annals of the Division of Russian Language and Literature of Sciences), Vols. XXIII-XXVII, St. Petersburg, 1881.

The additional literature on the tales has been referred to above, in the footnotes.

FOLK DRAMA

By the term "folk drama" we understand: (1) dramas which have been created for the people, or (2) dramas which are being created by the people. Here we shall speak of the popular drama only in the second sense of this term.

If the concept of drama is to be characterized as a dialogue intended for representation in action, then we shall find elements of the folk drama, in vast numbers, even at the very first stages of cultural development. The primitive syncretism (previously described), which is characteristic of the first stages in the creation of all peoples, by its very nature includes elements of the popular drama (as, for example, has been clearly shown in the classic works of Veselovsky). The incantation ceremonies of backward peoples, imitating hunting, fishing, and war for the purposes of husbandry and magic, are sufficiently graphic in their dramatic sense. To a very considerable degree, the survivals of primitive syncretism, with their dramatic elements, are preserved in the folklore of all European and non-European peoples.

In Russian folklore, elements of the popular drama are represented very extensively in the rituals connected with the calendar, and also in family ceremonies, especially those pertaining to marriage. In embryonic form the elements of the drama are found even in the most ordinary choral games of the countryside, the choral dances, where, furthermore, the dancers are frequently divided into two antiphonal sections.

That vast world of theatricalism which was cultivated by the Church was bound to influence the popular drama also. This influence, in fact, is to be seen in the language of the popular drama, as well as in its specific forms and certain of its stage settings.

But in the Russian folk drama this influence was considerably less than in the West, and was perceptible chiefly in the form of parodies (see, for example, the comedies *Mavrukh, Pakhomushka,* and the episodic roles of the priest in other plays).

[499]

The ecclesiastical influence upon the popular Russian theatrical creation is directly expressed as early as the end of the Middle Ages, in the territory influenced by the Catholic Church which advanced, first of all, through Poland, then into southwestern Russia. These influences were expressed through the southwestern religious school. Already in Poland, the Jesuit school drama which had elaborated biblical and legendary Church subjects according to all the rules of the scholastic Latin poetics, that had taken as its model the plays of Plautus and Terence, permitted the so-called *intermedii*.* The *intermedii* are comic scenes from everyday life, which were already being performed, not in the Latin, but in the vernacular tongue, frequently not even in Polish, but in Ukrainian or White-Russian. In these *intermedii* of the Polish school drama, one cannot help perceiving elements of the popular theater.

Scholars, students in the Jesuit colleges, provincials, sometimes of Ukrainian or of White-Russian origin, who were allied with the everyday life of the subordinate clergy and of the peasantry, on the one hand, introduced national, "plebeian" factors into the school dramas, and, on the other hand, contributed greatly to the popularization of the drama among the masses of the people, arranging—if in a simplified form—performances in the villages and hamlets. The *intermedii* of the Kiev Academy, and later also of other religious schools in the Ukraine, in White Russia, and even in Russia, still more intensified this process.

To the influence of the school theater, with its survivals of the medieval mystery plays and with the characteristic features of the comic *intermedii* which have just been mentioned, there must be credited the rise among us of the so-called "crèche play," called among the Poles "*shopka*," and among the White Russians "Bethlehem plays." The crèche performances consist of two sharply differentiated elements—the religious-biblical, and the realistic-comic. This division was emphasized and maintained by the very outward arrangement of the crèche stage—a box, divided into two parts: the upper, where plays were presented which were connected with the legend of

---

*Intermedio (Italian): a short comic piece, usually performed in the intervals between the acts of a musical production.—ED.

the birth of Christ in the manger at Bethlehem, and the lower, intended for the comic plays based on everyday life. Those who participated in the latter, in the Ukraine, were the traditional personages—peasants, soldiers, gypsies, Jews, and Poles, and also the Dnieper Cossack (who in the White Russian crèche play was frequently replaced by the figure of the policeman who accepted bribes).

This puppet theater which continued in existence down to the twentieth century, exchanged the puppet artists for living ones, and became the so-called "living crèche play," one of the forms of the folk drama in the proper sense of that word. The influence of the crèche play is reflected in *Tsar Maximilian* and other folk plays. The disseminators of the crèche theater were the democratic groups among the lower clergy, and the students in the theological seminaries, and after them the peasantry and the city bourgeoisie.

From the crèche theater there issued also the form known as the "peep show," which was diffused throughout Russia in the eighteenth and nineteenth centuries. The stage was replaced by little pictures, which were set in motion by a roller; the dialogue of the characters who participated was replaced by the explanations of the showman, which were chiefly of a comic nature, and in the form of verse. The content of the verses rendered by the showman frequently took on a social and popular character. Sometimes the authorities and the nobles were lampooned: "And here is the city of Paris; when you come in, then you lose your senses; our Russian nobility travel hither to squander their money; they start off with gold in a sack, and they come back on foot with a stick."

Close to the comic plays of the crèche theater and the discourses of the showman stand the *buffoon performances*, which, of course, have a common history with European buffoonery, but which in Russia developed their own buffoonish literary style, similar to the language of the showman. Unfortunately, the buffoon plays have been very inadequately studied.

One of the favorite types of buffoon entertainments was the puppet performance, the so-called "Petrushka" [Punch and Judy].

A performance of this show in Russia has been established by Adam Olearius as early as the year 1636. From Olearius' drawing, it is pos-

sible even to determine the subject of the scene which he saw. It is
the familiar traditional scene of the sale of a horse, by a gypsy, to
Petrushka. The scenes with the gypsy, and also the others—those with
the "doctor-physician, the apothecary from under the Stone Bridge,"
with the German, with the Tartar, with the ward police officer or with
the noncommissioned officer, and finally, with the little poodle dog,
in a number of variations—are basically quite well stabilized, and coincide in their episodes with the popular dramas, with which the theater of Petrushka had close mutual relations. Even the figure of Petrushka himself, apparently, through analogous figures in the German
theater, is derived from an Italian prototype, the famous Polichinelle,
taken over by the French popular theater, and also by the English.
In the latter, the name of the puppet hero is Punch. In the Czech
theater the corresponding figure of the buffoon is Kashparek. At the
present time, in the USSR, the puppet theater has been converted
to the cause of cultural development; it has had an especially broad
application in the artistic education of children. The content of the
plays which have entered into the repertory of the contemporary
puppet theater has little in common with the traditional folk theater.

However, an interesting variant of Petrushka, with certain interpolations belonging to the period of the revolution, was written down
in the year 1924 in Voronezh.[1] But this is a very rare instance.

We have enumerated above the elements of the drama: the ritual,
agricultural, and family activities of the peasants, the choral games,
the forms of the creative art of the buffoons, the church service, the
religious theater of the schools, with its *intermedii*, the crèche scenes,
the comments of the showman, the buffoon theater, and the theater
of Petrushka—all of this together gave the necessary dramatic material for the creation of the *folk drama* in the proper sense of the
word. The repertory of the Russian folk drama is not large: one may
reckon in all perhaps ten different subjects. But it is necessary to take
into account the improvisational character of this drama, leading to
a great number of variations of one and the same play. The best
known Russian popular drama, *Tsar Maximilian*, has been recorded

[1] Putivtsev, "Vanka," a contemporary popular puppet comedy, *Voronezh
Literary Proceedings, Annals*, I, 1925.

in more than two hundred variants, frequently differing very widely from one another.

The origin of *Tsar Maximilian* has not as yet been clearly established. Some investigators, V. V. Kallash for example, have conjectured that this play is a dramatic adaptation of the life of Nikita the Martyr, the son of the persecutor of the Christians, Maximilian, who subjected Nikita to tortures for his confession of the Christian faith. Others (P. O. Morozov and Academician A. I. Sobolevsky), basing their work on the foreign names in the play (Maximilian, Adolf, Brambeul or Brambeus, Venus, Mars), conjecture that this popular drama goes back to some kind of school drama of the first half of the eighteenth century, which in its turn is based upon a translated narrative of the end of the seventeenth and beginning of the eighteenth century. But out of these possible prototypes, the biographical narrative and the school drama, *The Comedy of Tsar Maximilian and His Son Adolf* could have preserved, in any case, very little; perhaps only the scenes where the pagan tsar demands that his Christian son shall bow down before the "idol gods." The remainder of its content is filled with scenes borrowed, apparently, from some kind of *intermedii* (one of these has already been established—"On Anik the Warrior and His Contest with Death"), with episodes from the crèche play, from Petrushka, and also from other folk plays, which are closely akin to *Tsar Maximilian*, for example, *The Ship's Boats*, *The Nobleman*, and so on. In addition, the text of *Tsar Maximilian* is filled to overflowing with fragments both from folk songs and from ballads, and also with quotations, with popular adaptations of the verses of Pushkin, Lermontov, and other poets. As we have seen, the principle of improvisation is utilized very widely in the plays.

In its original form, at the beginning of the eighteenth century, *Tsar Maximilian* could have been taken as a political witticism: in it (such are the conjectures or Shcheglov, Vinogradov, and others) contemporaries might have seen a satire on the relations between Peter I (who had married a Lutheran and warred against the traditions of the Church) and the tsarevich Alexis. According to the play, Tsar Maximilian marries a "heathen goddess" and demands of his son a renunciation of the traditional faith.

The second most widespread Russian folk drama bears various titles: *The Boat, The Ship's Launch, The Band of Robbers, The Cossack Chief,* or, in one of the complicated variants, *Mashenka.* In its main scene this play is very close to the traditional beginning of several of the robber songs (frequently linked with the name of Stepan Razin): it describes the boat sailing down the river (the Volga or the Kama), with the robbers sitting in it, and the chief standing in the middle. The content of the play consists of questions the chief asks the captain of the Cossacks about what he sees in the distance. In the different variants the drama is complicated by the interpolation of episodes, borrowed, for example, from a third popular play, *The Sham Nobleman,* or *The Naked Nobleman.*

The latter play is based upon a widespread folk anecdote of the nobleman and the bailiff (see above, in the chapter on the tales), who reports to the landowner that everything he has is in excellent shape, "only mamma has died, the house has burned down, the cattle have perished," and so on. The play *The Nobleman* presents a scenic parody on the nobleman's law court, on the nobleman's purchase of a horse, an ox, and peasants. The play apparently originated among the manorial servants. In the play *The Steed,* or *The Horseman and the Veterinary,* in the very entangled form of the dialogue between the rider (originally, the nobleman) and the veterinary, there is also a parodied description of the landowners and the various authorities. The play *Mavrukh,* presenting a popular adaptation of the song "Marlbro' s'en va-t'en guerre," contains a satire on the ecclesiastical burial service and on the mode of life of the clergy. Written down in the trans-Onega region by the scientific expedition of the State Institute of the History of Art, the play *Pakhomushka,* with all its outward crudeness, is very interesting as a parody upon the traditional peasant marriage ceremonies and upon the church wedding.[2]

With regard to their *composition and style,* the popular dramas may be characterized by the following features. The structure of each play is determined by the very faintly indicated "pivot" of the plot. (Still more clearly than in the others, this pivot is apparent in *Tsar*

[2] See "The Art of the North," *Peasant Art of the USSR* (Leningrad, 1927), No. 1.

Maximilian, where there is at least an indication of the intrigue of the conflict between father and son.) In *The Ship's Launch*, or *The Boat*, the somewhat marked characteristics of the plot are limited only to the motif of the journey of the robbers in the boat, and the encounters along the way with the Cossack captain, with the old men, and so on. In *The Nobleman* there is given only the motif of the comic purchase by the nobleman of various objects and people; in *The Steed* the plot revolves around the encounter of the veterinary with the horseman and the dialogue which arises thereupon; in *The Sham Nobleman* it is the encounter of the nobleman with the bailiff and the comic report of the latter as to the condition of the estate. Consequently, the dramatic interest of the plays is called forth, not by the complicated development and interweaving of the action, but either by the rapid changing of the scenes which are strung together one after another (in *Tsar Maximilian*) or else simply in the comic dialogue (in *The Nobleman* or *The Sham Nobleman*).

The comical quality of the dialogue is based on a few very simple devices, frequently emphasizing the acute class consciousness of the folk drama. One of its favorite devices is the so called "oxy-morons," built upon the combination, in one sentence or in several, of opposing concepts or figures, which can thereby create a comic impression of absurdity: "All of us, we fine fellows, were thoroughly soaked, so that there was not a single damp thread upon us, but all were dry" (*The Ship's Launch*). We often encounter, also, a still more formal device of humor—metathesis, that is, the changing of the places of words, in one sentence or in several, as a result of which the young lady "dies," the horse "passes away," and so on (*The Sham Nobleman*). Widely employed, also, is the device of a play of homonyms (words having the same sound, but different meanings) and synonyms (words closely related in meaning, but differing from one another in form). Often the play of homonyms is intensified and relieved by the motif of the deafness of one of the persons taking part in the tale.

On the latter device, for example, is based the entire scene with the two old gravediggers in *Tsar Maximilian*: "Vaska, old man, go to the Tsar!" "To what grasscutter (*kosár*)?" "No, not to the grasscutter, but to the Tsar," and so on. The device of the realization of metaphors is also used—the understanding in a literal sense of words that are figurative: "Is that the colonel?" "Exalt him higher still." "But isn't he the one who is already walking along the roof?" (*Tsar Maximilian*) These unstudied devices of comedy form a great contrast with the bombastically ornate speech of the majority of persons taking part in the action, and they thereby also produce a grotesque impression, not always realized as such by the actual participators and spectators of the popular drama. In the speeches of the Tsar Maximilian may be heard the echoes of the language of the Church and of the government offices.

With reference to the objects of *satire* in the popular drama, it must be said that its barbs are directed chiefly, as in Russian folklore in general, against two social groups: against the landowners and the clergy (see *The Nobleman, The Sham Nobleman, The Ship's Launch,* where the landowners are dealt with, and *Mavrukh,* where the priests are introduced). In certain variants of *Tsar Maximilian* and in other plays, there is episodic treatment of the officer class, and, comparatively seldom, of the merchant class, which again corresponds to the specific gravity of these personages in satirical folklore in general —in the tales and in the songs. The observations of the ethnographer-collectors on the content and style of the popular dramas lead us to assume that these plays, which perhaps had their origin among scholars, were most widely disseminated among the soldiers and those classes of the rural population who had left the village, chiefly for seasonal work. The conditions of life in the barracks or in the co-operative association (artel), owing to the concentration in one building of a great number of men without families, naturally contributed to the creation of ad hoc theatrical groups. The plays which had been learned in the city were then disseminated throughout the villages, being included usually among the Christmas entertainments, involuntarily absorbing thereby some of the traditional dramatic elements of the ceremonial folklore. In conclusion, we must not fail to note the numerous attempts to transfer the forms of the popular drama (particularly of *Tsar Maximilian*) to the school stage.[3]

[3] See, e.g., M. A. Rybnikova, *Tsar Maximilian.*

BIBLIOGRAPHY

Onchukov, N. E., *Severnye narodnye dramy* (Popular Dramas of the North) (St. Petersburg, 1911).

Vinogradov, N. N., "Narodnaia drama' 'tsar' Maksimil'ian' " (The Popular Drama "The Emperor Maximilian"), *Sb. Otdeleniia Russkogo iazyka slovesnosti Akademii Nauk* (Annals of the Division of Russian Language and Literature of the Academy of Sciences), Vol. XC, No. 7, St. Petersburg, 1914.

Remizov, A. M., *Tsar' Maksimil'ian* (The Emperor Maximilian) ed. of V. V. Bakrylova, with a bibliography (State Publishing House, 1920).

Vsevolozhskii, V. (Herrngross), *Istoriia russkogo teatra* (History of the Russian Theater) (Moscow-Leningrad, 1929).

Morozov, P. O., *Ocherki iz istorii russkoi dramy XVII-XVIII stoletii* (An Outline History of the Russian Drama in the Seventeenth and Eighteenth Centuries) (St. Petersburg, 1888).

Rovinskii, D. A., *Russkie narodnie kartinki* (Russian Popular Scenes), Vols. I-V (St. Petersburg, 1881).

Filippov, Vladimir, *Zadachi narodnogo teatra i ego proshloe v Rossii* (The Tasks of the Popular Theater and Its Past in Russia) (Moscow, 1918).

Perets, V. N., "Kukol'nyi teatr v Rossii" (The Puppet Theater in Russia), *Ezhegodnik imperatorskikh teatrov* (Yearbook of the Imperial Theaters for the Years 1895 and 1896).

Bogatyrev, P., *Cheshskii kukol'nyi i russkii narodnyi teatr* (The Czech Puppet Theater and the Russian Popular Theater) (Petrograd, 1923).

Veselovskii, Aleksei, "Starinnyi teatr v Evrope" (The Ancient Theater in Europe), *Istoricheskie ocherki* (Historical Sketches) (Moscow, 1870).

Piksanov, N. K., theatrical seminar, "Kul'tura teatra" (The Culture of the Theater), *Zhurnal Moskovskikh akademicheskikh Teatrov* (Journal of the Moscow Academic Theaters), No. 6, Moscow, 1921 (bibliographies).

LYRIC SONGS

If, as we have seen, the repertory of Russian storytelling is very great, the repertory of songs is inexhaustible. Scholarly collections have fixed in printed form a vast number of songs. It is sufficient to say that, for example, in the collection made by Academician A. I. Sobolevsky, *Great-Russian Songs* (seven volumes), there were 4,772 texts printed; in the collection of P. V. Shein, *The Great-Russian*, Vol. I, No. 1, there were 1,283; in the *Songs* collected by P. V. Kireyevsky there were 4,160, without even speaking of the numerous collections devoted to the songs of this or that specific region (for example, in the collection of the brothers B. and Y. Sokolov, *Tales and Songs of the Belo-Ozero Region*, there are 686 song items, without counting the popular rhymes).

But for all that, every investigator of the lyric song feels that the number of recordings we have is insufficient, since the texts of the songs have an especially great capacity for variation, much greater than that of the texts of the epics. Based more on the expression of emotions than on the exposition of a subject, the lyric song naturally gives a still greater scope than the epic song for the interpolation by the singer, or by the group of singers, of new feelings, concepts, poetic images. It may be asserted that the whole mass of the texts which have been printed is still insufficient for a judgment of the folk song. The wealth of the songs is, in reality, many times greater.

The number of the collected texts is also insufficient because many of the recordings have been produced without observance of scientific requirements, often without complete accuracy, so that the investigator's work upon them, whether from the viewpoint of history or from that of stylistics, is rendered exceedingly difficult.

The essential cause of the great number of variations in the lyric song is that, in contradistinction to the *byliny* or the religious verses, it is sung not by individual professionals, like the narrators or beggars, but by everyone—old and young, at home and in the field, singly and by an "association," that is, a chorus. Consequently, there is a greater opportunity to interpolate changes in the text, constantly to restore it, to adapt it to new moods and forms, and, in case of failure to understand it, or to learn it sufficiently well, to distort it.

The amount of talent of the performers of the song determines the degree of its artistic excellence. As among the disseminators of the other genres, so among the singers, there are those who are gifted, those who are mediocre, and those who are altogether lacking in talent. The genuine artist singer enjoys well merited popularity and attention.[1] One encounters certain masters of song who consider the text and the melody of equal importance, and who captivate everyone by the expressiveness of their performance. Others center their attention mainly on the melody, emphasizing its peculiarities, with particular distinctness, giving it an artistic individual interpretation; but with them the text often remains undeveloped. A third group, on the other hand, are conscious of the text above all. These singer poets rap it out, thinking relatively little of the melody, reproducing it as they have memorized it. These various types of artistry exert their own influence upon the specific character of the performance of the song. But in all cases the manner of the genuine master of lyric song can easily be distinguished from the mass of ordinary performances by the general run of singers, even though they may possess good voices.

This significant question of the creative work of the popular masters of the song has hitherto remained without sufficient investigation. The materials which have been collected on the singers are as yet very meager. Until the 1890's, the collectors paid no attention to the performers of the songs. Only in 1894 was there published, for the first time, a collection of songs with an indication of their performers.[2] The description of the actual manner of the singing

---

[1] As testimony on this point, one need only cite Turgenev's story "The Singers."
[2] *Songs of the Russian People, Collected in the Provinces of Archangel and Olonets in the Year 1886*, written down by F. M. Istomin and G. O. Deutsch (St. Petersburg, Russian Geographical Society, 1894).

did not begin until a still later period.[3]

There is a great diversity among the texts of the songs, and a great diversity in their social nature.

In the vast repertory of lyric songs, in the very first stages of the analysis, it is discovered that various social groups have taken part in the creation of the songs. Here, of course, the first place belongs to the basic agricultural core of the peasantry. But not only the basic stratum of the peasantry—the rural husbandmen, the plowmen—created songs, distinctly expressing in them their psychology and ideology, but also those classes of the rural population who did not find an outlet for their labor in the country, in cultivating the land, but who went away from the village, for long or short periods of time, to do other work, for the seasonal occupations. These groups created their own songs, reflecting both the conditions of their crafts, and the psychological changes produced by them. Such, for example, are the songs of the barge haulers, the songs of the wagoners, and so forth.

A very interesting attempt to reestablish the history of a certain barge haulers' song, which in its time was very widely disseminated, has been made by an investigator of the mode of life and folk creation of the Volga barge haulers, F. N. Rodin.[4] The song reproduces pictures of the hard life of the barge haulers, of their dreadful exploitation by the barge owners, but at the same time also conveys that instability of temperament which was so characteristic of the masses of the barge haulers—the violent transitions of the barge haulers, who "drudge" from their cheerless, heavy work to the reckless, drunken revels at their stops in the great harbors and cities.

The figure of the barge hauler, as conceived by the basic masses of the peasantry, is delineated in a somewhat dual and inconsistent aspect: the barge hauler was sharply differentiated from the monotonous throngs of the country people who were firmly bound to their

[3] Detailed and at times very acute observations as to the individual peculiarities of the creative performance of the songs by the artist singers have been made by one of the best collectors of song folklore, E. Lineva, *Great-Russian Songs in a Popular Harmonization*, Nos. 1 and 2 (St. Petersburg, 1909).

[4] F. N. Rodin, *History of a Barge Haulers' Song* (Saratov, 1929).

land and could not go far away from their own village. The barge
hauler is a man who has been everywhere, a man, as it seemed to
an outside observer, who is at liberty, who is free, who has experienced much and heard much (see the chapter on the tales). Hence,
too, the rural youth finds him of definite interest; but at the same
time the bitter reality constantly destroys the idealization: the
barge hauler frequently brings almost nothing home out of his
earnings (one recalls the proverb which we have previously cited,
concerning the barge haulers: "Necessity drives them downstream,
and bondage brings them back"). Therefore, both as regards history and everyday life, it seems to me that the following song contains a great deal of truth:

The free bird, the little quail,
Wherever she wished, thither she flew,
Wherever she took a liking to the place, there she alighted.
The free little bird alighted in the open country,
Beside the broad and splendid road that leads to Moscow,
Amidst the brilliant whiteness of the wheat,
She began to sing her mournful little song.
Do not moan, do not moan, ardent little heart.
Do not weep, do not weep, dear beautiful maiden!
It was not your papa nor your mamma who gave you in marriage—
It was you yourself, maiden, who conceived a desire
For the free barge hauler who came from down the stream.
People said: The barge hauler has lots of money.
He has one three-kopek piece in his knapsack,
And a stout cudgel across his shoulders.[5]

No less striking are the songs composed among the teamsters, or
stage drivers.[*] The *yamshchik's* or carrier's trade in the earlier years,
before the introduction of improved means of transport, played a
very great role in public and everyday life, and required the services of
a great number of persons. The driver's labor was attended with a
great deal of risk, owing to the bad condition of the roads and to all
the possible accidents on long journeys. The drivers often ended their

[5] A. I. Sobolevsky, *Great-Russian Popular Songs*, Vol. II, No. 396.
[*] The Russian word *yamshchik* includes various types of drivers of freight and
passenger vehicles.—ED.

lives far from their own homes and families. On this theme, also, is built the famous song, "The Mozdok Steppe":

> O you steppe of mine, steppe of Mozdok,
> Steppe of Mozdok!
> Far and wide, O steppe, you extend,
> You extend.
> From Saratov even to the town of Tsaritsyn,
> To Tsaritsyn.
> Along the way they stretched a great highroad,
> A broad highroad.
> Along it have traveled the young drivers,
> The fine young fellows.
> And their horses are all dun-colored,
> All dun-colored.
> And their collars are all of silver,
> All of silver.
> And their bridles are all inlaid,
> All inlaid.
> And their carts are all equipped with tires,
> All equipped with tires.
> And there happened to them a misfortune,
> And it was no small one:
> Their fine young man fell ill, he was taken sick,
> The young carriage driver.
> And he begged and begged his comrades,
> His comrades:
> "Oh, you, you my brothers, you my comrades,
> My comrades!
> Brothers, do not abandon my raven-black steeds,
> My raven-black steeds!
> But convey to my father, brothers, my profound respects,
> And to my dear mother my reverence,
> And to my little children impart my blessing,
> My blessing.
> And to my young wife her full liberty,
> Her complete freedom." [6]

Soldiers' songs comprise a special group. In this connection it must be remembered that the period of military service lasted for many years, and that consequently, during this time, the men would develop both a mode of life and a psychology that was all their own.

[6] *Ibid.*, Vol. I, No. 348.

The classless groups of society also created their own songs, for example, the robber gangs which of course were made up for the most part of peasant fugitives from serfdom. The basis of the poetics of the old robber songs is exactly the same as that of the peasant songs (the very same favorite figures of the wood and steppe and the broad field, the sun, the night, and so on), but in their own original application and aspect. Characteristic is that irony which is voiced in these songs with reference to the whole social structure, as well as to their own bandit profession, which has been produced by that order. The robber song utilized by Pushkin in *The Captain's Daughter*, where it is represented as being a favorite song of Pugachov's is a striking example. Pushkin borrowed it from Novikov's songbook (1780):

Do not rustle, mother, green grove of oak trees,
Do not hinder me, fine young fellow that I am, from thinking
    my thoughts,
That tomorrow I, fine young fellow that I am, must go for
    interrogation
Before a stern judge—the Tsar himself.
Furthermore the sovereign Tsar will ask me:
"Tell me, tell me, my fine sturdy fellow, son of a peasant,
Now how and with whom did you do your thieving, with
    whom did you ply your bandit trade?
And were there many comrades with you?"
"I will tell you, trustworthy Orthodox Tsar,
I will tell you all the truth, all the verity:
That with me there were comrades four:
And my first comrade was the dark night,
And my second comrade was my blade of tempered steel,
And as for my third comrade, it was my good horse,
And my fourth comrade was my tensely drawn bow,
And as for my messengers, they were tempered arrows."
And this is what the trustworthy Orthodox Tsar will say,
"Hail to you, my fine sturdy fellow, son of a peasant,
That you have known how to do your thieving, that you have
    known how to make a ready answer.
For this, my fine sturdy fellow, I will confer upon you
A lofty mansion in the midst of the field—
Two tall pillars with a crossbeam upon them." [7]

[7] *Ibid.*, Vol. VI, No. 424, pp. 331-332.

No small historical interest would attach itself to the songs of the former *manorial servants*, the household retainers. The earlier investigators rarely turned their attention to these "footmen's" productions. However, the songs of the household retainers both reveal their psychology and strikingly reproduce their mode of life, which sometimes in certain ways seemed incomparably more alluring than the mode of life of the peasant husbandman. A curious controversy on the theme, as to whose life is the better, furnishes us with the following song:

Oh, splendid is the life of the footman
At the nobleman's court:
They do not have to plow the land,
And they don't pay any taxes.
Oh, they do not have to plow the land,
And they don't pay any rent,
And they don't take the scythes in their hands.
Ah, you stupid peasants,
You can surely judge for yourselves.
Wherever they send you, you must run quickly,
So that their business may be prospered;
If you stand too long or loiter,
You have an interview with the mistress.
Look around behind you—
Someone is standing back of you, and threatening you with his stick.
You return home,
They take the caftan from your shoulders,
They lead you to the stable,
Behind you they carry a stick.[8]

In the vast repertory of the peasant lyrics, the majority of the songs grew out of the mode of life and the psychology of the peasant plowman, but at the same time we have a considerable number of those songs which, having originated among other social classes, were adapted and reworked by the peasantry in accordance with their own tastes and ideas. This serves to explain the great variety of sources, and the expression in the peasant lyrics of the styles of various classes. A noteworthy influence was exerted upon the peasant lyrics of the

[8] V. I. Simakov, *Popular Songs, Their Composers and Their Variants* (Moscow, 1929).

eighteenth to the twentieth centuries by the life of the city artisan and trading class. By means of oral transmission, through seasonal workers, "those who go to Petersburg," and workmen; through books such as the popular printed and manuscript songbooks, the satirical or sentimental ballad of the petty bourgeoisie penetrated into the masses of the peasantry, so that, when the folklorist has to familiarize himself with the song repertory of this or that country village, he soon discovers a considerable number of songs of the middle class. (The popular reworking of the ballads and songs of literary origin will be discussed below.)

We shall dwell for a time upon the more archaic songs, those which spontaneously expressed the peasant psychology and described the peasant mode of life. Many of the peasant lyric songs are the creation of women. For the most part it is precisely the woman's "feminine" lot that is reflected in them. Under the conditions of a natural economy, in the toilsome peasant mode of life, an environment was produced that was well adapted to such creation. Everyone knows, both from descriptions and from direct observations in the countryside, as well as from the content of many of the songs, how large a part was played in peasant life by evening gatherings, conversations, and spinning bees, when all the female members of a large undivided family, or the women from several homes of neighbors or relatives, got together to occupy themselves, during the long autumn and winter evenings, with spinning. In this occupation, and during many other kinds of work, a chorus of women, or individual singers, gave vent to their feelings, pouring them forth in songs which were traditional, but always adapted to their own case, and imperceptibly altered.

A very large part of the women's lyrics is devoted to a description of the heavy lot of the woman in a strange house. (Here there is a close connection of many of the lyric songs with the motifs of the wedding poetry; this is the reason that there is such an easy transition of the ceremonial wedding songs into the broad channel of the nonceremonial lyric.) Other songs speak of the misfortunes and unhappiness of marriage under the compulsory choice of a bridegroom, such as we have described in the chapter on the peasant wedding. (Such motifs, both in real life and in the song, are readily understandable.) Many songs speak of the domination of the husband, of the father-in-law and mother-in-law, of the machinations of the "taunting sisters-in-law." A countless number of songs mention the dear one who has been abandoned in one's own native district. The themes of a personal emotion of love and tenderness for an intimate friend, or, on the other hand, of jealousy and anger in the most diverse variations, are developed in the lyric songs, with their generally mournful, heart breaking refrains. In such songs the husband is often characterized in a very unflattering way. Sometimes, in the song, the woman makes a frank acknowledgment:

> The bird, the nightingale, sings her song,
> She does honor to the beautiful girls,
> She gives praise to the young married women.
>
> .   .   .   .
>
> Nor will she be joined in equal wedlock;
> Nor will a suitable husband turn up.
> He may be a thief, and he may be a drunkard,
> He may be old and wheezy,
> He may be young and unfriendly.
> He may be of your own age, and haughty,
> Always supercilious and stirring up trouble;
> And then he lies crosswise on the bed,
> And he speaks words that are crosswise too,
> And he commands you to loosen his girdle.
>
> .   .   .   .
>
> But I do not want to take off his shoes and his clothes,
> My heart is not inclined that way.
> For his feet, they are dirty,
> And my hands, they are white.
> My little hands are weary,
> And the golden seal rings are coming unsoldered,
> The gilded rings are coming unsoldered,
> They are coming unsoldered, they will get lost.[9]

[9] *The Peasant Lyric*, comp. by M. Hippius and Z. Ewald (The Soviet Writer, 1935), pp. 231-232.

Having been given in marriage against her will, joined in a church ceremony with a husband whom she did not love, the woman sang:

> Hushaby, you old devil,
> Either sleep, or die;
> Let me, in my youth, go out to play,
> Let me walk upon the street! [10]

Describing her reception into the family of her husband, the woman spoke of the unkind welcome given her by her new relatives:

> And there is a father-in-law and a mother-in-law,
> There are four brothers-in-law,
> And two sisters-in-law,
> And so the father-in-law says,
> "They are bringing a wrong doer."
> And the mother-in-law says,
> "They are bringing a spendthrift."
> And the brothers-in-law say,
> "They are bringing us a slattern,"
> And then the aunts say,
> "They are bringing a homeless girl."
> And the sisters-in-law say,
> "They are bringing us a good-for-nothing." [11]

Since we have no opportunity to enumerate even approximately all the diversity of themes in the peasant song lyric, let us try to give at least a very cursory analysis of the compositional structure and poetics of the lyric song.

In the song lyric we frequently encounter contaminated texts (that is, texts in which the definite traditional song is combined with other songs or with fragments of songs). The appearance of *contaminations* is frequently furthered by errors of memory. Highly significant, with reference to the contamination of songs by one another, is the identity or closeness of the refrains. The contamination is also furthered by the coincidence of imagery or specific formulas in the songs.

Since in folklore, as we have explained above while discussing its other genres, a very vast role is played by the traditional poetic

[10] P. V. Kireyevsky, *Songs*, new series, No. II, Pt. 2, p. 54, No. 1830.
[11] B. and Y. Sokolov, *Tales and Songs of the Belo-Ozero Region* (Moscow, 1915), No. 432, p. 433.

formulas (compare the *byliny*, tales, and laments), there are great opportunities for the contamination of the songs. It would, however, be altogether incorrect to think that one can reduce the whole process of the reworking of a literary text to such mechanical changes. Surely even the "mechanical" changes themselves can be called such only in a conditional way. Errors of memory, leading to substitutions, omissions, additions, and contaminations, are conditioned by the psychology of the social milieu which has assimilated a given text. Omissions and substitutions, upon a more detailed study, may prove to be not so accidental as they appear at the first glance. The very direction taken by the errors of memory corresponds to the psychological make-up, the experiences of daily life, and the ideology of the milieu which has accepted it. In the mass of material, the specific "errors" fit into an established picture, in which it is not difficult to discover what class has influenced them. Thus the "mechanical" changes are transformed into changes of an organic kind. What seemed on the surface to be a linking of associations, may have deeper roots in the psychology of the given social setting.

One of the basic devices of composition, utilized by the Russian peasant lyric, is the so-called *psychological parallelism*. Academician A. N. Veselovsky, in his work, *Psychological Parallelism and Its Forms As Reflected by Poetic Style*, has described the extensive utilization of this device in the lyric poetry of all nations, and has pointed out the roots of it in the animistic world concept of primitive man, who had come to know the outer world of nature through the pattern of his own mental and physical impulses. Primitive man imputed to surrounding nature the features of his own human life. Besides, Veselovsky comments,

the parallelism rests upon a juxtaposition of subject and object according to the category of movement, action, as an indication of voluntary self-activity. . . . Animals naturally appeared to be objects, they recalled mankind most of all . . . but plants, too, bore indications of the same resemblance: they were engendered and they blossomed, they grew green, they bowed before the force of the wind. The sun, as it seemed, also moved; it rose and set, the wind drove away the clouds, the lightning flashed, the fire enveloped and consumed the branches, and so on. The inorganic, immovable world was involuntarily drawn into this chain of parallelisms: it also lived.[12]

From such a parallelism there follow, genetically, many forms of imagery in language and in poetry, metaphors, metonymies, similes, symbols, and so forth.

Viewing the surrounding world in accordance with his own subjective state, seeing parallelisms everywhere, a resemblance of phenomena, primitive man was inclined also to comprehend his own subjective world by means of a comparison with the facts of the outer world; without having, as yet, developed the habit of abstract thought (although, according to Veselovsky's correct observation, even the latter cannot do without the familiar imagery which accompanies it), primitive man came to understand his own mental state by means of images drawn from the outer world.

This very psychological parallelism in the popular lyric is concealed not only in the use of metaphors and other forms of language imagery, but frequently forms the basis of the compositional structure of the whole song, possibly proving to be one of the most archaic forms of composition. From such a composition, as we shall see, there are easily produced also the actual facts and symbols in which the productions of the peasant lyric are so rich. Parallelism of composition is supported also by various other forms of parallelism—parallelism of sound, syntactical parallelism, and so forth—lending to the whole song an exceptional unity and harmony. Let us try to explain all this through the example of a single lyric, a so-called "household" song:

Down the little river, down the rapid river,
There a duck is swimming, with her is a drake.
Out in front is swimming the fine drake,
The fine drake, dove-colored and splendid,
And after him swims the little gray duck.
"Wait a minute, wait a minute, you dove-colored splendid **one**,
Oh, it surely would be better for us to swim together.
Yes, to swim together, not to drift apart.
Between us has flowed the swift river,
The swift river, my successful rival. . . ."
At our house, in the entrance, in the new passage,

[12] A. N. Veselovsky, *Collected Works*, Vol. I, p. 131.

There walked Stepan, and with him was Marya,
And in front walks Stepan the master
(Yes, Stepan the master, light of my eyes, Ivanovich),
And after him walks Marya, light of my life.
"Wait a minute, wait a minute, Stepan, my master,
Wait a minute, wait a minute, Ivanovich.
Oh, it surely would be better for us to walk together,
Yes, to walk together, not to drift apart.
Between us has come a strange woman,
A strange woman, my rival." [13]

On comparing the two parts of the song, we are easily convinced that its whole composition rests upon the strictly maintained parallelism, and that not merely of images, but also of syntax and even of sounds. The figures of the drake and the duck, swimming separately, and not together, along the swift river, give a striking representation of the discord between the husband and wife, into whose life a rival has intruded.

Again and again we are convinced of the organic unity, in the peasant folklore, of the poetic creations, with reference both to "content" and to "form": as in the *bylina* of the storytellers, so also in the laments of the wailers, in the proverbs and riddles, in the ceremonial and lyric songs, in the genuinely peasant creations the unity of form and content is very apparent.

The song which we have cited enables us easily to understand how the psychological parallelism had to lead to *symbolism* which so richly permeates the peasant lyric. Thinking with the aid of a comparison between the subjective and the outer world, that is, the utilization of parallelisms, was so habitual for primitive man, and even the comparisons themselves had become so well established, that naturally the capacity was developed for swiftly conjecturing the second part of the parallel from the first. Thus the symbol was developed. The symbol, according to the definition given by Veselovsky again, is genetically, in its own proper nature, the first member of a bimembral parallelism, with the omission of the second part of the parallel, or "unimembral parallelism."

[13] Sobolevsky, *op cit.*, Vol. III, No. 94.

We need only take, in the song which has been cited, the first part alone, without the second, and we have before us a complete symbol. For the man who is accustomed to the structure of the popular lyric, it is always easy, guided by the first part, to conjecture the content of the second, that is, the meaning of the lyrical symbolism. For such a man it will be instantaneously comprehensible, as soon as the traditional song mentions the drake and the duck, that it is speaking of the husband and wife, since these figure symbols have long ago become traditional in themselves. Here, in the traditional quality of the symbols, there is concealed also the reason why, from their viewpoint, some of the peasant songs appear to certain people, who have few contacts with the country mode of life and its folk creations, to be somewhat lacking in content, or in any event, not very intelligible. It must be borne in mind that the very image of the little river, at the beginning of the song, actually has, in itself, the power at once to dispose the rural singer and his hearers toward a definite emotional mood, since this image, in the popular poetry, is known to be an established symbol of sorrow, longing, and separation. In order to understand any work of art, one must know its artistic nature. This requirement applies, also, for understanding the phenomena of artistic creative work in folklore.

For the interpretation of the psychological genesis of the popular symbolism, a great deal has been accomplished by the works of A. N. Veselovsky; and for the unfolding of the meaning of specific symbolic images, much has been accomplished by the works of another eminent scholar, A. A. Potebnya, and a number of other investigators; [14] however, the social aspect of symbolism in the popular lyric has hardly been touched at all in the works that have appeared in print. A closer survey reveals: (1) The very great persistence of symbolic images, and (2) the relatively small number

[14] A. A. Potebnya, *The Crossing of Water as a Representation of Marriage* (Moscow, 1867), *On Certain Symbols in Slavonic Popular Poetry* (Kharkov, 1914), *On the Connection Between Certain Concepts in Language* (Voronezh, 1864); N. I. Kostomarov, "The Historical Significance of the South-Russian Song Creations of the People," *Collected Works*, Vol. XXI (St. Petersburg, 1905), Bk. 8; Avtamonov, "The Symbolism of Plants," *Journal of the Ministry of Public Education*, 1902, Bks. XI and XII; Vodarsky, "The Symbolism of the Great-Russian Popular Songs," *Russian Philological News*, Nos. 1-2, 1916.

of them (in comparison with the vast world of nature from which they are derived).

In the traditional peasant songs the number of symbolic images taken from the world of birds and plants is very limited. Furthermore, the symbols are quite strictly assigned in accordance with various aspects of peasant life: certain images are typical for songs of marriage and family life, others for songs connected with music and dancing, and a third group for humorous and satirical songs.

Without entering—because of lack of space—into a detailed analysis of the symbolism of the songs, we will limit ourselves to an enumeration of some of the most constant symbols, and an indication of their significance: The swan is the symbol of a bride; geese are the symbols of strange people, the bridegroom's relatives; the falcon and hawk are symbols of the young man and the bridegroom; the duck, of the married woman; the drake, of the husband; the dove and his mate are the symbols of a pair of lovers; the cuckoo is the symbol of a sorrowing woman and a widow; the oak, of manly strength and firmness; the birch and poplar, of the girl or young woman; the wormwood and nettle are the symbols of sorrow, woe, bitterness; the falling of the leaves, the bending of the trees, the end of the blossoming or the withering of plants, are the symbols of sorrow; another symbol of sorrow is muddy water; the crossing of a river is the symbol of marriage; the river, of separation; the snowball tree, the raspberry, the red currant, are the symbols of a girl just entering into marriage. The latter symbols, like many others, are based upon frankly sexual, erotic factors. The wedding song and the love lyric are filled with such images.

But in speaking of the constancy of symbolism in the songs, it is necessary to make a number of reservations. During many centuries the original meaning of many of the symbols has been quite lost, even at times by the persons who perform the songs corresponding to the tradition. This often explains, also, the blending, the confusion of the meanings of symbols which previously were altogether fixed.

In addition to the psychological parallelism, which contributes so much toward the understanding of the symbolism of the lyric song, one cannot fail to mention still another compositional device which may be observed in a considerable number of the songs. This device, like a number of others which are related to it, was discovered in the peasant lyric by Professor B. M. Sokolov, and explained by him in his article, "An Excursus into the Field of the Poetics of Russian Folklore." He called this device *"the gradual or progressive contraction of images."*

By this we understand that combination (internal coupling together of images) which takes place when the images progressively follow one after another in a descending series, from the image with the broadest scope down to the image with the narrowest scope as to content. We understand the scope in the sense of space for the representation of degrees of space. In the representation of family and social relationships, the "contraction" occurs in the sphere of the everyday traditional representations of the significance and importance of individual members of the family, or of classes of people on the social scale.

The last image in the series, the most "contracted" in its scope, when observed from the exact point of view of the artistic purpose of the song, is seen to be the most important. It is precisely upon it, properly speaking, that the attention is fixed. It is possible to say even more than this: the gradual descent of the preceding images has as its artistic function the bringing out of the final image, which stands on the very narrowest and lowest step of the series, with the purpose of fixing upon it the closest attention. Simultaneously, the transition from the broader images to the narrower, from the general to the particular, is a device for the gradual development of detail, which is necessary for the maximum concretization of this final image.[15]

The cases involving this device of the "gradual contraction of images" may be classified under the following headings: (1) the representation of nature (descriptions of garden, meadow, tree, birds on the tree); (2) the representation of dwellings (description of a chamber, a bedstead, a table and a feast, hand work; (3) the description of apparel (a costume or a headdress); (4) the representation of family relationships ("one's own family" and "a strange family"); (5) the representation of social relationships.

All that has been said above may be clarified through two or three examples. A representation of nature is given in the following song:

[15] *Artistic Folklore*, No. I, Moscow, 1926, pp. 39-40.

O valley, valley, you are green.
Through you, valley, there is a broad highroad,
A broad highroad, and a swift river,
A swift river with high steep banks;
And as for the high steep bank,
On it are yellow sands,
And upon the fine yellow sands
There are three little gardens.
So in the first garden
A little nightingale is whistling.
And in the second garden
A little cuckoo is calling.
And in the third garden
A mother with her son is grieving.
The mother was walking with her son,
The mother was questioning her son.[16]

The mother's questions as to who is dearest of all to her son are then given.

The gradual descent, from those natural phenomena which are wider in their scope to those which are narrower, is clear: the valley, the broad highroad, the swift river, the high steep banks, the high steep bank, the sands, on them the three gardens, in the third garden the mother with her son. The temporary slowing-down of the action by means of the three-membered parallelism serves to intensify the final aspect: in the third garden a mother is walking with her son. These are the concluding figures in the gradual series: the chief attention is centered upon them, and they (the conversation of the mother with her son) give the impetus for the development of all the remaining content of the song. Aside from the fact that all the images of the gradual descending structure belong to a single category of spatial concepts, they prove to be of the same kind with reference to symbolism and emotional trend. All these symbols which have become fixed in the popular poetic consciousness are of a lyrical, and mainly of a sorrowful, melancholy tendency, which is particularly emphasized by the epithets that are attached to them, and by the diminutive form of the actual names of the objects: "the valley," "the

16 Sobolevsky, *op. cit.*, Vol. III, No. 592.

swift little river," "the steep little bank," "the fine yellow sand," and even the "little gardens" with the "nightingale" and the calling "little cuckoo." All this gives the preparation and the inner justification for the words of the song: "And in the third little garden a mother with her son is grieving."

The formula "one's own family" preserves the following sequence of figures: father, mother, young brothers and sisters. Usually, according to the position of each of the members of the family, in the same gradually descending order, their activities, behavior, value, and so on, are described. For example:

> Receive us in love,
> With your fatherly blessing,
> With your motherly admonition,
> With your brotherly judgment,
> With your sisterly servility.[17]

In the formula "another family," the gradual series takes the following form: father-in-law, mother-in-law, brothers-in-law, sisters-in-law. Very often the two formulas, "one's own family" and "another family," by means of juxtaposition, or, more correctly, of contrast, in the same song, give, as it were, a twofold series with a progressive contraction, as in the song:

> Oh, alas, my woe, my great woe,
> Such great woe and sorrow,
> I was abandoned by my father when I was small,
> My mother I do not remember.
> Then my own dear brother nursed me and brought me up,
> My own dear sister cherished me.
> Oh, how my dear brother loves his sister,
> He takes his sister out in the evenings,
> He places his sister upon his knees,
> He strokes his sister's little head.
> "Do not marry, sister,
> Either in the city or in the countryside,
> Into a large family that is not willing to receive you.
> Do not give yourself to a father-in-law, sister, nor to a
>   mother-in-law,

[17] *Ibid.,* Vol. II, No. 183.

Nor to brothers-in-law, sister, nor to sisters-in-law."
But I, while yet a maid, acquired all these troubles:
And the first trouble is a strange land,
And the second trouble is a fierce father-in-law,
Yes, a fierce father-in-law, and an evil mother-in-law.
And as for the third trouble, there are the brothers-in-law,
There are the brothers-in-law and the sisters-in-law,
And the fourth trouble is a husband—a complete failure.
And I have no one at all with whom to share my thoughts,
Nor is there anyone with whom I can speak a word
in secret.[18]

In this song both formulas are present: "one's own" and "another's family," and besides, the latter is reiterated a second time, with the addition of characteristic epithets. The song has an introduction and an epilogue, both of a lyrical character, and in the middle are the progressive series of images, joined together by a transitional passage: "The brother is sorry for his sister, and advises her not to marry." It is obvious that the device of the "gradual contraction of images," in this song, is of dominating significance in the composition.

In the formula of "social relationships" the series of social concepts is given in descending order. Sometimes both formulas are even joined together, "social relationships" and "family relationships," organizing the two parts of the song. These progressive series in themselves govern the division of the song into stanzas. In the first part, at the beginning, the whole progressive series is given (boyar, tradesman, peasant), which is then subdivided, separating the song, as it were, into stanzas.

In the second part we have the formula "family relationships."

When at my own dear mother's
The three troughsful of dough had been kneaded,
Then her three daughters were spoken for.
And the first daughter was betrothed to a boyar,
And the second to a tradesman,
And the third daughter to a peasant.
The first daughter writes to her mother:
"Dearest mother, do not grieve over me.

18 *Ibid.*, No. 571.

Surely I am well off, living in the boyar's house:
Through all the dark night there are candles burning,
And while the candles burn, master workers sit there,
They sew and cut out silken dresses,
Wherewith to clothe my white body."
The second daughter writes to her mother:
"Dearest mother, do not grieve over me.
Surely I am well off, living in the tradesman's house:
Through all the dark night there are candles burning,
And while the candles burn, master workers sit there,
They sew and cut out rose-colored dresses
Wherewith to clothe my white body."
The third daughter writes to her mother,
And she does complain, she does shed tears:
"It is a hard thing for me to live in the peasant's house.
Through all the dark night there are candles burning,
And while the candles burn, master workers sit there,
They weave and plait silken lashes
To lash my white body."
The lash hissed in the air, and the blood splashed,
But even then I did not submit to my husband,
I bowed to my revered father-in-law:
'Sir, father-in-law, set me free
From this evil and angry husband.'
My revered father-in-law orders him to beat me harder,
He orders him to beat me harder, so that my blood may
    flow.
But even then I did not submit to my husband,
I bowed to my lady mother-in-law;
'Lady mother-in-law, set me free
From this evil and angry husband.'
My lady mother-in-law orders him to beat me harder,
She orders him to beat me harder, so that my blood may
    flow.
Then I bowed before the daughters-in-law,
And the daughters-in-law answered and said to me:
"It is not for us, sister, to be exalted above our husbands."
And then I submitted to my husband,
I bowed down before his right foot.[19]

[19] *Ibid.*, Vol. III, No. 5.

It is perfectly comprehensible that the formula of "family relationships," which was very frequently used in the peasant lyric, strikingly reflects the conditions of daily life and the dependence of the younger members of the family upon the elder. The formula of "social relationships" is still very closely connected with the feudal system and the social hierarchy of classes, which was based upon it. Thus the poetics of folklore is clearly conditioned by the nature of social life.

BIBLIOGRAPHY

COLLECTIONS

Chulkov, G. I., *Sobranie raznykh pesen* (Collection of Various Songs), Pts. I-IV (1770–1774); republished by the Academy of Sciences, Pts. I-III (1913).

Sobolevskii, A. I., *Velikorusskie narodnye pesni* (Great-Russian Popular Songs), Vols. I-VII (St. Petersburg, 1895–1902).

Shein, P. V., *Velikoruss v svoikh pesniakh, obriadakh, i pr.* (The Great-Russian in His Songs, Ceremonies, etc.) (St. Petersburg, 1898).

Kireevskii, P. V., *Pesni: Novaia seriia* (Songs: New Series), ed. M. N. Speranskii, Pt. II, Fasc. 1 (Moscow, 1918); Fasc. 2 (Moscow, 1929).

Lopatin, N. M., and V. P. Prokunin, *Sbornik russkikh narodnykh liricheskikh pesen* (Collection of Russian Popular Lyric Songs), Vols. 1-2 (Moscow, 1889).

Sokolov, B., and Y. Sokolov, *Skazki i pesni, Belozerskogo kraia* (Tales and Songs of the Belo-Ozero Region) (1915).

Lineva, E., *Velikorusskie pesni v narodnoi garmonizatsii* (Great-Russian Songs in a Popular Harmonization). Nos. 1-2 (St. Petersburg, 1909).

Istomin, F. M., and G. O. Deutsch, *Pesni russkogo naroda* (Songs of the Russian People) (St. Petersburg, 1894).

Istomin, F. M., and S. M. Liapunov, *Pesni russkogo naroda* (Songs of the Russian People) (St. Petersburg, 1899).

Pesni Pinezh'ia: Materialy Fonogramm-arkhiva, sobrannye i obrabotannye E. V. Gippius i Z. V. Eval'd (Songs of the Pinega: Materials from the Sound-Recording Archive, collected and edited by E. V. Hippius and Z. V. Ewald), Bk. II (Moscow, 1937).

ANTHOLOGIES OF POPULAR SONGS

Kartykov, M., *Russkie pesni: Pod redaktsii prof. N. K. Piksanova* (Russian Songs: Under the Editorship of Professor N. K. Piksanov) (Vologda, 1922).

Hippius, E., and Z. Ewald, *Krest'ianskaia lirika: Pod redaktsiei M. Azadovskogo* (The Peasant Lyric: Under the Editorship of M. Azadovsky, *Biblioteka poeta* (The Poet's Library: Minor Series) (Leningrad, 1935).

Sokolov, Y. M., *Narodnaia lirika* (The Popular Lyric) (Moscow, State Pedagogical Publications for Teachers, 1938).

RESEARCHES

Veselovskii, A. N., *Sobr. soch.* (Collected Works), Vol. I (St. Petersburg, 1911).

Potebnia, A. A., *O nekotorykh simvolakh v slavianskoi narodnoi poezii* (On Certain Symbols in Slavonic Popular Poetry) (Kharkov, 1914).

Kostomarov, N. I., "Istoricheskoe znachenie iuzhnorusskogo narodnogo pesennogo tvorchestva" (The Historical Significance of the South-Russian Popular Song Creations), *Sobr. soch.* (Collected Works), Bk. 8, Vol. XXI (St. Petersburg, 1906).

Avtomonov, "Simbolika rastenii" (The Symbolism of Plants), *ZHMNP* (Journal of the Ministry of Public Education), 1902, Bks. XI and XII.

Vodarskii, "Simbolika velikorusskikh narodnykh pesen" (Symbolism of the Great-Russian Popular Songs), *Russkii filologicheskii Vestnik* (Russian Philological News), Nos. 1, 2, 1916.

Sokolov, B. M., *Eksursy v oblast' poetiki russkogo fol'klora* (Excursus in the Field of the Poetics of Russian Folklore), *Khudozhestvennyi fol'klor* (Artistic Folklore), No. I, Moscow, 1926.

Finagin, A., *Russkaia pesnia* (The Russian Song) (Petrograd, 1923).

FOLK RHYMES *

❦

The folk rhyme or *chastushka* is the most widely diffused genre of the song poetry in Russian folklore from the end of the nineteenth century on. It has supplanted a great deal that, even a few decades ago, was so characteristic of the poetic creation of the countryside and of the city environs. The chastushka has become so dominant as an oral genre that among many people who are not skilled in the field of the special researches in folklore the impression has been created that, for instance, the country people in the decade preceding the revolution knew only the popular rhymes and nothing else. And because the popular rhyme responds very strikingly and promptly to the most diverse themes of contemporary life, it seems to many that this popular rhyme is altogether a product of this contemporary period. It is necessary, however, to weigh the questions: Is the popular rhyme really an altogether new genre? and what has called forth its great popularity during the past fifty years?

In the history of the chastushka there is revealed, in a most striking manner, the regularity of artistic processes, conditioned by the changes in social and economic life. In this creation of the masses, taking form in tens, possibly of hundreds of thousands of brief songs, there is revealed with special clarity the conformity to the established laws of the development of poetry. The poetic production of the masses, taken over a range of several decades, convincingly reveals the existing laws of the social conditioning of art.

The development of the chastushka represents a most interesting process, with complex meanderings and intertwinings, reflecting with great fullness and diversity both the historical life with its social conflicts and the dialectics of class conflict. The popular rhyme is a striking example of the poetic primitive, going back in its construction and psychological essence almost to the primitive archaic times;

* The Russian word is *chastushka*, a product of oral folk poetry, having four verses (or two verses with two half-feet in each verse), lyrical, comic, or dealing with daily life (Ushakov Dictionary).—ED.

[530]

and at the same time, it is frequently an expression of new ideas and attitudes among the masses of the people.

The popular rhyme, like many other genres of folklore, is at the same time both a memorial of the remote past and the loud voice of contemporary times.

As we shall see below, there are many popular rhymes which cannot be definitely assigned to any specific moment in history. The very same popular rhyme may have been in existence for decades, each time adapting itself, now to one and now to another manifestation of actual life, and being subjected sometimes to slight, sometimes to very extensive changes. That is why it is of such interest to watch the changing of the variants, the movement of the variable readings in the text.

Folklore apart from continuous variations is unthinkable. The capacity for variation, as we have seen many times, is one of the characteristic features of its creative nature. In the popular rhymes, as in other genres of folklore, the creation of words is by no means expressed each time in the creation of absolutely new texts, but very often only in a change in the form of a previously existing production. There are tens and hundreds of thousands of popular rhymes— this would mean that there are at least thousands of variations.

What then is the *popular rhyme as a genre?* It may be defined as a brief, generally four-line, rhymed song, enjoying a wide circulation among the great masses of the country and city population. Along with the four-line popular rhymes, there exist also (but in a considerably smaller number) popular rhymes which have six lines, and even those which have two. The two-line "agonies" constitute a special category of the popular rhymes.

In the form in which we know them, during several decades at the end of the nineteenth and the beginning of the twentieth century, the popular songs were in existence solely among the Russian population, so that they could be considered a distinctive feature of the Russian folklore. From the beginning of the imperialistic war, and then, much more markedly, from the beginning of the Great October Revolution, the Russian popular songs began to infiltrate into the Ukraine, into White Russia, and into the lands of the other peoples of the USSR. Furthermore, at first there was a direct borrowing of the Russian texts, with a slight revision, to make them conform to another national setting, often with the majority of the Russian words preserved. Later the revision became more thorough, the borrowed popular rhymes "were nationalized," and finally, using them as a pattern and preserving the rhythm, the four-line structure and the principles of rhyming, people began to create their own local, national folk rhymes. Among many nationalities, the borrowed genre was encountered along with the related, traditional genres of the national folklore; as a result of such mutual attraction, an original poetic diffusion took place and the national popular rhyme took on a distinct, new character, essentially corresponding, however, to the same social processes which, as we shall see farther on, had also produced, in their own time, the popularity of the Russian folk rhyme.

Unfortunately, in consequence of the small number of folkloristic scholars in the national republics, all this complex and exceedingly interesting picture of the origin and development of the popular rhyme, as a genre, has as yet received too little investigation. For example, in the field of the folklore of a number of peoples along the Volga (the Mordvinians, the Udmurti, the Mari, the Chuvashi), and among the Turkic peoples of Central Asia, the Russian popular rhyme found a fertile soil in the traditional, established forms of the four-line songs dealing with daily life (drinking songs, guest songs, and others); among the German colonists the Russian popular rhyme encountered something else which was very close to it both in form and in content—the *Schnaderhüpfl*. In the Ukraine and White Russia the folk rhyme became one of the prevailing forms of contemporary oral poetry, drawing close to the traditional *kolomyki*. The outward conditions of life during the period of war and revolution undoubtedly contributed toward such a deep penetration of the form of the popular rhyme into the various remote parts of the USSR. The life in the trenches, the enforced leisure in hospitals, on the part of men who had been brought together from the most widely separated corners of the land, contributed to the free exchange of the treasures of poetry and of customs. The period of the civil war, which joined the masses together in a common cause, still further intensified this process of the mutual interchange of poetry. Accordingly, one cannot be surprised that a single popular rhyme, which for some reason took people's fancy, should with the greatest swiftness have flown to the very borders of the land, being adapted everywhere to new places and to new peculiarities of daily life.

In view of the fact that the popular rhymes were disseminated not only among the masses of the country people, like the majority of the other genres of folklore, but also among the urban population (the proletariat, the craftsmen, and the bourgeoisie), there was an opinion, very widely current, that the popular rhyme, as distinguished from the other genres of folklore, had actually had its origin in the city, and had only later been transferred to the country. Not so long ago, many "connoisseurs" of folklore, who had been bred in the traditions of Slavophilism and nationalism, were inclined to consider the popular rhyme a manifestation of the city influence, which was also somewhat corrupting in nature, upon the poetry of the peasants.

The folk rhyme was regarded by many of these connoisseurs as to what was "truly of the folk," as an indication of the lapse in popular poetic tastes, the beginning of the disintegration of oral artistic creation. But, in the first place, we shall see further how incorrect it was to appraise the popular rhyme as a genre which was declining and lacking in artistic value, and on the other hand, how incorrect was the categorical assertion that the popular rhyme is a product of the city.

The folk rhyme, in its genesis, is a very complex phenomenon. Today, on the basis of numerous researches already made by folklorists (Academician A. I. Sobolevsky, Professor D. K. Zelenin, E. N. Yeleonskaya, and others), we may consider this point as firmly established, that in its form (its brevity and use of rhyme) the popular rhyme is of ancient origin, and in its source is closely connected with the traditional creative genius of the countryside. In fact, the investigators have pointed out several recorded peasant dancing songs of the end of the eighteenth and beginning of the nineteenth century, which are very close in their meter and structure to the chastushkas. However, the degree to which such songs played a part in everyday life was at that time comparatively small; the little songs played only the role of a dancing refrain, with a content that was chiefly of a merry and facetious nature.

> Lushka, yesterday you deceived me
> For the very first time;
> You just grabbed all my presents,
> But you did not come into my barn.

> It is sad for me, a young girl,
> To sit by my little window;
> My heart longs for the handsome youth,
> I am weary of looking out of the window.[1]

But in the latter half of the nineteenth century, or more exactly in the last quarter, the popular rhyme began to enjoy ever greater and greater popularity, and in the twentieth century, as we see, it came to occupy the first place in the song repertory of the country-side, from the viewpoint of quantity, far outdistancing the other forms of song creations, especially the so-called "long" and "extensive" songs.

The basic cause of such a vast demand for the popular rhyme is, beyond a doubt, the very great change in the social-economic condition of the countryside during the period of the development of industrial capitalism. The overthrow of the patriarchal foundations of the peasant life, which had grown up under the natural economy of feudalism, the greater ties between the countryside and the cities, the centers of industry and trade, had changed both the outward appearance of the countryside and the psychological tenor of its population. The swifter tempi of life and activity, the constant in-flux of new impressions, the frequent change of experiences—all this, naturally, must have decreased the demand for the old, deliberate poetic genres; must have given an impetus to the extensive employment, in the actual practice of poetry, of the brief, swift-moving form of the popular rhymes, with its conciseness of exposition and

---

[1] These little songs are from the book, *Russian Songs Composed in the Village of Spassky* (St. Petersburg, 1805), arranged by V. I. Chernyshev (*Annals of the Division of Russian Language and Literature of the Academy of Sciences*, Vol. 75, (St. Petersburg, 1904, Nos. 36 and 37). M. K. Azadovsky (*Literary Review*, 1939, No. 16) has expressed the theory that these are parodies in verse on popular songs.

swiftness of rhythm. The popular rhyme proved to be a very convenient form for swiftly and easily echoing all the diverse forms of personal and social life.

Consequently it is certain that between the manufacturing city and the development of the popular rhyme there is a deep inner bond. But this bond cannot be understood so literally and in such a simplified manner as one of the best known folklorists, A. M. Smirnov-Kutachevsky, is ready to accept it. In his article he has expressed the idea that the popular rhyme was born directly from the rhythm of the factory machines:

The birthplace of the popular rhyme is the factory: in place of the broad, expansive freedom of the fields and meadows, the Russian found himself at a factory bench, in the midst of the rhythmic drone of machines, the flashing of shuttles, the clanking of chain belts. His whole psychological world seemed to be caught and swallowed up by this rhythmic sound of work, by virtue of which his harmony of sounds must be subordinated to the measured tempo of the machinery. The popular rhyme, in its musical quality, is wholly permeated with the rhythm of the factory. Its sharply defined measure—a trochee or an iamb without unvoiced pyrrhics—matches the sharply defined rhythm of the factory machine.[2]

Without even speaking of the inaccuracy of the characterization of the measure of the popular rhyme, it is necessary to acknowledge the absolute impossibility of Smirnov-Kutachevsky's general assertion as to the rhythm of the factory as its direct source. As we have seen, the folk rhyme has its ancestors in the feudal countryside of the precapitalistic period. However, it would be absurd to deny the organic connection of the folk rhyme, this popular genre, with the development of industrial capital. But the form of the rhyme answered the demand for a lively song, in which it would be easy to find an echo of the swift changing of impressions. In conformity with the general economic upheaval which was taking place in the country, the folk rhyme, as a suitable poetic genre, was used by the most diverse social classes of the city and the countryside. The country

[2] A. M. Smirnov-Kutachevsky, "The Origin of the Popular Song," *The Printing Press and the Revolution* (1925), Bk. 2.

and city proletariat, the peasant middle class, the petty bourgeoisie of the country and the city (the artisans and traders) made use of the popular rhyme to suit their poetical and political aims. Being adapted to a new life and a new social function, the popular rhyme, with wonderful fullness and clarity, reflected the ramifications of the class conflict of the last decades before the revolution.

Having attained its fullest development under the powerful influence of the manufacturing city, the folk rhyme, nevertheless, did not lose its direct connections with its sources in the country. To a very considerable extent, contrary to the opinion of D. K. Zelenin,[3] it did not lose its connection with the dance. Genetically associated with the dancing refrain of the earlier period, it was also, in the new period, very often pressed into service in the capacity of a dancing song. For example, in the central manufacturing provinces, certain forms of popular rhymes themselves received the names of those dances of which they were the inevitable accompaniment: the "Ryazanochka," the "tsyganochka," the "Eletsky," and so forth. Frequently, also, the dance serves as the stimulus for very interesting improvisations. It happens very frequently that the "Ryazanochka" or the "tsyganochka" is transformed into an original competition between a pair of girls, in dancing, singing, and poetic creation. Striving to surpass her partner, each of the girls in the contest tries to astonish the audience by some kind of new figures in the dance, and by new popular rhymes. In this connection the girl either recalls, at the proper place, and very fortuitously, the songs which she has heard somewhere before, or else, in a burst of poetic inspiration, herself improvises new popular rhymes on the spot. Frequently the antiphonal chanting of the popular rhymes is transformed into an original and sometimes very artistic dialogue, for example:

> Dear friend Katya,
> Tell me your secret,
> When you were parting with your swain,
> Did your heart beat hard or not?

[3] D. Zelenin, "Das heutige russische Schnaderhüpfl (častuška)," *Zeitschrift für slavische Philologie* (Leipzig, 1924).

Her friend answers her:

> Dear friend Zhenya,
> I will tell this to you alone:
> When I was parting with him,
> My heart beat like a swelling wave.[4]

Here is another series:

> My darling bosom friend,
> My dear little flower;
> Carry my greetings,
> You know who my dear one is.

> It is not hard for me to carry your greetings,
> My dear little comrade,
> Only, will the one who is your delight
> Accept the greetings from you? [5]

Or a more complicated dialogue:

> I went down to the swift river,
> I went down upon my knees:
> Speak to me, river, two little words,
> What is a maiden like me to do?

> And the river answered me:
> "Dear little comrade,
> Respect him, and then he will not betray you,
> Your dear trifler."

> I do not want to pamper you,
> O you, my handsomest one of all,
> Let that girl pamper you
> Who is running after you.[6]

These series of popular rhymes, thematically connected with one another, are seen to be a transitional form between the popular rhyme and the song.

---

[4] Taken down in a factory in the former province of Tver, Archive of the State Museum of Literature.

[5] Y. M. Sokolov, *The Upper Mologa Region: Life, Language and Creative Art of the Populace"* (Tver Province, 1925), No. 2, p. 58.

[6] *Loc. cit.*

In the vast majority of cases, the folk rhyme is sung to the accompaniment of a small accordion. It must be noted, however, that
the connection between the text of the rhyme and the melody is
less fixed than in the case of the song. The same popular rhyme may
be sung to another tune. The accordion player is a favorite among
the young people of the countryside. Since all the merrymaking depends on him, the girls vie with one another in trying to cajole him;
each of the dancers considers it as her obligation to sing about him:

> What a handsome accordionist!
> My heart is stirred within me.
> Permit me, accordionist,
> To make your acquaintance.[7]

> I used to love an accordionist,—
> All my girl friends hated me;
> I cast aside my love, and ceased from it,
> All my girl friends grew fond of me.[8]

Folk rhymes are created by individual composers (in the country
villages and in the factories one frequently encounters specialists in
the composition of rhymed couplets; in recent times, more and more
frequently, these poets write down their productions in special notebooks); but often the rhymes are created collectively in companies
of young people, at the women's evening sittings over the spinning,
at evening parties, and at revels. Of course, usually in such a company there will be one person more inventive and resourceful than
the others, who gives the stimulus to the collective improvisation.
Very often, also, use is made, as it were, of memorized poetic phrases,
established poetic formulas, which are subject to numerous variations, revisions and restorations.

It happens with especial frequency that they begin to sing the
first line of some well known folk rhyme, and to this beginning attach various continuations. Let us take the manifold variations of
a rhyme with one and the same beginning:

---

[7] From the former province of Moscow, Archive of the State Literary Museum.
[8] From the former province of Tver, *ibid.*

> From heaven fell a little star,
> On the dew and on the mist.
> In all her life the maid had never known
> That in love there is deceit.[9]

> From heaven fell a little star,
> On a little shed made of planks;
> Give me, my darling, a little ring
> And your little pocket handkerchief.[10]

We find the same beginning also in a popular love rhyme of the former provinces of Saratov, Pskov, and others. But this same beginning is encountered also in popular rhymes for dancing and amusement:

> From heaven fell a little star,
> Landed right on Saratov.
> We will have now as our dancer
> Awkward Mishka, clumsy one.[11]

> From heaven fell a little star,
> On the earth it melted away.
> The priest was chasing his dear one,
> The priest's little wife was scolding.[12]

From the examples we have cited it will be seen with what originality the traditional beginning is adapted to various themes, and what an original use is made of the image contained in the beginning: sometimes the connection between the image symbol and the whole content of the popular rhyme is perfectly clear, sometimes it is obscured, sometimes it is transformed into a mere parody play with a pattern that is too hackneyed.

Still more frequently, the creation of new popular rhymes proceeds along a simpler line. The traditional popular rhyme, receiving a new adaptation, is subjected to a new revision. With special frequency there is encountered the change in personal names, the designations of country, village, or city events, and so forth. In all these cases even

9 From the former province of Kostrom, *ibid.*
10 From the former province of Ryazan, *ibid.*
11 From the former province of Ryazan, *ibid.*
12 From the former province of Kursk, *ibid.*

a slight alteration in the popular rhyme calls forth a new reaction among the singers, which heightens the effect of the little song.

During the past few decades, especially since the beginning of the imperialistic war (and then, with more force, after the revolution, of which we shall speak below), the repertory of popular rhymes began to be supplemented with a great influx of material from literature, from books. The popular rhyme was utilized for the purposes of political agitation and propaganda. This, too, is perfectly understandable, if we only consider how suited to these purposes the form of the popular rhyme is. Many poets—we may mention, in the first place, Mayakovsky—added to the vast mass a great number of popular rhymes, and part of these attained such an established position in the song repertory that, in some cases, it is altogether impossible to distinguish such an "artificial" rhyme from a "popular" one.

In this question of the "artificial" and "nonartificial" folk rhymes, it is necessary to make a distinction. Is it possible, and is it even necessary, for popular rhymes, which have been composed by authors and journalists, and through books have made their way among the masses of the people, to be included in collections of "popular" rhymes? The answer which must be given, in my opinion, is the following: if the popular rhyme enters into the repertory of one or another group of the population, then, regardless of the manner in which it entered into the specific milieu, it must be accepted as a fact of the mode of life of that environment. It is quite another matter if in some of the printed collections which are merely "potboilers" there are popular rhymes included which have been composed without adequate skill, in violation of the poetics of the given genre—in other words, falsified popular rhymes. But such popular rhymes generally do not have a very long life on the lips of the young people of the city or the countryside, and thus of their own accord pass out of the repertory.

Every social milieu produces an artistic and ideological selection in the songs which accrue in it, and this selection is in greater or lesser degree indicative of the poetic style of that milieu. In one setting a popular rhyme finds favor; in another, it will be altogether done away with, or subjected to revision. That is why it is so interesting to trace the life and wanderings of the popular rhyme, its constant changes, which correspond to the differences in the social environment and the vicissitudes of history. Some of the popular rhymes have been disseminated through the whole country, others have had a narrowly local significance, not passing beyond the limits of a single country town or factory. Some of the popular rhymes survive for several decades, others live for a very short period; very many are literally ephemeral. It is necessary to catch them in their flight, since they give, as it were, momentary impressions of a life which is swiftly changing. The folk rhymes constitute a kind of literary motion-picture theater.

The content of the folk rhymes is extremely varied. The greater number of the prerevolutionary popular rhymes were composed on the theme of the personal emotion of love. Love, jealousy, a quarrel with the loved one, separation (with all the shades of emotion, beginning with the tenderest, and ending with rage and cruelty) are expressed in these brief little songs. The vast majority of the popular love rhymes are the product of the creative art of girls and women, like the former old, drawn-out love song. Many of them are created in the course of a touching direct improvisation, impressionistically reflecting all the shades of one's mood:

> What a sharp saw
> Cut its way into the fir tree.
> What a foolish girl I was
> To fall in love with a boy,
>
> Look, my dear one, at the sky,
> Then, after the sky, look upon me;
> As the clouds pass over the sky,
> So the shadows pass over my heart.[13]

Some of the popular rhymes are filled with intimate emotion, which finds its expression, not by means of contrasts or comparisons, but only by pointing out some specific detail of a person's outward conduct:

[13] From the former province of Tver, *ibid.*

> Dear one, my dear one,
> How I was running after you!
> How fierce the frosts were,
> And I was wearing only my little jacket.
>
> I accompanied Kolenka
> Beyond the little old chapel;
> I shook my head:
> How thin Kolya had become! [14]

The motifs of love occupied the chief place in the repertory of popular songs of the countryside before the October Revolution, especially so because the popular rhyme was largely, as we have already said, a woman's song. These motifs were characteristic of the popular songs of the end of the nineteenth century, and also of the twentieth. The departures—which were constantly becoming more frequent—of the rural population to the city to earn money, afforded a ready stimulus for the development, in the popular rhymes, of the motifs of separation. During the periods of war, the Japanese, the [First] World War, and the civil war, the outward flow of the population, and especially of the young men, increased still more. The motifs of separation, during these years, are heard in the popular rhymes with ever increasing frequency. In the popular rhymes the girls expressed their longing to see again, however briefly, their dear ones who had been taken prisoners. And even without regard to the war, in daily life, separation after happy love was a regular occurrence in the countryside. Touching in its sincerity, the tone expressing the feeling of separation can, at times, even make unnoticeable the trite, even vulgar turns of phrase in the popular song, as, for example, the hackneyed introduction in the following popular rhyme:

> I was walking through the woods with interest,
> I was not rosy—I was pale.
> A little bird began to sing plaintively,
> "You are left alone, poor girl." [15]

The cause of the separation is frequently given as being the unfaithfulness of the loved one, and the successful rival may be one's own girl friend.

[14] *Ibid.*   [15] *Ibid.*

Among the popular rhymes dealing with love, there stands out a very interesting group concerning women rivals:

> The villainess is sitting
> Close beside the partition.
> How I wish the fancy combs
> Would fly out of her head!
> I always counted her my friend,
> I thought her a faithful friend,
> But now I have only just found out—
> She is the worst enemy.
> Don't be angry, my little friend,
> Don't be angry, you rich girl.
> The young man does not care for you—
> I am not to blame.
> Oh, my little friend, do not chide,
> And do not scold because of your friend.
> Buy a little iron-bound chest,
> Lock your darling in it.[16]

At times the girl conceals her feeling of jealousy, hiding it behind an assumed disdain:

> My dear one thinks
> That I am thinking of him.
> But he doesn't think of this—
> I've got seven or eight more besides him.[17]

The despair of the forsaken girl finds expression, for example, in such naïve popular rhymes as the following:

> On the Volga there is a thin film of ice.
> My dear one rode to the altar,
> But I stood on the bank and cried,
> "The priest shall not perform the ceremony."
> When my darling rides to be married,
> I will stand on the footboard behind the carriage:
> "Give back my handkerchief, give back my ring,
> Give back my gloves." [18]

Since the popular rhyme was composed (and is still composed) in the vast majority of instances by young people, so, naturally, the

[16] Archive of the State Literary Museum.
[17] *Ibid.*   [18] *Ibid.*

majority of these rhymes speak also of love and of its difficulties encountered before marriage. The number of popular rhymes describing family life is considerably smaller, and furthermore, those which do exist depict the family life from the point of view of these same young people: they describe the strictness of parents, the supervision, the reproofs, the punishments, the admonitions, and at times the relations of the parents to each other, and so forth. Here is a jestingly good-natured song about a father and mother, composed by an observing daughter:

> Papa is selling the bathhouse,
> Mamma cries, she won't give it up.
> Papa kisses Mamma,
> Mamma doesn't mind a thing.[19]

The vast majority of the prerevolutionary popular rhymes is made up of love lyrics, and also, in general, of echoes of the events of private, personal life. And nevertheless, the popular rhymes which deal with such private themes as these reflect the growth of the social consciousness of the countryside, and the deep changes in its mode of life and culture. If we compare the popular love rhymes in the nineteenth and twentieth centuries with the old-fashioned, long-drawn-out lyric songs, we shall easily be convinced that, in the sphere of personal emotion, vast upheavals have taken place, reflecting the more general upheavals in the whole philosophy of life of the peasantry. If in the languishing, old-fashioned songs there prevailed a feeling of frustration, conditioned by the insurmountable authority of family and social traditions (the authority of parents, the authority of the husband, the authority of the village talk and gossip), on the other hand, the personal and intimate popular rhymes, expressing all the changes of emotion, from the most tender to the most passionate and cruel, speak of the newly awakened freedom of emotion, even of the power of protest against institutions which were centuries old. Consequently, the popular love rhyme also is an index of the vast social upheavals in the countryside, a reflection of those profound social-economic changes which in the rural districts were the

[19] *Ibid.*

accompaniments of the development of industrial capitalism, and later of the radical overturn which was brought about by the Great October Socialist Revolution. Accordingly, it would be altogether incorrect to underestimate the significance of the popular love rhymes as clear indications of the changes in the social life of the countryside.

There were certain categories of popular rhymes which were composed also by the men among the rural young people. Here the distinguishing peculiarities, in comparison with the intimate and sometimes touching lyric quality of the girls' popular rhymes, were the features of deliberate coarseness in figures and words. The motifs of revelry, drunkenness, and rowdyism were very frequent in them. Such popular rhymes seemed at times to be indications of a breaking away from socially conscious, law-abiding society among certain strata of the peasantry. In others there sounded the notes of a kind of heartbreak, an everlasting despair, a helpless recognition of their own powerlessness to re-educate themselves, to restrict themselves, to subordinate themselves to the demands of intelligent society.

Such popular rhymes as these reawaken very many dark pictures of the prerevolutionary countryside with its constant fights, knifings, and drunken brawls. They enable us to re-create more distinctly that fathomless gulf which lies between the prerevolutionary and the Soviet mode of life of the rural young people, thanks to the progress of the cultural revolution, to the general collectivization, and to the work of the Young Communist League.

The satirical popular rhymes at first did not possess a broad public interest. These were mostly satirical mockeries by country girls of their lovers, and vice versa, and also satirical attacks by the young people of one country village on the young people of another. They made fun of outward manners, customs, mischievousness, rowdyism, drunkenness, peculiarities in dress, speech, the trifling incidents of rural daily life, for example:

> In 'Lexander's field
> There are two bay horses.
> Like 'Lexander's little boys
> They say their r's in their throat.

As for Andrew's village,
With what is it adorned?
With chairs and with vats,
And with drunken fellows.

Girls, do not marry anyone
From Ostashkov village,
There they have a funny speech
They say, "Hwy, hwy?" [20]

By the year 1905 the themes of the social-popular rhymes became more serious, more profound and extensive. We find in the popular rhyme echoes of strikes and the reflection of disturbances among the peasants:

Ah, *rat-tat, bang-bang,*
All the peasants are aroused.
They are cutting down the forests, they are burning the
     threshing floors,
They are all waiting to be free.

We have set fire to the hayloft,
And we stand and enjoy it.
The master has begun to tremble like a leaf,
The bailiff has grown thin.[21]

A series of popular rhymes satirizes the police, the clergy, and the tsar:

Softly, softly, softly, softly,
The district policeman sits on the roof
And cries, opening his mouth wide:
"The people have gone crazy." [22]

They say that the line of the Romanovs
Is descended from the rams.
Through Moscow the rumor has been borne,
Our peacemaker stinks.[23]

[20] *Ibid.*
[21] M. K. Babkin, *The Years 1905 and 1906 in the District of Mikhailovsk* (Ryazan, 1930), p. 31.
[22] *Ibid.*
[23] Recorded by V. Chicherov, Moscow, Archive of the State Museum of Literature.

The popular rhymes on specifically social themes were of great importance in the countryside previous to the October Revolution, but the nearer one draws to the Revolution, the greater is their place in the repertory of songs, and their relative influence constantly increases.

The imperialistic war could not help but be reflected in the thematics of the popular rhymes. The war began to weigh heavily upon the masses of the soldiers, the front and the rear began to do nothing but dream of seeing it brought to an end as quickly as possible:

> We are sick of it, we are sick of it,
> The German war.
> Maidens, pray to God
> That it may end in peace.[24]

The murmur grew, and criticism of the tsarist regime and of the imperial authority was aroused. In the countryside, and even at the front, in the trenches, despite the vigilance and strictness of the authorities, there sounded everywhere the notes of protest and censure, such as these:

> What have you done, you white Tsar?
> Out of time you have made war,
> Out of time and out of season,
> They have led us off to war.
> What have you done, Mikolasha?
> Our Russia is perishing![25]

Especially decisive are the protests of the young new recruits:

> Nikolasha, our white Tsar,
> Why have you made a new conscription,
> Why have you made a new conscription,
> And stirred up the anger of young lads?[26]

This familiar appeal to the tsar in the songs, combined with irony and scorn, is in itself characteristic of the rising dissatisfaction among

[24] From the former province of Kostroma, 1914, V. Smirnov, "The Role of the Countryside in the War," *Treatises of the Kostroma Scientific Society on Local Regional Studies*, No. V (Kostroma, 1916), p. 115.

[25] Y. M. Sokolov, *What Is Folklore?* (Moscow, *Peasant News*, 1935), p. 50.

[26] *Ibid.*

the masses. The way was prepared for the revolution, not only by the whole objective course of historical events, but also subjectively, through the mood of the masses.

BIBLIOGRAPHY

Sbornik velikorusskikh chastushek (Collection of Great-Russian Popular Rhymes), ed. E. N. Eleonskaia, with bibliography (Moscow, 1914).

Simakov, V., *Sbornik derevenskikh chastushek* (Collection of Popular Songs of the Countryside) (Yaroslavl, 1913).

——, Chastushki (Popular Rhymes) (Yaroslavl, 1915).

Sokolov, B. and Y., *Skazki i pesni Belozerskogo kraia* (Tales and Songs of the Belo-Ozero Region) (Moscow, 1915).

Sobolev, P. M., *K voprosy o ritmiko-metricheskoi structure chastushek* (On the Question of the Rhythmometrical Structure of the Popular Rhymes), Khudozh. Fol'klor (Artistic Folklore), Nos. 2-3, 1927.

Tufanov, "Ritmika i metrika chastushek pri napevnom ctroe" (Rhythmics and Metrics of the Popular Rhymes with a Melodic Setting), *Krasnyi zhurnal dlia vsekh* (Everybody's Red Journal), Nos. 7-8, Petrograd, 1923.

Kaletskii, P., "O poetike chastushki" (On the Poetics of the Popular Rhyme), *Lit. kritik* (The Literary Critic), No. 9, 1936.

SONGBOOKS AND
POPULAR ADAPTATIONS OF SONGS

❧

We have had occasion more than once to emphasize the point that between folklore and written literature there is no impassable gulf, that between folklore and artistic literature there has always existed, through the centuries, a close reciprocal interaction. Not only has literature been pervaded (sometimes to a greater, sometimes to a lesser degree) with the motifs of oral popular poetry, drawing up from oral poetry its invigorating force of emotion and thought, but conversely oral poetry, from the first stages of the development of literature, has felt the influence of that literature upon itself.

Even in ancient times, in the feudal period, when literacy was very greatly restricted (chiefly to the privileged classes), and during the domination of the narrow ecclesiastical trend in literature, the unwritten literature made its way among the masses of the people, and exerted no small influence upon their oral creation.

We have seen the effect of the ecclesiastical (canonical and apocryphal) prayers, legends, traditions, apocrypha, sermons, and aphorisms of other kinds of ancient Russian literature upon the popular incantation, upon ceremonial songs connected with the calendar (the *kolyadki*), upon the *byliny*, upon the most diverse groups of tales, upon the religious verses, upon the popular drama, upon the proverbs and sayings, upon riddles and divination, and so forth.

From the middle of the seventeenth century and later, in the eighteenth and nineteenth centuries, and in the twentieth, in proportion to the spread of literacy among the democratic classes of the people, the direct influence of literature upon oral poetry became ever more marked and more powerful.

In the first place, naturally, it was the oral poetry of the urban petty bourgeoisie which was exposed to this direct influence of books. Through the environment of the small trades-people, the lower bureaucracy, and the artisans, this bookish influence penetrated into the

milieu of the barely formed proletariat, and further into the surroundings of the declassed city poor. Through the trading and industrial
bourgeoisie, through the working people, still closely connected with
the countryside, through the soldiers, the manorial servants and the
hired domestics, as well as through the proletarianized and the upper
classes of the countryside, written (that is, literary) poetry comes to
be known among the broad masses of the peasantry, it comes to be
habitual with them, and is permanently incorporated into the repertory of folklore, becoming an organic and inalienable part of it.

We must emphasize anew, however, that it would be erroneous to
assume a mechanical borrowing, on the part of folklore, of literary
material. A comparative study of the literary source which serves as
the starting point for the researches, and of those sometimes numerous
variations, in which the song is disseminated in its oral form, gives an
always interesting picture of the radical changes which arise as a
result of the adaptation of a literary ballad or poem to the conditions
of oral creation, frequently, moreover, in a new social setting.

A comparison of the literary text and the oral variations very often
shows how the style of the piece gradually changes; how the new
social setting, into which the piece has found its way, brings about
a deformation of style in the whole, and eliminates that which is
unintelligible, or ideologically and psychologically alien, introducing
elements of its own customary class poetics and ideology. That is
why it is frequently so difficult, too, to discover in a song its literary
history. But during the last twenty years a good deal has already been
done in the work of establishing the literary sources of a number of
songs.

In Russia, researches in this direction began to be produced at the
beginning of the twentieth century. In 1903, a series of researches on
the literary origin of the songs which he had written down was made
by V. I. Chernyshev.[1] In 1909, A. A. Veselovsky, in his research on
The Love Lyric of the Eighteenth Century, and in 1912, M. N. Trubitsyn, in his extensive work *On Folk Poetry in the Social and Liter-*

---

[1] V. I. Chernyshev, "Information on Certain Dialects of the Tver, Klin, and
Moscow Districts," *Annals of the Division of Russian Language and Literature of
the Academy of Sciences,* Vol. LXXV, St. Petersburg, 1904.

ary Usage of the First Third of the Nineteenth Century, established
a number of indisputable facts with reference to the penetration of
aristocratic, bookish, pseudoclassical, and sentimental lyric poetry
into oral poetry. But these were all separate investigations, made in-
cidentally, in connection with other tasks which the authors of the
works mentioned had set for themselves. In 1914, A. S. Yakub [2] made
a detailed survey of those literary productions (poems and ballads)
which had entered into the repertory of oral popular poetry, to a
large extent by way of "songbooks" that had been compiled for general circulation. Later on, another series of literary sources for the
songs was revealed in the works of V. I. Simakov [3] and I. N. Rozanov.
A great deal of material is afforded for the study of this question by
the splendid book of I. N. Rozanov, *Songs of the Russian Poets.*[4] But
as yet we have no special piece of research devoted to the theme of
the creative adaptation, in oral song folklore, of a literary text, and of
the conformity to established principle, which must be revealed in
this process of the "folklorizing" of a literary production.[5] However,
one cannot help making, even now, a few general comments on this
process, on the basis of the observations which have been amassed by
the folklorists.

It is sometimes exceedingly difficult to determine the original literary form of a song because of the fact that, having become a part
of the repertory of oral folklore, the poem or ballad becomes a song,
with all of the song's inherent properties. Above all, they, like every
song, are subject to variations and adaptations. Consequently, for a
correct understanding of the source of a song, and the nature of its
early texts, it is necessary to have at hand a sufficient number of variants of it.

[2] A. S. Yakub, "Contemporary Popular Songbooks," *Annals of the Division of
Russian Language and Literature of the Academy of Sciences,* Vol. XIX (1914),
Bk. 1.

[3] V. I. Simakov, *Popular Songs, Their Composers and Variants,* with foreword
by Prof. Y. M. Sokolov, ed. (Moscow, 1929).

[4] I. N. Rozanov, *Songs of the Russian Poets* (18th and first half of the 19th
century), "The Poet's Library" (Leningrad, 1936).

[5] At the present time such an investigation is being prepared for publication
by A. M. Novikova, who has collected and systematized an enormous mass of
textual material.

These variants, through a comparative study, give us an opportunity of judging how there were gradually eliminated those elements of ideology and of poetics which were alien to that class setting into which the song had entered. This same comparative study of the variants can also show by what routes the song passed, before finding its way, for example, into the setting of the peasantry or the proletariat.

The reworking of the literary songs proceeds along the same lines, by which in general the changes are brought about in the text of a folklore song. These changes may be classified as changes which are, so to speak, mechanical, and those which are organic. In the first group may be included, above all, all alterations arising out of mis-understanding or mis-hearing of the text. A further vast role is played by errors of memory entailing the omission of words, and even of whole lines and stanzas. These errors of memory contribute to the appearance of so-called "contaminations," combinations of the song with other songs or with fragments of songs. The organic revisions in the literary songs are of greater significance.

On a purely theoretical plane, the historico-literary and historico-musical study of the popular revisions in the literary productions is very important for the science of ·folkloristics, because through the identification of the literary original of a song, the researcher discovers a point of departure for the arrangement of his work. Starting from that, it becomes possible to determine the governing principles in the development of the oral lyric with greater definiteness than, for example, in the cases of the *byliny,* the vast majority of the tales, and so on. The oral lyric of the feudal Middle Ages could not, in the same degree as the epic genres, come under the influence of books, since the secular bookish lyric hardly existed at all in Russian medieval literature (if we except the lyric elements in the epic and narrative genres of medieval literature—in the so-called "martial narratives," and so forth). The ecclesiastical, and in general the religious lyric, which flowered particularly toward the end of the Middle Ages, and the manuscript "psalms" and "canticles" were strikingly reflected, as we have seen, in the folklore of the lyric "spiritual verses" of the Church, of the Old Believers, and of the sectarians. With the in-creasing Europeanization of the ruling social classes, the secular lyric penetrated increasingly into the literature of the seventeenth and eighteenth centuries.

Certain of the productions of trivial poetry (apparently at first through the ecclesiastical surroundings of the seminary) penetrated also into the broader mass of the urban and village population, began to be sung everywhere, and to be transformed gradually into popular songs. Especially to be noted are the bookish sources of several of the humorous, jesting songs. Thus, for example, there is a humorous song which, even down to our own day, is still widely disseminated through the country villages:

> I lived with a gentleman the first year,
> And for this I earn from the master a pullet. . . .
> My little crested pullet
> Walks up and down the yard, leading her chickens.[6]

This proves to be a Russian oral version of a Polish song of the seventeenth century, which through Polish and Ukrainian manuscript songbooks has found its way into the oral peasant repertory, even in the Far North.

The seminary lyric of the theological students has infused into the repertory of living folklore no small number of other songs, too; compare, for example, a song which was still widely sung, even down to very recent times, among the village clergy, bourgeoisie, and the village intelligentsia, which in its bombastic, archaic speech, and in its ponderous imagery, betrays its seminary origin:

> The face of nature, the face of nature
> Has come alive anew, anew.
> With a tender smile the young growing things,
> In their wedding attire, have again appeared
> In our land, in our land.

But it is not this stream of the seminary lyric, noteworthy though it is, which holds our attention. Much more powerfully, in the oral lyric of the lower middle class, and later also of the peasantry, is revealed the influence of the bookish lyric of the nobility. This influence

---

[6] Sobolevsky, *Great Russian Popular Songs*, Vol. VII, No. 483.

began to be especially apparent in the last quarter of the eighteenth century.

In the second half of the eighteenth century, and also in the first quarter of the nineteenth, there is to be observed a lively exchange between bookish (literary) and oral (folklore) creations.

As one of the literary genres of the lyric of the nobility, which reflected the already mentioned movement of style in the direction of greater simplicity, there should be mentioned the genre of the "folk" or "Russian song," characteristic of the classicists of the eighteenth century (for example, K. G. Khovansky, I. I. Dmitriyev, N. P. Nikolev), of the sentimentalists (Y. A. Neledinsky-Meletsky), of the neoclassicists of the beginning of the nineteenth century (Delvig). In these ballads or "songs" there took place an interesting combination of elements of the poetics and the psychology of the nobility (representation of the refined, intimate emotion of love) with elements of the traditional poetics of peasant folklore (in symbolic patterns, use of rhythm, composition, vocabulary, traditional figures of speech, and so forth).

Many such literary productions of the nobility penetrated into the broad masses of the people, owing to the performance of lyric poems in the form of vocal ballads, partly by means of printed songbooks, which contributed powerfully to the popularization of this or that production. A considerable number of such ballads became a permanent part of the repertory of folklore. Of the best known ones, I need only mention the following poems of the end of the eighteenth and beginning of the nineteenth century: "Last Night I Was Walking in the Meadows," by Khovansky; "The Little Gray Dove Is Moaning," by Dmitriyev; "In the Evening a Beautiful Girl," by N. M. Ibrahimov (a Kazan poet, 1779–1818); "As I Go Out to the Little River," by Neledinsky-Meletsky; "Amid the Level Dale," and "Black-Browed, Black-Eyed, Dashing Fellow," by Merzlyakov; "Not the Fine Small Rain of Autumn," "Nightingale, My Nightingale, Sweet-Voiced Nightingale," and "The Little Bird Sang, and Sang, and Then Fell Silent," by Delvig, and others.

Among the other authors of the eighteenth and the beginning of the nineteenth century, whose productions were taken up into the repertory of folklore, one need only mention Lomonosov ("The Heavens Were Covered with the Darkness of Night"), Derzhavin ("Little Golden Bee" and others), Karamzin, Kheraskov. How great was the influence of the bookish lyric of the eighteenth century upon oral poetry, and how long this influence continued to be vital, even after many decades, is shown by the mere fact that a song which has been popular for the last forty years and is known by everyone, a song which has been sung in all the Russian country villages and in the suburbs of the cities—"Kindly Glances"—is directly dependent, genetically, upon a "song" by Kheraskov, "Separation." Following A. S. Yakub, I present for comparison the opening stanzas of both pieces.

Charming face, gracious glances! You are hidden from my eyes. Rivers, woods and mountains Will separate us for a long time to come.	Farewell, caressing glances, Farewell, my dear one, my darling. Valleys and mountains will divide us, I shall live now far apart from you.

A great influence was exerted upon the oral lyric by one of the genres of the classical style which was much favored in the eighteenth century, namely the so-called "pastorals," that is, brief little scenes and airs from the aristocratically stylized life of "shepherds" and "shepherdesses." The airs of these pastorals, since their music was simple, were well remembered, and quickly became popular. The pastoral, in spite of the fact that it was an expression of the refined and delicate emotions of love, in the conventional forms of idyllic simplicity and sincerity, by virtue of this striving toward even a conventional simplicity, naturally became mingled with elements of the genuinely simple and sincere peasant poetry. Consequently, in the pastoral, as in other forms of the love lyric of the eighteenth century, there is an obvious imitation of the folk song, with utilization of characteristic features of its poetics. This circumstance threw a bridge across from literature to the song folklore, and powerfully contributed to the penetration of very many airs, ballads, and poems, of an idyllic-pastoral character, into the repertory of the folk song. As an example we may point out a very popular "shepherds' " ballad of the eighteenth century, "Be Silent, Ye Pure Streams," and its adaptation, known in the songbooks of the end of the nineteenth and beginning of the twentieth century under the title "Seryozha the Shepherd."

As we have said, the so-called "songbooks," that is, the collections of songs and ballads, played a great role in the capacity of intermediaries between the oral and the bookish lyric, from the eighteenth century down to recent times.

The predecessors of such secular songbooks are the collections of "psalms" and "canticles," that is, verses having a religious content. These canticles and psalms were of Latin-Polish origin; through the Ukrainian clergy, minstrels and choir leaders, they penetrated into the Russia of the Moscow principality, and by the end of the seventeenth century had become very popular among the clergy, the nobility, and the merchant class, and called forth Russian imitations. The collections of psalms and canticles were chiefly in manuscript. Among the first, one must mention *The Rhymed Psalter* and *The Calendar in Verse*, by the well known Simeon Polotsky, which were set to music by the court chorister, the deacon Vasily Titov.[7] In the time of Peter the Great, and later, the collections of psalms and canticles also began to absorb canticles of a secular content, those of the courtiers and the nobility (for example, the songs of triumph and of love), and then gradually to be supplanted by the latter. At first, these secular songs, too, were in syllabic verse of a ponderous nature.[8] Such, for example, are the canticles in the manuscript collection (dated 1733) *The Chime of the Bells*, with tunes, like the following:

> But how joyful it is
> To pass the time
> Sweetly in love.

[7] See N. F. Findeisen, "Collections of Russian Songs of the Eighteenth Century," *Annals of the Division of Russian Language and Literature of the Academy of Sciences*, Vol. XXXI, 1926, p. 285; on the composition and sources of the collections of psalms and canticles, see the works of V. N. Perets, *Historico-Literary Researches and Materials*, Vol. I (St. Petersburg, 1900); *New Data for the History of the Ancient Ukrainian Lyric* (St. Petersburg, 1907), and others.

[8] On the development of this "versified" poetry in Russia, see I. N. Rozanov, *Verses*, "The Poet's Library": Minor Series (Moscow, 1935).

But soon such verse canticles were definitely replaced by the senti-mental-gallant, bucolic, pastoral-idyllic lyric. As we have already pointed out, in the second half of the eighteenth century there is es-tablished a mutual attraction between the book lyric of the nobility and the oral lyric of the bourgeoisie and the peasantry. The songbooks reflect this process with particular clearness. It must, however, be borne in mind that originally the printed songbooks did not strive to serve great masses of the population, in the way which was to become characteristic of the songbooks of a somewhat later period. The first songbooks were issued, first of all, in the interests of the court and the courtiers, and then for the broader circles of the nobility.

The first of such secular songbooks was the little book with music, *Leisure Between Tasks, or a Collection of Songs with Musical Ar-rangement for Three Voices: Music by G. T.* (St. Petersburg, 1759). The compiler of the songbook, who concealed his identity behind the initials G. T., was the tutor of Count Razumovsky, the son of the well known favorite of the Empress Elizabeth, Gregory Nikolayevich Teplov, the future privy councilor and director of the national china factory. The texts of the songs are mainly the gallant love verses of Sumarokov and other court poets; the music, which went through a great many reprintings in the later songbooks, was composed in the modes which were so fashionable among the court circle, those of the Italian Sicilianas, recalling the melodies of the barcaroles, the French minuet, the Polish polonaise and mazurka. These rhythms also continued to be characteristic of the majority of the ballads and literary songs; even of the so-called "Russian songs" of the whole of the eighteenth and the beginning of the nineteenth cen-tury.

The next large songbook with music was the *Collection of Simple Russian Songs with Tunes*, in four parts, which appeared in 1776, 1778, 1779, and 1795, compiled by F. V. Trutovsky, the chamber psaltery-player, who "was employed solely in the private apartments of Her Imperial Majesty for playing on the psaltery." Along with the genuinely popular, that is, traditionally peasant songs which, however, according to the compiler's own acknowledgment, had been "touched up" by him, there are a number of songs of literary origin. So far as their music is concerned, the songs of Trutovsky represent the traditional peasant motifs (Trutovsky himself was a native of the Ivanovsky suburb of Belgorod), with an obvious "veneer" of the foreign modes of vocal music mentioned above, which were fashionable in court circles.

Much more strict, in his observation of the ethnographic requirements, was the compiler of *A Collection of Russian Popular Songs, with Their Parts, Set to Music by Ivan Prach* (Parts I-II, first edition, St. Petersburg, 1790; second edition, 1818). As it has now been established with complete certainty, Prach is responsible only for the harmonizing of the songs, while the selection and recording of the tunes, and also the foreword to the collection, which is very interesting from the scholarly viewpoint, are the work of a member of the Academy of Fine Arts, the engineer, architect, and privy councilor N. A. Lvov, a great connoisseur and lover of songs.

These songbooks with music, both printed and in manuscript, were intended both for solo and for choral singing; both for the court notables themselves, and also especially for the numerous singers and musicians who lived at the imperial court, and at the courts and on the estates of the magnates (choruses of singers, horn players, psaltery-players, orchestras of musicians, theatrical troupes—all these were the almost obligatory appurtenances of the magnificent setting of the aristocracy. Along with such songbooks containing musical scores, there appeared also songbooks containing only the literary texts. These were gradually disseminated among ever widening circles of the nobility, then among the wealthy and the petty bourgeoisie, and finally even among the peasantry. As noted by the researchers, such songbooks by adapting new texts to the popular tunes served to refurbish the songs and ballads which had already begun to pall on the popular taste. In the songbooks, every now and then, we meet with indications that the song is sung to some well known "part" (this, at that time, was the designation of the tune or air).

The best known songbook, and the one which has an especially great significance for the historians of the Russian popular song, is the work of Michael Dmitryevich Chulkov (A *Collection of Various Songs*, Parts I-IV, with a supplement, 1770–1774).[9]

As in all of his exceedingly fruitful literary activity, in this collection, too, Chulkov oriented himself to a more democratic, chiefly urban petty bourgeois setting. Aligning himself with the "little" writers (see his preface to *The Scoffer*), Chulkov, the son of a court stove tender, who, however, had received a university education, felt humiliated in the midst of the court milieu of cultured society. He devoted the whole of his activity to the satisfaction of the artistic demands of the petty bourgeois, trader, and artisan masses. For a long time there was attributed to him the edition of the *Russian Songs* (ten parts, 1780–1783), constituting an original stylization of traditional tales, in imitation of the adventurous, magical, knightly romance which was much beloved by the bourgeois reader. With this same purpose he composed the collection of narratives, humorous tales, and anecdotes, under the title *The Scoffer* (four parts, 1766–1768)), which went through several editions. For this same circle, Chulkov wrote the adventure romance of daily life *The Comely Cook* (1770), and the realistic romance of daily life *Bitter Destiny*, and so forth.[10]

On the basis of all that has been said about Chulkov, it may readily be guessed that his *Collection of Various Songs* is, in fact, a collection of various songs, both traditional peasant songs and literary ones. As A. V. Markov has made clear,[11] Chulkov did not write down the texts of the songs himself, but employed chiefly the manuscript songbooks which came into his hands, with their characteristic feature—the mingling of the oral song repertory with the gallant-sentimental ballads. Moreover, Chulkov apparently—like P. V. Kireyevsky at a

[9] Pts. I-III only were republished by the Academy of Sciences in 1913.

[10] On Chulkov and his literary activity, see V. V. Sipovsky, *Outlines of the History of the Russian Romance*, Vol. I, Nos. I and II (St. Petersburg, 1909), and also V. S. Nechayeva, *The Russian Everyday Romance of the Eighteenth Century*; "M. D. Chulkov," *Scientific Annals of the Institute of Language and Literature*, Russian Academy of Popular Arts and Social Sciences, Vol. II, 1928. See also P. N. Sakulin, *Russian Literature* (Moscow, 1929), Vol. II, Chap. 6.

[11] A. V. Markov, "Chulkov's Songbook and Its Significance for the Great-Russian Popular Songs," *Annals of the Division of Russian Language and Literature of the Academy of Sciences*, 1917, Vol. XXII, Bk. 2, pp. 82-83.

later period—made use of recordings of songs which had been sent him by various persons in different parts of Russia. Especially notable are the rather large number of soldiers' songs, written down, apparently, for Chulkov as they were sung by soldiers' choruses. It is also possible that songs were recorded from citizens and merchants. Chulkov's songbook was republished by the author in 1776 in St. Petersburg, and in 1780–1781 in Moscow, by N. I. Novikov, under the title A *New and Complete Collection of Russian Songs,* with the addition of two more parts. Chulkov's songbook has a vast significance for the history of the Russian song lyric, since it gives the most abundant material for comparisons with the contemporary song repertory, and for conclusions as to the evolution of the song texts during the course of more than 150 years.

After the songbooks of Chulkov and Novikov there followed a long series of others, with very characteristic titles, indicating the aims which the composers had set for themselves, and the tastes of those whose demands were satisfied by these songbooks. Such, for example, are the titles: A *New and Complete Collection of Russian Songs: Including Love Songs, Pastorals, Comic Songs, Simple Folk Songs, Choral Songs, Wedding Songs, Christmas Songs, with the Addition of Songs from Various Russian Operas and Comedies; A Selected Songbook, or a Collection of the Best of the Old and the Very Latest: Songs of the Tender Passion, Pastorals, Christmas Songs, Wedding Songs, Choral Songs, Theatrical, Merry, Simple, Popular, Drinking, Martial, Little-Russian, Satirical, and Other Russian Songs* (1792); *The Pocket Songbook, or a Collection of the Best Secular and Simple Popular Songs* (1796); *Consolation for the Sorrowing, or Diversion for the Merry, or Toil in the Midst of Leisure for the Idler, or A New and Genuine Russian Songbook* (two parts, with frontispiece, Moscow, 1798), and so forth.

The tradition of compiling such songbooks passed over also into the nineteenth century, and extended into the first years after the revolution. Many songs from the songbooks of the eighteenth century are mechanically transferred into the songbooks of the nineteenth and twentieth centuries, others gradually fall away, being replaced by songs of the new order, or by adaptations of old songs. Furthermore, there is an obvious change in the social milieu for which the songbooks are compiled. With the growth of industrial capital, the increase and expansion of the bourgeoisie, with the increase in the number of literate persons, the songbooks become constantly more democratized. They are already oriented more and more toward the petty bourgeoisie and the peasantry. There is a gradual change, also, in the outward character of the books. If the songbooks of the eighteenth century were quite expensive books, appearing also in many volumes, and consequently, because of their price, within reach only of the well-to-do classes of the population, during the nineteenth century we see a greater and greater effort to lower the price, and at the same time, of course, a deterioration also in the quality of the publications themselves: the fat, multivolumed songbooks are gradually replaced by publications of a popular character, and toward the end of the nineteenth and in the beginning of the twentieth century they are transformed for the most part into thin little notebooks in folio or even half-folio, with a gayly colored, crudely drawn little picture on the cover. There is a gradual change, also, in the titles of the songbooks.

The link with the traditions of the eighteenth century still continued to be felt, however, for a long time, but, in conformity with the change in social life and culture, the content of the titles is changed. Here are several titles from various decades of the nineteenth century: A *Selected Songbook for Fair Maidens and Charming Women* (Moscow, 1816), A *Boudoir Songbook for Sweet Maidens and Charming Women* (Oryol, 1820), *The Latest Complete Songbook, or a Collection of Selected Songs of Every Kind* (four parts, Moscow, 1822), *Russian Songbook, or a Collection of the Best and Most Favored Songs*, published by K. Avdeyeva (two parts, St. Petersburg, 1848), *The Latest Complete Russian Songbook, Collected from the Popular Russian Songs and from the Works of Well Known Russian Writers* (four parts, Moscow, 1854), *Songbook, or a Collection of Selected Songs, Ballads, and Vaudeville Couplets,* (three parts, St. Petersburg, 1855), *Songs of the Tyrolese and Muscovite Grisettes, Sung by Them in the Tumanov, Zaytsev, Chasovnik, and Pegovoy*

Taverns, in the Cafés of Alexander's Garden, of the Tver Boulevard, and of the Wolves' Valley, with the Addition of Choral Songs by Osip (Moscow, 1860).

The very title of the songbook speaks of the social milieu in which it must have been eagerly purchased. We recall, from the memoirs of Ostrovsky, of Apollon Grigoryev, of Tertius Filippov, of Maksimov and others, how great was the increase, from the 1850's to the 1870's, in the creation of songs among all classes of the merchant population. The Moscow taverns were the nurseries, for the most part, of the pseudopopular Russian and also of the "gypsy" songs, which were disseminated throughout Russia. The tavern stage, and also all other kinds of open stages, produced and popularized all kinds of bourgeois songs, ballads, airs, and couplets. Compare these titles of songbooks: *A New Complete Songbook: A Collection of Selected Russian, Little-Russian, and Gypsy Songs . . . Ballads, Humorous and Satirical Poems, Airs, and Couplets . . . Collected by a Connoisseur* (second edition, enlarged, Moscow, 1874); *An Unexpected Present from the Young Men to the Fair Sex; I Want to Tell You a Story; Social Songs, Chansonettes, Couplets, Sung by the Artistes of Various Choruses . . .* (Moscow, 1878).

This bourgeois element, through stage performances and songbooks, was constantly filtering more and more into the song repertory of the countryside and of the factories and mills, obscuring and contaminating the genuine folk element. This was one of the manifestations of that "artistic culture" which capitalism brought to the masses.

As A. S. Yakub correctly remarked, these were not yet collections of a cheap "bast" character. But alongside of them, and gradually crowding them out, the enormous literature of the cheap popular songbooks began to breed and multiply. It was disseminated by the publishers of this popular type of literature, the so-called "literature of Nikolskaya Street" (these publishing houses were mostly located on Nikolskaya Street and on the Solyanka in Moscow). At the end of the nineteenth and the beginning of the twentieth century, there were in existence there such firms as the following, specializing in cheap "bast" literature: Morozov, Konovalova, which had replaced the firm of Abramov and Sazonov; Shalimov, Anisimova (replacing the Barkov firm), Sharapov, Gubanov, the very large Sytin firm, and on Trubnaya Square the firms of Maksimov and Balashov; in St. Petersburg, the firm of the Kholmushiny, formerly the Kuzin firm; in Kiev, the Gubanov firm, and so forth. (For information as to these publishing houses of so-called "bast" literature, see the previously mentioned article by A. S. Yakub.)

By the end of the nineteenth century, several of the firms that have been mentioned were bringing out songbooks at the rate of scores of thousands of copies (for instance, Sytin published, in 1894, 62,000 copies, and Gubanov 66,000). The titles of the popular songbooks are extremely diverse, but in general they fall into the following groups: songbook—"new," latest," "complete," "Russian," "popular," "martial"; collection or compilation of songs, ballads, couplets—"new," "the latest," "Russian," "selected," "the most select," "fashionable," "most favored," "soldiers'," "merry"; songs—"new," "popular," "merry." Very often these songbooks bore the title of one or another of the songs which might be popular at that particular time: "Marusya Has Taken Poison," "The Grave" (after the song, "Let the Grave Be My Punishment"), "The Golden Hills," "The Varangian," "Onward, Troika," "The Fire of Moscow Raged and Burned," "Ah, Wherefore This Night," "Hazel Eyes," "There Were Merry Days," "Ah, You Poor, Poor Little Seamstress," "This Last Brief Day," "A Dashing Fellow Is the Merchant," "The Transvaal," "My Camp Fire," "The Little Box," "I Lost My Little Ring," "Seryozha the Shepherd," and so forth. Some of the titles have a more general character: "The Merry Fellow," "The Forget-Me-Not," "Songs of the Vagabonds," "Convicts' Songs," "Prisoners' Songs," and also "Songs of the Drunken Alcoholics," "Songs of a Cuckold Husband," and so forth.

If we take into consideration all this enormous production of songbooks, both the popular ones and those of a more solid nature, it is easy to understand what a vast influence the songbooks must have exerted upon the oral song folklore of the urban merchant class, the bourgeoisie, the members of the intelligentsia, the workers, and the peasantry. Unfortunately, we do not as yet have any extensive, systematic research work on the history of the influence of the songbooks upon folklore. We do not even have, as yet, a complete and systematic survey of the songbooks themselves.

However, even a cursory study of the country song repertory of any locality, at the beginning of the twentieth century and today, shows the great percentage of songs which progress through the songbooks into literary poetry. The songbooks are interesting also in another connection: they frequently prove to be very important, dated documents for those changes which a literary ballad or song undergoes when it becomes a part of the oral repertory of the masses. The point is that the songbooks of the masses very often do not print the original texts as they come from the pen of the poet, but very remote revisions of the text, which have been produced as a consequence of the development of folklore. It must also be said that the attitude toward the author's text, in the vast majority of the songbooks, especially the cheap "bast" ones, was quite an unceremonious one. In the majority of cases, in the songbooks, the names of the authors are not indicated. Thus the songs lose their personal identity, and only through elaborate historico-literary researches have investigators succeeded in determining "the unknown author of a well-known song."

For example, not long ago, I. N. Rozanov [12] discovered who was the author of a very popular song which had in its time been part of the repertory of the famous vaudeville singer Plevitskaya, "The Fire of Moscow Raged and Burned." The author proved to be a little-known poet of the middle of the nineteenth century, N. S. Sokolov, who had printed, in the collection *Poetic Sketches: An Almanac of Verses*, published by A. M. Pozdnyakov and A. M. Ponomarev (Moscow, 1850), a poem entitled "He." We present for comparison both the original text by Sokolov and the variant as revised in the *Latest Songbook*, under the title "Stenka Razin," published by the company of the Publishers' Cooperative of Moscow Newspaper-Workers (Moscow, 1918), page 28.

[12] I. N. Rozanov, "The Literary Source of the Popular Song," *Artistic Folklore*, No. I, Moscow, 1926.

Text by N. S. Sokolov	Text in the Songbook
The fire of Moscow raged and burned,	The fire of Moscow raged and burned,
The smoke spread out along the river,	The smoke spread out along the river,
On the height of the wall of the Kremlin	And in the distance on the walls of the Kremlin
He stood in his gray coat,	He stood in his gray coat,
He saw the sea of fire;	And became thoughtful, the great one,
At first he was full of dark thoughts,	Crossing his arms upon his breast,
For the first time he comprehended woe,	He saw the sea of fire,
And his proud spirit was shaken.	
He dreamed of a wild island,	He saw the destruction before him.
He saw the destruction before him,	And concealing his reveries,
And became thoughtful, the great one,	He turned his gaze upon the flame,
Crossing his arms upon his breast,	
And he was sunk in revery,	And in the quiet voice of conscience
Turning his gaze upon the flame,	He spoke thus to himself:
And in the quiet voice of suffering	Why did I come to you, O Russia,
He spoke thus to himself:	Holding all Europe in my hands,
	Now with drooping head
Fate plays with man,	I stand upon the walls of the fortress.
She, the evil one, does this always,	All the troops, summoned by me,
Now she exalts you for a time—	Are perishing here among the snows.
Now she hurls you down to the depths of shame.	In the fields our bones decay
And I, who drew after me	Without burial or coffin.
The whole of Europe in chains,	
Now have bowed my head	Fate plays with man,
Upon these sorrowful walls!	She is always fickle,
	Now she lifts him up on high,
You too, guests summoned by me,	Now she hurls him into the abyss, without shame.
You too have perished among the snows—	
In the fields your bones decay,	
Without burial or coffin!	
Why did I come to you, Russia,	
Into your depths of snow.	
Here against the fateful stairs	
My bold foot has stumbled!	
Your vast capital—	
The last step of my dream,	
It is the tomb of my hopes,	
The mausoleum of my ruined splendor!	

In the adaptation given in the songbook we find a number of characteristic changes, in comparison with the original text. Here are some of them: the lines are omitted, in which we come upon literary and conventional turns of phrase, which would not be easily understood by the democratic reader of that time, such as (1) "The mausoleum

of my ruined splendor," or "Here against the fateful stairs," "the
tomb of my hopes." (2) The allegorical expression, "I, who drew
after me the whole of Europe in chains," is replaced by a simpler one,
more in accordance with colloquial usage: "Holding all Europe in my
hands"; also the bombastic metaphor, "Now she hurls you down to
the depths of shame," was thought to be too hard to understand, and
was replaced, with a change in the sense, by the simpler and more
comprehensible expression, "Now she hurls him into the abyss, without shame"; the sentimental and conventional epithet "sorrowful
walls," is replaced by the simple definition "fortress walls"; (3) those
details are removed which presuppose a knowledge of the personal
fate of Napoleon: the allusion to the banishment to the island of St.
Helena, "He dreamed of a savage island"; the indication of the diverse
racial origins of Napoleon's troops, the lines which we have already
mentioned, "who drew after me the whole of Europe in chains," and
"You, guests summoned by me."

On the whole, it cannot be said that the folklore adaptation proves
to be an inartistic distortion of the original; on the contrary, if we
remove one or two phrases (for example, "she hurls him into the
abyss, without shame," "the voice of conscience"), the adaptation
has heightened the expressiveness both of the chief figure and of the
main ideas of the production, on the uncertainty of fortune and of
human glory. The adaptation proves to be more powerful, also, with
regard to its composition: the line which expresses the basic sentence
("Fate plays with man") is transferred to the end of the production,
and seems to be made more emphatic. The example which has been
analyzed shows, I think, the methodological importance of a comparative study of the productions of folklore and of their literary
sources.[13]

We have dwelt in detail on the history of the influence of literary
poetry upon the oral lyric from the end of the seventeenth century to
the days of the October Revolution. We are convinced of the strong
mutual connection between oral and literary creative work. One of

---

[13] Valuable methodological observations have been made in the article by I.
N. Rozanov, "From Book to Folklore: the Kind of Verses That Become Popular
Songs" (*The Literary Critic*, No. 4, 1935).

the main routes for the penetration of literature into the repertory of popular songs was, as we have seen, through the manuscript and especially through the printed songbooks. Through the cheap, so-called "bast" publications there passed over into folklore many secondary, inartistic, and frequently coarse and commonplace productions. An attentive study of the adaptations shows that the popular taste, reared on the beautiful poetic tradition of many centuries, attempted a creative recasting even of this second-rate material, subjecting it, so far as possible, to its own esthetic standards (hence arise the numerous popular adaptations, often an improvement on the text); but, of course, one cannot help seeing also that damage which the popular art inevitably suffered from the influence of the capitalistic city with its taverns, its coffeehouses, and the commonplace publications of enterprising "hucksters."

But along with this dross of civilization, the city (and also, of course, the theater and the school) also brought into the artistic world of the popular masses productions of genuine art, both literary and musical. Even the cheap "bast" literature, in one way or another, whether in fragments or whether in careless, unverified reprints, nevertheless acquainted the broad masses of the people with the creative works of our best authors—Pushkin, Lermontov, Gogol, Nekrasov, L. Tolstoy, and many others.

We now already have at our disposal a sufficient quantity of data on the productions of the Russian poets from the eighteenth to the twentieth century (songs, ballads, verses), which took root permanently in the repertory of popular songs, along with the songs which had a purely folkloric origin.

It is very hard to enumerate all the songs which have their literary sources in the productions of the well known and less well known authors of the nineteenth and twentieth centuries. It seems to me, however, that it will not be superfluous to make a list of the most popular songs which go back to definite literary sources. The mere list of these may speak for itself, and testify to the power of the literary influence upon oral poetry. In making the present survey, I have availed myself (in selections) of those data which have been given in the article by A. S. Yakub, in the book by V. I. Simakov, and in the works of I. N. Rozanov.

Besides the songs by Merzlyakov and Delvig which have already been mentioned, among the works of the authors of the beginning of the nineteenth century (see above, page 554) should be mentioned the songs, very popular in their time, of Tryganov (1797–1831). Of his songs, the following enjoyed special favor: "Do Not Sew for Me, Dear Mother, the Red Sarafan," which was set to music by Varlamov; then, "Ah, My Little Silver Goblet," "Be Silent, Little Canary Bird," "Ah, Wherefore, Darling Masha," and others. Of the songs of Koltsov, those which were often sung and reprinted in songbooks, down to very recent times, included "The Little Farm," "I Saddle My Horse," "I Light the Candle of Unbleached Wax," "Do Not Rustle, O Rye, in Your Ripe Ears," "Do Not Tell Anyone Why, in the Spring, Through the Fields and Meadows, I Shall Not Gather Flowers," "Do Not Sing, Nightingale, Beneath My Window," "Embrace and Kiss and Caress and Fondle," "As the Winged Nightingale," "I Loved Him More Fervently Than Daylight and Firelight," "In the Field the Wind Is Howling," "The Winds Are Blowing, the Fierce Winds," and others.

Of Pushkin's lyrics, the following have made their way into the songbooks and, mostly through them, to the broad masses of the people, and have enjoyed an extensive diffusion, down to our own times: "The Black Shawl" (1820), "Toward Evening, in the Rainy Autumn" (1814)—these two are Pushkin's stylizations based on a savage ballad—"An Old Husband, a Menacing Husband" (1824), "The Prisoner" ("I sit behind the grating, in the damp dungeon," 1822), "The Talisman" ("There, where the sea splashes eternally," 1827), "A Winter Evening" ("The storm covers the sky with mist," 1825), "The Winter Road" ("Through the billowing fogs the moon makes its way"), "The Demons" (1830), "The Drowned Man" (1828), and others.[14]

From Lermontov: "I Walk Out Alone upon the Road" (1841),

[14] On the popular adaptations of Pushkin's poems, see N. P. Andreyev, "Pushkin in Popular Poetry," *The Literary Critic*, No. 1, 1937; I. N. Rozanov, "Songs of Pushkin," *The Young Collective Farmer*, No. 1, 1937.

"The Airship" (1840), "The Cossack Cradle Song" (1840), "Longing" ("Open the prison for me," 1840), and others.

From Zhukovsky: "The Night Review" (1836), and especially a fragment from "The God of Thunder" (1810).

From Nekrasov: "The Peddlers" (the fragments, "Ah, full to the top is my peddler's pack," and "It was well for a fine young fellow," 1861), "The Market Gardener" (1846), "The Troika" ("Why do you gaze so eagerly upon the road," 1841), "The Harvest Time Is at Its Height" (1863), "Caution" (1865), "Masha" ("The bright day dawned over the capital," 1851–1858).

From Nikitin: "From the Fair the Dashing Merchant Rode" (1858), "A Deep Pit Is Dug Out with the Spade" (1860), "The Stage Driver's Wife" (1854), "The Quarrel" ("Is it not time, Panteley, for you to be ashamed of the people," 1854), "The Song of the Lonely Peasant" ("Neither house nor home," 1850), "The Teamster's Departure" (1855).

Also the following must be mentioned: "My Camp Fire Shines in the Fog," "The Hermitess," by Polonsky (1846); "I Was Carefully Tended in My Mother's House," by Pleschcycv (1860); "The Convicts," "My Little Bells" (1854); "Do Not Ask, Do Not Search," and others by A. Tolstoy; "Here the Dashing Troika Whirls Along," by F. Glinka; "The Troika Whirls Along, the Troika Leaps," by Prince Vyazemsky (1834); "The Bell Rings and the Troika Whirls Along," by Malyshev; "Why Has the Clear Dawn Become Overcast," by Weltman (1831); "You, My Soul, Beautiful Maiden" (1841), by L. N. Ibrahimov; "Do Not Tempt Me When There Is No Need," by Baratynsky (1821); "The Death of Ermak" ("The storm roared, the rain made a noise"), by Ryleyev (1821), "The Lark" ("Between the sky and earth a song is heard"), by N. Kukolnik; "We Were Married, Not in Church," by Timofeyev (1832–1836), "Again I Stand Before You in Delight," by Krasov (1842); "The Swimmer" ("Our sea is not friendly"), by Yazykov (1828); "The Evening Bell," by Kozlov (1828); "Death of a Mother" ("Darling papa, where is my own dear mother," 1856), by Mey; "Not One Little Road Led Through the Field," by Krestovsky; "The Sacrifice of the Volga" ("From behind the island, in the channel," 1880), by Sadovnikov; "The Rock of

Stenka Razin" ("By the Volga there is a rock," 1864), by Navrotsky; "The Bandit Churkin" ("Among the drowsy woods the bandits are walking"), a translation of a poem by the German poet Freiligrath, made in 1846 by F. B. Miller; [15] "The Convicts" ("Open the window, open it"), by Vasily Nemirovich-Danchenko; "The Sun Rises and Sets," by Maxim Gorky; "Song of the Kamarin Peasant" (1867), "The Working Song," by Trefolev; "The Little Orphan" ("I grew up, like a blade of grass in the field," 1867), "At Mother's Grave" (1866), "The Poor Peasant's Lot" (1866), by Surikov; the adaptations of popular songs by Panov: "White Snowflakes, Downy Snowflakes" (1888), "Vanka the Steward" (1888), "The Mirthful Choral Dance," and others. Of the creative work of the "followers of Surikov," the bourgeois and peasant poets, by the end of the nineteenth century the following ballad songs began to attain vast popularity: "Do Not Chide Me, Dear One, That I Love Him So," by Razorenov; "Those Were Merry Days," by Gorokhov; "The Little Ring" ("I have lost my little ring, I have lost my love"), "The Wondrous Moon Floats Above the River," "Why, You Senseless One, Do You Destroy Him Who Was Enraptured by You," "Between Its Steep Banks Flows the River Volga," by M. I. Ozhegov.

Concerning the penetration of revolutionary songs of literary origin into the repertory of popular songs, we shall speak later, at the end of the chapter on the folklore of the factory and the mill prior to the October Revolution.

In our Soviet period may be observed, as we shall see further on, a still greater connection between popular oral creative work and artistic literature. Of the songs by Soviet poets and composers, which have penetrated deeply among the masses of the working people, we shall speak in the section devoted to Soviet folk poetry.

BIBLIOGRAPHY

Iakub, A. S., "Sovremennye narodnye pesenniki" (Contemporary Popular Songbooks) *Izvestiia Otd. russk. i az. i slov. Akad. nauk* (Annals of the Division of Russian Language and Literature of the Academy of Sciences), 1914, Bk. 1.

[15] I. N. Rozanov, "F. Freiligrath in Russian Folklore," *Literary News*, No. 2, 1936.

Simakov, V. I., *Narodnye pesni, ikh sostaviteli i varianty* (Popular Songs, Their Composers and Their Variants) (Moscow, 1929).

Findeisen, N. F., "Sborniki rossiiskikh pesen XVIII v." (Collections of Russian Songs of the Eighteenth Century), *Annals of the Division of Russian Language and Literature of the Academy of Sciences*, Vol. XXXI, 1926.

Rozanov, I. N., "Pesni russkikh poetov: XVIII v.—pervaia polovina XIX v." (Songs of the Russian Poets: from the Eighteenth to the First Half of the Nineteenth Century), *Biblioteka poeta* (The Poet's Library) (Leningrad, 1936).

Rozanov, I. N., "Literaturnyi istochnik populiarnoi pesni" (The Literary Source of the Popular Song), *Khudozhestvennyi Fol'klor* (Artistic Folklore), No. I, Moscow, 1926.

Rozanov, I. N., "Ot knigi v fol'klor: Kakie stikhi stanoviatsia populiarnoi pesnei (From Book to Folklore: The Kind of Verses That Become Popular Songs), *Literaturnyi kritik* (The Literary Critic), No. 4, 1935.

FOLKLORE OF THE
FACTORY AND THE MILL

As we have already noted several times in the preceding chapters, folkloristics in the nineteenth and at the beginning of the twentieth century was primarily concerned with a study of the folklore of the peasants and the countryside; the poetic creative work of the urban population, however, was not subjected to such a systematic study, nor even collected.

Especially characteristic is the ignoring, on the part of the old folkloristics, of the oral poetic creation of the urban proletariat. The causes of such inattention, or, more correctly speaking, contempt, lay in the class bases of scholarship and of the scholarly group, which guided this science during a whole century. The usual argument which justified scientific contempt for proletarian folklore was an allusion to the so-called "complete lack of artistry, vulgarity, and coarseness" of the oral creation of the "factory," to the harmful, corrupting role of the latter in the life of oral poetry, to the "deterioration" of poetic tastes not only in the city, but also in the countryside. It is clear to every contemporary investigator that all this argumentation was an expression of the class "tastes" of the former folklorists themselves. In the beginning the aristocratic and landowning background of the first collectors and researchers, and later the environment of the intellectual commoners, which was permeated with Populist * tendencies of various shades, naturally was bound to concentrate the attention of science upon the collection and study of the manifestations of peasant and rural folklore.

Everything that transgressed the boundaries of traditional peasant esthetics and ethics, or the limits of the poetry of the old feudal classes, was declared to be an indication of the decadence and corruption of poetic creation. With such an opinion, held by the old school with regard to urban folklore, and first of all to the "folklore

* Populist or "Narodnik" movement, which began in 1872, of Russian socialists to educate the peasantry.—ED.

of the factory," it is easy to understand the comparatively small amount of material which is at the disposal of folkloristics regarding the question of the history of proletarian oral poetry.

The facts adduced in the first attempts at research on this theme [1] are strikingly meager and fragmentary. In the old scientific collections of songs, "factory" folklore, the songs which either contain, in their thematics, aspects of factory life or else were written down in the factories and mills, are encountered sporadically—in fact, very rarely. In the largest collection of songs collected by P. V. Kireyevsky (containing 4,160 items), there are found not more than ten songs which can be assigned to the classification of the factory and the mill, and even these with a whole series of reservations.

With the material in such a condition, it was exceedingly difficult to work out a solution to the question of the sources and the first stages in the development of proletarian folklore. It was necessary to proceed by a circuitous method: to make a large collection of folklore material at the present-day factories and mills, and, comparing the repertory of various generations in the workers' environment at the same factory, and also the repertories at various industrial concerns, to reconstruct in retrospect a picture of the gradual changes in the wealth of songs of the factories during several decades. Unfortunately, even the work of just collecting the folklore of the factory and the mill did not begin until quite recently.

In 1925 I published a small article, "Songs of the Factory and the Countryside," [2] which was devoted to a characterization of the song repertory of the Kalinin china works, in the former Korchevsky district of the former province of Tver, based on materials collected by the students of the Tver (now the Kalinin) Pedagogical Institute. In 1928, P. M. Sobolev published an article, "On the Song Repertory of the Present-Day Factory," basing his observations on the folklore of

---

[1] P. M. Sobolev, "New Tasks in the Study of Folklore," *Revolution and Culture*, Bk. 1, 1929; "The Figure of the Factory Worker in the Song Folklore of the Nineteenth Century," *Literature and Marxism*, Bk. 2, 1930.

[2] Yury Sokolov, "Songs of the Factory and the Countryside," *The Educational News*, Bk. 4, 1925.

the factory population of Orekhovo-Zuyevo.[3] In the summer of 1929, the Folklore Subsection of the Institute of Literature and Language of the Russian Academy of National Arts and Social Sciences, together with the Folklore Office of the State Academy of Arts, made a special expedition to the factories and mills of the Urals, in order to record folklore. Unfortunately, these materials have so far remained unpublished.

In very recent years the work of studying the folklore of the factory and the mill has made noteworthy advances. In 1934 there appeared the book, *Folklore of the Factory and Millworkers*, with articles by P. M. Sobolev and V. I. Muravyev, which was reviewed in detail by A. L. Dymshits in *Soviet Folklore* (Nos. 2-3) for 1935. In 1934, in the magazine *Soviet Ethnography* (Nos. 1-2), A. M. Astakhova and P. G. Shiryayeva published an article, "The Old Working Song," with a number of new publications of song texts which had been written down in the factories and mills of Leningrad. In Volumes 19 to 21 of *The Literary Heritage*, devoted to the literature of the eighteenth century (Moscow, 1935), there was included an interesting publication by Dmitriyev, "The Folklore of the Working Class in the Eighteenth Century." A. N. Lozanova has published two articles on the history of the folklore of the factory: "The Song of Workmen and Serfs" in the magazine *The Cutter* (No. 13, 1934), and "Songs of the Factory and the Mill in Russia Under Serfdom" in the magazine, *Literary Studies* (Nos. 7, 8, 9, 1935). A considerable amount of information on the history of the song of the factory and mill is given in the book *Proletarian Poets*, Volume I, published by The Soviet Writer, 1935, with commentaries by A. L. Dymshits. See also the interesting article by A. L. Dymshits, "Folklore of the Working Class before the October Revolution," in *Literary Studies* (No. 1, 1936). The article has been reprinted in the book by A. L. Dymshits, *Literature and Folklore* (Moscow, 1938).

Among the local publications, a short article by I. Vlasov, "The Workmen's Chastushka," published on the basis of material from

[3] P. Sobolev, "On the Song Repertory of the Present-Day Factory," *Scientific Annals of the Institute of Literature and Language of the Russian Academy of National Arts and Social Sciences*, Vol. II, 1928.

the textile factories of the Ivanovsky industrial region, in the magazine *The Workmen's Region* (No. 12, 1935), is of interest. At the Sverdlovsk regional publishing house there was published in 1937 a large collection, *Prerevolutionary Folklore in the Urals*, compiled by the regional student V. P. Biryukov. A large amount of material on the revolutionary folklore of the workers before the October Revolution has been collected for the projected publication of the Folklore Section of the Academy of Sciences, *Songs of the Revolutionary Underground Movement* (a brigade * composed of S. D. Magid, P. Shiryayeva, V. I. Chicherov, M. S. Druskin). At the Triton publishing house there appeared a brochure by M. S. Druskin, *Revolutionary Songs of the Year 1905* (Leningrad, 1936). (See the review by Chernomordikov in the magazine *Soviet Music*, 1936.)

The Irkutsk folklorist A. V. Gurevich wrote a book entitled *"Folklore of Eastern Siberia* (Irkutsk, 1938). In it are presented valuable songs and tales of the events on the Lena in the year 1912.

In making an analysis of the proletarian folklore of the past, it is necessary to keep in mind that the working class did not represent a single solid mass.

The proletariat did not at once take form either as a class "in itself" or, what is more, as a class "for itself." In the everyday life, in the attitude toward the world, in the creative art of the laboring masses there were a multitude of ramifications, of nuances, all closely dependent upon the existence, in the past, of social strata within the proletarian class. Accordingly, the history of the folklore of the laboring man, naturally, stands in closest connection with the history of the formation and development of the proletariat and its relations with other classes and social groups.

The investigators of the folklore of the factory and the mill are faced with the enticing but very complicated task of uncovering, in the songs, tales, legends, and other genres of folklore, those phenomena which could have arisen, in the past, from among several groups: the serf workers in the manorial factories on the country estates; the workers in the possessional factories (peasants who were

---

* Soviet term broadened from its original military usage to denote any group of workers or scholarly workers engaged in a specific task.—ED.

attached to works owned by the State); the exiles and the convicts who had been conscripted to perform forced labor in government or private enterprises (mines or mills); the bond servants (the workers who were hired from among the quitrent-paying peasants, chiefly of the consuming provinces); the urban handicraftsmen and home artisans, as well as other strata of the lower middle class.

We must assume that all these classes of the working population, diverse in their social-economic, legal, and cultural type (from which the genuine proletariat was gradually formed), contributed their specific element to the enormous repertory of song and tale of the national folklore. Now, in selecting material from the general mass of folklore, one finds, as yet, comparatively little that could be directly linked with the mode of life and the state of mind of any particular one of the classes of the working population which have been enumerated above. But later on, with a greater accumulation of material, and with the perfecting of methods of class analysis, we may assume that there will emerge a clearer and fuller picture of the folklore of the first stages in the formation of the proletarian class itself.

Of great historical interest are the songs of the workers in the mines and foundries of the eighteenth century. These songs, which, unfortunately, have been preserved in only a few recordings, are valuable commentaries on the historical information concerning the terrible conditions of work at that time, the incredible forms of ruthless exploitation of the laborers, whose ranks were filled up either from the possessional and ascribed peasants, or from among the exiles and the convicts. It must be kept in mind that the situation of the exiles and convicts at the mines and mills was even more difficult than in the prisons. There are authenticated instances of the deliberate committing of criminal offenses, with the aim of escaping from the mines and mills and getting into prison. Such was the depth of woe and despair among the "working people" of the Urals.

One of the songs popular at that time, which had its origin around Barnaul, at the Zmeyevsky mine, gives a very good indication of the song repertory of the workers of the period. The mine was militarized. The work was carried on under the supervision of the military authorities. The song contrasts the free and idle existence of the officers with the heavy convict labor of the laborers. In this song the workers' recognition of social injustice is already apparent, and social antagonism is sharply expressed. In its language and style the song obviously bears the influence of the bookish speech of that period.

Oh, that work in the mines!
We say, the work in the mines,
It makes trouble for everybody!
To be an officer is not boring—
And besides, they don't have to live parted from
  their loved ones.
But our inspector and gentlemen officers,
When they have put everything in good order,
They stayed for a while, then went away.
Alas for you, poor peasants,
Miners of the first division;
You all know anxiety;
How the bells call us to work,
The gong drives us to work, it disturbs us.
We cannot object.
Oh, you, who bathe us in our own sweat—
The Zmeyevsky foundry!

The detailed enumeration of the tools of labor, and the description of the process of production, are very characteristic, as the song progresses further. This feature, as A. N. Lozanova has correctly noted, is typical of the songs of the factory and the mill from their very beginnings. In these impressions of the craft interests of the workmen, there is revealed one of the marked peculiarities which distinguish the songs of the workmen from the songs of the peasants, with which they are connected in their origin. The song continues:

Oh, you, who bathe us in our own sweat,
The Zmeyevsky foundry!
Sharply, loudly she beats on a board,
And invites people to visit her.
Beside the cord, the side,
There is a trough and a rake,
A poker, a hammer;
We pour a charge into the furnace
Of four hundred poods * in weight;

* Approximately seven tons.—ED.

When we have put in the four hundred poods in
    weight—
In one shift we will burn it all up.

Like many other songs of the workers in the factories, mills, and
mines, this song also emphasizes the arbitrariness and cruelty of the
foremen and other overseers and administrators, their taking of bribes,
and other forms of exploitation. Like many other workmen's songs,
the song calls these actual persons, whom it exposes, by their own
names. This indicates that the song bore a concrete fighting character
for that time, in a specific mill; the satire was right out of real life,
and therefore biting.

The foreman walks about, making sure
That the slag is not rich *
Let us strive, friend and brother,
So that Pravdin may be rich.

From the variants of the song it is easy to determine that Pravdin
is the surname of the foreman, the one who assigns the tasks, and
this office made it possible for him to receive bribes on a large scale.
Certain passages in the song refer to the military, prisonlike regime in
the mine, to the practice of corporal punishments, to the whole
nightmare of forced labor, coerced by the fear of severe physical
punishment. The workers were divided into commands (sections),
many being confined, as in prison, behind gratings, and kept under
the constant observation of overseers.

Alas, for you, poor paupers,
Poor fellows of the fifth division!
You all know anxiety,
When the bells call you to labor.
They drive you to labor, they disturb you,
We cannot object.
Now we hear again
How they strike five o'clock.
They begin to clang on the gratings,
Your heart is despondent.
We must get our tools!
Hammers and rabbles,

* And therefore wasteful of metal.—ED.

Sledge hammers.
Through the fountains they will start the water flowing,
They let our heart out too
We set ourselves to work
To get out the golden ore.
Let the contractors not cast upon us
An angry glance of their eyes,
Let them not threaten us with their hands,
Let them not frighten us with the rod.[4]

It is interesting that in one of the variants (the one given by Blümmer) the song is concluded with a kind of defiantly ironical ending, having an acute class significance:

> When we have finished our lesson,
> They'll let us all go home.
> We will walk along the street,
> Loudly will we sing a song,
> How the authorities love us.

But there was also another ending, more obscured, evidently meant to mislead (the variant given by Paramonov):

> When we finish our lesson,
> Then they will let us go home.
> And when we are going home,
> Loudly will we sing a song.
> Past Meder's we will go,
> Past Kenig's we will go,
> To the little bazaar we will go,
> We will take some loaves for a half-kopek,
> And we will have breakfast.

The Meder and Kenig mentioned in the song are some kind of persons in authority, from the mine administration, or German foremen. The ending of the song is curious from the viewpoint of everyday life and social psychology: it indicates the class-organizing role

----

[4] This song was taken down by E. I. Paramonov at Barbaul, from a former Zmeyegorsky workman, and published in the *Tomsk Provincial News* for the year 1865, Nos. 17-18. Another variant of it was given in the book by V. I. Semevsky, *From the History of Compulsory Mining Labor in Siberia* (Irkutsk, 1897). A third variant was published in the sketch-romance of Blümmer, "On the Altay." On the song, see the article of A. N. Lozanova, "Songs of the Factory and Mill in Russia Under Serfdom," *Literary Studies*, Nos. 7-8, 1935.

of the workers' collective. It is only necessary to gather together, to walk in a gang; then boldness increases, as well as the consciousness of their own strength, the song becomes clearer, sharper, more insolent. When they are all together, then even the authorities are not so formidable. The somewhat obscured variant, too, carries echoes of class mockery. The deliberately prosaic last verse of the song cannot possibly be taken in any other way than as a mockery of the authorities and their spies, in view of the renown of the other variant.

No less curious, also, is another song-poem, reproduced in the *Works Concerning the Siberian Mines and Mills*, by Ivan Herman (Part I, St. Petersburg, 1797). This song is also connected with the Zmeyegorsky mine. It was composed by workers who were under age, who had been sent to the mine "to pick ore." On this task, I. Herman writes as follows:

For the sorting of ore they make use of those workers who, because of extreme age, injury, or illness, cannot endure the work in the mines and mills; but the greater part of them was made up of the workers' children, who, from all the mills, were sent out to the mines in the month of May, and in October were again returned to their homes and fathers. . . . The pay for such workers was calculated at from three to seven kopeks per working day.[5]

The song is very significant in that from it one can readily see what a hatred grew up, even from the years of childhood, for the heavy forced labor, and consequently also for the mill, factory, or mine.

Here are a few extracts from this historically valuable song of the young workers at the end of the eighteenth century:

> They send us to pick ore,
> They whip and abuse us very much,
> Not knowing themselves for what sins,
> They send us into distant lands.

The song further enumerates (in a manner somewhat resembling that of the parallel barge haulers' songs) those places through which the youths had to make their way to the Zmeyegorsky mine:

---

[5] I. Herman, *Works Concerning the Siberian Mines and Mills* (St. Petersburg, 1797), Pt. I, pp. 269-270.

> Let us go to Bel-Mesov,
> Let us sing a merry song,
> Let us go to Shadrin,
> Let us pull the foreman's hair,
> Let us go to Sáushka,
> We will ask the old woman
> To give us all we want to eat and to drink,
> And to put us to bed.
> In the morning we will rise,
> We will get our little bags,
> We will eat some dried bread,
> And we will look into the distance,
> We see—on a high hill,
> Above the high dam, above the water,
> Stands the Zmeyev gold mine,
> And what a repugnant sight it is to us! [6]

This ejaculation, which bursts forth from the very hearts of the children, breathes its own unfeigned sincerity. In the fragment which has been given, we cannot but notice the reminiscences of the tale—which are very characteristic of the creative work of children—in the words, "We will ask the old woman to give us all we want to eat and to drink, and to put us to bed," there is clearly heard an echo of the tale of the old witch Baba-Yaga, who, at his request, gave the noble youth Ivan the Tsarevich "all he wanted to eat and to drink, and put him to bed."

A profound truthfulness and a genuine realism pervade the description of the frightful picture of the children's work in the mine. Irregular in their phrasing, rhythmically inharmonious, the lines of the song-poem literally reverberate with the truth of their words:

> At the place for panning gold
> There is a diabolical foreman.
> He comes, he fixes his eyes on us,
> He makes us work.
> He walks along—he beats us with birch rods,
> And tears the hair upon our heads.
> And on a holiday he makes us work hard,
> And he himself does not know for what sins.

[6] *Ibid.*, p. 169.

We do not know to whom we can complain,
Only to God alone,
But He is high above us,
And the Tsar is far away:
And we say: Oh, ho, ho!
Our life is a bad one!
We live in barracks.
We live only on bread and water.
If we run away from work,
And for whole days we lie in the bushes,
They catch us, and then
They flay and work us to death.[7]

In speaking of the songs of the Ural mineworkers of the period of serfdom, one cannot help referring to still another type of song which was widely disseminated in its time: to the songs which described the workers' dreams of fleeing from the mine as soon as their wounds are healed after the corporal punishments, after their passage through the "green garden," that is, through the lines of soldiers (running the gantlet):

The winter has passed away, with the frost,
We were set free from all dangers,
The only hard thing that remains for us
Is to pass through the green garden.
The garrison stands in order,
The drummers at the ends;
They engrave designs on the back and shoulders,
They lead us off to the hospital,
They wind us with wet rags,
It seems, they want to cure us. . . .
We rose from our bunks,
Thinking one thought:
Now there is an end to the sickness,
There is no reason why we should be ill.
Let us as quickly as possible, brethren,
Take to our heels.[8]

[7] *Ibid.*
[8] Printed by Ponomarev in the article "What the People of the Urals Sing about Themselves," *The Northern News*, No. 11, 1887; reprinted in the above-mentioned article by A. N. Lozanova, p. 174.

This song later passed over into the category of the prison and convict songs.

The mining enterprises in the Urals—the mills and mines—which belonged in very considerable part to the well known, wealthy Demidov family, have left a deep and gloomy memory among the workmen of the Urals. In 1936, E. M. Blinova took down from a seventy-eight-year-old woman in Sverdlovsk a song which clearly reproduces all the horror of the cruel exploitation of the mineworkers in the eighteenth century, the horror which compelled the workers to flee into the woods and mountains, to become members of bandit gangs. Here is this song:

> Permit us, sir and master,
> In your house,
> In the lofty mansion,
> To leap and dance,
> And tell of all the cities,
> Of all the Demidovs.
> In the Demidovs' mill
> The work is hard,
> Ah, the work is hard. . . .
> Ah, our poor backs are aching!
> They set us at the convict labor of the mine,
> Ah, and they do not let us out.
> There they kill us with hunger,
> Ah, they give us nought but cold water!
> O you mountains, and you high mountains,
> And you dense forests upon the mountains!
> Hide the noble youths, the fleeing men,
> Hide the poor bandits,
> Oh, hide the men from Demidovs'.[9]

The great service which V. P. Biryukov and E. M. Blinova have rendered to the cause of Soviet scholarship lies in their recording of the most valuable productions of the ancient folklore of the workmen in the Urals. The recordings which they have produced and published have in very great degree filled up the lacunae which formerly existed in our information as to the oral creation of the proletariat of the factories and the mills.

[9] V. P. Biryukov, *Prerevolutionary Folklore of the Urals*, p. 273.

In this book by V. P. Biryukov, *Prerevolutionary Folklore of the Urals*, the second section, compiled and annotated by E. M. Blinova, is devoted to the oral creative art of the Ural workmen. Apart from a number of newly discovered workmen's songs, a great deal of attention is paid in the collection to the "secret tales" of the Ural workmen, that is, to the legendary-historical accounts of specific episodes in the violent class conflict of the workers and the insurrectionist "bandit" groups with the fierce exploiters—the owners of the mills, the mill managers, and the other representatives of the mill administration. These workmen's tales were called "secret" in the Urals, since people had to relate them secretly, without the knowledge of the millowners and the tsarist police. These secret tales indisputably played a great role in political agitation and in revolutionary propaganda.

The Secret Tale of the Golden Commander was written down in a number of variants. The basis of the tale is an actual episode from the history of the workmen's uprisings in the Urals in the second half of the eighteenth century. Shortly before the Pugachov revolt, a great impression was produced upon the working masses of the Urals by the insurrectionary activity of a peasant serf who later became a foundry worker, Andrey Stepanovich Plotnikov. Compelled to flee, he joined one of the numerous gangs of robbers in the Ural Mountains. He soon became well known under the nickname of Ryzhanka, or the Golden Commander. In 1771 he killed one of the cruelest millowners of the Urals—Shiryayev. Soon after this event, Ryzhanka was captured and, after terrible tortures, was executed. The legend of the Golden Commander ascribes to him a multitude of noble exploits. For example, according to the legend, while he was still an ordinary member of the bandit brigade, he killed his commander, Pribytov, with his own hands, because the latter, it seems, wanted to violate a young girl who had been taken captive, the niece of the millowner Shiryayev. After this, Ryzhanka was chosen as commander; the figure of the girl whom he had saved has been adorned by the popular legend with all the trappings of romantic fantasy. According to the legend, the girl gave the commander a miraculous seal ring, and also imparted to him a secret "valuable word" which was possessed of a magic power to open before the commander all locked doors, and even to lay open before him mountains and the bowels of the earth.

How popular such secret tales were among the workers, and how keenly they were caught up by the audience in that early time, is indicated by the following narrative of a Ural workman, the aged A. L. Eroshin (the account was written down in 1935):

From my grandfather I had already heard that Pokhodyashin, the master, had built our copper foundry upon bones. On bones, too, they blew in the blast furnace. They washed the gold with blood, and there is a tale about that. Only I have forgotten the tale, but the song you can write down. [He gives the song.] The other songs I don't remember—I've forgotten them, but they used to sing them. They would strike up a plaintive air, but they composed more obscene songs against the stewards and the managers. . . . But the tales that we related were exact. There lived with me in the barracks a certain aged workman—they called him Kostochka. As soon as he began to tell tales of the leader Ryzhanka, the fellows would make him tell them three times in an evening. When he came to the place where Ryzhanka spoke the precious word, and the iron doors opened before him, and the master, that is, the millowner, I've forgotten what they called him, fell on his knees before Ryzhanka and besought him with tears that the commander would let him go, saying that he would no longer make sport of the working people, and the commander thought it over—when Kostochka would tell about that, then no matter how many times the fellows had heard it, they would begin to abuse that master, and our own master in the bargain, with filthy language. They didn't want to believe that Ryzhanka, I mean, was making a fool of himself and would not kill that reptile. Then Kostochka himself began to tell the story another way. Only everyone wanted to know what Ryzhanka would do with the master.[10]

In the secret tales of Ryzhanka, or the Golden Commander, there are a good many artistic motifs which are known to us from the legends of Stepan Razin and Pugachov (in particular, the motif of the treasure hidden till the given time has come), but the workmen's secret tales have, in the majority of cases, a greater social acuteness than the peasant folklore about Razin and Pugachov.

[10] *Ibid.*, p. 214.

As the legends of Razin and Pugachov (and in our days, as we shall see, some of the legends of Chapayev) repudiate the thought of the death of these popular heroes, so the secret tales of the Golden Commander also express confidence that he has only hidden himself for a time on Mount Azov, the access to which is guarded by the maiden whom he saved (in a number of legends she has been nicknamed the Maid of Azov).

One variant of the tale ends as follows:

I know very well that they did not put the Golden One to death; they tried and tried to catch him, but they could not succeed in catching him. And, to tell the truth, how could one catch him here, when he had his miraculous ring with him? As soon as they began to overtake him—twenty men they were who were chasing him—then the Golden One brought them to Mount Azov, and he turned down the stone [in his seal ring]. The stone glittered. The mountain opened up, and the commander disappeared. In that cave, there in Mount Azov, a beautiful maiden guards the gold, and a great many weapons are piled up there. And Omelian Ivanych also came thither to the commander, and then they made war together. But that they executed the Golden One, and drove the people from all the factories out to see the execution—that is nothing but tales. It was another that they executed, not the Golden One.[11]

According to another narrative, "The Precious Name" (heard by the collector P. P. Bazhov in 1894–1895 from a talented narrator, the workman V. A. Khmelinin), the mountain also hid both the gold and the maiden. How many people have tried to open up the mountain and find the gold that is hidden in it, but they could not:

No, apparently, a powerful spell had been cast over that matter. Until the appointed hour comes, Mount Azov will not open. Only once was there a sign. This was when our little father, Omelian Ivanych, made his appearance again, and the working people began to gather on Mount Dumma. So, our old men have related, it seemed as though at that time a song was heard from Mount Azov. It was as if a mother was playing with her child, and singing him a cheerful lullaby. And since that time it has not been heard. Everything is groaning and weeping. . . . And I see that I cannot wait for the

---

[11] *Ibid.*, pp. 188-189. This variant was written down by E. M. Blinova in 1936, from a former workman, a 76-year-old man, A. B. Kuznetsov.

time when Mount Azov will open up. If only it might have happened that I heard a rather more cheerful song from there! But you, young fellows, may perhaps live to see that time. But it cannot be that the gold has lost its power. That Solikamsky [the hero of the legend] spoke cleverly. One must understand this. Whoever it may be of us that lives until that time, he will look upon the treasure of Mount Azov. He will learn also the precious little name, by means of which these riches are unlocked. And so this is no simple story. One has to use his brains, evidently, as to what's what.[12]

As we see, such secret tales of the workmen clearly incarnated the "expectations and longings of the people," the dreams of that time when the riches of the earth would become the property of the toiling masses.

In the majority of the songs of the factory and the mill, written down at the end of the eighteenth and in the first third of the nineteenth century, there is definitely felt a still closer connection of the factory worker with the countryside. The workman of that time, in the vast mass, as we have seen from a brief survey of the social classes of which the factory population was made up, was a peasant, who had not lost, in his daily life, the attitudes and the psychology of his blood kinship with the rural economy and with the whole country life. It must also be noted that the factory itself, at that period, still was in the nature of a manufactory, where the work was mainly produced by hand, and not by machines. And this circumstance also toned down the difference between the workman and the peasant, who was accustomed to various domestic handicrafts and home industries.

In the factory-manufactory, the serf, the possessional worker, and even the hired workman, still felt himself in many ways to be a peasant. Between him and the owner of the enterprise, patriarchal personal relationships might exist, in which the worker had as yet a very slight consciousness of class exploitation and of its social-economic nature. Accordingly, it was natural that a song could be composed (perhaps as late as the end of the eighteenth century), such as the one recorded in 1833 by P. V. Kireyevsky, in the village of

12 *Ibid.*, p. 195.

Voronky, in the Zvenigorodsky district of the province of Moscow, in which it is said that the bitter complaint of the factory workers as to the difficult conditions of their work had been met on the part of the master with the magnanimous promise to improve these conditions, with regard to the workmen's quarters, new weaving looms, and an increase in wages.

It is difficult, from the context of the song, to judge whether we have an account of some definite instance that actually took place, in which the master satisfied the complaints of the workers, or whether the song has only utilized the device of narration (as to the master's promise to fulfill the requests of the workers) in order to express their ardent, even if primitive, dream of an improvement in their situation. We think that the latter assumption is the more correct, since the whole structure of the song (the introduction, the emotional description of the type of the workmen, the great number of diminutives and caressing words, and the whole minor key of the song) is not attuned to a joyful mood. The poetics of the song, furthermore, are wholly confined to the customary framework of the traditional long songs of the peasants, with their themes of the hard life of the soldier, of a foreign country, of the bitterness of fate. The introduction of the song contains the traditional images of village poetry, with the emotionally emphasized symbol of sorrow—the broken-down little bushes:

> You, my woods, little woods, my dark woods,
> You, my bushes, little bushes, little osier bushes,
> Why is it, little bushes, that you are all broken down
>   already?
> The fine young fellows, the factory workers, have their
>   eyes all red with weeping.
> When there came to meet them, the factory workers, the
>   chief owners,
> The chief owners of Grach Skarnaukhov.[13]

[13] Here the reference is to the owners of the well known manufactory near Moscow, Grachev and Karnaukhov. The Grachevy and Karnaukhovy were merchants who had had their origin among the peasant serfs. See A. Stepanov, *The Peasant Manufacturers, the Grachevy*; on the characteristics of the serf capitalists of the latter half of the 18th and the beginning of the 19th century, see *Annals of the Historico-Social Division of the State Museum of Russia*, Leningrad, 1928.

Do not weep now, fine young fellows, fine young factory
    workers.
I will build for you, my children, two bright new rooms,
Automatic looms, heavy threads for the warp,
And I will give to you, children, a fine high price,
A fine high price, napkins at a ruble apiece.[14]

It is difficult to say with absolute certainty what class of workers
the composers referred to here. It was most likely composed by possessional peasants, since it speaks of the fine young lads of the merchant's factory. The presence of the motif of peasant folklore, in
this song, is completely understandable.

Another song, a variant of which was also written down at Voronky
by P. V. Kireyevsky (*Songs*, new series, Petrograd, No. 1584), is
known also from a recording which dates from the end of the eighteenth century. It was published in the *New Russian Songbook* in
1791, Vol. III (see the reprinting in A. I. Sobolevsky, *Great-Russian
Popular Songs*, Vol. VI, No. 553). We give this variant of the
eighteenth century:

Near, near to the little town,
Near to the little green garden,
Near to the green garden,
Near to the city of Yaroslavl,
Not far from the river,
From the suburb that has been begun
On the beautiful and handsome,
On the high hill,
There stood a great factory.
In that factory are the workers—
Dashing, fine young fellows,
Dashing and young,
Unmarried, bachelors.
The lads gathered together
From that factory to go walking
To the beautiful and handsome,
To the high hill;
They sat down by the edge of it,
Near the green garden,

14 P. V. Kireyevsky, *Songs*, No. 1578.

Near the green garden,
Near the city of Yaroslavl.
They sat down, they sang songs,
They ordered the nightingales to whistle:
"Little nightingales, whistle!
We have come to you to have a good time!"
The little nightingales whistled,
And cheered up all the fine young fellows.
How it was with us, lads,
In the city of Yaroslavl,
In the suburb of Tolchkova,
In the house of the soldier's widow
There were fine girls.
There was Vasilushka the son,
A master hand at weaving carpets;
He weaves the carpets, he weaves designs in them,
And he collects the recruits:
He is clever at writing letters,
Clever at reading writing.
He appears before the company,
He himself plays on the violin.
They began to play on the violin
To win the heart of the beautiful maiden,
For her who was schooled and well mannered,
For Pashenka the widow's daughter.
Her mother spoke to Pasha,
And her brother tried to persuade her:
"Enough, Pashenka, stop it,
Don't go out with the young fellows!
The boys will lead you astray,
Into an evil reputation!"
"Even though I gain an evil reputation,
Yet I will go out with them all!"

This song was obviously created among a stratum of people who were connected, not with the countryside, but with the city; specifically, among the urban lower middle class, from whom, as we have already said, there came the domestic craftsmen and the "master workmen" of the factories. The connection of the latter with the factory-manufactory was of various kinds: some were skilled workers, others had a less subordinate existence, ranging all the way up to the position of the independent owner of a small establishment.

In the above song, according to our view, we have a description of the factory worker, Vasilushka, who is one of the petty bourgeoisie, who knows both "how to weave carpets" and "how to write letters" and "read documents," to entertain company, "to play the violin," and thereby to give pleasure to his sister, the "schooled and well mannered" Pashenka. The song emphasizes the outward culture of Vasilushka, since it makes him, along with his mother, caution his sister against being led astray by the young fellows at the factory. Here there is delineated the figure of the master workman at the factory, contrasted to the other "young fellows at the factory" or "factory boys," as that of a worker who is at once more skillful and more cultured. In this light it becomes comprehensible why the factory people come to visit the master workman, and why he associates with them, though he also warns his sister with reference to their conduct. In its ideology and poetics this song is more closely connected, not with the country, but with the city artisan class.

The song is known in two old variants (one of the eighteenth century [1791] and one dating from the 1830's). In the first variant there are definite indications of the place where the song was composed: there is mention made of Yaroslavl and of its suburb Tolchkova. In the variant given by Kireyevsky, these concrete references to time have already been lost. The name Vasilushka remains, but the name of his sister has been changed. The relationships, on the whole, remain substantially as they were before. Perhaps, in the latest variant, there is a heightening of the expression of sympathy for the young fellows in the factory. This ending of the song, affirming the attractiveness of the company of the factory lads, made this song popular in the factory repertory. Not without reason did it survive at least four decades.[15]

In another song, written down by Kireyevsky at Voronky (No. 1573), there is given a summary picture of the work and the recreation at the factory. There we see both the young fellows of the

---

[15] P. Sobolev, "The Figure of the Factory Worker in the Song Folklore of the Nineteenth Century," *Literature and Marxism,"* Bk. 2, 1930.

factory, and the master workmen, with the apprentices, who are engaged both in teaching the young lads and in fine work. It is curious that this song, too, is connected with Yaroslavl, where, it may be supposed, it had its origin:

> In the city, in the town,
> In the town of Yaroslavl,
> In Market Row,
> There the main offices are situated,
> The hand looms are set up
> In three sections—after the German fashion;
> Here stand young fellows, Turks.[16]
> They stand by the table,
> The masterworkmen teach them to write.
> The apprentices and the master workmen
> Have made the fine clothing,
> They have woven the towels,
> The towels all of the same size,
> The little shuttles move in time with the reed of the loom,
> Like little chains of gold.
> The lads from the factory
> Began to play their game,
> For silver
> They consoled, they cajoled
> The beautiful girl into the mansion.[17]

In the songs which were composed among the working people who had not lost their connections with the countryside, the figure of the "young fellow at the factory," of the "factory boys," who are gay, full of fun, generous in their merrymaking, their carousing, and their dandyism, is extremely idealized. The city more and more is becoming the magnet which draws them; it is more and more taking possession of the thoughts and dreams of the young man who is half workman and half peasant.

Such an idealization, of course, was especially characteristic of the workmen who were hired from among the free peasants or those who paid quitrents. Kireyevsky wrote down, at Voronky, a very interesting variant of a peasant song which had previously been very widely dif-

---

[16] It may be that the Turks were prisoners of war.
[17] Kireyevsky, *Songs*, New Series, II, Pt. 1, No. 1573.

fused, "Vanya's Mother Sent Him to Reap in the Field of Summer Corn." A new ending has been added to the song, clearly depicting the very powerful attraction which drew the young fellow from the countryside to the city. We give, in its entirety, the variant taken down by Kireyevsky:

> Vanya promised to live in the country,
> And to perform his work
> With the country peasants.
> But the country labor
> Is nothing but boredom and anxiety:
> They get little sleep at night,
> They hurry, one after another,
> In order to get the crops in from the field quicker,
> So that the storm cloud may not descend upon them,
> So that the heavy rain may not come.
> Vanya's mother sends him
> To reap in the field of summer corn.
> "Go, my dear Vanya, and reap."
> Vanya went out on the little porch,
> He placed his scythe upon his shoulder,
> In no joyful mood he went forth.
> Vanushka reaped the whole day through,
> But he reaped only a single sheaf,
> He stood around with the young mistress.
> Was it perhaps from boredom with her
> That Vanya cut his hand—
> The blood flowed in a stream.
> The young mistress came running up,
> With her handkerchief she bound his hand
> So that the blood might not flow.
> His father and his mother chide him,
> All the workers are angry
> That Vanya reaps so lazily.
> His father and his mother looked at him
> And waved their arms,
> They shout: "Vanya, go home,
> Go home, Vanushka,
> Go home, dear boy, and go to sleep."
> Vanya ran, he hurried,
> He sat down behind the oaken table,
> He began to sharpen his pen,

Vanya sharpened the pen very fine,
He began to write a letter.
Vanushka writes to the kingdom of Moscow,
To the government at Petersburg,
He cursed the countryside:
"The village of Voronkovskaya
Is an accursed settlement.
I may call it a prison."
Vanya was born at Voronky,
But he was christened at Archangel.
"Now I live in Moscow,
In Moscow I live, and have my abode;
I am not indifferent to the beautiful girls,
And I go to the tavern with them." [18]

The manufacturing town was attractive to the rural youth because of the greater freedom of its life, outside the bounds of the patriarchal, family conditions of village life, together with the wages paid in cash, and the opportunity of passing one's time gaily in the company of friends. Here is a delineation, in a song dating from the 1830's, of the factory workers, and what it is that makes their life attractive and enviable:

In the little wood, in the little wood, a little river ran through
     the sands,
To our mother Moscow, to the factory courtyard.
As for the factory workers—they are clever people,
Clever people, they have powdered faces;
They weave carpets and napkins in various designs.
They have woven and rewoven, they have remade them into
     caftans.
The caftans aren't worth much to us, but there might be
     money in the pocket;
The silver rubles in the purses don't give us any chance
     to sleep at night:
At midnight the money rattles, it calls us to go to the
     public house.
Young tapster, unlock the new public house,
Let in the girls and fellows—fill up the goblet fuller,
Do not spare our money.[19]

18 *Ibid.*, No. 1570.   19 *Ibid.*, No. 1489.

As we have seen, the barge hauler in certain of the Volga provinces was the object of a dual attitude toward himself on the part of the rural young people: he attracted them by the relative freedom of his life (in comparison with that of the countryside under serfdom), by his experience, and his opportunity to enjoy himself on the money he had earned. But at the same time, everyone realized the instability of the barge hauler's fortune, since in the end he would generally return home without a farthing in his pocket. When he returned to the countryside, the barge hauler lamented unceasingly for his life away from home. It was hard to hold him in the country. The same thing was true also with the factory workers.

In this respect the following song is very characteristic:

> I was such a handsome fellow,
> I myself lived at the factories,
> I used to print various kinds of calico.
> I received no small amount of money—
> As much as eight hundred rubles a year;
> And out of this I was short
> Sixty rubles for taxes.
> I had a reckoning with my master,
> And I didn't get anything out of it.
> I went out of the office,
> I wiped the tears away with my fist.
> When I had wiped away the bitter tears
> I started off on a long journey.
> As I traveled the whole long way,
> I kept lamenting over the account:
> Where had I put the money?
> Where were the ten silver kopeks, where was the ruble,
> What had become of the two rubles and fifty kopeks?
> But when I got home,
> All ragged and gaunt,
> Like a common crook . . .
> "Now you live in the country,
> Have a sup of the plain cabbage soup,
> And wear torn bast shoes!" [20]

Just as the country girls had quickly come to recognize the undesirability of marriage with a barge hauler, "who has one three-

[20] Sobolevsky, *op. cit.*, VI, No. 550.

kopek piece in his wallet, and a cudgel of elmwood across his shoulders," so they came to regard as unenviable the fate of the peasant girl who has fallen in love, to her sorrow, with a dashing young fellow from the factory:

If I fall in love, girl that I am, with such a fine young fellow,
With such a dashing, swaggering factory worker,
With a swaggering factory worker, curly-haired Vanusha,
Curly-haired Vanusha, with the white skin and the rosy cheeks.
You, my swaggering factory worker, what have you done to me?
What have you done to me, to my life?
The thief has tortured me, he has tormented me, he has come
    to know strange places,
In a distant foreign region he has fallen in love with another,
And me, the sorrowful one, the unfortunate one, he has forgotten
    forever.
He left me, he, the thief, the bandit, to sit forever among the
    maidens,
Forever among the maidens to sit, suffering a bad reputation.
No one will take me for his wife, poor me, unfortunate me:
Neither an old man, nor a young man, nor a man of my own age
    who is a terrible drunkard.[21]

The decline of the feudal countryside and the development of capitalistic relationships pushed the peasants into the city, to the factory. At times the factory itself lured the peasant to it, tempting him with wages paid in money, more freedom than he had in the country, and good company. The dark and difficult aspects of factory life, furthermore, were frequently forgotten in the countryside. At the factory itself, however, motifs were composed, as we have already seen in the example of the song about the weavers of Grach Skarnaukhov, which were far from being always joyful. With the development of the mechanization of production, with the intensification of industrial capitalism and all its inherent forms of exploitation, along with the growth of the workmen's critical attitude toward the life that surrounded them; with the growth of the proletarian self-consciousness, and of protests against exploitation, there is an intensification of the notes of criticism and protest in the folklore of the

[21] Kireyevsky, *op. cit.*, No. 1577.

factory. In a song which was taken down in 1877, in the province of Kazan, there is already heard, not a complaint of one's own bitter lot, but a malicious irony and class hatred for the exploiter, the owner of the enterprise:

> Thank God, our master:
> Things are being put right;
> Out of the bast sack, in the bast mat,*
> He will fly up the chimney with the smoke!
> This is why he will fly up!
> In the morning he wakes us early.
> He doesn't give us tea to drink,
> He cooks poor the cabbage soup for us:
> Without cabbage, without any meal—
> Just some lukewarm water!
> We took a little sip of the water,
> But we didn't get a scrap of beef!
> We worked through all the holidays—
> Our master has no money.
> If we shall ask him for money—
> He will always squint up his eyes.
> Now the devil take you, master,
> With this work of yours,
> With this work of yours,
> With your wicked steward,
> With your wicked steward,
> With your precious apprentice! [22]

In the second half of the nineteenth century, more songs are constantly appearing with a clearly and definitely expressed condemnation of the ruling order in the factories. Thus, in a certain song, written down in the Moscow district in 1888, it says:

> The beautiful summer is passing,
> The frosty winter is at hand,
> The frosty winter is at hand,
> The factory workers' hearts are sinking.
> The worker rises soon after midnight,
> He hastens to his work.
> He fell asleep over the machine,

---

* Out of the frying pan into the fire.—Ed.
[22] Sobolevsky, *op. cit.,* Vol. VI, No. 562.

And it tore off his right arm.
They sent him to his father and mother.
His father and mother come out,
Their tears flow in three streams.
And among the people they are talking,
They are all blaming the factory owner:
Ah, you shameful mill,
You have ruined all the people.
You have ruined them, you have spoiled them—
No one will marry among them,
Neither a gentleman, nor a merchant,
Nor a factory worker.
Only that one will marry among them
Who feeds the swine in the forest.[23]

Analogous motifs are encountered also in the popular rhymes of the factory and the mill at the end of the nineteenth and beginning of the twentieth century. Such, for example, are the chastushkas which were written down by Beloretsky at the factories in the Urals, and the following, which even textually closely approximate the factory song which we have just given: [24]

This accursèd mill of ours
Has ruined all the people:
Some have lost a finger, some have lost two,
Some the arm as far up as the elbow.

No less characteristic, also, is another chastushka of the Urals:

I have smashed in my chest twice
At the open hearth furnaces,
I am blinded in both eyes—
It almost took the head off my shoulders.

The chastushkas of the factory workers were full of pessimism:

It is hard, brothers, fellow workers,
It is hard to live in the world.
So then surely, brothers,
Let us drown our sorrow in drink.

[23] *Russian Reports*, No. 21, 1888; reprinted in Sobolevsky, *ibid.*, No. 563.
[24] G. Beloretsky, "Poetry of the Mill," *The Russian Treasure*, No. 11, 1902, p. 41.

Nor did the workman, worn out with his heavy and unendurable toil, expect anything good for his son, either:

> When I look upon my son:
> My heart is torn,
> The same bitter, evil fate
> Will be passed on to him.

And the workman is ready to envy the peasant, who seems to him a free man:

> In the summer, at his work in the field,
> He is his own master.
> In the winter he sleeps like a log without waking,
> Like a great lord.

As we already know from the chapter which was devoted to the peasant lyric, the theme "For whom is life easier?" was one that had been widely diffused. To the peasant plowmen it seemed that life was much easier for the house servants than for them. But the house servants, in their own song, reveal just how easy and cheerful their life is. The same song was recast, in the Urals, in the form of a controversy between the peasants and the miners at the foundry:

> Peasants, you peasants,
> In a word—you are fools!
> You have not spent your time in the mines,
> You have not seen need and woe.
> You have not spent your time in the mines,
> You have not seen need and woe.
> Just come down into the mines with us,
> And then you will find out all about it.
> Come down into the mines with us,
> And you will find out all about it.
> Then you will find out all about it—
> About the miner's way of life.
> The miner does not plow the land,
> He does not take the scythe into his hand,
> He does not take the scythe into his hand,
> He does not put his money into the treasury.
> He does not take the scythe into his hand,
> He does not put his money into the treasury.

> The miner knows cold, the miner knows hunger,
> He has neither bread nor water.
> The miner knows cold, the miner knows hunger,
> He has neither bread nor water.
> He has neither bread nor water.
> He has no liberty whatsoever.[25]

But it would be incorrect to think that the song of the factory and the mill, at the end of the last century and the beginning of our own, was limited exclusively to pessimistic strains. Among the chastushkas written down by Beloretsky at the mills of the Urals, there are some in which there prevails the feeling of conscious class hatred, both for the industrial exploiters and for their henchmen.

Beloretsky presents a series of bitter local satires, which sharply delineated the attitudes of the workmen and their relationships to the factory administration:

> The splendid Beloretsky mill,
> Stands on the bank of the White River.
> Our chief manager
> Keeps looking up with one eye.
> The damp earth shook,
> The rivers flowed back into the mountain:
> The devils threw off from the horse
> The madam who weighs a hundred poods.
> The engineer (Pokotilo)
> Had his mug burned with steam,
> We are sorry, brother workers,
> That he was not burned all over.[26]

Characteristic also is the song "As in the Evening Time," taken down by Y. A. Samarin in the summer of 1931 from a workman in the Alapayevsky mill, Efrem Grigoryevich Zyablin, who was forty-one years of age. This song was sung by the workmen in the late nineties of the last century.

> As in the evening time
> By the factory gates

[25] Biryukov, *Prerevolutionary Folklore of the Urals*, p. 281.
[26] G. Beloretsky, "Poetry of the Mill," *The Russian Treasure*, No. 11, 1902. p. 43.

All the people gathered together,
All the people gathered together,
As at a splendid choral dance.
Ah, no, and no, ah, but no, indeed!
All the people gathered together.
They see our foreman coming,
And he brings the master with him.
Ah, but yes, ah, but yes, indeed!
And he brought the master with him.
The master made a speech as follows,
Ah, he spoke, he spoke, he spoke, indeed!
"Now disperse, you men,
To your quarters, to your houses,
For I will not give you a ruble!
Ah, shall I give, I will not give!
But if you do not go to your houses,
To your quarters, to your corners,
Then I will give an order,
Ah, shall I give, yes, I will give!
And they'll seize you by the necks!" [27]

The song obviously speaks of strikes, of collective protests, of an organized struggle for an increase in wages. Unfortunately, because of the absence of variants, it is impossible to judge what was the outcome of the episode depicted by the song.

At the end of the nineteenth and beginning of the twentieth centuries, more and more there arises the fashion of composing new songs of the factory and the mill upon the motifs of popular songs and ballads. Such, for example, is the new version of "The Little Box," a song created by the "gold seekers" of the Urals, in the goldfields, and depicting the difficult life of the gold seekers:

The little box is full to overflowing
With gold dust,
And when you remember your sweetheart,
Then longing gnaws at your soul.
At night you will go out into the distant mountain,
You will work all day long,

[27] Taken down by Y. A. Samarin from an old man, a gold seeker in the village of Sinyachikh, near the city of Alapayevsk, in 1931, *The Literary Critic*, No. 10, 1935. p. 161.

And you will come home sorrowful,
And hungry, like a shadow.
Although my little box is full,
And surely the seal is strong,
Still you cannot get hold of gold dust
For your sweetheart.
As soon as you come from your work,
In a flash you hurry to the lessee,
At once you give him the little box,
And you hurry home alone.
Without a kopek, you live in misery,
Nor do you make any profit at all,
But with your work as a gold seeker
You have enriched the district chief.
For I have put forth no small strength,
When I was getting the gold dust.
And then, all this money
Our master has squandered on drink.
Although my little box is full,
Yet I don't get any good of it, not even a half-kopek,
My sweetheart will have to go forever
Without a patterned kerchief.
I myself shall be a gold seeker forever,
I shall never have enough to buy some wine;
My sweetheart will have to caress
My sorrowful face forever.[28]

I must refer to one more revision of a song—"At the Nizhnetagilsk Mill."

At the Nizhnetagilsk mill,
Above the old big mine,
A fateful misfortune befell
That poor young fellow.
In those years, the master's paws,
Like claws, held us all,
And Vazhgin the artel member seized everything,
And without even counting it a sin
He took both the money and the bread,
And the granulated sugar.
With the money that we had bought with our blood

[28] *Ibid.*, p. 160.

He built himself a house.
He built himself a mansion
Out of fine large bricks,
Every one of us was poor
And worked for him through many nights.
Vazhgin, at the command of Pavlukha,
Came into the house of each one of us,
And drove each one to work
With a big horsewhip
And all of us, till the time came,
Had to be in subjugation to him.
And we all went to work,
The whole year through, from one sunrise to another.
But the time came, and there appeared
Among us that daring poor fellow,
He never prayed to God,
And he addressed us all as follows:
"Comrades, my brothers,
You have had enough of breaking your backs
So that the masters, the devils,
Can take their ease upon your toil.
That terrible time is past. . . .
Pavlukha will not always be the manager.
We ourselves will obtain justice,
We will not work for the noblemen."
But as he was speaking, Pavlukha,
And with him Vazhgin the drinker of blood,
Sent half a hundred Cossacks,
And they had received only one command:
To shoot, without sparing ammunition,
If they had to move against us.
They issued the order.
The sergeant gave the command.
But they took the poor young lad
And shackled him in fetters.
And, not allowing him to take leave of his family,
They conducted him along by the prison wall.
From the mill, by halting stages,
They drove him away beyond Lake Baikal,
And the poor man died there, without anyone knowing,
Among those cheerless crags.

And at home there remained his father
And his old, feeble mother.
And let us all together, men,
Remember him and wish him peace! [29]

In that case the song "Through the Wild Steppes Beyond Lake Baikal" served as a model. The author of the revised version, according to information collected by Y. A. Samarin, was a certain political exile. He composed this revision in 1907, describing in it an actual event of the life at the Nizhnetagilsk mill. The Pavlukha and Vazhgin who are mentioned in the song are real persons: Vazhgin was a member of the artel, and Pavlukha is the nickname of the owner of the mill, P. P. Demidov-San Donato (who died in 1908). The song actually reflects an episode in the conscious class conflict of the workmen, and delineates the figure of the party organizer of the workers' movement. The song obviously had a propagandist function and, it would seem, performed it very successfully, inasmuch as it has been preserved in the memory of the working people down to our own time.

Some of the songs of the workers in the factory and the mill are striking in their realistic exactness, in their precise reflection of the conditions of life in the mill, of the relationships of the workers with the owners and administrators, their unmasking of class politics as carried on by the factory owners. A song which is thus interesting, by virtue of its almost documentary character, is the "Song of the Famous Factory of Chesher" (printed for the first time in the *News of the Working Men and Women of the Fiber Industry*, No. 1, 1907):

When at Chesher's factory
The work was going on prosperously,
The good gentleman Chesher
Always was nice to the workers.
And ended the matter thus,
That he added five kopeks a day.
He does not talk much,
He turns directly to writing,

[29] Taken down by Y. A. Samarin in 1931.

And then he said, "By God,
I will take it all away, little by little."
For his own profit
He puts them all to work on sateen;
In order to make up all the losses
He started using rotten threads.
With clay alone he sizes
And then the siphons blow;
Though all the people fall ill,
Nevertheless Chesher has his profit!
But when your feet begin to ache,
Then they promise to fire you.
So that the warmth might not get out,
There were no ventilators.
From the workmen, Semyonov the idiot
Continually draws sweat;
Frankly he will say to the stoker
That he must put on more steam;
He himself goes straight to the office to sleep,
And does not want to know a thing.
And the only thing he knew, even before,
Was to sweep out the polishing room;
But for his odious suggestion
He received promotion.
Now it is perfectly evident
That everything is entrusted to him:
In the weaving, also the knitted fabric,
And the whole fourth floor.
And that there should not be flaws in the web,
For that, the blind Semyon is used:
He won't even pass the lining,
He examines everything, to the smallest fold,
But as for the flaws, and as for the dirt,
He had an arrangement with Volodya.
But Volodya is not clever—
He believes what Semyon has said.
As soon as they find out a subverter,
Then at once they will fire him,
But if it is a "Russian man," [30]
Him they will not drive away, no never.

[30] A "Russian man" was a member of the Black Hundred (ultramonarchists) of the "Union of the Russian People."

It is curious that by its realistic, documentary character this song of the twentieth century in many ways recalls those early songs of the workers in the eighteenth century, of which we spoke at the beginning of this chapter; there is the same attention to the details of the manufacture, to the workmen's surroundings in the business; there is the same concrete quality in the satire, with the indication of names and surnames of their nearest class enemies. But, in spite of all the likeness in the basic features of the workers' style, there should be noted also a great difference: the songs of the twentieth century speak of the boundless growth of the class and political consciousness of the proletariat.

Many of the songs and chastushkas which we have quoted or referred to attest to the fact that the soil was very well prepared for the inclusion in the proletarian song repertory of a number of songs, hymns, marches, and poems taken from the literature of the revolution. A very interesting example of the inclusion in the folklore of a poem by a proletarian poet has been pointed out by I. N. Kubikov.[31] In the illegal publication *The Workers' Thought* (No. 7, 1899), there was published a satirical poem, "The Story of the Priest and the Devil," lampooning a priest who terrified the workers with threats of hell, and then was himself transported by the devil to a metallurgical works which was not a whit less terrifying than hell in any particular. This poem, according to the testimony of the proletarian writer Jacob Shvedov,[32] was a popular song at the Moscow mill of Guzhon, being subjected, in its oral transmission, to changes and additions. Many of the revolutionary songs composed by the writers and musicians of the revolutionary intelligentsia became so much a part of the daily usage of the working masses that it is not possible to separate them from proletarian folklore. A valuable effort at a survey and analysis of the folklore revisions of literary songs among the workers has been made by the above-mentioned ar-

[31] I. N. Kubikov, "Proletarian Poetry in the Illegal and Trade Union Press" (period of the 1890's and the 1900's), *Literature and Marxism*, Bk. 3, 1931, pp. 83-85.
[32] *At the Steel Furnaces* (1928), p. 10.

ticle of A. L. Dymshits, "Workers' Folklore Before the October Revolution."

The following songs of revolutionary purpose entered into the permanent repertory of workers' songs: "The International" (E. Pottier, translated by A. Y. Kotz); "The Warsaw Song" (by Sventitsky, adapted by G. M. Krzhizhanovsky); "Boldly, Comrades, Keeping Step" ("The Battle March," by L. P. Radin); "The Boundless World Is Full of Tears," "The Red Standard," (by Akimev-Makhnov); "Funeral March," "You Fell as a Victim in the Deadly Combat" (Arkhangelsky), "The Blacksmiths" (F. Shkulev), "The Convicts" (A. Tolstoy), "Tortured in Heavy Bondage" (G. A. Machtet), "The Working Song" (Dubinushka, Bogdanov, and Olkhin), "The Crag on the Volga" (Navrotsky), "The Prisoner" (Pushkin), "The Cart Dashes Along the Dusty Road," "The Sun Rises and Sets" (Gorky), "Glorious Sea, Sacred Baikal" (Davydov), and others.[33]

The collection, recently begun by the folklorists of eastern Siberia, of folklore materials dealing with the shooting of the gold mineworkers on the Lena in 1912 is of great historical and social interest.[34] This event was vastly important in the history of the revolutionary movement of the working class (for the shooting on the Lena, according to the words of Lenin, was the event which gave rise to the transition from the revolutionary *mood* of the masses to the revolutionary *rising* of the masses); but its echoes in folklore were for a long time left unnoticed by the folklore collectors. But during recent years a systematic collection of this most valuable material has been begun. Now it is known that there was in existence a series of songs composed by those who participated in or witnessed these events, the workers of the Lena. The songs were of an accusatory character. They held up to fierce ridicule and imprecation those who took part in the shooting: the district police officer Galkin and the overseers of the mines, Belozerov and Savinov, and in particular the one who had charge of the shooting, the villainous cavalry captain Treschenko.

[33] The revolutionary songs have been reprinted in the collection *Fifty Russian Revolutionary Songs*, comp. and ed. by M. S. Druskin (State Museum Publishing House, 1938).
[34] A. V. Gurevich, *Folklore of Eastern Siberia* (Irkutsk, 1938).

A. G. Gurevich succeeded in taking down (in fragments) an extended song from the former woman worker in the Lena Gold Mines, F. K. Druzhinina.

She was no longer able to recollect the song in its entirety, but even those fragments which were preserved in her memory are clear evidence of the general mood that was expressed in this song:

> Treschenko—the executioner—
> Drank his fill of blood at the Putilov works *
> And returned to the Lena.
> On the Lena he drank his fill of blood
> And returned to Putilov.
> And they rewarded him for this:
> They poured out a barrel of gold for him.
> But as for the fact that he killed workers—that is no
>   misfortune:
> The earth will soon produce more of them.

The song comes to an end with a menacing curse upon Treschenko:

> Grandsons and great-grandsons
> Will curse the name of Treschenko,
> As for you, you villains,
> You cannot escape destruction,
> If not your children,
> Then your grandsons,
> If not your grandsons, then your great-grandsons,
> Will have to drink
> Of this bitter cup
> Which you have given to drink
> To the workers in the Lena gold fields.

A. V. Gurevich is altogether right in urging further search for songs and stories dealing with the Lena tragedy of 1912, not only by the folklorists of eastern Siberia, but also by the folklorists of the whole USSR, since the workers in the Lena mines were from various provinces of old Russia, and after the shooting, many of them went back to their homes in their native regions.

Besides the songs about the events of the Lena, there were many oral "tales" taken down, recollections which clearly reflect the mood

---

* In St. Petersburg.—ED.

of the workers, who had come to know what they might expect from the government of the tsar and from the factory owners, and who had become imbued with a feeling of class vengeance and a desire for revolutionary upheaval. The songs and tales of the workers on the Lena expressed the deep conviction that the evil doings of the tsar and the capitalists would not go unpunished, that the time for popular vengeance was coming. With historical accuracy and profundity Comrade Stalin said, in his address to the workers of the Lena in 1927, on the occasion of the fifteenth anniversary of the shootings on the Lena:

The shooting of the workers on the Lena, in April, fifteen years ago, was one of the bloodiest crimes of the Tsarist autocracy. The bold struggle of our comrades who fell in the distant Siberian forests, beneath the bullets of the Tsar's men, has not been forgotten by the victorious proletariat. Looking back on the path which they have traveled, the workers of the Union can say: "Not a single drop of the workers' blood of the people of Bodaibo* has been shed in vain, for the enemies of the proletariat have received their retribution, and the proletariat has already obtained its victory over them. Now, free from Tsarist and capitalist oppression on the banks of the Vitim, you have the opportunity to mine gold, not for the enrichment of the parasites, but for the increase of the power of *your own* workers' government, the first one in the world. Honor and glory to those who fell in the struggle for the victory of the working class!" [35]

BIBLIOGRAPHY

Sokolov, IU. M., "Pesni fabriki i derevni" (Songs of the Factory and the Countryside), *Vestnik prosveshcheniia* (Educational News), 1925, Bk. 4.

Sobolev, P. M., "O pesennom repertuare sovremennoi fabriki" (On the Song Repertory of the Contemporary Factory), *Uchenye zapiski Instituta literatury i iazyka RANION* (Scientific Annals of the Institute of Literature and Language of the Russian Academy of National Arts and Social Sciences), Vol. II, Moscow, 1928.

——, "Novye zadachi v izuchenii fol'klora" (New Problems in the

* Gold-mining center.—ED.
[35] J. V. Stalin, "To the Workers of the Lena," *The Lena Miner*, No. 57, 1927, reprinted in the collection, *The Mines of the Lena* (Moscow, 1937), p. 348.

Study of Folklore. *Revoliutsiia i kul'tura* (Revolution and Culture), Bk. 1, 1929.

——, "Obraz fabrichnogo rabochego v pesennom folklore XIX v." (The Figure of the Factory Worker in the Song Folklore of the Nineteenth Century), *Literatura i marksizm* (Literature and Marxism), Bk. 2, 1930.

Astakhova, A. M., and P. G. Shiriaeva, "Staraia rabochaia pesnia" (An Old Workers' Song), *Sov. etnogr.* (Soviet Ethnography), Nos. 1-2, 1934.

Shiriaeva, P. G., "Materialy po rabochemu fol'kloru" (Materials on the Workers' Folklore), *Sov. fol'klor* (Soviet Folklore), Nos. 2-3, 1935.

Dmitriev, S., "Rabochii fol'klor XVIII v." (Workers' Folklore of the Eighteenth Century), *Literaturnoe nasledstvo* (The Literary Heritage), Nos. 19-21, Moscow, 1935.

Lozanova, A. N., "Fabrichno-zavodskie pesni krepostnoi Rossii" (Songs of the Factory and the Mill in Russia in the Period of Serfdom), *Literaturnaia ucheba* (Literary Studies), Nos. 7, 8, 9, 1935.

Vladimirskii, G., "Rabochie pesni XIX veka" (Workers' Songs of the Nineteenth Century), *Lit. Donbass* (Literature of the Donetz Coal Field), No. 1, 1936.

Pesni i skazki na Onezhskom zavode (Songs and Tales in the Onega Mills) (Petrozavodsk, 1937).

Blinova, E., *Pesni ural'skogo revoliutsionnogo podpol'ia* (Songs of the Revolutionary Underground in the Urals) (Sverdlovsk, 1935).

——, *Skazy, pesni, chastushki* (Tales, Songs, Popular Rhymes) (Chelyabinsk, 1937).

Biriukov, V. P., *Dorevoliutsionnyi fol'klor na Urale* (Prerevolutionary Folklore of the Urals) (Sverdlovsk, 1937).

Druskin, M. S., *Revoliutsionnye pesni* (Revolutionary Songs of the Year 1905) (Leningrad, 1936).

Sobolev, P. M., and A. L. Muravev, *Pesni rabochikh* (Workers' Songs) (Smolensk, 1935).

Dymshits, A. L., "Heudachnyi opyt" (An Unsuccessful Effort), a review of Sobolev and Muravev's *Sovetskii fol'klor* (Soviet Folklore), Bks. II-III (Leningrad, 1935).

——, *Literatura i fol'klor* (Literature and Folklore), collection of articles (Moscow, 1938).

Gurevich, A. V., *Fol'klor Vostochnoi Sibiri* (Folklore of Eastern Siberia) (Irkutsk, 1938).

SOVIET FOLKLORE

SONGS AND CHASTUSHKAS

1. SONGS

The Great October Socialist Revolution brought about most vital changes in the creative art of oral poetry. But these changes did not come about all at once. Certain processes took form only gradually, in proportion to the increasing power of the Soviet regime and the development of Soviet folklore; and they did not always attract the attention of folklore collectors and researchers in time or as fully as they merited. However, even now it is possible to determine the outlines of the changes which have been going on in folklore.

These changes have to do not only with thematics, the distinctive peculiarities of which in Soviet folklore catch the eye at once, but also with artistic forms which may be discerned only by a more detailed analysis. Furthermore, these changes in the artistic forms took place gradually. This is true both of the changes in the folklore style as a whole (with reference to poetic diction, imagery, and compositional devices), and of the changes in the life of specific genres— the dying out of some, the transformation of others, the birth of yet others.

The main, basic genre, which distinguishes the oral creative art of the period following the October Revolution from that of the pre-revolutionary years, was and still is the martial *revolutionary song*. This song, after the October Revolution, took the first place in the oral poetic repertory of the factory and the mill, and then became, as we shall see further on, the fundamental form also in the folklore of the countryside.

[611]

Here, it is not important that the actual number of revolutionary texts at the beginning was still not so very great; nor is it important that the favorite and most widely disseminated songs in the first years of the revolution were songs which, for the most part, had been created in the periods of preparation for the revolution, such as "The International," "The Warsaw Song," "Boldly, Comrades, Keeping Step," "The Funeral March," and a number of other songs which we have enumerated in the preceding chapter dealing with the pre-revolutionary period in the workers' folklore. Characteristic changes were made, however. In the "Funeral March," in the line "The time will come, and the people will awaken," the future tense has been changed into the past, "The time has come, and the people have awakened"; and again in the "International," "This is our . . ." is in place of "This will be the last and decisive battle."

What is important is that these songs, which previously had been sung by comparatively small groups of the advanced sections of the working class, began to be performed with enthusiasm by millions of workers, and also of peasants; they occupied the most prominent place in the daily singing and musical life of the masses of the people. The folklore collectors often make an error when they characterize the folklore of this or that period, of this or that class, on the basis merely of a general calculation of the number of different texts, and fail to take into consideration, above all, the relative importance of this or that song in the everyday life of the masses, the force of the public demand for this or that text. For if we compare, for example, the songs which were sung by the young people in the factory and the mill before the revolution with those which comprise the current repertory among the gatherings of young people in our own time, then the distinction will be found to be very great.

A song which was composed a long time before the revolution, "The Blacksmiths," by F. Shkulev ("We are blacksmiths and our spirit is young; we forge the keys of happiness"), and which was frequently encountered in the song repertory of the workers even in the years preceding the October Revolution, became one of the most widely disseminated songs only in the years which immediately followed it.

But it was not only the old revolutionary song that was, as it were, resurrected to a new life. During the period of the revolution and the civil war, the repertory of revolutionary songs among the proletariat—first of all, of course, among the progressive young people —was greatly enlarged through the inclusion of new songs.

We may mention next "The Budyónny March" * by A. D'Actille; "The Execution of the Communards"; "Ever Higher and Higher" (words by Herman, music by Khait); the partisan song "Through the Valleys and the Hills," by Alymov; "There In the Distance, Beyond the River, Lights Began to Gleam"; "Boldly Will We Go to Fight for the Power of the Soviets"; "The Seaman" (with the refrain, "Over the seas, over the waves"); "The Young Guards," to the words of Bezymensky ("Forward to meet the dawn"); "The Budyónny Cavalry," "The First Cavalry" (in both, the words by Aseyev, music by Davidenko); "The Mounted Troops," by Surkov, "Song of an Encounter," by Shostakovich, "Green Meadow," by Gusev; "Kakhovka," by Svetlov, "Song of the Motherland," "March of the Merry Fellows," and many other songs by the recipients of honorary decorations, the composer Dunayevsky and the poet Lebedev-Kumach, and so forth.

Of the contemporary poets who have written songs that have been disseminated among the masses, N. Aseyev, E. Bagritsky, A. Bezymensky, M. Golodny, V. Gusev, A. Dzerzhinsky, A. Zharov, S. Kirsanov, V. Lebedev-Kumach, V. Mayakovsky, A. Prokofyev, M. Ruderman, M. Svetlov, I. Selvinsky, A. Surkov, N. Tikhonov, I. Utkin, I. Frenkel, and others should be mentioned. Of the composers who have worked on the creation of songs for the masses, and consequently have exerted an influence in one way or another upon the musical creativity of the people, we may mention: Alexandrov, Bely, Vasilyev-Buglay, Davidenko, I. Dzerzhinsky, Dunayevsky, Knipper, Koval, Kompaneits, Krasev, Novikov, Shebalin, Schechter, Chembergi, and others.

All the songs which have been enumerated are performed not only by the urban proletarian, but also among the broad masses of the

* Sometimes spelled "Budenny" in American periodicals.—ED.

peasantry on the collective farms. A great role in their popularization has been played by the Red Army.[1]

We have excellent grounds for considering these songs, the majority of which are the work of writers and composers, as an integral part of the contemporary folk creation, since they have become a permanent part of the repertory of the masses of workmen and peasants, and have been frequently subjected to changes in text and melody,[2] like any popular song, and exert a great influence upon the musical and literary

[1] The publishing of Soviet songbooks for the masses was, until recent years, poorly organized. At first they republished songbooks which either were repetitions of those in use before the revolution, or were basically patterned upon the same type. During the past few years the publishing houses have begun to devote more attention to this important work. In 1930 the State Publishing House issued a songbook, *The Red Standard*, with a foreword by A. V. Lunacharsky, which had a circulation of 200,000 copies; in 1935 there appeared a collection of songs compiled by A. Shafir, edited by N. N. Aseyev and Y. M. Sokolov. In this connection the regional publishing houses also have been active. Thus in that same year, 1935, the Sverdlovsk Regional State Publishing House issued, under the editorship of E. M. Blinova, *Songs of the Socialist Motherland*, and the Western Regional State Publishing House at Smolensk published, under the editorship of Prof. P. M. Sobolev, *Songs for the Masses*; at the same time, too, there appeared at Irkutsk a "Songbook" compiled by A. Gubanov. But these and other songbooks like them gave only the words of the songs. A considerable need existed, however, also for songbooks with musical notes. The State Museum Publishing House published only separate songs, or very small songbooks, like *Thirty Songs of the Pioneers*, and only in very recent times has it begun the publication of more extensive songbooks. A very successful effort at the publication of a songbook which is elegant in its format, and excellent in its choice of songs, has been made by the Gorky Publishing House, which issued in 1935 *Songs and Chastushkas*, selected by N. G. Biryukov. In the collection the melody is given for the text of each song. Vastly significant for the popularization of the songs of the masses (both literary and popular) have been two publications, with music, by the Military State Publishing House: *Russian Popular Songs*, Vols. I-III (Moscow, 1936–1937), and *Songs of the Red Army* (Moscow, 1936). A detailed bibliographical list of the songbooks for the masses which have been published since the October Revolution, has been compiled and prepared for publication by V. M. Sidelnikov.

[2] On these changes, see the articles by A. A. Surkov, "Singers, Front and Center!" *The Standard*, No. 8, 1934; and I. N. Rozanov: "From Book to Folklore: The Kind of Verses That Become Popular Songs," *The Literary Critic*, No. 4, 1935; "Songs of the Soviet Poets," *The Literary Critic*, No. 12, 1937; "Old Soldier Songs and Our Songs of the Red Army," *Literary Studies*, No. 2, 1938; "A Book of Songs by Lebedev-Kumach," *The New World*, No. 5, 1938; "Elijah Frenkel's 'The Seamen,'" *The New World*, No. 7, 1938; "Contemporary Russian Poetry and Song Folklore," *Literary Studies*, No. 6, 1938.

poetic creations of the laboring people. It is true that in the majority of cases the process of change and variation in these revolutionary songs goes on at a much slower rate than in any other kind of songs, whether old or new; but this is to be explained by the fact that the texts of the revolutionary songs were established by numerous printings running into millions of copies, and through frequent performances by organized choruses at demonstrations, in clubs, and at meetings. In speaking of the creativeness of the Soviet people, however, one cannot help taking account of the very great role played by the songs mentioned, and others like them, in the life of the working people after the October Revolution.

The song creation of the masses of workmen and peasants at first developed in an altogether spontaneous way. The revolutionary fighting ardor at the time of the October Revolution, the revolutionary enthusiasm, the heroic moods at the time of the civil war sought expression for themselves. The chief means of such expression were, as we have just now said, the popular, widely diffused revolutionary hymns, marches, and songs of the proletariat, both those which had been composed before the October Revolution, and also certain productions of Soviet poets and composers; but the masses were not satisfied with this. Naturally, the demand arose for the creation of local songs connected with the concrete events on the fighting fronts and in the various parts of the structure of Soviet culture, of the new way of life. Local songs began to appear. Some of them endured for quite a long while, and at times attained a rather broad diffusion, but very many of them remained within the narrow limits of the milieu which had produced them, and, reflecting the concrete events of the local region, thus did not extend beyond its boundaries. Their historical significance is very great, but, unfortunately, at the time they were not written down in as large numbers as they should have been, and it must be assumed that many of them have disappeared forever.

In the majority of cases the new songs are found to be a revision of these or other popular songs of the former, prerevolutionary time. The new content of the texts was usually connected with the accustomed musical motifs. In this respect, many of the partisan songs are very characteristic.[3]

Certain of these appear to be adaptations of old soldier songs. Such, for example, is the song of the northern partisans, "The Clouds Are Dark, the Clouds Are Menacing." [4] Not only was it sung to the tune of an old soldier song, but in its text, too, it appears to be a paraphrase of it. In place of the words of the old song:

> It is hard, it is hard for us, fellows,
> Before Warsaw, to take the town;
> And it is still harder than that
> When we have to run up under cannon fire
> When we ran [with our rifles] up under the cannon,
> We all shouted out, "Hurrah!"

the partisan song was sung this way:

> It is hard, it is hard for us, fellows,
> To make war with the Whites,
> But it is still harder than that
> For us to run up under the cannon.
> We ran up under the cannon guns,
> We all shouted out, "Hurrah!"
> The accursed Whites
> Ran away, each one wherever he could.

The song of the Siberian partisans about the struggle with Kolchak's party, "Kolchak, the Contemptible Tsar of Siberia," [5] was sung to the

[3] For the texts of the partisan songs, see the collection *Partisans* (Chita, 1929); A. P. Georgyevsky, "Folklore of the Coastal Region," *Russians in the Far East* (Vladivostok, 1929), Sec. IV; the collection of V. Senkevich, *Songs of the Siberian Partisans*, with foreword by A. A. Surkov (Moscow, State Museum Publishing House, 1935); the articles of S. F. Baranov, "Songs of the Partisans of Eastern Siberia," *Annals of the Society for the Study of the Eastern Siberian Region*, Vol. I (LVI), Irkutsk, 1936; and "On the Songs of the Partisans of the Trans-Baikal Region," *Annals of the Irkutsk State Scientific Museum*, Vol. II (LVII), Irkutsk, 1937; A. M. Astakhova, "Folklore of the Civil War," *Soviet Folklore*, No. 1, Leningrad, 1934; A. N. Lozanova, "Songs of the Civil War Among the Collective Farms of the Northern Caucasus," *ibid*. Many of the partisan songs have been reprinted in the book by V. M. Sidelnikov, *Red Army Folklore*, Y. M. Sokolov (Moscow, 1938).

[4] This was originally printed in the collection *Soviet Folklore*, No. 1, p. 24, and reprinted in Sidelnikov, *Red Army Folklore*, p. 133.

[5] Sidelnikov, *op. cit.*, p. 128.

tune of a song which had been popular in the period before the revolution, "The Fire of Moscow Raged and Burned." The songs of the Far Eastern partisans, "The Cold Winds Are Blowing," "Hover Not, Sea Gulls, Above the Sea," [6] are sung to the tune of a prerevolutionary song which described the destruction of the cruiser *Varangian* in the Russo-Japanese War, "The Cold Waves Are Breaking." The song "Hover Not, Sea Gulls, Above the Sea" was written down by the composer A. G. Novikov, also in the northern Caucasus, and its text was adapted to the events of the local partisan war.

In spite of the borrowing of musical tunes, and at times the imitativeness of literary and rhythmic forms, the partisan songs could not help but have a great historical significance. They appear as striking testimonies to the stirring experiences of the proletariat and the revolutionary peasantry during the period of the civil war and the conflict with the interventionists. The songs speak also of the unexampled heroism of the partisans; of the exceptionally difficult conditions of the conflict with the splendidly armed adversaries; of the furious curse upon those who betrayed and were traitors to the cause of the working class, and of the passionate devotion of the heroic warriors to the Soviet motherland. While waging their intense struggle with the enemy, the partisans knew that the revolutionary mother country would highly value their exploits.

> Soon the whole world shall come to know
> Of the doings of the partisan detachments.
> Kite, bear to the Soviet motherland
> Our partisan greeting!

So runs the concluding couplet in the Far Eastern variant of the song "Hover Not, Sea Gulls, Above the Sea." [7]

The civil war produced a great many of the most poignant psychological clashes. The idea of the class conflict was sometimes embodied in song, for greater expressiveness, in the figure of a conflict between two brothers, one being on the side of the proletariat, the other on

[6] See A. P. Georgyevsky, *Russians in the Far East*, No. IV (Vladivostok, 1929), reprinted in the collection *Red Army Folklore*, p. 124.
[7] See A. Novikov, "An Expedition in Search of Songs of the Civil War," *Soviet Music*, No. 2, 1936, p. 21.

the side of the Whites, the bourgeoisie. In this connection, in the new songs, a device is employed which was widely utilized in the old folklore when it was necessary to contrast the rich man and the poor man, the kulak (rich peasant) and the farm laborer. (Compare, in the chapter on tales, the tales of the two brothers, of destiny, of fate. See page 484.) Such is the subject of a song which was written down in the North:

> In a settlement, in a little peasant hut,
> Two brothers lived peacefully with their father.[8]

Certain of the partisan songs, through the use of a very simple melody, attain an extreme expressiveness, reflecting deep faith in the justice of the revolutionary exploit and in the victory over the class enemy. Such, for example, is the partisan campaign song which was written down in the northern Caucasus:

> Through the Sedinsky forests and valleys
> Passed the partisan detachment.
> They marched, they fought for freedom,
> The working people came to help them.
> The bourgeoisie began to wish to drink their fill
> Of the blood of the proletarian workers,
> The bourgeoisie will not succeed in drinking their fill
> Of the blood of the proletarian working class;
> But the bourgeoisie will have to perish
> At the mighty hand of the working class.[9]

Of interest is the Ural variant of the same song:

> Through the mountains and valleys of the Urals
> Passed the partisan detachment.
> They marched, they fought for freedom;
> The working people came to help them.
> The bourgeoisie began to wish to drink their fill
> Of the blood of the proletarian working class.
> The bourgeoisie surely will not succeed

[8] First printed in the collection *Soviet Folklore* No. I, p. 27; reprinted in *Red Army Folklore*, p. 94. A variant of this song is given in the article by Y. M. Sokolov, "Songs and Tales of the Collective Farm Village," *The Collective Farmer*, No. 2, 1935.

[9] See A. Novikov, *op. cit.*

In feasting in the sumptuous palaces,
But they will certainly be compelled
To pass the winter in damp cellars.
And against the Whites, the fine rifle of the Reds
Will fire without ever missing.

The variants of this song, as of others, show how great was the demand of the masses for a creative expression of their revolutionary feelings. A song had only to spring up somewhere along the front, and it was passed on to other sectors of the civil war and subjected to various adaptations: to additions or abridgments, interpolations, substitutions, while the basic idea of the song, and the mood expressed by it, remained unchanged.

According to the correct observation of the poet A. A. Surkov,[10]

like any other artistic production, the partisan song conveys the striking impressions of an era, and in the character of its musical technique, and in the form of its text, it reveals the peculiarities of the social setting which gave birth to it. That is why an attentive study of the material of the partisan songs makes it possible, by secondary indications of literary and musical derivation, to determine the social personality of the nameless authors of these songs.

Thus, in the repertory of the Red partisans, there is perceptible a marked dependence upon the soldier songs of the prerevolutionary era. This is perfectly understandable, since the partisan detachments were formed mostly of peasants who had already taken part in the World War. A partisan song which was written down in Siberia:

But the cannon, the cannon were thundering,
Our machine-gun was crackling,
And the Whites, the Whites were advancing.
Comrades, forward!
The Siberian partisan
Is not afraid of the Japanese cannon.
For the power of the Soviets we will fight,
The power of the workers and peasants.[11]

[10] See the foreword by A. Surkov to the collection *Songs of the Siberian Partisans*, by V. Senkevich (Moscow, 1935), p. iv, State Music Publishing House.
[11] *Ibid.*, p. v.

—appears to be a revision of a well known song about Churkin, and other partisan songs are imitations of ballads which were popular in their time, exerting, as we have already said above, a strong influence on the songs of the peasantry and of the factory and the mill during the prerevolutionary period.

Here, for example, is a song of the Far Eastern partisans, "On the Death of Pogadayev," composed to the tune of, and in imitation of, the ballad "The Sea Gull" ("Now the morning has dawned red, the waters are growing rosy, above the lake flies a swift sea gull").

We give this partisan song:

> Now the morning has dawned red, we have occupied Sretensk,
> And with fighting the enemy has withdrawn from the town—
> But we have lost the commander of the regiment.
> The corpse of the slain man—we could not find it.
> All night long we wandered there in battle, among the mounds,
> In the ravines, standing waist-deep in the cold snow,
> And toward morning we gained the heights and the mountains,
> Only one station was a stronghold for the enemy.
> Then, with fifty men, there rushed to the attack
> Our unforgettable leader, against the enemy station.
> The attack was repelled, but our commander was lost,
> His frenzied horse bore him off to the enemy,
> And a bullet pierced the champion of freedom,
> And carried off the leader of the seventh regiment.[12]

In specific instances the words, figures, and rhythms are drawn by the partisan poets from the stores of the traditional old peasant song. Curious in this respect, for instance, is a song that was written down in Krasnodar, from former members of the cavalry partisan detachment of 1918–1920, glorifying the commander of the detachment, who was greatly loved by the fighting men:

> Our commander, the commander,
> Our commander is a fine fellow.
> Our commander is a fine fellow,
> He is not married, he is a bachelor.
> Under him is a fine raven-black horse,

[12] First printed in the collection *The Partisans* (Chita, 1929); see also the collection *Red Army Folklore*, p. 118.

And the splendid saddle is like silver.
The cap that he wears is laughing,
And his gloves are speaking to us,
His gloves are speaking to us,
They do not allow us to marry.
It does not suit us to marry,
It is better for us to live as bachelors.[13]

The images and rhythms of this song are prompted by the traditional peasant wedding songs, the songs of tribute to the "chiliarch" and to the "bachelor" guest.

However the question may be decided as to just what specific traditional song served as the direct source for any given partisan song, in any case it is beyond doubt that the partisan poets created their song on the basis of an excellent knowledge of the poetics of the traditional peasant song.[14]

Many of the partisan songs, naturally, were modeled upon the popular revolutionary songs—such, for example, as the song composed by Rebrov-Denisov, who took part in the fighting before Ust-Kut. It is a curious thing that this song was distributed by headquarters on the

[13] A. Novikov, *op. cit.*
[14] In the Belo-Ozero variant of the song of tribute to the "commander" there occur, among others, the following lines (from B. and Y. Sokolov, *Tales and Songs of the Belo-Ozero Region* [Moscow, 1915], p. 380, No. 263):

The high commander is a handsome fellow,
He is a pleasing fellow.
As for the sheepskin coat that the commander wears,
It is made of raccoon.
As for the girdle that he wears,
It has golden ornaments.
Then he has a hat with a feather,
And his gantlets are adorned with silver.
And the hat he wears is laughing,
And his gantlets are speaking,
His gantlets are speaking,
They want to make presents to the girls.

The partisan song which we are analyzing altered the text of a traditional wedding song, adapting it to the creation of the figure of the army commissar. Hence comes the change, in place of "gantlets with silver" (in the wedding song a veiled allusion to the fact that the commander, in response to his song of tribute, must requite the girls with money), to "a saddle made like silver," and the corresponding change of the country "gantlets" to "gloves," etc. Other details of the partisan song were prompted by the wedding song of tribute to the

northeastern front, along with the communiqué, to all the military units. It was written in imitation of a well known revolutionary funeral march, "You Fell as a Sacrifice in the Deadly Combat":

> Farewell, comrades! Eternal rest!
> You have been taken away from us forever.
> Fateful for you was the combat before Ust-Kut,
> But bravely did you fight with the enemy.
> You gave up your life for a sacred ideal—
> Your motto was: Death or liberty.
> Eternal glory to all those who fell as a sacrifice
> For the happiness of their own people.[15]

In general it must be said that very many of the partisan songs were created in direct connection with actual episodes in the civil war, and for that reason they have an incontestable historical significance. Unfortunately, the songs of the civil war began to be collected quite late, and many of them have disappeared forever. During the past few years, especially in connection with the great public interest in the history of the civil war, the work of collecting them has been intensified. The first extensive, although, it is true, still incomplete summary of all that has been collected and published in this field,

---

bachelor guest or best man at the wedding (see *Songs Collected by P. V. Kireyevsky: New Series*, No. I [Moscow, 1911], No. 282):

> But who is the bachelor among us, and who is not married?
> Sergey is the bachelor among us, Mikhalych is not married.
> He mounts his horse, and beneath him the horse rejoices,
> He waves his whip, and the horse dances beneath him. . . .
> When he rides out to the meadows, the meadows grow green,
> When he rides out to the meadows, the flowers begin to bloom,
> The flowers begin to bloom, the birds begin to sing.
> When he rides along the street, the whole street grows bright.

The figure of the fine young bachelor riding on his horse and by his very aspect making all surrounding nature glad, in conjunction with the figure of the elegantly dressed commander, whose "hat even laughs" and whose "gantlets speak," is so familiar in the wedding songs that it rose up in the memory of the poets of the partisan detachment, who were peasants in their origin, when they wanted to pay tribute to their beloved commander.

There might recur to their memory not only wedding songs, but also playing and dancing songs, in which there is a loving delineation of the ideal figure of the handsome young fellow, cleverly bestriding his horse, and by his aspect delighting the eyes of all around him.

[15] See the collection *Red Army Folklore*, p. 126.

has been given by V. M. Sidelnikov in the book *Red Army Folklore*. Now we have at our disposal a considerable body of folklore material dealing with the period of the civil war and the struggle with the interventionists.

Songs were composed on all the fronts during the civil war—the north, east, south, and west. They were composed usually by the fighters themselves, the direct participants in the events which are mentioned in the songs. The names of the composers, in the majority of cases, have not been preserved, but a goodly number of the authors have been identified. Some of the authors had obviously had a certain amount of literary experience; others appeared to be, in the true sense of the word, self-taught, and to a great extent were groping their way, as we have seen, very often failing to select the appropriate poetic model. Some of the songs of the unknown partisan and self-taught poets of the Red Army attained a vast and enviable popularity throughout the whole Soviet land; others had only a local circulation. The song "The White Army, the Black Baron," which had its origin in the first years of the civil war, and made the round of all the fronts of the Red Army, and later of the whole Soviet Union, achieved great popularity. Still greater popularity was gained by the song with the refrain:

> Boldly we will go to battle
> For the power of the Soviets,
> And as one we will die
> In the struggle for this power.

This song became, and remains up to the present time, one of the favorite songs of the masses during the time of any popular demonstrations.

And how puny now seem the attacks upon this and other songs of the masses, on the part of the representatives of the RAPP * and the RAPM,† who strove by decisive measures to drive these songs out of the song repertory of the masses, on the ground that, for instance, in the song under consideration, there were distinct features of the

* Russian Association of Proletarian Writers.—Ed.
† Russian Association of Proletarian Musicians.—Ed.

tune of the prerevolutionary ballad, "The Fragrant Clusters of the White Acacia." We have already seen that not only this song, but also a considerable number of other songs of the partisans and of the masses of the Red Army, during the first years of the revolution and the civil war, by their tunes, and by their literary-poetic structure, were connected with the prerevolutionary song heritage, but it would be altogether incorrect to ostracize such songs on that ground alone. Surely it must not be forgotten that with these songs the proletarian and peasant masses went to war against their class enemies, with these songs they took heart, and with these songs they conquered. These songs became precious remembrances for those who took part in the civil war, and they have high significance as artistic and historical documents, although many of them are far from displaying musical or poetic perfection.

Many songs were composed about the heroes of the civil war, about the glorious leaders who guided the Red Army to victory—Stalin, Voroshilov, Ordzhonikidze, Frunze, Budyónny; about Chapayev, the legendary general of the Volga provinces and the Urals; about Shchors, the "Ukrainian Chapayev"; about the heroic Don Cossacks Podtelkov and Krivashlykov, about the Red partisans beyond Lake Baikal, Lazo, Zhuravlev, and Pogadayev, and about the other heroes, well known and less well known. It is necessary, for the period nearer to our own, by means of a systematic interrogation of those who took part in the war, to collect these songs, and in this way to save them from oblivion.

Great popularity has been enjoyed, throughout the Soviet Union, even up to the present time, by the "Partisan Song" ("Through the valleys, over the mountains, the division moved forward"), which was composed by some unknown Siberian partisan who perished in the war with the Whites, and which was disseminated through the whole country, in the adaptation made by S. Alymov.

Not so long ago there was published (in *Pravda*, 1937, No. 53) a beautiful song, "The Town on the Volga," dedicated to the heroic defense of Tsaritsyn and Comrade Stalin's leadership of the front:

Denikin's men left the siege,
Journeying to the town on the Volga
Where the warriors of the Tenth Red Army were fighting
On the muddy spring roads.
There rose up from the horizon
A hurricane of Cossack spears,
To the headquarters of the Tsaritsyn front
There came an armored car from the Kremlin.
Comrade Stalin arrived at headquarters.
And he led the troops forward,
And the warriors of the Tenth stood
Firmer than a breed of stone. . . .
And the Volga tells the story,
Lapping against its banks,
How we repelled the enemy,
Who was like a ravening wolf!
The warriors went through a shower of stars,
Among the holes in the road.
The town on the Volga became
A Bolshevik stronghold.[16]

A very considerable group of songs is devoted to Budyónny and his famous Red cavalry. In addition to the "Budyónny March" of A. D'Actille, and the "Budyónny Cavalry Song" of Aseyev, which quickly entered into the repertory of the masses of the people and became known to everyone, there were many songs about Budyónny composed by the actual fighters, or by unknown poets. Such, for example, is the song "Budyónny," beginning with the words, "And the battle with the Cadets raged and thundered" (which, as one can judge even from the first line, was composed after the pattern of "The Fire of Moscow Raged and Burned"), though it is true that this did not attain a very wide circulation; or the song, having a great many variants, with the well known verse:

> Ask Tsaritsyn, ask Ukraina,
> Ask Perekop or the Don,
> With what daring and with what heroism
> Semyon fought for the motherland.[17]

[16] Reprinted in *Red Army Folklore*, p. 57.
[17] *Ibid.*, p. 62.

Exceptionally great popularity was won by a song about the Budyónny reconnaissance (the author of which is still unknown):

> There, far away, beyond the river,
> The fires were kindled,
> The red light flared up in the clear sky—
> A hundred young warriors
> From Budyónny's troops
> Galloped off, to reconnoiter in the fields.

There are also songs about Chapayev; but concerning this favorite of popular legends there have been preserved, as we shall see, more oral narratives and legends than songs. There have been more songs but fewer legends preserved about the Ukrainian division commander Shchors, than about Chapayev. One of the songs, composed by the fighters of the famous Bogunsky regiment, which was commanded by Shchors, thus formulates the attitude of the masses of men in the Red Army toward the brave general:

> We did not know the way back,
> The Bogunsky men do not go back!
> Forward: against the Polish gentlemen, against Petlura!
> With Shchors, indeed, we only go forward! [18]

The song creation of the years of the civil war, and of the conflict with the interventionists, perhaps, is not always brilliant in its artistic finish. This, naturally, could not help but lag behind the tempestuous aspiration of new ideas and attitudes. Frequently it renders with great power the pathos of the revolution, the feeling of hatred for the enemies of the revolution and of the people, the supreme bravery, daring, and self-sacrifice of the leaders and of the common soldiers. These songs, mostly composed by the actual participants in the civil war, and in part preserved until the present time in the song repertory of the masses, serve as a splendid means of public training in the spirit of Soviet patriotism and heroism.

But it was not only the civil war and the life of the Red Army which furnished food for the song creation of the masses. The whole life of

[18] Collection, *Narratives About Shchors* (Young Guard, 1937), No. 11; reprinted in *Red Army Folklore*, pp. 74-75.

the country at the time of the revolution, all the stages of consolidation and further development of the Soviet regime, found poetic echoes in the songs of the masses. In these, just as in the songs about the civil war, and as in general in all the song folklore of the period following the October Revolution, there is observable the powerful influence of the book, of literary productions. And even the very creativeness itself, at times, proceeded along both channels: frequently a song would be composed in its written form, and would then quickly attain a wide circulation orally.

Exceedingly characteristic of the period following the October Revolution is the ever greater fusion of the written and oral poetic creation. From the very first years of the revolution, there was observable the powerful enthusiasm, felt by the young people of the city and the country, for the writing of verses. But these verses, if they were suited to the taste of the circles nearest to the poet, would soon be transformed into a song. At first, however, before the development of the workers' and peasants' correspondent movement,* before the expansion of the broad network of systematically functioning literary circles at the factories and in the country villages, the art of song writing was of an elemental character, with almost no one to guide it. And, accordingly, it is not surprising that the lower ranks of poets and singers frequently chose, as models for imitation, works which were far from first-class in quality. The lower quality of song creation proceeded mostly along the line of adaptations or revisions of this or that popular poem, of this or that song which for some reason had attained popularity.

As a very significant, characteristic example (though, it is true, not from the first years of the revolution, but from the beginning years of the New Economic Policy) one may cite the numerous adaptations of "The Little Bricks," which had at one time been exceedingly popular. This song made its appearance in 1924–1925. Over the period of a number of years it was fated to be one of our most popular songs.

---

* Workers' and peasants' correspondent movement: Established in the early 1920's to include the participation of workers, peasants, and Red Army men in the Communist press, and to supplement the work of the Communist Party in building Socialism (*Malaia sovetskaia entsiklopediia*).—Ed.

The State Music Publishing House and other publishing firms have distributed the song in millions of copies. The song held a firm place in the programs at all kinds of concerts. A motion picture was built around the theme of "The Little Bricks." The song was widely disseminated among the masses, entering into the song repertory of the factories, mills, and the countryside, and calling forth numerous imitations and adaptations among the most diverse social strata of the proletariat, among various groups of the peasantry, among the remnants of the urban petty bourgeoisie, and among the declassed criminal groups.

These adaptations were very diverse, both in their content and in their artistic merits, reflecting the distinctions in the social psychology of various classes. A very large majority of the adaptations of "The Little Bricks" had their origin among the working people. Quite independently of their artistic value, the presence of these revisions gave evidence of the great attraction of the proletarian masses toward poetic and musical art; of the striving to reflect in song the phenomena and the problems of contemporary life. The only pity is that they employed as an artistic model works which were not of high poetic value.

In many adaptations of "The Little Bricks" we are dealing with an independent composition and an independent revision of the models, standing sometimes close to, and sometimes further away from, the original text. Besides, there is observed the characteristic striving of every new variant to adapt the song to the local setting, to its own factory, mill, mine, or coalpit. This made the song still more popular among the workmen of a given concern. Beyond a doubt, some of the revisions of the original text are better in quality than their source: historically, they are more concrete, and from the artistic standpoint they are frequently more expressive.[19]

For example, in one of the revisions of "The Little Bricks" coming from the Donets coal field, the action is transferred to another setting, as compared with the original text: in place of the brick works, there is quite a detailed and distinct description of the charac-

[19] For a series of popular revisions of "The Little Bricks," see the article by V. U. Beletskaya, "Miners' Songs," *Ethnographic News*, Bk. 5, 1927.

ter of life and work in the coal mines, a more detailed description of the class conflict in the prerevolutionary era, and there is introduced a detailed description of the civil war, the starting point of which was this very Donets coal field. There is a picture in concrete detail of the revival of the workers' life in the mines; but the general treatment of the subject has remained almost exactly the same as it was in the. original version of "The Little Bricks."

Revisions of "The Little Bricks" were produced not only among the workers in industrial concerns, but elsewhere. There were peasant revisions, and there were no small number of revisions among the urban bourgeoisie also, and at last, revisions in the "thieves' argot." The latter circumstance involved a great vulgarization of the content and motif of the song. The song could not help becoming a bore in the end, and by 1930 there began to appear various parodies of it and of its different adaptations. Soon "The Little Bricks" began to disappear from the song repertory. At the present time "The Little Bricks" has almost entirely disappeared from the song life of the working people, yielding place to productions which are much more interesting from the viewpoint of art as well as of ideas. Only here and there, in the culturally retarded regions, people still amuse themselves with renderings of "The Little Bricks," and even with the composition of new variations; but this is no longer characteristic of the folklore of the country as a whole.

As a result of the development of the Socialist offensive, with the liquidation of the kulaks as a class; with the progress of industrialization, and of collectivization in the rural economy; with the large-scale progress of the cultural revolution, especially during the course of Stalin's two glorious Five-Year-Plans, great changes manifested themselves in folk creative art, and most frequently in song.

The songs of a number of Soviet poets, especially the hearty songs, full of the joy of living, and permeated with the sense of Soviet patriotism, by Dunayevsky and Lebedev-Kumach ("March of the Merry Lads," "Wide Is My Native Land," and many others), became the favorite songs of young people all over the Soviet Union. They not only began to be sung on all the collective farms and at all the industrial and commercial enterprises, but were also translated into almost all the languages of the peoples of the USSR, and were imitated by all the humbler poets and musicians.

And even in general, the artistic level of the so-called "poet of the masses" was greatly altered, in comparison with the first years of the revolution. With the growth of secondary and higher education, both in schools and by correspondence, there grew up everywhere a numerous new Soviet intelligentsia. Every working man and collective farmer who had ever felt a poetic talent within him, or at any rate the wish to create works of art, is now writing, and has the opportunity to become directly acquainted with the best monuments of contemporary and of earlier literature, and to develop himself both artistically and politically. From this, naturally, came the heightened and constantly increasing blending of oral poetry with literature. Sometimes even a local poet creates a poem which bears the obvious impress of literary influences, but which becomes a local, and sometimes even a widely popular song of the masses, fully in tune with the popular moods of the time.

It is interesting in this connection to note the curious fact that frequently a beautiful poem attracted general attention only when it passed over from a book, newspaper, or manuscript into the mouths of the people, and became a popular song.

Of such songs which have become widely popular, the authors of which have not even been determined, we may give, for example, a song which was written down for the first time in 1936, from a chorus of workmen in the Frunze mill at Penza, but which during the last year and a half or two years has become one of the most popular songs of the Russian masses. It is a song about the beloved Stalin:

> From land to land, over the summits of the mountains,
> Where the free eagle makes his flight,
> Of Stalin the wise, our own, and beloved,
> The people compose a beautiful song.
> This song flies swifter than a bird,
> And the world of the oppressors trembles wickedly.
> This song is not held back by posts and frontiers,
> It is not held back by anyone's boundaries.
> It is not afraid of scourges or bullets,

This song sounds in the fire of the barricades,
The rickshaw and the coolie sing this song,
The Chinese soldier sings this song.
And lifting up, like a standard, this song about Stalin,
The ranks of the united front march forward.
The menacing flame burns and blazes up,
The nations arise for the final conflict.
But we sing this song proudly,
And we praise the grandeur of Stalin's age—
We sing of life, splendid, happy life,
Of the joy of our fortunate victories.
From land to land, over the summits of the mountains,
Where the airplanes hold their colloquies,
Of Stalin the wise, our own, and beloved,
The peoples sing a beautiful song.[20]

Such new folk songs of the masses speak for themselves. They testify to the high development of the political and artistic culture of the people in the Soviet land.

But, with all the artistic and ideological value of the new folk songs of the masses, the question arises, how we may direct the composition of new songs into the channel of utilization of the rich artistic heritage which has been left to us by the many centuries of folk song creation. At the present time many Soviet poets, working at the creation of songs for the masses, are attentively studying the traditional song culture of the people. A great deal is also being done today to bring the folk-song heritage back to the toiling masses. (See, for example, the publications of *Russian Folk Songs* by the State Military Publishing House, the activity of the Red Standard Ensemble with the Red Army songs and dances, under the direction of Professor A. V. Aleksandrov, and many others.) It may be assumed that we shall soon have new songs, on a profoundly folk and national basis, with reference to their artistic form. The song "Little Field, O Field," by the poet V. Gusev, must be considered one of the most successful results of the creative attention of the contemporary poet to the popular song; this is a song for the masses, composed upon the motifs of the popular traditional lyric—indisputably one of the best in the Soviet repertory.

[20] *Creative Art of the Peoples of the USSR* (Pravda, 1937), p. 159.

2. CHASTUSHKAS

The independent song creation of the laboring masses is revealed most fully in the Chastushka. This form was suited, more than the other song forms, to the expression of the various repercussions of numerous phenomena, great and small, of revolutionary life. The cause of this is hidden in those characteristic properties of the popular rhyme as a genre, of which we have spoken in the chapter on chastushkas in the prerevolutionary period. The brevity and mobility of the form, the opportunity for a swift reaction to every new fact, to every new occurrence of the national or local life, the ready assimilability and, consequently, the ease of transmission from one person to another, the adaptability of the chastushka form in the interests of agitation and propaganda made the chastushka the most widely diffused and the dominant song genre in Russian folklore following the October Revolution. The basic difference between the post revolutionary chastushka and that of the prerevolutionary period consists in the intensification of social and political motifs in its content. And this involved, in the last analysis, considerable changes also in its form, and first of all in its composition.

The February Revolution and the overthrow of the autocracy had already given a powerful stimulus to the expression of still more distinct and direct social protest than we had had earlier. Besides, in the popular rhymes heard in the country villages and on the military fronts, there quickly began to resound the motifs not only of conflict with the tsarist regime, but of social conflict, of class conflict with the bourgeoisie.

Without a Tsar, without a sovereign,
We shall live in freedom.
We will stab all the bourgeois,
We will kill all the bourgeois.
We will educate the bourgeois:
We will take off their galoshes and make them wear bast shoes.[21]

[21] V. Semyonovsky, "Popular Songs of the Ivan-Voznesensk Province," *The Red Soil*, No. 1, 1921.

The October Revolution found a much louder echo in the chastushkas than did the February Revolution.

In the chastushkas of the October Revolution, the class consciousness and the social-economic demands of the proletarian and peasant masses found broad expression. The chastushkas record the fact that the October Revolution brought not only a change in authority, but decisive alterations in the relationship of the class forces:

> They deceived us long,
> But now we have awakened.
> We have driven out many masters,
> We ourselves have become like Tsars.[22]

There was a powerful change in the attitude of the masses toward the war, as soon as it passed into civil war:

> As soldiers, lads,
> Willingly we will go,
> For the Soviet power, lads,
> We will shed our hot blood.

The attitude of the Red new recruit toward the call is entirely different from what it was in the earlier period toward the tsarist recruitment:

> Do not weep, somebody's aunt,
> And do not be sorrowful, my own mother.
> I will kill the White Guardsmen,
> And I will come home again.[23]

The Red Army conquers people's sympathies; in it they see not only a military force, but also a great force on the side of culture. Here, for example, are the reasonings of girls, as a chastushka marks them:

> What matter that the sun has set,
> Tomorrow a new one will arise;
> What matter that they drafted my friend,
> He will come back educated.[24]

[22] V. Y. Struminsky, "Popular Rhymes of the Orenburg Region," *Proceedings of the Society for the Study of the Kirghiz Region*, No. 2, Orenburg, 1922.
[23] *Red Army Folklore*, p. 168.   [24] *Ibid.*, p. 169.

The civil war gave birth to many chastushkas, marking specific facts, skirmishes, battles, and heroic exploits. Many of them record victories over the Whites, and often they deride the enemy. Here, for example, are chastushkas which were composed in the region beyond Lake Baikal, at the time of the struggle in 1919–1920 with the White Cossack leader Semyonov:

> Ataman Semyonov,
> He led the troops;
> But now in the woods
> He runs with the wolves.[25]

Or still another series of chastushkas from the period of the civil war:

> I will play louder on my accordion,
> Listen, brothers and friends.
> Kolchak has drowned in Siberia,
> And Yudenich in Luga.
>
> Do not spare for the Whites
> Either the butt or the bayonet:
> The White soldier will be thrown into the grave,
> The longed-for peace will appear.
>
> We have met with well aimed bullets
> Those who wore golden epaulets,
> And to overtake them have galloped
> The ranks of the Red cavalry.
>
> Shkuro ran off to the Don—
> A useless effort,
> And after him in pursuit pressed
> The iron cavalry.
>
> The rifles sounded: *tuk-tuk*,
> And the Reds were right on hand.
> The machine-guns spoke: *tra-ta-ta*,
> And the Whites ran away.[26]

[25] Archive of the State Museum of Literature.
[26] *Red Army Folklore*, pp. 46-48.

Everyone remembers the special series of chastushkas about the "little apple," so called because each of the rhymes in this series began with the verses:

> Oh, little apple,
> Whither are you rolling?

This introductory verse of the popular rhyme grew out of the favorite prerevolutionary chastushka:

> Oh, little apple,
> And where is it rolling?
> Oh, dear mama,
> I want to get married.
> Not to an old man,
> Not to a little one;
> To a fine soldier,
> Bold and daring.[27]

The following Ukrainian prerevolutionary chastushka must be regarded as the original song, the ancestor of all the "little apples" that were to follow:

> Roll, little apple,
> Whither you may roll.
> Give me in marriage, papa,
> Wherever I may wish.

At the time of the civil war, both warring camps made use of variations of the chastushka about the "little apple." There were "little apples" both on the White side and on the Red. In the historical scheme, this fact is very interesting; it emphasizes the political role of folklore, its significance as a means of agitation.*

The various complications of the civil war, especially in the south, the change of authorities and regimes, are reflected in the different variations of this chastushka:

> Ah, you little apple,
> You have rolled away.
> The power of the Cadet party †
> Has been overthrown.

[27] D. Zelenin, *Outlines of Russian Mythology*, p. 357.

* Agitation—Here, political agitation to rouse the masses to action.—Ed.

† Constitutional—Democratic party formed in 1905 by Paul Milyukov, and representing Russian liberal elements.—Ed.

Ah, little apple,
You have rolled along,
And the power of the Soviets
Has been strengthened.

Ah, little apple,
Now it has grown ripe.
The proletariat of all lands
Is united.

Ah, little apple,
On one side it is green.
Kolchak is not allowed
To pass beyond the Urals.[28]

The title "The Little Apple" came to be applied also to those songs which, although they did not have the introductory verse, "Ah, little apple," were constructed rhythmically on the same scheme, for example:

General Krasnov,
Whither are you stamping?
When you come near to Tsaritsyn,
You will stop a bullet.

Ah, young cadet,
Whither are you rushing?
When you run into the First Cavalry,
You will not return!

The steamer is coming,
The waves are in coils,
We will feed the fish
With the Volunteers.*

The steamer is coming,
The waves are in coils;
Be filled, O fleet,
With the Konsomols.[29]

[28] *Creative Art of the Peoples of the USSR*, pp. 219-222.
* Volunteers: In this case reference is to the Volunteer Army, an anti-Bolshevik force organized in 1917–1918.—ED.
[29] *Ibid.*, pp. 220-221.

Another series of popular rhymes, also widespread at the time of the civil war, is known as "The Barrel." The folk songs which were included in this series began with the line, "I am sitting on a barrel." The initial variant goes back also to the prerevolutionary repertory of lyric chastushkas; this time, however, not to the Ukrainian, but to the North Russian:

> I am sitting on a barrel,
> The barrel is rolling.
> Now my darling does not love me,
> Later he will miss me.[30]

In the revolutionary period the first line of this chastushka became the first line for those rhymes which reflected either domestic troubles caused by differences in political opinions or general discords for political reasons:

> I am sitting on a barrel,
> And on the barrel is a bird.
> My husband is a Haydamak,*
> But I am a Bolshevist.
> I am sitting on a barrel,
> The barrel is turning around.
> I was enrolled in the Commune,
> Makhno † is angry.[31]

By the aid of adaptations, variations of the same song which for some reason had become popular, it was convenient to adjust it to fit the swiftly changing political events, and to please the authorities. In the variations of a chastushka were expressed the political stratification of the populace at the time of the civil war. If we had, among the hundreds of variants, copies of one and the same chastushka arranged chronologically, and by locale and class, we should possess graphic historical documents telling of the course of the

---

[30] E. N. Yeleonskaya, *Collection of Great-Russian Popular Rhymes* (Moscow, 1914), No. 21.

* Haydamak: soldier of special cavalry detachments of the Ukrainian national army under Petlura at the end of 1918.—Ed.

† Makhno: leader of anarchical peasant bands in the civil war.—Ed.

[31] D. Zelenin, *op. cit.*, pp. 364-365.

civil war, following the peculiarities of the moment, the times, and
the mutual relations of the class forces.

The political significance of the chastushka frequently underwent
a change, not only from the variations of its text—of lines or individual words—but sometimes merely by a change in the intonation.
Especially characteristic, in this respect, are the chastushkas about
the representatives of the poor peasant class who have risen to power.
The poorer class wove into such rhymes a feeling of class pride at
those decisive changes in social life which the revolution had brought
with it; while the kulaks and the counterrevolutionary elements of
the countryside, on the other hand, set forth such facts with a feeling
of class hatred and malicious mockery:

> Formerly he was a workman,
> He used to sweep away the snow from the entrance,
> Now he is chairman
> Of the village district council.[32]

The peasant poor, however, very definitely laughed at the rich
men who sometimes, by cunning, had slipped into a place in the
local administration:

> A commissar became Fadey,
> The wealthy man in the village,
> But he did not long adorn his post—
> He fell into the hands of the special police.[33]

Long before the revolution, there had existed in the rural villages
folk songs which harshly lampooned the clergy. Under the conditions of tsarist censorship, and also as a result of subjective selections by the earlier collectors, most of these songs failed to make
their way into the printed scholarly collections and into the popular
songbooks. With the revolution, and with the development of antireligious attitudes, the anticlerical and antireligious chastushkas
greatly increased in number. Some of these rhymes unquestionably
made their way into the villages (and into the factories) through
newspapers, antireligious magazines and brochures, and from the

[32] V. Y. Struminsky, *loc. cit.*
[33] Archive of the State Museum of Literature.

speaking platforms in clubs, but this does not alter the essentials of the picture: wherever such chastushkas may have come from, in making their way into the song repertory of the village and the factory, once a great demand for them arose among the masses, it testified to the process which was going on, of critical reexamination of the traditional world view. True, this reservation must be made: the number of antisacerdotal, anticlerical popular rhymes during the first years of the revolution was a great many times larger than the number of antireligious chastushkas in the genuine sense of the word. This observation fully coincides with the information that we have about a similar correlation in the thematics of other genres of folklore at that time—the tales, anecdotes, and songs.

Here are a few of the antisacerdotal popular rhymes of the first years of the revolution:

> There is no one in the world more vile and wicked
> Than the potbellied priests.
> They steal without compunction
> From the country peasants.

> But the new priest
> Really has some conscience:
> From everyone he takes
> Two rubles for their sins.[34]

> At the house of Peter the priest
> They found three buckets * of beer.
> In the possession of his young wife
> They found ten buckets of vodka.

> At St. Nick's they have bells,
> And at St. Saviour's they have cast-iron ones.
> At St. Nick's the priests are thieves,
> And at St. Saviour's they are wizards.[35]

Vast popularity was enjoyed, from the earliest years of the revolution, by this chastushka:

[34] *Ibid.*
* Bucket (*vedro*)=2¾ gallons.—Ed.
[35] V. Y. Struminsky, *loc. cit.*

Our God, you, our God,
What are you doing?
You sit in the heavens,
You do not work.[36]

The chastushkas noted that church attendance had fallen off a great deal:

Only the old, old women
Frequent the temple of God.
The young people think
That the saints are trash.[37]

Instead of prayer, the young people prefer study:

Sunday has come,
I will not go to pray.
For me this time has passed,
I will go to study.[38]

The chastushkas of the first years of the revolution give a lively and clear picture of the organization of the Young Communist League in the countryside, and of that conflict which the progressive young people had to wage for the strengthening of their organizations, a conflict both with society and with their families. Some parents (of the wealthy or culturally backward class) were ready to permit their sons to play cards and to go out reveling, if only they did not attend meetings of the Young Communist League, or engage in political activity. Here is a characteristic chastushka which records such facts:

Tell us, young Komsomol,
What do they say there at home?
"At my card playing they don't say a word;
But for going to meetings, they scold me." [39]

It is interesting that similar acknowledgments are heard, to an even greater extent, from the young girls. The parents were ready to load their daughter with presents, if only for the future she would keep away from the Young Communist League:

36 Archive of the State Museum of Literature.
37 *Ibid.*   38 *Ibid.*   39 *Ibid.*

They bought me a white dress
And said, "Don't soil it";
And what else did they say?
"Don't go out with that fellow from the Young Communist
League." [40]

Under such conditions as are depicted in these chastushkas, it is readily understandable what an impression must have been produced by the bold, open acknowledgments by the girls that they were breaking with the old social traditions, and entering upon a new mode of life.

In general, the girls felt themselves to be more independent, they began to believe more in their own powers; but even so, in the rhymes was often echoed the girl's acknowledgment that this independence could not be won all at once, but the girl was following in the steps of her sweetheart. It was he who usually pointed the new way to her; he influenced her outlook upon the world, and it was only following in his footsteps that the girl entered the Young Communist League:

They say that I am a Komsomolka *
But I was not a Komsomolka.
I began going out with a boy from the Young Communist League,
I became a Young Communist League girl.[41]

The member of the Young Communist League had a great deal of work to do in order to raise the cultural level of his girl-friend. He strove to enlighten her, to educate her, to raise her up to his own level.

> The whole of the sixth anniversary
> I spent sitting with Manya.
> I unfolded to her the whole picture
> Of how people live in Germany.[42]

[40] Y. Sokolov, "The Upper Mologa Region: Social Life and Creative Art of the Population," *The Tver Region*, No. 2, 1925.
* Komsomolka: girl member of the Young Communist League, feeder organization for the Communist Party; Komsomolets: boy member; Komsomol: Young Communist League.—ED.
[41] Y. Sokolov, *loc. cit.*
[42] *Ibid.*

Love for a Communist, or for a member of the Young Communist League, introduces much that is new into the commonplace personal life, it broadens the mental horizon, it leads to new interests.

> I am now no longer yours,
> I now belong to Senya;
> He took me to the Soviet
> To hear the speeches of Lenin.

> I am now no longer yours,
> I now belong to Senya;
> I fasten upon my breast the emblem
> Of Comrade Lenin.[43]

The disparity of development, of tastes, of interests, of everyday habits, between husband and wife, which was so frequently encountered during the first years of the revolution, was the cause of many disagreements. In the first period after the October Revolution there was a chastushka that was very widely disseminated, which briefly formulated the causes of these discords:

> My husband is a Communist,
> And I am an Independent;
> That is why our love
> Is not getting anywhere.[44]

Love for a Communist requires a great break in traditional habits and customs:

> If you love a Communist,
> You must walk purely.
> If you do not walk without reproach,
> You will not be able to wash yourself clean.
> If you love a Communist,
> You must change altogether:
> You must not wear the cross and chain,
> You must not pray to God.[45]

The decrees of the Soviet Government concerning new forms of marriage, divorce, and so forth, produced a great impression upon

[43] V. Y. Struminsky, *loc. cit.*
[44] Archive of the State Museum of Literature. [45] *Ibid.*

the countryside. In the rural communities which had been bred for centuries in traditional, patriarchal family principles, in the absolute submission of the children to their parents, of the wife to the husband, the opportunity for a free ordering of one's personal destiny was bound to find striking expression in the creation of songs and chastushkas. The new life had its way. The country village not only adapted itself to the new order, but even began to defend it fervently.

The chastushkas of the first years of the revolution give clear delineations of the most diverse phenomena of the changing social life. There are noted both the fundamental phenomena, which entered deeply into life and changed it radically, and also the sporadic and temporal phenomena, product of the circumstances of the moment. Thus, in the great number of rhymes, there found expression a great many now forgotten pictures of the years of economic collapse, of the civil war, and of War Communism.

A multitude of scenes from the daily life of the recent past were etched in the rural chastushkas. All the social and economic factors of the time of economic collapse were noted by the chastushka which was like an instantaneous photographic plate. The lack of goods, speculation, the peasant "black market," and the struggle with these, and all the other phenomena of the years of War Communism, are etched in these four-line popular rhymes. Here is a momentary glimpse of a scene at the railroad station, during the years of the peasant "bagmen"; * the crowd of passengers stands waiting for the train, the train draws near, but in it there is not a single free place, either inside or outside; even the engine is covered with black marketeers carrying bags; the train passes by the station without having taken anyone on. Some inventive author thereupon composes, on the spot, the following humorous chastushka:

> Locomotive, locomotive,
> Aren't you ashamed
> To be so loaded with profiteers
> That no one can see you? [46]

---

* Bringing food in from the country for sale on the black market.—ED.
[46] *Ibid.*

The countryside, no matter how strong the wave of new ideas, opinions, and attitudes, still could not, all at once, completely shake off the burdensome heritage of the old way of life. Not immediately, but only after stubborn resistance, did the old way of life give way to the new. The old lack of culture still made itself felt for a long time. The chastushka recorded, as before, the drunken revelry, the rowdyism, mischief, fights, and knifings. The countryside, in the first period, was still not sufficiently provided with institutions of political enlightenment. Part of the countryside was under the considerable influence of the kulak ideology. The kulak class was ready to support even the drunkenness and revelry of the young people, if only they did not join the hateful Young Communist League, and did not become permeated by the new world view. In the first years of the revolution, the group among the young people which was not politically conscious, belonging chiefly to the kulak class, became infected with rowdyish, decadent attitudes, which, by the way, were very similar in nature to many of the motifs expressed in Yesenin's works during those years. These mental states in Yesenin's lyrics, which are generally blamed on the urban literary Bohemianism, in reality had their social roots in the psychology of the corrupted upper strata of the countryside. The rowdyish chastushkas developed those same motifs which are already known to us from our survey of the rural chastushka before the October Revolution.

During the years of the Five-Year Plans a great decrease is notable in the rowdyish motifs in the chastushka repertory of the countryside. This circumstance is undoubtedly connected with the profound changes which were going on in the rural mode of life during the reconstruction period and the period of the development of the Socialist organization during the Stalin Five-Year Plans. There were the strengthening and the development of the Party and Young Communist League organizations, the enormous progress of school organization and of the extensive work of the Board of Political Education. There was the enormous influence upon the countryside of newspapers, brochures, and books, along with the corresponding increase in the number of village reading rooms. There was the progress of clubs and of the amateur theater, and the expansion of the radio network which penetrated into the most remote corners of the land. There was the vastly important work of the Board of Political Education of the Red Army, which poured into the rural communities every year more and more new contingents of educated personnel. There was the great movement of rural workers into the city, drawn thither by the mighty growth of industrialization and of the Socialist organization. And finally, there was one of the most important phenomena, which had an incalculable influence upon the growth of political consciousness and culture in the rural regions. This was the collectivization of the rural economy, which introduced a system of organization and the cultivation of social labor, and of labor discipline.

All these and many other things knocked the foundations out from under the rowdyish and decadent anarchistic psychology; all this re-educated the country youth; all this awakened new motifs in their poetry, particularly in the repertory of the chastushka. Life brought forward new phenomena and new demands during these years, the years of the two Stalin Five-Year Plans, and these were echoed in the chastushkas. No longer do we find in the rhymes the burden of the imperialistic war, the heroism of the civil war, nor the pictures of life from the period of War Communism, the years of collapse and hunger, nor the timid declarations of a break with the old prejudices and habits. We now find straightforward, firm, full conviction in the expression of their devotion to the work of Socialist construction, of their active participation in it, their readiness, at the first word of the beloved leader, to rise to the defense of the motherland. And, above all, the themes of the great economic revolution which had been accomplished in the countryside, the themes of the victory of the collective farm organization—all these are strikingly brought out in the repertory of the period of the two Five-Year Plans.

But the victory did not come all at once. It was necessary to endure the fierce opposition of the class enemy, the kulak class. The chastushkas of the year of the great crisis, and of the years close to it, vividly reflect this conflict with the enemy kulaks.

The rhymes of that period are striking documents of class conflict which developed with the progress of collectivization. The kulak attentively followed what was going on among the young and not yet well established collective farms, noting the slightest failure or fault.

For example, the collective farmers of the kolkhoz * known as the Red Star (Likhoslavl district, formerly in the Moscow, now in the Kalinin province) frequently sang a chastushka which they had composed (with the help, it is true, of one of the old introductions), which is joyous and full of confidence in the success of the kolkhóz:

> Soon, soon the snow will melt away,
> From the mountains the water will come rolling down;
> Every month our Red Star
> Grows stronger and stronger.[47]

When the neighboring kulaks spoke ironically, taking malicious advantage of temporary setbacks in the new collective-farm movement, the collective farmers did not yield, but, overcoming the difficulties, triumphantly sang again:

> At the kolkhoz, at the kolkhoz,
> Everything turns out right.
> At the kolkhoz good fortune piles up by the cartload,
> Rising into a mountain.[48]

The class enemy who favored the backwardness and lack of culture of the countryside ended by being beaten. The collective farmers realized all the advantages of the collective-farm organization. The peasant woman who had previously been oppressed both in society and in the family, felt her independence, her power:

> My husband drove me away, and my father beat me,
> My stepmother was not kind to me.
> But in the collective farm I became,
> Like all the others, a free woman.[49]

To the malicious kulak agitation against the collective farms, the kolkhoz chastushka answered with a decisive rebuff. It played a large

---

* Kolkhóz: a collective farm; kolkhóznik: a member of a collective farm.—Ed.
[47] *Ibid.*   [48] *Ibid.*
[49] *Chastushkas of the Collective Farm* (Kuibyshev, 1936), p. 46.

role in the conflict with the kulak power and its intrigues, noting with satisfaction its failures, the groundlessness of its gloomy predictions, the unsuccessfulness of its agitation:

> The kulak was lying when he said
> That the summer wheat is not coming up.
> For the wheat, only see,
> Is up as high as a man's chest.[50]

> We have put forth a great deal of strength,
> We have endured very much,
> In spite of all the kulaks' bellowing,
> The collective farms have grown up! [51]

The chastushkas proclaim the failure of the kulak agitation, the setting free of the peasantry from the power of the kulak:

> It's enough: we have bent our backs,
> We have fed the spider sufficiently.
> Now we have joined the collective farm,
> And we will drive the kulak to the devil! [52]

In the chastushkas, the class hatred of the toiling peasantry for the kulak, and the consciousness of victory over the class enemy found formidable expression:

> The little samovars reached the boiling point,
> The little teapots started to clatter,
> All the collective farmers began to sing,
> The kulaks burst into tears.[53]

The chastushkas of the collective farm, however, advise the people not to be satisfied with the progress they have made in the war with the kulaks, but summon them to redoubled vigilance, emphasizing the resourcefulness and cunning of the class enemy, and his capacity for assuming all kinds of disguises.

> See, the kulak, is wearing a new skin,
> Humbly craves admission to the collective farm.
> His poor old shirt is all torn. . . .
> The bloodsucker is just pretending! [54]

[50] *Ibid.*, p. 22.   [51] *Folklore of the Volga* (1937), p. 145.
[52] *Creative Art of the Peoples of the USSR*, p. 351.   [53] *Ibid.*
[54] Y. Sokolov, *What Is Folklore?* (Moscow, 1935), p. 61.

The kolkhoz organization went on developing. The collective farm was changing the daily life of the peasant. In fact, every month brought something new: now they would open a public dining hall, now day nurseries for children, now a village reading room; now they would procure a new machine or tractor, now they would set up a new radio receiver, and so on. All this raised their spirits, and the chastushka cheerfully records every new conquest of culture:

> Play, play, accordion,
> Now it is a new age.
> We do not eat dry food—
> Now we have a dining room.

> We have evened off all the strips,*
> All the boundaries we have wiped out.
> And great harvests
> We are receiving from the earth.[55]

The chastushka reflects the vast rise of culture in the village. The contemporary rhymes of the collective farm are shot through with allusions to schools, clubs, the movies, village reading rooms, the radio, and the earnest desire of the kolkhozniks for the mastery of letters, science, and technical knowledge:

> I am very seldom at home now:
> I am sitting in the club over a book.
> I am not wasting my time,
> I am following political events.[56]

> On the mountain stands a birch tree,
> It was clothed in green,
> And the collective farmers
> Were very eager to study.[57]

> When in our village reading room
> They hung up a linen screen,
> Even the old, old women
> Came together to see the movies.

---

* Strips into which the land was formerly divided among individual peasants.—Ed.

[55] *Chastushkas of the Collective Farm*, pp. 32, 34.

[56] *Ibid.*, p. 37.

[57] Y. Sokolov, *op. cit.*, p. 60.

> In the field there are resting places
>   everywhere.
> If you want to take a breathing spell,
> You can listen to the radio
> And read the newspaper a while.[58]

The contemporary rhyme of the collective farm devotes special attention to the tractor. The tractor, like the combine and other highly perfected machines, contributed to the rapid solidification of the collective economy and to the full acknowledgment of its advantages by the peasantry. The tractor evokes first astonishment, then delight:

> The tractor keeps up with everything:
> It plows, it sows, it harvests,
> It saws trees, it grubs out stumps.
> The only thing you have to do is watch it.[59]

> In the field are forty, in the field are forty,
> In the field are forty dessiatines *
> One good fellow, on a tractor,
> Plows and harrows all of them.[60]

The man, and later on the woman, who runs the tractor gradually becomes one of the favorite heroes of the life and poetry of the collective farm. From the chastushkas it is easy to follow the gradual changes in the attitudes of the collective farmers toward the machine which was destined to play such a tremendous role in the economic revolution of the countryside.

> The tractor drives along the road,
> And the girls shy away from it.
> At first they were afraid of it,
> But then they got used to it and liked it.[61]

> I did not love the tractor driver,
> I was not a tractor driver myself.
> But when I got behind the wheel myself,
> I fell in love with the tractor.[62]

[58] *Chastushkas of the Collective Farm*, pp. 32, 28.   [59] *Ibid.*, p. 56.
* Dessiatine=2.7 acres; forty dessiatines=108 acres.—ED.
[60] *Creative Art of the Peoples of the USSR*, p. 366.
[61] *Chastushkas of the Collective Farm*, p. 56.   [62] *Ibid.*

And here is a touching confession:

> The tractor driver is so handsome,
> I will bewitch him!
> Upon his tractor by night
> I will place two daisies! [63]

The girl herself dreams of becoming a tractor driver, and her dream frequently comes true:

> All around is the field, all around is the field,
> And on the field is the tractor.
> And is it not possible that some day
> I shall be a tractor driver's wife? [64]

The last two lines of this rhyme are sung differently in other variants, according to the progress of the desires of the collective-farmgirl:

> And is it not possible that some day I shall be
> A tractor driver myself.

The girl's dreams are fulfilled, and a new rhyme observes:

> Broad is the road that leads into the field.
> Over the field a light wind is blowing.
> Our tractor driver's name is Pasha,
> She wears a bright red kerchief.
> There behind the tractor's wheel
> The girl is sitting like a king.
> Her tongue is very sharp,
> She is a real brigadier. [65]

A lovingly attentive, protective attitude grows up toward the tractor. A cultured approach to the machine is fostered, a consciousness of responsibility for it:

> From the machines you expect to get help,
> Then see to it that you don't spoil them.
> You are receiving a machine,
> Then look to it, and answer for it. [66]

[63] *Creative Art of the Peoples of the USSR*, p. 354.
[64] Archive of the State Museum of Literature.
[65] *Creative Art of the Peoples of the USSR*, p. 353.
[66] *Chastushkas of the Collective Farm*, p. 16.

In the chastushkas of the collective farm, now and then there stand in opposition to each other the new comrade of the peasant on the collective farm—the tractor—and his old foster mother, "mother wooden-plow," which has now become the symbol of the woe and heavy toil of life in the previous time, before the revolution:

> Farewell forever, O tears,
> O wreck of a wooden plow!
> We are working on the collective farm,
> Under the regulations of Stalin.
>
> Among the linden trees, on the moss,
> We have buried the wooden plow,
> And on the other side
> We have buried the wooden harrow.
>
> Ah, the wooden plow has lain down to rest,
> Now the tractors do the plowing.
> I only wish I could get to see Stalin,
> I surely would be a happy woman!
>
> Oh, you little field of the kolkhoz
> I have fallen in love with you!
> It is you, Comrade Stalin,
> Who have given us our seat upon the tractor.[67]

A great deal of space is devoted, in the chastushkas, to the work of the shock brigadiers, socialist competition, and in the most recent period, to the Stakhanovite movement. And it must be said quite definitely, that the chastushka of the collective farm was widely utilized in the development of these grand movements among the working people, in which there has been so powerfully expressed the labor enthusiasm of the workers in the fields, who had learned labor discipline and organization. The various forms of the kolkhoz chastushka were stamped with socialist competition among brigades, links, and individual workers.

> Do not call, cuckoo
> Do not call, crook-backed bird.
> I am now a shock worker,
> I am now a wealthy woman.

---

[67] *Creative Art of the Peoples of the USSR*, pp. 366-367.

We have lots of firewood in our forest,
And plenty of brush.
Do not be a loafer,
But follow the example of a shock worker.

Formerly, at home, I was always thought
A good-for-nothing worker.
But now, on my own collective farm,
I earn five hundred working days a year.

I am a brigadier on the kolkhoz,
My heart, ah, my heart is thrilled!
My first brigade
Is competing with the third.[68]

We, milkmaids on the collective farm,
Will swiftly turn out our work:
We work in the shock-brigade fashion,
We want to live in the Stalin way.[69]

The kolkhozes increase, they become Bolshevist, and the kolkhozniks grow wealthy, and the chastushkas observe joyfully:

Now everybody is happy
In our own ancestral land.
All the collective farmers among us
Have a fine cow apiece.[70]

How the lads on the collective farm
Are beginning to grow rich!
They are building houses, covering them with planks,
It is interesting to watch them! [71]

The thoughts of the collective farmers are continually directed toward Lenin and Stalin, the organizers of the new life. Their words, their instructions, their counsels are preserved in the memory and in the heart of every genuine kolkhoznik. Not without good reason are the numerous references to the beloved leaders, in the rhymes of the kolkhoz, so spontaneously sincere:

[68] *Ibid.*, p. 394.
[69] Archive of the State Museum of Literature.
[70] Y. Sokolov, *What Is Folklore?* p. 60.
[71] *Folklore of the Volga*, p. 130.

Life is prosperous on the collective farm—
It does not elude our grasp.
So Comrade Stalin has said,
Our beloved leader and friend.[72]

I will buy a portrait of Lenin,
And put it in a little gold frame.
He brought me out into the light,
Ignorant peasant woman that I was.[73]

From one window to another
I have moved the flowering plant
So that there might be light on the portraits
Of Lenin and Stalin.[74]

The rhymes touchingly combine the names of Lenin and Stalin, emphasizing the fact that Stalin is leading the country along the path laid out by Lenin, and putting into practice the legacy of Lenin:

According to the legacy of Lenin,
According to the legacy of Stalin,
We have established the collective farm—
The true way of life for the peasant.[75]

There is a very curious chastushka which in a strange manner echoes the vital and absorbing problem of the obliteration of the boundary lines between the city and the country. On those foremost kolkhozes, where the great work of collectivization was especially successful, the young people no longer want to consider themselves "country fellows," as they are customarily called. They are acutely conscious that the collective farm is very far from being what used to be called the rural village, and they formulate their thoughts in a chastushka:

There are no rustic lads any more.
This is the way we have decided the question:
There is no village, there is no countryside,
There is only the prosperous collective farm! [76]

[72] *Chastushkas of the Collective Farm*, p. 5.
[73] *Creative Art of the Peoples of the USSR*, p. 437.
[74] *Ibid.*, p. 396.   [75] *Ibid.*, p. 351.
[76] Y. Sokolov, *op. cit.*, p. 62.

Up to this point we have been speaking of the peasant chastushka, and chiefly that of the collective farm, during the period following the October Revolution; but it would be incorrect to think that the chastushka, after the October Revolution, was created and existed only in the countryside. The chastushka after the October Revolution, as well as before it, existed and exists not only in the country, but also in the city; not only among the peasantry, but also among the urban workers. Even more than that: after the October Revolution, the chastushka of the city workers exerted a considerably greater influence on that of the peasantry than it had before the revolution. This is especially true with reference to the rhymes on social and political themes. The ideology of the advanced revolutionary class, the ruling class, exerted a continual organizing influence upon the ideology of their associates, the toiling peasantry. The poetic creation of the city proletariat drew in its train the poetry of the peasants. This was particularly expressed in the chastushka. This form of rhyme was, and remains, one of the favorite forms of song creation in the Soviet factory and mill. Widely diffused not only among the workmen, but also among the kolkhoz peasantry are rhymes dealing with the two dominant themes of Soviet folklore in general: those concerning the country's defense and the closely related themes of Soviet heroism, as manifested by the daring Soviet aviators, frontier guards, seamen, and particularly the conquerors of the Arctic.

While listening to the repertory of chastushkas sung during the last few years on the collective farms and in factories, or in collecting material with the help of special folklore expeditions and excursions, one cannot help noticing how many rhymes deal with the readiness of the Soviet people to defend their Socialist motherland, and with their longing to emulate the renowned heroes of the Red Army, of the fleet, and of the air force.

The Soviet youth frequently recall, in their chastushkas, the heroic figure of Chapayev. The figure of this man, as nurtured in the popular songs, legends, and tales, is well suited to fire the spirit to heroic exploits. A young Soviet patriot pledges himself to wage war, like Chapayev:

Play, my accordion,
Play with all your power.
Like Chapayev, I will fight,
If the enemy comes against us in war.[77]

The warriors are confident of victory, since at the head of the Red
Army there stands the well tried Red general Voroshilov:

If the bourgeois attack us,
They will receive a devastating blow:
Voroshilov, the Commissar,
Is preparing us for the defense.

Our forces are on the defensive.
If the enemy plunges into battle,
Then our beloved Voroshilov
Will lead us after him.[78]

The Soviet masses of the laboring people profoundly accepted the
ideas of the leader of the peoples, Comrade Stalin, that the Soviet
Union is not aspiring toward the conquest of any foreign lands whatever; the Soviet Union is striving for peace, but if the enemy should
attack, then "not one inch of our land will we yield up to anyone."
Numerous folk chastushkas repeat the words of Stalin, expressing
complete agreement with them:

Henceforth, with a watchful eye,
We shall observe our boundary.
We do not need any other land,
But our own land we will not yield.

Toward the Eastern boundary
The white reptile crawls again.
Only we will not give him
Our land to trample upon.

Whoever pokes his swinish snout
Into our Soviet vegetable garden,
We will beat that idea out of him at once;
Let him not poke in his snout! [79]

[77] *Red Army Folklore*, p. 182.
[78] *Ibid.*, pp. 180, 181.   [79] *Ibid.*, pp. 183, 184.

Folk songs gave a very vivid and striking response to the exploits of the Soviet aviators and seamen. The epic voyage of the *Cheluskin*, the aviators who rescued the *Cheluskin's* men from the icebergs, Papanin's men, the heroes of the Soviet Union, the aviators who made the flight to America by way of the North Pole, the numerous records of Kokkinaki, and the many other famous and distinguished Soviet persons who have astonished the world with their heroism, daring, and endurance have been extolled a countless number of times in chastushkas which express all the diversity of shades of feeling, of rapture, pride, and tender love for the brave men who have brought added glory to the Socialist motherland. For lack of space, we will give only a few examples. They prove how close the heroes' names were to every Soviet citizen.

> Ah, we have such aviators,
> Aviators who are brave young fellows!
> They have added glory to the whole land,
> They have brought back the *Cheluskin's* crew!

> I will close the door of the oven,
> So that the cake may get brown.
> To me, a simple young girl,
> Vodopyanov has sent his greetings.

> My heart has been smitten
> By the aviator Kamanin.
> Oh, that I might be among the icebergs,
> And that he alone might fly out!

> Today I dreamed a dream,
> What a delightful dream it was!
> Molokov fell in love with me
> And invited me to come to Dickson!

> Our aviators are heroes!
> There's not a day but this is what we hear:
> Kokkinaki has gone up high,
> Alekseyev has gone up higher still! [80]

[80] *Creative Art of the Peoples of the USSR*, p. 457.

Inspired by the examples of outstanding courage and Soviet patriotism, Soviet young people, both boys and girls, dream of becoming aviators, glider troopers, paratroopers, tank drivers, Arctic explorers, and frontier guardsmen. And all this is strikingly reflected in thousands of chastushkas.

The form of the chastushka was widely utilized for social-political agitation, in campaigning, and in propaganda for higher production. Hence arose those gradually accumulated features which basically distinguish the chastushka of the postrevolutionary period from that which preceded the revolution. These include, above all, a much closer connection than formerly with the literary speech (in vocabulary and in turns of phrase), a much greater concern with public questions. The percentage of chastushkas with social themes, in comparison with those of the prerevolutionary period, has increased several times over, though the love theme still remains, even down to the present time, the predominant one in this genre.

In the contemporary chastushka there is observed a gradual changing of the old accustomed repertory of this genre, for example, the gradual disappearance of the favorite compositional device of the old chastushka, as in general of the traditional peasant lyric—the device of "psychological parallelism." The many traditional beginnings, with figures taken from the world of nature, which made up the first part of the psychological parallelism, and symbolically expressed that which was set forth in the second part, have been transformed into a stereotyped poetic pattern. This pattern, in a purely mechanical way, often only with the help of external alliterative assonances, is joined to the remaining part of the chastushka. On the other hand, in our time there have appeared a great number of these rhymes, all the lines of which center about a single logical thought.[81]

This process of transformation of the chastushka genre testifies to the decisive changes in the general culture of the masses of the people to the swiftly developing habit of abstract theoretical thought. At the same time, musicians observe also significant changes in the

[81] See the article by P. I. Kaletsky, "On the Poetics of the Popular Rhyme," *The Literary Critic*, No. 9, 1936.

whole musical structure of the chastushkas, and also in the correlations between the text, the melody, and the role of the instrumental accompaniment. That sensitive connoisseur of musical folklore, E. V. Hippius, correctly remarks that the former syncretism of the literary art, of the song melody and the instrumental music, is being replaced by a very clever synthesis of the differentiated arts, which also bears witness to the vast progress that has taken place in the artistic culture of the toiling people.[82]

One cannot fail to note, in addition, the very frequent use made by contemporary Soviet poets of the rhythms and composition of the chastushka. Instances are constantly being multiplied in which the chastushkas of a poet permeate the masses and enter into the general repertory of such rhymes, being subjected to all those processes which are characteristic of any song that is transmitted orally.

Songs and chastushkas—these are the traditional genres of folklore which, reflecting the new life in an artistic form, and being subjected to a considerable transformation, have assumed and continue to occupy a prominent place in the popular creative art of Soviet Russia. Some of the traditional genres of folklore altogether disappear from view, as, for example, religious verse, the ceremonial song, the charm, the superstitious tale, and so forth. The dying out, in our time, of these genres which had grown up on the soil of feudal relationships is altogether natural: there no longer existed any of the necessary prerequisites for them, and above all, there was no longer that faith in the supernatural, that mythological character of the animistic world view, on which they had originated and continued to exist.

[82] See E. V. Hippius, "Elements of Intonation in the Russian Popular Rhyme," *Soviet Folklore*, Nos. 4-5, 1936.

PROVERBS AND TALES

1. PROVERBS

Many of the traditional genres of folklore continue to be developed. These include *proverbs, sayings,* and *riddles.* But numerically there are still, of course, not so many of the new proverbs and sayings, in comparison with the general vast store of the ancient ones, which have been accumulated in the course of centuries, and even of millennia. Proverbs and sayings—these are, as it were, the deposited formulas of the age-long observations and reflections of a people. But even so, the experiences of life during twenty years of the Soviet regime have already yielded a number of most valuable conclusions of the popular wisdom, which have penetrated deeply into the consciousness of the people, and have found expression in proverbs. Such, for example, are the proverbs and sayings dealing with the civil war, its historical significance and results: "He did not trust the Bolsheviki, he put his faith in the noblemen's guns"; "There are no more masters, the masters are swimming in the Black Sea"; "Petlura ran into the woods, and the devil took Denikin"; "The atamans and the noblemen fought with us—and they lost their trousers"; "Makhno perished a long while ago, and of Petlura, not even his skin remains"; "The roads are now grown over with grass, where the noblemen's feet used to pass." [1]

Strikingly imprinted upon the popular proverbs and sayings are the struggles with the kulak class, and there are warnings to be vigilant: "The kulak went out the gate of the collective farm—and that was the end of him"; "That time is past, in which the kulaks' fat sides used to bulge"; "Don't let a thief get up to the cart, and don't let a kulak get into the kolkhoz"; "Such a quiet little voice, but such devilish thought"! [2]

Like the chastushkas, the popular proverbs and sayings strengthened the relation of the people to the kolkhoz, to the conquests of the

[1] *Creative Art of the Peoples of the USSR,* p. 260.
[2] *Ibid.,* p. 364.

[659]

new agricultural technique, to the advantages of collective labor: "When a man lived alone, he went around in rags; but when the collective farm came, he found a caftan"; "Wealthy is that collective farm in which harmony reigns"; "A good kolkhoz has all its horses nice and plump"; "'Take a rest, little plowshare,' said Grandpa Timoshka, 'it is not your time now, we have a tractor.'"

A great many proverbs and sayings are being composed on the theme of national defense, testifying to the constant anxiety of the people for the inviolability of the boundaries of the Socialist motherland, to their readiness to defend it, to their love for the Red Army and their belief in its power. "Great is the power of Klim Voroshilov"; * "If you serve in the Red Army, you have nothing to worry about"; "Budyónny is our cavalry commander"; "If the collective farmer is also a crack horseman, it means he is one of Budyónny's men." [3]

Specific utterances of the leaders Lenin and Stalin have entered into the popular Soviet speech as proverbs. Such, for example, is the well known aphorism or watchword of Lenin, "Quality above quantity," or his words on the decisive character of the conflict with capitalistic elements in the public life and economy, expressed in the question: "Who will get the best of whom?" Many old folk proverbs or aphorisms of earlier writers have acquired a new sense and significance, and have become popular among the masses of the people, because they have been cited in the leaders' speeches. Such, for example, are the proverbs used by Comrade Stalin in his pre-election speech about people who cannot make up their minds on political matters: "He's just a so-so man, neither fish nor flesh"; "Neither a candle for God nor a poker for the devil"; or, following Gogol, "Neither a Bogdan † in the city nor a Selifan † in the village."

---

* Kliment Yefremovich Voroshilov, one of the early Bolshevik leaders, hero and commander of the Red Army victory at Tsaritsyn, Minister of the Army 1925–1940, member of the Politbureau.—ED.
[3] *Red Army Folklore*, pp. 162-163.
† Characters in Gogol's *Dead Souls.*—ED.

2. FOLK TALES

Among the traditional narrative genres of Russian folklore, the folk *tale* continues, in our time, to live a full life. The observations of folklorists indicate that the folk-tale creation has even gained in power as compared with prerevolutionary years. The artistic mastery of a number of talented storytellers has somehow developed. This has been especially noticeable during the last few years, the years of the Five-Year Plans. Here there is definitely expressed in a very high degree the general moral self-consciousness of the storytellers, in the majority of cases collective farmers who had experienced in themselves the improvement of material and spiritual life and the influence of the over-all growth of Soviet culture. A large role is also played in the elevation of artistic creation by the great attention which the Soviet public devotes to folk creation and to its masters. Many of the popular narrators have begun to feel as if they have grown wings, and have devoted themselves to their art with great love.

Not without reason, during the past few years, have there appeared such talented Russian storytellers as the Voronezh storyteller Anna Kupryanovna Baryshnikova; the northern storyteller (from the Karelian Autonomous Soviet Socialist Republic) Matthew Mikhailovich Korguyev; the storyteller from the Moscow province, Vasily Ivanovich Bespalikov; Ivan Fyodorovich Kovalev, from the Gorky province, and many others. As we have said in the proper place, from some of these storytellers there have been written down a very large number of tales (from Kupryanikha, Korguyev, and Kovalev, about a hundred apiece). Special publications have been devoted to some of them—a fact which in itself is also sufficiently indicative of the public attention to the folk creative art and to its outstanding representatives.[4]

[4] See the books *Tales of Kupryanikha,* with articles and notes by A. M. Novikova and I. A. Ossovetsky (Voronezh, 1937); *White Sea Tales, Related by M. M. Korguyev,* ed. A. N. Nechayev (Leningrad, 1938); *Tales of I. F. Kovalev,* with articles and commentaries by E. V. Hofmann and S. I. Mintz (State Literary

After examining the records of the tales produced in the Soviet era, especially during the last eight or ten years, one becomes convinced of the fact that in the general character of the transmission of the traditional tale subjects, very obvious upheavals are now in progress. First of all, with the majority of the storytellers there is apparent (though in a varying degree) a curtailment of the themes of the fantastic, miraculous tales in favor of the realistic tales—those of everyday life, and those of a social-satirical nature. Contemporary storytellers (not only the young ones, but even the old) devote a great deal of attention to the satirical tales against the nobles and priests, especially the latter. As we know, these social-satirical motifs in the folk tales were very widely diffused also in the old, prerevolutionary folklore; but at the present time, after the October Revolution, when the antipopular, exploiting role of the landowning class and of the clergy is recognized with a distinctness previously unheard of, the popular satire becomes still sharper and more striking. Much that under the conditions of the old regime had not been sufficiently thought out or expressed can now be fully and completely discussed. Beyond a doubt such tales as these, with their social-satirical content, played a great role in propaganda and agitation in the general process of the revolutionary destruction of the old mode of life and ideology.[5]

The general tendency toward realism in the contemporary tale is also reflected in the fact that a multitude of realistic details of everyday life, and frequently details already taken from the new Soviet mode of life, have actually been introduced into the tale of a miraculous, magical character.

Here is the comment of A. N. Nechayev, the investigator and publisher of the tales of the storyteller M. M. Korguyev:

Museum). In addition to these, see the collections of tales, compiled in the Soviet period: I. V. Karnaukhova, *Tales and Legends of the Northern Region* (Moscow, 1934), and *Tales of the Krasnoyarsk Region*, comp. M. V. Krasnozhenova, ed. M. K. Azadovsky and N. P. Andreyev (Leningrad, 1937).

[5] See, on this point, the correct observations of N. P. Andreyev in the introductory article to the collection *Tales of the Krasnoyarsk Region* by M. V. Krasnozhenova (Leningrad, 1937), pp. 20-23.

All, or in any case the majority, of his tales are distinguished by the tendency of the storyteller to paint the traditional motifs in the realistic and psychological colors of everyday life. This, without detracting from the interest of the subject, endows his tales with a great freshness, an excellent compositional agreement, and, as it were, removes them from the magical plane to the plane of reasonable explanation. The heroes of his tales have been humanized. Their actions are motivated and psychologically justified. . . . Realistic sketches of the details of everyday life, depicted in intimate lyrical tones, are very characteristic of Korguyev's tales. In giving a fresh adaptation to a traditional outline, in fashioning a new composition and introducing a great quantity of contemporary material, Korguyev corrects many of the old concepts, and thereby connects the tale organically with our contemporary period. He replaces the wooden eagle, upon which the hero of the tale usually does his journeying, by a two-seated airplane, with levers for steering "to the right" and "to the left." Unusual, also, for the tale, is the hero's refusal, on principle, to marry the daughter of the tsar or prince; and the great number of new words (comrade, manager, subway, bookkeeper, airplane, and so forth) and the contemporary phraseology. All of this, taken together, endows Korguyev's tales with an exceptional vitality, interest, and cognitive value.[6]

Much of what has been said about the White Sea storyteller Korguyev can also be applied to the Voronezh woman narrator Kupryanikha, as well as to Kovalev, the storyteller of the Gorky province, and to other contemporary storytellers, who involuntarily reflect, in their language, figures, and their treatment of the traditional popular tales which have been handed down to them, our contemporary Soviet period, the internal upheavals in men's consciousness, and the external changes in everyday life.

The contemporary Soviet period, however, is even more directly and strikingly reflected in the tales of the Soviet storytellers. The many talented Soviet storytellers do not confine themselves to the transmission, even though in a new treatment, of the traditional tales; they strive to compose *new tales*, with the clearly formulated artistic purpose of expressing, in the forms and figures of the tales,

---

[6] A. N. Nechayev, *White Sea Tales, Related by M. M. Korguyev,* pp. 8-10.

their own new world view, their attitude toward the October Revolution, and toward the whole Soviet regime.

In this connection, great social and artistic interest is attached to the tales which were written down in 1937 from several talented Russian storytellers, by the editorial staff of *Pravda*, and printed in the well known volume *Creative Art of the Peoples of the USSR*: "The Most Precious Thing," by the Onega narrator, F. A. Konashkov; "Three Sons" and "The Little Scarlet Flower," by V. I. Bespalikov; "The Hill of Ice," by I. F. Kovalev; "How the Hunter Fyodor Drove Out the Japs." by G. I. Sorokovikov (of Siberia); "Chapayev Is Alive," by A. I. Filonina (from the Kuibyshev province), and "The Death of Chapayev," by M. M. Korguyev.

Konashkov's tale is based on one of the popular themes in Russian traditional folklore, which was also utilized by Nekrasov—the theme of wandering in search of truth. Three collective farmers had a dispute with one another as to the question, "What is the most precious thing in life?" and they decided to go wandering through the land to find the correct answer. After a long journey through the Soviet land (a motif which afforded the storyteller an opportunity to give a description of the great attainments of Soviet culture), the wayfarers arrive in Moscow, happen upon Stalin, have a talk with him, and come to the general conclusion that "the best and most precious thing we have on earth is the word of Comrade Stalin." In the language of Konashkov, who is not only a storyteller, but, as we have mentioned several times above, a well known narrator of *byliny*, there are many echoes of the poetic speech of the *byliny* and of the traditional tales: "Then the Ratai say: We will sow the rye and barley, and when it has ripened, we will harvest the grain, we will pile it up into stacks, we will drag out the stacks, and thresh it at home, we will prepare the malt, and brew the beer. Without grain, no one can possibly live!" Or we have another description of a journey through the Soviet land:

They are going along by themselves, and they marvel. Where formerly the rivers rose up over the ford, and there was no passageway either on foot or for carts, there they have built bridges across the rivers, half a verst in length: they have driven in piles, they have laid planks, and have set up balustrades upon them. Where under the old government there were swamps that no one could crawl through, and there was no passageway either on foot or for carts, they have laid splendid paved roads. Along these roads there pass various kinds of machines, and by Lake Onega itself there stands an airplane. You can either go on foot, or take your place in a machine and ride, or you can get into the airplane and fly. Where there were dense woods that could not be passed through, they have laid fine broad roads, the whole surface is smoothed over, and lanterns have been placed along the route. If you travel by day, it's light, and if you travel by night, it's light.[7]

In Bespalikov's tale "Three Sons" we have a vivid echo of the newspaper accounts of the heroic death of the frontier guard Lagoda, and of his self-sacrificing brothers, who took his place in the service for the protection of the frontiers. Only, in the tale, the first brother did not perish. When they reach the frontier region, his brothers revive him, sprinkling his tortured body, as is the fashion in tales, with spring water, which they have succeeded in procuring in the mountains.

Another tale by Bespalikov, "The Little Scarlet Flower," tells how the kulaks attacked a leading collective farmer, a certain Paul Zhukov, and buried him in the earth, but he was dug up out of the ground and saved, owing to the fact that from the red Order on his breast there grew up, miraculously, a little scarlet flower. This is a very successful utilization of the traditional tale motif of the miraculous plant, which grows up on the grave of one who has suffered unjustly.

Kovalev's tale "The Hill of Ice" is devoted to the conquests of the Arctic.

Of great historical and social interest are the tales about the popular favorite, the hero of the civil war, Chapayev, whose figure, as we have seen, is delineated in many poetic genres in the creative art of the Soviet people. According to the popular tales, Chapayev, or, as the tales and legends frequently call him, Chapay, did not die.

This is the way the Kuibyshev narrator A. I. Filonina ends her tale about him:

[7] *Creative Art of the Peoples of the USSR*, p. 97.

Only it is a lie that Chapayev was drowned. The general's men killed Chapayev's men, that is true, but Chapayev remained alive. Wounded, all covered with blood, he staggered along. His comrade, Petka, supports him:

"What are you going to do alone?" Petka says to him.

But Chapayev could no longer speak, from weakness. Petka loaded him on his back, and he carried him to the Ural River, and he carried him through that river, on his back. And he brought him back to health.

Chapayev survived, and changed his name, and was no longer called by the nickname of Chapayev, but by some other kind of name. This was because of his error, I mean, so that there might not be any shame upon his people. And even now people tell the story that Chapayev is alive, that he has become a great commander, and he is so very just and kind.[8]

In another tale, which was written down in the province of Saratov, from the collective-farm stableman F. B. Buzayev, there is also introduced the persistent idea that Chapayev did not perish. According to this tale, he was hidden by some old man, a Kirghiz, who for this was brutally tortured by the Whites. According to the words of the storyteller, Chapayev often, by his sudden appearance, rescued the Red Army detachments from harm:

Here now the detachment is about to perish, for its forces are very few, and also it has no cartridges. At any moment the brutal Whites will cut down our good men—and suddenly, no one knows from where, Chapayev will appear. He flies upon a fiery horse, as on a bird; he brandishes his silver sword, and the skirts of their cloaks are scattered upon the wind.

"Follow me, boys!" he shouts, and straightway falls upon the Whites.

The fear of the Red Army men disappears, their hearts are set on fire, and they rush to the attack, along with Chapayev. And they lay about them to such good effect that there is not one living soul among the enemy remaining.

And then, when they recollect themselves, they look around, and Chapayev is not there. And they could not believe that he had in truth been there. But many of them assure that they saw Chapay.

[8] *Ibid.*, pp. 230-231.

Only, on his breast there was not one, but there were three battle Orders.[9]

One of the very best tales about Chapayev is the tale by M. M. Korguyev, first printed in the volume *Creative Art of the Peoples of the USSR*, and printed for the second time in the collection *White Sea Tales, Related by M. M. Korguyev*. Here is what A. N. Nechayev, the specialist in Korguyev's creative art, has to say about this new heroic tale:

Here Korguyev has made use of his customary device—the blending of various elements in a new composition. This attempt to create a new tale based on contemporary material is curious not only because of the outward conditions under which it was created [Korguyev composed the tale directly after he had listened to the *bylina* of the narrator P. I. Ryabinin, on Chapayev.—Au.], but besides giving an indication of the author's broad creative scope, the tale "About Chapayev" presents a wealth of interesting material for the study of Korguyev's mastery of his art. In working out a new subject, he drew from the traditional tale material only two motifs, and furthermore, with a great artist's delicacy of perception, he selected only those features of the motifs which most closely corresponded to the legendary-heroic representation of Chapayev. The amazing martial exploits of the hero of the civil war, and his unusual popularity, have been combined by Korguyev in the traditional figure from the folk tale of the knight who fights with serpents, who is invincible in combat, because of the talisman-ring which he has in his possession. This is approximately everything that he takes from the folk-tale motifs in his reworking of the material.

However, the production bears all the features of the folk-tale tradition. This is achieved both by the development of the subject, the composition, and by the whole style of the narrative: here, too, are the customary formulas, such, for example, as the beginning: "Not in a certain remote kingdom, not in a certain far-off state, but in this very one in which you and I are living—once upon a time there lived a peasant," or in the description of a battle: "And he began to beat down Kolchakov's men and Denikin's men, as one sickles down the grass"; or, "And he cut him down with the sword, and he pierced him with the spear, and he swept away like the whirlwind," and so forth. Here also is the trinity, so familiar in the tale: the hero, the

[9] *Red Army Folklore*, p. 108.

youngest of three brothers, fights with increasing intensity in three battles. Certain episodes are borrowed in their entirety from the magical and heroic tales, but in the new composition they have a modern ring. Thus, for example, even the folk-tale formula in the description of a fight is bound up with the contemporary period: "He tried to slash him with the sword, pierce him with the lance—but had to fire his revolver." A new type of weapon is introduced into the traditional description of the fight, and this at once creates an organic tie between the imagery of the fairy tale and contemporary life.[10]

There has not as yet been sufficient material gathered on the contemporary tales, but even the amount of material which has already been collected reveals how organic is the union, in the Soviet tale, between the old tradition and the vital feeling of the contemporary period.

[10] *White Sea Tales*, p. 7.

LAMENTS, POEMS, TALES

❦

1. LAMENTS

One of the ancient traditional genres of folklore, the *popular lamentation*, or *wailing*, has also been further developed in the Soviet era.

The civil war afforded material for the "recruiting" lament (to use the old terminology), and for the funeral lament.

For all their closeness to the traditional poetics of the popular lamentations, the laments of the Soviet era very often—and with increasing frequency as one approaches the more recent years—are altogether lacking in that ecclesiastical-religious coloring which was inherent in the prerevolutionary lamentations, and are filled with new ideas, with civil and revolutionary motifs.

The following two Siberian lamentations from the period of the civil war are characteristic in this respect.[1] In one of these, the "Lamentation of a Mother for Her Son, Killed by the Japanese" (during the period of the Intervention), after the interrogatory exclamations which are traditional in the popular lament:

And whither then, my dear son, are you going away from us,
And for whom then do you forsake your aged parents? . . .
And who now will give us food and drink in our old age?
And who will bury us, as we have buried you?

a significant explanation is given, very characteristic of that time, as to the motives which stirred the young hero to go to war:

But you, our own darling, turned away from us,
And went into the woods and mountains to gain freedom.
But you did not gain a bit of freedom, but only death
    for yourself,
And for us, in our old age, woes and sorrows.

[1] Originally published in *Materials for the Study of Partisan Poetry* (Irkutsk, 1926), reprinted in *Red Army Folklore*, by V. M. Sidelnikov, pp. 129-131.

The enemy have consumed us, they have plundered everything,
And have snatched you, in your youth, out of the world. . . .
They did not give you a chance to live until freedom came,
And they did not give you a chance to get acquainted with
the new life.

In another lament, "The Lamentation of a Wife for Her Husband
on Seeing Him Off To Join the Partisans," again, at the beginning,
there come the questions which are traditional in the "recruiting"
lament:

To whom have you left your beloved wife,
And to whom then have you left your dear little children?
Alas, and what then shall I do with them,
Being a woman ignorant and uneducated?

The last line is characteristic of the mode of life of the first years
after the revolution, when the country woman still frequently felt
her cultural backwardness as compared with her husband who was
absorbed by progressive ideas and heroic moods.

The lament comes to an end with the motif which is so new for
the "recruiting laments," delineating the revolutionary attitudes of
the progressive peasantry, who with heroic self-sacrifice defended the
revolution:

Do not weep, beloved little wife. . . .
How can I forget you,
And how can I forget my little children?
And when the dear children shall ask you:
"Where is our dear papa, or is he no more?"
Then tell them, dear wife,
"He is fighting to obtain freedom."

The lamentations reach still greater ideational and artistic heights
when their traditional form is used by the talented women poets of
the people to express the people's feelings in connection with the
death of the greatest men of the era. Such is the lament, wonderful
in its artistic expressiveness and its depth of feeling, of the White

Sea woman narrator M. S. Krukova on the death of Lenin: "Moscow, the City of Stone, Is All in Tears." [2]

In the chapter on the traditional folk lamentations, we saw that the lamentation, especially in the North, was performed not only as an expression of narrowly personal and bitter grief, but frequently— for example in the creative work of the famous wailer Fedosova— served as a poetic form for the expression of social attitudes and ideas, and at the same time included striking pictures of family and social life.

In the chapter on historical songs we have observed that from the beginning of the eighteenth century on, elements of the poetics of the lamentation were interwoven into the genre of the historic song. Such, for example, are the song laments for the death of Peter I, which were imitated by similar later historical song laments of the eighteenth and even the beginning of the nineteenth century.

M. S. Krukova, a splendid connoisseur of the oral poetic tradition, a performer of *byliny* and historical songs, a composer of laments, as we have already observed, is distinguished by a great gift of improvisation. On the basis of the traditional poetics of the laments and historical songs, with which she was so familiar, M. S. Krukova also composed her own lament for Lenin, a work which is original and, at the same time, of an authentically folk character.[3]

The first lines of Krukova's lament recall the typical beginning of many of the historical songs of the seventeenth and eighteenth centuries.

> That's how it was in our Moscow, the city of stone,
> A great misfortune has occurred there. . . .
> Moscow, the city of stone, is all in tears.

[2] In addition to M. S. Krukova, laments were also composed by other peasant poetesses of the North. Eight laments, including the lamentation of M. S. Krukova and a translation from the Karelian of a lament by M. M. Khoteyeva, have been published in a small but valuable book, *Tales and Laments for Lenin* (Petrozavodsk, Karelian Institute for Scientific Research, 1938).

[3] M. S. Krukova's lament was published for the first time in the volume *Creative Art of the Peoples of the USSR*, pp. 52-55.

Thus Krukova begins her lament.

> That's what happened in our Moscow:
> At midnight, the bells began ringing,
> And our Moscow merchants burst into tears.

The above lines are the beginning of the historical song lament (written down in the year 1619 by Richard James) on the occasion of the death of the provincial governor, Skopin-Shuysky.

"That's how it was in Moscow, the city of white stone," is the first line of the historical song on the resolution of the Muscovites not to give up their native city of Smolensk to the Poles. And the beginning of the song on the death of Peter I runs as follows:

> When among us it happened, brothers, in Holy Russia,
> In Holy Russia, in Moscow the city of stone.

And if thus, line by line, we analyze Krukova's lament for Lenin, we can recall a multitude of parallel expressions, images, turns of phrase which are encountered in the traditional historical songs and laments. But, as a genuine poet, Krukova, remaining historically within the limits of the traditional poetics of the popular lament, creates her own original poetic work, introducing into it both the motifs of her own personal life impressions (in particular, details which can be explained primarily by the mode of life and interests of the northerners dwelling by the sea), and the motifs of our own time.

For example, Krukova utilizes the traditional poetic formula of the popular lament: the question addressed to the departed as to whither he is journeying. This question is usually given, in the traditional popular laments, in approximately such a form as this:

> But whither are you journeying?
> And whither have you fitted yourself out to go?
> And what way and road are you taking?

M. S. Krukova develops this traditional poetic formula into an extensive picture of our Soviet land (from a point of view, it is true, which is typical of an inhabitant of the northern seacoast) and of the strenuous work of the leader who guided the whole of its political and economic life. Owing to the concrete nature of the facts enumerated by Krukova, her entire work becomes unusually striking and artistically convincing:

> And whither is he journeying among us?
> On what way, and on what road?
> Is it a distant path, and a sorrowful one?
> And is he going to foreign, Western lands?
> Is he going on the blackened great ships,
> On the steamers, or the steamships?
> Or is it possible that he is going to the Eastern lands,
> And to cities that are far away?
> He is not going to any of our cities that are in the East,
> And he is not going on the blackened great ships,
> Nor is he going on our steamers that run by steam:
> Nor is he going across our deep seas,
> Nor indeed is he going to watch the icebreakers,
> How they ply, how they penetrate
> Into the winters, the cold winters,
> Nor is he going across the White Sea,
> As if to see, as if to examine things there.
> All have found out, they have guessed,
> All, from the oldest to the youngest,
> That he has gone away from us, he has withdrawn himself,
> Not beyond the steep mountains of the Sparrow Hills,
> Not across the River Mother-Moscow,
> Not beyond the dark and dense woods.
> When he went away from us, he disappeared here,
> Like a mighty leader, our dear comrade,
> But still Lenin was the father of all Russia,
> Still Vladimir Ilyich was our light.

At times some one specific realistic detail, which Krukova introduces with great artistic taste into the traditional fabric of the lament, gives it a warm and touching quality. In the following words Krukova describes how Lenin lies in the mausoleum (she composed the lament immediately after her first visit to his resting place):

> His clear eyes are gently closed,
> His sweet lips have just become silent,
> His white hands are relaxed.
> In his short military jacket
> He sleeps soundly, and will not awaken.

This realistic, concrete reference to the "short military jacket," inserted into the traditional poetic formula of the popular lament, shows what a real poet Krukova is, and how skillfully she utilizes her talent as a narrator-improviser, writing sincerely and penetratingly.

As is characteristic of a great poet, not a single detail escaped the keen observation of Krukova on her visit to Lenin's mausoleum. She remembered the sorrowful and stern faces of the Red Army men who stood on guard at the entrance to the mausoleum. Krukova tried to penetrate into their feelings and thoughts. And she creates the remarkable image of Red Army men who guard the precious dust of Lenin, and through them, she creates a poetic image of the whole Red Army, which guards the whole land of the Soviets:

> They watch him day and night,
> Young recruits of the Red Army,
> And in their hands they all hold rifles,
> Shining rifles, with strong locks.
> They stand, and they become thoughtful,
> They become thoughtful, and grow sorrowful:
> And their thoughts are much agitated,
> And their sighing is profound.
> Sleep peacefully, dear Ilyich,
> The Red Army is very powerful,
> Very powerful and very loyal.

The lament for Lenin comes to an end with a thought which, as we shall see further on, is repeated in a multitude of works of the most diverse peoples of the Soviet Union—that Lenin's work is left in the faithful hands of his illustrious pupil and friend, Stalin:

> All his works he has entrusted and bequeathed
> To the unswerving leader of all of the people,
> His illustrious friend Stalin.
> He is all the time thinking his thoughts with Ilyich,
> He is thinking his thoughts, and speaking these words to him:
> "We are with you, Ilyich, we will not part,
> We will not part, we will not separate ourselves from you,
> Eternal will be the memory of you."

The form of the ancient popular lament was often utilized by the talented representatives of the contemporary creative art of the people—and not of the Russian people alone. The lament for Stalin's favorite pupil and fellow worker, Sergey Mironovich Kirov, who was villainously murdered by the enemies of the people—a lament composed by the remarkable Mordvinian woman narrator E. P. Krivosheyeva [4]—has deservedly attracted the widespread attention of the entire Soviet people.

2. POEMS

We have seen that a number of the old traditional genres of Russian folklore continue their life also in the Soviet folk creation, subject to very great changes with regard to their ideational content and their artistic form.

A question that is altogether legitimate is frequently raised in the public press: Is there such a thing as a *Soviet bylina?* Is the epos of the *byliny* still in process of creation?

I have already had occasion to give a brief answer to this question, in the chapter on the *byliny*. It should be remembered that the *byliny*, constituting a poetic genre which was closely linked with the age of feudalism, ceased to be composed, as new creations, as early as the end of the sixteenth century. (There are a very few exceptions, which need not be taken into account.) During three centuries and a half, the creative art of the *byliny* has been confined to artistic versions, variations of subjects which had been composed earlier. Not without reason had the *byliny* long and aptly been called, among the people, "ancient tales." In other words, the genre of the *byliny* was looked upon, both by the narrators themselves and by their audience, as a narrative dealing with events that had occurred long ago, in a period of great antiquity. Modern times, from the end of the sixteenth century on, found almost no echo in the *byliny*. We have seen that this function was performed by the so-called "historical" song—and that only to the beginning of the nineteenth century. Fantastic in character, based to a very considerable extent upon a profound faith in the miraculous, the *bylina* could not rise

---

[4] "Lament for Kirov," *Creative Art of the Peoples of the USSR*, reprinted in the collection *Russian Laments* (Leningrad, 1937).

anew and develop, in view of the radical changes in the general world view of the people. It was not without reason that the ancient *byliny* continued to be related only in the very distant borderlands, where the power of the old traditions and views was much stronger.

But, none the less, the vast poetic heritage of the popular *byliny* has been utilized by several contemporary narrators, in their efforts to give an artistic response to the events of our modern Soviet life, in the forms of the old epos of the *byliny*.

But here, frequently, we do not have a genuine artistic *bylina*; in place of the *bylina*, we have only a stylization imitating the *bylina*. So, for example, the well known narrator of the trans-Onega region, Peter Ivanovich Ryabinin-Andreyev, composed the *"Bylina* of Chapayev,"[5] and performed it from manuscript in a number of the higher-school auditoriums in Moscow. (Ryabinin is literate, and writes down his productions himself.) And even with all Ryabinin's mastery of the rhythm and tune of the *byliny*, for all his strict and even pedantic use of the traditional formulas, epithets, and threefold repetitions which characterize the *byliny*, his *"bylina"* cannot be regarded as successful. There is too great a contrast between the old form and the new content: with Ryabinin, there is no organic connection between the form and the content.

Martha Semyonovna Krukova's poetic experiments have been crowned with much greater success. One must take into consideration Krukova's great gift of improvisation, which is characteristic of her, and of which we have already spoken. It must also be said that Martha Semyonovna did not set herself the task, as Ryabinin did, of creating a *bylina* in the absolute sense. She broadly utilized, for her epic productions on contemporary themes, the poetics of several traditional genres which were well known to her—the poetics of the ancient *byliny* (more than one hundred of which were taken down from her lips), of the historical songs, the lamentations, and the ancient, so-called "sostenuto" lyric songs. As a result, we have something new, original, independent, which in certain specific aspects (for example, in the verse, in the traditional formulas, and so on)

[5] Printed in *The Standard*, No. 5, 1937.

even recalls the "ancient songs," but as a whole is sharply distinguished from them, particularly by its great sustained lyric quality, by the free plan of its composition, by the presence of general arguments, by the emphatically political tendency of the production. The poet herself senses the distinction between her new productions and the "ancient songs," and, contrasting her works with the latter, she calls them "new songs." This particular genre of legendary poems is one of the manifestations of the Russian folk epos in the new stages of its development.

When reading the "new tales" of Krukova, it is necessary, however, to bear in mind one circumstance connected with the process of her creative work in producing them: she works with the help of the writer V. A. Popov. Popov supplies M. S. Krukova with books, newspapers, and magazines. Krukova has been literate from childhood, and is a passionate lover of reading; that is why, even in her "ancient tales," one so frequently finds reminiscences of books. He tells her many stories, and frequently accompanies the narrator in her travels. In particular, Krukova recently made a trip to the Caucasus, accompanied by Popov and his wife. With reference to the part Popov plays in Krukova's creative process, he himself says:

My part in the transcription and revision of the actual legends has been limited to assisting her to place certain events in their correct historical sequence; in eliminating abstractions which have no direct relation to the basic theme; in the considerable curtailment of superfluous repetitions, and of descriptions which at certain points were too long drawn out, and which created a disproportion in the different parts of the production; and in the elimination of the peculiarities of the White Sea dialect" [Mainly phonetic, not lexicological or morphological.—Au.].[6]

Popov wrote down the following of Krukova's "new tales," or "legendary poems": "Long-Beard and the Bright Falcons" (a legend of O. U. Schmidt and the epopee of the Cheluskin); "Chapay";

[6] *Legends and Poems of Martha Semyonovna Krukova,* transcr. and rev. by Victorin Popov (Archangel, 1937), p. 16.

"A Tale of the North Pole" (on the exploits of Papanin's men); [7]
"A Tale of Lenin." [8]

The tale of Lenin is a poetic version of the biography of Vladimir Ilyich, with an extensive description of the revolutionary events of the years 1905 and 1917, and of the civil war. In order to give some idea of the general character of the exposition, and the style of the "Tale," I give a brief selection from the chapter devoted to the beginning of the civil war:

> When thereupon the dark cloud arose
> Above that land, above our Soviet Russia,
> Then there was a roar as of loud thunder,
> Then a great storm began to rage,
> The sky was covered with clouds from all four sides,
> The generals and sergeants gathered together,
> The landowners and the factory owners gathered together.
> The princes and the noblemen gathered together,
> The merchants, very wealthy men, gathered together,
> They crowded into a secret place,
> A place that was secret and hidden,
> And they spoke among themselves such words as these:
> "What is this that has happened in the dear land of Russia?
> We cannot endure the new order,
> We cannot live in such a life.
> We cannot get along with them. . . .
> Let us assemble our generals and our majors,
> Let us assemble the whole of the White druzhina,
> Let us fall upon the force of the Red Army.
> Let us kill and destroy them, and trample them all into
>   the dust."
> And Lenin, the leader, takes his usual walk in the Kremlin,
> With his hand he is smoothing his head,
> With anxiety, he paces rapidly up and down the room,
> His zealous heart is troubled:
> "Alas, they are all ravening lions,
> Ah, they are all dishonorable dogs,
> The dogs do not give us a chance to rest,

[7] *Ibid.*

[8] "A Tale of Lenin, by Martha Semyonovna Krukova," written down and revised by Victorin Popov (Moscow, The Soviet Writer, 1938). All the books have been reprinted in *Legends of M. S. Krukova* (Moscow, State House for the Publication of Artistic Literature, 1937).

To handle our affairs, and to put them in order.
We shall have to wage war with them, to contend with them,
We will take them in battle, in bloody combat,
We will leave none of them for seed!" [9]

Here we see again, as in the "Lament for Lenin," a very skillful introduction into the traditional style-structure of the details and facts of our own time, even including the realistic individual delineation of the figure of Lenin: his characteristic movement when agitated, his swift gait.

Or here is still another example of portrait painting, in the organic blending of realistic individual features and elements of the traditional epic poetics: the idealizing hyperbolism, the constant epithets, and so forth. Krukova thus draws the figure of Comrade K. E. Voroshilov, mounted on his horse:

How white his mane is, and how it streams,
And how his white tail curls,
How from the horse's mouth flame and smoke billow out,
How from the horse's eyes sparks pour forth,
And on the horse sits a wondrous knight,
He holds the reins in his left hand,
In his right hand he holds a telescope.
And on the horse sits our bright falcon,
And his name is Klim Voroshilov, our light. [10]

A great part of Krukova's legendary poems deals with the theme of the conquest of the Arctic. And this is altogether comprehensible in the creative work of a narrator who lives by the northern seacoast. For her, the epopee of the *Cheluskin* and the heroic life of Papanin's men on the icebergs are very near and dear themes. She, being an inhabitant of the White Sea Coast, knows well the heaped-up blocks of ice, the caprices of the sea and of the Arctic Ocean, the dangers which lie in wait for the seamen at every step. That is why she composed with such love the poem "Long-Beard and the Bright Falcons" (by these she means the glorious hero-aviators, who rescued the men of the *Cheluskin* from the iceberg), the "Legend of the North Pole," and a poem which has not yet appeared in book form, but has been

---

[9] "The Tale of Lenin," pp. 41-42.   [10] *Ibid.*, pp. 42-43.

printed several times in newspapers, on the safe return of Papanin's men to Moscow. Krukova is the poet of the North. She is attached to her own White Sea region with a passionate devotion.

Popov wrote down from Krukova the following poetic improvisation, which she composed in reply to the invitation extended her to move permanently to Moscow or Leningrad from her native town of Zimnyaya Zolotitsa ("Winter Gold"), on the shore of the White Sea:

> There is nothing more delightful in the North
> Than the White Sea.
> It is always with us here, our glory.
> Very lovely, as it stands before us when it is quiet,
> Then it stands, and does not ripple,
> Not a wave of the sea overflows—
> Then it is good to look upon the White Sea!
> But, when the wild winds blow,
> The tempestuous winds of the North,
> Then the mighty waves arise,
> Then the White Sea begins to roar,
> It drives all the waves in to the shore,
> Upon the yellow sand.
> Like white sea gulls, the waves fly upward,
> The waves will rush toward the shore,
> Then the gray rocks will begin to thunder,
> The sea will roar and be troubled.
> It is good to look upon the White Sea
> When it is ruffled by the stormy weather.[11]

An excellent connoisseur of the multitude of legends, tales, and songs about Peter I who astounded the imagination of the coast dwellers, two centuries ago, by his inexhaustible energy in the building of the fleet, Krukova speaks with still greater rapture of the efforts and successes of the Soviet mariners, aviators, the scholars who are working to subjugate that formidable element, the sea; about the organizers of all these labors and victories—Lenin and Stalin.

More recently, Martha Semyonovna has been occupied with a great creative work, the composition of a long poem on J. V. Stalin.

[11] *Legends and Poems of M. S. Krukova*, pp. 14-15.

The trip to the Caucasus, where she visited Gori, the birthplace of the leader, and admired the Caucasus Mountains and the Black Sea, produced a very powerful impression upon her, which will undoubtedly be strikingly reflected in her poem.

In Krukova's example we see how, in the Soviet Union, the popular narrator of the old-time *byliny* is transformed into an authentic contemporary poet, who devotes his talent to the expression of the ideas and emotions by which the whole country lives. The social significance of the artistic activity of the popular narrators is so great that the most talented of them (M. S. Krukova, M. M. Korguyev, F. A. Konashkov, A. K. Baryshnikova Kupryanikha, I. F. Kovalev) were recently (August 9, 1938) elected to the body of the Congress of Soviet Writers, as full members.

3. TALES

In surveying the Russian folklore of the Soviet period, one must definitely draw the conclusion that the folklore of Soviet Russia has a predominantly realistic character. The remote past, hoary antiquity, fantastic figures which lead us back into the heart of the centuries or into the regions beyond the clouds hold considerably less interest for the contemporary composers and performers of folklore than they did before the revolution. Contemporary life, its characteristics, its affairs both great and small, the life of contemporary society and of the individual member of that society, in all its reality—these are the things which are of paramount interest to the popular poets. The life of every modern man, whatever position he may occupy in society, proves to be much more interesting than an imaginary life, or than the life of distant eras. Every man, over the revolutionary years, has lived through so much of joy and sorrow, so much that is new, that to come to know one's self, the life of the surrounding people, the life of one's own factory, of one's own collective farm, is a great necessity.

And not without reason, in our own time, is there observed in folklore a leaning toward the oral "tales," toward the biographical narratives and memoirs, toward stories about one's self, about one's own life, about events in which one has had a part, about remarkable people whom one has had occasion to meet or to work with. In the last few years the Soviet folklorists have already collected quite a large amount of material from the oral tales of workingmen and peasants about the revolution, the civil war, the heroic restoration of the economy destroyed by war, and all the further stages in the development of the Socialist construction.

It is true that this narrative genre, or, to speak still more correctly, these genres, still stand, to a considerable extent, on the periphery of folklore; the justification for their inclusion within the body of material known as folklore is still being disputed by certain investigators. They point to the fact that the tales, at times, are related without any special pretensions to artistic merit; some of the tales are in the form of a single, solitary fact; many of them do not pass from mouth to mouth, they do not attain any permanent form.[12] However, the majority of Soviet folklorists assign a great importance to the recording of oral tales, since they give valuable material for judgments as to the birth of a new poetic genre. Perhaps, indeed, not all of them, but at any rate—as the observations of folklorists have established—many such narratives of personal experience, thanks to frequent repetitions by one and the same storyteller, have taken on permanent form. Some of them begin to be retold by the listeners, and thus the single story begins to live its life as folklore. Certain of these tales are obviously connected, in style and composition, with the traditional folk stories, the realistic fairy tales and anecdotes. And the historical significance of the oral autobiographies and memoir tales is obvious to everyone.

In 1925 an attempt was made at an extensive collection of auto-

---

[12] The theoretical arguments on the nature of the oral tale, as a folklore genre, and on the methods of writing it down are illuminated in an article by P. Bogoslovsky, "On the Soviet Revolutionary Epos, and the Methods of Its Collection and Study," *Soviet Regional Studies*, No. 7, 1934; and also the article by A. Gurevich, "How to Record Oral Narratives" (on the question of the methods of writing down and revising oral narratives), *Annals of the Society for the Study of Eastern Siberia*, Vol. I, 1936. A summary report on the problem of the oral tale was read at the session of the Institute of Ethnography of the Academy of Sciences of the USSR in June, 1938, by N. D. Komovskaya. The report is being prepared for publication.

biographical narratives.[13] From the year 1928 on, the writing down of oral tales takes on a systematic character.[14] A great collection of oral narratives was compiled by Comrades Mierer and Borovik, who wrote down from the Ural workmen their recollections of their participation in the Civil War. These narratives, in respect of their ideological and artistic character, are very diverse, and for this reason they are not of equal value. Many of these tales are infectious in their martial heroic enthusiasm, they make us feel the pathos of the conflict for the bright Socialist future; others reveal terrible pictures of the terrors of the civil war, all kinds of atrocities perpetrated by Kolchakov's men upon the workers; some are striking in the exactness and businesslike quality of their historical narrative; some interpolate expository matter into the customary flow of the traditional tale of everyday life or anecdote. An attentive study of these and similar recordings will enable us in the future to draw essential conclusions as to the genre or genres of the oral memoir. In any case, a new and important problem has been revealed for folkloristics.

The systematic and large-scale recording of the oral narratives of workmen and peasants may also yield a vast store of material for writers, as striking documents taken from life. Folklorists have more than once had occasion to comment on the very evident fact that frequently a magnificently gifted narrator, who can set forth his oral tale in an interesting, artistic, and convincing manner, becomes altogether powerless when he takes up the pen. By means of writing down oral narratives, fixing upon them the attention both of the

[13] N. Yurgin, "The Collection of Peasant Autobiographies," *Artistic Folklore*. Bks. IV-V, 1929.

[14] S. Mierer and V. Borovik, "Oral Narratives of the Ural Workmen Dealing with the Civil War," *The Revolution*, with a foreword by Y. M. Sokolov (Moscow, State Literary Press, 1931); R. S. Lipets, *Life of the Collective Farmeress Vasyunkina* (Moscow, State Literary Press, 1931); A. M. Astakhova, "Folklore of the Civil War," *Soviet Folklore* (Leningrad, Academy of Sciences of the USSR), No. 1, 1934; V. M. Sidelnikov and V. U. Krupyanskaya, "Oral Poetic Creative Works Dealing with Chapayev," *The Literary Critic*, No. 12, 1936. See also the material in the book by V. M. Sidelnikov and V. U. Krupyanskaya, *Folklore of the Volga*, with Foreword and ed. Prof. Y. M. Sokolov (Moscow, 1937); V. M. Sidelnikov, *Red Army Folklore*, ed. Prof. Sokolov (Moscow, 1938); V. Paimen, *Chapay: A Collection of Popular Songs, Tales, Stories and Reminiscences of the Legendary Hero of the Civil War* (Moscow, V. I. Chapayev, 1938).

narrator himself and of those who surround him, it is possible to attain great results for the stimulation of literary creation and for the enrichment of the artistic language of Soviet literature.

One of the favorite themes of the contemporary workers' and peasants' tales seems to be: "How we used to live (that is, before the October Revolution) and how we live now (under the Soviet regime)." Such narratives have great historical and social interest, furnishing, as it were, a graphic illustration of A. M. Gorky's idea that "The better we know the past, the more easily, the more profoundly and joyfully we shall understand the great significance of the present which we have created." [15] "Tales" of such a kind unfold before us the inner growth of the Soviet people, all the diversity of ways which brought them to a break with the past, and to the working out of a new philosophy. Here is a fragment of a characteristic oral tale, written down in 1930, in the province of Moscow, from an elderly collective farm woman, by V. I. Chicherov.[16]

I have been living with my husband for twenty-two years. The first year I lived with my husband, I had no particular harmony with him. And I did not even understand whether it was harmonious or not. I had a child born, and I stayed with this child three weeks at my mother's house. I got him accustomed to a lamp. I came back to my husband, but here they don't give me any light. I say that I will buy a lamp with my own money and light it. But they say to me: "You will not buy it, and you will not light it."

Then they began to spin. I had a pood of seed. And from this seed I shod and dressed my husband, my child, and myself. And at home they sowed eight poods of seed, and I worked it all alone. To me myself they did not give any flax: not a pood, not even a thread, not a single fiber did they give to me. I did the spinning, with nothing but the leavings, and that without any light. They would not give me a light. Sometimes my husband comes from a session with the men, he brings some snuff, he makes his way to the bed, to put some snuff in my nose for fun; he does not find me, he does not see that I am at the window. It is so dark. My mother-in-law would never give me any light at all. . . .

We were having the summer holidays—St. John's Eve. And my

---

[15] M. Gorky, *On Literature* (Moscow, 1937), p. 481.
[16] See Y. M. Sokolov, "Songs and Narratives of the Collective Farm Village," *The Collective Farmer*, No. 2, 1935.

husband says to me: Now our men are carousing these nights. See to it that you don't come after me if you want your mug in one piece. Well, I was obedient to his words, and I did not go after him. I did not go, but still I did not sleep—I waited. He is coming. He asks his mother: "And where is my wife?" Then I came out. Well, he so humiliated me, that you wouldn't think it possible. I didn't know how to please him. He says: "When you lie down, don't lie down; when you stand, don't stand; when you walk, don't walk; and when you sit, don't sit." In this way the whole night passed. No one knew what had happened. Even I did not understand. As they said to me before: "Be submissive to your husband, you must obey him, in whatever he may command. . . ."

At my sister-in-law's wedding my husband got dead drunk. He got up, and he says: "And what does my foot want?" I already know his custom, I come out, I bow myself on my knees at his feet. But he says to me: "This is not enough for me! Throw yourself down flat before me, like a fish!" My tears began to roll down. I threw myself at his feet like a fish. He had not thought of the fact that I was about to give birth! Looking upon me, all the people were disturbed, pitying me, with such an abdomen. But what was to be done, it was that government. . . .

But now the Soviet government has pressed his wings down, like those of a little sparrow after rain. Now I am very well satisfied with the Soviet government. And from that time on I have stopped going to church, I have stopped praying to God, I have not had the children baptized, I have stopped carrying my dead to the church.

From this narrative, artless, but moving in its sincerity and truthfulness to life, it is seen that the stupid willfulness and despotism of the husband, and in general the slavelike position of woman in the old peasant patriarchal family, were with perfect correctness linked, in the peasant woman's ideas, with the whole of the old regime ("it was that government"). And the deliverance from family bondage, experienced first of all by the downtrodden woman in the revolution, served as the beginning of a complete reversal of her world view, led to deliverance also from bondage to the church, and led to the proud self-consciousness of the Soviet woman citizen, who can always find protection for her rights at the hands of the Soviet government.

Such oral "tales," dealing, as it appears at first glance, with the private life of an individual, inconspicuous person, are in reality splendid documents of our era.

Of course, an even greater social and historical significance attaches to the oral "tales" of outstanding people in the Soviet land, for example, of the heroes of the civil war, of Chapayev and others. We have seen that the figure of the favorite, popular hero found echo in the most diverse genres of Soviet folklore (in the song, the chastushka, the tale, the legend, and the poem written in the style of the *byliny*). A multitude of oral tales, also, have been devoted to him. It is enough to say that the folklore expedition, "In the Steps of Chapayev's Division," conducted in the Kuibyshev and Saratov provinces in 1936 under the leadership of V. M. Sidelnikov, recorded as many as four hundred oral tales from the former men of Chapayev's division, or from those who had witnessed the exploits of Chapayev.

There are certain, even very brief "tales" of Chapayev, which pass on to us only specific episodes from his life, but at the same time strikingly delineate the figure of the hero as he impressed himself upon the popular artistic memory.

Such for example, is the "tale," written down in Saratov Province, under the title "A Lecture of Chapayev's About How One Man Need Not Be Afraid of Seven." [17]

Vasily Ivanovich was a cheerful-spirited, manly, wonderful fellow. With him, even the coward became brave, and the sullen man was cheerful.

In a certain battle, several young fellows fled from the adversary. They were cowards, to put it more simply.

Vasily Ivanovich found out about this after the battle, summoned them all, and proceeded to read them a lecture to the effect that one man need not be afraid of seven.

"It is a good thing for one man to fight against seven," said Chapayev. "It is hard for seven to fight against one. Seven men need seven hillocks to fire from, but all you need is one. One little hillock you can find anywhere, but it certainly is hard to find seven hillocks. Then you alone lie down and start firing: you kill one, six will be

[17] See V. M. Sidelnikov and V. U. Krupyanskaya, "Oral Poetic Works on Chapayev," *The Literary Critic*, No. 12, 1936; reprinted in *Red Army Folklore*, p. 99.

left; you kill two, five will be left. When you have killed six, then the last man surely must be frightened of you. Make him put his hands up, and take him captive. And when you have taken him captive, then lead him before the staff."

The remarkable *Workmen's Tales of Lenin* are of great interest.[18] "Every workman reminisces in his own way; in the reminiscences there are contradictions, but on the whole they give a remarkable reflection of that general mood, which at that time gripped the workmen [the reference is to the meeting with Ilyich at the Finland Station]. . . . The recollections of the workmen are valuable for the reason that, having been collected at various factories, they give a complete and unified picture of Lenin," says N. K. Krupskaya.

A great artistic truthfulness, a sincerity, and a touching quality emanate from the tales of Lenin which were printed in the volume *Creative Art of the Peoples of the USSR*, published by the editorial staff of *Pravda*: "How Theodosia Nikitishna Went to See Lenin," written down in 1928 on the Northern Railway; "The Button," written down in 1927 in Archangel; "The Guest," written down in the village of Kashino, in the Volokolamsky district of the Moscow province; "The Bees," from the village of Yam, near Gorok, in 1937, and others.[19]

Especially characteristic is the tale "The Button," which has caught the spirit of tenderness that the people have toward the memory of Ilyich.

Lenin comes to visit us at the factory. They shout at me, "Natorova, you take his coat!"

It was hot in the club. Lenin began to speak. He threw his overcoat on a chair. I seized it and put it in the cloakroom. I see that on the left side the middle button is missing. I pulled a button off from my own jacket and sewed it on Lenin's coat with strong thread, so that it would stay on a long time. He went away and did not notice. But the button didn't quite match. And I am so flattered, and keep my secret.

Then quite a lot of time went by. I was walking along Liteiny Pros-

---

[18] *Workmen's Tales of Lenin*, transcripts by S. Mierer and V. Borovik, foreword by N. K. Krupskaya, introductory article by Yemelyan Yaroslavsky (Moscow, Trade Union Publishing House, 1934).

[19] *Creative Art of the Peoples of the USSR* (*Pravda*,) pp. 37-50.

pect, and in the window of Phoenix, the photographer, there was an enlarged portrait of Lenin. He was wearing the very same overcoat. I gazed fixedly at it, for there on his coat was that very same button —*my* button.

That very same winter he died. At the photograph shop on Liteiny Prospect I bought a memorial portrait.

I have it now, near my mirror, in a frame.

Every day I go up to it, I look at it, and I cry a little.

Still, there is my button, sewn on his coat.[20]

Along with the stories about Lenin, stories about encounters with Stalin are widely diffused among the people. To see and to hear Stalin is the dream of every Soviet citizen. If anyone has the joyful opportunity of seeing, much more of talking with Stalin, he is obliged to relate, a multitude of times, all about his encounter with the great man. These stories nourish the creative fancy, and so there is built up, before our very eyes, the epos of Stalin and similarly the epos of Lenin, not only in the Russian creative art, but in the creative art of all the fraternal peoples of the Soviet Union.

20 *Ibid.*, p. 39.

FOLKLORE OF THE PEOPLES OF THE USSR

❧

It is difficult to survey the Russian folk creation of the Soviet era apart from the creation of all the fraternal peoples of the USSR.

Even in the past, both the recent and the remote past, Russian folklore absorbed into itself the artistic influences of the culture of neighboring and even of distant peoples of the West and East, and in its turn it enriched many other peoples by the wealth of its poetry. In the first part of this course we have had occasion to speak at some length concerning the researches of scholars on the question of the cultural intercourse of the West and the East, an intercourse in which the Russian people have played a very vital part. We recall, likewise, what has been said about the presence of a very great number of "migratory" motifs in the Russian *byliny*, religious verses, tales, and so forth. As we have seen, a great role was played in the poetic exchanges by the professional popular poets and artists of ancient Russia—the buffoons and the jesters.

Observations upon the history of folklore among the other (non-Russian) peoples of the USSR indicate that among them, also, oral poetry frequently broke down the artificial barriers which had been established among the various peoples by the efforts of the Church and the governmental authorities, and which stirred up chauvinism and sectional hostility. Popular poetry frequently took no account of the boundaries of states or of languages or of religions. An outstanding example is the activity of Sayat Nova, the famous *ashug* of the Transcaucasian region in the eighteenth century, who can justly be claimed as their own national poet not only by the Armenians, but also by the Georgians and the Azerbaijanians. He did his creative work in three languages, and contributed a great deal toward the poetic exchange among the three peoples who had often been enemies. Such is the activity of many of the *ashugi* of Daghestan with its many tribes; their songs quickly passed over from one language into another, as, for example, the songs of Suleyman Stalsky, even in the period before the revolution. Such is the activity of many of the *akyny* and

[689]

zhirshi of Kazakhstan and Kirghizia, in particular the activity of Dzhambul Dzhabayev, whose songs have been spread abroad not only through the Kazak villages, but also far beyond the boundaries of Kazakhstan.

But none the less, the development of the national poetry of each of the peoples of former tsarist Russia was accomplished, on the whole, in an isolated manner, without organic connection with the poetry of other lands. This is not what we see now, in our socialist land, where such a powerful impression has been made upon all of life and culture by the great friendship of the peoples, established by the genius of Lenin and Stalin.

The oral creative art of the peoples of the USSR is a striking manifestation of genuine internationalism, and at the same time of the national culture of each country.

The Soviet folklore of all the peoples of the Soviet Union is a most valuable historical document, an indication of the close union in which all the peoples of the socialist motherland live. Through a survey of the thematics of the oral poetry of the most diverse Soviet peoples, may be clearly seen the unity of moods and experiences, expressed in works of the greatest diversity of language and form, yet permeated with common ideas and emotions.

The October Revolution awoke the creative powers of the laboring masses among all the peoples of the Soviet Union. Even as early as 1918, Lenin wrote of the "splendid scope which the great revolution had given to popular creative art," [1] and also wrote of the "independent, historical creation of the majority of the population, above all, of the majority of the laboring people." [2] These words of the great leader referred, above all, to the social life, to the political and economic structure, but, beyond a doubt, they can be extended also to all the aspects of Soviet culture, including folk art, and in particular popular oral poetry.

Concerning the creative flights of the laboring people as a result of the victories of the October Revolution, and with regard to the birth of new songs and the decisive changes in the character of the

---

[1] V. I. Lenin, *Collected Works*, XXII, p. 376.
[2] *Ibid.*, p. 440.

popular poetry, that folk poet of Kazakhstan, Dzhambul, wearer of
the Order,* has beautifully said:

> My joy came in the October Revolution,
> The Moscow Decree brought me joy,
> With a new song I came to the assembly,
> And along with Dzhambul, Kazakhstan burst into song.
> Since that time, like a youth, I am burning with happiness;
> I am giving my best songs to my motherland.[3]

In the history of the world, it is not possible to point out another
stupendous event which could be compared with the October Revolution, in the power of its influence on the creative art of the toiling
masses of the people. In the history of the world, it is impossible to
find any other event which, in such a short period of time, has
brought about such profound changes in the existence of popular
creation. The old narrow social and national barriers have been broken
down. The working people have drawn their breath in freedom, filling their lungs with the fresh air of the vast and boundless spaces
which have been opened up before the peoples of the USSR. With
beautiful picturesqueness the Tadjik singer and workman Alimdzha-
nov has expressed these feelings:

> You have opened to us all the doors of the world,
> Great Lenin, the giant of the ages.[4]

During the twenty years of the socialist regime, there have been
extremely powerful changes in the world view as expressed in the
popular poetry.

The profound talents of the laboring people revealed themselves
in all their brilliance at the time of the collapse of the old regime of
oppression and violence, which had embittered the folk consciousness
and the folk poetry in every way.

The masterly national-minority policy of Lenin and Stalin liberated the numerous peoples of tsarist Russia from a twofold oppression—that of the tsarist autocracy, and that of the power of the local

---

* Order of Lenin, civil order of merit bestowed for exceptional public service.
—Ed.

[3] Dzhambul, *Songs and Poems* (State Literary Press, 1938), p. 85.

[4] *Creative Art of the Peoples of the USSR* (*Pravda*, 1937), p. 179.

national aristocracy and bourgeoisie. Now, summing up the total achievements of the Soviet regime, we may state that among all the peoples of the USSR there exists a new Soviet poetry, "national in form and Socialist in content" (J. V. Stalin). This very great flowering of the popular poetry, which is taking place before our very eyes, is deeply realized by its actual creators—the folk singers, whether they be Russian narrators or Caucasian *ashugi*,* Kazakh and Kirghiz *akyny*, † Uzbek *bakhshi*, ‡ or Yakutsk *olongokhuty*. § The Kirghiz *akyn*, Moldobasan Musulman-Kulov, sings:

> Stalin has resurrected us,
> He has enlightened the ignorant people.
> He has rallied together into the collective-farm army
> All the poor and scattered people.
> He has given us power to glory
> In an Olympiad of singers.
> He has called forth to life
> The talent of all the people.
> For the backward, ignorant tribes
> He has created an age of happiness,
> Under his wise supervision
> Man has become a man.[5]

During the existence of the Soviet regime, the works of folklore of the peoples of the USSR reflect the most striking aspects of Soviet social and everyday life. In its ideational content and high artistic quality, the popular poetry of this great period of twenty years testifies to the vast cultural growth of the laboring people, in comparison with the time prior to the October Revolution.

The thematics of Soviet folklore are exceedingly diversified and distinct in essence from the thematics of the time prior to the October Revolution. At that time, as in the prerevolutionary folklore of all nations, there predominated either the themes of remote antiquity

---

* People's bard poet in the Caucasus, composing or improvising his own song, sung to the accompaniment of a stringed instrument.—ED.

† "Name of a popular poet bard in Central Asia. He improvises verses to the accompaniment of a stringed instrument (dowry)."—*Slovar' poeticheskikh terminov*, A. P. Kviatkovskii (Moscow, 1940).—ED.

‡ Name of Uzbek people's poet and storyteller.—ED.

§ Or *olonkhosud*, a Yakutsk people's poet and storyteller.—ED.

[5] *Ibid.*, p. 119.

(in the epic), or the themes of personal emotion and narrow family life (in the song lyric). In the oral creation of our own era, popular interests have definitely shifted from antiquity to the contemporary period, from a world bounded by narrowly personal experiences and family relationships, to the vast expanses of nation-wide and international political questions and problems. Contemporary interests have assumed the first place in the emotions and reflections of the laboring people. As we have already said, the numerous observations of Soviet folklorists have established a curious fact—the tendency, widely developed among the popular narrators, to speak in their creative work of things which they personally have seen or experienced. The grandeur of the events of the revolution, of the civil war, of the struggle with the Interventionists, the unprecedented rise of the working people, their active participation in the socialist organization both in the city and in the country, in the newly erected industrial plants and on the collective farms—all these have relegated the ancient thematics to the background in the creative art of many of the popular narrators and singers.

One of the favorite themes in the Soviet folklore of all peoples is the contrast between the old and the new mode of life. On this contrast between the old and the new are based a multitude of the women's songs of the Soviet East. Among many of the peoples of the East, prior to the October Revolution, the position of women was still more difficult than it was in the Russian countryside. Women were bought and sold, in the fullest sense of the word, like slaves. Here is a song of a Soviet Turkmenian woman:

Now the time has come to break the tent of slavery—
Now you all may drink the delicious sherbet of liberation.
But it was long ago that our women friends were sold to the enemy,
Long ago they were thrown into the well, bound both hand and foot.
Anyone who had boundless wealth would buy four or five of them.
Now there has come, at last, the day of liberation,
The October Revolution has brought us liberty, it has saved us from
  the ancient bondage,
And our new rights are now forevermore in our own hands.[6]

[6] Rhymed transl. by V. A. Dynnik, following text in *Soviet Folklore*, No. I, 1934, pp. 141-142.

Or here is the way a Kirghiz singer contrasts the past and present:

> How did the Kirghiz live formerly?
> Their teaching was the Koran.
> Nobody considered them to be a people.
> The fog enshrouded them:
> Without enlightenment, night and day
> They languished in woe. . . .
> Tyrants trampled us down,
> They kept us in the dark—
> The poet could not speak
> Of his own bitter fate.
> In order to please the rich men,
> He hid his woe within himself.
> Without learning, amidst the wild steppes
> Our people lived beneath the yoke of darkness.
> We never heard any songs
> Of joy from the singers.
> But now the free *akyn*
> Is a son of our joyous native land.[7]

The composer of the remarkable lament for S. M. Kirov, the Mordvinian poet-improviser E. P. Krivosheyeva, in another of her productions, "Remember the Past," speaks thus of the burdensome life of the Mordvinian women in the past:

> I will sing of you now, women of Mokshan.
> I will sing of you now, women of Erzyan.
> Or, woman of Mokshan, do you not know, do you not understand,
> How in your need you were consumed and tormented?
> Or you, oppressed woman of Erzyan,
> Was not your womanly lot just as bitter?

This song, addressed to her daughters and granddaughters, is brought to a close by the aged singer with the following words about the new life, which proceed straight from her heart:

> I have raised you, I have raised you for these bright days,
> You will remain and live on, children of my blood.
> Now you will never see such misfortune:
> The era of the Soviets is happy and joyful.[8]

[7] *Creative Art of the Peoples of the USSR*, pp. 118-119.
[8] *Ibid.*, pp. 304-307.

In the songs of the women of the Soviet East, a great deal of space is devoted to the *parandja*,* that symbol of the recent bondage of woman, of her woe and degradation:

Oh, sisters, enough have you hidden the beauty of your faces behind the heavy veil,
Enough have you swallowed the blood of sorrow, and wept in the corner! [9]

In the Soviet folklore of the fraternal peoples, many songs and legends have been devoted to the civil war, which confirmed the victory of the October Revolution and the deliverance of the peoples from all kinds of bondage. The peoples of the Soviet Union, each in accordance with its own national poetic traditions, have delineated the figures of the leaders of the Red Army—Lenin, Stalin, Ordzhonikidze, Frunze, Voroshilov, and others.

The Kazakh *akyn*, Utep Ongarbayev, sings as follows about Frunze:

From the eyes of the knight streamed a flame of fire—
He came riding to shatter destiny.
His sorrel horse had tinkling bells on its bridle,
And a white spot on its forehead.
He rode through the salt marshes, over the grass,
Over the yellow hillocks of sand.
Behind him swayed, in a dense steel-blue mass,
Thousands of shining bayonets. . . .
His swords and bayonets were multiplied!
The whole of Kazakhstan is enveloped in dust:
All the shepherds and all the farm laborers
Started off on the long expedition.
A son of poverty, he shattered destiny,
He burst the links of the chains,
He stirred for the great conflict
All the poor people of the steppes.
How should we not know his bright blue eyes?
How should we not remember his face?
The bands of the Whites, and the landowning nobles,
He has utterly destroyed.[10]

---

* Veil worn by Mohammedan women.—ED.
[9] *Ibid.*, p. 440.   [10] *Ibid.*, p. 169.

Or the collective farmer of Kabarda, the singer Sizhazhev, composes the following song of congratulation for the fiftieth birthday of Sergo Ordzhonikidze, recalling his military services in the civil war and in the conflict with the Interventionists:

Sergo, light of our eyes!
Beloved deliverer of your native Caucasus!
Here in the Caucasus you have raised the Red standard,
And it floats above us unchangeably,
Today and tomorrow, and will float forever!
With the living word of Lenin,
With the living speech of Stalin,
Sergo visited the Caucasus!
The birds of prey flew together,
With a greedy cawing they called together the evil black flock,
The black birds of prey with their sharp iron beaks were tearing the
    mountaineers of the Caucasus.
But you have delivered us from the enemies,
Envoy of the great Lenin!
In those terrible days in the Caucasus, Sergo fought and conquered.[11]

The Red Army and its heroic leaders constitute one of the favorite themes of all Soviet folklore, both among the peoples of the Caucasus and Central Asia, and among the peoples of the Far North. A Saam (Lapland) collective farmer and shepherd affirms in his song:

If Stalin and Voroshilov say war has come,
And the enemies want to take our land away, we will all go to fight.
We will take the rifles, we will begin to fire, we will defend our tundra.
On the tundra the snow is deep, there are no roads.
But we are not afraid of the snow, we know how to travel through it
    everywhere—
Our reindeer run swiftly.
On the reindeer we will carry guns, ammunition, and food,
The reindeer will help us with meat and skins.
We with our reindeer will help the Red Army,
We will conquer the White enemies.
We will defend our land, our lakes, our reindeer.[12]

In Soviet folklore all forms of Socialist construction and all the achievements of Soviet technology which had been put into practice

[11] *Ibid.*, p. 210. [12] *Ibid.*, p. 290.

in the economic and cultural life of the country found expression. The Socialist competition, the shock-brigade work, the powerful Stakhanovite movement occupy a prominent place in the thematics of Soviet oral poetry. The names of the best Stakhanovites have become popular in the songs of the people, along with the names of the heroes of the Red Army. Tractors, combines, motorcars, airplanes, "Ilyich's little lamps" (Lenin's electric-light bulbs), and radio receivers have become an inalienable part of the poetic lexicon of Soviet folklore, affording a striking contrast with the mode of life reflected in the old songs.

The new implements of peasant labor, the latest achievements of progressive technology, which brought a great alleviation of peasant toil, are described with rapture, joyful astonishment and love in the popular poetry of all nationalities in the USSR.

Typical is the following Turkmenian song, which transmits in the most spontaneous manner the impression of a fairy tale coming true in reality—an effect which was produced upon the people by the new and hitherto unprecedented technological inventions:

I have seen the interesting works of the Bolshevik:
I have seen how the machine flies up into the clouds;
I have seen how the automobile runs along the road!
You just have time to shout "Look there!" and it's past you, nothing
    left but a cloud of dust.
And another machine came out to our camp, I have seen it,
"Grr-grr-grr!" it cries angrily, like a devil—I have seen it,
In it there is living water—I have seen it—and there is fire:
This horse plows the earth day and night for the local peasants.
But there is still one more wonder of wonders, I have seen it,
It comes to us to sing songs from the sky—I have seen it,
Below is a pipe, above is a tall mast, I have seen it,
And it sings about the interesting deeds of the Bolshevik.[13]

The radio, the movies, the club, the village reading room, the circles for independent artistic activity, the Olympiads of the arts, and many other features of the new Soviet culture have become a permanent part of the thematics of the folk poetry among all the peoples of the

[13] *Ibid.,* p. 348.

USSR. The popular poetry is a vital and convincing testimony to the vast changes in the social and domestic mode of life of the toiling masses of the people of all the fraternal nationalities.

Soviet folklore not only afforded an artistic reflection of the new phenomena of social life, but was itself, constantly, a keen weapon in the social conflict. Soviet popular poetry was compelled to wage a great conflict with the folklore of the enemy class both in the period of the civil war and during the years of the collectivization of the rural economy. The kulak at that period was trying to utilize the oral creative art to further his own counterrevolutionary purposes. But the laboring people gave a powerful rebuff to the intrigues of the kulaks. Besides, the conflict was being waged also by means of the written word. This was the state of affairs throughout the country. The new Soviet songs were one of the striking and productive forms of political agitation and propaganda, one of the means of the conflict for solidifying the socialist regime. The role of Soviet folklore on the anti-religious front is also very great, especially in the exposure of the priests' exploitation and obscurantism. The popular songs, chastushkas, satirical tales, and anecdotes about priests, mullahs, and rabbis, which had had a very long continued tradition in the folk creative art, were given a new and militant sharpness in Soviet folklore.

But if the folklore of the peoples of the USSR was expressive of the people's wrath and sarcasm toward their enemies, at the same time, however, popular creative art expressed the people's fervent love for the organizers of the new socialist life.

The figures of the great leaders, Lenin and Stalin, are drawn, in Soviet folklore, with particular love, pride, and tenderness.

No matter how highly poetic, striking, and majestic may have been the figures of the old popular epos, no matter how powerfully there may have been set forth in them, according to Lenin's expression, "the hopes and expectations of the people," still, in the great majority of cases, they were the creation of the poetic and social dream of the people, and not the direct reflection of actual persons who had had their existence in historic reality.

But this also is fully understandable, since reality itself, marked by social injustice, arbitrariness, oppression, and ignorance, could not produce the kind of people who could fully correspond to the popular ideal. The laboring people could only dream of the future, creating poetic visions, incarnating them in the figures of fictitious heroes.

We see something quite unlike this now, in the Soviet folklore, in the oral creative art of the peoples of the Soviet Union.

Our Soviet reality itself has proved to be richer, more interesting, more attractive than poetic fiction. There has never been such a store of rich and diverse material as that which, from every aspect of real life, has faced the masters of the poetic art. Soviet folklore is altogether based on impressions which have been fostered by the living, contemporary period. Life itself has become miraculous.

It was no longer necessary to invent heroes. Heroes, the bearers of the popular ideals, those who embodied these popular ideals in their own life, were all around. Popular heroes were created by the October Revolution, by the conflict with the interventionists, the enemies of the people, which followed it; and by the Socialist regime.

"Leaders, captains, produced by the people, who yesterday had been farm laborers, weavers, miners, locksmiths, had now become famous warriors, the commanders of daring regiments and armies. And over them all, as fathers, as wise teachers, as fearless leaders, were Lenin and Stalin. . . .

"What wonderful material for the popular creative art, for the talented storyteller!" [14]

And the folklore of all the Soviet peoples created a multitude of legends and songs about Lenin, Stalin, Voroshilov, Ordzhonikidze, Budyónny, Chapayev, Shchors, and many other heroes of the Soviet land; about the daring aviators, shock brigadiers, and Stakhanovites.

The figures of the leaders of the socialist revolution, Lenin and Stalin, are many-sided and many-hued. The poetry of the Soviet peoples has raised a stately monument in their honor. The songs composed by the peoples about their beloved leaders will be passed on throughout the centuries.

In a certain Oirotian legend it is related how the poor hunter Anchi, having been plundered by a rich landowner, a *zaysan* (steward), and

[14] *Ibid.*, Foreword.

a *shaman* (priest), starts out to journey through the wide world on a search after truth:

I will go and traverse
The sixty peoples living in the Altai,
And I shall find an answer.
Without deceit, without crafty deceptions,
I will go and find out:
Is there such a power in the world, in the wide world,
That the *zaysan* might stand dumb before it?
Will there ever be such a time in the world, or not,
When the rich landowner, not having a farthing to pay for his dinner,
Will long for a rancid biscuit?
And will such wisdom ever be found, and in whom,
That the sage may prove to be a fool before it? [15]

And then, having traversed the whole of the Altai Mountains six times, and having passed seven times through the whole earth, Anchi heard, upon Mount Altai, the powerful voice of a knight, proclaiming the end of the rule of the *zaysans*, the rich landowners, and the *shamans*, summoning the poor to join in a harmonious, brotherly family in order to build a new life.

To the perplexed question of Anchi, as to who this knight may be, the people who surround the knight make answer:

He did not come down to us from heaven, veiled in clouds,
Not from the bowels of the earth did he come forth into the light—
He is a son of our own people, possessing boundless might,
For the people he fought—I cannot count how many years.
He destroyed the enemies. His exploits are imperishable.
His great name is—Lenin! [16]

In the same way, numerous heroes of the folk creation of other nationalities in the USSR search for the truth and find it in Lenin, in his teaching and in his deeds. The White Russian tale "Lenin's Truth" tells the story of two brothers, poor men, who went wandering through the earth and seeking after truth—first from a nobleman, then from a priest, then from a merchant and a manufacturer; nowhere do they find this truth—until the time when they have recourse to Lenin.

[15] *Ibid.*, p. 4.   [16] *Ibid.*, p. 8.

The theme of wandering through the world in the search for truth and happiness belongs to the traditional thematics of the old Russian tales (for example, the tales of Marko the Rich and Vasily the Unfortunate, of truth and falsehood, and so on). In its roots it goes back to remote antiquity. We find it in the creative art of many peoples. But in Soviet folklore the problem is solved differently.

All the peoples of the Soviet Union sing of Lenin as the deliverer from oppression, injustice, want, and poverty. But the popular creation is always very concrete. The folk singers and storytellers (the Russian narrators, Caucasian *ashugi*, Uzbek *bakhshi*, Kirghiz *akyny*, Kazakh *zhirshi*, Tadjik *gafizy*, Yakutsk *olongokhuty*, and other masters of popular poetry, whatever they may be called) re-create with great precision the dark picture of the earlier national life, that grievous life from which the people were set free by the leader of the October Revolution—Lenin. This is the way the old Uzbek *bakhshi* Ergash begins his oral poem "Comrade Lenin":

Lenin sees: only the rich men are powerful.
To the wealthy executioners the enemies are not formidable.
That man is powerful who has his purse well lined.
The rich man cannot hear the words of the poor peasants,
And the rich man does not even look upon the poor.
And to the rich men they, the poor peasants, are laughable.
Lenin sees: for the laboring people there is nothing but toil.
The poor man has worked and worked, and then the rich men take
    everything away,
But one has to work harder than a slave.
The poor peasants have to bend their backs like slaves.[17]

After describing the difficult life of the poor peasants in the pre-revolutionary era, the Uzbek poem passes into a rapturous hymn to Lenin:

> We ought to celebrate in song
> Every one of the words of Lenin!
> And his glorious works
> We must sing of everywhere!

[17] Zarifov, "Soviet Folklore in Uzbekistan," *The Literary Critic*, No. 2, 1935, transl. in verse by V. A. Dynnik.

Lenin's thoughts were with those
Who suffered and were oppressed.
When the people are set free,
We must celebrate Lenin!
He gave his powers and his life
For the poor, hungry people,
So we must follow after Lenin,
And walk in his ways!

The Oirotian poem about the poor peasant Anchi also comes to an end with a joyous ascription of praise to Lenin:

After the endless tears,
After a thousand dark
And joyless years,
Those who were born in the depths of bondage
Have now received joy,
Have seen the light,
Now they have been set free
From the violence of their enemies.
To thee we sing a song,
A song of honor and glory,
Lenin! [18]

Lenin is the friend and protector of the poor peasants says a certain Kazakh song:

All his life he shone, giving light to the dark earth,
His heart ached for the poor, as for his own child.[19]

Lenin united all the poor peasants, all the laboring people, in the conflict with the rich, with the tsars, and the doers of violence.

At the summons of Lenin, as related in the Armenian popular poem "Lenin the Leader":

The warriors are coming from the four corners of the land:
The workmen have come—thousands of thousands!
The jobless have come—thousands of thousands!
The landless have come—thousands of thousands!
The waterless have come—thousands of thousands! [20]

[18] *Creative Art of the Peoples of the USSR*, p. 9.
[19] *Ibid.*, p. 58.   [20] *Ibid.*, p. 22.

And Lenin, with the help of the working people, has conquered:

> Lenin, the leader, laid down the law of the Bolsheviks.
> From those who were rich he took away everything,
> He made the rich men poorer than cats,
> To those who had nothing he gave everything.
> He clothed and shod the poor, and made men out of them.[21]

Lenin is called the friend of the poor in the songs and tales of all the peoples of the Soviet Union.

In the Tadjik "Song of Lenin" the people praise the leader as the deliverer from coercion and poverty, and the words of the song swell into a hymn of joy:

> The glory of your rule is a hundredfold!
> In it are just laws and wise concord.
> There is no poor man who did not rejoice at it—
> Our Lenin is our brother and leader!
> The world was dark with violence.
> Lenin was at one with the poor,
> And Violence has been interred—
> Our Lenin is our brother and leader! [22]

Lenin delivered the working people from poverty. He accomplished also another great work. He reconciled the peoples who had previously been hostile to one another. He united them into a single family. The popular *ashugi* of the many tribes of the Caucasus revert to this theme with particular frequency. The singers of Azerbaidjan, a region which had suffered so much in the past, where blood flowed in streams during the Turkish-Armenian massacre, observed in their songs, at the establishment of the Soviet government:

Not so very long ago the peoples were destroying one another, as the hunters destroy wild beasts.

Our hope—the young people—was perishing among the howling beasts.

Then the peoples rose up against this evil and disgrace.

[21] *Ibid.*, p. 24.
[22] V. Samarin, "Songs of Soviet Tadjikistan," *The Literary Critic*, No. 5, 1935, transl. in verse by V. A. Dynnik.

Long live the Communist Party!
Long live the Red Army, which has brought us peace!
Long live Lenin, who has accomplished such great deeds! [23]

The concept of Lenin is so closely connected in the consciousness of the popular poets with the life of the poor, that in the poetic imagination of the peoples of the USSR, the great emancipator of the working people is himself pictured as a poor man, and is invested with an imaginary biography of a poor man. Thus, for example, an Armenian poem relates:

Then Lenin the leader arose from his place and stood up,
He spoke, face to face, to the Sultan and to the rich men:
"I am the son of a poor man, and brother to all who are poor,
Come out, we will fight in a life-and-death struggle!" [24]

Thus in the poetic figure was expressed the profound consciousness, present in all the working people, of the blood relationship and organic connection between Lenin and the laboring people.

The figure of Lenin, as it took poetic form in the artistic consciousness of the peoples of the USSR, preserves in the oral creative art of our land a number of persistent, permanent features which create a new tradition in folklore. In the figure of the great leader of the revolution, the popular poetry always emphasizes his wisdom, humanity, and delightful simplicity. We have seen this in the Russian "tales" of Lenin.

And at the same time the people realize that this simple and, to borrow the expression of a certain tale, "human" man, embodied in himself a vast strength, the strength of the people itself. This circumstance serves to explain why, along with the exact delineation of the real personality of Lenin, one frequently also encounters in Soviet folklore Lenin represented as a knight, a giant. Not only that—the figure of Lenin takes on at times, in the popular poetry, a literally cosmic character:

And Anchi saw: before him is a knight,
Among the boundless spaces filled with people,

23 *Pravda*, No. 22, 1930.
24 *Creative Art of the Peoples of the USSR*, p. 18.

Shaking the whole land by a single word,
In his aspect he is kindest of the kind, and strongest of the strong!
His brows are like the mountain ridges!
His eyes burn with a blinding flame!
It seemed that the whole world was ready to rise without delay
And follow his scarlet standard! [25]

In the popular songs and legends, especially in the poetry of the Soviet East, Lenin is sometimes called "equal to the clouds" (a Tadjik song), sometimes it is said of him that "Lenin is as tall as the snow-capped mountains" (A Kazakh song); again, in a multitude of songs of the most diverse peoples, he is compared to the sun (in Armenian, Georgian, Turkmenian, Tadjik, Tazakh, Evenkian, Ukrainian, and Russian poetry).

And, indeed, how could one help comparing the great leader of the peoples with the sun, the source of light and warmth! Surely, thanks to Lenin, the peoples who such a short time ago lived in dark gloom and absolute shadow have seen the genuine light of social justice, education, and culture. The peoples of all parts of the Soviet land sing of Lenin the Sun.

In the cold north the Evenkian singer, greeting the morning's dawn, turns to Lenin in his thoughts and his heart:

> Now it has grown light upon the mountains,
> Now the night is diminishing.
> Now the Evenkian arises,
> Now he has put on his gantlets,
> Now he gazes in all directions,
> Now he has looked upon the mountains,
> Now he beholds his sun,
> Now he sees it—the rays of Lenin,
> Now he beholds it—it is his Party.[26]

In hot Kirghizia the Dunganian singer echoes his distant northern comrade. He also sings of Lenin the Sun, who has enlightened the darkness and dispersed the black gloom:

In the night, above the dark earth, suddenly the dawn appears and glows,

[25] *Ibid.*, p. 6.   [26] *Ibid.*, p. 27.

"What kind of magical gleam of light is this?" people say, rising.
The winds are howling, the rain is pouring, but still the light shines—
Lenin is braver and brighter than the sun! For Lenin there is no
  night!
Wonder of wonders! All the poor people have become one family,
Let the people govern themselves wisely and justly,
Such a sun the earth has never seen in its time.
Lenin has said: Let the poor man reach out to the poor man a broth-
  erly hand.[27]

When the terrible news of Lenin's death shook the whole family of
Soviet peoples, the popular poets and singers responded to the death
of the beloved leader with a great number of sorrowful songs and
poetic laments. And again, many of the popular poets had recourse
to the figure of Lenin the Sun. The sun, the source of light and symbol
of eternity, again was blended with the figure of the leader of the
people.

For all the grievousness of the loss that had been sustained, the
popular songs expressed the inexhaustible optimism of a people who
had conquered, and their faith in the unshakable solidity of that
which had been won by the laboring people under the banner and
guidance of Lenin.

A certain Georgian peasant singer has beautifully expressed the
feelings and thoughts of the peasants and working people. He, who so
deeply felt and understood all the power and significance of the sun
in a worker's life, has with great artistic conviction sung of the two
suns. ("Two Suns" is the title of his song.)

> Sun, sun, enough of tears!
> Let the day shine over woe.
> Ilyich was a friend to you—
> Dress him now in diamonds!
> The seas cannot contain our tears,
> No one can count our tears;
> Smile, coming out of the clouds,
> And do not echo the sobs of the earth! . . .
> Before Ilyich came,
> We had only you to console us,

[27] *Ibid.*, p. 16.

No one loved us then,
Only you gave us warmth.
We warmed our bodies in your rays,
But surely our soul was frozen within us!
Who can count up how many of us perished,
Hurrying to procure a crust of bread? . . .
There are two suns—you give us warmth and light,
You give color to our life;
To extinguish your deathless rays—
There is no power in the universe which can do that! [28]

The death of Vladimir Ilyich left the laboring people thunderstruck. The grief of the people was outpoured in the beautiful works of the folk poets. The death of Lenin served as the basis for a multitude of popular traditions and legends. Both Suleyman Stalsky and Dzhambul Dzhabayev composed their heartfelt songs on the death of Lenin; also the Russian narrator of the North, Martha S. Krukova, composed her touching lament.

It is highly significant that in the songs and laments composed by the popular singers on Lenin's death, for all the force of the people's grief as expressed in them, there is no despair. In all the folk songs is heard a note of confidence in the immortality of Lenin's work. This confidence is strengthened by the thought that Lenin's work has passed over into the trustworthy hands of his gifted pupil and friend— the great Stalin.

In the creative perception of the folk singers, the figures of both leaders—Lenin and Stalin—are joined with one another, just as in actual life the work of Lenin and of Stalin was one.

The vow of Stalin at the bier of his teacher is reflected in many songs of the various peoples of the Soviet Union.

A movingly beautiful account of Stalin's great vow is given in a song composed in Ossetia, which presents the thoughts and emotions of all the laboring people:

Many wise people had died before Lenin,
But the death of Lenin struck terror into our hearts.
We followed the bier with our standards lowered.
The people do not recall a time of severer frost. . . .

[28] *Ibid.*, pp. 61-62.

The mountain paths were covered with ice,
The hail beat upon us, the snowstorm swept over us. . . .
The sky grew dark, but we went on to our goal.
Lenin had left us his warmth.
He, dying, had entrusted our fate
To his friend and brother, Stalin.
"My brother, protect the poor men from the rich,
And reorder their lives, as I have taught you."
Stalin recovered from his sorrowful thoughts,
He restrained his tears for the sake of the thousands of people,
He touched the heart of his teacher,
And set us at rest with his vow.[29]

The oral poetic creation of all the peoples of the Soviet Union produces a great number of tales about Stalin as the incarnation of the peoples' expectations and hopes.

In speaking of Russian contemporary folklore, we have had occasion to note the theme, which is very often treated in the songs and stories, of encounters with Stalin, and the expression of the dream of seeing the leader and conversing with him. The same motifs are to be found in the contemporary folklore of all the Soviet peoples. Everyone in the Soviet Union has this yearning toward Stalin.

A Laksian song expresses this thought as follows:

Rivers rush toward the sea,
Iron is attracted to the magnet,
Plants reach toward the sun,
Birds strive to reach the south.
But human beings yearn for happiness,
They strive for truth,
Their hearts are drawn toward friendship,
Their thoughts turn to you!
I would like to be a swallow,
A swallow with swift wings,
Light and shapely in body,
That I might visit the Kremlin,
That I might see, though only once,
How Stalin would smile,
Hearing the speech of the new people
That have been created by him.[30]

[29] *Ibid.*, pp. 83-84.　　　　　[30] *Ibid.*, p. 87.

The poetry of the peoples observes in Stalin, as it observed in Lenin, his charming simplicity, and at the same time his greatness, the greatness of his works, of his projects.[31]

The images which are most frequently applied to Stalin in the poetry of very many peoples are those of the sun and the eagle. There is a very powerful representation of Stalin as an eagle, in a song composed by the Tadjik ditchdigger Ali Ibrahim Safarov:

Where can you find, in the Pamir mountains, such a great eagle,
Who has millions of faithful and bold eaglets?
There is no such eagle on the mountains!
There is such a happy eagle, far away beyond the mountains:
They call him Stalin.
Where can you find, on the mountains, thousands of thousands of
    eaglets,
That, as soon as the elder eagle summons them, will come flying?
There are no such bold eaglets on the mountains.
There are such eaglets in the factories and in the villages,
Without rest, they fly for thousands of versts upon their wings of
    iron!
If the elder eagle summons them to fight, they all come flying, as
    one.
Every eaglet is a son of the great Stalin.
What does the old eagle teach his young fledglings?
The eagle teaches his young fledglings to search for food.
Stalin the eagle teaches the eaglets to win happiness and glory.
Stalin the eagle teaches the eaglets to create a new earth,
Why are the snakes hissing beyond the River Pyandzh, on the farther
    bank?
Because they have seen that there, beyond the river, are many fine
    calves.
Why are the kites sitting in a flock, and crying, and screaming, and
    whistling?
Because our splendid eagles have driven them away from the flocks.
In Afghanistan the jackals howl with jealousy and anguish.
The jackals see how well we have begun to live, beyond the river.
The Afghan girls weep bitterly: can it be, they are calling us?
They see how cleanly and warmly the Soviet girls live.[32]

[31] From the collection *Old Workmen's Tales of the Great Leader* (Tiflis, Dawn in the East, 1937).
[32] *Creative Art of the Peoples of the USSR*, p. 123.

The greatness, the wisdom, and the iron will of Stalin are beautifully expressed in a song by the Kurdish singer Ahmed Mirezi. The song "I See Stalin" comes to an end with this clear and vigorous stanza:

You are the most beautiful and bright flower of the basil!
You are the best and greatest pupil of Engels, Marx, and Lenin!
You are met and accompanied by the rejoicing cries of the people!
With all their heart, the people understand your wise language!
You are powerful, you are firm, we love you! You are great! [33]

A multitude of songs have been composed about Stalin throughout the entire Soviet Union. But the best singers about Stalin, by general acknowledgment, are found to be two very striking, talented representatives of the folk creative art, the famous poets and recipients of the Order, the Lezgian Suleyman Stalsky and the Kazakh Dzhambul Dzhabayev.

SULEYMAN STALSKY (1869–1937)

With the name and the figure of Stalsky there is closely linked that magnificent manifestation of Soviet culture which is known as the creative work of the peoples of the USSR.

No one who was in the Hall of Columns of the House of the Unions at the time of the First All-Union Congress of Soviet Writers, at the end of 1934, will ever be able, to the end of his life, to forget the impression which was produced by the appearance on the platform of this lank old man in the long Caucasian coat (*beshmet*), who did not speak but sang his greeting.

The death of the popular poet of Daghestan, the wearer of the Order, Suleyman Stalsky, who had been nominated by the people as a candidate for representative on the Supreme Council of the USSR, deeply stirred every Soviet reader.

Suleyman Stalsky was a striking representative of oral folk poetry, an indication of the height which it can attain in the creative work of the best of its masters.

The figures of the wise leaders of the people, Lenin and Stalin; the figure of Gorky, "the herald of the tempests"; the figure of the

[33] *Ibid.*, p. 114.

working class, "which raised its sword in that October hour"; and the figures of the writers, "the young singers," looking "into the face of the future," were fused together, in this greeting, into a general picture of the new socialist life, "fresh as mountain air":

> Our day is fresh as mountain air.
> Through the years of hopes accomplished,
> In flaming purple dressed,
> We have reached the age of youth.
> My great country
> Has been set free from bondage.
> We have awakened from our evil sleep,
> We have awakened—and hither have we come.[34]

Even his own appearance at the Congress of Soviet Writers was accepted by Suleyman Stalsky not as a literary event, not as a moment in his own personal biography, but as an event of profound social significance:

> Through the vast spaces of the mountain lands
> The token of greeting was given to the poet,
> And here am I, Suleyman Stalsky,
> Come to the glorious congress of singers.[35]

The illiterate singer Suleyman Stalsky revealed here great social perception. Through the instinct of a genuine folk poet, he understood what at that time was still far from being realized, even by many of our highly educated writers and critics: that the very fact of the appearance of a popular singer-*ashug*, in this literary setting, in the capacity of a member with equal rights, and an honored guest, was in itself an event of great historical importance.

With the appearance of the Lezgian *ashug* at the All-Union Congress of Writers, a decisive emphasis was given to that constant and close connection which had always existed between artistic literature and popular oral poetry, and which has been particularly manifest in our own days.

It seemed to be symbolic that Suleyman sang his song of greeting with his face turned toward a portrait, that hung not far from the

[34] S. Stalsky, *Poems and Songs* (State Literary Press, 1938), p. 71.
[35] *Ibid.*, p. 71.

platform, of Taras Shevchenko, the popular poet of the Ukraine, who had based the whole of his creative art on folk songs.

With Suleyman Stalsky's appearance at the Congress of Writers, there begins a new stage of his creative activity: the *ashug* of Daghestan now becomes well known not only in his own land of Daghestan; his songs are read by all the peoples of the USSR; his songs and his simple, but at the same time original, figure of a folk poet have become popular throughout our multilingual and multinational land. And do we not have a living indication of Suleyman Stalsky's popularity in the message in the form of a song which was addressed to him, not so very long before his death, by another folk poet, the Kazakh *akyn* Dzhambul, wearer of the Order?

The appearance of Suleyman Stalsky at the First All-Union Congress of Writers, the fervent reception accorded to him by the writers, the references to Suleyman's speech in the newspapers proved to be the beginning of a wide public interest in the masters of folk art in all the republics and provinces of the Soviet Union. From that time on, with ever increasing frequency, the name of the Kazakh *akyn* Dzhambul began to appear in print. Soon he too becomes an All-Union celebrity (since the time of his arrival in Moscow during the ten-day celebration devoted to Kazakh art). At that time, many other talented Kazakh *akyny* and *zhirshi* were not only registered by the Union of Writers, but the most gifted of them were even made members of the Union.

In Buryat-Mongolia the rhapsody-singer A. Toroyev is assured broad public recognition. Several *bakhshi*, popular singers and narrators of Uzbekistan, are included in the body of the Uzbek Union of Soviet Writers. Not long ago, as reported in the newspapers, a similar admission of the masters of oral folk poetry into the Union of Writers took place in Azerbaidjan: a group of five talented Azerbaidjanian *ashugi* became members of the writers' organization. These and similar facts demonstrate how deeply the thought has penetrated into the popular consciousness that the creators of oral poetry are just as much poets as their literary colleagues. Suleyman Stalsky had the honor of being the first to demonstrate the right of the masters of the popular literary art to an acknowledgment of their great role in the development of Soviet artistic culture.

How great has been, and is, the significance of the popular singers in the day-to-day life of the working people may be seen from the biography of Suleyman Stalsky himself. From his youthful years, even up to the end of his life, he was creating his songs in constant, vital intercourse with the people. Having himself learned the poetic art from the *ashugi* who visited his native village of Ashag-Stal, Suleyman never composed his works for himself alone; but, when he had created a song, he immediately sang it to his fellow villagers, sitting with them somewhere under a tree, or even as they walked along, returning from their work in the fields. And the poet, in later times, could not even recollect at what moment his songs had become the common possession of his native village and district. This direct intercourse of the poet-singer with his audience not only contributed to the popularity of his songs, but was also reflected, in a most beneficial manner, in the whole of his creative art. Suleyman's listeners were not a passive audience; their responses to the songs of the poet compelled him to test himself, to verify the thoughts and emotions which were included in the song, the effectiveness of the poetic figures and language. According to everyone who knew the Daghestan poet, he had an altogether exceptional memory. Having once composed a song, he had it firmly fixed in his memory. But even so, it would sometimes happen that he forgot certain lines, and then his fellow villagers, several voices at once, would prompt him with the forgotten words of his own song. Such facts as these are also one of the evidences to the authentic folk character of his creative art.

But the popular character of Stalsky's poetry is revealed most profoundly in his productions themselves. The foundations of the revolutionary creative art of Suleyman had already been laid in the prerevolutionary period. The illustrious poet of Daghestan had experienced, in his own case, all the burden of the life of a poor peasant. Born outside of the parental home, from which Suleyman's mother, in her pregnancy, had been driven forth by her husband because of another woman; abandoned thereafter at the threshold of his own father, given out to be brought up by a strange woman; then, at the whim of his father, falling into the hands of an evil step-

mother, the future folk poet came to know much of sorrow and injury, even in his early childhood. As a boy of thirteen, he had already
gone out of his native village to work as a farm laborer. The work
on the English plantations in Gandzha, the dread malaria, the heavy
toil of a workman building railroads in Central Asia, in the oil industries of Baku, up to the age of thirty; his return to his native
places, and his marriage to a poor orphan; and from that time on, to
the revolution itself, his almost uninterrupted sojourn in Ashag-Stal—
here is the *curriculum vitae,* simple and undramatic, but full of toil
and suffering, of the popular poet, up to the time of the October
Revolution.

The motifs of Stalsky's prerevolutionary poetry are closely connected with his lot as a poor, hard-working man. In his poetry one
hardly ever encounters the lyric of contemplation; in his poems he
is either the poet of the people's sorrow or else the poet of the
people's wrath. Characteristic, in this sense, is one of his early productions, "The Nightingale." These verses begin with two figures
which are traditional in eastern poetry—that of the nightingale and
that of the blooming garden. But how unexpectedly and originally
Suleyman treats these traditional figures, which have usually been
developed in the style of the erotic lyric:

> You sing of the blooming garden,
> Your world is green, O nightingale.
> Enamored to distraction of the flowers,
> Is it possible you do not notice
> The sufferings, the torments of the poor,
> Their laments and groans, O nightingale?
> Your melodies grate harshly on the ear,
> O nightingale enamoured of the flowers.[36]

Here one hardly knows what to wonder at most—the boldness and
novelty of the artistic interpretation of the customary poetic motifs,
or the way in which the poet so clearly perceives the social tasks which
lie before a work of creative art. "The sufferings, the torments of the
poor"—that is one of the basic themes of the prerevolutionary poetry
of Suleyman. Indignation at social injustice, inequality, the contrasts

[36] *Ibid.,* p. 23.

of poverty and wealth—this is expressed with great acuteness in his early verses. Besides, Suleyman knows how to find for his social protest not only the declaratory and rhetorical forms, which are so characteristic of the poetry of the East, but also the living figures, taken directly from the common life of every day, which have been suggested to the peasant poet by his customary use of concrete and visual imagery. Characteristic, in this respect, is the poem dedicated to the samovar, which was regarded by the poor peasants as the symbol of plenty, and which had become the object of constant envy and naïve rapture among the poor:

> You drink water, you heal the whole world,
> And the tea is sweet, and there is cheese with the bread.
> But I am quite bereft of a samovar—
> The samovar and I are not on friendly terms. . . .
> This is the news that went out among us:
> You only show honor to the man
> Who has money to count over;
> For the poor—the frosty cold is their only samovar.[37]

The social indictment, which is so bold and decisive in the songs of Suleyman, is also very concrete: it is directed at those with whom the poor peasants had to come into direct conflict—at the village elder, the judge, the mullah, the wealthy kulak. Besides, Suleyman often has specific persons in view, and mentions their names. This would make the effect of the song upon his listeners, who were of the same village, all the more powerful. But, for all its local coloring, the song did not sacrifice any of its typical character or its social significance. In the song "The Village Elder" Suleyman stigmatizes the wicked *aksakal* (elder) of his village, Hassah:

> They say that Hassah is even ready
> To betray us, at the end of all.
> But his staff is too severe,
> He is just like a piercing thorn, O people.
> Whither shall one flee from these misfortunes?
> There is no recourse against the *aksakaly*.
> Thus Suleyman has spoken, the poet,
> For surely he has suffered too, O people.[38]

[37] *Ibid.*, p. 28.   [38] *Ibid.*, p. 26.

The last line is extremely characteristic: the popular poet does not separate himself and his own sorrow from the life and sufferings of the rest of the poor peasants. Even in his own consciousness he remains unalterably the poet of the people.

With great wrath he attacks the Mohammedan clergy, and indicts the systematic pillaging of the peasants (in the poem, "The Mullahs"). In these antimullah, anticlerical motifs, Suleyman's poetry is also very typical of the attitudes of the peasant poor of any nationality.

> There is no truth in the eyes of a mullah.
> You are only a hearth of envy.
> Having thrust your lever deep in the earth,
> You want to blow us up, mullahs.[39]

At times Suleyman expresses hatred for the oppressors of the people, of whatever kind they may be, in the form of malicious sarcasm. Even the outward habits of the mullahs, the officials, the wealthy men are hateful to Suleyman. His natural love for his native Lezgian tongue is outraged by the servile imitation, on the part of the local rich men, of the speech of the Russian officials, the treason to their own national speech. The observant poet remarks how the local national bourgeoisie betray the interests of the people, maintaining a constant friendship with the imperial appointees, the Russian officialdom:

> See: for bags of money
> The officials have become your friends.
> They walk along, they do not see the poor people,
> They have become arrogant donkeys.
> Toadies! Timeservers!
> You do not answer us "Salaam,"
> But "G'morning." . . . Absolutely a disgrace!
> You have become dandies in your speech. . . .
> You follow after bribes and ranks,
> And do not give us a chance to breathe.
> "Get out! Get out!" you shout at the poor men,
> Such proud rascals you have become! [40]

Aroused by the oppressions of the rich men, the clergy, the administration, the judges; by their contempt for the working people,

[39] *Ibid.*, pp. 25-26.   [40] *Ibid.*, p. 33.

and by their plunder, the folk poet foresees that requital which the seething wrath of the people is preparing for all the exploiters. In the poem "The Judges," composed by Suleyman Stalsky a year before the World War and four years before the revolution, there are such prophetic stanzas as these:

> Enough of plundering everything and everybody!
> Enough of waiting for earthly consolations.
> Terrible is your transgression!
> A great punishment awaits you, judges.
> For centuries you have plundered us, for centuries!
> You have pillaged the poor man long enough!
> From Suleyman's bow there flies against you
> The powerful arrow of indignation, judges.[41]

Thus, with integrity, fully, decisively, boldly, the Lezgian poet-singer expressed his state of mind, blending his personal feelings with the emotions of the oppressed people.

At first one is struck by the very clear revolutionary purposefulness of the poet; but on recalling the stages of his life as a poor laboring man, one understands how the steel for the sharp-edged songs of Suleyman was tempered.

The folk poet was fully prepared for the acceptance of the revolution. With fervent, passionate joy he heard the news of the fall of the tsarist autocracy, of the arrest of the tsar, of the popular justice meted out to the generals. During the first period, Suleyman, like many of the peasants, believed that real liberty had come; the poet was ready to give himself up to the illusion:

> Into my village the morning light has brought
> The news of the overthrow of the Tsar.
> Not without reason did they throw down the tyrant—
> And today the Duma is ruling. . . .
> The people have driven out the officials,
> And they are fleeing in all directions.
> They babble foolishly, although they have not taken into
>   their mouths
> A single drop of anything.

[41] *Ibid.*, pp. 34-35.

How refractory and proud your spirit was!
When you had stripped the people bare,
Leaving them to rot in prison, depriving them of their
    rights,
You drove out those who sought to present their grievances.
You shouted at them, as if they had been dogs, "Get out!"
Oppressive was your kulak, oppressive was he!
Now you have become soft as silk,
And caressing in your speech.
Now you see, Suleyman,
Life has become easier for the peasants,
Now the invitation to freedom has been given—
Now a different time has come.[42]

But soon the bandage fell from Suleyman's eyes. He, like all
the poor people, saw that the liberty which had been established by the
February Revolution was illusory and ephemeral. Essentially, in the
countryside, everything remained as it had been under the old regime:
the rich men did just as much plundering, the very same flock of
crows kept circling over the heads of the laboring people; only, to
everything else there was added the carousing of the bourgeois-na-
tionalistic conflict in the Caucasus, under the cloak of pompous
phrases:

> Every day we have a new prince over us—
> He wants to plunder the Caucasus.
> More than once has the thorn bush pierced us
> With its thorns, now in broad daylight.
> And they all speak fairly,
> But they diffuse a deadly poison:
> The she-goat, which brings forth young,
> Is now being replaced by the he-goats.
> I, Suleyman, have caught a glimpse of life,
> It bids me to forsake the assembly.
> There is no top to them, and no bottom,
> Now it is nothing but talk and talk.[43]

The keen gaze of the popular poet was able to penetrate the deceit
of pretty words, and Suleyman in disgust turned away from that
which others were ready to acknowledge as genuine freedom.

[42] *Ibid.*, pp. 35-36.   [43] *Ibid.*, pp. 37-38.

Still greater was Suleyman's disillusionment in the succeeding years (1918–1919), until the establishment of the Soviet regime in Daghestan.

Everything that Suleyman observed during that period led him to the irrefutable conclusion that the people were being cruelly deceived:

> Yes, Suleyman, you are right, you are right—
> They have deceived us, and robbed us! [44]

A most moving impression is produced by the song which Suleyman composed in protest against the Jewish pogroms perpetrated by the bourgeois-nationalist cliques. The poet of the laboring people reveals to the poor of Daghestan all the hideousness of the hunting down of the Jews, refutes the lie of the conflict "for the faith," and wrathfully lays bare the rapacious instincts which prompt the pillaging of Jewish dwellings, and which are played upon by the nationalist bourgeoisie in inciting the people.

On reading this song of Suleyman Stalsky's, one bows in admiration, both before the clearness of his social thought, his class consciousness, and also before that boldness with which he rushed to the defense of the poor Jewish people against the fury of chauvinistic wickedness. This song proves, once more, how vast may be the social and educational significance of the activity of the folk poet-singers, the *ashugi*, who such a short while ago were hardly noticed, and were not regarded as being of any account, either by the writers or by the critics. Addressing himself to those who participated in the pogroms, Suleyman said in his song:

> I will speak out my opinion:
> You are absolute crooks!
> You know how to destroy a Jewish dwelling,
> And drag the bedding out, laughing the while! . . .
> No, it is not for the faith that you are hostile to them:
> Your own inhumanity—there lies the trouble!
> You know how to catch all their chickens, without fear
> And without any trouble whatever.
> Suleyman, the poor peasant, knows everything,
> But he cannot in any possible way convince you.

[44] *Ibid.*, p. 42.

Forgetting where the real enemy lies,
You know how to kill the Jews at once.[45]

Suleyman already knew where the real enemy lay. By that time, having been taught by everything that he had observed, he had already come to a definite conclusion as to the way which must be traversed by the poor people of the countryside. This was the way of the revolutionary proletariat. In the development of this conviction, it seems to us, a role was played also by Suleyman's recollections of his work on the English plantations of Gandzha, and as a railroad worker in Samarkand, and as a worker in the oil industries of Baku. Suleyman the farm hand and Suleyman the workman were never once forgotten by Suleyman the peasant.

What was going on in the Caucasus stirred up the soul of the poet:

You give your word to everybody,
But that word is nothing but a lie.
You are lying, you are just like a saddle,
Which serves everybody, you wicked Caucasus.[46]

Suleyman was waiting for decisive changes. He was dissatisfied with the life which he observed all around him. With the instinct of the artist and of the observer of the people's life, through his constant meditation Suleyman had come to understand what salvation consisted in; namely, in a radical reconstruction of society. But the doctrine of the revolutionary proletariat was still unknown to him.

"At that time I still did not know anything about the Bolsheviks," Suleyman reminisced in the "Account of Myself," taken down from his dictation in 1936 by Kapiev Effendi.

I did a lot of thinking. People came riding past my hut, and they used to ask my advice. But I didn't always hurry with my answer. I knew that the tongue is not the foot: if you make a slip of the tongue, you are often left lying on the ground, without strength to lift yourself up again.

One day the interventionists came to Kassum-Kent, and they hanged three of my fellow villagers. What for? It turned out that they were Bolsheviks, and had come from Baku to help us.

---

[45] *Ibid.*, pp. 43-44.   [46] *Ibid.*, p. 45.

Oho! thought I, the land is ours, the mountains are ours, and the people they are killing are also ours. What in the world is this? It means that the Bolsheviks are we ourselves, and here alien people are lording it over us.

That very same day, on the street, I met my former master.

"Suleyman," said he, "why didn't you compose a song in honor of Khassim Bey, or are you keeping it for the Bolsheviks?"

I was silent.

"This world is a wheel," added my master; "everything's turning around."

"It's turning around the wrong way," I took him up.

"Wait a minute, wait a minute, surely your neck isn't asking for the noose yet?"

"No," I answered. "The noose loves fat, and my neck is nothing but skin and bones!"

That day, one small drop of my blood began to speak, the first time, like a Bolshevik. I didn't try to hinder it, I let it have its way. Its voice became my very own.[47]

This drop of blood, which "began to speak, the first time, like a Bolshevik," became a living ferment which reanimated and strengthened the whole spiritual being of Suleyman Stalsky who had already been prepared, by the whole of his personal and creative life, to become the poet of the socialist revolution. And soon Suleyman spoke out with the full power of his voice.

In his song he calls down a passionate curse upon the old world, that long-time enemy of his:

> We know your purposes,
> Perish, old world!
> We are your long-time enemies,
> Perish, old world!
> The pain of all peoples and tribes,
> As tribute, as tax, you have exacted from us,
> Explode, with those rusty laws of yours,
> Go up in smoke, and disappear from our eyes!
> Perish, old world! [48]

Stalsky is constantly more and more confirmed in his consciousness of the vast role of the working class in the revolution. Suleyman has

[47] *Ibid.*, p. 19.   [48] *Ibid.*, p. 49.

given poetic formulation to his thought in the triumphant hymn "The Workman":

> Labor is the beginning of all beginnings.
> Laying bare his dagger for brotherhood,
> The father of labor, the workingman,
> Has won freedom for us.
> From his cradle he has had
> A blood tie with the peasantry.
> That is why the first helper
> Of the peasant is the workingman. . . .
> You are not clever at deceit,
> You see the truth, Suleyman—
> Though his garment be soiled and torn,
> Strong in spirit is the workingman.[49]

Suleyman accepts in its entirety the socialist revolution which was achieved under the guidance of the proletariat. He gradually becomes the fervent singer of Soviet Daghestan, of the Soviet Caucasus, of the Soviet Union; he becomes the triumphant singer of Socialist construction, of the ever increasing friendship of the peoples, of the new forms of collective work.

Suleyman was greatly shaken by the death of the leader of the revolution, Lenin. Following his custom of always finding concrete images for the expression of his emotions, Suleyman Stalsky combines the conveying of his sorrow with the description of a cold winter day. The song attains a high emotional tension:

> Lenin, our father, has passed away,
> And the cold day is dead today.
> The wise man has departed. O pain at the heart!
> What a cold day it is today.
> Death has come to one man, but thereby
> The whole vast world has become small to us.
> This cold day, today,
> Has brought us enough anguish for many and many a day.
> There has fallen from the mighty trunk
> The purple leaf. Death has borne away
> Our leader, our teacher, our eagle. . . .
> And indeed—it is a cold day today.

[49] *Ibid.*, p. 51.

And Suleyman's grief oppresses him.
He sings a sorrowful song.
And with him the laboring people
Are afflicted. . . . It is a cold day today! [50]

But, along with all the laboring people of the Union, Suleyman finds consolation for himself in the fact that Lenin's work has been placed in the loyal and reliable hands of Lenin's great pupil—Comrade Stalin:

> When he went away, when life was extinguished
> For Vladimir Lenin—in the hour of despondency
> The great world became narrow for us,
> And the flame is in our hearts even now.
> And the horde of flattering enemies
> Was rejoicing at that time.
> But our government is always strong—
> A master builder is with us now.[51]

Suleyman Stalsky takes a passionate and direct part in the decisive struggle for the socialist reconstruction of the countryside, for the collectivization of the rural economy, in the struggle with the enemies of the cause of the collective farm, and with the kulak class. Furthermore, as in his early verses, the struggle with the enemy is absolutely concrete. Suleyman's songs are, in the first place, an attack upon that enemy whom he sees before him, at home in his native land, in his native village. And at the same time the figure of this concrete enemy takes on certain type-features. Suleyman insists upon carrying the conflict with the enemy to the very end, never trusting him, nor giving up to his cunning and his trickery. To this point he devotes a poem with the characteristic title "An Old Enemy Can Never Be a Friend":

> No, an old enemy is not a brother to you—
> He cannot but be harsh.
> When the day breaks, you will not be glad,
> Kindness cannot come from such a one as he. . . .
> On his old wounds—such is my advice—
> Strike him, strike him back.
> In the bog, which has been rotting for three hundred years,
> There cannot be any wholesome water.

[50] *Ibid.*, p. 52.   [51] *Ibid.*, p. 55.

> Slam your door shut in the kulak's face,
> And put no faith in his trickeries.
> With him you may expect nothing but losses—
> With an enemy, it can't be any other way.[52]

The popular poet of Daghestan seems, as it were, to echo Gorky, with his well known maxim: "If the enemy does not yield, they annihilate him."

In general, Suleyman Stalsky had a great deal in common with Maxim Gorky. Besides the rich experience of life, which had been acquired in the toil of their burdensome and grim youth; besides the feeling of a very close connection with the masses of thc laboring people, they are united by the firmness of their faith in the powers of the working people, their inexorableness in the struggle with their enemies. Their memorable encounter at the Congress of Writers also served as the beginning of a personal friendship. Suleyman was stirred to the very depths of his soul by the attention which the great writer showed him. That is why the verses which were called forth by this encounter are so direct and sincere:

> My heart was fired with joy
> At the honor which he showed me.
> O profound mind, O kindly aspect!
> The conversation was a genial one.
> I thought: For the pattern of my rhymes
> He has shown me this honor. . . .
> I turn anew to my songs, and fervently
> I sing of workmen and of peasants.
> And Suleyman has become young again—
> Gorky has shown me such honors.[53]

Here, in these lines, it is not Suleyman's ambition that is speaking, but the touching pride of a national poet in the fact that his poetic labors have received acknowledgment, and that, consequently, he has not toiled over his songs in vain.

In one of his works Suleyman Stalsky acknowledges that the composition of verses is a great and strenuous task for him:

[52] *Ibid.*, p. 63.   [53] *Ibid.*, p. 72.

I, Suleyman, have no knowledge of books,
But there is one thing that I have thoroughly grasped—
Verse comes with difficulty, with difficulty,

and that is why, with him, "There cannot be a single empty verse." [54]

In his songs Suleyman speaks with love and tenderness of the young people, of the students, of the Young Communist League. Being himself illiterate, Suleyman rejoices at the fact that now the young people of the peasant working class have gained access to books and education.

Stalsky's biographers relate the following episode. Soon after the popular poet's return from the Congress of Writers at Moscow to his own land, Suleyman was riding around to the neighboring villages. (They all wanted to see him, and to hear his speeches and songs about Moscow, about Stalin.) At the gates of a certain school he was met by a group of school children, and one of them opened a book with a portrait of Suleyman, and with a joyful smile began to point him out to everyone: "That is the man who comes riding. He is here. We know him!" Stalsky then turned to the youngster with the following words: "See how fortunate you are: Suleyman used to talk to you, even before this." And then, with a heavy sigh, he added, "But books do not talk to me that way."

It is clear to everyone who has any knowledge of the poetry of Stalsky, with what rapture he greeted the Stalin Constitution which confirmed for every citizen of the Soviet Union the right to labor, to rest, and to receive an education.

To everyone who has any knowledge of Stalsky's poetry, it is clear with what fervent love, with what devotion he regards the creator of the Constitution, the leader of the peoples, who has strengthened their great friendship—Comrade Stalin.

The song of the national poet of Daghestan on Stalin is widely known throughout the Soviet Union. In the form which is customary with him, that of a finely chased Oriental quatrain, with the first three lines always bound together by the same rhyme, and then finishing off with a refrain (in the fourth), Suleyman Stalsky gives us a

[54] *Ibid.*, p. 63.

masterly work of art, of great power and expressiveness. One feels that Stalsky is speaking not only for himself, but for the whole people which has given him the right to be called its national poet.

> Briskly moving forward,
> The party leads the mighty ones.
> The laboring people are on the march—
> And you are their standard, Stalin.
> To all the laboring people you are like a light
> That glows for them from the years of youth,
> Leading us where there is no sorrow,
> Where there is only joy, Stalin.
> The years are passing by—year after year
> You preserve us from misfortunes,
> And the distant vault of heaven
> Is visible to you, our supreme one, Stalin.[55]

Dzhambul Dzhabayev
(Born 1846)*

The whole of the Soviet Union recently observed the seventy-fifth jubilee of the creative activity of the national *akyn* (singer-poet) of Kazakhstan, the aged Dzhambul, who is nearly a hundred years of age.

The very fact that the whole country honored, not a writer, but a singer-poet, a folk storyteller, is in itself exceedingly significant. Such an event as this could take place only in the country of victorious socialism; it would have been altogether unthinkable in prerevolutionary Russia. There was too much neglect of, and at times even conscious contempt for, folk art on the part of the ruling classes and their government. The representatives of folk art were regarded, at best, as something eccentric and exotic, the object of a superficial and far from serious curiosity. Only the very narrow circles of scholarly specialists, a small number of writers and musicians, and the more enlightened and democratically inclined teachers and literary men, displayed a genuine and profound interest in folk art.

No less significant is the fact that the whole Soviet land was honor-

[55] *Ibid.*, p. 134.
* Died 1945.—Ed.

ing a popular poet who belonged, not to the Russian nationality, but to one of the nationalities of Central Asia, to one of those nationalities concerning whose life—to say nothing of their poetry—hardly anyone knew anything before the revolution.

The jubilee of the Kazakh popular poet Dzhambul, wearer of the Order, was a great holiday in the Soviet Union, and was a new and convincing proof of the magnificent success of the wise nationality policy of Lenin and Stalin, the result of the strong and tested friendship of the peoples of the USSR.

The Great October Socialist Revolution revealed the natural riches of the country; it revealed also the poetic riches which lay hidden among the masses of the people. The October Revolution made clear, and revealed to all the world, what vast and diverse talents are to be found among the working people of all nationalities who constitute one united brotherly family of Soviet peoples. The names of the Lezgian *ashug* Suleyman Stalsky and of the Kazakh *akyn* Dzhambul Dzhabayev have become near and dear to every conscious Soviet citizen, no matter where he may live or to what nationality he may belong.

Dzhambul is at one and the same time both an *akyn* and a *zhirshi*, that is, he is not only a poet-improviser, but also a performer of the old traditional works of the national folklore. According to testimony of persons well acquainted with the life and creative art of Dzhambul, he possesses an exceptionally well stored memory, and is an outstanding connoisseur of the Kazakh popular poetry, especially of epic and lyrico-epic poems. He remembers well and recites splendidly the old poems of the sixteenth and seventeenth centuries, such as the poems about the national heroes, the knights Koblandy, Er-Sagyn, Er-Targyn, Shora, or the famous romantic poems on the love of Koza-Korpesh and the minstrel Slu, and Kyz-Zhibek.

Dzhambul knows also the heroic poems of a later period, poems dealing with the popular uprisings against the oppression of the tsars and the khans, the poems of the nineteenth century; for example, the poems on the uprising of Isatay, on the uprising of Beket the knight, and also the poems on the prerevolutionary uprising at the time of the

World War, the uprising of the Kazakhs in 1916, the songs about the hero of that uprising, the famous Amangeldy-Imanov.

This surpassing knowledge of the history of his native land, of the national historical traditions, of all the wealth of many centuries of folk poetry, reveal to us the soil out of which Dzhambul's poetic creativeness grew. Dzhambul's poetry is bone of the bone and flesh of the flesh of the folk art of Kazakhstan.

But it is not only in this respect that Dzhambul is a typical *zhirshi* and *akyn*. He is simply the most striking representative of the popular poets. Many of the Kazakh *akyny* and *zhirshi*, as well as the Uzbek *bakshi* or the Caucasian *ashugi*, are characterized by a knowledge not only of their own national poetry, but also of the poetry of many other peoples, especially the neighboring ones. Dzhambul has an excellent knowledge of the creative art of the Kirghiz, who are related to the Kazakhs; in particular, he remembers long passages of the immense Kirghiz epic poem *Manas*. He knows the songs of the Uzbek and the Turkmenian. He is well acquainted with the poetry of the Tadjiks and the Persians. Throughout the ninety-two years of his life, the Kazakh *akyn* has performed on the bass lute a multitude of motifs from the song treasury of the entire Near East.

Long ago it became necessary to disabuse one's self of the idea that the folk poets were creators and performers only of so-called "poetic primitives." The best of the popular singer-poets have been, and are now becoming, with ever increasing frequency, the creators and performers of valuable works of a high artistic level. In former times, because of the imperfect development of literacy, the folk poets were the fundamental disseminators of artistic culture. Such were the *aedists* and rhapsodists of ancient Greece, the jongleurs of medieval France, the *ashugi* of the Caucasus, the "merry fellows," the artists of ancient Russia—the "buffoons." Certainly it is not without reason that in one of the beautiful Russian *byliny*, that of the unsuccessful marriage of Alyosha Popovich, there is a description of the appearance of Dobrynya Nikitich in the role of a psaltery (*gusly*) player and buffoon, who makes use both of the native national motifs and also of the musical and poetic motifs of other lands and peoples:

The beggar began to play on the gusly,
On the beautiful gusly,
And he took some of his dances from Novgorod,
And others he took from Tsargrad.[56]

The creative art of many of the *akyny* of Kazakhstan is similarly rich in diversity of sources. It is especially rich in the case of a singer so outstanding, both in the excellence of his creative memory and also in his gifts as a singer, as Dzhambul.

Dzhambul's importance lies not only in the fact that, as we shall see, he is a striking exponent of the popular ideas of our era and of our land, the ideas of socialism and communism. The significance of his creative work is also great because of the fact that through him the poets and readers of all peoples of the Soviet Union are brought closer to the poetry of the Near East. It is possible to affirm with absolute certainty that no writer or scholar has done so much for the popularization among the masses of the Russian people of a knowledge of the nature of Oriental poetry as Dzhambul, and also, of course, Suleyman Stalsky. It is through them that the average Russian reader has come to feel the originality of the Oriental poetic art, and to comprehend it organically, not in the abstract. Dzhambul and Suleyman have done a great deal, by their own poetic practice, for the mutual interchange of the national artistic treasures of the various peoples.

Dzhambul's own poetic work, like that of many other Kazakh *akyny*, is closely linked with traditions of poetic style found in Oriental poetry. It is only necessary to listen a bit attentively to the rhythms and motifs of Dzhambul's songs to observe the most characteristic of his compositional devices, the selection and linking of poetic figures, and there will at once become clear the close bond between Dzhambul's poetry and the many centuries of tradition of the poetry of the other peoples of Central Asia, the Transcaucasus, Iran, and even of the whole Near East.

In examining carefully the favorite images used by Dzhambul, the reader involuntarily recalls the Oriental poets, beginning with the renowned master workmen of ancient Iran in the twelfth century,

[56] A. F. Hilferding, *Onega Byliny* (1873 ed.), p. 538.

Khayyam and Nizami; in the thirteenth century, Sa'adi; in the fifteenth century, Djami; the great Georgian of the twelfth century,
Rustaveli; and the Armenian-Georgian-Azerbaidjanian poet-*ashug* of
the eighteenth century, Sayat-Nova. In spite of all the dissimilarity
among all the poets mentioned here—in thematics, ideas, and psychology—there are certain features in their creative art that connect
their poetics which has been conditioned by many centuries of tradition, and by the long-continued cultural intercourse of the countries
which produced them.

Let us survey Dzhambul's poetic and figurative stock in trade, how
he loves to have recourse to the figure of the nightingale, finding
certain resemblances between the nightingale and the poet in general,
and particularly those poets of whose creative work Dzhambul was especially fond. This is the way he speaks of Pushkin:

> Not one of your songs can be forgotten.
> You, Pushkin, are near and dear to the heart of the people!
> We all live better and more happily because of you,
> Roll on then, deathless as life, O Nightingale! [57]

Dzhambul calls his colleague Suleyman Stalsky a "nightingale":

> Ashug Suleyman,
> Nightingale of Daghestan,
> Pour forth your joyful trills at dawn. . . .
> Everywhere is the nightingale's song of yearning.
> Not in cages—
> On the fresh branches of the poplars,
> In the mountains of Daghestan, in the gardens of Kazakhstan,
> The nightingales sing more merrily every day.[58]

Dzhambul also has recourse to the figure of the nightingale in his
well known reply to the poet Hasem Lakhuti, wearer of the Order:

> Through your lips the Tadjik people
> Sing their nightingale's song.[59]

And the Tadjik poet, too, began his address to Dzhambul with the
figure of the nightingale and the rose, so traditional in Oriental
poetry:

[57] Dzhambul, *Songs and Poems* (State Literary Press, 1938), p. 85.
[58] *Ibid.*, p. 92.   [59] *Ibid.*, p. 87.

Flutter and rejoice, free nightingale,
Over your happy rose! [60]

Dzhambul mentions roses, tulips, poppies, and flowers in general a great number of times.

In accordance both with his own fervent love of nature and at the same time with the poetic tradition which he so profoundly made his own, he loves to speak of an enormous, blooming, joyous garden, of the flowers of legendary Gulistan: "Before the Fatherland the flowers of Gulistan fade"; "The joyous garden of my Fatherland is all in bloom"; "Kazakhstan is blooming like an enormous garden"; "Look, Lakhuti! The garden is growing profusely"; "The tulips and roses are murmuring in the garden." [61]

In the spirit of the profound poetic tradition of the East, Dzhambul very often makes use of the figures of precious stones, valuable gems, gold, silver, and pearls, for the representation of pictures of nature, or in the expression of his own rapture before the spiritual beauty of man. Emeralds, sapphires, rubies, turquoises, diamonds, brilliants, and also amber and pearls are scattered in handfuls through the lines of Dzhambul's songs: "Above us glows the turquoise of the heavens"; "The dewdrops lie in a chain of pearls"; "The flowers are gleaming with the fire of precious stones"; "The roses are flaming like enormous rubies"; "The pearly rivers run through the valleys"; "The grain is ripening, more golden than amber"; "The meadows are covered with turquoise flowers"; "Every little leaf the plane tree is a brilliant." [62]

The address to Pushkin, which we have already mentioned, begins with the following lines:

You burn like a diamond and bloom like a ruby,
O mighty *akyn* of Russian poetry.
Pearls of song you have created for the world,
Out of a black century your genius has shone forth. [63]

Dzhambul is very fond of comparing songs with precious stones: "The songs burn, like a great precious stone"; [64] or of A. M. Gorky:

[60] *Ibid.*, p. 86.
[61] *Ibid.*, pp. 52, 56, 88, 93.
[62] *Ibid.*, pp. 42, 55, 68, 71, 82, 88.
[63] *Ibid.*, p. 85.
[64] *Ibid.*, p. 93.

He brought us songs of conflict
Of empearled and gleaming words.[65]

On the other hand, Dzhambul has an altogether different image
for songs, but one which is also drawn from the Oriental poetic
tradition: A song is honey. "The words in it are fresh and fragrant
as honey." [66]

In the style of Oriental poetics, Dzhambul frequently has recourse
to the figures of silk, satin, velvet, brocade, and all rich materials and
also of carpets:

The warm winds make a rustling like silk. . . .
There the spring is wandering, spreading all around
Carpets of grasses bursting into bloom.[67]

The figures of all kinds of precious substances, of gold, silver,
precious stones, pearls, sumptuous fabrics, carpets, delicate fragrances
and sweet savors, and also of tender flowers and plants, are recalled
by the lines of the Persian, Georgian, and Armenian poets. Dzhambul obviously drew his figures not only from surrounding nature, but
from something else that was no less dear to him than nature—from
the poetry of his own native land of Kazakhstan, and from that of
other peoples of the East.

Dzhambul also employs a number of other images which are
widely diffused, in general, in the poetry of the East. Thus Dzhambul loves to recall, in his works, the legendary heroes of Oriental
tradition. In the well known "Poem on Voroshilov," Dzhambul contrasts the Soviet marshal to the legendary captains of antiquity, who
are popular in the poetry of Oriental lands: Genghiz Khan, Ali,
Iskander (Alexander the Great), Rustem, Manas, and Kene Khan.

Dzhambul often mentions the favorite fantastic figures of the
Kazakh folklore tale—the winged horse Tulpar, the miraculous bird
Sunkar. Continuing the tradition of many Kazakh *akyny*, Dzhambul
works over afresh one of the favorite themes of the poets of Kazakhstan: the theme of the search for the happy land, "Zher-uyuk," a
theme which has recently been developed in detail by the *akyn* Bek
in the "Song of the Eternal Dream of Asan Kaiga." As a develop-

[65] *Ibid.*, p. 91.   [66] *Ibid.*, p. 50.   [67] *Ibid.*, pp. 98, 99.

ment of the same theme, Dzhambul composed the poem "Utegen the Knight."

It would be fascinating to establish the dependence of Dzhambul's poetry upon the genre-compositional forms of the ancient poetry of Kazakhstan, and also on the poetry of other peoples of the East. But this can be done only by Orientalists, and chiefly by specialists in the literature of Kazakhstan, since the existing translations of Dzhambul, for all the excellence of many of them, still cannot give us an exact representation of the peculiarities of structure, much less a rhythmic picture of the original productions.

But for all the close connections which Dzhambul has with the poetic tradition of his native land, and of the other lands of Central Asia, the Caucasus, and the Orient beyond our borders, it would be absurd not to see in Dzhambul's creative art, above all, his own personal response to the impressions received from nature and from the whole life of his native Kazakhstan. Dzhambul deeply absorbs impressions of life and of nature. His creative memory retains them all permanently. His keen observation and strong feeling for nature are revealed as the source of a multitude of the most delicate little sketches of all that the poet, in the course of his long life, has noticed in the natural phenomena of his native land and in the life of its people. On reading Dzhambul's songs, even a man who has never been in Kazakhstan will come to have a feeling of the land and of the life of the people, both past and present. The importance of artistic perception in Dzhambul's works is very great.

In Dzhambul's songs one senses the poet's fervent love for his native land, his devotion both to the mountains of Alma-Ata and to the boundless spaces of the Kazakh steppe, with the odors of the plants, the brilliance of the flowers; with the freely pasturing droves of horses, the enormous herds of sheep; with the passing caravans of camels; with the eagles soaring above the steppe, and the hissing snakes that hide themselves in the grasses; with the flocks of wild geese, swans, and cranes that come flying past. By day the whole steppe is flooded with the bright gold of the sunshine; by night, the vast spaces of the steppe are covered with a canopy of stars. In the beautiful, lyrical "Cradle Song" Dzhambul paints a most wonderful picture of the steppe in slumber:

> That you, my lad, may go to sleep,
> Dzhambul sounds his lute.
> He fingers the strings
> With a good grandfatherly hand
> He rocks your cradle
> And softly sings a song;
> That peace may come winging to you,
> A blue star is dreaming.
> On the *dzhailau* * the flocks are slumbering.
> The downy little kids are sleeping,
> The little camels are sleeping in the steppe,
> The golden foals,
> The calves with their high foreheads,
> The little lambs with their soft fleece.
> You, my little one, must also sleep.
> The grasshoppers are sleeping in the grass,
> The little fishes are sleeping in Amu-Darya.
> Listening to the deep stillness,
> Above the river sleeps the reed.
> The flowers are sleeping, and the lakes, and the lands.
> Then why are you not sleepy too,
> My black-eyed little one? [68]

Dzhambul knows his native region from one end to the other; he knows where the best grass is, where the best pastures are. The cattle-raising collective farmer of his country appeals to him, as to the best judge of the land, when, with the approach of spring, the necessity arises of transferring the flocks to the summer pasture, the *dzhailau*. Dzhambul thus describes this migration:

> The collective farm Er-Nazar awakened from sleep.
> The weather had grown cool and clear.
> The collective farmers came to me with a request.
> "Lead us, father, to the *dzhailau*—thither,
> Where the grass is growing and the water is blue,
> Where the warm winds rustle like silk. . . ."
> I got up and said, "Very well."

---

* *Dzhailau:* summer pasture.—ED.
[68] *Ibid.*, p. 72.

I mounted my horse, and led out the drove of horses.
The leaping steeds began to neigh, when they scented the
     wide spaces.
After me, carrying his nomad tents,
Rode my kinsman, the jolly kolkhoz.
I saw, in excitement and with heart afire,
How the dew was steaming, and how to Karakol
There flew the white-shouldered eagle;
How on the resounding great height above me
Ala-tau was glowing in its pearly white turban,
And I heard, as somewhere it fell from cliffs,
A waterfall roar with the rolling of stones.
I know this land for thousands of versts—
Couch grass and wormwood, *saksaul* * and *kuray* †. . . .
With my eyes shut I can find the *dzhailau*,
I lead the flocks along the paths.[69]

And indeed, how could Dzhambul help knowing his native region
of the steppes! Summarizing the total results of his ninety years of
life, in his magnificent poem "My Native Land," Dzhambul says
of himself:

    . . . For ninety years the herds have pastured,
    For ninety years the feather grass has blown,
    For ninety years the cranes
    Have carried their songs up to the clouds.
    For ninety years the stirrups have jingled.
    Ninety years have bowed me down.
    For ninety years I have kept a horse,
    So that I might ride into the new days.[70]

Throughout his long life, Dzhambul studied all the changing
shades of nature in his native land, all the colors, all the hues, all
the odors. He feels keenly, and knows how to convey to his hearers,
the agitation which is experienced by all of nature, and by man,
with the approach of spring in the steppe. The poet's rapture is
quivering in his every line:

Saddle my horse! The tent is too narrow for me!
Over the steppe floats the bright blue spring!

* *Saksaul:* haloxylon.—Ed.   † *Kuray:* saltwort.—Ed.
[69] *Ibid.*, pp. 98-99.   [70] *Ibid.*, p. 140.

The black-eyed girls have begun to sing by the tents,
The delicate sweet kumiss * has begun to foam.
The merry birds are hovering over their nests,
And with neighing the mares are calling their foals.
And the white swans are floating in the sky
Above the steppe, that is green as emerald.
O blooming steppe! Thou art more enchanting than a dream!
The flowers are gleaming with the fire of precious stones!
The purple poppies are blazing like a flame.
The tulips of the steppe are sparkling in every petal.
Like enormous jewels, the roses are glowing,
And the white lilies pour out their fragrance.[71]

For poetic similes and metaphors Dzhambul very often makes use
of typical phenomena of the Kazakh life of the steppe, and of nature. This makes his imagery particularly concrete: "My blood, like
kumiss, began to bubble, ringing in my ears"; "When our blood
filled the *aryks* . . ." † [72]

Like the waves of the Aral Sea in breakers,
Strong is our land.[73]
The snows of Ala-Tau are clothed in the sunset,
In the last rays of the sun they are glowing like rubies.[74]
When I grew white-haired, like the snows of Ala-Tau,
Then I came to know that wonderful word "Soviet."[75]

Dzhambul's poetry, as we see, is exceedingly organic: its roots go
back into the depths of the artistic traditions of the East; it is nourished by the living springs of the national Kazakh art; it has absorbed
into itself the beauty of nature in the Kazakh steppe, and in the
folkways. Dzhambul's poetry is, from beginning to end, a poetry of
the people.

And it is all the more precious, it is all the more significant that
the great folk-singer *akyn*, inheritor and possessor of the poetic riches
of his national artistic culture, became the ardent singer of the new
way of life, the singer of the October Revolution, of socialism and

---

* Kumiss: fermented mare's milk.—ED.
[71] *Ibid.*, p. 42.
† *Aryks*: irrigation ditches in Turkestan and other parts of Central Asia.—ED.
[72] *Ibid.*, pp. 23, 62.   [74] *Ibid.*, p. 37.
[73] *Ibid.*, p. 60.   [75] *Ibid.*, p. 25.

of communism. The organic character of all of Dzhambul's creative work, from his earliest years down to our own days, is a striking testimony to the thoroughness with which the October Revolution has been accepted by the masses of the people of Kazakhstan.

Characteristic of Dzhambul's creative work after the October Revolution is his favorite theme: the contrast of the old with the new, the continual meditation of the poet on those world-shaking changes in the mode of life, world view, and economic life of the Kazakh people, and even in nature itself in Kazakhstan—in the Kazakh village, in the Kazakh landscape. Dzhambul, like the ancient Boyan, loves celebrating the glory of the new life in his songs, to "weave the fabric of the [present] time."

Dzhambul is not like some old men who are ready to idealize the ancient times, and to bewail their own long-vanished youth. For this poet, almost one hundred years of age, real youth has arrived now, with the coming of youth for his country. He joyfully hails the October Revolution and the changes it has brought, both in the life and in the economy of the Kazakhs. He is delighted with the change in the whole aspect of his native land. It is not without reason that one of Dzhambul's best songs, universally acknowledged as such by the whole Soviet Union, is his famous "The People's Greeting," addressed to V. M. Molotov. In this song the poet conveys with great power the emotions that move him. The song produces a powerful impression by its profound sincerity and simplicity. These lines give a striking picture of Kazakhstan as transformed by the October Revolution and the Stalin Five-Year Plans:

> Songs were born in the villages of the steppe,
> Songs of a land torn by slavery
> Songs that slipped through the centuries like the sands,
> Songs of sorrow, need and anguish.
> Seventy years I sang through my tears,
> In the ragged tents, among the hungry throng,
> In the cold huts, and in the needy villages,
> Of life that was heavy, like a load of *saksaul,*
> Of life that was steep, like the mountain of the deer,
> My cracked lute sung.[76]

[76] *Ibid.*

And following this description of the gloomy past there come these vigorous and triumphant lines:

My joy came with the October Revolution
The Decree of Moscow brought me joy.
With a new song I have come to the assembly,
And along with Dzhambul, the whole of Kazakhstan began to sing.
From that time, like a youth, I am glowing with joy;
To the motherland I am giving my very best songs.[77]

And further on, Dzhambul, with a deep feeling of patriotism, enumerates the riches of a regenerated Kazakhstan, blending with the regeneration of the country his own spiritual regeneration.

Like the garden of Gulistan, the steppe has burst into bloom,
Life has given me a tent abundantly supplied,
It has spread for me a miraculous carpet
From Sin-Tszy to the Ural Mountains.
It has smoothed out wrinkles upon my brow.
Dzhambul walks as one who has grown young again.
To his people have been given forever
The riches of a great and happy land.
The copper of Karsakpay, the lead of Kara-Tau,
The valleys of blooming Ala-Tau,
The hoards of white Altaian ore,
And the black gold of Karaganda,
The gushing fountains of the oil of Emba,
The rivers, seas, and forests of Kazakhstan,
The cotton of Chimkent, the wealth in flocks of sheep,
The fragrant apples of Alma-Ata.
And my eyes have no more encountered
The woe, need, and sorrow of the past.
The hands of the steppe dweller have guided trains
Into the limitless deserts of Betpak-Dala.[78]

Dzhambul, as a fervent Soviet patriot, was inexpressibly delighted that the achievements of socialist industry penetrated into Kazakhstan, that the Kazakhs of the steppe were successful in mastering the new techniques. He is an ardent admirer of the Turkestan-Siberian Railway, and very often mentions the railway in his songs. He delights in it, takes pride in it, and poetically compares it with the

[77] *Ibid.*　　　　[78] *Ibid.*, p. 26.

traditional figure—so dear to the cattle-rearing people of Kazakhstan —of the horse of the steppes.

> And in Kazakhstan, heavy-maned and splendid,
> As with a million hoofs
> The fiery, raven-black Turksib *
> Sounds its shrill whistle through the steppes.[79]

The wise Dzhambul does not contrast the "iron cavalry" to the horses of the steppe, as did Sergey Yesenin, who, not understanding the course of history, did not to the very end accept the revolution. But with living joy Dzhambul and the whole Kazakh people greeted this wonderful guest.

The Kazakhs fell in love with their railroad. The Turkestan-Siberian Railway became a popular favorite. The people came to love the music of the engine whistles, of the rails, and of the wheels.

> The song of the rails and the pounding of the wheels
> Every Kazakh village knows.[80]

The engine whistles and the measured revolutions of the wheels became firmly interwoven with the harmony of the sounds of the steppe. And the popular poet joyfully hails this new combination of sounds. The ear of the poet discerns in them a new beauty.

The new phenomena, in general, are so sensitively and organically perceived by him that they begin to be an integral part of his system of imagery, which, as we have seen, is based on many centuries of poetic tradition. And Dzhambul accomplished this so cleverly that there is no stylistic break whatever. The following lines are characteristic in this respect:

> A snake can never expect to reach the clouds,
> And a camel can never fly like an eagle,
> And a locomotive can never cross the waters of the sea,
> And a steamboat cannot run on dry land.[81]

Accepting the new life with his whole soul, the poet every now and then returns in his thought to the difficult life of the past, before

* Familiar abbreviation for the Turkestan-Siberian Railway.
[79] *Ibid.*, p. 33.   [80] *Ibid.*, p. 45.   [81] *Ibid.*, p. 63.

the revolution. Dzhambul continually contrasts that which existed in the past with what the bright present offers us:

> "Look," said I, "and believe the *zhirshi*,
> The summer pastures all around us are fair as a dream,
> Only, it was not always that we were able
> To pasture herds and flocks upon them.
> I remember: twenty years ago,
> Right here, boiling up, there foamed a waterfall,
> And the rainbow shone so brightly in the distance,
> And the juicy herbs grew here. . . .
> But we, poor people, could not pasture our flocks here. . . .
> The grass and the coolness, the flowers and the water—
> They were all counted part of the rich landowner's property,
> And the rich landowner was fiercer than a ravening wolf.
> He was encouraged in his cruelties by the Tsar,
> He trampled down the poor people with his wild horse,
> He struck them hard with a whip, without pity,
> And with his fierce dogs he chased them.
> And the poor people went, cursing their fate,
> In the hungry years, to the salt marshes,
> Where the salt, seeping out, shone white in the distance,
> Like bitter tears of the earth. . . .
> But today—look and admire, my friends
> The collective-farm lands are too boundless to be measured!
> In our land are pastured millions of head
> Of sheep, of mares, and of cattle." [82]

There is a touching appeal in Dzhambul's song addressed to his pioneer * grandson (over whose happy childhood the aged poet cannot rejoice enough). And again the recollection of the hard past makes him still more alert, still more keen to feel the whole significance of the new conditions under which the Soviet young people are growing up:

> We grew up in an altogether different way.
> We were held in, like dogs.
> And when, beneath the sun of May,
> The silken flag of the Pioneers
> Nods to me like a scarlet poppy,

[82] *Ibid.*, p. 100.
* Communist Children's Movement. Pioneers are normally 10 to 16 years old.—Ed.

Then the unaccustomed tears
Quiver in the old man's eyes.[83]

Carefully surveying the new life, comparing it with what went on in the country before the revolution, the Kazakh *akyn* addresses himself with fervent gratitude—both his own personal gratitude and that of his whole people—to the men with whose names this new life will forever be linked in the consciousness of all mankind—Lenin and Stalin.

The songs of Dzhambul, inspired by a visit which he made to the mausoleum of the body of the great leader of the revolution, are permeated with a profound devotion to the memory of Lenin. What great heights are attained, in these songs, by the social consciousness of the poet! How sincerely and ardently Dzhambul conveys the feeling of friendship among the peoples of the whole Soviet Union—a friendship which had been established by the genius of Lenin! The Kazakh *akyn* profoundly appropriated Lenin's ideas of a glorious internationalism! Before the mausoleum on Red Square, Dzhambul came to feel with particular power the whole significance of the great friendship of the peoples.

The mausoleum stands in the very center of the land,
The peoples, like rivers, have flowed up to it.
The Tadjik and the Oirot and the Kazakh are coming
With love in their hearts and with sorrow in their eyes.
The Afghan comes, and the Persian and the Arab,
Like children to a father, like warriors to their staff
    officer.
And I come along with them, in deep emotion,
I lift up my eyes, and eagerly look.
And I see—he lies in the tomb as if alive,
Peaceful and wise, simple and dear.
The standards have dipped above him with love.
The peoples pass, but he is motionless,
He does not hear, when I, bent and white-haired as I am,
Whisper to him in the Kazakh tongue my filial greeting,
And whisper him my oath—that I will be a follower of Lenin,
That I will think and fight and live after Lenin's manner,
And will tell all my children and grandchildren and great-
    grandchildren,

[83] *Ibid.*, p. 74.

Both in songs, and in the stanzas of poems,
That Lenin, like the sun, gives life to this planet,
That the genius of Lenin burns on in Stalin.[84]

A great many of Dzhambul's works are dedicated to Stalin. It may be asserted with absolute certainty that the figure of Stalin is the fundamental and central figure in all of Dzhambul's postrevolutionary poetry. In the figure of Stalin is incarnated all the rapture of the aged *akyn* with the new Soviet socialist life; with the name of Stalin are linked all of his best feelings and thoughts. Stalin is the direct and foremost pupil of Lenin, the continuer of his revolutionary work. Stalin is the sun of a new life, enlightening the whole world. Stalin, the creator of the great Soviet Constitution, is the fountain of happiness, both for the poet personally and for all the peoples of the Soviet Union.

I am the happiest singer on earth—
I have seen Stalin in the Kremlin at Moscow.
I stood beside the leader of all the peoples,
And strongly pressed his powerful hand,
That hand which has firmly guided
A hundred and seventy-five million people
For two decades, forward, ever forward,
In the radiance of happy and sun-bright days.[85]

Dzhambul is a passionate champion of the work of Lenin and Stalin. He has composed beautiful songs on the faithful comrade-in-arms of Stalin—Molotov, Ordzhonikidze, Voroshilov, Kaganovich, and others. On the other hand, with what wrath his songs are filled when he speaks of the enemies of the people, of the Trotsky-Bukharin grovelers, of those who wanted to do harm to the Soviet land! Dzhambul's songs are a sharp-edged weapon directed against the enemy:

Happiness is dear to us, and honor is dear,
With our blades we will cut the enemy to pieces. . . .
Life won with blood is dear to us,
We will trample down the enemy into the hot earth.
The beloved motherland is dear to us—
We will cut down the enemies in our lands.

[84] *Ibid.*, pp. 20-21.   [85] *Ibid.*, p. 21.

We will cut them down, in the heat and in the rain
    and in the snow,
Until the enemy is completely annihilated.
So that Stalin, stroking his mustache with his hand,
When he hears of the victory may exclaim, *"Zhak-sy!"* * [86]

As a genuine Soviet patriot, Dzhambul verifies his every step, his every public act, by the thought: Would it deserve the approbation of the leader? Stalin is the supreme standard of social behavior. Dzhambul also rears the Kazakh young people in this conviction.

> Let the Kazakh Pioneer remember—
> Stalin is the highest example,
> The wisest of all the wise men,
> The best father of all fathers.[87]

Returning in his reminiscences to the past, the poet asks of himself and of the Kazakhs:

What have we known? Anguish, poverty, and darkness.
What have we seen? Chains, the whip, and the bayonet.
The rich men kept us down, worse than dogs,
In the darkness our stifled cry died away.
But as the sun, on rising, dispels the darkness,
You have come, and the peoples have been saved by you.
And we have forged our emblem, and we have lifted on high
    the flag
Of the brightest and happiest land.
Stalin, the Sun! Burn on, without being consumed, in the
    Kremlin.
To thee we bring our songs and hearts and flowers.
On all the immeasurable planet of this earth,
There is no man the people need more than you! [88]

The *akyn* Dzhambul, who belongs to Kazakhstan and to the whole Soviet Union, in the national form of his art as a singer, has expressed with the greatest fullness and truthfulness the emotions and thoughts of all the patriots of the socialist motherland.

---

* *Zhaksy*—Kazakh word meaning "good."—ED.
[86] *Ibid.*, p. 165.   [87] *Ibid.*, p. 71.   [88] *Ibid.*, p. 24.

CONCLUSION

❧

The poetry of the people is at present enveloped by the warm care of the Party, the Government, and the whole Soviet public. A great deal of attention is devoted to folklore by all the literary organizations, beginning with the Union of Soviet Writers and ending with the literary circles in the industrial establishments and on the collective farms. Throughout the land the work of collecting folklore is going on exuberantly. Literary museums and archives, during the past few years, have accumulated vast collections of folklore, gathered by scholars on their expeditions.

It is necessary to emphasize with particular vigor the great attention which is being devoted to questions of folklore by the central and the local press. And this has given a great deal of new life to folklore itself, exerting a most beneficial influence on the creations of workmen and collective farmers. The immense publishing ventures instigated by the great proletarian writer A. M. Gorky, especially the work of the *Pravda* staff in preparing, for the twentieth anniversary of the Soviet power, the volume *Creative Art of the Peoples of the USSR*, contributed a great deal toward attracting public attention to folklore. The central organ of the party, *Pravda*, as a further development of its work in preparing the volume *Creative Art of the Peoples of the USSR*, published in the newspaper itself a great many productions of Soviet folklore, both Russian and also that of the other peoples of the USSR.

District, Republic, and provincial newspapers, even those of wide circulation, sometimes include articles on folklore, sometimes information on the work of collecting folklore, sometimes brief instructions as to what should be gathered and how, but most of all, they contain actual folklore material: chastushkas, songs, tales, legends, proverbs, and so forth. This contributes a great deal to the elevation of the popular creation itself to a higher ideological and artistic level. One cannot refrain from pointing out that a great role in the collection and dissemination of folklore is being played by the workers' and peasants' correspondents. The central magazines, which serve as a guide to the local subordinate press, carry appropriate instructive and informational articles, making clear how folklore is used, and how it should be used, in the press.

It must furthermore be added that the central and local newspapers are staging competitions more and more frequently for the best songs by the people.

In the enrichment of folklore with new productions, and in the popularization, throughout the land, of local folklore, in the best examples of the old and of the new (both Russian and that of other nationalities), the radio plays a tremendous role. It presents folk songs in the harmonic arrangements of composers and as performed by professional artists; it also presents the genuine, unchanged works of folklore as performed by the actual popular singers, narrators, and storytellers.

Phonograph records are of similar importance. The activity in the manufacture of phonograph records, in recent times, is in no small measure linked with the popularization of folklore. Thus, for example, there has recently been a great work accomplished in the recording of Russian, Ukrainian, Uzbek, Kazakh, and other songs.

In the popularization of folklore the sound film is beginning to take an increasingly large part. Thus, by direct order of Comrade Stalin, the well known producer Dovzhenko, in making the motion picture about the "Ukrainian Chapayev," Shchors, utilized the Ukrainian folklore of song and story to a great extent.

A place of exceptional importance in the history of contemporary folklore must be assigned to the All-Union, Republic, district, regional, collective-farm, and sometimes factory Olympiads for amateur art. During the past few years these Olympiads have revealed hundreds and thousands of talented musicians, dancers, singers, storytellers, narrators, and other performers and creators of folklore. The Moscow ten-day celebrations devoted to national art have made a magnificent contribution.

All these forms of public attention to folklore, which we have briefly enumerated, all these means for the popularization of folklore: the literary organizations, the press, radio, motion picture, the Olympiads for amateur art, the ten-day celebrations devoted to national art, the state theatrical stage and concert platform, the various forms of club work, and so forth, provide innumerable opportunities to give broadly organized help to the development of folk creation, to contribute to its further ideological and artistic growth, and to uncover all its innumerable treasures.

To the oral poetry of the masses a period of great flourishing has arrived. Now there can be no instance in which outstanding popular talents will remain unnoticed or unfostered by the public. Now we have all the prerequisites for the broadest development of the talents of the people. For the creative art of the people there has begun the most propitious and brilliant era, illumined by the genius of Stalin.

All the more fascinating, and at the same time all the more responsible, have become the tasks which lie before the Soviet study of folklore. All the more vital must be the stream of new research personnel in the field of folkloristics. Before the Soviet folklorists there has been opened a broad and honorable way of service to the people, that service of which Comrade Stalin has spoken in his address on the progress of science.

RUSSIAN TRANSLITERATION TABLE

(Based on the new Russian orthography)

This scheme is designed for the convenience of readers who do not know Russian. It is intended primarily for the rendering of personal and place names—mostly nouns in the nominative case.

The aim is to produce words as "normal" in appearance as possible, without the use of diacritical marks, superscripts or apostrophes, but at the same time to approximate the sounds of the Russian words, so that if spoken by an educated American they would easily be identified by a Russian.

Names which are a part of English cultural tradition, such as Moscow, Archangel, Tolstoy, Tchaikovsky, are given in their customary English spelling.

Extended phrases or entire sentences involving verb forms and case endings, which occur in footnotes for the convenience of students who know Russian, are given in a somewhat more complex transliteration which is reversible.

Russian		*English*	
А	а	*a*	
Б	б	*b*	
В	в	*v*	
Г	г	*g*	except in genitive singular where it is *v*, as in Tolstovo.
Д	д	*d*	
Е	е	(1) *ye*	when initial, and after ь, ъ, and all vowels, except ы, и: Yekaterina, Izdanie, Nikolayev.
		(2) *e*	elsewhere, as in Lenin, Vera, Pero.
Ё	ё	*yo*	but after ж and ш = *o*.
Ж	ж	*zh*	
З	з	*z*	
И	и	*i*	but after ь = *yi*, as in Ilyich.
Й	й	*y*	in terminal diphthongs, but *i* medially, as in May, Kochubey, Kiy, Tolstoy, but Khoz*yai*stvo.
К	к	*k*	

Russian		*English*		
Л	л	*l*		
М	м	*m*		
Н	н	*n*		
О	о	*o*		
П	п	*p*		
Р	р	*r*		
С	с	*s*		
Т	т	*t*		
У	у	*u*		
Ф	ф	*f*		
Х	х	*kh*	*as in*	Kharkov.
Ц	ц	*ts*		Tsargrad.
Ч	ч	*ch*		Chapayev, Vaigach.
Ш	ш	*sh*		Shakhta.
Щ	щ	*shch*		Shchedrin.
Ъ	ъ	Omit		
Ы	ы	*y*		Mys, Tsaritsyn.
Ь	ь	Omit		
Э	э	*e*		Ermitazh.
Ю	ю	*yu*		
Я	я	*ya*		

ADJECTIVAL ENDINGS

Singular	ЫЙ, ИЙ	ый, ий	both simply *y*, as in Dostoyevsky, Grozny.
Plural	ЫЕ, ИЕ	ые, ие	both simply *ie*.

The English letter *y* serves both as vowel and as consonant (as it does in English): (1) as a vowel *within* words, as in Mys, Tsaritsyn, and also (2) as an adjectival terminal vowel, as in Khoroshy, Razumovsky, May, Kochubey, Tolstoy, and (3) with consonantal force to soften vowels, as in Istoriya, Bratya, Yug.

INDEX OF AUTHORS' NAMES

(COLLECTORS AND INVESTIGATORS OF FOLKLORE)

❦

(These indexes are translations of those in the Russian edition.)

751

* The initial "E" is pronounced "Ye" in Russian.—ED.

INDEX OF NAMES OF MASTERS
OF THE POPULAR CREATIVE ART

❧